The NEW ENCYCLOPEDIA *of* SOUTHERN CULTURE

VOLUME 20 : SOCIAL CLASS

Volumes to appear in
The New Encyclopedia of Southern Culture
are:

Agriculture and Industry	*Law and Politics*
Art and Architecture	*Literature*
Education	*Media*
Environment	*Music*
Ethnicity	*Myth, Manners, and Memory*
Folk Art	*Race*
Folklife	*Religion*
Foodways	*Science and Medicine*
Gender	*Social Class*
Geography	*Sports and Recreation*
History	*Urbanization*
Language	*Violence*

The NEW

ENCYCLOPEDIA *of* SOUTHERN CULTURE

CHARLES REAGAN WILSON General Editor

JAMES G. THOMAS JR. Managing Editor

ANN J. ABADIE Associate Editor

VOLUME 20

Social Class

LARRY J. GRIFFIN & PEGGY G. HARGIS
Volume Editors

Sponsored by

THE CENTER FOR THE STUDY OF SOUTHERN CULTURE

at the University of Mississippi

THE UNIVERSITY OF NORTH CAROLINA PRESS

Chapel Hill

This book was published with the
assistance of the Anniversary Endowment Fund
of the University of North Carolina Press.

© 2012 The University of North Carolina Press
All rights reserved
Designed by Richard Hendel
Set in Minion types by Tseng Information Systems, Inc.
The paper in this book meets the guidelines for permanence and
durability of the Committee on Production Guidelines for Book
Longevity of the Council on Library Resources.
Library of Congress Cataloging-in-Publication Data
Social class / Larry J. Griffin & Peggy G. Hargis, volume editors.
p. cm. — (The new encyclopedia of Southern culture ; v. 20)
"Published with the assistance of the Anniversary Endowment
Fund of the University of North Carolina Press."
"Sponsored by The Center for the Study of Southern Culture at the
University of Mississippi."
Includes bibliographical references and index.
ISBN 978-0-8078-3559-3 (cloth: alk. paper)
ISBN 978-0-8078-7232-1 (pbk.: alk. paper)
ISBN 978-0-8078-8254-2 (ebook)
1. Social classes—Southern States—Encyclopedias. 2. Southern
States—Social conditions—Encyclopedias. I. Griffin, Larry J.
II. Hargis, Peggy Griffith, 1955– . III. University of Mississippi.
Center for the Study of Southern Culture. IV. Series.
F209 .N47 2006 vol. 20
[HN79.A13]
975.003 s—dc22
2011533004

The *Encyclopedia of Southern Culture*, sponsored by the Center for
the Study of Southern Culture at the University of Mississippi, was
published by the University of North Carolina Press in 1989.

Tell about the South. What's it like there.
What do they do there. Why do they live there.
Why do they live at all.

WILLIAM FAULKNER

Absalom, Absalom!

CONTENTS

General Introduction *xiii*
Introduction *xix*

SOCIAL CLASS IN THE AMERICAN
SOUTH *1*

Agriculture *57*
American Revolution *61*
Antiunionism and Right-to-Work
   Laws *66*
Asian Americans *71*
Black Elite and the Black Middle
   Class *78*
Civil Rights Movement *80*
Collective Memory *85*
Crime and Punishment *87*
Demagogues *92*
Education *97*
Environment *101*
Ethnicity *105*
Foodways *109*
Free Blacks *112*
Gender *118*
Honor *122*
Humor *128*
Industrialization and
   Deindustrialization *136*
Industrialization, Employment, and
   Organized Labor *140*
Jews *144*
Labor, Geography of *146*
Latinos *152*
Latino Workers *156*
Literature *162*
Lynching *166*
Middle Class, Development of *172*
Migration *176*
Music *181*
Place and Space *186*
Political Behavior *190*
Populist Movement *198*
Poverty *201*
Race and Labor, since 1865 *209*
Racial Attitudes *213*
Radicalism *222*
Radio, Television, and Film *227*
Reconstruction and Redemption *230*
Religion *235*
Secession, the Confederacy, and the
   Civil War *239*
Sharecropping and Tenancy *242*
Slaveholders, Black *247*
Slavery as a Class System *251*
Social Reform, 1932–1954 *255*
Southern Identity *260*
Sports *263*
Stereotypes, Female *267*
Stereotypes, Male *272*
Sunbelt South *276*
Tourism *283*
Upper Class, White *287*
Urbanization *290*
Voting Rights *295*
Welfare and Charity *301*
Women, White, Working-Class *303*
Women and Labor *306*
Working Class, Black *310*

American Federation of Labor 313
Anti-Semitism 315
Appalachia 317
Artisans 319
Bacon's Rebellion 321
Black Belt 322
Bluegrass Music 324
Blues Music 326
Braden, Carl, and Anne McCarty 328
Campbell, Will 330
Child Labor 332
Citizens' Councils 333
Civic and Historical Pageants and Pilgrimages 334
Clubwomen 337
Coal and Iron Workers 339
Congress of Industrial Organizations 341
Convict Lease System and Peonage 343
Country Music 346
Desertion during the Civil War 348
Fraternal Orders 350
Freedmen's Bureau 351
Gated Communities 353
General Textile Strike of 1934 357
Geophagia and Pica 357
Global South 358
Greenbackers 361
Hamer, Fannie Lou 363
Highlander Folk School / Highlander Research and Education Center 365
Hillbillies, Crackers, Rednecks, and White Trash 367
Horton, Myles 370
Hunting and Fishing 372
Indentured Servants 373

Indian Removal, 1800–1840 375
Industrial Workers of the World 376
In-Migration 378
Jacksonian Democracy 379
Jazz 381
Kester, Howard Anderson 383
King, Martin Luther, Jr. 385
Knights of Labor 386
Ku Klux Klan and Other White Racist Organizations 388
Longshoremen 390
Lumber Workers 391
Lumpkin, Grace 393
Lumpkin, Katharine Du Pre 393
Mardi Gras 394
Mason, Lucy Randolph 399
Memory, Appalachian 400
Migrant Workers 402
Military Academies 403
Mine, Mill, and Smelter Workers 407
Mitchell, H. L. 409
NASCAR 410
New Deal 412
New South, 19th-Century 414
1938 Economic Report on the South 415
Oil Workers 417
Operation Dixie 419
Ozarks 421
Pellagra 423
Poultry Workers 425
Railroad Workers 427
Raper, Arthur 430
Rap Music 431
Readjusters 434
Regulator Movement 436
Rock 'n' Roll 437
Service Workers 439
Shape-Note Singing 441

Share Croppers' Union and Southern
    Tenant Farmers' Union 443
Socialism and Communism 444
Southern Conference for Human
    Welfare / Southern Conference
    Educational Fund 446
Southern Regional Council 448
Southern Student Organizing
    Committee 449
Spiritual and Gospel Music 451
Steelworkers 455
Textile Workers 457

Timber and Naval Stores 459
Tobacco Workers 462
Washington, Booker T. 464
Wells-Barnett, Ida B. 466
West, Don 468
Williams, Claude 469
Yeomanry 471
"You Might Be a Redneck If . . ." 472

Index of Contributors 475
Index 477

GENERAL INTRODUCTION

In 1989 years of planning and hard work came to fruition when the University of North Carolina Press joined the Center for the Study of Southern Culture at the University of Mississippi to publish the *Encyclopedia of Southern Culture*. While all those involved in writing, reviewing, editing, and producing the volume believed it would be received as a vital contribution to our understanding of the American South, no one could have anticipated fully the widespread acclaim it would receive from reviewers and other commentators. But the *Encyclopedia* was indeed celebrated, not only by scholars but also by popular audiences with a deep, abiding interest in the region. At a time when some people talked of the "vanishing South," the book helped remind a national audience that the region was alive and well, and it has continued to shape national perceptions of the South through the work of its many users—journalists, scholars, teachers, students, and general readers.

As the introduction to the *Encyclopedia* noted, its conceptualization and organization reflected a cultural approach to the South. It highlighted such issues as the core zones and margins of southern culture, the boundaries where "the South" overlapped with other cultures, the role of history in contemporary culture, and the centrality of regional consciousness, symbolism, and mythology. By 1989 scholars had moved beyond the idea of cultures as real, tangible entities, viewing them instead as abstractions. The *Encyclopedia*'s editors and contributors thus included a full range of social indicators, trait groupings, literary concepts, and historical evidence typically used in regional studies, carefully working to address the distinctive and characteristic traits that made the American South a particular place. The introduction to the *Encyclopedia* concluded that the fundamental uniqueness of southern culture was reflected in the volume's composite portrait of the South. We asked contributors to consider aspects that were unique to the region but also those that suggested its internal diversity. The volume was not a reference book of southern history, which explained something of the design of entries. There were fewer essays on colonial and antebellum history than on the postbellum and modern periods, befitting our conception of the volume as one trying not only to chart the cultural landscape of the South but also to illuminate the contemporary era.

When C. Vann Woodward reviewed the *Encyclopedia* in the *New York Review of Books*, he concluded his review by noting "the continued liveliness of interest in the South and its seeming inexhaustibility as a field of study." Research on the South, he wrote, furnishes "proof of the value of the *Encyclopedia* as a scholarly undertaking as well as suggesting future needs for revision or supplement to keep up with ongoing scholarship." The two decades since the publication of the *Encyclopedia of Southern Culture* have certainly suggested that Woodward was correct. The American South has undergone significant changes that make for a different context for the study of the region. The South has undergone social, economic, political, intellectual, and literary transformations, creating the need for a new edition of the *Encyclopedia* that will remain relevant to a changing region. Globalization has become a major issue, seen in the South through the appearance of Japanese automobile factories, Hispanic workers who have immigrated from Latin America or Cuba, and a new prominence for Asian and Middle Eastern religions that were hardly present in the 1980s South. The African American return migration to the South, which started in the 1970s, dramatically increased in the 1990s, as countless books simultaneously appeared asserting powerfully the claims of African Americans as formative influences on southern culture. Politically, southerners from both parties have played crucial leadership roles in national politics, and the Republican Party has dominated a near-solid South in national elections. Meanwhile, new forms of music, like hip-hop, have emerged with distinct southern expressions, and the term "dirty South" has taken on new musical meanings not thought of in 1989. New genres of writing by creative southerners, such as gay and lesbian literature and "white trash" writing, extend the southern literary tradition.

Meanwhile, as Woodward foresaw, scholars have continued their engagement with the history and culture of the South since the publication of the *Encyclopedia*, raising new scholarly issues and opening new areas of study. Historians have moved beyond their earlier preoccupation with social history to write new cultural history as well. They have used the categories of race, social class, and gender to illuminate the diversity of the South, rather than a unified "mind of the South." Previously underexplored areas within the field of southern historical studies, such as the colonial era, are now seen as formative periods of the region's character, with the South's positioning within a larger Atlantic world a productive new area of study. Cultural memory has become a major topic in the exploration of how the social construction of "the South" benefited some social groups and exploited others. Scholars in many disciplines have made the southern identity a major topic, and they have used a variety of methodologies to suggest what that identity has meant to different social groups. Literary critics have adapted cultural theories to the South and have raised the issue of postsouthern literature to a major category of concern as well as exploring the links between the literature of the American South and that of the Caribbean. Anthropologists have used different theoretical formulations from literary critics, providing models for their fieldwork in southern communities. In the past 30 years anthropologists have set increasing numbers of their ethnographic studies in the South, with many of them now exploring topics specifically linked to southern cultural issues. Scholars now place the Native American story, from prehistory to the contemporary era, as a central part of southern history. Comparative and interdisciplinary approaches to the South have encouraged scholars to look at such issues as the borders and boundaries of the South, specific places and spaces with distinct identities within the American South, and the global and transnational Souths, linking the American South with many formerly colonial societies around the world.

The first edition of the *Encyclopedia of Southern Culture* anticipated many of these approaches and indeed stimulated the growth of Southern Studies as a distinct interdisciplinary field. The Center for the Study of Southern Culture has worked for more than three decades to encourage research and teaching about the American South. Its academic programs have produced graduates who have gone on to write interdisciplinary studies of the South, while others have staffed the cultural institutions of the region and in turn encouraged those institutions to document and present the South's culture to broad public audiences. The center's conferences and publications have continued its long tradition of promoting understanding of the history, literature, and music of the South, with new initiatives focused on southern foodways, the future of the South, and the global Souths, expressing the center's mission to bring the best current scholarship to broad public audiences. Its documentary studies projects build oral and visual archives, and the New Directions in Southern Studies book series, published by the University of North Carolina Press, offers an important venue for innovative scholarship.

Since the *Encyclopedia of Southern Culture* appeared, the field of Southern Studies has dramatically developed, with an extensive network now of academic and research institutions whose projects focus specifically on the interdisciplinary study of the South. The Center for the Study of the American South at the University of North Carolina at Chapel Hill, led by Director Harry Watson and Associate Director and *Encyclopedia* coeditor William Ferris, publishes the lively journal *Southern Cultures* and is now at the organizational center of many other Southern Studies projects. The Institute for Southern Studies at the University of South Carolina, the Southern Intellectual History Circle, the Society for the Study of Southern Literature, the Southern Studies Forum of the European American Studies Association, Emory University's SouthernSpaces.org, and the South Atlantic Humanities Center (at the Virginia Foundation for the Humanities, the University of Virginia, and Virginia Polytechnic Institute and State University) express the recent expansion of interest in regional study.

Observers of the American South have had much to absorb, given the rapid pace of recent change. The institutional framework for studying the South is broader and deeper than ever, yet the relationship between the older verities of regional study and new realities remains unclear. Given the extent of changes in the American South and in Southern Studies since the publication of the *Encyclopedia of Southern Culture*, the need for a new edition of that work is clear. Therefore, the Center for the Study of Southern Culture has once again joined the University of North Carolina Press to produce *The New Encyclopedia of Southern Culture*. As readers of the original edition will quickly see, *The New Encyclopedia* follows many of the scholarly principles and editorial conventions established in the original, but with one key difference; rather than being published in a single hardback volume, *The New Encyclopedia* is presented in a series of shorter individual volumes that build on the 24 original subject categories used in the *Encyclopedia* and adapt them to new scholarly developments. Some earlier *Encyclopedia* categories have been reconceptualized in light of new academic interests. For example, the subject section originally titled "Women's Life" is reconceived as a new volume, *Gender*, and the original "Black Life" section is more broadly interpreted as a volume on race. These changes reflect new analytical concerns that place the study of women and blacks in broader cultural systems, reflecting the emergence of, among other topics, the study of male culture and of whiteness. Both volumes draw as well from the rich recent scholarship on women's life and black life. In addition, topics with some thematic coherence are combined in a volume, such as *Law and Politics* and *Agriculture and Industry*. One new topic, *Foodways*, is the basis of a separate volume, reflecting its new prominence in the interdisciplinary study of southern culture.

Numerous individual topical volumes together make up *The New Encyclopedia of Southern Culture* and extend the reach of the reference work to wider audiences. This approach should enhance the use of the *Encyclopedia* in academic courses and is intended to be convenient for readers with more focused interests within the larger context of southern culture. Readers will have handy access to one-volume, authoritative, and comprehensive scholarly treatments of the major areas of southern culture.

We have been fortunate that, in nearly all cases, subject consultants who offered crucial direction in shaping the topical sections for the original edition have agreed to join us in this new endeavor as volume editors. When new volume editors have been added, we have again looked for respected figures who can provide not only their own expertise but also strong networks of scholars to help develop relevant lists of topics and to serve as contributors in their areas. The reputations of all our volume editors as leading scholars in their areas encouraged the contributions of other scholars and added to *The New Encyclopedia*'s authority as a reference work.

The New Encyclopedia of Southern Culture builds on the strengths of articles in the original edition in several ways. For many existing articles, original authors agreed to update their contributions with new interpretations and theoretical perspectives, current statistics, new bibliographies, or simple factual developments that needed to be included. If the original contributor was unable to update an article, the editorial staff added new material or sent it to another scholar for assessment. In some cases, the general editor and volume editors selected a new contributor if an article seemed particularly dated and new work indicated the need for a fresh perspective. And importantly, where new developments have warranted treatment of topics not addressed in the original edition, volume editors have commissioned entirely new essays and articles that are published here for the first time.

The American South embodies a powerful historical and mythical presence, both a complex environmental and geographic landscape and a place of the imagination. Changes in the region's contemporary socioeconomic realities and new developments in scholarship have been incorporated in the conceptualization and approach of *The New Encyclopedia of Southern Culture*. Anthropologist Clifford Geertz has spoken of culture as context, and this encyclopedia looks at the American South as a complex place that has served as the context for cultural expression. This volume provides information and perspective on the diversity of cultures in a geographic and imaginative place with a long history and distinctive character.

The *Encyclopedia of Southern Culture* was produced through major grants from the Program for Research Tools and Reference Works of the National Endowment for the Humanities, the Ford Foundation, the Atlantic-Richfield Foundation, and the Mary Doyle Trust. We are grateful as well to the College of Liberal Arts at the University of Mississippi for support and to the individual donors to the Center for the Study of Southern Culture who have directly or indirectly supported work on *The New Encyclopedia of Southern Culture*. We thank the volume editors for their ideas in reimagining their subjects and the contributors of articles for their work in extending the usefulness of the book in new ways. We acknowledge the support and contributions of the faculty and staff at the Center for the Study of Southern Culture. Finally, we want especially to honor the work of William Ferris and Mary Hart on the *Encyclopedia of Southern Culture*. Bill, the founding director of the Center for the Study of Southern Culture, was coeditor, and his good work recruiting authors, editing text, selecting images, and publicizing the volume among a wide network of people was, of course, invaluable. Despite the many changes in the new encyclopedia, Bill's influence remains. Mary "Sue" Hart was also an invaluable member of the original encyclopedia team, bringing the careful and precise eye of the librarian, and an iconoclastic spirit, to our work.

INTRODUCTION

Social class is one of the fundamental analytical categories for studying southern cultures. Exploring southern society as the context for cultural life is an enduring concern of scholars from such disciplines as sociology, social history, anthropology, social psychology, and political science, among others, and this volume shows the vital public policy connections to scholarly issues of social class. The topic brings to mind social typologies long associated with the region—elite planters, whether Cavaliers or cotton snobs from the lowlands; sturdy yeomen farmers from the Upcountry; antebellum slaves; textile hands and mill owners; Depression-era black and white sharecroppers; and small-town merchants. The relationship between social class concerns and race relations has been especially central, and many articles herein examine ways supposed racial solidarity has affected social class divisions. Southern society surely offers examples of social orthodoxy working to suppress social conflicts and divisions and to promote a status quo structure. But just as surely, those conflicts and divisions have been deep seated, compellingly expressed at times, and the source of notable reform efforts. The South's long dominant biracial population, with origins in Western Europe and West Africa, has provided a particular context for the development of social classes in the region, and the recent increased demographic diversity from immigration is providing dramatically different contours for contemporary social class development.

The *Social Class* volume of *The New Encyclopedia of Southern Culture* looks at macro- and microlevels of social class formation. The overview essay has two parts. The first provides a historical narrative and looks at theoretical frameworks that can inform the larger understanding of class relationships and identities in the South and elsewhere. The second part offers sociological perspectives, outlining broad forces shaping southern social class development and raising issues of social status, mobility, work environments, and agrarian and industrial contexts. The second part draws from rich sources of census and survey data to provide timely contemporary information to supplement the historical grounding of the first part of the overview. Thematic and topical entries provide in-depth information on key historical events, including Bacon's Rebellion, Indian removal, the Civil War, the Populist movement, the New Deal, and the civil rights movement. Many of these stories are told elsewhere in *New Encyclopedia* volumes, but the sharp focus here is on their significance for understanding social class. The same is true for our coverage of such major themes as education, politics, religion, sports, and gender—all turn out to be essential for understanding how social class formations have been experienced in the region. Separate articles detail major social classes, whether the upper class, yeomanry, artisans, the working class, or the middle class. Stereotypical hillbillies and crackers are part of the social class story, and readers will discover how they became so associated with the South. The editors have paid special attention to ways that creative expressions in the South have had social class dimensions, seen in articles on literature, film, radio and television, and all sorts of music, from jazz and country to spiritual and gospel music, to contemporary rap. Shorter topical entries provide details on a variety of organizations, including the Southern Conference for Human Welfare, the Highlander Folk School, the Freedmen's Bureau, the Citizens' Councils, and clubwomen. Work is a major theme, with entries that chart the role of unions and other working-class organizations, including the American Federation of Labor and the Congress of Industrial Organizations, the Knights of Labor and the Share Croppers' Union, the Mine Mill and Smelter Workers Union, and textile unions. Readers find out about timber workers, longshoremen, indentured workers, convict lease workers, steelworkers, oil workers, and the region's growing number of service workers.

This volume appears at a time of dramatic social and economic change in the South, with the region connected to national and international developments more than ever before. Appreciation of the role that social class has played in the southern past is essential to charting emerging social relationships in the newest South.

The NEW ENCYCLOPEDIA *of* SOUTHERN CULTURE

VOLUME 20 : SOCIAL CLASS

SOCIAL CLASS IN THE AMERICAN SOUTH
HISTORICAL PERSPECTIVES

One of America's most cherished ideals is the notion that any person who strives hard can be successful. The possibility of social and economic mobility attracted millions of immigrants and sustained the "American Dream." In no region is this idea more widely believed than in the South, and no section more thoroughly scorns Marxist notions of a society rigidly divided into hostile classes on the basis of economic relationships. In reality, the South exists somewhere between its own idealistic myth of free and easy access to opportunity and the Marxist perception of an impenetrable class structure. Whether phrased in terms of a harsh concept such as "class" or a more acceptable one such as "status," the reality of social differentiation has contradicted the noble ideals of social equality and equal access to opportunity. Class identification involves a great deal more than one's rank in the economic order. It is related to the entire social structure, although the nature of that relationship is hotly debated. One's status may depend on family, occupation, or self-perception, and it may be expressed in one's education, place of residence, political identification, church, or even depiction in literature.

Interpretations of Social Structure. Attempts to apply class interpretations to the South's social structure may be divided into three categories. The most familiar was expounded by Karl Marx and divided society into two classes engaged in mortal conflict. The prevailing system of economic production created a struggle between those engaged in the production of wealth and those who profited the most from its inequitable distribution. Economic struggle between classes determined all social relationships and political roles. Although some have attempted to apply rigid Marxist interpretations to the South, the more influential studies derive from a modification of Marx that deemphasizes economic determinism in favor of the cultural domination of one ruling elite over all others.

Max Weber, though influenced heavily by Marx, added two elements to the economic notions implicit in "class." "Status," as a concept of social honor or prestige, recognized that one's standing is partly determined by the consciousness of individuals, both that of their own position and that of others. "Party" added the idea of political or legal power as a component because Weber observed that social stratification was a manifestation of the unequal distribution of power. Position in society was not determined solely by which economic group one belonged to but by the power that group could command compared to the power held by other groups.

Finally, an American, W. Lloyd Warner, expanded the concept of "status" and applied it specifically to American society. The social position one held depended not so much on economic criteria as on how a person lived, who his family was, and how people in the community judged, interpreted, weighed, and compared these factors. America contained not Marx's simple two-class structure, but a complex six-layer system existing not in mutual hostility and conflict but in relative harmony.

Complicating all these considerations was the presence of large numbers of blacks in the South. Constituting a caste rigidly divided first by slavery and later by segregation, blacks developed a separate class system sometimes paralleling and at other times conflicting with the white structure.

Colonial Era. The colonial South produced conflicting patterns of landownership and class tension. Earlier historians attributed such conflicts as Bacon's Rebellion in Virginia to class tensions between wealthy seaboard aristocrats and poorer backcountry farmers, although such explanations appear now to be excessively simplistic. Actually the colonial patterns varied from one southern colony to another. For instance, the trustees who established Georgia banned slavery and prohibited ownership of more than 500 acres of land in an attempt to create a democratic region for the "worthy poor." But ambitious Georgia settlers thwarted such noble intentions, pointing to the greater prosperity of South Carolina and Virginia as precedent for introducing slavery and the plantation system. The success of plantation agriculture widened the chasm between classes and created strong antiroyalist sentiments among the upland farmers who would soon earn the title of "crackers." But land policy in Georgia remained generous throughout the colonial period; almost any male head of household could qualify for virtually free land. Although the Revolutionary War had a leveling effect in some ways, it also reflected class tensions. Officers in the state militias came from aristocratic stock. They commanded southern units often composed of unpropertied, poor recruits. South Carolina units contained sharp distinctions in dress, lodging, and food that led to desertions, neglect of duty, insolence toward officers, and general misbehavior.

Antebellum Era. Applying class theories to the antebellum years has produced exciting new interpretations and furious arguments. White society was divided into at least three major groups: planters, yeoman farmers, and poor whites. What united these three classes was a common commitment to the racial superiority of whites, common kinship ties that often existed between planters and yeomen, and belief in the possibility of movement into the upper class if one sought good land, worked hard, and subscribed to community values. Each group also contained substantial variety. Among planters the range extended from small farmers with less than five slaves who lived more like yeomen than feudal lords to legendary barons with thousands of acres who constructed Greek Revival mansions, acquired extensive libraries, and ruled their domains with paternalistic concern for their hundreds of subjects. To those of Marxist persuasion, the planter class appears not to have been so much a capitalist class as precapitalist or even anticapitalist. Planters were hostile to all manufacturing except industry that complemented agriculture, such as the textile industry. They feared the rise of cities because both the urban bourgeoisie and the white working class that would develop there were quite beyond planter control. Moreover, their wealth was concentrated in land and slaves, and credit served their agrarian interests, leaving little money for speculative industries. Their values—honor, gentility, a highly ordered social structure, and an easygoing, relaxed society—were contrary to the capitalist values of northern businessmen and explain the South's inability to sustain manufacturing on any extensive scale. Planters typically belonged to Episcopal churches and were conservative in politics, often supporting the Whig Party.

The yeoman class was by far the largest of the three major social groups. Unlike the planter who grew commercially marketable products such as cotton and tobacco, the yeoman was a self-sustaining farmer who worked in his own fields, produced extensive crops of corn and wheat, and maintained herds of livestock that roamed free in woodlands adjacent to his fields. He obtained rudimentary education in one of the hundreds of academies, cast his vote for Jacksonian Democrats, especially the ones who advocated easier access to public lands, and typically belonged to emotional religious sects such as the Baptists or the Methodists. Yeomen were often related to planter families by either kinship or marriage, aspired to enter that class, and were often successful when cotton prices were high and their lands fertile. When unsuccessful, they were a highly mobile group, moving westward in search of better land. Slavery provided them a means of controlling social and economic competition with blacks and a sense of class identification with other whites.

Even poor whites, the most elusive and enigmatic of the classes, generally accepted the plantation ideal, though they participated only peripherally in the economic system. Producing neither commercially marketable staples nor extensive food crops and livestock, they barely existed by hunting, fishing, harvesting sparse crops on poor land that usually did not belong to them, or working for minimal wages as farm laborers or in the cotton mills and urban industrial jobs that began to develop in the late antebellum years. Illiterate, transient, sickly, they were often despised by blacks and other whites alike, stereotyped by the comic southwestern humorists, and dismissed as "po' white trash." Actually poor whites varied from wretched ne'er-do-wells to substantial but landless farmers with stable families. Few of the economic benefits of the plantation system leaked through to them, and their only pride was the color of their skin, praised publicly by planter and yeoman alike, but of little practical value.

The notion that racial solidarity prevented internal dissension between white classes is not supported by the historical facts. Conflict occurred at many points within the social order. There was sectional strife between Upcountry farmers, living on small farms with few slaves, and Lowcountry planters. Economically the classes differed about free and easy access to land, taxation, and education. Politically they divided between Whig and Democrat.

Religious divergence according to class inspired a famous description of denominationalism more concerned with social status than theology: a Methodist was a Baptist who wore shoes; a Presbyterian was a Methodist with a bank account; an Episcopalian was a Presbyterian who lived off his investments. Such good-humored stereotyping obscured more fundamental conflicts. During the years immediately following the American Revolution, religious strife developed in the Virginia Tidewater. Separate Baptists held mass gatherings where itinerant preachers proclaimed the depravity of man, the terrors of hell, and the glories of redemption. They denounced finery of dress, cockfighting and gambling, fiddling and dancing—the very values by which the aristocracy demonstrated its superior status. Worse than that, they opposed taxation to support a state church and demanded separation of church and state. Drawn from the lower economic groups, the Separate Baptists created a popular, nonhierarchical, participatory system of association and authority, an "egalitarian world of humble men seeking their own ultimate meaning according to their own lights." In the following years Separate Baptists moderated their fierce Calvinism, but other disputes within the religious community replaced this one. The rise of new sects, such as the Disciples of Christ and the Cumberland Presbyterians, and the bitter struggle between missionary and antimission Baptists had distinctive class aspects.

Literature also reflected the differences in social status. Most southern writers were drawn from the gentry or professional classes, and they created a substantial literary tradition by describing the foibles, eccentricities, shrewdness, and humor of poor whites. Characters such as Augustus Baldwin Longstreet's "Ransy Sniffle" or Johnson J. Hooper's "Yellow-legs" satirized and stereotyped the white lower class.

Daniel Hundley, born into the Alabama planter elite, was one of the first southerners to describe systematically the region's class structure. His 1860 volume, *Social Relations in Our Southern States*, devoted chapters to "The Southern Gentleman," "The Middle Classes," "Cotton Snobs," "The Southern Yankee," "The Southern Yeoman," "Poor White Trash," and "The Negro Slaves." His description of poor whites was particularly harsh. Attempting to refute abolitionist charges that poor whites were the inevitable residue of a slave society, Hundley traced the class to paupers, convicts, and indentured servants, people explained by bad blood, not economic environment. Such "lazy vagabonds" preferred to live in rude log cabins on sterile soil where their yellow-faced women dipped snuff, smoked pipes, and raised large broods of "dirty, squalling, white-headed little brats" amid squalor, superstition, and slavish adherence to the Democratic Party. Their only redeeming quality was support of slavery and even that was the result of ignoble motives—"downright envy" of the planter and "hatred of the black man."

Although the world of blacks was fundamentally different from that of poor whites, internal variations occurred there also. Standing at the top of the social ladder were free blacks, who in 1860 numbered 262,000 and constituted 12.8 percent of the black population in the Upper South and 1.5 percent in the Lower South. Often of mixed racial ancestry and frequently residing in towns or cities, they developed job skills and relatively independent churches, schools, and fraternal societies. In 1860 one-sixth of Richmond's bricklayers and blacksmiths and half its plasterers and barbers were black. Protected from white competition by the stigma of "nigger work," some free blacks became substantial property holders. In the years following the Civil War, many leaders came from this class, including nearly half of the 22 blacks who served in Congress between 1869 and 1900.

Differentiation by class is harder to measure among slaves. Whatever their advantages over their fellows in job skill, skin color, or literacy, free blacks remained bound to the slaves by the "peculiar institution." Nonetheless, a hierarchy did exist, with house servants, ministers, and skilled artisans at the top and field hands at the bottom. Adaptation to white culture also varied, with some slaves maintaining strong African elements and others quickly adopting American forms.

Impact of the Civil War. All class arrangements were affected by the Civil War, but no consensus exists concerning the extent of change. Class tensions—which had been somewhat confined during the antebellum years by common kinship and folkways, the ideology of white supremacy, the availability of land, rapid economic mobility, and the nonelite origins of the planter class—underwent subtle change during the Civil War. In the initial phase of conflict, yeomen and poor whites rallied to the Confederate cause despite frequent hill country opposition to secession. Most military units contained a cross section of economic classes and elected their own officers, a process considerably more democratic than in the Revolutionary War. But as the war progressed, yeomen and poor whites bore the worst effects. Drought, draft, and taxes-in-kind fell heavily on common whites in hill counties and piney woods. The families soldiers left behind faced grievous problems by 1862–63, causing southern states to levy taxes on wealthy planters in order to distribute food to the poor. But for this relief, unrest would have been even greater. As it was, desertion by yeomen and poor whites increased dramatically by 1863, and southern hill counties experienced growing anarchy. Poverty, desertion, resistance to Confederate policy, and growing peace sentiment were closely related.

The appearance of discontinuity after the Civil War was certainly greater than the reality. Although planters lost their slave work force, they retained control of economic and political life and in some states adjusted quickly to the New South drive for industrialization. In Alabama and North Carolina, planters apparently not only survived but participated actively in the manufacturing enterprises that flourished in the Piedmont and in bustling industrial towns such as Birmingham and Anniston. In other states, leaders in the rapidly growing textile industry were urban professionals and businessmen, with planters and farmers playing little role. In South Carolina, the rise of Upcountry towns had more to do with the development of manufacturing than did the survival of the plantation system.

The New Industrial Order. Whatever the origin of the new industrial order, several elements are clear. The planter class retained a major share of influence and power, although it had to compromise its opposition to towns and factories. The promise of Emancipation, which offered blacks such bright hope in 1865, dimmed amid agricultural poverty. Nor was the black dream the only casualty of the last years of the century. New South exponents could proclaim the dawn of a different world, but economic reality defied their pronouncements. In 1900 the South remained the poorest, most technologically backward, most rural, least industrialized region of America.

A Mississippi Delta plantation owner (foreground), 1930s (Dorothea Lange, photographer, Library of Congress [LC-USF-34-9599C], Washington, D.C.)

Because their expectations were so great, blacks were the most disappointed of southerners. As a symbol of their emancipation, tens of thousands of former slaves temporarily left the land, filling towns to overflowing with their tent cities. Wartime devastation not only prevented them from obtaining work but necessitated the Freedmen's Bureau's providing rations to them and to poor whites in order to prevent mass starvation. Gradually most freedmen drifted back to the land, some to purchase their own farms, but most to work as day laborers or as tenants. For blacks accustomed to slavery, even the sharecropper system represented a step toward freedom. Though often cheated, they could negotiate their own contracts, function at least theoretically as equals, and operate their farms without the constant supervision of owners. But in terms of health, diet, and general economic well-being, the status of many black sharecroppers declined even from that of a slave.

For whites who had barely survived on the periphery of the antebellum economy, tenancy added social insult to economic injury. Thousands of poor whites left their remote pine barrens and mountain hollows for small plots on former plantations only to discover that falling cotton prices, advancing boll weevils, and sometimes unscrupulous owners and merchants provided no better life. Out of preference or under pressure, tenants often grew cotton because it was one of the few crops that could be marketed for cash. In this way their lot declined from that of the subsistence food producers of the antebellum years. As agricultural conditions worsened, ever larger numbers of yeoman farmers fell through the land tenure system into some form of tenancy: of all southern farms, 36.2 percent were operated by tenants in 1880, 49.2 percent in 1920, and 55.5 percent in 1930. Poor diet, ill health, and illiteracy doomed one generation after another to sharecropping.

The landless poor searching for a better life were often seduced by the allurements of the industrial South. Although white tenant farmers were vaguely aware that they shared their economic bondage with blacks, some of the new industrial jobs reinforced that knowledge. Many of the industries—notably lumber, iron and steel, and mining—employed a biracial work force in which the major distinction was the white man's pride of race.

Although the intent of employers was not necessarily to exploit workers or create rigid class distinctions, that was the effect of industrialization. Workers of both races lived in company houses, sent their children to company schools, purchased goods from company commissaries, and worshiped in company-built and company-subsidized churches. Newly arrived rural families placed little value on education, barely survived economically, and pressured their children into mines or mills where they often grew up stunted and illiterate. When supplies of free labor lagged, owners contracted with sympathetic state officials to lease convicts.

The notable exception to this new biracial world of lower-class workers was the textile industry. Although blacks held menial jobs as loaders or janitors, cotton mill operatives generally were white. Attracted by the advantages of lower transportation costs, cheap nonunion labor, and abundant water and steam power, the textile industry moved rapidly south from New England between 1880 and 1930. In 1860 the South contained only 10,152 mill workers, but by 1890 there were 36,415, and by 1900, 110,015. Salaries in the 1890s in North Carolina averaged only 50¢ a day, and 70-hour workweeks were common. By 1900 the industry employed 25,000 children below the age of 15, most of them working in the states of Georgia, Alabama, and the Carolinas.

Child labor owed its existence to pressures both from the family and from industrial society. Farm parents relied heavily on child labor and often put little stock in formal education. Hence, when parents left the land for the mill village, they seldom hesitated to allow young children who chafed under the discipline of the local schoolteacher to enter mill employment. Although 90 percent of working children under 15 were employed in textile mills in 1900, increasing numbers worked in coal mines and glass factories, as Western Union boys, and in various other occupations. Their numbers had tripled in the decade between 1890 and 1900. Other regions shared the problem but none to the extent of the South, and from that region came early organization to abolish child labor. Unfortunately, many of the South's industrialists, though by no means all of them, opposed reform. They had become accustomed to the "family wage," a salary for the male head of family that was so low it required all family members to work. During the textile boom between 1900 and 1915 expansion of the industry required an enormous increase in labor, and much of this addition came from children under the age of 16. Industrialists claimed that children also learned factory routine more easily, and their hands were quicker and more agile. Furthermore, idle children were troublesome children, and work at an early age bred habits of thrift and industry. The results frequently were illiteracy and cyclical poverty.

At first the urban middle class felt little threatened by the growth of this large white working class, even praising the conservative religious and family values that made rural whites preferable to either newly arrived European immigrants or recently emancipated blacks. But as industrial conditions worsened and labor unrest increased, it began to view workers as a dangerous and disruptive element.

Organized Labor and Populism. Even though labor unions existed in the urban antebellum South, unionization had made little headway until after the Civil War. The first glimmer of the new direction of labor came in the years from 1873 to 1877 when freedmen, stereotyped as submissive, conducted a series of strikes. The Greenback-Labor Party provided the framework for biracial unionization and political action. This early labor activity in the postbellum South was fundamentally different from such disruptions in other regions, not only because it involved a coalition of blacks and whites, which exposed the movement to charges of racial iconoclasm, but also because it was often sustained by a deeply religious perception that cast the conflict more in terms of striving for human justice and right than in Marxist-style confrontation of economic classes.

The failure of the Greenback-Labor Party effort in the 1870s was the prelude to a long succession of disappointments for labor. Organizing efforts by the Knights of Labor beginning in 1885 recruited 45,000 members of both races and succeeded in controlling city governments in some southern cities, but these gains were wiped out by the depression of the 1890s.

Organization of farmers proved more immediately successful as the national depression multiplied agricultural problems in the 1880s and 1890s. The Farmers' Alliance at first sought to unite middle-class farmers into marketing collectives. However, rapidly escalating rural poverty carried many farmers further into radical agrarian politics. Primarily a movement of small farmers and rural professionals alarmed by their downward mobility and declining social status, the Populist Party also attracted support from lower-class tenants and industrial workers. At the other end of the economic spectrum, prosperous farmers often deserted the alliance when it moved into the political stage of Populism, frightened by its biracial political appeals and its quasi-socialistic demand for public ownership of railroads. Like the southern labor movement, Populism drew its vision of the impending apocalypse more from the Bible than from Karl Marx or Pierre-Joseph Proudhon. This was a distinctly southern brand of radicalism in which religion played a central role, even furnishing the vocabulary for public debates; Populists seldom used class terms, preferring instead words with moral connotations such as "robbed," "stolen," "injustice," and "evils." Religious imagery and Christian metaphors abounded.

Although Populism ultimately foundered upon a sea of criticism, white and black Populists seldom exceeded the prescribed limits of southern society. White Populists were willing to include blacks in common political efforts, but they were as opposed to racial equality as Democrats. Nonetheless, Populism was a landmark in southern history because it vigorously advocated economic justice for the lower middle class and for poor people of both races.

The demise of Populism forced many whites back into the Democratic Party. Together with the return of middle-class farmers, who had left the Farmers' Alliance earlier, these forces were strong enough to change the Democratic Party, which previously had been dominated by large farmers and industrialists. Reform of party rules allowed a direct role for ordinary white voters but also restricted the franchise through the imposition of poll taxes and other strictures.

As a result of these changes, southern politics became democratized, whether or not it became more liberal. The Socialist Party briefly thrived in the remote farmlands of Oklahoma and Texas and in the cigar factories of Tampa and Key West. Within the increasingly class-conscious populations of mill towns and mining camps, angry voters joined poor rural farmers to elect racial demagogues who promised far more reform than they enacted. Except for the psychic good it did them to abuse the "better classes" symbolically by electing such men as Cole Blease, Sidney Catts, and Theodore Bilbo, they realized few improvements in their lives.

The poor established more enduring patterns in their efforts at unionization. The United Mine Workers conducted organizing drives that resulted in a number of strikes between 1900 and 1921. The Brotherhood of Timber Workers united some 35,000 white and black lumbermen and poor farmers in Louisiana and Texas during the same years. Most strikes were defeated by better-organized and better-financed companies that usually had the support of the state press, the governor and state militia, farmers, and the urban middle class. Frustrated by their defeats, most whites left both unions.

The violence of these strikes alarmed the thriving middle class. Already aware of abuses and injustices thanks to the educational efforts of ministers, social workers, and reform-minded journalists, urban professionals and businessmen sought to slow class polarization. Winning allies from among enlightened businessmen who saw reform to be in their own best interest, this coalition backed political candidates who favored moderate reforms that did not substantially threaten existing class arrangements. Supported by a middle class acting from a variety of motives—economic self-interest, genuine religious and humanitarian concern for economic and social justice, desire for social control of the lower classes—these progressive politicians challenged the more demagogic representatives of poor whites as well as the conservative Bourbons who had dominated the years after Reconstruction. The most advanced reformers endorsed woman suffrage, built settlement houses, favored labor reform, and even organized an interracial movement designed to reduce racial tensions. Their hegemony temporarily broken, conservative landowners and industrialists waited for the reform mood to pass. Their wait was not long.

Progressive Era reforms were moderate and often assisted businessmen as much as or more than workers. Disillusioned by the betrayal of politicians whom they elected, by the impotence of their labor unions, and by worsening agricultural and manufacturing conditions in the 1920s, poor whites often directed their frustrations at helpless blacks. The very reform mood that had brought modest progress for whites resulted in worsened conditions for blacks. The American Federation of Labor acquiesced in the exclusion of blacks for skilled jobs. Black workers, abandoned by organized labor and by their white coworkers, became understandably cynical. They desperately sought any jobs available, even if the work involved acting as strikebreakers. Natural economic hostility between workers competing for the same jobs was compounded by racial animosity, making the years from 1880 to 1930 the most racially violent in American history. Lynchings, labor violence between strikers and "scabs," and pitched battles between whites and blacks spread across the region. The ideal of working-class solidarity became a mockery in a world where color of skin obscured all other considerations.

Impact of the Great Depression and the New Deal. The maelstrom of the Depression both heightened class divisions and introduced important new elements into southern life. The steady deterioration of agricultural conditions during the 1920s drove many blacks off the land and more and more whites into tenancy. During the 15 years from 1920 to 1935, the number of white tenant families increased by 300,000, whereas the number of black families in similar circumstances declined by 70,000. Of the South's 1,831,000 tenant families in 1935, nearly two-thirds were white. In Mississippi nearly half the state's total population lived as tenants. Layoffs, wage reductions, and stretch-outs propelled textile workers and coal miners into a wave of strikes beginning in 1929. The most famous of these disruptions, the textile strike in Gastonia, N.C., and the miners' strike in Harlan County, Ky., involved communist organizers and unions, to which workers turned when more conservative unions either deserted them or proved ineffectual. Such actions by white workers who were often among the most religious and traditional people in their communities constituted less a proletarian uprising than a desperate outburst against a society that neither understood nor very much cared for the plight of its lower class.

Although it made few converts, the Communist Party established a southern headquarters in Birmingham and even published the *Southern Worker*. It dared to challenge the South's racial taboos by defending nine black boys unjustly accused of raping two white women on a train near Scottsboro, Ala. It also organized a small sharecroppers' union among black tenants south of Birmingham and gained a foothold in the Mine, Mill, and Smelter Workers Union, which organized Birmingham area iron ore miners of both races.

In the Arkansas Delta, H. L. Mitchell, J. R. Butler, and E. B. McKinney began the Southern Tenant Farmers' Union (STFU) in 1934. A biracial union that enrolled both former white Klansmen and blacks, the STFU attracted national attention and challenged New Deal agricultural policies. Although New Deal reforms were well intentioned, powerful forces in the Farm Bureau, the state agricultural extension agencies, and the U.S. Department of Agriculture administered policies in such a way that most benefits went to landowners who were encouraged to reduce acreage and thereby dislocate thousands of tenants. The extent of such dislocation is uncertain, but early Roosevelt policies obviously did little to improve agricultural conditions among tenant farmers.

Rural rehabilitation through the Resettlement Administration provided temporary assistance, as did state relief administrations that created jobs for the unemployed. Some workers were hired to build new subsistence communities where hard-hit industrial workers could farm small plots and live in decent housing.

The boldest New Deal initiative came in 1937 with the passage of the Bankhead-Jones Farm Tenancy Act. Delayed for two years by Roosevelt's ambivalence and emasculated by intensive conservative opposition, the act provided modest loans to tenants for equipment and seeds. Unfortunately, the most visionary element, federal loans to tenants so they could purchase their own land, was so underfunded and selectively administered that only the most successful, responsible, and promising tenants received loans. Among the millions of southern tenants, only a tiny fraction received land purchase loans, and in the 1940s even this modest effort was destroyed by a conservative Congress.

Other attempts to help were more successful. An internal division within the labor movement and a national administration sympathetic to organized labor created new opportunities for workers. Already aided by New Deal minimum wage legislation, southern workers drew the attention of the Congress of Industrial Organizations (CIO). The CIO attempted to organize all workers within an industry rather than dividing them according to crafts or skills. Its commitment to biracial unions and flirtation with left-wing politics caused middle- and upper-class southerners to brand it a communist threat to southern institutions. It sent organizers south and trained southern workers, especially at the Highlander Folk School in Tennessee. The result was fierce and often violent struggles to organize Birmingham iron and steel workers, rubber workers in Gadsden, Ala., and textile operatives across the South. Thanks to national publicity and timely help from the federal government, some of these efforts were successful, though the attempt to organize the textile industry was a notable exception.

The descent of many middle-class people into poverty provided tenant farmers and industrial workers with welcome allies. People who had never before faced real want suddenly found themselves quite as helpless as the poorest sharecropper, without job, food, or home. The New Deal provided employment, and frightened middle-class folk joined their impoverished neighbors to elect New Deal congressmen. Conservatives retained enough power to make southern congressmen the least loyal of Democrats to the New Deal, but FDR found the general population of no other region of America more receptive to his programs. Downplaying race and emphasizing economic reforms for all, Roosevelt won the South's affection.

Support for Roosevelt and the New Deal brought together liberals from throughout the region. Liberals, including CIO organizers, state Democratic leaders, social workers, ministers, college professors, and reform journalists, tried to solidify their gains through organizations such as the Southern Conference for Human Welfare. New Democratic leaders, often with strong religious backgrounds, such as Olin Johnson in South Carolina, Brooks Hays in Arkansas, and Hugo Black in Alabama, combined white and black, middle- and lower-class support to win office. Unlike earlier candidates elected by poor whites, these men actually advocated significant reform programs in state houses and in Congress.

Impact of World War II. Owing both to reforms and to the location of military bases and war industry in the South between 1940 and 1945, unprecedented changes swept through the region. The rate of tenancy, especially among whites, declined as industrial jobs lured tenants off the land. Union strength and federal law raised industrial wages to the point that coal miners and steel workers earned more than schoolteachers and could no longer be categorized as poor whites. Increasingly comfortable in lower-middle-class suburbs or in their own houses newly purchased from mine or mill, they soon forgot about the people left behind. When black outrage erupted among returning Negro servicemen encountering the old racial barriers, such people often became the worst and most violent opponents of change. Shrewd conservative leaders from affluent backgrounds did nothing to prevent such conflict and often fueled it, dividing unions along racial lines and defeating liberal politicians by shackling them with charges of "nigger lovers" or "communists."

Turmoil also occurred within the black community. Older, traditional black elites had coexisted with racism in uneasy but practical compromise. Conservative, upper-class whites had tried to restrain lower-class violence, and blacks had sought economic opportunity without threatening to disturb social inequality. But the small black middle class of teachers, ministers, businessmen, and small-farm owners was swept aside by angry urban residents. The most liberal of the older professional classes, especially ministers, teachers, and labor leaders, provided articulate and courageous leadership, and the modern civil rights movement was born.

Threatened as it was by the aspirations of blacks, the white lower middle class reacted stridently. Rallying to the leadership of conservative politicians who threatened to close integrated public schools or interpose the state between white citizens and unpopular Supreme Court rulings, it posed a primary barrier to implementation of desegregation. As the years passed and black boycotts of businesses and passive disobedience disrupted one community after another, many merchants, newspaper publishers, and business leaders bowed

Mechanic at work, Knoxville, Tenn., 1943 (Esther Bubley, photographer, Library of Congress [LC-USW-3-38103E])

to the inevitable and accepted black demands. But this only unleashed some poor and lower-middle-class whites to a frenzy of violence.

They accepted the leadership of conservative business people when it was available, but angry white workers found their favorite spokesman in the self-proclaimed populist George C. Wallace of Alabama. Combining a frankly racist rhetoric with a prounion advocacy of the "little man," Wallace proved to be the shrewdest and most enduring southern politician since Louisiana's Huey Long. Although repudiated by AFL-CIO leadership, Wallace remained popular among the white rank and file, especially in the building trades. Capable of changing positions according to altered circumstances, he even survived the racist politics of the 1960s and 1970s, and won the governorship of Alabama in 1982 by class appeals to a biracial constituency of black and white workers and farmers in a state with the nation's second highest rate of unemployment.

Nearly forgotten in the giddy affluence of the war years and after was another South that profited little from the currents of change sweeping south of the Potomac. The mountains of Appalachia proved too stout and high a barrier. Of course, changes did occur, particularly in the valleys of the Tennessee River watershed where government dams and cheap power fueled an economic miracle. But higher in the mountains and up the remote hollows poverty persisted. Among a people of immense pride, independence, fierce family loyalty, fatalism, and rich cultural heritage, the new era intensified problems. Technological change in the coal mining industry cost the region 265,000 jobs in just nine years between 1950 and 1959. In some eastern Kentucky counties three of every four miners lost their jobs. In the entire Appalachian region, more than 600,000 jobs were lost in mining and farming during this one decade. Internal migration seemed the only solution, and more than 2 million people left the southern highlands for industrial cities between 1940 and 1970. There they carved out ethnic enclaves, established their own storefront churches, and retained their distinctive culture. Stereotyped by local media and citizens, they suffered as badly at the hands of blatant bigots or misguided reformers as blacks had before them. Cynical and bitter, longing for old places and ways, they persisted in their subculture with rare tenacity.

Whatever their woes, migrants were better off than the folks they left behind. Within 340 Appalachian counties in 1960, one of every three families lived on an annual income of less than $3,000; of those over 25 years of age, only 32 of 100 had finished high school. In Kentucky 20 percent of the population was eligible for surplus federal food.

The Appalachian Development Program, the Job Corps, and President Lyndon B. Johnson's War on Poverty made some progress toward resolving the South's enduring poverty. At first, middle-class southerners provided lukewarm support for such initiatives, though even this reservoir of goodwill began to run thin as escalating expenditures and black participation cost the Kennedy-Johnson programs many white allies.

Paradoxically, the success of federal programs and private economic investment swelled the middle and upper classes and reduced concern for the people who remained behind. Even status-conscious, upwardly mobile blacks tended to desert old neighborhoods, churches, and institutions in search of newer and more prestigious environments. For those trapped down the lonely dirt roads or in the urban shacks, life still seemed hard indeed.

The Modern South since World War II. In many ways the South after 1945 converged with the nation. Following the war, race—the single most distinctive social relationship defining the region for more than three centuries—quickly emerged as the nation's most significant economic, legal, moral, political, and social dilemma. As the civil rights movement redefined every aspect of southern life, it also brought the region more fully into the national mainstream. Southern exceptionalism declined as the North coped with its own racial problems, and hostility toward the South waned as apartheid receded. The Republican Party began a passionate courtship of the region that culminated in marriage. The white South, without ever substantially modifying its political or cultural conservatism, nevertheless switched political allegiances, becoming the GOP's chief bastion. And the black South, now politically empowered and mobilized, became the most reliable ally of the national Democratic Party.

Sunbelt prosperity for the first time since the Civil War led not only to a net in-migration of African Americans but to continued low taxes, anti-unionism, and a "favorable business climate," which appealed to conservative northern and overseas corporations as well as to Rust Belt retirees. Per capita income as a percentage of the national average rose in every southern state. The two largest high-tech research centers in America sprouted up in the research triangle linking Raleigh–Chapel Hill–Durham, N.C., and in Huntsville, Ala. Mechanization of agriculture transformed thousands of family farms into giant agribusinesses. Displaced rural blacks spread their poverty to southern and northern cities. Slightly better-off rural whites bought pickup trucks and headed for blue-collar jobs in adjacent cities.

Growing prosperity, urbanization, and immigration (including large numbers of Latinos by century's end) changed entrenched social patterns. Palm Beach, Broward, and Dade counties in Florida became home to nearly 650,000 Jewish residents by the end of the 20th century (the second largest concentration outside New York City). The South's percentage of Catholic residents doubled. Mormon, Moslem, Buddhist, and Hindu worship centers tracked other immigrants.

Perhaps the greatest effect of these changes fell on the white middle class. Sociologist John Shelton Reed emerged as the best and most prolific interpreter of this burgeoning sector of the South's population. Finding evidence for both southern convergence and continuing exceptionalism, Reed focused on the iconic rituals and institutions taking form: new golf clubs and gated communities, beach condos, *Southern Living* magazine, regional foodways, changing cultural patterns, even unique depictions of southern coeds who posed for *Playboy* magazine. His social typology ("southern folk, plain and fancy" as he described them) became a classic. Reed's prolific scholarship represented both the widening and the deepening of scholarly attention to southern class relationships following the war. Once dominated by sociologists, economists, and historians of class conflict, new generations began to study the more intricate and complex social intersections of health, professionalism, religion, gender, music, folklife, and sport.

Health remained an intractable problem long after racial distinctions declined. Earlier in the South's history, hookworm and pellagra attracted attention. By century's end, rates of maternal and infant mortality, obesity, diabetes, sickle cell anemia, stroke, heart attack, and cancer took center stage. In the 1980s the American Cancer Society began to study elevated rates of cancer morbidity as an ethnic problem. But it soon became obvious to researchers that high rates of mortality from the disease owed more to poverty than to ethnicity. The South's abnormally high incidence of black and white poverty accounted for most of these heightened risks: unhealthy diet; religious fatalism; lack of health insurance; absence of health care professionals in poor, rural counties; late diagnosis; poor education.

Even the professional training of teachers, health professionals, and social workers magnified class differences. Professionals were drawn mainly from middle-class families with little understanding of the people at the bottom of the socioeconomic ladder. Often patronizing in their interactions with the poor, many professionals became more agents of social control than of empowerment. They also treated symptoms more than they sought to change the structural barriers constructed by affluent and powerful people to protect their wealth, property, and social standing.

Women's studies noted that southern females bonded in some ways across class and racial boundaries, whereas on other issues (civil rights notably) they continued to divide along caste and economic lines. Middle-class women both black and white sought out churches and social clubs reflecting their own economic and social mobility. Even when they were not able to pass into higher echelons of social status, they could at least separate themselves from the clamoring throngs beneath.

Similar differentiation occurred among males where masculine identity within class and racial categories changed considerably. As men abandoned jobs that paid too little to support their families, women often took their places. Conversely, when salaries in predominantly female occupations (schoolteachers, music and educational ministers in churches, nurses) began to rise, men often replaced women or at least carved out significant male enclaves. Male affinity for religion often depended on whether ministers proclaimed and organized their church programs around softer, more communal aspects of Christianity or tougher, more competitive, masculine themes. "Rednecks" and "good old boys" (working-class and rural white males) once were the subject of negative outsider stereotyping and ridicule. By end of century they relished the stereotypes, which were celebrated in numerous television sit-coms, Hollywood movies, and even presidential campaigns.

Country music—a characteristic component of white, male, working-class culture—found a place not only in the hearts of its partisans but also in the literature of cultural historians and folklorists. If one traveled from east coast to west, from Canada to Mexico, the unifying radio format seemed to be either National Public Radio for the effete and educated or country music for the common man and woman. In ways profoundly important, the folk religion, music, and art of the South's common people reached an audience substantially beyond the region that birthed it once the negative yoke of racism slipped a bit.

The same could be said of sport. Stock car racing, particularly its slick commercial manifestation in NASCAR, transcended its southern origins and working-class white audience to establish beachheads in all regions. Racial integration of southern college football and basketball teams turned the Southeastern Conference (SEC) into an athletic juggernaut. SEC schools might treat graduation rates and NCAA compliance rules casually, but they warred in earnest on gridiron and hardwood, dominating major college athletics (they also hastened interregional migration by enlarging their recruiting base nationwide).

Virtually no southern social institution escaped racial change and economic modernization. And by the 21st century the region's class system worked pretty much as the nation's did, despite occasional reminders of a more painful past.

J. WAYNE FLYNT
Auburn University

SOCIAL CLASS IN THE AMERICAN SOUTH
SOCIOLOGICAL PERSPECTIVES

Scholarly inquiry into the history and culture of the American South has centered squarely on race: narratives of racial exploitation, oppression, and redemptive collective action generally trump those of social class. So deeply ingrained is the South = Race identity, for example, that the true title of the 1963 March on Washington, "The March on Washington for Jobs and Freedom," with its explicit economic trajectory, has been effectively forgotten. The reasons for all of this are easy enough to understand. The region's racial regimes, whether that of slavery or Jim Crow, were understood to be different from how race was handled in other parts of America—codified in law, harsher, and more bloodthirsty. And the workings of race distorted the South's institutions and cultural patterns, resulting in retarded urbanization and industrial patterns, a subsequent lack of economic opportunity, undemocratic one-party politics largely devoid of class dynamics, and ethnic homogeneity among whites. Thus, race was the basis of "the South" as a distinct social formation that had begun to take shape in the 18th and 19th centuries.

Moving into the 21st century, race remains the root of black and white southerners' personal and group identities. It has channeled their ambitions for themselves and their children; it shapes their patterns of sociability, mating rituals, and places of residence; it has defined their "duty," their moral sensibilities, and their legal and cultural place; and it has privileged whiteness with a degree of political presence, economic advantage, and honorific obeisance unparalleled by all else that socially constituted women and men in the South. Race was the primary prism through which southerners saw and understood their world, the ground on which they walked, the air they breathed. Past, present, and possibility are all interwoven with race, and all are interpreted, vitally if not exclusively, in racial terms. In a culture such as the American South, one premised on and organized by racial meanings and practices, one in which literally no facet of human existence escaped profound racial coloration, explanation, and trajectory—be it religion, economics, gender roles, popular culture, or politics—race seemed the key to unlocking the enigma that was the South, its central theme and master narrative. Race even, it was thought, explained the region's peculiar class structure, relations, and conflicts: poor and working-class whites continually put their racial interests, which were generously served by institutionalized white supremacy, ahead of their class interests in economic and political action, and so were usually unwilling to join their even more impoverished African American brothers and sisters in a sustained cross-racial alliance of the economic have-nots. Racial solidarity defeated class solidarity every time.

Scholars of the South, social scientists especially, have tended to view class and race as analytical categories fixed in meaning and defined in such a way to be directly mapped onto, or directly extracted from, social structure. Understanding each of the categories thusly, the penchant of many South-watchers has been to try parcel out the independent effects of race and class and attribute causal primacy and "relative explanatory importance" to one or the other. And in this scholarly contest, class has almost always lost.

As both the many essays in this volume and Wayne Flynt's historical overview make clear, however, the American South has always been a class society and its history has always been made and expressed, at least in part, through the relations, tensions, and compromises within, between, and among the region's various classes. There is precious little in the experience of southerners that is not importantly touched, to one degree or another, by social class. Race and class, conjoined in a plantation system of production, are responsible for the colonial South's very existence, first through indentured servitude and then through racial slavery. Slavery's defense also entailed the melding of class and race. So deeply had antebellum white southerners internalized America's self-idealization as land of freedom and equality, for example, that slavery—incontrovertibly a class system of enormous economic and power differentials—was understood by its defenders and critics alike in racial rather than class terms. Organizations built around class grievances and interests—labor unions, for example, or the local Chamber of Commerce—obviously owe their very existence to class awareness and inequalities. Educational, occupational, and economic opportunities and circumstances, of course, are powerfully affected by the class positions southerners occupy, as are their opinions about equality and inequality. So, too, though, are sexual relations; the use of leisure time and recreation preferences; attitudes toward war, race, foreign aid, abortion, and national priorities; understandings of the proper role of women; health; family patterns; religiosity; music tastes; political action; and much, much more. Trying to make sense of the region without recourse to some form of class analysis therefore is as impossible as is trying to understand it without using the notion of race or, and as the scholarship of the past few decades has revealed, gender as well. The analytical difficulty for observers of the region, then, is to bring class, gender, and race together in a coherent interpretive frame—that is, to make gender and race work *with* rather than *against* class—that permits a deeper and more thorough comprehension of southern history and culture.

The anthropologist Marshall Sahlins has noted that "people act upon their circumstances according to their own cultural presuppositions, the socially given categories of persons and things." In the South, these "socially given categories of persons" surely included race and gender, as well as class. Beginning well before the publication of the original *Encyclopedia of Southern Culture* in 1989, and most certainly intensifying since, scholars have increasingly turned from debating the finer points of Marxian and Weberian theories of social inequality to conceptualizing class, race, and gender as articulations of status, privilege, power, and cultural difference that are (a) historicized as materially and symbolically inscribed sets of impositions, practices, and personal and collective identities and meanings; (b) simultaneously constitutive of and constituted by social relations and institutional arrangements; and (c) subject to contestation, redefinition, and change. Each analytical category or status marker thus molds self-conceptions (as "female" or "male," as "worker" or "manager," as "black" or "white"), structures relationships and therefore institutions, permeates understandings of group interests and grievances, and normatively empowers or constrain action. In placing each of the three categories on an equal analytical plane, so to speak, this conceptual reformulation, in turn, has pushed scholars away from questions about the relative import of class versus racial or gender oppression, or about whether racism, sexism, or class exploitation "really" drove southern history. They increasingly ask, instead, how gender, class, and race in the South were (and likely continue to be) so interpenetrated in appreciation, meaning, and signification—so fused, in a word—that attempts to disentangle them may be impossible and that efforts to subsume one form of oppression (class, say, or gender) under another (say, race) is fruitless.

Social inequalities in the region, of which class inequalities are one form, are now being studied in an analytical frame that takes as given the power of this fusion of identity, interests, and position to mold consciousness, action, and the social organization of institutional life. Research emphasis, correspondingly, has shifted from efforts to parcel out the unique effects of race and class (and, again, we would add gender) to understanding and explaining their interpenetration in specific historical circumstances, to why and how they fused as they did, and to the consequences of this. By asking such questions as how gender practices were expressed and conveyed in class and racial interests, for example, or how class was experienced in gendered and racial forms, or how gender and racial grievances derived from both work and nonwork settings could be addressed through class organizations such as unions, or how class conflict between and among whites was displaced onto and at the expense of African Americans, scholars have offered innovative, intellectually productive interpretations of regional patterns ranging from racially discriminatory actions against African American steel workers in Birmingham in the 1940s to the defeat of crucial aspects of the War on Poverty in the 1960s, from the lynching of Leo Frank in 1915 and opposition to lynching by middle- and upper-class white women throughout the region in the 1920s and 1930s to the organization and subsequent disorganization of black, female tobacco workers in North Carolina in the late 1940s and early 1950s and the use of gender stereotypes, particularly female stereotypes, as a working-class strategy during militant union organizing drives in the mountains of east Tennessee during the Depression.

Future scholarship on the region is likely to extend these "fusionist" analytical impulses by bringing in both religion and ethnicity and interrogating them about how their historically shifting meanings and unfoldings are woven into gender, class, and race and about how they are expressed through the language of class, race, or gender. Such scholarship may at times be inelegant, messy, and, doubtlessly, almost always complex. If so, it will well mirror the region it attempts to comprehend.

In his historical overview, Wayne Flynt rightly notes that Marxist approaches to social class, assuming as they do the inevitability of conflict between two great classes with irreconcilably inimical economic interests, have been scorned in the South (and, we would add, in the United States generally) both by analysts and by everyday southerners, whatever their class or status position. No doubt the main reason for this attitude is that Marxism has been both fatally tainted by its association with socialism and communism, "isms" that most Americans have long rejected as un-American, and further discredited by the abject failure of the communist project in Eastern Europe.

There is, however, another, more pragmatic reason for its disuse in much scholarship (although one perhaps not entirely unrelated to a generalized abhorrence of Marxist thought). State, local, and federal governments do not use Marxist categories, such as "capitalist," "bourgeoisie," and "proletariat," when collecting information about precisely how people make their living, about their economic circumstances, or about their relationship to what Marxists call the means and forces of production. With few exceptions, the official data that are collected and organized by U.S. governments at all levels, instead, have a broadly (if implicit) Weberian logic because the categories assessing the extent of socioeconomic inequality are anchored in status, prestige, skill, and income differences, often in such a way that these differences are represented as steps on a ladderlike hierarchal continuum, with many finely distinguished rungs situated close together rather than as a structure with a few distinct, even opposing, social groupings. New classification schemes for industrial and occupational titles inaugurated by the Census Bureau in the last 20 to 30 years, as well as actual shifts in the organization and nature of work, moreover, partially obscure the traditional manual-nonmanual, blue-collar–white-collar occupational differences often used in past research as a proxy for social class. Social surveys and public-opinion polls permit greater flexibility on this score, primarily because some of the most widely used surveys assess class awareness, consciousness, interests, and identity, but generally they, too, downplay explicit Marxist imagery in their questions and in how responses are categorized.

None of this is to suggest that studying social class with census-type information or survey or polling data is impossible. But it does imply that what can be learned with such data, particularly census data, is limited and, in a precise sense, biased toward Weberian rather Marxian forms of explorations and explanations. Owing to these conceptual and methodological difficulties, as well as to the complexities induced by race and gender noted earlier, there are no simple answers to such questions as What was/is the profile of the southern class structure? or How many classes were/are there in region? or What have been/are the consequences and correlates of class inequalities? Still, as many of the contributions to this volume effectively attest, analysis of survey and U.S. Census data can richly inform our understanding of southerners' objective socioeconomic circumstances, their subjective understandings of their place and class position in society, and the relationship between the two.

Shaping the Southern Class Structure. Among the many forces that have structured the region's class relations and dynamics, six are particularly significant because of their sweeping historical scope and far-reaching significance in shaping the region's contemporary labor force. Both their consequences for social classes (e.g., for class formation, consciousness, actions) and how they mediate the effects of class are multivalent, interdependent—sometimes working in complimentary ways, at other times working in contradictory ways—and usually spatially and temporally uneven.

Industrialization. The first factor of import, and one permitting much that followed, is industrial diversification, notably a profound shift from agriculture to, first, manufacturing and, more recently, to service-sector industries. Nothing so distinguished North from South, or so thoroughly dominated

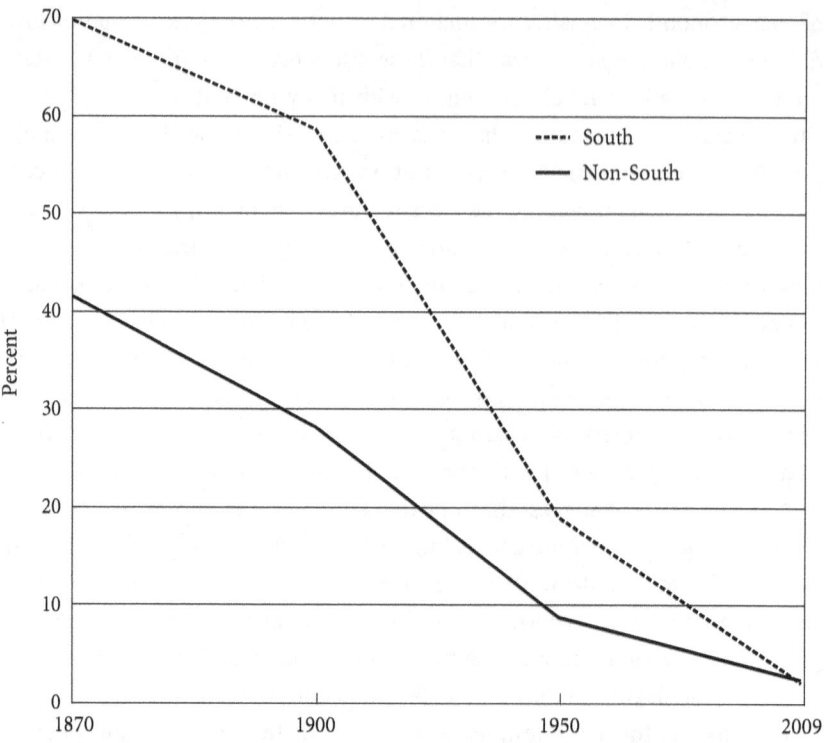

FIGURE 1. Agricultural employment as percentage of civilian labor force in the U.S. South, 1870–2009.
Source: Analysis of U.S. Census data available from Steven D. Ruggles, J. Trent Alexander, Katie Genadek, Ronald Goeken, Matthew B. Schroeder, and Matthew Sobek, Integrated Public Use Microdata Series: Version 5.0 [Machine-readable database] (Minneapolis: University of Minnesota, 2010).

southern life for so long, as did the region's commitment to agriculture, particularly the production of such staple crops as cotton, tobacco, sugar, and rice. Out of 10 southerners in the labor force in 1870, seven were in agriculture (see Figure 1), and almost 60 percent continued to be so employed in 1900: at that time, 38 percent of employed southern whites were farm owners, tenants, or managers, and another 18 percent were farm workers of one sort or another. Comparable statistics for African Americans in the region were 25 and 32 percent, respectively. Agrarian life was experienced by many whites and most African Americans as sharecropping, a form of tenancy that frequently left croppers debt ridden, impoverished, and without trade-union bargaining rights or political voice. Fifty years later, in 1950, more than 40 percent of Mississippi's labor force was still rooted directly in agriculture. The statistic for the

South as a whole was 19 percent (9 percent in the North). Yet by 2009, only 2 percent of the region's workers were engaged in agriculture, a slightly smaller proportion than stamped the non-South. At that time, Mississippi had proportionately fewer farmers and farm workers than Minnesota.

Education. Second is the gradual increase in the literacy and educational attainment of southerners of all races, with African Americans and other peoples of color, though on the whole still less credentialed than whites, enjoying especially rapid gains. Education is a crucial indicator of social class and is, itself, heavily conditioned by the class position of an individual's family of origin: it is, for example, the best single expression of cultural capital (essentially competitively advantageous values, dispositions, knowledge, presentational and linguistic styles, and behavioral routines) — and a major determinant, through both skill enhancement and credentials, of other dimensions of class, most particularly occupational placement and income attainment. In 1870 a quarter of whites, and more than 85 percent of black southerners, were unable to read, or to write, or were completely illiterate (see Figure 2). That African Americans throughout the South were at that time largely illiterate is of course a direct consequence of the slave owners' opposition to the education of their enslaved populations. Literacy was more pervasive in the non-South. By 1930, the last year literacy data were collected by the U.S. Census, virtually all whites in both regions and African Americans in the North were functionally literate; 20 percent of southern blacks, however, remained illiterate.

Segregated education, inferior schools, and governments' poor enforcement of compulsory education laws (all southern states had such laws, at least nominally, by 1918) continued to take their toll on African Americans' educational attainment in the South (see Figure 3). In 1960, for example, 48 percent of blacks (and 40 percent of members of "other," mostly Asian and American Indian, races) had completed less than six years of formal schooling, while fewer than 5 percent had any college education. Comparable statistics for southern whites were 27 and 14 percent, respectively. Northerners of all races in 1960 still benefited from an appreciable education advantage, but a half century of steady gains in the South has largely eliminated that regional (but not racial) imbalance.

Occupational Shifts. Occupational differentiation (rooted, again, in the movement of capital and labor out of agriculture and into other economic sectors) and occupational upgrading — that is, the growth of managerial, professional, and technical jobs that require more education, are (by most but not all standards) more skilled, and are certainly more prestigious and better paying than most jobs in the past — is the third important element molding contempo-

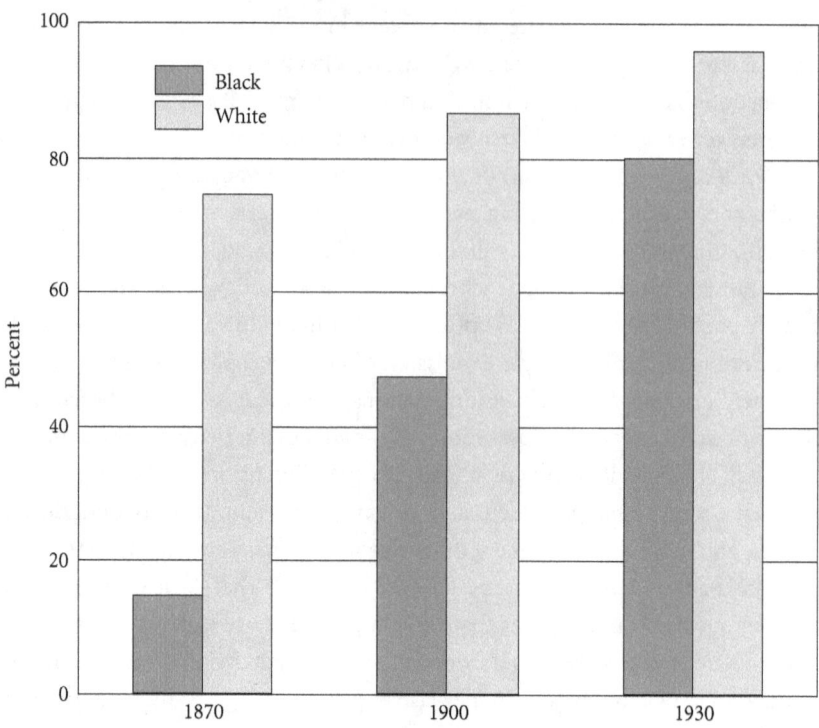

FIGURE 2. Literacy rates in the U.S. South, 1870–1930.
Source: Analysis of U.S. Census data available from Steven D. Ruggles, J. Trent Alexander, Katie Genadek, Ronald Goeken, Matthew B. Schroeder, and Matthew Sobek, Integrated Public Use Microdata Series: Version 5.0 [Machine-readable database] (Minneapolis: University of Minnesota, 2010).

rary class relations. Almost 30 percent all southerners in the labor force in 2009 were either professionals or managers-administrators (see Figure 4). In 1870 fewer than 5 percent were in either occupational group, even using antiquated, overly generous occupational classifications. The 2009 statistics, moreover, almost perfectly mirror the presence of these high-status jobs in the North. To be sure, there is considerable heterogeneity in the prestige and average earnings of the dozens of specific occupations labeled professional or managerial, and white males continue to be privileged in the positions they occupy within professional and managerial occupations. The South's African Americans and Latinos, especially, are underrepresented in higher-paying, more skilled jobs and overrepresented in occupations at the bottom of the occupational-status hierarchy. This is true as well for women of all races. Still, southerners of all races and in all states in the region have witnessed, if not equally, occupational

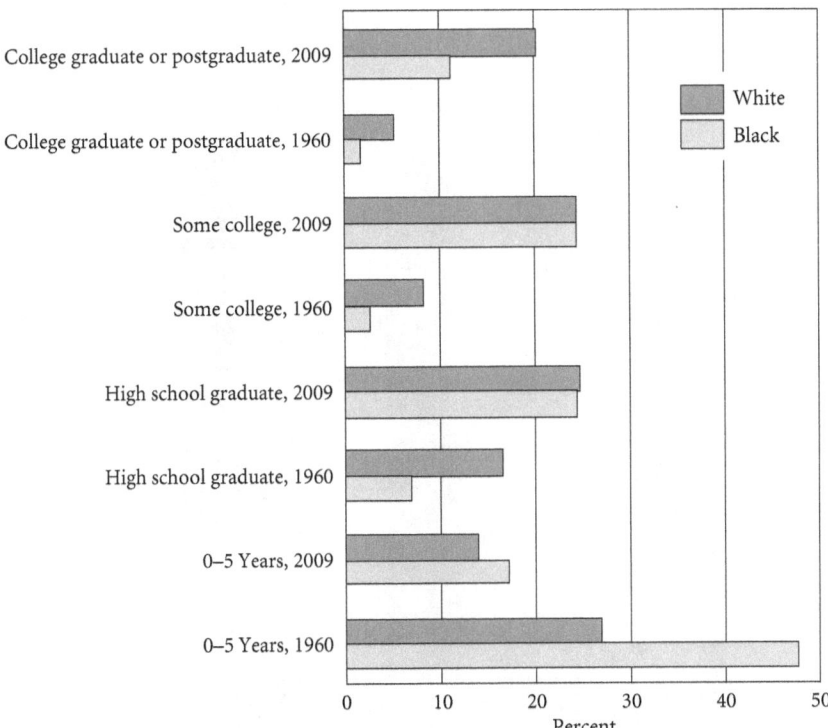

FIGURE 3. Educational attainment in the South, 1960–2009.
Note: Entries represent percentage of southerners at each educational level.
Source: Analysis of U.S. Census data available from Steven D. Ruggles, J. Trent Alexander, Katie Genadek, Ronald Goeken, Matthew B. Schroeder, and Matthew Sobek, Integrated Public Use Microdata Series: Version 5.0 [Machine-readable database] (Minneapolis: University of Minnesota, 2010).

upgrading: in 2009 the percentage of managers and professionals in the employed civilian labor force, for example, ranged from 32 in the South Atlantic states (e.g., Virginia) to 28 in the East South Central (e.g., Tennessee) to 29 in the West South Central (e.g., Texas).

Urbanization. Industrialization made occupational and education upgrading both possible and necessary. Occupational and education changes, in turn, were codetermining, each both contextualizing and spurring further change in the other: an increasingly literate and educated labor force induced the importation or indigenous development of more skill-intense jobs, and the availability of more skilled jobs, many with educational requirements for entry or advancement, pushed educational attainment or certification upward. All of these changes have transformed the South, steering it from an overwhelmingly

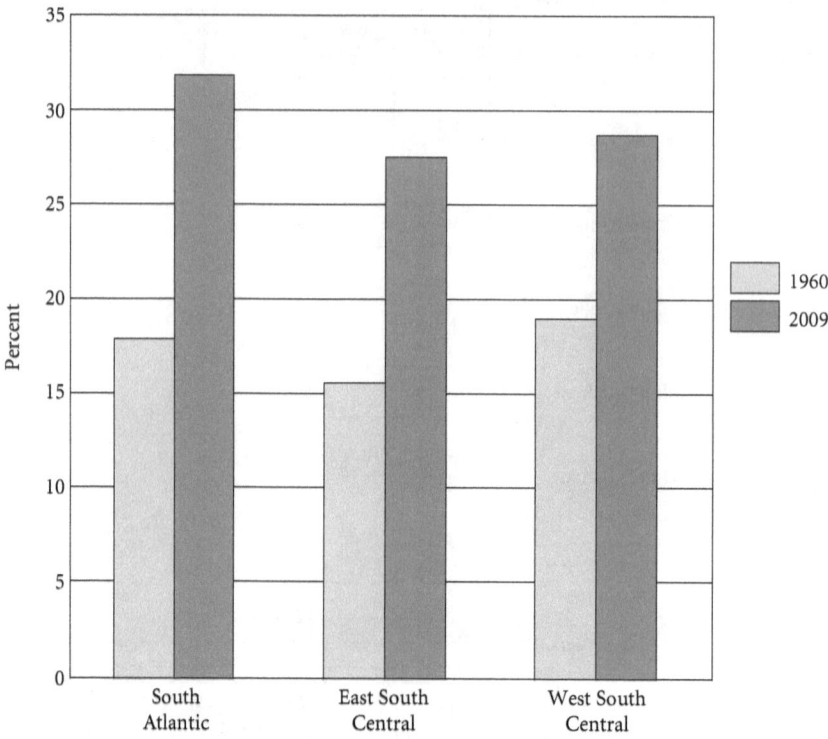

FIGURE 4. *Professional and managerial occupations in the U.S. South, 1960–2009.*
Note: Entries represent percentage of all employed southerners in professional and managerial occupations.
Source: Analysis of U.S. Census data available from Steven D. Ruggles, J. Trent Alexander, Katie Genadek, Ronald Goeken, Matthew B. Schroeder, and Matthew Sobek, Integrated Public Use Microdata Series: Version 5.0 [Machine-readable database] (Minneapolis: University of Minnesota, 2010).

rural, agrarian society to a largely urban one, a fourth change of huge significance. Not until 1910 did more than 10 percent of southerners reside in metropolitan areas (the non-South had reached that threshold by 1850). The South began to urbanize rapidly in the 1950s, and by 2009–10 approximately 82 percent of its population lived in metropolitan areas (compared to 86 percent in the non-South).

Civil Rights Movement of the 1950s and 1960s. Fifth is the success of the civil rights movement in removing many (but most emphatically not all) racist barriers to education, skill enhancement, employment, trade-union membership, and income generation, thereby allowing African Americans and other southerners of color to both contribute to and benefit from the educational, indus-

TABLE 1. *Occupational Segregation by Race, U.S. South, 1960–2009*

	1960	2009
Chief executives/public administrators	1.4	5.6
Civil engineers	1.2	7.5
Physicians	2.0	7.7
Registered nurses	8.6	14.6
Lawyers	2.3	7.4
Real estate salespersons	2.6	7.6
Payroll/timekeeping clerks	2.1	16.7
Bank tellers	~0	15
Electricians	2.0	9.6
Tool/die makers	<1	7.7
Butchers/meat cutters	10.3	20.2
Laundry workers	57.7	33.2
Construction workers	47.1	27.3
Average	18.8	17.7

Source: Analysis of GSS data from James A. Davis, James A., Tom W. Smith, and Peter V. Marsden, *General Social Surveys, 1972–2008* [Cumulative File] [Computer file], ICPSR04697-v4 (Storrs, Conn.: Roper Center for Public Opinion Research, University of Connecticut; Ann Arbor, Mich.: Inter-university Consortium for Political and Social Research [distributors], 2009-12-04). doi:10.3886/ICPSR04697

Note: Entries are percentage of the occupation that is African American. Only members of the employed civilian labor force (ECLF) are included in the analysis. The entry labeled "Average" indicates that 18.8% of the ECLF in 1960 was African American; in 2009, that statistic was 17.7%.

trial, and occupational changes of the past half century and to acquire considerable political clout, especially in the South's large cities and rural Black Belt. Table 1 shows one aspect of this process—occupational upgrading of African Americans since the civil rights era. Poverty rates for blacks, for example, were also much lower in 2009 than in 1960, though obviously much steeper than for whites even at the latter date (see Figure 5). Racial gaps persist into the second decade of the 21st century in all of the region's opportunity structures and reward hierarchies, however, particularly so in earnings and income at all levels of employment and of schooling (see Figure 6). But structural changes in the economy, enforcement of civil rights legislation and subsequent government racial policies, the now visibly fraying social safety net, and African American

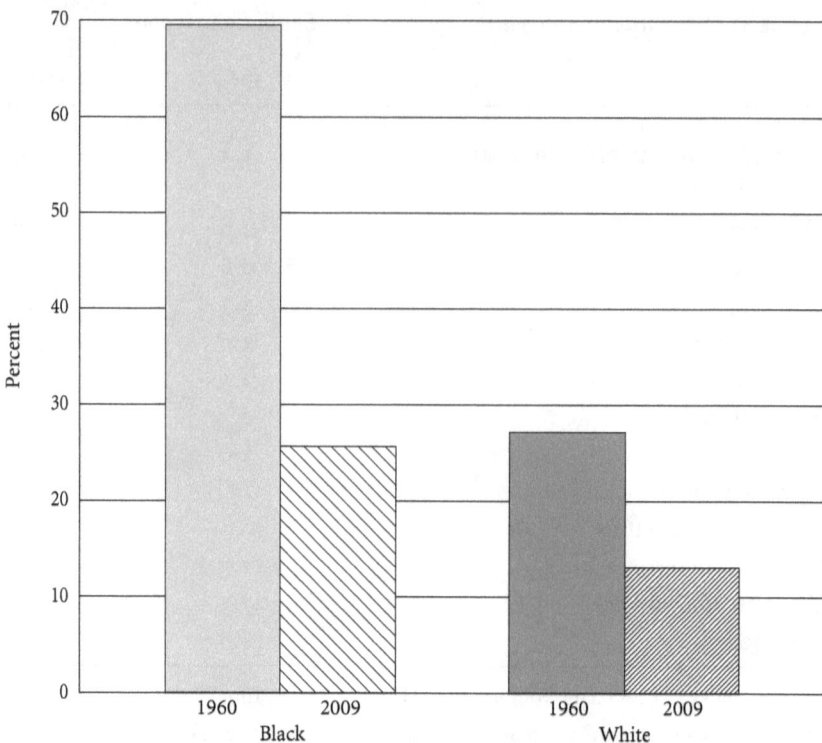

FIGURE 5. *Poverty in the U.S. South, 1960–2009.*
Note: Entries represent percentage of southerners below poverty line.
Source: Analysis of U.S. Census data available from Steven D. Ruggles, J. Trent Alexander, Katie Genadek, Ronald Goeken, Matthew B. Schroeder, and Matthew Sobek, Integrated Public Use Microdata Series: Version 5.0 [Machine-readable database] (Minneapolis: University of Minnesota, 2010).

agency have, together, resulted in both the growth of a large, educated black middle class and, particularly for this stratum, increasing socioeconomic opportunity and advancement. (Figures 7 and 8 demonstrate this for occupational placement more generally and reduced income disparities.) The contours of the class structures of whites and blacks are now broadly similar with a top, middle, and bottom, and, since the 1970s, African Americans share (if less efficaciously) the same routes of intergenerational class mobility long enjoyed by whites in the region, with education of paramount importance in this process.

Female Labor Force Participation. The sixth component of import is the soaring participation of women (especially white women) in the South's paid labor force, and the resulting gendered division of labor in the workplace, feminization of particular occupations, and continuing sex differences in overall

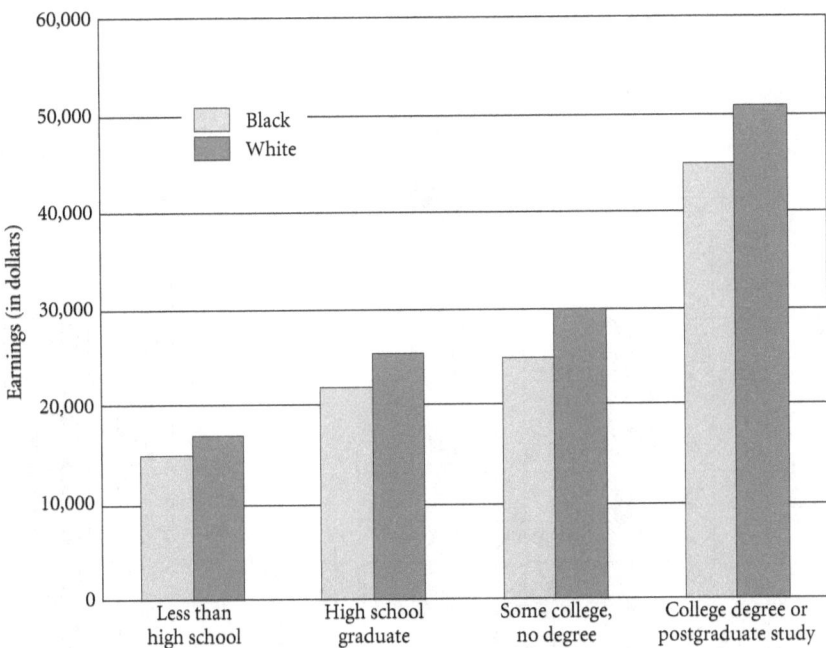

FIGURE 6. Median earnings by race and education in the U.S. South, 2009.
Note: Entries represent median earnings of the employed civilian labor force with positive earnings.
Source: Analysis of U.S. Census data available from Steven D. Ruggles, J. Trent Alexander, Katie Genadek, Ronald Goeken, Matthew B. Schroeder, and Matthew Sobek, Integrated Public Use Microdata Series: Version 5.0 [Machine-readable database] (Minneapolis: University of Minnesota, 2010).

compensation. In 1870 the labor force participation rate of the region's white women was roughly 7 (i.e., 7 percent of adult white women were either working for wages or looking for such work; see Figure 9); for African American women, it was 41. Almost a century later, in 1960, less than a third of eligible white women were in the labor force. By 2009, however, the labor force participation of white women in the South had increased sharply (with a rate of 57); the rate also increased for African American females, though less abruptly (64). (The comparable rates for African American and white males were 64 and 76, respectively.) Females constituted just less than half of both the South's and the non-South's employed civilian labor forces in 2009.

Participation hardly means equality, however. Even in 2009 the occupational structure remained heavily sex typed (see Figure 10), with certain occupations in the South (and throughout the nation), whether white- or blue-collar, seemingly the preserve of (often white) males (e.g., electrical engineers, fire fighters,

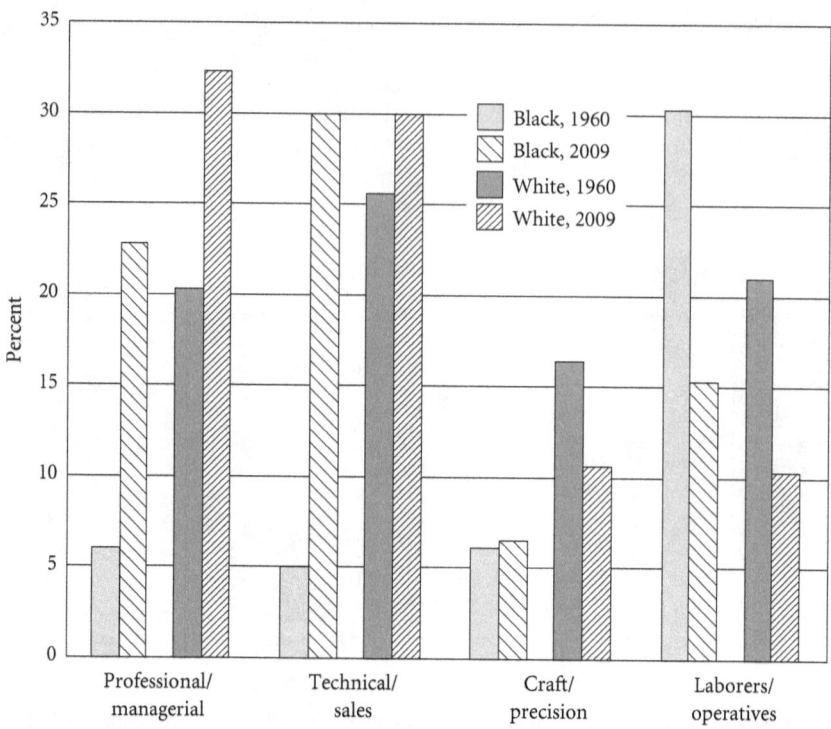

FIGURE 7. Race and occupational position in the U.S. South, 1960–2009.
Note: Entries represent percentage of southerners in selected occupations.
Source: Analysis of U.S. Census data available from Steven D. Ruggles, J. Trent Alexander, Katie Genadek, Ronald Goeken, Matthew B. Schroeder, and Matthew Sobek, Integrated Public Use Microdata Series: Version 5.0 [Machine-readable database] (Minneapolis: University of Minnesota, 2010).

machinists, and craft and precision workers generally), and others almost completely feminized (e.g., registered nurses, dietitians, secretaries, kindergarten or early school teachers). Occupational segregation and labor markets split by gender (and, as we have seen, by race as well)—whereby women and men (and blacks and whites) often do not work in, or compete for, the same jobs—in turn, translate into earnings inequalities. For every $100 white men who worked 40 hours or more per week earned in the South in 2009, comparably employed white females and African Americans of both sexes earned appreciably less—$74 for white women and black males and $64 for black females. (These ratios are based on the median earnings of full-time workers; use of mean earnings indicates greater racial and gender inequalities. Both sets of statistics are presented in Figure 11.) In no state or subregion in the South, in

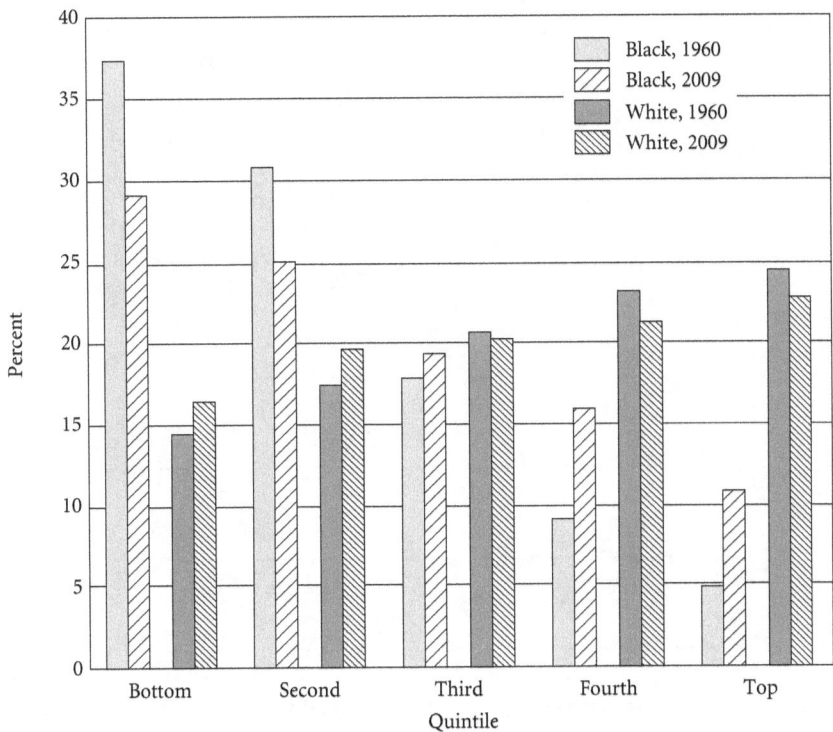

FIGURE 8. Distribution of income by race in the U.S. South, 1960–2009.
Note: Entries are percentage of southerners in each income quintile.
Source: Analysis of U.S. Census data available from Steven D. Ruggles, J. Trent Alexander, Katie Genadek, Ronald Goeken, Matthew B. Schroeder, and Matthew Sobek, Integrated Public Use Microdata Series: Version 5.0 [Machine-readable database] (Minneapolis: University of Minnesota, 2010).

fact, does gender or racial parity or even near parity in earnings exist. In this, unfortunately, the region is hardly alone: such inequalities continue to characterize the entire nation.

Reinforced by fundamental and (often closely related) political changes in the region, these trends, when taken together, have effectively eroded the material basis of southern exceptionalism and lifted the overall income level of southerners to near equality with the rest of the nation (see Figure 12). Two additional factors, more recent in occurrence and consequence, also bring North and South closer together. Suggesting the demographic and spatial limits of the educational and occupational upgrades that mark much of the South's labor force, deindustrialization and the loss of manufacturing jobs in both the metropolitan and the nonmetropolitan areas of the region have sev-

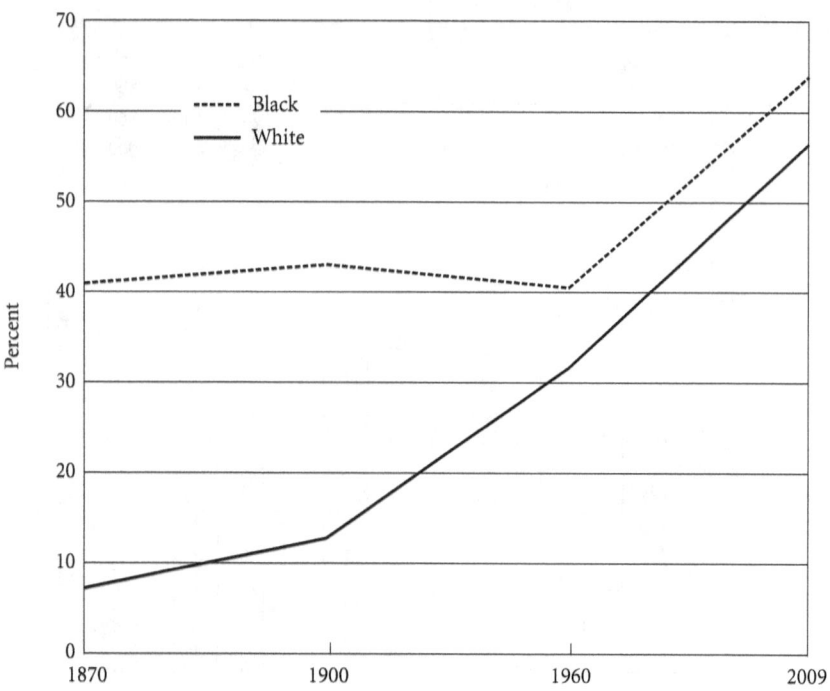

FIGURE 9. Female labor force participation in the U.S. South, 1870–2009.
Note: Entries represent percentage of adult women in the labor force.
Source: Analysis of U.S. Census data available from Steven D. Ruggles, J. Trent Alexander, Katie Genadek, Ronald Goeken, Matthew B. Schroeder, and Matthew Sobek, Integrated Public Use Microdata Series: Version 5.0 [Machine-readable database] (Minneapolis: University of Minnesota, 2010).

ered the ties many southerners had to meaningful work offering a living wage, further isolating and impoverishing them and their children. Additionally, the partial Latinization of the region's labor force, as millions of migrants from Mexico and points farther south moved into low-wage construction, landscaping, and other occupational niches, has destabilized traditional class and racial relations. Both trends are also national in scope. Unlike, say, in 1930, the South's class and status hierarchies, mobility patterns, and ways in which class "works"—at least as we can gauge them from available data—now look very much like what we know of the non-South.

Moving into the 21st century, wageworkers and salaried employees in the American South are, on the whole, increasingly urban, educated, skilled, and prosperous, but are also fragmented—divided by gender, race, ethnicity and national ancestry, documented and undocumented status, occupation, in-

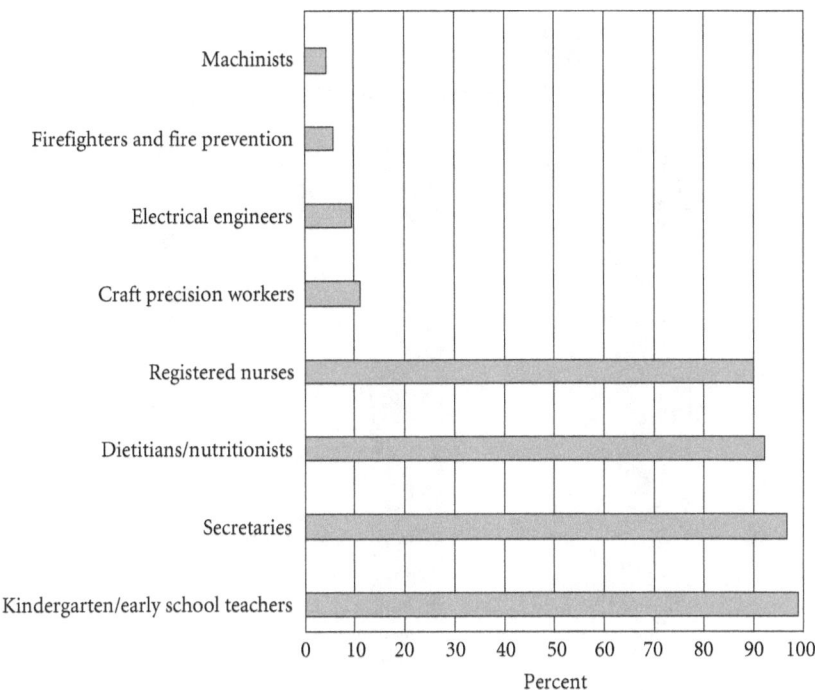

FIGURE 10. *Sex-typing of selected occupations in the U.S. South, 2009.*
Note: *Entries represent percentage of occupation employees who are female. Only members of the employed civilian labor force are included in the analysis.*
Source: *Analysis of U.S. Census data available from Steven D. Ruggles, J. Trent Alexander, Katie Genadek, Ronald Goeken, Matthew B. Schroeder, and Matthew Sobek,* Integrated Public Use Microdata Series: Version 5.0 *[Machine-readable database] (Minneapolis: University of Minnesota, 2010).*

dustry, and labor market (including access to work). Everything about social class in the region—exactly how it is expressed, how it is experienced, what it does to people, and its fissures and tensions—inevitably has been imprinted by both the trends that have shaped the South's modern labor force and the divisions in it. America's politicomythic self-image as egalitarian and the pervasiveness of the Horatio Alger or Log Cabin sensibility toward social mobility (i.e., opportunity + hard work = success) combine with the contemporary southerner's greater skill, enhanced opportunity, and material comfort, on the one hand, to dilute workers' solidarity, obscure class in its many guises, or, in collective understanding, render all southerners "middle class" and thereby essentially classless. On the other hand, some of these trends, such as industrialization and the entry of African Americans into skilled and semiskilled blue-

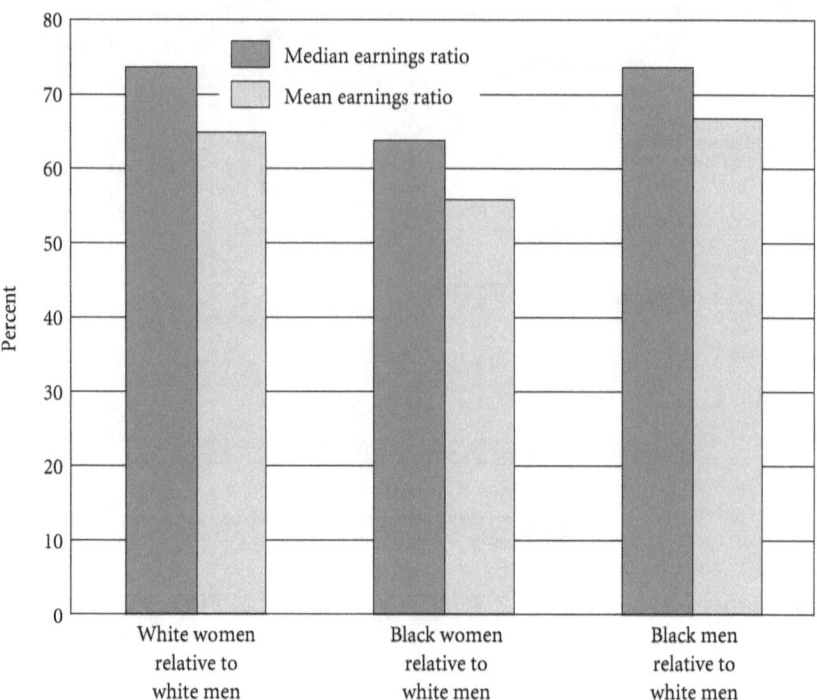

FIGURE 11. *Relative earnings of full-time wage and salary workers by race and sex in the U.S. South, 2009.*
Source: *Analysis of U.S. Census data available from Steven D. Ruggles, J. Trent Alexander, Katie Genadek, Ronald Goeken, Matthew B. Schroeder, and Matthew Sobek,* Integrated Public Use Microdata Series: Version 5.0 *[Machine-readable database] (Minneapolis: University of Minnesota, 2010).*

collar jobs, could spur heightened class and trade-union sensibilities. Additionally, both poverty rates and income inequality in southern states are still somewhat higher than in other regions. In 2009, 16 percent of southerners (and 26 percent of black southerners) were "officially" poor (see Figure 5), and, with income from all sources less than half the poverty level, 7 percent were "hyperpoor" (comparable statistics for the non-South were 13 percent and 6 percent). Poverty is considerably more prevalent in the lower South and in the Appalachian parts of the region than elsewhere in the region. Moreover, of the 15 states with the highest "top-to-bottom" income ratio in 2004–6 (i.e., the ratio of the average income of the top 20 percent of families in the income distribution to the average income of the bottom 20 percent of families), seven were southern. Of the 20 most unequal states by this measure, 11 were in the South. Alabama, with a top-to-bottom income ratio of 8.5, was the second most unequal state in

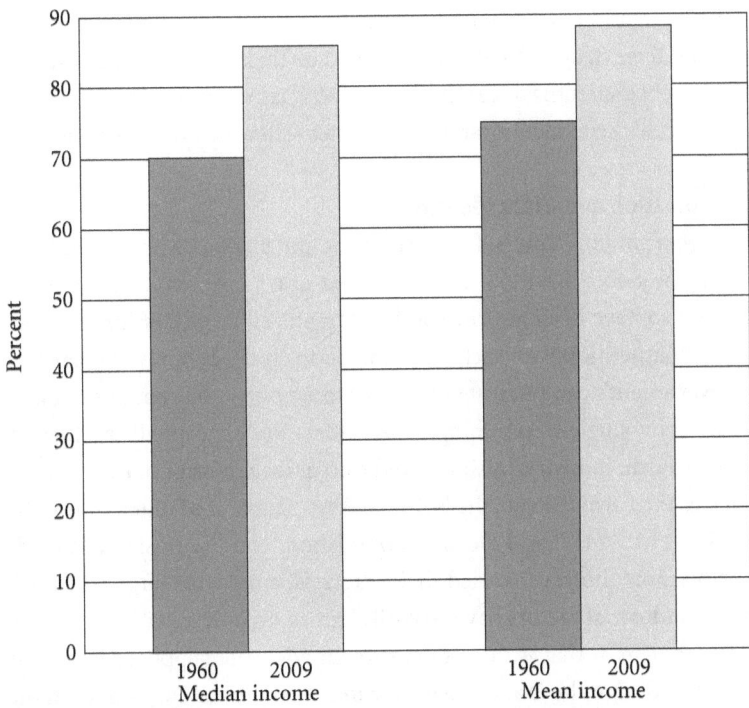

FIGURE 12. Regional divergence/convergence in family income, 1960–2009.
Note: Entries are ratios of South/non-South average family income.
Source: Analysis of U.S. Census data available from Steven D. Ruggles, J. Trent Alexander, Katie Genadek, Ronald Goeken, Matthew B. Schroeder, and Matthew Sobek, Integrated Public Use Microdata Series: Version 5.0 [Machine-readable database] (Minneapolis: University of Minnesota, 2010).

the country. (New York was ranked the most unequal, with a score of 8.7.) Such visible privations and inequalities, as well as consumer indebtedness, the lack of health insurance, the indignities and insecurities of low-wage work, and the experience or fear of job loss, might push southerners toward class awareness, and, possibly, class consciousness of the sort that leads individuals both to believe that their own and their group's economic hardships result from the privileges of others and to join trade unions or other class organizations to express their grievances.

The South's history suggests that southerners are deeply ambivalent about the idea of social classes, seemingly both denying their existence (or their saliency) and embracing and acting on them, even if by class they have generally meant something quite different from that envisioned by Marx. Still Marx, more than other critics, highlighted the interdependence of unequal economic arrangements existing "out there," the inner worlds of people who experience those inequalities, and their struggles to organize and act on their subjective understandings and objective circumstances. It is to those class organizations and inner worlds—especially class identity and its correlates—to which we now turn.

Class Organization and Class Identity

Class Organization. Planters, factory owners, and businesswomen and businessmen in the South have not always shared exact economic and political interests, and so have been at times both disorganized as a class (or class faction) and in competition with each other for labor, credit, commodity markets, and the government's ear. But just as often, or more often, they have been organized, if not in a single overarching peak association of "capitalists," then in more specific farm, industry, business, and CEO associations of one sort or another, such as the Farm Bureau, the National Association of Manufacturers, the National Right to Work Legal Defense Foundation, and the Business Roundtable. Furthermore, however varied their interests, employers large and small and from all industrial sectors have typically agreed on how to solve or contain the "labor problem"—that is, how to ensure an adequate supply of low-wage workers and to design the labor process for maximal profitability—and on the necessity of governments at all levels to create or maintain a healthy "business climate," one conducive to investment and profit making. Political parties and associations have, on occasion, also served as organizational functionaries of powerful economic interests: the Jim Crow–era Democratic Party, for instance, was largely controlled by white planters and it, in turn, functioned to maintain their class (as well as racial) hegemony in the region.

Solving the labor problem means, usually above all else, keeping "forced" or "compulsory" unionism, as it is called, banned from the fields, off the shop floor, far from the sales counter, and out of the office. Agriculture and rurality were not fertile soil for trade unions, and the history of the agrarian South is littered with failed farmer movements and thwarted efforts to organize farm workers. Although, as economist Ray Marshall has noted, labor unions have long had a presence in the region, racial divisions and competition, economic dependence, overt (even violent) hostility from planters, political powerlessness (especially among disfranchised, impoverished rural African Americans), and government repression all played their part in keeping the southern rural proletariat disorganized and unorganized.

But as the region urbanized and industrialized, and as its workers moved out of agriculture and into towns and cities with increasing numbers of blue-collar factory jobs, the prospects for unions, and hence for collective bargaining rights, workplace voice, and better wages and working conditions, brightened. Amid much labor militancy, concerted organizing drives, and favorable national policies and legislation (e.g., the National Industrial Recovery Act of 1933, the Wagner Act of 1935), workers in textiles, coal, steel, oil, automobile, and other industries across the South fought successfully for union representation in the 1930s. By 1939, according to data collected by economist Leo Troy, more than 900,000 union members lived in the South, accounting for roughly 13 percent of the region's employed nonagricultural wageworkers. Organization was unevenly distributed throughout the region: more than 40 percent of West Virginia's wageworkers were in unions (many in the biracial United Mine Workers), for example, while barely 4 percent of South Carolina's and North Carolina's workers were organized (see Table 2). Tight labor markets, union pressure, and a generally sympathetic federal government during World War II expanded union membership still further, and in 1946 the Congress of Industrial Organization launched a seven-year organizing drive in the South. Known as Operation Dixie, the movement ultimately failed for a variety of reasons— passage of the antiunion Taft-Hartley Act of 1947, so-called right-to-work laws in most southern states, anticommunism, implacable employer resistance, and racial divisions among manual workers, among others—leaving southern workers the least organized in the United States at the time. Still, almost one in five nonagricultural wageworkers in the region were unionized or covered by union contracts by 1953, again with large state-to-state variation patterned much like that observed in 1939. (With about 40 percent of their workforces in unions at that time, the Midwest and the Pacific states were the most heavily organized regions in the country.) Labor's numerical strength for most states in the region remained more or less steady until the 1970s.

With the coming of what sociologist Daniel Bell called postindustrial society, however, employment in manufacturing, mining, and other traditional blue-collar occupations has markedly declined since then. In the past several decades, the South (and the nation, of course) has lost hundreds of thousands of such jobs to the knowledge, health, and financial service sectors of the economy (and, given the relative ease of capital mobility, to even cheaper labor abroad). Although such industries and occupations are not in any categorical sense unorganizable by labor unions (e.g., the example of Finland, which has exceptionally high white-collar and professional unionization rates, demonstrates this), they traditionally have been more difficult to unionize in the South and elsewhere, and employers across the country seem determined to keep it that way. Despite successful organizing efforts among state and municipal employees and some smaller-scale (and often tenuous) union victo-

TABLE 2. *Labor Union Density in Southern States, 1939–2010*

	1939	1953	1970	1985	2010
Alabama	16.1	24.9	22.8	15.9	10.2
Arkansas	12.7	21.5	15.7	11.5	4.1
Delaware	7.8	18.4	27.4	16.6	11.5
District of Columbia	21.7	21.2	18.8	16.6	9.0
Florida	11.3	16.2	13.9	9.4	5.6
Georgia	7.0	15.0	13.7	10.2	4.0
Kentucky	22.5	25.0	25.4	17.0	9.0
Louisiana	9.6	19.5	17.9	9.7	4.4
Maryland	12.0	25.2	25.2	16.8	11.6
Mississippi	6.5	14.7	15.0	9.5	4.5
North Carolina	4.2	8.3	8.8	6.5	3.2
Oklahoma	10.4	16.1	16.8	10.6	5.5
South Carolina	4.0	9.3	9.1	4.6	4.7
Tennessee	15.3	22.6	23.8	13.3	4.7
Texas	10.3	16.7	13.8	7.5	5.5
Virginia	12.8	17.4	16.7	9.8	4.7
West Virginia	41.7	44.1	34.9	22.8	14.8

Source: For 1939 and 1953 data, see Leo Troy, "Distribution of Union Membership among the States, 1939 and 1953," Occasional Paper 56, *National Bureau of Economic Research* (1957). For 1964, 1985, and 2010 data, see Barry T. Hirsch and David A. McPherson, "Union Membership and Coverage Database from the Current Population Survey: Note," *Industrial and Labor Relations* 56, no. 2 (January 2003): 349–54. Annual Updates may be found at http://unionstats.gsu.edu. The decline in the absolute number of unions members discussed in the text is found in the U.S. Census Bureau, *Statistical Abstract of the United States*, 2011, table 665, and Bureau of Labor Statistics, "Economic News Release: Table 5. Union Affiliation of Employed Wage and Salary Workers by State" (21 January 2011), http://www.bls.;gov/news.release/union2.to5.htm.
Note: Entries represent percentage of private and public nonagricultural workers organized in trade unions.

ries among workers in textiles, aircraft production, and catfish and pork processing, the labor movement's membership and political clout in the region (and, again, in the country as a whole) have steadily fallen. According to the U.S. Bureau of Labor, Tennessee lost a staggering 121,000 union members (and 140,000 workers covered by collective bargaining contracts) from 1985 to 2010.

Georgia (with 86,000 fewer unions members by 2010), Virginia, Kentucky, Louisiana (with union losses of more than 70,000 each), and Arkansas and North Carolina (roughly 50,000 fewer union jobs each) also registered large decreases in union membership since 1985. Unions did increase their rolls in a very few southern states, but even here union density—that is, the proportion of wage and salary workers organized into unions—was, as Table 2 shows, stagnant (South Carolina) or actually declined (Texas). Consequently, the South remains the least-organized region of the country: eight states in the region had union density rates of less than 5 percent in 2010, the regional average was less than half that of the non-South, and, in most states, union density was below— in some cases far below (e.g., Kentucky, Tennessee, and West Virginia)—1939 levels. Public-sector unionization, a crucial source of remaining union membership and strength (e.g., only 1.5 percent of private-sector workers in North Carolina are unionized), is also under assault in many states, as state and local government officials use the Great Recession of 2008–11 to undermine the right of state and municipal employees to bargain collectively. Perhaps as both cause and consequence of unions' diminished role in the workplace and the polity, labor quiescence and defensiveness rather than assertiveness are now generally the rule.

Industrial and occupational trends and political postures, however, establish only the broad range of possibility; they are not in and of themselves dispositive. Ultimately, the fate of the trade-union movement in the South will depend on the dynamic between workers and their employers, governmental and legislative responses to this dynamic, and, because it influences how governments act, public opinion about workers' right to organize and bargain collectively. On the last point, polls are somewhat mixed. Some suggest a recent uptick in support for unionization; others are less sanguine. Since 1964 the American National Election Studies (ANES) has asked one of the most widely used questions about how Americans view a variety of groups and social institutions, including labor unions. Called the "feeling thermometer," it asks respondents to rate the degree of their warmth toward unions on a scale of 0 to 100, with higher scores indicating greater warmth. Southerners, again, are divided by race on this issue (but not so much by gender). African Americans in the region, who are proportionately somewhat more organized in trade unions than whites, have considerable warmth for unions (see Figure 13): since the mid-1970s, their thermometer reading has averaged in the high 60s. Whites in the region, on the other hand, have been tepid about unions—their score has been approximately 50 over the same time period, down slightly from the mid-1960s. (By way of comparison, in 2004–8 southern blacks' and whites' warmth for the Democratic Party was

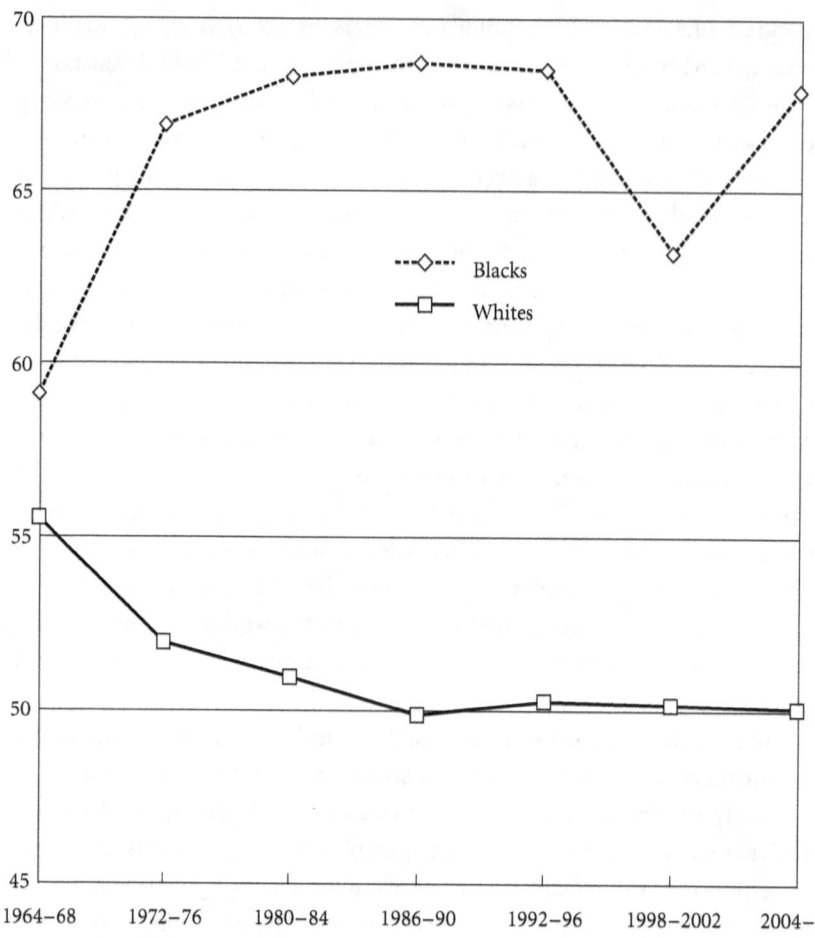

FIGURE 13. Southerners' expressed warmth toward labor unions, 1964–2008.
Note: Entries represent the average degree of warmth toward unions on a scale of 0–100 expressed by blacks and whites.
Source: Analysis of The American National Election Studies (www.electionstudies.org). The ANES Guide to Public Opinion and Electoral Behavior (Ann Arbor: University of Michigan, Center for Political Studies [producer and distributor]). These materials are based on work supported by the National Science Foundation and a number of other sponsors. Any opinions, findings, and conclusions or recommendations expressed in these materials are those of the author(s) and do not necessarily reflect the views of the funding organizations.

77 and 49, respectively; for big business, 63 and 54; for southerners and the middle class, mid-70s for each group; and for the military, high 70s/low 80s for both.) More distressing for future organizing efforts in the South is the lack of warmth currently expressed by one of unions' natural constituencies: the white working classes. In what appears to be a "class disconnect—that is, individuals acting against their own class interests—the thermometer reading for white southerners who self-define as working class (see the following "Class Identification" section) in the ANES was only 52 in 2004–8, little different from the average for all whites in the region. (The score for "middle-class" southern whites was lower, 48; black southerners' reading was 68, whether "working" or "middle" class.) Coupled with continuing structural changes in the economy, further deindustrialization, well-financed employer hostility, and government "neutrality" or outright opposition, a lukewarm or indifferent public, particularly indifference by its large, white "middling" status groups, poses further challenges to unions' long-term viability as a significant mechanism for advancing the well-being of working- and middle-class southerners of all races and as an important expression of their grievances and aspirations.

Class Identification. Two ongoing social surveys are particularly valuable for the study of class identification, the American National Election Studies (ANES) and the General Social Survey (GSS). Each tells us something the other cannot. Since 1948, the ANES and its predecessors fielded by the University of Michigan have asked representative samples of Americans, over 40,000 in all, if they were members of either the working class or the middle class. Sixty-eight percent of those who responded to the question readily acknowledged they were members of one of these two classes. Respondents who initially said they belonged to neither class were pressed to answer either middle or working class with a "Well, if you had to choose . . ." type probe. Another 30 percent of respondents subsequently claimed a class identity. The ANES then asked respondents who claimed to be members of either the middle or working class if they were part of the "average" stratum or the "upper" stratum of the class with which they identified. It also recorded "volunteered" responses indicating that interviewees were either members of "other" classes, such as the upper class or the lower class, or dismissed the notion of classes entirely. The GSS, which is housed at the University of Chicago, has queried randomly chosen Americans, almost 50,000 since 1972, about whether they "belonged" in the lower class, the working class, the middle class, or the upper class. It, too, noted if respondents denied the existence of classes.

Less than 1 percent of respondents in the ANES spontaneously rejected the idea of classes (only one respondent in the GSS did so), and even if all of those who said they did not know their class position or otherwise could not answer the class identity question did so because they had no clear idea of what social class was, the percentages remain very small, no more than 3 percent or so. There were no regional differences here. Nor, in the ANES, were regional differences seen either for respondents' claim to a class identity only after use of the "if you had to choose" probe or in volunteering a class other than working or middle. (Only about .5 percent of all ANES respondents said they were either lower class or upper class; another 1 percent or so volunteered some "other" class.) Proportionally more respondents in the GSS identified with either the lower class (6 percent over the years 1972–2008) or the upper class (3 percent over the same time period), probably because the GSS permitted these categories as explicit response alternatives. Reflecting historical patterns of discrimination as well as extant racial inequalities, African Americans in the GSS were more than twice as likely as whites to embrace a lower class identity (11 percent for blacks over the entire 1972–2008 period, less than 5 percent for whites). There were no important regional dissimilarities, and, minor fluctuations aside, "lower-class" identity claims for respondents of both races and from both major regions were constant through time. Both the GSS and the ANES, then, reveal that relatively few Americans (and, very clearly, few whites), North or South, see themselves as (or are willing to acknowledge themselves to be) other than working or middle class, and fewer still appear to reject the existence of classes.

The ANES and GSS surveys are also in complete agreement on four significant patterns. First, southerners and other Americans have never viewed themselves as exclusively or even predominately middle class. This is true for men and women and blacks and whites. Since the GSS first asked its version of the class identity question in 1972, proportionately almost as many white southerners have claimed to be part of the working class as part of the middle class—for both identities, over the past 35 years, the percentages of the region's whites who chose one or the other range from the low 40s to the high 40s. Self-defined working-class black southerners, furthermore, have outnumbered "middle-class" African Americans in the GSS by a margin of two to one (e.g., in 2004–8, 56 percent of the region's blacks claimed a working-class identity; 28 percent claimed a middle-class identity). The ANES tells a very similar story (see Figure 14): since the mid-1950s, African Americans in the South have been much more likely to describe themselves as working rather than middle class, and, until the most recent surveys, southern whites have opted for either an "average" or "upper" working-class identity more often than they have chosen any form of middle-class identity. (Only about 10 percent or so of both whites

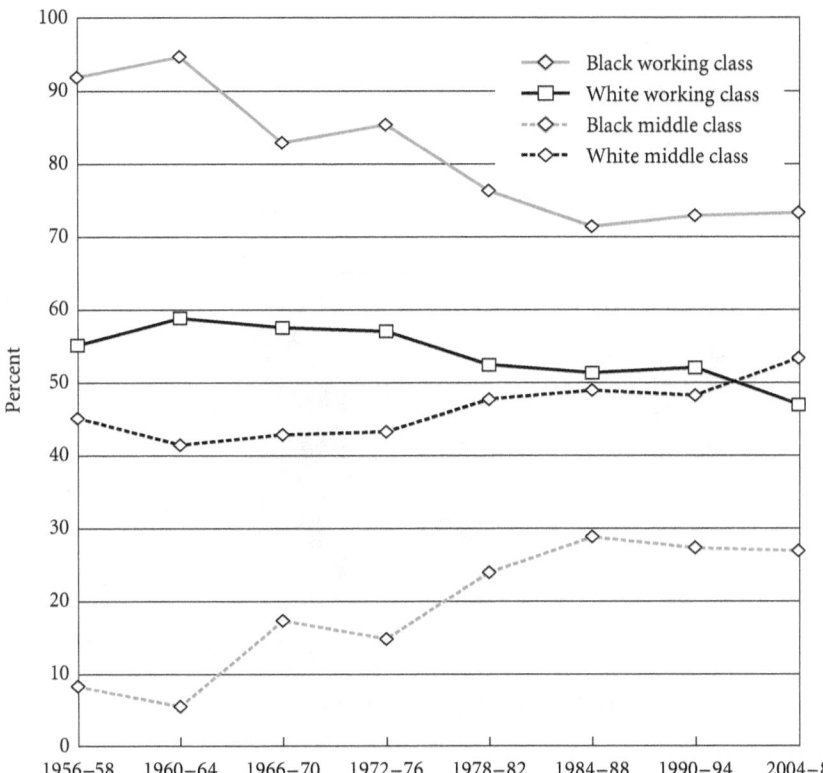

FIGURE 14. *Class identification by race in the U.S. South, 1956–2008.*
Note: Entries represent percentage of respondents identifying with each class.
Source: Analysis of The American National Election Studies (www.electionstudies.org). The ANES Guide to Public Opinion and Electoral Behavior (Ann Arbor, MI: University of Michigan, Center for Political Studies [producer and distributor]). These materials are based on work supported by the National Science Foundation and a number of other sponsors. Any opinions, findings, and conclusions or recommendations expressed in these materials are those of the author(s) and do not necessarily reflect the views of the funding organizations.

and blacks place themselves in the "upper" tier of either the middle or the working class.) The long-term implications of the atypical 2004–8 ANES results, which point for the first time to a white preference for middle class (53 percent) over working class (47 percent), is unclear. That we found no evidence of similar identity shifts by southern whites in the GSS of 2004, 2006, and 2008 suggests that the inversion may be a statistical anomaly rather than a harbinger of future defections from white southerners' working-class identities. Regional differences in both surveys were generally small, and those of any import were usually because of the larger presence of African Americans in the South.

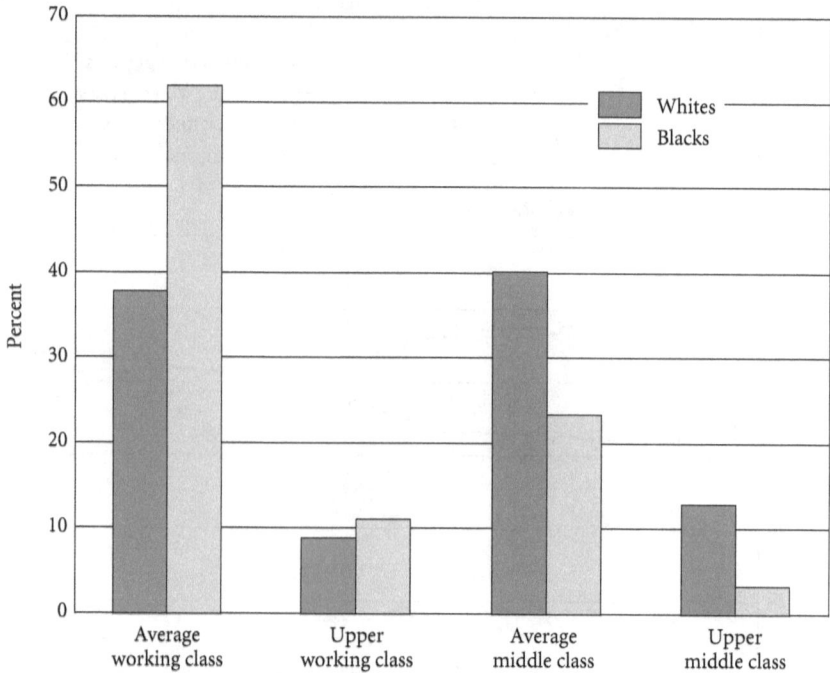

FIGURE 15. Class identification by race in the U.S. South, 2004–2008.
Note: Entries represent percentage of respondents identifying with each class or class faction.
Source: Analysis of The American National Election Studies (www.electionstudies.org). The ANES Guide to Public Opinion and Electoral Behavior (Ann Arbor, MI: University of Michigan, Center for Political Studies [producer and distributor]). These materials are based on work supported by the National Science Foundation and a number of other sponsors. Any opinions, findings, and conclusions or recommendations expressed in these materials are those of the author(s) and do not necessarily reflect the views of the funding organizations.

The second pattern seen in both the ANES and the GSS is that, on average, blacks and whites differ in where they position themselves in the southern class hierarchy, with African Americans in the ANES noticeably more likely than whites to describe themselves as working class and less likely to view themselves as either "average" middle class or "upper" middle class. (See, again, Figure 14.) Again echoing continuing racial inequalities in economic opportunity, material circumstances, and life chances, roughly three out of four southern blacks in the 2004–8 ANES, for example, claim membership in one segment or another of the working class (and 85 percent of them chose "average" rather than "upper" working-class status). Fewer than half of southern whites say they are members of any part of the working class. African Americans and whites in the region

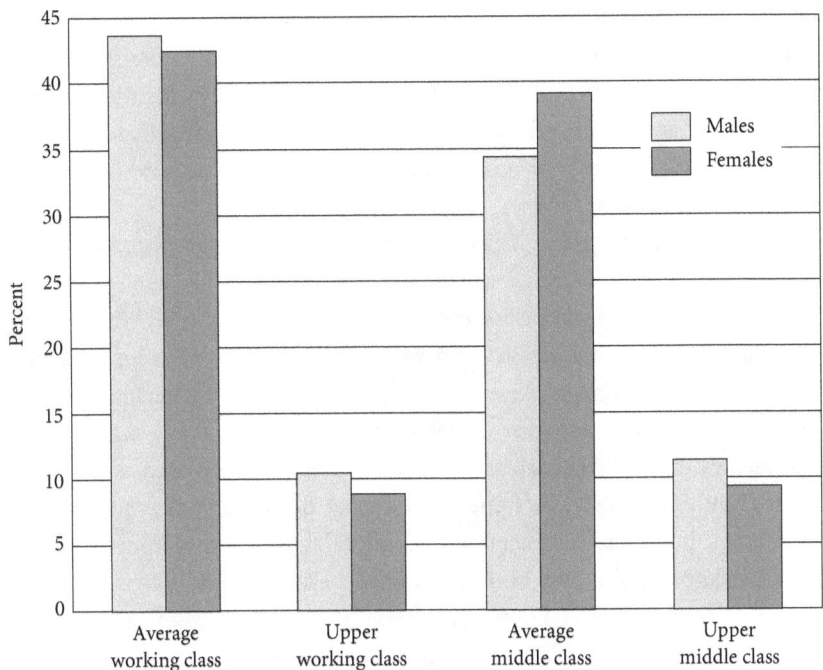

FIGURE 16. Class identification by gender in the U.S. South, 2004–2008.
Note: Entries represent percentage of respondents identifying with each class or class faction.
Source: Analysis of The American National Election Studies (www.electionstudies.org). The ANES Guide to Public Opinion and Electoral Behavior (Ann Arbor, MI: University of Michigan, Center for Political Studies [producer and distributor]). These materials are based on work supported by the National Science Foundation and a number of other sponsors. Any opinions, findings, and conclusions or recommendations expressed in these materials are those of the author(s) and do not necessarily reflect the views of the funding organizations.

thus are no closer to identifying with the same classes in the first decade of the 21st century than they were a generation earlier, a fact making cross-racial class alliances all the more difficult to achieve and sustain (see Figure 15).

The third noteworthy pattern, seen again in both the GSS and ANES surveys, indicates social consensus rather than dissensus. Despite occupational segregation by gender, the sex typing of jobs, and the large pay differences between men and women, few systematic gender differences in class identification are evident (see Figure 16). In the 2004–8 ANES, 43 percent of southerners of both sexes identified as "average" middle class, and an additional 10 percent or so (again of both sexes) saw themselves in the upper stratum of the middle class. In the GSS, 42 percent of both males and females claimed middle-class status.

Gender differences in working-class identity claims in either poll are small. Race is not a factor here: there were few systematic gender differences for either black or white southerners. These patterns were also virtually identical outside the South. That women and men understand themselves generally to be in the same social classes may be because they often contribute to and "share" the same household class position.

Finally, results from the ANES from mid-1950s to the late 1970s and early 1980s, presented in Figure 14, show a modest, gradual movement of African Americans out of working-class and into middle-class identities. This may be a social-psychological reaction by many southern blacks to the consolidation and institutionalization of the successes of the civil rights movement, successes ranging from redefining what it means to be black to opening school, firm, and factory doors. Whatever its exact cause, it has neither been undone nor subsequently deepened; the trend line here has been essentially flat since the early 1980s. Indeed, southerners' class identity claims (whether from women or men, blacks or whites) have been stable since the late 1970s in both the GSS and the ANES, with no cyclical movement and little sensitivity to macroeconomic conditions or structural shifts in the economy over the past 30 years or so (see Figure 14).

Although subjective, class identity is neither ephemeral nor disconnected from the materiality of peoples' existences: it is, in fact, very much embedded in social structure and rhythms of their daily routines, in economic circumstances, and in apperceptions of (and no doubt aspirations for) their "place" in the social fabric. Compared to respondents from households with no trade-union member in the 2004–8 GSS, for example, those from union households both less frequently place themselves in the lower class (3 percent vs. 8 percent) and more frequently identify as working class (55 percent vs. 47 percent). Highly educated southerners in the same set of surveys, and those in the top third of the income distribution, moreover, are more than twice as likely to claim a middle-class status than those without a high school degree or in the bottom income tercile (see Table 3). Professionals and managers in the GSS self-identify as middle class much more often than working class (61 to 32 percent), and blue-collar workers, as would be expected, do the opposite: 63 percent of craft workers say they are members of the working class; barely a quarter of them assert a middle-class identity. All of these patterns are quite similar for men and women. However, as seen in Table 4, African Americans' class identities, especially the transition from lower to middle class, while conditioned to a degree by their socioeconomic achievements, are less sensitive to class indicators than are those of whites. This likely results from continued institutional barriers to

TABLE 3. *Education, Family Income, and Family Social Class Identification, U.S. South, 2004–2008*

	Education	
	Did Not Complete High School	College Graduate or Postgraduate
Lower class	18%	2%
Working class	54%	28%
Middle class	27%	63%
Upper class	2%	8%
	Income Tercile	
	Bottom Third	Top Third
Lower class	17%	<1%
Working class	55%	25%
Middle class	27%	65%
Upper class	2%	9%

Source: Analysis of GSS data from James A. Davis, Tom W. Smith, and Peter V. Marsden, *General Social Surveys, 1972–2008* [Cumulative File] [Computer file], ICPSR04697-v4 (Storrs, Conn.: Roper Center for Public Opinion Research, University of Connecticut; Ann Arbor, Mich.: Inter-university Consortium for Political and Social Research [distributors], 2009-12-04). doi:10.3886/ICPSR04697

the cultural and economic integration of blacks, even those who have clearly "made it" by American middle-class standards, and, too often, their treatment by white Americans as indistinguishable members of a common racial group rather than as individuals fully differentiated by social class and economic advantage or disadvantage. These racial differences again signify now in a different, racialized way, the anchoring of class identities in realities and rhythms of southerners' lives.

Thanks to survey research and public polls, we can dispel some inaccuracies about what is believed known about class identification. Analysis of the GSS and ANES data demonstrates that despite the real or assumed diminution of traditional class differences, occupational upgrading in the region, the affluence (at least by historical standards) and growing educational qualifications of many of its inhabitants, and all of the other changes the South has witnessed

TABLE 4. *Education, Family Income, and Family Social Class Identification of African Americans, U.S. South, 2004–2008*

	Education	
	Did Not Complete High School	College Graduate or Postgraduate
Lower class	26%	6%
Working class	43%	54%
Middle/upper class	31%	40%
	Income Tercile	
	Bottom Third	Top Third
Lower class	21%	0
Working class	52%	53%
Middle/upper class	27%	47%

Source: James A. Davis, Tom W. Smith, and Peter V. Marsden, General Social Surveys, 1972–2008 [Cumulative File] [Computer file], ICPSR04697-v4 (Storrs, Comm.: Roper Center for Public Opinion Research, University of Connecticut; Ann Arbor, Mich.: Inter-university Consortium for Political and Social Research [distributors], 2009-12-04). doi:10.3886/ICPSR04697

in the past half century or more, southerners nonetheless are aware of class differences, believe some form of class hierarchy exists, and can place themselves, more often as working class rather than middle class, within that structure. That members of the more vulnerable, dependent, and exploited classes do not always recognize their economic interests, that they seldom possess the organizational capacity to act on those interests, once recognized, and that they too often are not permitted the cultural space and political opportunity to maneuver through and around obstacles to self-determination, dignity, and opportunity are, themselves, irreducible features of the region's structures of privilege and power rooted not only in class but also in gender and race.

Methodological Note. For the most part, we adhere to the U.S. Census definition of the American South, which consists of 16 states and the District of Columbia situated in three subregions: the South Atlantic (D.C., Delaware, Florida, Georgia, Maryland, North Carolina, South Carolina, Virginia, and

West Virginia), the East South Central (Alabama, Kentucky, Mississippi, and Tennessee), and the West South Central (Arkansas, Louisiana, Oklahoma [since 1900], and Texas). With few exceptions noted below, the statistics we present are from our original analyses of different datasets rather than from published sources. This method permits us greater flexibility and precision in addressing the issues important to our discussion. The data on the characteristics of the U.S. labor force—education, industry and occupation, family income, and so on—are drawn from the 2009 American Community Survey (ACS), from samples of a number of federal decennial censuses, especially those of 1870 (1 percent sample), 1900 (5 percent sample), 1930 (5 percent sample), 1950 (1 percent sample), 1960 (1 percent sample), 2000 (5 percent sample), and, in the case of urbanization for the years 2009–10, from the Current Population Survey. All are also administered by the U.S. Census. These data have been collected and made freely available in machine-readable form by the Integrated Public Use Microdata Series (IPUMS) at the University of Minnesota. This is a unique, extraordinarily useful resource, one allowing us and other researchers to access and analyze Census and ACS information on literally millions of individuals. The complete reference to IPUMS is Steven Ruggles, J. Trent Alexander, Katie Genadek, Ronald Goeken, Matthew B. Schroeder, and Matthew Sobek, *Integrated Public Use Microdata Series: Version 5.0* [Machine-readable database] (Minneapolis: University of Minnesota, 2010). The specific statistics we report may differ from those published in government reports for a variety of reasons: the use of different surveys (e.g., the Census Bureau's Current Population Survey rather than the decennial censuses); different sampling frames; differences in the population or groups used to compute percentages (e.g., nonagricultural labor force vs. the entire civilian labor force, or wageworkers vs. all wageworkers and salaried workers); differences in the use of weighted or unweighted data; differences in how missing data are handled; and differences in industrial and occupational classifications, among others. As a rule, we specify our target group or population in the text, tables, and figures and, when analyzing census data, report results with data weighted to make them more representative of the U.S. population. We also analyze data from two ongoing social surveys or public polls, the American National Election Studies (ANES) and the General Social Survey (GSS). The ANES is collaboration between Stanford University and the University of Michigan (see www.electionstudies.org). The GSS is housed at the National Opinion Research Center at the University of Chicago (see www.norc.uchicago.edu/GSS+Website). We usually "pool" or combine surveys to increase the number of respondents in the analysis (particularly important when focusing on subgroups defined by region, race and gender) and thus the stability and reliability of our results; for example, we pool GSS respondents for the years 1972–75 and 2004–8 and ANES respondents for 1956–58 and 2004–8. The number of survey respondents in any specific analysis is a function of the exact question we analyze (e.g., some questions are asked on only half of the respondents) and the group or subgroup under consideration, and it varies from several hundred to several thousand. We report weighted results from the ANES and, for technical reasons, unweighted results from the GSS. Data on unionization are directly taken from published and online reports and referenced in Table 2. State-level income inequality data are also directly taken from Center on Budget and Policy Priorities and Economic Policy Institute, *Pulling Apart: A State by State Analysis of Income Trends* (2008).

LARRY J. GRIFFIN
PEGGY G. HARGIS
Georgia Southern University

Fred A. Bailey, *Class and Tennessee's Confederate Generation* (1987); Numan V. Bartley, *The New South, 1945–1980: The Story of the South's Modernization* (1995); Edward H. Beardsley, *A History of Neglect: Health Care for Blacks and Mill Workers in the Twentieth-Century South* (1987); Daniel Bell, *The Coming of Post-Industrial Society* (1973); Edna Bonacich, *American Sociological Review* (October 1972); F. N. Boney, *Southerners All* (1984); W. Fitzhugh Brundage, *The Southern Past: A Clash of Race and Memory* (2005); Kathleen Canning, *American Historical Review* (June 1992); James C. Cobb, *Industrialization and Southern Society, 1877–1984* (1984); Robert Coles, *Migrants, Sharecroppers, Mountaineers* (1971); Allison Davis, Burleigh Gardner, and Mary Gardner, *Deep South: A Social Anthropological Study of Caste and Class* (1941); John Dollard, *Caste and Class in a Southern Town* (1937); Alan Draper, *Conflict of Interests: Organized Labor and the Civil Rights Movement in the South, 1954–1968* (1994); Anthony P. Dunbar, *Against the Grain: Southern Radicals and Prophets, 1929–1959* (1981); Cynthia M. Duncan, *Worlds Apart: Why Poverty Persists in Rural America* (1999); Elizabeth W. Etheridge, *The Butterfly Caste: A Social History of Pellagra* (1972); John Ettling, *The Germ of Laziness: Rockefeller Philanthropy in Public Health in the New South* (1981); Barbara J. Fields, *New Left Review* (no. 181, 1990); Gary M. Fink and Merl E. Reed, eds., *Race, Class, and Community in Southern Labor History* (1994); J. Wayne Flynt, *Dixie's Forgotten People: The South's Poor Whites* (1979), *Poor But Proud: Alabama's Poor Whites* (1989); Tami J. Friedman, *Journal of American History* (September 2008); Eugene D. Genovese, *The Political Economy of Slavery: Studies in the Economy and Society of the Slave South* (1965); Richard Godden and Martin Crawford, eds., *Reading Southern Poverty between the Wars, 1918–1989* (2006); Lawrence Goodwyn, *Democratic Promise: The Populist Moment in America* (1976); David M. Gordon, Richard Edwards, and Michael Reich, *Segmented Work, Di-*

vided Workers: The Historical Transformation of Labor in the United States (1982); Elna C. Green, ed., Before the New Deal: Social Welfare in the South, 1830–1930 (1999), This Business of Relief: Confronting Poverty in a Southern City, 1740–1940 (2003), The New Deal and Beyond: Social Welfare since 1930 (2003); Larry J. Griffin and Larry W. Isaac, Encyclopedia of American Studies (2001); Larry J. Griffin and Robert R. Korstad, Social Science History (Winter 1995); Margaret J. Hagood, Mothers of the South: Portraiture of the White Tenant Farm Woman (1939); Jacquelyn D. Hall, Revolt against Chivalry: Jesse Daniel Ames and the Women's Campaign against Lynchings (1979), Journal of American History (September 1986); Evelyn B. Higginbotham, Signs (Winter 1992); Michael Honey, Southern Labor and Black Civil Rights: Organizing Memphis Workers (1993); Angela M. Hornsby-Gutting, Journal of Southern History (August 2009); Daniel Hundley, Social Relations in Our Southern States (1860); R. Douglas Hurt, ed., The Rural South since World War II (1998); Mary R. Jackman and Robert W. Jackman, Class Awareness in the United States (1983); Matthew Frye Jacobson, Roots Too: White Ethnic Revival in the Post–Civil Rights America (2006); Dolores Janiewski, Sisterhood Denied: Race, Gender, Class in a New South Community (1985); Charles S. Johnson, Shadow of the Plantation (1935); Charles S. Johnson, Edwin R. Embree, and Will W. Alexander, The Collapse of Cotton Tenancy: Summary of Field Studies and Statistical Surveys, 1933–1935 (1935); Jacqueline Jones, The Dispossessed: America's Underclasses from the Civil War to the Present (1992), Journal of Southern History (August 2009); Robin D. G. Kelley, Journal of American History (June 1993); V. O. Key Jr., Southern Politics in State and Nation (1949); Lewis M. Killian, White Southerners (1970); Jack Temple Kirby, Rural World's Lost: The American South, 1920–1960 (1987); Robert Rodgers Korstad, Civil Rights Unionism: Tobacco Workers and the Struggle for Democracy in the Mid-Twentieth-Century South (2003); Annette Lareau and Dalton Conley, eds., Social Class: How Does It Work? (2008); Edward J. Larson, Sex, Race, and Science: Eugenics in the Deep South (1995); Earl Lewis, In Their Own Interests: Race, Class, and Power in Twentieth-Century Norfolk, Virginia (1991); William A. Link, The Paradox of Southern Progressivism, 1880–1930 (1992); Edward Magdol and Jon L. Wakelyn, The Southern Common People: Studies in Nineteenth-Century Social History (1980); Jay Mandle, Roots of Black Poverty: The Southern Plantation after the Civil War (1978); F. Ray Marshall, Labor in the South (1967); Monica McDermott, Working-Class White: The Making and Unmaking of Race Relations (2006); Timothy J. Michin, Journal of Southern History (November 1999), Journal of Southern History (August 2008); Marc S. Miller, ed., Working Lives: The Southern Exposure History of Labor in the South (1980); Robert Norrell, The House I Live In: Race in the American Century (2005), Journal of American History (December 1986); Eduardo Obregón Pagán, Journal of American History (September, 2010); Jill Quadagno, The Color of Welfare: How Racism Defeated the War on Poverty (1994); Roger L. Ransom and Richard E. Sutch, One Kind of Freedom: The Economic Consequences of Emancipation (1977); Arthur F. Raper, Preface to Peas-

antry: A Tale of Two Black Belt Counties (1936); John Shelton Reed, *The Enduring South: Subcultural Persistence in Mass Society* (1972), *Minding the South* (2003), *One South: An Ethnic Approach to Regional Culture* (1982), *Southern Folk, Plain and Fancy: Native Social Types* (1986), *Southerners: The Social Psychology of Sectionalism* (1983), *Surveying the South: Studies in Regional Sociology* (1993); Leonard Reissman, *Class in American Society* (1959); Marshall Sahlins, *Historical Metaphors and Mythical Realities: Structure in the Early History of the Sandwich Islands Kingdom* (1981); Todd L. Savitt and James Harvey Long, eds., *Disease and Distinctiveness in the American South* (1988); Anne Firor Scott, *The Southern Lady: From Pedestal to Politics* (1970); Joan W. Scott, *American Historical Review* (December 1986); Byron E. Shafer and Richard Johnston, *The End of Southern Exceptionalism: Class, Race, and Partisan Change in the Postwar South* (2006); Robert E. Shalhope, *Journal of Southern History* (November 1971); Harvard Sitkoff, *The Struggle for Black Equality, 1954-1980* (1981); Barbara Ellen Smith, ed., *Neither Separate Nor Equal: Women, Race, and Class in the South* (1999); Melvyn Stoker and Rick Halpern, *Race and Class in the American South since 1980* (1994); Tom E. Terrill and Jerrold Hirsch, eds., *Such as Us: Southern Voices of the Thirties* (1978); George Brown Tindall, *The Emergence of the New South, 1913-1945* (1967); Donald Tomaskovic-Devey and Vincent J. Roscigno, *American Sociological Review* (August 1996); Keith Wailoo, *Dying in the City of the Blues: Sickle Cell Anemia and the Politics of Race and Health* (2001); Jonathan M. Wiener, *American Historical Review* (October 1979), *Social Origins of the New South: Alabama, 1860-1885* (1978); William J. Wilson, *The Declining Significance of Race: Blacks and Changing American Institutions* (1978); Jamie Winders, *Progress in Human Geography* (December 2005); Elizabeth Wisner, *Social Welfare in the South: From Colonial Times to World War I* (1970); C. Vann Woodward, *The Origins of the New South, 1877-1913* (1951, 1971), *The Strange Career of Jim Crow* (1974); Robert H. Zieger, *For Jobs and Freedom: Race and Labor in America since 1865* (2007).

Agriculture

As in urban areas, class status in the rural South derived in part from one's income level or access to capital. Throughout most of southern history, race also shaped class definitions with whites defining themselves in large part by the fact that they were not people of color. Common bonds built from dealing with the weather and the commodities market and the common experience of working the land created some sense of shared identity among farming folk, a factor that blurred class boundaries somewhat. So did the rural "culture of personalism," a phrase coined by historian Mark Schultz to describe the way in which the face-to-face relationships and densely woven kinship networks in small rural communities created cross-class networks of mutual aid. Class definitions are not stable, however; they shift over time, and they vary from place to place across the region.

Before the Civil War, southern whites clustered into three rough categories. At the top of the hierarchy were planters, the powerful landowners who held large numbers of slaves and occupied positions of political power. The middle ground was occupied by a group of yeomen farmers and small slaveholders whom historian Frank Owsley termed "plain folk." Most plain folk earned their living through a combination of livestock herding and small-scale subsistence and market-oriented crop production. From the time of Bacon's Rebellion in 1676 Virginia, planters had used a "divide and conquer" strategy to prevent poor and middling whites from making common cause with African Americans. By emphasizing the superiority of whiteness, they discouraged the development of class-based solidarity among poor whites and blacks. Yet class identity was more complex than simple race consciousness. Men among the plain folks derived their identity largely from their whiteness and from their pride in their independence from planter control as well as their power to control the dependents in their households. At the bottom were desperately poor whites who existed at the margins of antebellum southern society as share tenants or renters. The ranks of the poorest whites grew after 1837 when the Specie Circular Act made it more difficult for the poor to acquire land, especially in the wake of a decline in cotton prices. Class tensions grew among whites in the 1850s.

African Americans occupied the space below poor whites in the antebellum class hierarchy. While most southern blacks were enslaved, free blacks also lived in the countryside. In spite of laws that restricted their physical and economic mobility and sometimes threatened their free status, many free blacks earned livings as skilled craftsmen and enjoyed the protection of elite whites.

The convulsions of the Civil War and Reconstruction sparked a protracted redefinition of class categories. Some former planters descended into genteel poverty, although these people often retained both their landholdings and their positions of political leadership. They were joined at the top of the class ladder by newly wealthy whites who purchased land or by the hired managers of corporately owned plantations. Elites used their power to maintain their own status, resisting changes that might dilute their power. Most of all, elites sought to maintain a plentiful, cheap, and tractable labor supply.

Planters achieved this labor supply control through manipulation of the sharecropping system. Sharecropping emerged as a negotiated solution to newly freed African Americans' need to access land for farming and cash-strapped plantation owners' struggle to find willing laborers. Typically, a landowner provided the sharecropper and his family with a plot of land and a small house in exchange for a share of the crop or, sometimes, a cash rent payment.

Elite and middling farm families usually explained the poverty of sharecroppers as a result of laziness and the lack of ambition or "management" skills. Texan Etta Carroll said, "Some of them didn't work enough, and some of them were not good managers, and that made a lot of difference." But sharecroppers themselves understood that the system re-created many of the most exploitative features of the antebellum plantation system, offering widely varying levels of autonomy. Because crops were sold once a year, sharecroppers needed a way to obtain food and supplies in the intervening months. They acquired these supplies through "furnishing" merchants (often the planter himself) who advanced the sharecropper supplies, securing the debt with a lien against the future crop. Thanks to this crop lien system, landless farmers became dependent on the landlord for all of their material needs, giving even the fairest and most benevolent of landowners considerable control over the lives and fortunes of sharecroppers. Tenants who challenged the landlord's control could face arrest, eviction, or violence. At its best, the sharecropping system provided the landless with access to land and an opportunity to accumulate savings and thus climb the agricultural economic ladder. At its worst, sharecroppers remained powerless against grasping landowners.

In its earliest stages, most sharecroppers were black, but as the South's farm economy stagnated in the late 19th century, many whites were sucked into tenancy and the crop lien system. By 1900 about one-third of white farmers and three-quarters of black farmers in the South worked land they did not own.

Though many plain-folk whites fell into tenancy in the late 19th and early 20th centuries, middling white farm families continued to thrive in many areas of the South. As in the antebellum period, the middling folk usually owned small amounts of land. Some were unusually prosperous tenants. Members of the community generally characterized them as ambitious, law abiding, and hardworking, but they were less likely to hold the reins of power in rural communities than their more powerful landowning neighbors were.

A class hierarchy was also evident among blacks in rural communities in the late 19th and early 20th centuries. Whites defined some blacks as the "better sort" on the basis of their adherence to white standards of appropriate behavior. Kenneth Young, the child of black Alabama landowners, noted, "Back in those days and even now, not much respect was given to black folks who didn't own their homes and very few did. Most of them were tenants on white folks' places. If you were what you considered a prosperous black person, owned your home and owned your land, the whites respected you, liked you better than they did that black man who had nothing."

African Americans themselves characterized prosperous blacks as hardworking and ambitious. Lonnie Graves, of Satin, Tex., explained, "There were a group of black people in this community, and as I'm sure in other communities as well, who had a lot of pride, who worked hard, who earned their living, who made their land pay off. And they could spend their money for what they wanted. They bought new cars, just like the white people did. Sent the kids off to finish school in Marlin and Waco or Austin or wherever. And they did this in spite of, you know, the hard things, the disadvantages that they had to live with."

New Deal era reforms, government intervention during the World Wars, agricultural modernization, and rural industrialization generated a new round of alterations in rural southern class relations. Many landless of both races rose to middle-class status by taking off-farm jobs, and millions headed to southern and northern cities for work during the middle decades of the 20th century. For those left behind, however, things often grew worse, largely because of elite whites' ability to manipulate government programs to their own advantage. In his 1936 study of two Georgia Black Belt counties, sociologist Arthur F. Raper noted that though New Deal programs had provided the income to rejuvenate the plantation economy, "Many tenants are being pushed off the land while many others are being pushed down the tenure ladder, especially from cropper to wage hand status [because] the various federal resources which come into this region tend to be spent in conformity with the plantation, the philosophy and practices of which root back into slavery. New techniques of exploitation have evolved." Studies of southern Texas found that wealthy white ranchers used similar strategies to control their Mexican workforce as those used by white planters over landless blacks. Moreover, agricultural mechanization and the shift to the use of expensive chemical fertilizers and hybrid seeds tended to push middling and poor farmers off the land.

It might seem surprising that antebellum plain folk and post–Civil War middling farmers and sharecroppers did not develop a class consciousness similar to that developed by urban working classes. Such a sense of shared class interest might have facilitated organizing to combat exploitation and marginalization. A number of factors undermined the potential for rural southerners to develop a working-class identity. The noneconomic aspects of rural class status, especially race and gender, led small to middling white farmers to identify themselves with the planter elite, even when the elites worked in ways that harmed the plain folk. Stephanie McCurry has demonstrated the yeomen in the antebellum South Carolina Lowcountry remained committed to the slave regime, not just because they shared a racial identity with their planter neighbors but also as a means of defending their own right to be "masters of small worlds"—to dominate the dependent wives, children, and slaves in their households. During the Great Depression, black and white sharecroppers in northern Alabama and in the Arkansas Delta organized to combat planter exploitation and abuse, but they rarely made common cause with white small landowners who instead identified their ambitions and interests as similar to those of elite planters. And after World War II, many farm people came to share the interests and ambitions of the larger middle class. They wanted to build comfortable and attractive homes, drive late-model cars, take vacations to interesting locations, and send their children to college. Most believed their best hope to achieve these ambitions lay in embracing the tenets of industrial agriculture.

Whites who remained on the land after World War II embraced the promise of industrial agriculture, but they faced more and more forces beyond their control, particularly the unpredictable global commodities market. In many rural southern communities, the landowning elite lost control of local government to a rising middle class that prospered in manufacturing and the service industry; a rural elite persists, but it does not exercise the power it once did. Many farmers, including those descended from the ranks of elite landowners, lost their land in the farm crisis of the 1980s. Thousands of black farmers, victims of decades of discrimination from federal officials, joined a successful class action suit against the U.S. Department of Agriculture, but the settlement of that lawsuit came too late to help most stay on the land. Today the wealthiest southern farmers often derive the bulk of their incomes from nonagricultural activities. The majority of southern farmers are defined by the USDA as part-time farmers, but in some parts of the South, a new group of entrepreneurial farmers is moving to the country, growing organic crops, and catering to the national sustainable agriculture movement. Today the class hierarchies of the southern countryside are again in flux.

MELISSA WALKER
Converse College

Stanley Aronowitz, *How Class Works: Power and Social Movements* (2003); Pete Daniel, *Lost Revolutions: The South in the 1950s* (2000); Cynthia M. Duncan, *Rural Sociology* (Winter 1996); Lacy K. Ford, *Origins of Southern Radicalism: The South Carolina Upcountry, 1800–1860* (1988); Steven Hahn, *The Roots of Southern Populism: Yeomen Farmers and the Transformation of the Georgia Upcountry, 1850–1890* (2006); Samuel C. Hyde Jr., *Plain Folk of the South Revisited* (1997); Stephanie McCurry, *Masters of Small Worlds: Yeomen Households, Gender Relations, and the Political Culture of the Antebellum South Carolina Low Country* (1995); Frank L. Owsley, *Plain Folk of the Old South* (rev. ed., 1982); Arthur F. Raper, *Preface to Peasantry: A Tale of Two Black-Belt Counties* (1936); Mark Roman Schultz, *The Rural Face of White Supremacy* (2005); Melissa Walker, *Southern Farmers and Their Stories: Memory and Meaning in Oral History* (2007); Mark V. Wetherington, *Plain Folk's Fight: The Civil War and Reconstruction in Piney Woods Georgia* (2005); David Williams, *Bitterly Divided: The South's Inner Civil War* (2008); Nan Elizabeth Woodruff, *Journal of Southern History* (May 1994).

American Revolution

Popular views of the American Revolution tend to emphasize accounts of a people united in a common cause. In the southern colonies, wealthy and educated gentlemen led their patriotic liberty-loving neighbors into a revolt against tyrannical British rulers, waged a successful war for independence, and founded a new nation. Yet, like all political movements, the American Revolution originated in and was shaped by divisions among colonists as much as animosity toward Britain. Many of these divisions stemmed from conflicts between different social classes within the southern colonies. The differing expectations of diverse groups of people and the new demands they made during the imperial crisis profoundly altered the Revolutionary settlement.

Though we often think of the southern colonies as slave societies, divided only by white masters and their African bondspeople, in the late 18th century the colonies were rather societies with slaves. Though there was tremendous variation in different regional pockets, most people were not slave owners. Those who did own slaves commonly engaged only one or two at most. Throughout most of the southern colonies, enslaved Africans formed but only the bottom of a hierarchical edifice that included male and female convict and indentured servants (laborers from Britain who were bound to a certain term of labor as punishment, or to pay their passage), apprentices, free wage laborers and overseers, tenant farmers and nonslaveholding smallholders, poorer slaveholders and substantial landholders, and, finally, local and cosmopolitan elites, some of whom owned dozens of slaves, others of whom held hundreds of Africans in bondage and owned thousands of acres of land. Even within some of these apparently monolithic social blocs, many, sometimes overlapping layers of differences helped complicate social relations within and between different classes. As any self-respecting gentleman, backcountry farmer, or enslaved African would know, the southern colonies were deeply divided and hierarchical societies in which social and economic inequalities were on conspicuous display.

Many of these divisions quickly came to the fore when Britain began reforming its imperial governance in order to help pay for the tremendous cost of the Seven Years' War. Even as colonial leaders tried to forge new cross-class alliances with artisans and urban laborers to oppose the Stamp Act, enslaved Africans began making demands for their own liberty. Though running away and insurrections were not new tactics for black communities in the southern colonies, the cry of "liberty" began to resonate widely, encouraged by rumors that the British would free the slaves if there was a rupture. When more and more slaves took advantage of the increasing tension between London and the colonists to launch their own bids for independence, whites divided in their responses. Some redoubled their efforts to oppose British legislation and tried to channel anxiety into anger. Others believed that anarchy would result from further resistance and stayed at home.

At the same time, thousands of poorer whites in the backcountry regions of the southern colonies demanded liberty from the control of wealthy eastern elites. Regulators in North Carolina—many of whom were inspired by a new evangelical religious radicalism—wanted an end to unfair taxes and corrupt local officers imposed on them by the same patriot elite who opposed Britain. Along with Baptists and other dissenters in Virginia, many of these Regulators also demanded greater religious liberty. Four years before the "shot heard round the world" was fired at Lexington in 1775, farmers in North Carolina took up arms in defense of their liberties. More than 20 were killed in the ensuing battle. Six more were hanged. Patriot leaders in eastern North Carolina cheered the end of the Regulator movement as they were now free to pursue their grievances against Parliament. But it was unsurprising that many backcountry farmers refused to support the patriot movement.

Arguably, some of these divisions helped turn resistance into armed conflict with Britain. All along the James River, enslaved Virginians began to mobilize in early April 1775 as the colony was shaken by rumors and reports of insurrections. The Royal governor Lord Dunmore took the opportunity to seize all the powder in the Williamsburg magazine and told patriot leaders he did so because he feared rebellious slaves would capture it. Though nervous patriot leaders tried to calm the situation, angry white Virginians poured into the capital and harassed Dunmore's troops even as hundreds of slaves made their way to British lines. Emboldened by black support and angered by militant patriots, Dunmore eventually issued his famous—though limited—proclamation offering freedom to slaves and servants of rebel masters who could reach him. In Virginia, enslaved Africans began the Revolution.

As Dunmore's proclamation made clear, hundreds of indentured and convict servants also took advantage of the start of hostilities to make their own bids for liberty. All across northern Virginia and Maryland, including on George Washington's own plantation, Mount Vernon, servants slipped away and made for British lines. Some banded together with black slaves to make their escape. Others found themselves fighting alongside free whites who had cast their lot with the British. Though stereotypes of American loyalists tend to depict them as wealthy, conservative, and unthinking supporters of the crown, many patriot leaders complained that it was the "lower sort" who most often aided the British. Certainly a high percentage of poorer farmers could be found in many of the places where there were concentrations of loyalists such as the Georgia backcountry, the Carolina Piedmont, and the Eastern Shore of Delaware, Maryland, and Virginia, but loyalists could be found throughout the southern colonies. Many people who supported the British had expressed previous complaints against patriot leaders.

Other groups joined the patriot movement but in return made demands on patriot leaders, even in the midst of the conflict. Tenants in northern Virginia refused to pay their rents while there was no market for their crops and they had to serve in the militia. Others demanded the right to elect their own militia officers and many complained of the exemptions from military service allowed to planters who owned more than four slaves. Many made more overtly political demands. In Virginia, Baptists told patriot leaders they would gladly join them in the conflict with Britain if they promised religious freedom. On Maryland's Eastern Shore, poorer laborers and others who owned little or no property demanded universal male suffrage, or at least suffrage for any man willing to bear arms in defense of independence. Across the southern colonies, too, small farmers, artisans, and laborers made inroads on the committees that were originally dominated by local elites, and then helped elect delegates to the assemblies who would support independence. Even before Thomas Paine's *Common Sense* convinced many elites to support independence, thousands of ordinary colonists in the South had already made that decision. They wanted new governments that were more responsive than the old; or, as some conservative patriots feared, they wanted independence from the rule of their genteel neighbors.

The intensifying divisions along with the new demands made by diverse groups in the first year of the conflict with Britain ironically also helped convince many wealthy and conservative planters to support independence. As John Page—a friend of Jefferson's—argued, independence would allow patriot leaders to restore the rapidly diminishing authority of government. If they moved quickly enough, they could create new constitutions that would be similar to the old ones. Radical leaders such as Page convinced many foot-dragging colleagues to support independence precisely to stop what they called the "rising Disorders" in the colonies. Without independence and a new government, they warned, the situation would be even worse.

In trying to restore their authority, though, many patriot leaders may have helped undermine the long-term war effort. The war for independence lasted for seven years. It was one of the longest and bloodiest wars in America's history. The per capita equivalent of the number of casualties in the Revolution would today mean the death of perhaps as many as 300,000 Americans. And yet it was not such a long and bloody war merely because the might of the British armed forces was brought to bear on the hapless colonials. It was because of the many divisions among Americans themselves over whether to fight, what to fight for, and who would do the fighting. It was by any measure the first American civil war. This was nowhere more clear than in the southern colonies.

In Maryland, for example, conservative patriot leaders supported independence but erected the most conservative new form of government in the union. Over the demands of their neighbors, they merely lowered the property qualification for voting (which still left out half the adult white male population of the state) and maintained high property qualifications for office holding (only 11 percent of the population had enough property to sit in the lower house). When it became clear that the Maryland patriot elite would offer few concessions in the new constitution to those they expected to enlist in their defense, angry lower-class whites laid down their arms or joined the British. Many more abandoned the cause when it became clear who would have to do most of the fighting. In Virginia, thousands of patriot farmers turned away in anger when new draft laws targeted the poor and vulnerable. Others tired of continued call-outs of the militia while their wealthy neighbors were classed as invalids and exempted from service. Many actively protested and disrupted all efforts to draft soldiers for the Continental Army.

Those who were disillusioned by the limits of Revolutionary change and angered by the terms and conditions of the war joined a growing number of neutrals and loyalists. Some areas, such as the Georgia backcountry, Carolina Piedmont, and the Eastern Shore, were plagued by chronic and persistent internal violence and strife between loyalists and patriots. But everywhere the British went, they were aided in some degree by local residents. Such support encouraged the British and prolonged the war. Yet active supporters of the crown were merely the tip of the iceberg. Many hundreds of thousands of people in the southern colonies decided there was little in the contest for them and simply kept their heads down. They did so either by tacking back and forth between support for the new state governments and the British or by simply lying low. They ignored calls to turn out in the militia. They refused to pay taxes. They harbored deserters. They made the best terms they could. Some even fought to stay neutral. In sum, they added to the growing numbers of people who defended local autonomy and criticized the intrusions of higher authorities, whether they were British officers or Continental officials. Resistance to the war effort brought mobilization to a standstill throughout all of the new states, prolonging the conflict and making it far more divisive, bloody, messy, and complicated than it might have been—and certainly more so than many patriot leaders had initially envisioned.

Historians have not yet come to terms with the divisive nature of the Revolutionary War and its political and social consequences. But the conflicts and divisions that wracked the new states during the Revolutionary War had profound and far-reaching effects. The long war exhausted and demoralized many hundreds of thousands of people. It gave rise to new divisions as southern states complained they had been abandoned by the northern states when the British invaded late in the conflict. The war also gave rise to conflict between Continental authorities and state officials, and between state and Continental officials and new citizens in the states. The constant demands for men and supplies entrenched for some a bitter desire to defend local autonomy, while resistance to these efforts left many yearning for greater centralized control. Paradoxically, the Revolution that created a new nation may have also laid the basis for a growing antipathy toward the newly established federal government.

MICHAEL A. MCDONNELL
University of Sydney

Ronald Hoffman, *A Spirit of Dissension: Economics, Politics, and the Revolution in Maryland* (1973); Ronald Hoffman, Thad W. Tate, and Peter J. Albert, eds., *Uncivil War: The Southern Backcountry during the American Revolution* (1985); Woody Holton, *Forced Founders: Indians, Debtors, Slaves, and the Making of the American Revolution in Virginia* (1999); Marjoleine Kars, *Breaking Loose Together: The Regulator Rebellion in Pre-Revolutionary North Carolina* (2002); Allan Kulikoff, *Journal of the Historical Society* (Spring 2002); Michael A. McDonnell, *The Politics of War: Race, Class, and Conflict in Revolutionary Virginia* (2007); Jerome Nadelhaft, *Disorders of War: The Revolution in South Carolina* (1981); Gary B. Nash, *The Unknown American Revolution: The Unruly Birth of Democracy and the Struggle to Create America* (2005); Jim Piecuch, *Three Peoples, One King: Loyalists, Indians, and Slaves in the Revolutionary South, 1775–1782* (2008).

Antiunionism and Right-to-Work Laws

Scholars and observers of organized labor have long pointed to the American South as inhospitable to unions. Race, religion, and resistance to change imposed from the outside have all, at one time or another, been used to explain this antipathy. The public policy choices of states seem to reflect this antiunion stance. All southern states have right-to-work laws in effect, which increase the costs of collective action by forbidding the union shop, and most pose significant restrictions on public-sector union organizing. To this day, unions remain weaker in the South than in other regions.

Far from inevitable, the current state of unionism and labor policy in the South owes much to the organizing struggles of the 1940s—struggles where the outcome was by no means predetermined. Here race certainly weighed heavily on unions and political representatives alike, though labor's setbacks were shaped in part by its own tactical blunders as opposed to a regionwide distaste for unionism. Nonetheless, by the takeoff of the southern civil rights movement in the 1950s, unions were weakened and legally circumscribed. The later spillover between civil rights and public-sector union organizing would prove to be short-lived.

Slavery, the Civil War, and the subsequent later industrialization of the region no doubt slowed the early development of class-based organizations. There were, however, notable early experiments. The Knights of Labor (KOL) made significant inroads in the region during the 1880s, scoring political victories in several states. The Knights were open to workers of any skill, trade, or race. Some KOL local unions organized black workers alongside whites; many were race specific. By 1888 there were more than 100 KOL local unions in North Carolina, 65 in Louisiana, and 64 in Alabama. In 1887 and 1888 KOL unions claimed credit for electing city councilmen in Lynchburg, Va., city and county officials in Macon, Ga., and mayors in Jacksonville, Fla., Anniston, Ala., and Vicksburg, Miss.

KOL gains sparked considerable local opposition and their organization faltered as the region pushed back against Populist challenges. The American Federation of Labor (AFL), which took off after the decline of the Knights, offered a narrower version of trade unionism. With much of its growth coming in the post-1900 period of enforced segregation, it abandoned any of the racial liberalism of the Knights. AFL unions did make notable gains in the region during World War I, as did unions everywhere. But here the response of southern employers was especially swift. Local chambers of commerce sponsored free employment services to break union strongholds in the skilled trades and organized resistance to labor spread across states from Texas to North Carolina. Few of the wartime union gains were sustained into the 1920s.

While labor unrest in textiles shook the South in the early 1930s, the New Deal put union struggles squarely into the political process. The Wagner Act, passed in 1935 and upheld by the Supreme Court in 1937, gave federal backing for unionism. The act ruled many of the favored employer tactics illegal by establishing a set of unfair labor practices, it stipulated uniform election procedures, and it established the National Labor Relations Board (NLRB) to oversee its administration. Union membership increased substantially in this newfound favorable environment.

In lieu of any immediate overhaul of Roosevelt's national labor policy, many employers and their associations began to target labor unions throughout the states. Spearheaded by groups such as the Southern States Industrial Council, the Farm Bureau, and many local affiliates of the Chamber of Commerce and the National Association of Manufacturers (NAM), these efforts first concerned restrictions on union organizing and picketing because the Wagner Act contained no such limits. Supreme Court rulings in the *Senn* and *Thornhill* cases of 1937 and 1940 protected peaceful picketing from legislative attack. In response, many organizations campaigned for "antiviolence" statutes that fell within the policing powers of states but that similarly limited labor picketing. Texas was the first state to pass an antiviolence law in 1941, followed by Mississippi in 1942, with Arkansas, Florida, and Alabama all passing variants of it the following year. Though these early laws often proved constitutionally dubious, they nonetheless put unions on the defensive and forced them to expend resources in costly court battles.

Union growth and employer resistance exploded during the war years. In exchange for a no-strike pledge, the National War Labor Board (NWLB) backed union security arrangements in defense industries in 1942, whereby workers in unionized plants were required to remain in the union and pay dues for the length of the collective bargaining contract. This federal backing combined with an incredibly tight labor wartime market proved to be a boon for labor organizations and particularly for the new Congress of Industrial Organization (CIO) unions. Union membership doubled in the South during the 1940s, a growth rate surpassing that of any other region. Although southern unions were still weak compared to their counterparts in the industrial strongholds of the Midwest, states such as Alabama and Tennessee ranked in the middle of the pack, hovering around 20 percent of the nonagricultural workforce belonging to unions in the mid-1940s. The growth of wartime industry throughout the region fueled large membership gains in several states.

In this context, employers turned their attention to right-to-work laws that banned the union shop. After winning an election, unions were legally bound to collectively bargain for wages and benefits for all workers covered by the contract. In a right-to-work state, however, unions (or the NWLB) could not compel all workers to eventually join and pay dues, which made organizing and sustaining a union much more difficult. The Christian American Association out of Houston was the first in the nation to champion the "right to work" as a full-blown political slogan. Its director, Vance Muse, took the phrase from an editorial in the *Dallas Morning News* and ceaselessly promoted it throughout the decade, particularly across southern states. The face of employer opposition during this period was mostly that of small business, although larger firms often contributed resources through the NAM and their state affiliates. Arkansas and Florida were the first states to adopt right-to-work rules in 1944. As Table 5 shows, early right-to-work activity had a distinctively southern feel. Some 14 states adopted right-to-work laws by the spring of 1947. This encouraged congressional conservatives to protect state right-to-work laws in section 14(b) of the Taft-Hartley Act, passed in June of that year.

What is more, for labor, the highly publicized postwar southern union organizing campaigns—particularly the CIO's "Operation Dixie"—quickly faltered. Despite a million dollars and 200 organizers devoted to organizing the region, the campaign was a thorough failure. The labor setbacks were not widely anticipated at the time. As late as 1946 *Fortune Magazine* saw the complete unionization of the South as inevitable. And there were indeed some notable gains. For example, during the 1940s, a liberal-labor coalition in Texas effectively took over the state Democratic Party and appeared well situated to advance a progressive political agenda. This did not last.

Many scholars attribute the union fallout to the persistence of racism and

TABLE 5. *Antiunionism or Right-to-Work Activity in the 1940s and 1950s*

Year of Right-to-Work Passage	State(s)
1944	Arkansas, Florida
1945	South Dakota
1946	Arizona, Nebraska
1947	Delaware, Georgia, Iowa, New Hampshire, North Carolina, North Dakota, Tennessee, Texas, Virginia
1951	Nevada
1953	Alabama
1954	Louisiana, Mississippi, South Carolina
1955	Utah
1957	Indiana
1958	Kansas

Note: Delaware, Indiana, and New Hampshire later repealed their laws. Louisiana repealed its law in 1956 and then adopted it again in 1976.

the inability or unwillingness of unions to mount a regionwide, interracial campaign. Unionization, particularly the brand of unionization promoted by the early CIO unions, threatened to upend the racial order of the 1940s South. Consistent with this type of threat-based explanation, the timing of right-to-work laws across southern states is strongly correlated with the pace and location of union organizing. The role of public antiunion sentiment in the labor setbacks is more difficult to assess and impossible to separate from the larger structural obstacles facing unions. Blacks were systematically disenfranchised, and rural districts were overrepresented in state legislatures, diminishing potential sources of union support. Gallup Poll data from the period, mostly reflecting this shrunken electorate, show the region to be less supportive of unions as a whole. Yet support for the open shop (right to work) was actually less pronounced in the South than elsewhere.

Differences in union and employer strategies were notable. AFL and CIO union factions remained hopelessly divided and refrained from political coalition work while they competed over workers in union elections. The CIO separated its union organizing and political operations to appeal to the allegedly more conservative white workers in textiles, whom they targeted most heavily. Employers by contrast were adept at balancing union resistance at the factory gates with political advocacy across southern state legislatures. Indeed, in the spring of 1947, while the president of the NAM lauded the political mobilization of southern employers for right-to-work rules, CIO general counsel Lee Pressman still had to alert labor leaders of the mounting campaigns for union regulation, as unions were literally being routed at statehouses across the South.

If the causes underlying the rise and setback of unions in the South are complex, the outcome of the decade is clear. By the dawn of the civil rights movement, southern unions were legally circumscribed and weaker than they were prior to the highly publicized organizing drives. Some states went further to outlaw public-sector unions, the dues checkoff, and certain forms of picketing among other restrictions. As historian Nelson Lichtenstein notes, to organize the South during these years required "a massive, socially disruptive interracial campaign . . . a campaign not dissimilar from that which the modern civil rights movement would wage in the 1960s." Despite pockets of civil rights–labor organizing during the 1940s, these movements would largely miss each other for another two decades.

Labor organizing had ground to a halt by the takeoff of the southern civil rights movement. Yet during the late 1960s and early 1970s the civil rights impulse took hold in public-sector union organizing. Martin Luther King Jr.'s final days were with striking sanitation workers in Memphis. A year later mostly female, African American hospital workers in Charleston waged a nationally publicized strike against the Medical University of South Carolina in which the Southern Christian Leadership Conference (SCLC) organized protests alongside the Retail, Wholesale, and Department Store Workers Union local 1199B. But the spread of such labor protest faced steep obstacles. Most states explicitly forbade public-sector unions. Indeed, despite the interest in the Charleston case, and the supposed breaking of the "magnolia curtain" with the strike settlement, the local union was never recognized. The employer had no legal mandate to do so. The SCLC and the national union 1199 moved on to other projects, and organizing ceased the following year.

Given that union gains have come almost entirely in the public sector in recent decades, the lack of affirmative public-sector bargaining laws across the region in conjunction with right-to-work laws has served to dampen labor activity. To date, only Florida has collective bargaining provisions that extend to most public employees. The southward movement of industry and population in the postwar years was thus largely a union-free development. Louisiana was the last of the former Confederate states to adopt a right-to-work law in 1976, after repealing the law in the 1950s. As the South undergoes a significant demographic transformation with increasing numbers of immigrant workers, unions face new sets of obstacles and opportunities. Polling data showed a general uptick in union support in the region at the end of the 20th century, yet any renewal of union organizing will take place in a political environment that decidedly favors employers rather than unions. This fate is owed to the struggles of the 1940s.

MARC DIXON
Dartmouth College

Terry Boswell, Cliff Brown, John Brueggemann, and T. Ralph Peters, *Racial Competition and Class Solidarity* (2006); William Canak and Berkeley Miller, *Industrial and Labor Relations Review* 43:2 (1990); Daniel B. Cornfield, The Gallup Organization (1999); Marc Dixon, *Journal of Policy History* 19:3 (2007), *Social Problems* (May 2010); Leon Fink and Brian Greenberg, *Upheaval in the Quiet Zone: 1199SEIU and the Politics of Health Care Unionism* (2009); Larry J. Griffin, Michael E. Wallace, and Beth A. Rubin, *American Sociological Review* (April 1986); Michael Honey, *Southern Labor and Black Civil Rights: Organizing Memphis Workers* (1993); Larry Isaac and Lars Christiansen, *American Sociological Review* (October 2002); V. O. Key Jr., *Southern Politics in State and Nation* (1949); Robert Rodgers Korstad, *Civil Rights Unionism: Tobacco Workers and the Struggle for Democracy in the Mid-Twentieth-Century South* (2003); Nelson Lichtenstein, in *The Rise and Fall of the New Deal Era*, ed. Steve Fraser and Gary Gerstle (1989); F. Ray Marshall, *Labor in the South* (1967); Frederic Meyers, *Southern Economic Journal* (May 1940); Leo Troy, *Southern Economic Journal* (April 1958).

Asian Americans

The South, as a region, now has the second-largest population of Asian Americans in the United States; only the Pacific Northwest can claim more in number. The history of Asian Americans in the South goes back at least two centuries, but the major growth in population occurred after Congress passed the Immigration Act of 1965. The arrival of immigrants coincided with social and economic forces that changed the face of Dixie. The civil rights movement and federal legislation broke down racial barriers, while new economic opportunities for both native and newcomer served to make southern destinations more appealing.

The emergence of Asian communities in the South over the past four decades shows an ironic trend from both Asians and native southerners when we consider notions of class and status. Although patterns of adaptation among Asian Americans show some uniformity, such as the value given to religious community, networking among associations, shifting family structures, and rural/urban/suburban relocations, one can identify differences and diversity.

Certain occupational trends have emerged: Indian Americans with hotel management, Japanese with biotech businesses, Vietnamese with manicurist salons, Hmong with hosiery mills, and Filipinos with nursing homes. But these stereotypes also overlook the variations in profession and lifestyle that can be found within each group of Asian southerners.

In the antebellum era, Filipinos may have been the first Asians to arrive in the South. They were sailors from Spanish ships who made their way via Mexico to the Louisiana territories in the second half of the 18th century. A Filipino settlement in Jefferson Parish named Manila Village became home for fishermen. The first significant presence of an Asian group in the South, however, came in the postbellum period, when Louisiana, Texas, and Mississippi courted Chinese laborers, so-called coolies, to work sugar and cotton plantations. In 1870 a labor agent named John G. Walker started a company in New Orleans that promoted Chinese workers. He disparaged both Negro and Caucasian workers, but described the coolies as "able-bodied, docile, and experienced agricultural laborers to be drawn from the interior China provinces whose climate most nearly resembles that of the cotton and sugar regions of the South." The importation of (mostly male) coolies, however, conflicted with a Reconstruction ideology of emancipation and created ambiguity within the expected dualities of race and status.

In Mississippi, Chinese families eventually opened and operated grocery stores, which were patronized mostly by blacks. Despite the disadvantage of knowing little English, the Chinese were able to become capable "middlemen" in the biracial Delta culture. They found in the Baptist church educational, recreational, and financial resources that enabled some degree of assimilation, even if social status often remained uncertain. Beginning in the 1970s, however, chain store companies and new career options began to undermine the stability of Chinese grocery and hardware stores that had been in families for three and four generations.

In the past four decades, Asian groups have helped shape the character of southern suburbs. Koreans in the Atlanta suburb of Duluth represent a good example of this development. In Georgia, there are about 40,000 Koreans; the majority live in Duluth, also known as "Korea-town." On Buford Highway, one passes miles of shopping centers, grocery stores, restaurants, and churches with Korean signs. When Korean auto manufacturer Kia Motors looked at sites for a new plant in the United States, Georgia obviously held appeal, and in 2009 Kia opened its West Point, Ga., plant. Also, the fact that many Koreans were Christian (mostly Presbyterian) has helped assimilation in the Protestant South.

During World War II, some 17,000 Japanese were interned in two Arkansas camps. After the war, almost all chose to locate elsewhere. In recent decades, however, Japanese have had a significant impact on the business sector. Japanese companies made major inroads in places such as Austin, Tex., and the Research Triangle Park in central North Carolina, both of which are home to numerous high-tech industries. Japanese expatriates working with transnational companies have tended to live in suburban, gated communities that sharpen the social and economic disparity with poor Carolinians living nearby. These transient residents occupy what one scholar describes as a "globalized hybrid space": living in comfortable, almost bubblelike settings, but still vulnerable to global economic changes.

The trend in Asian American interracial marriage, which in the South frequently involves notions of status, also deserves comment. In a 2000 study, Texas and Florida were listed among the 10 states (all with large Asian American populations) with the highest percentage of people who identified themselves as multiracial. Though color lines have shifted with the presence of new immigrants from Asia and Latin America, researchers have noted that Asians and Latinos prefer to identify themselves as white rather than black. In the case of Asians especially, a new "color line" seems informed by an upwardly mobile status affected by such variables as education, income, religious identity, and language skills. A *New York Times* article (30 January 2011) reports that, compared to other regions of the country, the South in 2009 had the highest rate of Asian American intermarriage. The greatest number of these intermarriages was between Asians and non-Hispanic whites. About 75 percent of Asians who intermarry are women, following a familiar gender and race pattern.

Second-generation Asian youth in the South (and generally in America) have further complicated the idea of status, race, and culture with a self-awareness of hybrid identity. While young people have often insisted on identification with American middle-class society, they also increasingly embrace the diaspora immigrant culture and its strong regard for family, community, and religion. Racial identity may not always be clear, but social success (especially among Asian Indians, Koreans, and Japanese) rivals that of non-Hispanic whites. Asian American youth may, in fact, see advantages to the dual or "in-between" status.

In the South, Asian Indians represent the largest group. From 1990 to 2000 the rate of growth among Indians nationwide exceeded any other Asian group, with a population increasing from 815,447 to 1,899,899. In 2009 the population had increased to over 2,200,000. In the South, Asian Indians number about 750,000. In nine out of 12 southern states, Indians represented the largest number of Asians. Today, Texas ranks fourth among all states in number of residents of Indian background (221,823), with its heaviest concentration of Indians in the Houston area. Florida (118,550), Virginia (90,379), and Georgia (83,753) were also listed among the 10 states with the largest population of Asian Indians. Even in southern states in which Indians represent a small percentage of the voting population (Table 6), they have produced some accomplished politicians, such as governors Bobby Jindal of Louisiana and Nikki Haley of South Carolina.

According to a recent Allied Media Corporation study, Asian Indians had the highest annual medium household income (over $60,000) of all U.S. ethnic groups. Sixty-four percent had at least a bachelor's degree. More than 5,000 Asian Indians are faculty members in higher education. Along with academics, many are doctors, real estate agents, computer scientists, engineers, and businessmen. The *Austin Business Journal* reports that, since 1960, a minimum of 25,000 Indians educated at Indian Institutes of Technology have settled in the United States. According to some estimates, Asian Indians manage about 50 percent of lodges and 35 percent of hotels in the United States. The Indian immigrants who began arriving in the South in the past 50 years usually came from high-caste social groups and from families with adequate financial resources. Many originally came to attend universities and eventually found work in the states as physicians, computer scientists, and engineers.

Like the Chinese before them, Indians complicated the standard black and white racial categories. They arrived in the mid-1960s during the last gasps of Jim Crow, but soon enough to experience its inequities. An old-timer might recall the barber who refused to cut his hair or the restaurant owner who denied him service. But by and large, Asian Indians have managed to effectively navigate the prickly surface of social interaction. In comparison with other Asian groups, the Indian immigrants' more extensive educational background and greater facility with the English language worked to their advantage. They have made homes largely in the suburbs of growing metropolitan areas such as Atlanta, Houston, and the Raleigh-Durham area. Consequently, they have often been heavily involved with land development. Like the Japanese expatriates mentioned earlier, many live in neighborhoods where divisions between the prosperous suburbs and the rural depressed South become quite clear.

The size and fluid character of the Asian Indian community require caution in making generalizations. Adaptations over three generations, among the thousands of families, have happened in multiple ways. For instance, the children of the first families, who were less numerous, often quickly took on the accents and habits of southern life. New, successful, growing suburban communities could effectively create resources that promote Indian ethnicity and inhibit

TABLE 6. Population of Asian Southerners, by State, 2009

State	Total	Indian	Cambodian	Chinese	Filipino	Hmong	Japanese	Korean	Vietnamese
Alabama	46,868	12,320	2,714	10,720	4,547	106	3,353	7,589	5,519
Arkansas	24,566	4,911	0	2,448	4,755	2,917	1,084	3,477	4,974
Florida	380,548	118,550	6,687	66,079	87,504	3,010	13,356	27,202	58,160
Georgia	256,129	83,753	6,006	41,960	18,024	4,542	8,502	48,798	44,544
Kentucky	38,196	10,628	670	8,817	4,080	0	4,986	5,413	3,602
Louisiana	57,708	8,103	82	8,600	7,047	0	977	4,598	28,301
Mississippi	21,901	5,205	143	4,331	3,802	0	1,165	1,581	5,674
North Carolina	164,909	51,338	5,864	30,300	16,994	7,052	6,349	20,680	26,332
South Carolina	48,500	11,110	818	10,228	9,138	716	3,612	5,372	7,506
Tennessee	71,323	19,796	1,692	13,958	9,160	542	4,859	10,257	11,059
Texas	757,337	221,823	13,285	141,518	103,001	394	17,346	57,967	202,003
Virginia	333,426	90,379	6,778	51,532	61,199	276	11,347	64,653	47,262

Source: 2009 U.S. Census.

assimilation. Divisions can develop between families with a long-term commitment to the area and those who are considered transitory. In the analysis of Asian American assimilation, one also should not overlook the role that Indian families have played in small towns throughout the South, which remains a largely unexplored area of diaspora research. In rural counties of South Carolina, for example, Indian families have run profitable motel and quick shop businesses, and Indian physicians and medical technicians have contributed significantly to the improvement of medical services. In small towns, the Indian physician may obtain a kind of status taken for granted in the new suburb.

Whereas Indian Asians often arrived in the South with good social and economic resources, immigrants from the lands of Southeast Asia (Vietnam, Laos, and Cambodia) came with few. Four hundred thousand Vietnamese live in the South, out of a total of over 1 million Vietnamese in the United States, the greatest number in Louisiana, Texas, and Florida. Vietnamese first began arriving after the fall of Saigon in 1975, and waves entered after the epic journey of the so-called boat people in 1978. After the Amerasian Homecoming Act of 1987, about 30,000 so-called *bui doi* (dust of life), a name for the children of Vietnamese mothers and American fathers, were brought to the United States; many found homes in the South. The Vietnamese formed tight-knit communities in which Vietnamese often continued to be the household language. Enterprising families started small businesses, such as restaurants and manicure salons. In the past decade, many Vietnamese (along with Hmong, Laotian, and Cambodian) southerners have been pursuing a more agriculturally based lifestyle. The Carolinas and Georgia have seen a marked increase of Vietnamese farming. A large number have taken up poultry farming, but fruit, peanut, and plant nurseries are also becoming well represented. Of the more than 57,000 Asians who live in Louisiana, at least 28,000 are Vietnamese. In the coastal and delta areas, many became involved with the fishing industry and the oil industry. In politics, Vietnamese in Louisiana, like Indian immigrants, can point to the success of one of their own. For instance, in 2008 Joseph Cao became the first Vietnamese American elected to Congress.

Among Asians, the Montagnards (Mountain People) offer one of the most uniquely southern cases, since North Carolina has the largest concentration (about 5,000) outside of Vietnam. The Montagnards are from the central highlands of Vietnam and during the war allied with U.S. forces. Having supported the United States, many Montagnards lost their land and became displaced once the Americans left. Through contacts with former veterans and military personal in North Carolina, arrangements were made for settlement in the state. Montagnard immigrants were employed in service jobs, landscaping, and manufacturing. Such employment was physically demanding but required minimal language skills. The Montagnards live in moderate-income subdivisions located on formerly rural landscapes. Increasingly, both husbands and wives work outside the home and share childcare. The Montagnards are predominately Christian. While the community continues to finds ways to preserve the distinctiveness of Montagnard culture, it stresses the importance of obtaining language skills and education for success in the United States; these two goals, however, can be difficult to balance.

About 15,000 Hmong live in North Carolina. Like the Montagnards, they helped American forces and suffered persecution when the war ended. In the 1990s hundreds of families migrated to the Catawba Valley and began working in hosiery mills that had a demand for unskilled labor. Like the white migrants from Appalachia who first came to work in the mills, the Hmong have internally nurtured the ties of family, religion, and community. As is the case with many Asian groups, care of children involves all generations. Grandparents who live with their children often take on the responsibility for childcare while both parents work. But, like the Appalachian mill workers' descendants, college-educated Hmong children increasingly choose other professions and do not return home.

Throughout the American South, Asian southerners have been agents of economic, social, and cultural change. Their impact on the southern cultural landscape goes beyond the usual recognition of the "model minority" stereotype. Often praised for their effective embrace of the values of self-sufficiency, hard work, and reliability, Asian southerners have also played a crucial role in complicating the categories of race, class, and religion. And, like many southerners who seek the American dream, they find way to keep the circles unbroken.

SAM BRITT
Furman University

Christina Chia and Hong-an Truong, *Southern Exposure* (Summer 2005); James C. Cobb and William Stueck, eds., *Globalization and the American South* (2005); Lucy M. Cohen, *Chinese in the Post–Civil War South* (1984); Moon-Ho Jung, *Coolies and Cane: Race, Labor, and Sugar in the Age of Emancipation* (2006); Stephen L. Klineberg, in *Asian American Religions*, ed. Tony Carnes and Fenggang Yang (2004); James L. Peacock, Harry L. Watson, and Carrie R. Matthews, eds., *American South in a Global World* (2005); Susan Saulny, *New York Times* (30 January 2011); Christine So, *Economic Citizens: A Narrative of Asian American Visibility* (2007); Charles Reagan Wilson, "Chinese in Mississippi: An Ethnic People in a Biracial Society," *Mississippi History Now* (2002, online, 25 March 2011).

Black Elite and the Black Middle Class

Elite status in a social system generally requires landownership and other markers, although there have been some exceptions. Black elites in America attained their status sometimes with but most often without landownership, great wealth, education, or even their freedom. This class qualification speaks to the fortitude and agency of African Americans and is also representative of the oppressive structures that have created social classes based on race. Although many black Americans have achieved middle-class and elite status, the historic problems of race and class still affect their social mobility. Despite these obstacles, black middle class and elite in the South continue to rise in economic and political power.

Europeans brought a diverse group of Africans with them as they explored and conquered the Americans. Not all Africans coming to colonial America were enslaved, although most were brought against their will. Once they entered the emerging colonial structures, almost all lost connections to previous status and became part of a strict racialized class system. Throughout the colonial and antebellum years, African Americans in the South were relegated to the lowest social order with castelike rigidity. Despite the wrath of slavery and institutionalized oppression, blacks achieved elite status among themselves in an internal social organization, some designed by slave owners and some of their own making. Mixed-race and other privileged slaves were frequently given the best household positions on the plantation. These house servants had access to better clothing, health care, and valuable information. Those with privilege often supervised other slaves, further complicating class divisions among the enslaved community.

The inhumane treatment of enslaved African Americans and the subsequent racial dictatorship of the Jim Crow era created a social structure that heavily influenced the expression of social class in the South. Like other parts of the country, southern society is still complicated by the long-lasting effects of slavery. Because the South experienced less social fluidity than other regions, many African Americans have yet to fully overcome the complications caused by racism and segregation. Social mobility for black southerners coming out of slavery emerged alongside the struggles for equality and greater access to freedom. African Americans created universities, established religious organizations, and erected business networks to support the growing demand for black-owned products and services.

In the aftermath of slavery and the decades that followed, many of the region's black elite and middle class left for better opportunities, but some remained. In many cities throughout the South, "aristocrats of color," light-skinned wealthy blacks, were at the top of many industries directed at black customers. These elite blacks were well educated and well traveled but, most importantly, held claim that they were not descendants of slaves. Even though they were elite among African Americans, black elites frequently remained the object of ridicule by whites who scoffed at the notion of an "aristocrat of color." Nevertheless, many black elites in cities such as New Orleans and Charleston lived in luxury and prestige.

From the Progressive Era onward, as more African Americans began attending colleges and professional schools, middle-class and elite black families put a tremendous amount of pressure on young adults, especially females, to adhere to strict codes of behavior lest the entire family lose its standing in the social class. In addition to high academic and moral standards, black women faced strong expectations that they should give back to the families and their communities in a "lift while you climb" philosophy. With this in mind, black Americans used black social clubs, fraternities and sororities, and professional organizations to strengthen their positions in society.

Blacks and whites alike gave special status to African American preachers and social activists because of their influence over propriety within the community. As they have in other social rights movements, the black middle class and elite have been a primary resource for leaders and volunteers in the NAACP and other rights groups as well. The voices of prominent black leaders including those of the Harlem Renaissance and other movements of the early 20th century introduced the world to the "New Negro." The outspoken notable blacks of the era emboldened and inspired black southerners, many of whom expressed themselves through music, art, and literature.

Both world wars changed labor, gender, and race relations in America, bringing many more African Americans into factories or military service. Black home ownership increased, propelling more blacks into the middle class, although they rarely received the same advantages of middle-class whites. Blacks in the military, especially black officers, were considered part of the black elite, particularly if they were highly decorated. Their steady, albeit substandard, pay enabled them to gain some financial stability and perhaps notoriety as well.

In each era, with rare exception, the highest levels of American social class have remained outside the grasp of even the black elite, despite the strides made by the generation before them. Oprah Winfrey, with her total net worth reaching into the billions as of 2011, is the only African American to break into the Top 400 of America's richest people. In his 2000 song "Country Grammar," southern rapper Nelly demands "Bill Gates, Donald Trump, let me in now." For most black southerners, this mantra speaks volumes about the elusive nature of elite status for many in this country.

RHONDA RAGSDALE
Rice University

William B. Gatewood, *Aristocrats of Color: The Black Elite 1880–1920* (1990); Lawrence Graham, *Our Kind of People: Inside America's Black Upper Class* (1999); Michael Omi and Howard Winant, *Racial Formation in the United States: From the 1960s to the 1990s* (1994); Stephanie J. Shaw, *What a Woman Ought to Be and to Do: Black Professional Women Workers during the Jim Crow Era* (1996).

Civil Rights Movement

Race was clearly front and center in the civil rights movement, but social class was also important in several significant ways. First, class relations in the South structured the conditions for the emergence of the movement. Second, class relations shaped the dynamics of the movement during its heyday. Third, the civil rights movement and its legacy generated important class-based consequences. Much is missed if class is neglected in our understanding.

It is no secret that slavery played an essential role in the historical development of the United States. American slavery was primarily a class-based institution designed to cruelly extract surplus value from a dehumanized subject population to benefit a purportedly superior class of white, property-owning men. From the early 1600s, slavery fueled development in both the North and the South. In the South, slaves were exploited on plantations. In the North, they worked as domestic servants and in a variety of trades. While slavery began to fade in the North toward the end of the 18th century, it continued in the South, especially as cotton became the dominant crop.

The antebellum South was a white supremacist slave society, an economic racial apartheid. In the North, black and white workers were often at loggerheads as European immigrants often shoved black workers aside in labor market competition. Capital frequently found the racial and ethnic heterogeneity of the U.S. working class useful for lowering labor costs and undermining solidarity by pitting one ethnic group against another. Black workers in some cases acted as strikebreakers, earning the hatred of many white labor organizations. Racism was endemic in both the North and the South and kept black and white workers segregated and the potential power of their union fragmented and wasted.

After the Civil War, slavery was dismantled, yet soon supplanted by a different form of racial subjugation integral to the crop lien and debt bondage system of sharecropping. Although the Populist movement, the Knights of Labor, the International Workers of the World, and New Orleans waterfront workers provide examples to the contrary, it was not until the late 1930s and early 1940s that a concerted attempt was made to incorporate black workers into the labor movement. Until then, blacks who dared question, agitate, or organize against the conditions of their labor faced intimidation, violence, or murder. In some cases white unions led the charge. This changed in 1930s, however, with the efforts of the Congress of Industrial Organizations (CIO). Because African Americans composed a significant portion of the growing unorganized mass-production workforce, the CIO could not ignore them as the American Federation of Labor had so often done. Yet the interest of the labor movement in civil rights for African Americans was short-lived.

World War II had a tremendous impact on the civil rights movement. As Jack Bloom writes in his *Class, Race, and the Civil Rights Movement*, the war "opened up jobs for blacks, took them off farms, and set them in the cities, it put guns in their hands and trained them to use them; the war exposed blacks to education and to the world and made them more cosmopolitan." Yet after the war, many blacks found themselves to be worse off. Black workers were typically channeled into the most menial labor at lowest pay, locking them into conditions of hardship and poverty. Cotton had been responsible for the expansion of the slavery in the early 19th century, and its decline in the 20th century played a huge role in the emergence of the movement. Technological changes in agriculture accelerated during the 1950s and drove tenant farmers and sharecroppers from the land to the cities. In the cities, many blacks faced job discrimination, few educational opportunities, and obstacles to job prospects as automation and cybernation grew in industry. As southern blacks became more urban, black church rosters swelled. In turn, the economic and political power of these churches grew, and with the help of movement ministers, congregations became increasingly concerned with social and economic justice. Yet during this time—the height of the Cold War—the labor movement purged itself of its most left-leaning and racially progressive members and consequently ceased to be an aggressive ally of those fighting for civil rights. Movement activists looked beyond labor, finding sustenance in religious and educational organizations instead.

In the decades predating the civil rights movement, blacks in the South had played a central role in the region's economic infrastructure but were barred from equal access to the South's social structure. Although the movement did have roots in, and took many of its cues from, working-class struggles of the 1930s and 1940s, the movement from the mid-1950s to the mid-1960s was heavily based in the black middle class. Black ministers, teachers, and especially students formed the shock troops in this phase of the movement.

Although organized labor was largely absent from the movement during its early period (though it did play a role in a variety of early events such as the 1963 March on Washington, as well as events in the later 1960s), the strategies and successes of the movement nonetheless depended on a number of class-related issues and concerns. The civil rights movement overturned the white supremacist planter aristocracy, and it did so through a robust, class-based coalition of forces that included "Southern business and middle classes, the Northern middle class, the national Democratic party, and the federal government," as Bloom puts it in his *Class, Race, and the Civil Rights Movement*. Various forms of economic sanctions and tactics were used by both the movement and its opponents in this historic struggle.

The countermovement against the southern civil rights movement also had important class dimensions. One of the most important resistance organizations, the Citizens' Council, formed on 11 July 1954 and constituted, along with the Ku Klux Klan, one of the key organizations of white southern resistance to the movement. At its peak, more than 150,000 strong, across Mississippi, Georgia, South Carolina, and Louisiana, its membership consisted of leading citizens, including governors, congressman, judges, physicians, lawyers, industrialists, and bankers. The council used many tactics to combat the civil rights movement, including intimidation, vandalism, and various forms of economic warfare. It withheld advertising and other revenues from businesses and organizations that might threaten solid South white supremacy. Boycotts were organized against businesses that did not share the council's ideological stance, and much harsher tactics, such as denial of credit, goods, and services, cancellation of insurance policies and mortgages, job loss and eviction, were used against blacks involved in the movement.

Not only were forms of class warfare used by the white resistance, but they were also used by the movement itself. In Orangeburg, during a 1955 school board desegregation drive, economic power was used against the black activists, but blacks countered by launching their own boycott against white merchants who were leading the resistance. Bus boycotts were used effectively by the movement in Montgomery and Tallahassee. In Greensboro in February of 1960, commerce was disrupted to protest segregated lunch counters. In Nashville the local movement used lunch counter sit-ins, theater and library stand-ins, and a successful economic boycott of the downtown white-owned business district.

After the 1965 Watts riots, King and the movement became much more interested in economic justice, and King tried to rebuild bridges between the movement and organized labor that had been broken in the 1940s and 1950s. Jack Bloom writes that "King and the SCLC embarked upon a serious campaign that involved them in strikes and union organizing in Atlanta; Memphis; Detroit; Birmingham; St. Petersburg, Florida; and Charleston, Georgetown, and Florence, South Carolina." It is King's legacy as an economic radical that is left out of the standard stories told about his leadership. He became acutely class-conscious and very active against class injustices between 1965 and 1968. King believed that the Civil Rights Act of 1964 and the Voting Rights Act of 1965 were simply the first steps in a longer journey and that a radical redistribution of the wealth in the United States was necessary for the country to experience real democracy. King died supporting the strike of sanitation workers in Memphis. Less than two weeks after his assassination, the striking black sanitation workers obtained a settlement. This victory inspired the Southern Christian Leadership Conference to support black hospital nurses in Charleston in a contentious two-month strike from March to July 1969. The strike ultimately won for the nurses much needed pay increases, a grievance system, and a credit union. These victories signaled that civil rights unionism was a winning strategy. The successes of the movement in the 1960s were to become even more influential in the years ahead.

The civil rights movement in the South was clearly successful in a number of respects—its abolition of the Jim Crow system of racial apartheid, providing the call to action behind the Civil Rights Act of 1964 and the Voting Rights Act of 1965, and perhaps most importantly for creating a new culture of racial pride and dignity among African Americans. The civil rights movement was also the major catalyst for a rejuvenated culture of activism in America. It was the movement leader that stimulated a massive wave of reform movements (student, women, antiwar, environment) that emerged in the 1960s and 1970s. Even older movements that had become highly institutionalized and stagnant were, at least for a time, revitalized in their militancy and movement activism by the civil rights movement.

The movement led to a number of sustained institutional achievements. Politically, the movement was key to rebuilding the Democratic Party and elimination of one-party rule in the South. Today, largely because of the movement, the black middle class is larger and has more resources than ever before. Expansion of educational opportunities has been important, allowing blacks to take advantage of a host of programs, smaller classes, and superior personnel and facilities. The number of black students enrolled in college or university and attaining professional jobs has increased dramatically. Unlike their relatives who shunned the South decades before, many blacks have been returning to the region.

There is little doubt that the civil rights movement produced some very momentous, if partial, changes in American society. Yet there have been setbacks, and many blacks still encounter serious obstacles with persistent racism leading the list. Racism reduced and altered in form as a result of the civil rights movement is integrally tied to contemporary class dynamics in a host of disturbing ways: resegregation of public schools, hypersegregation of some inner cities, extreme unemployment rates among black and Latino youth, erosion of voting rights in some areas, weakening of the labor movement, unraveling of the social safety net, malignant growth of the prison industrial complex with its enormous black male incarceration rate, ever-increasing ability of placeless capital to move at will, discriminatory subprime lending that was partially a product of the failure to enforce civil rights laws and a major factor in the U.S. housing crisis, and wealth and income inequalities that approach pre–New Deal levels. As Cynthia Griggs Fleming writes in *In the Shadow of Selma*, among the collective voices appearing nowhere in national conversations about racial injustice and civil rights legacy are those of the southern rural blacks, many of whom were on the front lines of the civil rights movement during its heyday. The benefits of movement change have largely passed them by. Their everyday life is a constant struggle for basic civil rights, and the contingencies of class are crucial for understanding this condition.

The mass southern civil rights movement began with a boycott in Montgomery and ended with a strike in Memphis. In the midst of the movement many observers often saw nothing but race-based chaos rather than one of the largest working-class uprisings in American history. Class relations were central to the movement throughout its history. Now with soaring deficits, a global recession, and a failure of leadership in Congress, there is a real danger that many of the gains resulting from the civil rights movement are slipping away. The attitude of many blacks in the South (and perhaps some whites, too) might be summed up in the words of Andrew Broadnax, a southern labor organizer, "Everything changed, but ain't nothin' changed." Although there have been significant social and cultural changes in the South (and the nation generally), the power structures responsible for and representative of the political economy of the region are in some ways quite similar to those found in earlier times. The "Third Reconstruction" and new forms of social movement leadership have yet to materialize. Outsourcing and capital flight have left much of the South without a viable manufacturing sector and years behind the rest of the world in informational and "green" technologies. With few decent jobs, a crumbling educational system, and failing infrastructure, it is hard not to conclude that existing patterns of racial and class stratification in the South might endure for years to come. When the historical sociology of the long civil rights movement is finally written, social class will be a significant part of the story.

DANIEL M. HARRISON
Lander University

LARRY W. ISAAC
Vanderbilt University

Lawrence Bobo and Ryan A. Smith, in *Beyond Pluralism: The Conception of Groups and Group Identity in America*, ed. Wendy F. Katkin, Ned Landsman, and Andrea Tyree (1998); Clayborne Carson, ed., *The Autobiography of Martin Luther King, Jr.* (1998); Jack Bloom, *Class, Race, and the Civil Rights Movement* (1987); Alan Draper, *Conflict of Interests: Organized Labor and the Civil Rights Movement in the South, 1954-1968* (1994); Philip Foner, *Organized Labor and the Black Worker* (1974); Michael Goldfield, *WorkingUSA* (September 2008); Jacquelyn Dowd Hall, *Journal of American History* (March 2005); Michael Honey, *Southern Labor and Black Civil Rights: Organizing Memphis Workers* (1993), in *Southern Labor in Transition, 1940-1995*, ed. Ron Zieger (1997); Larry Isaac and Lars Christiansen, *American Sociological Review* (October 2002); Larry Isaac, Steve McDonald, and Greg Lukasik, *American Journal of Sociology* (July 2006); Joseph Luders, *American Journal of Sociology* (January 2006); Aldon D. Morris, *The Origins of the Civil Rights Movement* (1984), *Annual Review of Sociology* (August 1999); Sarah C. Thuesen, *Southern Cultures* (Fall 2008); Steve Valocchi, *Social Problems* (August 1994).

Collective Memory

Social class acts on memory both by structuring access to the resources needed to establish, disseminate, and maintain memory and by structuring alliances and conflicts within and between classes that influence memory. Those who have been in control of greater resources and greater social and political authority have exercised disproportionate power over public space and the versions of history that get inscribed there. Public spaces in the South's cities such as Jackson Square in New Orleans or Marion Square in Charleston tend to have been named for members of the elite, as were streets. The many controversies over renaming streets for Martin Luther King that flared up in the late 20th century only emphasize this point. With the exception of monuments celebrating the Confederate common soldier and those erected later in the 20th century, most monuments in the South, as elsewhere, were put up by the elite, of the elite, but for everyone.

As publishing became more widespread in the 19th century and a mass media arose in the 20th, elites were able to use these means to encourage some memories and suppress others. A subtler connection between social class and memory can be seen in education. The South lagged behind the rest of the nation in the provision of public education, so until Reconstruction, education was largely a privilege of the upper class, along with the expanded sense of the world and one's relation to it afforded by education. The educated were more able to place their own experiences in a broader context, to have a historical memory in which they themselves were significant actors. Finally, given the importance of oratory in southern culture, the social elites, better able literally to make their voices heard at political occasions and commemorative events, had greater ability to shape public memory.

However, this points us toward another key feature of memory in the South. To the extent that the South long had a less urban population, lower levels of formal education, and higher rates of geographic persistence across time, the importance of oral communication has been greater in the South than in other regions. Oral tradition allowed lower classes to maintain, at least among themselves, very different memories from those perpetuated among their betters. This phenomenon is most clearly seen in relation to the experience of slavery; former slaves and their descendants told their families the truth of enslavement for decades while social elites celebrated it as a benign institution. The existence of these subaltern countermemories has sometimes led to strong public debates once the lower class maintaining them finds the power to introduce these countermemories to public discourse, as has happened with greater frequency toward the end of the 20th century in the aftermath of the civil rights movement and as changes in the agricultural and industrial economies loosened old patterns of deference. On the other hand, elites for generations used memory of the Civil War and Reconstruction to attempt to gain the support of poorer whites for white supremacy, even though their historical experience and contemporary interests might have pointed toward class-based hostility instead.

BRUCE E. BAKER
Royal Holloway, University of London

Derek H. Alderman, *Professional Geographer* (November 2000); Bruce E. Baker, *What Reconstruction Meant: Historical Memory in the American South* (2007); W. Fitzhugh Brundage, *The Southern Past: A Clash of Race and Memory* (2005);

Gaines M. Foster, *Ghosts of the Confederacy: Defeat, the Lost Cause, and the Emergence of the New South, 1865–1913* (1987).

Crime and Punishment

England was the basic source of the colonial South's legal systems, and migrants to the colonies carried English criminal law with them to protect property, suppress disorder, and defend morality. Local courts headed by justices of the peace (or their equivalent) dealt with minor crimes, whereas higher courts, with their grand juries and petit juries, dealt with felonies. Deviations from English standards were usually in the direction of leniency; many crimes that carried the death penalty in England were punished more mildly in America. The great majority of those found guilty paid small fines, but other punishments included whipping, branding, or exposure in the stocks.

England, though, had no law of slavery, and each colony spelled out crimes that applied only to slaves and established special courts to try them. Slave codes also introduced new crimes that applied to whites, such as trading with slaves or aiding slave insurrections; white women could face harsh punishments for having sexual relationships with slaves or free blacks. Yet, whites could not be convicted on the basis of black testimony, and many acts that would have been crimes against a white victim were not crimes, or were crimes of less severity, if blacks were victims. In North Carolina, for example, killing a slave was not considered murder until 1774.

The actual patterns of crime in the colonial era are difficult to measure, in part because punishment of criminal acts by servants and slaves was often left to masters. Surviving records of North Carolina and Virginia courts show that, unlike New England courts, they dealt with a higher proportion of crimes of violence than of property crimes and crimes against morality. The most reliable data on crimes concern homicides, on which records were kept. Historian Randolph Roth has shown that the broad trends in homicides over time were basically similar in all the colonies, with homicide rates extremely high in the earliest years and declining irregularly until the era of the American Revolution. In the Chesapeake colonies, for example, the rates of adult homicide (the number killed per year per 100,000) were about 30 in the 1650s, declined to between 10 and 15 by 1700, and fell to about five by the 1750s.

The absolute rates in the Chesapeake colonies were significantly higher than rates in New England and perhaps twice as high as those in Pennsylvania. There seems little doubt that the sharper class differences in the Chesapeake, with its many slaves and white servants, helped to produce these higher homicide rates.

Homicides and assaults often involved masters attacking servants, or vice versa; Roth estimates that more than half of homicides in the Chesapeake in the 17th century were connected directly to white servitude. Many property crimes involved servants charged with theft from masters, and other crimes were specific to servitude. Both female and male servants, for example, could be sentenced to extra time in service for illegitimate births. More generally, the law in action favored the propertied. In 18th-century North Carolina, among those charged with property crimes such as larceny, accused laborers were twice as likely to be convicted as property owners accused of the same crimes. The overriding need for white solidarity, however, probably diminished the impact of social class among whites on crime and its punishment. The conviction rate for those accused of crimes in 18th-century North Carolina was just 32 percent overall, and for those charged with assault, the propertied and the unpropertied were convicted at about the same rate. Juries often prevented death sentences by convicting on a lesser charge.

In the 1760s, as government authority came under challenge, crimes of violence rose throughout the colonies. Vigilante "Regulators" in the North Carolina backcountry forced the closure of courts considered to be corrupt, and Regulators in the South Carolina backcountry, angry over the failure of the courts to control crime, seized and punished accused criminals. The Revolutionary War brought bitter partisan fighting in the southern colonies, and the homicide rate soared and remained high for many years. Yet, after the Revolution, criminal codes became less harsh and the use of the death penalty was sharply limited. After 1796 in Virginia, only murder was punishable by death. Inspired by Enlightenment ideas calling for the rehabilitation of criminals, every southern state except South and North Carolina built prisons before the Civil War, and prison terms replaced branding, whipping, and other forms of punishment. Into these prisons went mostly white men, mainly poor and disproportionately foreign-born, who had been convicted of property crimes.

In the early 19th century, patterns of crime—at least of violent crime—in the South began to diverge sharply from national norms. Following the War of 1812, homicide rates outside the South fell to historic lows, ranging from one murder per 100,000 adults in New England up to six in other northern states. In the slave states, though, homicide rates never returned to the lower, prerevolutionary level; they ranged from eight to 28. Before 1810, for example, homicide rates in the plantation regions of Georgia were about 1.5 times those in rural Ohio, but by 1820 they were almost three times as high. In this same period the southern states gained their reputation as places of primitive violence. Travelers and humorists told tales featuring lower-class bullies who kept one fingernail long, the better to gouge out eyes in drunken hand-to-hand battles, or gentlemen who dueled with pistols after elaborate exchanges of formal messages. Although northerners occasionally dueled—Abraham Lincoln almost did so in 1842—and poor men in the North brawled to demand respect and defend their masculine honor, personal violence was more widely accepted and practiced in the southern states. As before the Revolution, courts in the North dealt mainly with property crimes, whereas those in Georgia and South Carolina dealt most often with crimes of violence or disorder. Sympathetic juries treated such crimes leniently and, except for outsiders such as Irish immigrants, seldom sentenced white men to long prison terms. In local courts in those states, from 63 to 90 percent of those accused of violent crimes were either not indicted or ultimately acquitted.

Dueling often involved politicians and newspaper editors for whom the trading of public insults was the stock-in-trade. The practice was condemned by evangelical clergymen and members of the growing urban middle class, and several states outlawed duels, but duelists were rarely brought to court. The Alabama legislature more than once exempted members from the requirement to swear an oath that they had not participated in a duel. While dueling, with its elaborate etiquette, was supposed to distinguish gentlemen from those in the lower orders, many of the conflicts between rich men or public figures took the form of street brawls or murders from ambush.

Participants in these roughly class-based forms of violence shared a culture of honor under which a man should resent every public insult or hint of disrespect. Historians have attributed this culture to the frontier or to the Scots-Irish heritage of many southerners, but neither of these explanations fits the geographic patterns that have been uncovered. In the era of the Revolution, for example, the Shenandoah Valley of Virginia had very low levels of homicide, and in the antebellum era, counties in the mountain South had homicide rates that approached the extremely low rates of New England; both were areas of heavy Scots-Irish settlement. Instead, Roth has concluded, southern violence was "most strongly linked to the presence or absence of slavery." In a land where "mastery" was defined in uniquely evident ways, no white man wanted to be treated like a slave or to appear to be mastered by another. Vigilantism in the South also was intertwined with slavery. Hundreds of blacks and a number of alleged white "instigators" were killed during insurrection scares, and, despite the obvious threat to the property rights of slave owners, more than 50 slaves were killed for alleged crimes by lynch mobs before the Civil War. Vigilante mobs also drove out, and occasionally killed, suspected abolitionists, especially in the 1850s.

The Civil War, even more than the Revolution, altered the patterns of crime and the criminal justice system in the South. In the mountain areas, previously the most peaceful, ugly conflicts erupted as Confederate dissenters—most of them nonslaveholders—resisted the draft or joined the Union army. Killings and destruction or theft of property soared, sometimes directly because of the war, and sometimes not. These regions were plagued for decades with self-perpetuating cycles of vengeance killings.

Most consequential was the destruction of slavery, and with it the slave codes. White southerners hoped to protect their power with a distinctive set of "Black Codes" that would have criminalized many forms of ordinary economic behavior by African Americans, but this effort was squelched by the Civil Rights Act of 1866 and the Fourteenth Amendment. In response, legislatures spelled out more property crimes in statutes and sharply increased penalties, so that the theft of a single hog might bring a long prison sentence. Vaguely written vagrancy statutes allowed local officials to round up workers in times of labor shortages.

Local courts now devoted themselves more to crimes against property, mainly by black defendants. To defray the cost of soaring prison populations, all southern states eventually turned to the leasing of convicts to private employers, and many local jurisdictions did the same. The convict lease system, especially in the lower South, provided forced labor to politically favored industrialists or planters. Overworked, underfed, and whipped into obedience, convicts in these sometimes appalling camps died in great numbers. Whites were potentially subject to the same penalties as blacks under ostensibly color-blind laws, but in fact whites were still protected by the need for white solidarity, and juries were reluctant to convict whites of crimes that might put them on a chain gang with blacks. In Alabama, for example, in the late 19th century 94 percent of state-leased convicts and 96 percent of county convicts were African Americans.

Not satisfied with the regular legal system as a way of controlling black labor and black behavior, whites turned more often than ever before to extralegal action. During Reconstruction, white vigilantes, in the form of the Ku Klux Klan and similar groups whose members included a broad cross section of white society, attacked, and sometimes killed, both blacks and whites who supported the Republican state governments or in other ways threatened white hegemony. Homicide rates soared to levels not seen since the 17th century: in Piedmont Georgia they reached 25 per 100,000, compared to 10 before the war, and in Louisiana perhaps as high as 90. After the restoration of Democratic rule in southern states the homicide rate declined sharply in most places, but both measurable crime rates and perceptions of those rates again rose in the 1890s, a decade of political turmoil and economic depression. Vigilante crowds, including both rich and poor whites, lynched hundreds of African Americans accused of crimes or, sometimes, simply of failing to defer. Although many whites in the growing urban middle class publicly deplored lynchings for their lawlessness, their main response was to build a system of legal segregation that would, they hoped, restore order and prevent conflict by separating the races.

As long as this violence operated in support of white supremacy, whites could act largely without fear of punishment, and coroners' juries typically concluded that lynch victims had come to their deaths "at the hands of parties unknown." White vigilante violence, however, could and did meet strong resistance when it threatened the interests of other whites, as it did when "whitecappers" in Mississippi attacked black tenants and small farmers to attempt to drive them from the labor market. And it should be kept in mind that lynchings of black men by white mobs, while dramatic and powerful, account for only a small part of the rise of homicides in the South (about 2.4 lynchings per 100,000 when southern states' overall homicide rates ranged from 10 to 30). Whites killed whites, and blacks killed blacks, in large numbers, and in the late 19th century the black homicide rate for the first time in history began to exceed the white rate.

In early 20th century, private leasing of convicts gradually disappeared. In Tennessee, where convicts were used to keep wages down and break strikes, miners attacked the prisoner stockades of Tennessee Coal and Iron and released the prisoners; convict leasing was ended there in 1894. In other states, Progressive reformers fought against convict leasing following exposés of horrific conditions. Even after leasing was abandoned, however, convicts continued to work in chains under state or local control, building roads and levees, growing cotton at places like Parchman Farm penitentiary in Mississippi, or digging coal for the state of Tennessee. Improved conditions for convicts may have actually made whites more eligible for conviction and imprisonment. By 1927, 27 percent of Georgia's convicts were white, as compared to less than 10 percent in 1908, the last year of convict leasing.

Since World War I, at first very gradually, southern patterns of crime and punishment have moved toward national norms. Lynchings declined, in part as a result of campaigns by the NAACP and white reformers such as Jessie Daniel Ames, until they had become rare by 1940. The Supreme Court began to enforce national norms of criminal procedure in the states and to forbid such blatant forms of discrimination as all-white juries, and federal prosecutors began to go after vigilante groups that attacked civil rights workers.

In the early 21st century the South is the region with the highest official rates of crime (both violent and property crime) and with the most conservative views on punishment. No southern state has abolished the death penalty, and of the 10 states that have executed the most prisoners since 1976, eight belonged to the Confederacy (and the other two, Oklahoma and Missouri, were slave states or territories in 1860). Yet much evidence points toward a lessening of regional differences. In the 1920s the murder rate in most southern states was two or three times the national average; currently the rate in the South is about 22 percent above the national average. Further, according to annual population surveys of victims of crime, southerners are *less* likely to be assaulted than other Americans. Incarceration rates for African Americans are actually lower than the national average in seven of the 11 former Confederate states. Historically, what has stood out as exceptional about the South in both crime and punishment has been their entanglement with race and slavery. Now, in these spheres, as in politics, economics, and others, we may be witnessing the end of southern exceptionalism.

J. WILLIAM HARRIS
University of New Hampshire

Edward L. Ayers, *Vengeance and Justice: Crime and Punishment in the 19th-Century American South* (1984); Scott P. Culclasure, in *The Confessions of Edward Isham: A Poor White Life of the Old South*, ed. Charles C. Bolton and Scott P. Culclasure (1998); Michael Stephen Hindus, *Prison and Plantation: Crime, Justice, and Authority in Massachusetts and South Carolina, 1767–1878* (1980); Alexander C. Lichtenstein, *Twice the Work of Free Labor: The Political Economy of Convict Labor in the New South* (1996); Randolph Roth, *American Homicide* (2009); Donna Spindel, *Crime and Society in North Carolina, 1673–1776* (1989).

Demagogues

In the antebellum South, electoral politics was a contested affair with both Whigs and Democrats maintaining a viable presence in a variety of local, state, and national elected offices. The parties often differed on key matters, including tax policy and internal improvements such as infrastructure and railroad development, but agreed that the preservation of slavery was the most critical matter even as they occasionally bickered on the best way to protect the peculiar institution. When the Whig Party fractured and eventually died in the years before secession, the Democratic Party controlled politics through most of the South. Disagreements within the one remaining party were then largely focused on whether slavery could be best protected from within the

Union—cooperationists—or within the confines of a new and separate nationality. Much of the political discourse of the Confederate era revolved around wartime issues of supply and resources, keeping the home front protected, and matters of military strategy.

With the unconditional surrender at Appomattox, southern politics pivoted toward a new coalition of freed slaves, blacks who had been free before the war, and other Republicans including carpetbaggers and scalawags. This new political structure minimized the whites who had previously dominated the economic and political spaces and places of power. The massive unpopularity of Reconstruction led to the rise of Redeemers, white southerners who wished to regain control of the South in the name of white supremacy, the Democratic Party, and, to a lesser extent, a mixed economy of agriculture and industry. By early 1877, Reconstruction was over in the South, and the Redeemers worked feverishly to solidify their power. Along with the rise of the Redeemers and their conspicuous ideas about race and gender came the rise of the demagogue—a politician whose notoriety was gained by inflaming the passions and prejudices of the voters without much interest in problem solving or comprehensive policy achievements.

In the rural, overwhelmingly agricultural, poverty-laden South, electoral politics became the first spectator sport for white southerners decades before college football and NASCAR became cultural passions. Demagogues, in this political culture, became headline acts. Political rallies provided gathering opportunities for southerners whose lives were often isolated and defined by work and family. These campaign events often featured food, live music, and a host of speeches by lesser-known politicians. Demagogues such as Cole Blease and Ben Tillman (South Carolina), James K. Vardaman and Theodore Bilbo (Mississippi), Eugene Talmadge (Georgia), Jeff Davis (Arkansas), Tom Heflin and later George Wallace (Alabama) were the most popular attractions and gave raucous speeches, usually placing the blame for the problems of the day on two time-tested villains: blacks and the federal government. The most successful demagogues in gaining and maintaining elected office tended to be charismatic speakers whose rallies were eagerly anticipated by southern whites for both style and substance.

From the late 19th through the mid-20th century, southern demagogues flashed particularly hateful rhetoric toward blacks. Bilbo once challenged "every red-blooded white man to use any means necessary to keep the niggers away from the polls." Davis called black voters an "ever-present eating cankerous sore" and proclaimed that blacks were capable of neither higher education nor moral culture. Tillman assured his voters that any person who "doubts that civilization depends on white supremacy is a fool and a knave." Vardaman told Mississippi voters that "the way to control the nigger is to whip him . . . and another is to never pay him more wages than is actually necessary to buy food and clothing." While some politicians, newspaper editors, and progressives complained about the vociferous attacks, the hard-edged racial appeals proliferated primarily because dynamic demagogues were more likely to win than lose.

Racial demagoguery not only provided a scapegoat for ordinary southerners in a venue that pleased them but assured whites of all classes that their status would be protected. Demagogues promised to limit the spaces and places where blacks could live and work, and vowed never to allow blacks to enter into schools or other public areas where whites, particularly white women, could be found. "The nigger cannot live in the same country with the white man on terms of social and political equality," Vardaman once noted. "It is one of the impossible things. One of the other of the races will rule. They will not mix." And demagogues called southern whites to action if blacks even attempted sweeping integration. "There's not enough troops in the Army," South Carolina governor Strom Thurmond declared, "to force the southern people to break down segregation and admit the Negro race into our theaters, into our swimming pools, into schools, and into our homes."

Miscegenation, or race mixing, was a constant theme of demagogues who invoked pseudoscientific research findings to support the belief that blacks were untrustworthy, more likely to retrogress than progress, and driven by a voracious sexual lust for white women. Some scholars argue that this particular motif served not only to limit blacks but to restrict white women who, demagogues and their followers believed, needed the constant protection of vigilant white men in order to prevent their debasement. In an impoverished South where men struggled to achieve the societal charge to provide economically for their families, the call to protect white women created a virtual mania about marauding black sexual predators that surfaced in literature, in sermons, and in political discourse. In order to protect the honor of fragile delicate southern women—a characterization demagogues traded in regularly—southern men were called to action. Failure to protect society from sexually aroused black men was often described in terms tantamount to ceding control of one's own household.

Most demagogues publicly endorsed lynching as a responsible form of action, particularly when it occurred in response to an allegation of sexual assault perpetrated on a white woman. Beyond stump speech endorsements of lynching, demagogues generally looked the other way when trials invari-

Senator James Vardaman of Mississippi at the Democratic National Convention, 1912 (Harris & Ewing photographers, Library of Congress [LC-H261-1506])

ably exonerated those accused of murdering blacks under the guise of righteous violence. Many lynchings were not the product of sexual assault—either real or imagined—yet rape became the single most common way to justify the practice. Rather than simply characterize lynching as a distasteful but essential action undertaken by emotional whites, some demagogues like Blease called the practice "necessary and good." This distinction indicated that demagogues viewed violence as not only an acceptable option but a preferable one in many cases. "If it is necessary," Vardaman once bellowed, "every Negro in the state will be lynched; it will done to maintain white supremacy." On the national level, southern congressmen and senators prevented Congress from passing a federal antilynching law, in part because of the popularity of home-state demagogues.

If virulent castigations of blacks were staple acts of demagogues on the hustings, attacks on the federal government were not far behind. Strom Thurmond headlined the 1948 Dixiecrat presidential ticket largely under the twin banners of states' rights and opposition to civil rights. Thurmond warned voters that the national Democratic Party and federal government officials were conspiring to overturn southern traditions like segregation and hand power and access to blacks. Dixiecrats blasted President Harry Truman's civil rights plank, predicted the eventual rise of a police state, cautioned against anti–poll tax and antilynching legislation, and characterized southern whites, not blacks, as the true victims of nefarious conspiracies to limit their lives. "For our loyalty to the party," Thurmond explained to the Dixiecrat political convention, "we have been stabbed in the back by a president who has betrayed every principle of the Democratic Party in his desire to win at any cost."

Twenty years after Thurmond won four states, despite not even being on the ballot in roughly half of the country, Alabama Governor George Wallace won five in his own third-party campaign, this time under the banner of the American Independent Party. Wallace reached the governorship with a series of defiant attacks on civil rights initiatives, vowing to "stand in the schoolhouse door" to prevent integration and promising in his 1963 inaugural address to stand for "segregation today, segregation tomorrow, segregation forever." He further elevated his regional and national appeal by blasting the 1964 Civil Rights Act, federal judges who he occasionally noted needed a "barbed wire enema," court-ordered busing to achieve racial balance, and other "social engineering" plans set in motion by the federal government. Wallace's actions and words gained surprising purchase in some northern strongholds such as south Boston and Milwaukee, indicating that many Americans distrusted both the federal government and the intentions of civil rights workers.

Demagogues often mixed their contempt for blacks and the federal government with a healthy dose of economic Populism. In Louisiana, Huey Long's Share the Wealth program advocated redistribution of income from the rich and capping maximum annual income, and completed a massive statewide infrastructure revitalization program largely through increased corporate taxes. Some of the most ambitious road-building programs for rural areas came from demagogue administrations, as did reforms limiting convict leasing, modernizing barbaric prisons, expanding mental health treatment, and providing old-age pensions. "Jesus Christ, Sears-Roebuck, and James K. Vardaman are the only friend a poor man has," Mississippians said of their demagogue senator and governor. Scholars disagree on the level of authenticity of demagogues who accentuated these working-class appeals, though it is clear that progressive legislation was enacted in most every southern state while demagogues governed.

Southern demagoguery seemed to shift gears by the 1970s, giving way to a more covert series of code phrases and ideas. Overt descriptions about black inferiority morphed into less transparent attacks on "welfare queens," criticism of wasteful federal spending, and calls for more "law and order" on the streets. Southern demagogues championed private schools as a better alternative than integrated public ones, called for lower property taxes, and occasionally championed the continued flying of the Confederate battle flag as a reflection of heritage, not hate. Most scholars see the rise of viable two-party politics across most of the South, a growing black, Latino, and urban voting presence, the softening of traditional racial ideas, and the broader reach of the media as factors limiting overt demagoguery as the South approached the 21st century.

JEFF FREDERICK
University of North Carolina at Pembroke

William Anderson, *The Wild Man from Sugar Creek: The Political Career of Eugene Talmadge* (1976); Dan T. Carter, *The Politics of Rage: George Wallace, the Origins of the New Conservatism, and the Transformation of American Politics* (1995); Jeff Frederick, *Stand up for Alabama: Governor George Wallace* (2007); William F. Holmes, *The White Chief: James K. Vardaman* (1970); Stephen Kantrowitz, *Ben Tillman and the Reconstruction of White Supremacy* (2000); Chester M. Morgan, *Redneck Liberal: Theodore Bilbo and the New Deal* (1985); Richard D. White Jr., *Kingfish: The Reign of Huey P. Long* (2006); T. Harry Williams, *Huey Long* (1969).

Education

Social class lies behind the institutional and curricular development of private and public education in the South, both the class structure as it was and is and the class structure as southerners have thought it should be. Always mediated by constructions of gender, race, religion, and region, social class has often determined which southerners had access to education, for how long, and for what purpose, as well as the content of educational programs. Southern states still tend to be (although the South is not the sole region represented) at the bottom of charts for education statistics—reflecting the enduring legacies of class as well as race in southern history.

Education was a badge of elite status in the colonial and early national periods. Wealthy white families in southern colonies hired private tutors for their children and patronized denominational schools such as Ursuline Academy in New Orleans (1727). Some sent their young men to the College of William and Mary (chartered in 1693) or to the North or Europe to complete the classical education expected of gentlemen. The politics of nationalism and then regionalism, as well as the economic changes wrought by the Market Revolution, spurred an expansion of the region's educational institutions and opened their doors to some of the middle ranks in the early 19th century. Southern states erected their own universities, such as the University of Tennessee (1794), the University of North Carolina (1795), the University of Georgia (1801), the University of South Carolina (1805), the University of Virginia (1825), the University of Alabama (1831), and the University of Mississippi (1848). At such institutions, and at private colleges such as Transylvania University (1780) and Emory University (1838), young white men not only completed their classical training but learned to balance self-striving for economic success with expectations that they would maintain elite leadership in politics and elite white male social authority in the household and community. Institutions such as Georgia Female College (1839) and Tennessee's Mary Sharp College (1853) strove to offer similar academic training to buttress elite status for white women.

The antebellum South's academy movement opened up educational opportunities for not only the planter and political elite but the expanding southern gentry composed of well-to-do households headed by merchants, professionals, and market-oriented farmers. The Virginia Military Institute (1839) served as a model for other state and private military academies that blended the traditional academic program with applied science and engineering. Similarly, private academies for young men and women of the white middle class proliferated throughout the rest of the antebellum period.

Antebellum southerners of all ranks understood that their educational attainment was an important signifier of their social class. The region's common schools increased in number in this period, but their association with "poor schools" and exclusion of black youth limited their reach. Reformers made public education a responsibility of state and local governments and called for universal white education to extend the literacy and numeracy skills needed by a dynamic market economy, much in the same way as reformers in the northern common school movement. Yet whites of all social classes were reluctant to increase taxpayer support for schools that might erode either elite power or white male authority in the household. Common schools might run for a few months on public funding, then continue by subscription for children whose parents could afford to pay or forgo their children's labor. The limited schooling available to free black children in private schools generally reinforced their place in the urban working class while also offering a chance for economic advancement in the long term, making them especially vulnerable to white opponents in the 1850s.

The Civil War, Emancipation, and Reconstruction challenged southerners to rethink and rebuild their social structure and brought greater attention to education as a tool of class advancement and status. African Americans led the drive for private and public schools of their own and for the South's first systems of universal public education. Most newly freed black southerners were working-class people, and though the South's universal public school systems would quickly become segregated by race, working-class whites would potentially benefit as well. As Reconstruction state governments fell, however, so did state support for education.

Enough of the common school system survived, albeit crippled by discriminatory funding (or nonfunding) of schools for black children, to fuel not only a rapid increase in the numbers of children attending school and in literacy rates but also renewed calls for action. Farmers' organizations and agrarian politicians included improved public education and broader access to higher education in their agendas. From the other end of the political and class spectrum, the region's educational elite at southern colleges and universities began reshaping higher education itself by incorporating more of the scientific and technical subjects that could train a new generation of elite leaders for a modern industrialized South. New state universities, such as the University of Arkansas (1871), Mississippi State University (1878), and the Georgia Institute of Technology (1888) specialized in such subjects and began training new generations of young white men and women for middle-class and professional careers in business, commercial farming, and the region's growing education systems. At the same time, African American southerners also sought advancement into middle-class and elite status through higher education. Some attended private institutions such as Fisk University or Hampton University that dated back to the 1860s. More attended new public institutions of higher education initially restricted to vocational and teacher training, such as Florida Agricultural and Mechanical University (1887).

Although the New South business and planter classes remained suspicious of state-funded public schooling for whites and blacks, as did large numbers of lower-class white southerners, the alliance of school advocates with an increasingly vocal southern middle class and northern philanthropic foundations brought massive changes to education in the South during the early 20th century. Progressive Era debates over funding, content, and control of public education in the South often focused on race and produced public school systems that systematically benefited white rather than all children and young people. Social class was a less dramatic but integral part of Progressive education reform. Progressive educators updated earlier ideas about manual training to encourage learning by doing on the one hand and vocational education as a means of economic development on the other. Measures such as the Smith-Lever Act (1914) and Smith-Hughes Act (1917) entrenched vocational education in agriculture, mechanical trades, and home economics. Intended to produce better-skilled industrial and agricultural workers, as well as middle-class professionals, when applied in black schools "industrial education" programs were more oriented to low-skilled and service occupations and served to make black public education more acceptable to both upper- and lower-class whites. Meanwhile, African American southerners used such programs as leverage to increase access to elementary and secondary education that could propel them into the ranks of landowners, business operators, and professionals.

The Great Depression and New Deal brought increased federal attention to the South—"the Nation's No. 1 economic problem"—and its schools. Federal Emergency Relief Administration, Works Progress Administration, and National Youth Administration dollars helped to preserve the South's existing class and racial structure while also undermining it by allocating federal resources, however unevenly, across the region's still-developing universal education systems. The Tennessee Valley Authority pointed to the significance of federal investment for regional economic growth that would require southern schools to train students for an even more industrialized and technologically advanced economy. During and after World War II and then the Cold War, the Oak Ridge National Laboratory, military bases, and NASA installations have helped to channel federal funding for public higher education and research to southern universities. With further support from the GI Bill and other federal educational benefits programs, southern colleges and universities expanded enrollments and graduate programs for the Sunbelt's expanding ranks of workers in high-tech industries as well as academia. One of the many forces behind the mid-20th-century movement to desegregate education was the recognition that legalized discrimination in education would continue to prevent African American advancement within this rapidly modernizing class structure.

Yet educational quality and equity have remained elusive, for southerners as for all Americans. In the 1980s a new generation of southern governors, led by Bill Clinton of Arkansas and Lamar Alexander of Tennessee, called yet again for increased educational funding and standards as tools for both social and economic advancement. Late 20th-century education reforms broke down old barriers and brought southerners' levels of educational attainment, measured in terms of high school graduation and college degrees, closer to national averages. Nevertheless, in the early years of the 21st century the standardized testing and performance-based funding used as tools of reform have brought renewed recognition of the ways that social class continues to divide southern students and their schools and leaves those who learn and teach in inner-city and rural districts at a disadvantage.

MARY S. HOFFSCHWELLE
Middle Tennessee State University

James D. Anderson, in *The American South in the Twentieth Century*, ed. Craig S. Pascoe, Karen Trahern Leathem, and Andy Ambrose (2005), *The Education of Blacks in the South, 1860-1935* (1988); Fred Arthur Bailey, *Class and Tennessee's Confederate Generation* (1987); Charles W. Dabney, *Universal Education in the South* (1935); Thomas G. Dyer, in *The American South in the Twentieth Century*, ed. Craig S. Pascoe, Karen Trahern Leathem, and Andy Ambrose (2005); Christie Anne Farnham, *The Education of the Southern Belle* (1994); Dan R. Frost, *Thinking Confederates* (2000); Jennifer R. Green, *Military Education and the Emerging Middle Class in the Old South* (2011); James L. Leloudis, *Schooling the New South: Pedagogy, the Self, and Society in North Carolina, 1880-1920* (1996).

Environment

According to historians of the colonial South, the environmental conditions faced by early European settlers fostered a degree of rough social equality, at least in the sense that masters and servants found themselves working side by side in often dangerous and grueling conditions as they built their settlements in the swamps and forests of the Atlantic seaboard. The tools of colonization, too, blurred social distinctions, as the use of free-ranging cattle and feral pigs not only aided in the clearing of forestlands but also provided an important source of food to those who shared the large commons. As they struggled to carve a living out of the wilderness, early settlers of all classes inhabited similar, rough-and-tumble dwellings or even shared them. The need to supplement food crops with hunting and fishing, both of which also served as social bonding activities; the need to defend settlements from American Indian hostility; the fear and loathing of the large predators and snakes that abounded on the coastal plain; the indiscriminate ravages of diseases and natural disasters; and the inclination to see in these the hand of God—all cut across class lines to such an extent that they at least blunted the sharp class distinctions that so defined southern society in subsequent eras.

As settlements became more stable and populations grew, society in the colonial South rapidly became more hierarchical; social, political, and economic leadership came to be concentrated in the hands of a relatively small elite of large landowners and slave owners. In environmental terms, this meant not only that those at the top of the social hierarchy owned the most land and the most fertile land but also that they owned the land adjacent to the waterways that facilitated transportation, controlled the facilities—such as sawmills and turpentine stills—that processed the resources drawn from the environment, monopolized information and knowledge regarding nature and its proper uses, and had access to the financial and social capital that enabled them to enlarge their already substantial operations. The tobacco planters of the Chesapeake, the rice planters of South Carolina and Georgia, and those who harvested and processed naval stores in southeastern North Carolina thus imposed on nature the same kind of mastery, domination, and control that increasingly characterized social relations in the South. In the process, they used their political influence to define as "improper" and "wasteful," and thereby marginalize and often criminalize, the environmental practices of the lower classes. Colonial laws that prohibited hunting by fire at night, hunting out of season, taking naval stores from the longleaf pine forest without a legal land claim, or setting the woods on fire to fertilize lands reflected the colonial elite's understanding of what constituted "proper" use of nature as well as its desire and ability to impose its view on colonial society. This drive for mastery, too, fostered the cultural association of the South's wild and uncultivated places—dense forests, pine barrens, and especially swamps—with elements and activities that challenged the established social order: brigandage, pirates, runaway slaves, race mixing, crime, and a lack of religion. In addition, elitist detractors of the South's "poor whites" pointed to the debilitating effects of the region's climate and uncultivated environment as the causes for lower-class whites' sloth, laziness, squalor, and moral degeneracy.

Several factors mitigated the potential for class unrest over access to, and control over, the environment: the ideology of white supremacy in a slave society, the continued existence of a large and bountiful commons, and the increased availability of land as the United States expanded westward after the states became independent. This state of affairs continued into the antebellum period and only grew more dominant as white southerners, emulating the eastern elite's drive for mastery over wild nature and subordinate humans, spread slavery and cotton across the southern half of the United States. Although the romantic mythology of the Old South likes to depict planters and plain folk alike as down-home people rooted in the southern soil while transient and money-grubbing Yankees visited the destructive forces of industrial capitalism on the northern landscape, the environmental havoc wreaked by white southerners of all classes was, if anything, greater than that caused by the industrializing North. Extensive soil exhaustion and erosion, deforestation, the hunting of species to near extinction, ramshackle dwellings that reflected the transience of much of the southern population, the preponderance of destructive feral hogs, the often careless use of fire in agriculture—these were the hallmarks of much of white society in the antebellum South. Elite planters continued to dominate politics, the economic infrastructure, the information and knowledge necessary for successful operations, and the networks that provided social and financial capital, but class unrest remained sporadic as long as hunting, fishing, private property, the commons, cotton, and slaves fostered a common culture of domination and exploitation, especially among men. In fact, historians of the Civil War argue that one of the Confederacy's advantages during the early years of the war was the greater familiarity and skill among southern men with firearms, horseback riding, and outdoor survival.

In the decades following the Civil War, various developments turned the southern environment into a battlefield that often divided southerners along class lines. Industrialization brought to the South entrepreneurs who, encouraged and often joined by southern boosters and industrialists, coveted the region's wealth of untapped natural resources. This sudden increase in value, boosted by increased monocropping of tobacco and cotton on southern farmlands, unleashed on the southern landscape a torrent of economic development. The lumber industry cut millions of acres of southern forest and left vast stretches of "cutover" in its wake. The South's railroad network expanded rapidly and added to the growing demand for lumber and other resources. In Texas, the oil industry emerged as a major force of economic growth and environmental destruction. In Appalachia, the lumber industry was joined by the coal mining industry in what is often referred to as its "assault" on the southern environment. Industrialization also transformed the harvesting of naval stores in the remaining longleaf pine forests of Georgia and Florida, as well as the oyster fisheries of Maryland. Common southerners did not object to this rapid industrialization, but typically provided the necessary labor and welcomed the opportunity to supplement the fruits of their rural existence with wages. However, the hardships of sharecropping and the crop lien often drove them to rely exclusively on industrial labor for their livelihood, and they were often subject to low wages, dangerous working conditions, and brutal treatment. And because southern industry was largely extractive and therefore transient, companies often departed when the resources ran out—a practice known as "cut and run" in the lumber industry—and left the local population with the ravaged, depleted, and polluted land. Within this context, class strife about the environment and its uses explicitly manifested itself in violent clashes between coal miners and strikebreakers in Kentucky and West Virginia. Historians also link the famous feud between the Hatfields and the McCoys to the unsettling effects of modernization and economic development.

Moreover, the increased value of the South's natural resources, combined with the fear that rapid industrialization would deplete them, inspired political and economic elites to implement a range of protective measures that criminalized traditional environmental practices and often denied the lower classes access to what had once been a large and abundant commons. Subsistence hunting, market hunting, gathering firewood, and burning crop fields close to woodlands were among the common activities that came to be defined as "wasteful," their practitioners as "spoilers" who may find even the law turned against them. One of the most controversial developments in this large-scale move toward progressive conservation of natural resources was the closing of the open range in the late 19th century, which mandated that farmers pen in their hogs in order to protect not only other farmers' crops but also the pine forest, where hogs devoured tons of mast and feasted on longleaf pine seedlings. The hog, a mainstay of the southern diet and in many ways an icon of southern culture, came to be considered "an enemy of the pine," and the long-standing practice of letting hogs roam the woods came to a hotly contested end. Combined with the relentless move toward ever more acreage devoted to cash crops such as tobacco and cotton, the closing of the commons opened the door for industrial meat production in the American South, with the lower classes—who had for so long depended on the southern swamps, forests, and waterways for access to food and resources—reduced to serving as wageworkers in the burgeoning chicken and pork industries.

In the course of the 20th century, these class divisions continued to manifest themselves even as modernization and industrialization reshaped the relationship between southerners and their environment. Political and economic elites, often with the support of lower-class workers, created a business climate that favored corporations and discouraged unions and environmentalists, and the South became home to industries that are among the worst offenders in terms of poor working conditions and environmental pollution. Where the lower classes used to suffer disproportionately from diseases such as pellagra and hookworm, they now bear the brunt of the adverse effects of air pollution, run-off from coal mining, coal sludge lagoons, pig waste lagoons, and the waste dumped into the region's waterways by large pulp and paper companies. They are also affected disproportionately by the ill health effects of obesity, fostered by the practices of the modern food and tobacco industry. Health experts argue that tobacco and Krispy Kreme Donuts from North Carolina, Coca-Cola from Atlanta, and Kentucky Fried Chicken have contributed greatly to the development of a "stroke belt" that stretches from Virginia to Texas across the South. Poorer neighborhoods are also hit disproportionately by the devastation wrought by natural disasters, as witnessed during and after Hurricane Katrina in 2005 and the BP oil spill in 2010. What is currently referred to as "eco-racism" is most often an issue of social class as well. Much of what used to be the commons has been privatized, deforested, and turned into so-called golf communities and commercial areas; governed by laws that continue to exclude the traditional uses and practices that historically characterized common usage of the environment, what remains of it often serves the tourist industry, the lumber industry, and other corporate and government interests.

Still, insofar as there is a common southern culture that continues to blunt the sharp class distinctions that have long characterized southern society, it is very much a shared understanding of the region's environmental legacy and character. The South is a physical place, a geographic region to which is attached a cultural identity. The Republican Party's dominance in much of the South is rooted, in part, in a shared hostility toward "tree-huggers" and other environmentalists. There is a widespread and entrenched shooting, hunting, and fishing culture that continues to serve functions of social bonding and intergenerational transmission of tradition and identity. And country music, together with other expressions of southern culture such as *Southern Living*, continues to celebrate and romanticize the beauty and simplicity of living close to the land, being rooted in the soil, and having a sense of place. Even in places where environmental destruction and class division went hand in hand—such as Harlan County, Ky., Ducktown, Tenn., and much of West Virginia—people's collective memories cut across class lines to sustain fierce loyalty to, and romantic nostalgia for, the extractive industries and destructive practices that laid to waste so much of the southern landscape.

TYCHO DE BOER
St. Mary's University of Minnesota

Robert D. Bullard, *Dumping in Dixie: Race, Class, and Environmental Quality* (1990); James C. Cobb, *Industrialization and Southern Society, 1877-1984* (1984); Jack Temple Kirby, *Mockingbird Song: Ecological Landscapes of the South* (2006).

Ethnicity

The modern concept of ethnicity grew out of the 18th-century classification system developed by the Swedish botanist Carl Linnaeus. His book *Systema Naturae* (1735) provided a basis for the modern taxonomic system that identified people as *Homo sapiens* but did not clearly differentiate the color or race of people. In Victorian England, Herbert Spencer helped to further identify human races and used color as a key factor in social development. He formulated his theory of Social Darwinism to explain how the "white" Anglo-Saxon race evolved into the most advanced people in the world, while categorizing "black" Africans as least developed and therefore in the need of guidance from European colonialists. These ideas emerged in the United States in works such as Lothrop Stoddard's *The Rising Tide of Color against White World-Supremacy* (1920), in which he identified five distinct races on the basis of skin color that included white, yellow, red, brown, and black.

The work of the racial theorist provided a basis for a new way to define the people and territory of a country amid the rising movement of European nationalism. The late 19th-century German sociologist Max Weber defined a new term called "ethnicity" to describe how people distinguished themselves from their neighbors. Weber differentiated ethnic groups by their self-identified shared ancestry, community, and collective cultural rules. Issues such as skin color, language, and religion did not affect this united population. Rather, he coined the term "social closure" to describe how diverse peoples excluded some of their neighbors to form a distinct ethnic group. Thus, in a southern context, Weber's ideas identified former slaves as racially black, yet ethnically American.

During the 20th century, Weber's ideas of ethnicity became helpful tools in examining the diverse American immigrant populations in the polyglot nation. By the 1950s, ethnicity became a commonly used term to describe where peoples' ancestors originated in the world. Historians such as Oscar Handlin in *The Uprooted* (1951) sought to explain how a Polish or Hungarian immigrant transformed into an ethnic American. Handlin proposed that immigrants survived the traumatic Americanization process by forming new social, political, and religious affiliations in the United States. This "melting pot" theory provided a monolithic model by which all immigrants acquired American culture and then became citizens. While the book provided an easily understood assimilation process, Handlin did not include a way to address the regional, religious, or political differences found within ethnic groups.

In the 1964 article "Contadini in Chicago: A Critique of the Uprooted," Rudolf Vecoli countered Handlin's "melting pot" theory and started a continuing debate by proposing that ethnic groups retained aspects of their original culture after becoming American. Vecoli argued that, once in the United States, Italian immigrants re-created many aspects of their native life including churches, aid societies, traditional festivals, and parochial enclaves. All of these characteristics led Vecoli to conclude that Americanization had not fully enveloped Italian immigrant life.

Over the past five decades, Handlin's assimilationists slowly merged with Vecoli's cultural pluralists as historians sought to describe the retention of Old World folkways, as immigrants Americanized, among increasingly diverse populations in the southern states. During the colonial era, immigrants from Great Britain and African slaves dominated the South. After the American Revolution, relatively small enclaves of German, Irish, Mexican, and Cuban immigrants moved to the region as job competition with slaves diminished the need for foreign workers. Once the Civil War ended, plantation owners brought in groups of Chinese workers as a source of cheap labor. By the early 20th century, significant numbers of Italians, Welsh, Croatians, and Poles moved to urban and mining regions. After the First World War ended, immigration declined because of new regulations that fostered the Americanization of ethnic groups already living in the country. Only after the 1960s did policies change, which in turn led to new waves of Cuban and Mexican workers, refugees from Ethiopia and Bosnia, along with Chinese and Indian immigrant groups.

For most ethnic historians, ideas of social hierarchy also played an important role in immigrant integration. The closer the ethnic group conformed to middle-class English or Anglo-Saxon political, religious, cultural, and racial norms when they arrived in the Americas, the sooner they integrated in society. The process began when the initial wave of 17th-century English settlers arrived in the South. They set precedents that allowed Anglo-Americans to dominate subsequent immigrant and slave populations. Anglo-American control of the tobacco, indigo, and rice trade allowed them to control the coastal regions politically and economically. For example, members of the Virginia House of Burgesses or South Carolina's Grand Council created both laws and cultural norms for their communities. After independence from England in 1783, the scions of the coastal families moved inland, where they bought up land for new cotton plantations that fed a growing number of American factories as the nation industrialized. In the process, the Anglo-American population spread social, political, and economic control over the entire South.

Anglo-American domination of the region meant that both working-class immigrants and slaves had to conform to standards set by a powerful middle-class minority in the country. Scots-Irish and Irish immigrants rebelled against Anglo-American domination and moved inland where they established semi-independent communities along the interior. However, issues such as intermarriage, shared political ideals, and support first for slavery and then racial superiority formed bonds among the former inhabitants of the British Isles, which in turn helped to integrate the ethnic groups in America. Ronald Lewis's *Welsh Americans* demonstrates how religious and linguistic ties, combined with political support and racial similarity, allowed the Welsh to quickly integrate in the West Virginia coalfields.

The German or Polish Jewish populations, Italians, Croats, and Chinese immigrants endured a longer period of conflict with Anglo-Americans before they achieved social acceptance. A confluence of religious prejudices against Catholics and Jews, racial identification of these groups as nonwhite, and disdain for people active in social reform and labor unions provided ample reasons for southerners' misgivings about the new immigrant groups. The distrust of foreign ethnic groups manifested in events such as the 1891 lynching of 11 Italian immigrants suspected of murdering a sheriff in New Orleans and the 1915 lynching of Leo Frank, a Jewish businessman from Georgia. During the First World War, the Ku Klux Klan experienced a revival in popularity by suppressing "enemy-aliens," especially anarchists, syndicalists, and communists from the new immigrant communities. As a result of the prejudices and violence, many of the Southern and Eastern European ethnic communities did not integrate until after the Second World War.

In the modern era, the South has entered into a period of widespread immigration by diverse ethnic groups from around the world. Individuals from Mexico and Cuba arrived in the greatest numbers as they sought political freedom and economic prosperity. Over the past few decades, Latinos have transformed the ethnic makeup of the United States with a population in 2006 that burgeoned to 44 million people. Smaller groups of approximately 1.6 million Asian Indians, 1.4 million Chinese, 423,000 East Africans, and 113,000 Bosnians moved to the United States. Many settled in Texas, Virginia, Georgia, and Florida, where they have established new ethnic enclaves. Southerners had a mixed reaction to the latest immigrant populations. Whereas some individuals held on to their traditional beliefs about white racial superiority, others embraced the new diversity of southern society. The influx of skilled workers, laborers, and refugees has also led to a rise in both ethnic and religious conflicts for Asian, Middle Eastern, and African immigrants. Muslims from these regions experienced a public backlash against mosque construction as seen recently in Murfreesboro, Tenn. At the same time, Latinos came under increased scrutiny over the issue of illegal immigration. All these groups have been in the process of integrating into American society and finding social acceptance from the middle-class Anglo-American populations, a process that continues to this day.

Each of these ethnic groups has a body of literature dedicated to its unique Americanization process; however, the *Harvard Encyclopedia of American Ethnic Groups* provides an excellent starting point for any research on the subject. Within the subject of ethnic integration, new works have also emerged, dedicated to the role women played in the construction of immigrant communities. Donna Gabaccia's *From the Other Side: Women, Gender, and Immigrant Life in the U.S., 1820–1990* develops the idea that women faced social exclusion on the basis of both their gender and ethnicity. In order to fully participate in society, women had to transcend their traditional family roles, while simultaneously conforming to middle-class Anglo-American culture. The dual process slowed the integration of women as they sought to redefine their role in American society.

Whether viewed as a single or dual process, integration or Americanization studies have developed over the past few decades to encompass the majority of immigrants who chose the southern United States as their new home. Regardless of ethnic origin, immigrants in the South encountered an Anglo-American population that expected universal conformity to their middle-class values. Each ethnic group has struggled to obtain recognition of their middle-class status, while maintaining vestiges of their cultural heritage. In the process, the immigrants expanded ideas of inclusion to embrace simple food staples such as pasta, tortillas, and lamb to more complex social issues. Differences in race, religion, and political affiliation remain divisive issues that defy any quick solutions. However, the South has been changing with the rapid introduction of diverse populations, and their integration process will continue over the next few generations.

PAUL LUBOTINA
Middle Tennessee State University

Daniel Arreola, *Tejano South Texas: A Mexican American Cultural Province* (2002); Myron Berman, *Richmond's Jewery, 1769–1976* (1979); Lucy Cohen, *Chinese in the Post Civil War South: A People without a History* (1984); Donna Gabaccia, *From the Other Side: Women, Gender, and Immigrant Life in the U.S., 1820–1990* (1994); Solomon Addis Getahun, *The History of Ethiopian Immigrants and Refugees in America, 1900–2000* (2006); David Gleeson, *The Irish South, 1815–1877* (2001); Ronald L. Lewis, *Welsh Americans: A History of Assimilation in the Coalfields* (2008); James G. Leyburn, *The Scots Irish: A Social History* (1989); Anthony Margavio and Jerome Salamone, *Bread and Respect: The Italians of Louisiana* (2002); Gary Mormino and George Pozetta, *The Immigrant World of Ybor City: Italians and Their Latin Neighbors in Tampa, 1885–1985* (1998); Stephan Thernstrom, ed., *Harvard Encyclopedia of American Ethnic Groups* (1980); Milos Vujnovich, *Yugoslavs in Louisiana* (1974).

Foodways

During the early 20th century the South ranked dead last nationally in every conceivable economic category, and when the Great Depression gripped the country in 1929, many southerners grimly joked that they did not notice any difference in their circumstances. In the 1930s President Franklin D. Roosevelt described southern poverty as the most serious economic problem facing America.

Wife of tenant farmer cutting a piece of ham in smokehouse near Pace, Miss., 1939 (Russell Lee, photographer, Library of Congress [LC-USF34-032054-D], Washington, D.C.)

At the dawning of the New Deal economic recovery program, the majority of the South's African American population and about half of its whites subsisted on a hunger diet. "It seems indisputable that the condition of the poor, whether sharecroppers in the black belt, millworkers in the Piedmont, or scratch farmers in Appalachia, began to reach its nadir about 1925," writes Joe Gray Taylor.

As it had been during much of the South's past, from the early colonization of Virginia, pork continued to be a mainstay on the region's tables well into the 20th century and at the same time a symbol of the inequitable distribution of food products. The phrase "eating high on the hog," used to describe periods of prosperity, had its converse in the scraps of fatback and gristly ham hocks allocated to slaves for 200 years on the plantations and dispensed to white and black patrons alike at general stores and company commissaries. Pigs have played a central role in southern survival largely because they are one of the most efficient sources of food, as their weight can increase 150-fold in the first eight months of life, and most of the animal is edible.

One of the great paradoxes of the southern table is the fact that African Americans, the southerners subjected to the worst forms of class as well as race discrimination, have made some of the greatest contributions to the region's cookery. African slaves enriched the diet of the South by introducing products from their homeland such as okra, collard greens, black-eyed peas, and benne, or sesame, seeds. The kitchen was one of the few places where displaced and enslaved Africans could exercise their creativity, raising common, often even discarded, foods to grandeur. "It is difficult to reconcile the glory of the feast with the ignominy of slavery," writes John Egerton. Ironies continued after the end of slavery. In the Jim Crow South, from the end of the Civil War into the 1960s, blacks who cooked in restaurant kitchens were not allowed to step out front and eat in the dining room. Poverty created class deprivation for many blacks to confront as well as racial oppression. Writer Richard Wright dwelled on sheer hunger from lack of family resources for food as a child, as well as racial limitations.

With Emancipation, blacks were no longer classified as slaves, but many remained just as economically dependent on whites, who employed them as cooks, maids, and servants, at extremely low wages. Black cooks, according to Egerton, "turned pork fat and flour into rich gravies, stale bread and cold rice into sweet puddings, leftover meats and vegetables into soups and stews and baked dishes." Likewise, the food cooked and served on Pullman railroad cars, primarily by black men, rivaled that served by the best southern hotels, yet until the end of segregation, those same black men could not ride with white passengers.

The image of the frilly-frocked southern belle, presiding over a table set with silver and porcelain, is a marked contrast to the hardworking lives of so many plantation matrons and especially to the hardscrabble existence of countless southern farm women, who sold eggs to supplement the family income and turned used cotton chicken-feed sacks into curtains and clothing. Until recently, the cooking of the aristocratic, planter class was preserved in southern cookbooks, to the exclusion of the marginalized. Most southerners never owned slaves.

Half the poor families in the United States, one-seventh of the white poor and two-thirds of the nonwhite, lived below the Mason-Dixon Line as late as 1966. Throughout the first half of the 20th century, the meat in the diet of poor southerners in the Appalachian region consisted largely of fatback—very little bacon or ham—and cornbread or flour biscuits, all low in protein and vitamins and resulting in the proliferation of such nutrient-deficient diseases as pellagra. By the end of World War II, milling companies had begun to fortify their flour and cornmeal with vitamins, which brought a significant improvement in the health of southerners.

Amid troubles and triumphs, economically disadvantaged southerners of all races have resourcefully combined the lowliest of foodstuffs—the simple fare of field and farm—to create some of America's most memorable dishes: lard-seasoned soup beans and cornbread flecked with pork cracklings; redeye gravy, a simple combination of grease, water, and perhaps some leftover coffee; and pain perdu, "lost bread" or "French toast," an ingenious way of using leftover bread as dessert, perked up with precious sugar and spices. Hard times resulted in clever ways to preserve meat, vegetables, and fruit. Country hams, cured with salt and smoke, apples boiled down into apple butter, and green beans strung and dried as "leather britches" all grew out of necessity.

Southerners have pickled watermelon rinds, made wine out of corn cobs, stewed mudbugs, killed spring lettuce with vinegar and bacon grease, and sautéed dandelion greens, thereby creating America's most diverse indigenous cuisine, appreciated all the more because of the hardships from whence it has come.

FRED W. SAUCEMAN
East Tennessee State University

John Egerton, *Southern Food: At Home, on the Road, in History* (1987); Lu Ann Jones, *Mama Learned Us to Work: Farm Women in the New South* (2002); Joe Gray Taylor, *Eating, Drinking, and Visiting in the South: An Informal History* (1982).

Free Blacks

Free blacks lived in the American South from the early years of English colonization in North America through the Civil War, though they were outnumbered in most times and places by enslaved members of their race.

Africans in Virginia, site of the first permanent English settlements, almost always arrived as slaves, and in small numbers, through much of the 17th century; the entire black population of the colony was only some 2,000 at the time of Bacon's Rebellion (1676). More than a few people of African origin brought skills and cosmopolitan backgrounds; some, through assiduous labor, managed to purchase their freedom, and occasionally to acquire land and slaves or indentured servants of their own. In Northampton County on Virginia's Eastern Shore, nearly a third of the black population had attained its freedom by 1668, and 10 black men—nearly one-fifth of the county's black male population—were landowners. Economic status rather than color or nationality determined these men's social position; they associated freely with whites and pursued their interests in court.

When enslaved Africans gradually replaced indentured Englishmen as the principal source of plantation labor in the late 17th century, the Chesapeake colonies adopted laws that reinforced a growing tendency on the part of whites to equate blackness with slavery and degradation. Opportunities for enslaved blacks to attain freedom were nearly eliminated.

The colony of Carolina was settled beginning in 1670, nearly three generations after the colonization of Jamestown, largely by men who brought enslaved black laborers with them. Some blacks managed to purchase or otherwise obtain their freedom. Yet in Carolina, as in the Chesapeake, the rise of a plantation economy based on enslaved black labor snuffed out any prospect of attaining liberty for most bondpeople by the early 18th century.

Self-purchase was not the only source of the South's free black population during the colonial era. Fraternization between blacks and whites was common, especially among agricultural laborers, and children born to white women were spared a life in bondage even if the father was a black slave. The white mother of such a child in some colonies could be indentured as a servant for a period of years or see her existing term of service lengthened, and her children might be bound out as servants until they reached adulthood. Ultimately, however, these women and their children became free, and they produced new generations of free brown people. (In much of the South, whites' habit of distinguishing "blacks" or "Negroes" from "mulattoes" or persons of mixed race fell largely into disuse by about 1800. The categories "free people of color" and "free Negroes" now encompassed most people with discernible African ancestry, and the term "free black" in this entry parallels this usage.)

The Enlightenment ideals of the American Revolution, along with antislavery convictions among Baptists, Methodists, and Quakers, promoted significant growth in the Upper South's free black population during the latter 18th century. Virginia, always the largest slaveholding state, in 1782 gave masters the right to manumit slaves. Those who opposed this measure never managed to rescind it, but they did secure a new law requiring any slave liberated in Virginia after 1806 to leave the state within one year unless granted a waiver by the state legislature (or, later, by the county court). Laws of this kind, replicated in other southern states, were rarely enforced, but they were used against the occasional free black individual whom officials deemed undesirable.

Masters concerned about their slaves' individual welfare were the ones most inclined to manumit and, at the same time, most daunted by the possibility that those they liberated might be forced away from family, friends, and homeland. Nevertheless, a modest but significant wave of private manumissions in the late 18th century did not wholly abate in the 19th. Some masters liberated only one or a few favored slaves, whereas others, such as George Washington, freed all their slaves, usually by will. Sometimes emancipators tried to equip those liberated for life in freedom. Planter Richard Randolph wrote a will, carried out by his widow, Judith, at considerable sacrifice, that manumitted more than 90 slaves and conveyed land in Prince Edward County, Va., to many of them.

The free black population of the southern states thus rose by 1810 from a tiny (and unrecorded) number to more than 100,000—8.5 percent of the region's black population. By 1860 one in every eight or nine black Virginians was free; so were half the blacks in Maryland, as the northern and western parts of the state moved informally toward a system of wage labor. The free African American population of the South at large had risen to more than a quarter of a million—augmented in the preceding half century far more by natural increase of the existing free population than by new manumissions. Some masters still released large numbers of blacks—but, influenced by state laws requiring newly liberated blacks to leave and by the general discrimination free Afro-Southerners faced, some now provided for the resettlement of those they emancipated either in the free states (which themselves discriminated severely against blacks) or in Liberia.

While many free blacks in the Upper South, or their forebears, thus received their freedom from masters who acted on principle, the small populations of free blacks in most of the Cotton Kingdom contained a higher percentage of people fathered by white slaveholders who then freed them and sometimes tendered them money, protection, and perhaps some education. This difference between subregions can be overemphasized, however. Many of Alabama's free black population in the 19th century, for example, were children of stable unions between black men and white women which, though frowned on in theory, were often tolerated by whites.

It is reasonable to view the free black population of the South as having become by about 1800 a distinct caste in society; this caste in turn was stratified by income and occupation. Free blacks in most times and places, whatever their economic status, were denied the right to serve on juries, join the militia, testify against white defendants in court, or vote (exceptions on the last point include North Carolina, where blacks voted in numbers until, over considerable white objection, they were disfranchised in 1835). At least in theory, free blacks throughout the South were also required to register with local authorities and to produce on demand copies of their registration. Sometimes they had to pay special taxes. Other laws sought to limit or deny free blacks' right to own firearms, receive schooling, preach the Gospel, or assemble without white supervision.

Nevertheless, a typical textbook statement that "one slip, or any ignorance of the law, could send [a free black] back into slavery" describes (and even overstates) the letter of the laws aimed at free blacks rather than actual practice. John Hope Franklin wrote of North Carolina that "the seeming harsh and illiberal laws . . . were often softened by those who interpreted and administered them" to the point that "often, there was no enforcement at all." Many free blacks lived in states—Virginia, North Carolina, and Alabama, to name three well-documented examples—that allowed them to own and dispose of property and to pursue civil lawsuits against whites. The ability to file, and sometimes win, such suits helped compensate for the inadmissibility of black testimony incriminating white aggressors in criminal trials. Meanwhile, the free black property holder, in Franklin's words, "could be fairly sure that the courts would stand by him during his period of possession" and often gained "the respect—somewhat disquieted, perhaps," of his (or her) white fellow citizens. White and free black individuals often did business with one another, and sometimes they harvested crops and founded churches together or even joined in spousal unions.

In southern Louisiana and other areas along the Gulf Coast, the free Negro caste included many mixed-race, well-to-do *gens de couleur* (or *créoles de couleur*) who traced their freedom back to the period of French and Spanish rule; here, and in Charleston, the colored upper echelon carefully segregated itself from the black population, most of whom remained enslaved. In various parts of the South, some free people of color, usually through hard work and enterprise and sometimes through inheritance from white fathers who manumitted them, acquired considerable wealth; William Ellison, a cotton gin maker in South Carolina and one of the South's dozen wealthiest free blacks, owned more than 60 slaves by 1860. Whites recognized social differences among free Afro-Southerners. They casually spoke of a class of "respectable" free blacks— "men of industry, intelligence, and general good character," as the *Richmond Dispatch* put it in 1853. Yet even these people were subjected to civil disabilities and stereotyping, as in the allegation of proslavery apologist Thomas R. Dew that free blacks were "the very drones and pests of society."

One-third of free Afro-Southerners lived in cities and towns by 1860, and scholarly investigations of free black life have tended to focus on this urban population. The majority of free Afro-Southerners lived in the countryside, however, and many were farm laborers who, having begun their life in freedom with few material assets, lived and reared families in modest or impoverished circumstances. Local governments' practice of binding out poorer children of both races, but especially free blacks, as apprentices to whites has typically been depicted in recent times as a kind of quasi enslavement. In fact, as Franklin writes and others have shown, apprenticeships became in many instances "an effective method of training free Negro children to become proficient workers and intelligent citizens."

Free Afro-Southerners often fraternized and intermarried with slaves. Some free blacks purchased their enslaved spouses or children and kept them in nominal bondage rather than face even the remote possibility of their expulsion under laws such as the one Virginia adopted in 1806. Free blacks also fairly frequently became the spouses of fellow blacks who remained the property of some white person; such families confronted the danger that the enslaved partner would be sold or bequeathed to a master who lived far away.

In much of the Lower South, the option of manumitting blacks was severely limited or denied during the several decades that preceded the Civil War. The percentage of blacks who were free remained minuscule in the Lower South outside of Louisiana, Charleston, and a few other enclaves. Free blacks in several states of the Lower South were required to have white "guardians" to vouch for their good behavior and to conduct their business transactions. Although the requirement was insulting, these guardianships fairly often turned out to be pro forma arrangements between people who were well acquainted with one another. Kidnapping of free blacks for sale into slavery, probably the most fearsome peril facing free Afro-Southerners, appears to have been more frequent in the southernmost free states than in those where slavery was legal.

The Nat Turner slave rebellion and the emergence of northern abolitionism in the 1830s prompted new levels of anti-free-black invective and a proliferation of restrictions on free blacks in the South; a similar crescendo occurred in the 1850s. Even so, property holding by southern free blacks expanded as never before during the same period—a trend that likewise accelerated in the decade before the Civil War. The status and attainments of free Afro-Southerners look different depending on the standard one applies. While historian Brenda Stevenson writes of black women who were relegated to washing clothes for "only a few cents a day," Loren Schweninger shows that more than 300 of these free black clothes washers in the Upper South earned and saved enough to purchase nearly $200,000 worth of real estate in the 1850s. All in all, historians tend to exaggerate both the wave of relative white liberalism and black optimism that followed the American Revolution and the tide of repression that began by the early 1830s.

The discrepancy between aggressive racist rhetoric and legislation on the one hand and often-tolerant day-to-day treatment of free blacks on the other constitutes an abiding theme in southern history, reflecting both ambivalence on the part of white individuals and overt differences of opinion among southern whites. Few if any white southerners advocated full citizenship for free blacks, yet some quietly but consciously undermined certain restrictions that the state imposed upon free people of color. Elements within the Baptist Church in Virginia, for instance, continued to allow blacks to preach and run many of their own church affairs even after state law ostensibly prohibited both in 1832.

The North-South conflict over slavery during the 1850s did produce a hardening in white attitudes toward free blacks in the South, though not always in ways that are readily understood today. A law of 1856 in Virginia allowing self-enslavement is often cited as an expression of whites' desire to return all blacks to bondage, and indeed the existence of such a measure reflects no credit on white Virginia and its political leadership. Yet the self-enslavement law was not adopted to rid the state of free blacks. Rather, the legislation affected a small but growing number of black individuals, probably between 100 and 200 persons over the following eight years, who were actually threatened with expulsion from Virginia; applying for self-enslavement could avert that eventuality. The law placed formidable barriers in front of anyone who sought a white master; and in fact, as legislators anticipated, the few free blacks who did apply to enslave themselves often selected masters they already knew well—people who apparently had no intention of treating the black petitioners as actual slaves.

White hard-liners across the South in the same decade vociferously demanded that free blacks be enslaved or expelled en masse—a development that caused much anxiety among free Afro-Southerners. But "most" white southerners, as historian Ira Berlin writes, "shrank back in horror" from such proposals, and these initiatives were rejected almost everywhere. Ironically, it appears that life in a slaveholding society had instilled in white southerners a reverence for freedom so powerful that they were loath to revoke the liberty even of free blacks, whom, as a group, whites excluded from true citizenship and habitually belittled.

White attitudes toward free blacks, never uniform or consistent, varied also under the Confederacy. Some whites touted the loyalty and competence of "good and true men" in the free black community, while others regarded free Afro-Southerners as potential subversives. Almost from the beginning of the war, free black men were impressed (in effect, drafted) to do manual labor for the Confederate armies. They were often paid, and their terms of services were supposedly limited. Still, free blacks' wartime experience often amounted to one of forced labor.

After general emancipation in 1865, the term "free black" lost its earlier meaning as it came to encompass all Afro-Southerners. Even so, blacks who had been free before the Civil War, particularly those who had attained literacy and some economic security, supplied a significant portion of both the small Afro-Southern middle class and the black leadership during Reconstruction, especially during the first few years of that period.

MELVIN PATRICK ELY
College of William and Mary

Ira Berlin, *Slaves without Masters: The Free Negro in the Antebellum South* (1974); T. H. Breen and Stephen Innes, *"Myne Owne Ground": Race and Freedom on Virginia's Eastern Shore, 1640–1676* (1980); Thomas E. Buckley, S.J., *Virginia Magazine of History and Biography* (July 1994); Reginald Dennin Butler, "Evolution of a Rural Free Black Community: Goochland County, Virginia, 1728–1832" (Ph.D. dissertation, Johns Hopkins University, 1989); Melvin Patrick Ely, *Israel on the Appomattox: A Southern Experiment in Black Freedom from the 1790s through the Civil War* (2004); Barbara Jeanne Fields, *Slavery and Freedom on the Middle Ground: Maryland during the Nineteenth Century* (1985); John Hope Franklin, *The Free Negro in North Carolina, 1790–1860* (1943); Nancy M. Hillman, "Between Black and White: Race and Reform in the Baptist Churches of Southeastern Virginia, 1800–1870" (Ph.D. dissertation, College of William and Mary, 2012); Luther Porter Jackson, *Free Negro Labor and Property Holding in Virginia, 1830–1860* (1942); Michael P. Johnson and James L. Roark, *Black Masters: A Free Family of Color in the Old South* (1984); Suzanne Lebsock, *The Free Women of Petersburg: Status and Culture in a Southern Town, 1784–1860* (1984); Edward Maris-Wolf, "Liberty, Bondage, and the Pursuit of Happiness: The Free Black Expulsion Law and Self-Enslavement in Virginia, 1806–1864" (Ph.D. dissertation, College of William and Mary, 2011); Gary B. Mills, *Journal of American History* (June 1981); Christopher Andrew Nordmann, "Free Negroes in Mobile County, Alabama" (Ph.D. dissertation, University of Alabama, 1990); Loren Schweninger, *Black Property Owners in the South, 1790–1915* (1990); Brenda E. Stevenson, *Life in Black and White: Family and Community in the Slave South* (1996); Peter H. Wood, *Black Majority: Negroes in Colonial South Carolina from 1670 through the Stono Rebellion* (1975).

Gender

Class positions, relations, and conflicts are deeply imbued with gender. Insofar as class position may be defined primarily by occupation (and, especially for women, by the occupation of one's spouse), the relationship between gender and social class is relatively direct. Occupational segregation channels women and men into different types of jobs and employers; associated pay gaps and gendered care-giving responsibilities render female-headed households at special risk for poverty. In these and many other ways, class position and the material realities of class manifest differently for women and men.

Social and cultural expectations for appropriately feminine and masculine behaviors also vary widely by social class, and they influence the content of class-related solidarity, the prospects for class conflict, and the exercise of class power. Masculinity, for example, has been an important element of working-class solidarity in male-dominated industries such as coal mining, where gendered expectations of virility and toughness have in some contexts reinforced workers' militancy. And paternalism, a gendered (and racialized) form of class domination, was used to justify slavery and later characterized employers' strategies for securing authority and legitimacy in key southern industries such as textiles.

The southern political economy has shaped employment opportunities and thereby the gendered class structure of the region. The early 20th-century significance of labor-intensive manufacturing, for example, meant that white women and men (and children) often worked in the same factory, albeit at distinct jobs and rates of pay. Drawn by the prospect of earning their own wages and anticipating greater cultural freedom, rural farm women in southern states such as North Carolina flocked into the new textile mills and, during the heydays of textile employment, attained some of the highest rates of female labor force participation in the United States. However, women remained vulnerable in the monoeconomy of company towns, where loss of a husband's higher wages or falling out of favor with their boss could spell destitution.

The exclusion of working-class African Americans from manufacturing also had gendered implications. Up until the civil rights movement, the single most significant source of employment for African American women (outside of family-based agriculture) was domestic service, which placed them in a complicated household relationship with the white women and men who were their employers. African American women in some cases acquired considerable authority and respect, albeit constrained by racial hierarchy, in white families. At the same time, however, relegating "women's work" to African American women consigned them to the lowest paid of jobs, made them vulnerable to male sexual advances in the seclusion of white households, and reinforced the low value attached to all women's domestic labor. Meanwhile, the restriction of working-class African American men to a narrow band of hard labor jobs reinforced dominant images of black masculinity as intensely physical and larger than life—to be envied, feared, and controlled by white men.

Women of all races from middle class and more privileged backgrounds also faced class-specific constraints related to gender. Those who pursued professional training and employment were able to do so within a narrow range of professions, above all, nursing and teaching. Not only were such occupations subject to the masculine authority of physicians and administrators; they also carried, and continue to carry, cultural connotations of nurture and self-sacrifice that inscribe those who perform them as "feminine." The social implications have been contradictory and include both limitations and certain forms of authority. In segregated African American communities, for example, female nurses and teachers enjoyed considerable esteem for their education, service to the community, and roles in racial uplift.

Class-related rules of decorum and propriety, which function in part to establish distance from lower classes and make class superiority visible, even self-evident, are also gender specific. Codes of chivalrous behavior among gentlemen and chaste purity among ladies are icons of a southern past that set elites apart in the idealization if not always the realities of their behavior. Although the cultural authority of such codes has waned, relative formality in dress, manners, language, physical comportment, and, for women, proper sexual distance from men continues to communicate a cultural refinement that enacts and legitimizes class hierarchy. For African American middle-class women in particular, the "politics of respectability" has required demonstrations of moral commitment and ethical behavior that distance them from stereotypes of lascivious black women and, in a more contemporary frame, from those who are presumed lazy, promiscuous, and welfare dependent.

Expectations of feminine propriety and morality have also shaped women's strategies for class-related solidarity and protest. Suffragists and middle-class reformers emphasized women's moral superiority to justify their expanded involvement in politics. Working-class women have drawn on the moral authority of motherhood to enhance their political legitimacy; the union organizer Mother Jones is a classic example. In potentially violent strike settings, women have walked picket lines armed with brooms, tomatoes, and other household "weapons," relying on cultural prohibitions against assaulting women as they taunt strikebreakers and sass police and company guards. Other "disorderly women" have openly defied gender conventions, adopting masculine dress and affect as they protest their treatment in the workplace.

Even as some women have shrewdly utilized motherhood and femininity as political resources, however, the ultimate incompatibility between female subordination to masculine authority and the powerful public roles women have collectively claimed has also generated contradictions and backlash. Married women of all classes who become activists have in some instances experienced domestic violence, divorce, and threats to their access to their children. Female labor activists, even in prounion community settings, have found their organizing goals trivialized and their strikes condemned, on the basis of sexist arguments that their labor force participation is temporary, their earnings unnecessary, and their employment (especially in care-giving fields such as nursing and teaching) ideally motivated by feminine compassion rather than financial necessity.

The contemporary political economy of the South continues to structure class in gender-specific ways. The burgeoning service sector, which relies disproportionately on female labor, offers new opportunities to middle-class urban women (as well as men) with professional training. The lower end of the service sector has also expanded, however, and frequently provides below-subsistence wages to a heavily female labor force of retail clerks, office workers, restaurant servers, and others. Meanwhile, the strongholds of male working-class employment in mining, manufacturing, and construction have dwindled, and working-class men increasingly find their status as family breadwinners, a crucial element of heterosexual working-class masculinity, threatened; not surprisingly, such men's resentment at their economic decline in some instances finds expression through hostility to feminism and calls for a return to conventional gender relations in which men are unequivocally head of the household.

Indeed, gendered representations of class have become an important staple of contemporary political culture. In the post–civil rights movement, post-9/11 era, the cultural trappings of southern, white, working-class masculinity—guns, hunting, hard work, informal dress, manly affability—have become in the hands of would-be populists the true markers of "the people," the heart of a nation embattled by "foreign" ideas, peoples, religions, and military threats. This strategy is not new. From Theodore Bilbo to George Bush, from Eugene Talmadge to Jim Webb, southern politicians of various political stripes have positioned the white working class as their core constituents and appealed to it in implicitly gendered, frequently racist terms.

Thus the nexus of gender and class is currently shifting in important ways, particularly with the erosion of a family wage system that briefly permitted heterosexual, working-class, white (and, to a limited degree, black) southern men to install themselves and deeply identify as family breadwinners and heads of households. Despite patently insufficient wages and widening gaps in income and wealth, class position in contemporary political culture and dominant systems of representation is more about cultural affect and identity than about occupation, income, or economic resources. Class inequality continues to be enacted through gendered expectations and codes of behavior, but today these work to legitimate class hierarchy in large part by obscuring it.

BARBARA ELLEN SMITH
Virginia Tech

Michelle Brattain, *The Politics of Whiteness: Race, Workers, and Culture in the Modern South* (2004); Jacquelyn Dowd Hall, *Journal of American History* (September 1986), Hall, James Leloudis, Robert Korstad, Mary Murphy, Lu Ann Jones, and Christopher B. Daly, *Like A Family: The Making of a Southern Cotton Mill World* (1987); Evelyn Brooks Higginbotham, *Righteous Discontent: The Women's Movement in the Black Baptist Church, 1880-1920* (1993); Jacqueline Jones, *Labor of Love, Labor of Sorrow: Black Women, Work, and the Family from Slavery to the Present* (1985); Rebecca R. Scott, *Feminist Studies* (September 2007); Virginia Rinaldo Seitz, *Women, Development, and Communities for Empowerment in Appalachia* (1995); Stephanie J. Shaw, *What a Woman Ought to Be and to Do: Black Professional Women Workers during the Jim Crow Era* (1996); Barbara Ellen Smith, ed., *Neither Separate Nor Equal: Women, Race, and Class in the South* (1999); Jim Webb, *Born Fighting: How the Scots-Irish Shaped America* (2004); Michael Yarrow, in *Bringing Class Back In: Contemporary and Historical Perspectives*, ed. Scott G. McNall, Rhonda F. Levine, and Rick Fantasia (1991).

Honor

In the agrarian slave South, honor had more than casual significance in the life of the whites, rich and poor alike. African Americans, free and slave, also knew the uses of honor. Courage and reputation were not considered separate notions but a unity to which most members of the social classes adhered. Men were expected to uphold the virtues of valor, defend their families, properties, and personal integrity, and prove true to their family's traditions. To lose signal regard in the eyes of others was something to be feared. In small, rural communities, everyone knew or tried to know everything about their neighbors. In more urbanized places privacy could be better guarded. For most white southerners, though, the dictum "always dread dishonor" fell naturally from a father's lips to warn a son or daughter.

Honor was based on a mixture of physical characteristics and degrees of wealth. With regard to the former, the ethic established the hierarchy of social life: male over female, white over black, age over youth, traceable lineage over obscurity, and wealth, achieved or inherited, over penuriousness. Social rankings rested on those features. They largely determined the community's assessment of an individual's character and behavior. The higher one's reputation for gallantry, honesty, open-handedness, and family and community loyalty, the higher was one's place on the social ladder. As they still do today, judges, generals, cabinet officers, and others held respect under that rubric. Deference to those with such rank was greater than is customary now. No prouder title, southern planters often thought, was so gratifying as the designation,

"Colonel" or "General." Honor, after all, is a martial code, and the southern males, planters or yeomen, were jealous of their skill with arms. Mistrusting strangers and jealous of their rights, they were supposed to do all in their power to protect hearth and home, be it grand or humble.

For all the social classes, honor figured in many aspects of civic, political, and social life. It was not just confined to the rich and powerful, who displayed the principles of the "cavalier spirit." We tend today to identify this venerable ideal merely in the battle flourishes of a J. E. B. Stuart or the southern literary infatuation with the verses of Lord Byron and the novels of Sir Walter Scott. David O. Selznick's film *Gone with the Wind* offers a romantic view of the pre–Civil War South. The opening scenes reveal happy, submissive slaves, belles in hoop skirts, and gentlemen in fashionable attire sipping mint juleps. That fantasy did not represent the darker realities of southern life. The slaveholding planter elite was very small in numbers, although nearly a third of all white families owned one or more slaves. Yet, at every level of political life, members of the upper class controlled the offices, whether they were Whigs or Democrats, the chief parties of the day. They easily convinced poorer folk that their white skin conferred a sufficient degree of honor and superiority over all slaves and free blacks.

Eloquence accorded the well-educated spokesmen in the political arena high marks on the honor scale. As a public notable, the aspiring office seeker was expected to mount the rostrum, silence the rowdy, gesture grandly, and speak words that all could understand and appreciate. It helped his political aims if, in his election campaign, he also provided a lavish barbecue and generous amounts of liquor. Hospitality had its benefits. The votes of the less well off were thereby won in an unspoken gift exchange with the local leader.

Orlando Patterson, the Harvard sociologist, points out that all slave societies, from the dawn of time, have adopted some form of the honor ethic. It was the moral basis of that social order along with the sources of the Old and New Testaments as slavery was common in the ancient Middle East. Under this regime, the American slave was therefore obliged to acknowledge the master's honor with appropriate, deferential, and cheerful words. That was a reassurance that the world was revolving as it should.

By no means, however, was the control of human property quite as secure as their owners would have liked. The slaves, too, sometimes asserted themselves in ways that defied their owners. For instance, Frederick Douglass was a Maryland slave who later escaped to become a leading abolitionist. As a teenager, he had decided no longer to submit to the frequent whippings that a cruel farmer named Covey gave him. He struck back. The pair fought for over two hours, but

Covey lost blood and the battle. The victor was unscathed. After that, Douglass reported, he felt no more the sting of the cart whip. Covey wanted no repetition of his former fate nor risk becoming the subject of local white mockery. The great fear among whites was the prospect of slave revolt.

Actually, slaves also had their own code of honor, confined though it was to their cabin quarters. Slave men prevailed over their women, the elderly were to be respected, being a good singer or spellbinding storyteller gave a commendable reputation—all were among the means to maintain an inner dignity and enjoy prestige within their quarters. Occupational skill was also a means to slave esteem. Expertise at fishing, hunting, trapping, sailing, or some other occupation won the approval of other slaves and sometimes whites as well. William Elliott, a renowned South Carolina sportsman, was the proud owner of a slave named May who was an accomplished harpoonist of devil fish. Honor especially accrued to male slaves who might have a capacity to think, talk, and act fast. To sharpen their talent, they might take up the game of "playing the dozens." The object was to insult another slave who then had to retort with a greater insult, with onlookers clapping and groaning over the words exchanged. Those with the greatest gift for the exercise could win honor among their fellows, especially when they sought to fool the master or overseer. The game had originated in West Africa but proved most useful in black relations to their owners. With admirable serenity, some slaves could "jive," as the term still in use, declares. That was particularly so with house servants who had frequent contact with the master class. They knew how to talk to the white people. The unprepared slave, out of a fear that paralyzed the tongue, could not manage the technique. That failure might cause the black community real trouble from an irate white man. Such slaves lost respect and were labeled "fools" by their fellow slaves. The linguistic maneuvers that slaves could create grew from their very vulnerability, their powerlessness in a white-dominated world. Clearly, the slave system set severe limits on black autonomy.

To return to the honor of the gentry class, nothing mattered so much as the safeguarding of personal and familial repute. In a largely oral environment like the Old South, words spoken to taunt or insult struck the recipient as hard a blow as if he had received a slap in the face. If accepted, it would permanently scar his self-regard. The duel, usually with pistols in America, was, for some, the preferred way to restore one's self-esteem and the applause of others. Only those bearing the manners of gentlemen were eligible for the honor of shooting an opponent. Principals, that is, the dueling participants, had to be of equal footing in society. Seconds, also of the same moral and social rank as their principals, arranged the time and location. These friends were also supposed to seek reconciliations, a mission that sometimes did succeed. A surgeon was ordinarily present along with a presiding officer to give the appropriate signal. The seconds stood by to advise their principals and assure the fairness of the proceeding. Given the class-based nature of the duel, the purpose was not necessarily to obliterate the foe. Rather, the aim was to demonstrate the bravery of the gentlemanly challenger. By and large, members of the bar, military officers, and newspaper editors, many of whom were involved in politics, were the most likely to challenge and fight. (Clergymen, bankers, and town merchants were far less inclined to seek vindication with guns.)

An example of politicians so engaged was the fight in 1825 between Henry Clay, secretary of state, and the belligerent Sen. John Randolph of Virginia. They fired twice at each other but what a relief it was, they discovered, when none of the bullets had struck the other. In another case, by orders from President Sam Houston, Gen. Joseph E. Johnston was about to assume command of a Texas Republic regiment in 1838. His predecessor, the ousted Gen. Felix Huston of Natchez, Miss., demanded satisfaction. He felt insulted by his demotion. The pair fired ineffectively at each other several times. Finally, Johnston was struck in the thigh. Huston approached his opponent, struggling from the ground, and shook his hand. No hard feelings ensued.

Only 14 percent of encounters terminated in death, but dueling was thought to be a civilized means to prevent ambushes, feuds, and careless words in conversation. Also, it must be added, the practice was losing favor as the South became more evangelical in the 1840s and 1850s. Protestant preachers railed against the un-Christian tradition. Antidueling societies sprang up, but the general view was echoed in the words of Sen. Seargent S. Prentiss of Mississippi: "I am no advocate of duelling." Yet, he continued, "when a man is placed in a situation where if he does not fight, life will be rendered valueless to him, both in his eyes and those of the community," his only choice was to meet the challenge.

Defense of personal and family honor was not confined, though, just to the small number of antebellum southern gentlemen with hot tempers. Males of inferior status fought with knives, fists, and teeth in barroom brawls. Rivals would be mocked, however, in their neighborhoods if they had tried to imitate the lethal rituals of their betters. A clergyman traveling through Virginia backcountry was horrified that men in combat "bit one anothers lips and Noses off" and plucked eyes out and kicked each other in the groin, "to the Great damage of many a Poor Woman," wife of the victim. "Rough and tumble" fights were matters of honor, with no holds barred. "To feel a feller's eyestrings, and make him tell the news" was a matter of pride to the aggressor and a reason for laughter for those egging on the fight.

Men without the prestige of being deemed gentlemen nevertheless maintained a sense of honor. (To be sure, prostitutes, professional gamblers, and criminals defied the code and acted in a defiantly shameless, honorless manner.) Hard-minded farmers could be most resentful of their social superiors. For one from the upper ranks to insult a yeoman's honor or show haughty indifference could lead to reprisals—the burning of a barn, the shooting of a favorite stallion, the whipping of slaves belonging to a reviled slaveholder. Under such circumstances, planters were generally careful about how to greet and deal with less fortunate neighbors. In her diary the wealthy Mary Chesnut of South Carolina mused on the subject. "The meanest citizen," she observed, having the right to vote, exercised far too much power. After a sumptuous dinner, her well-to-do guests relaxed on the piazza, smoking. But in their midst sat one "Squire MacDonald, the well-digger." Fully at ease, he puffed on his clay pipe and "leaned back luxuriously" in his chair. Shoeless and sockless, he placed his muddy, well-digging toes on the porch railing. The women guests whispered that Mary's husband, James, was solemnly listening to McDonald's ungrammatical conversational monopoly. "Oh, that's his way," one lady remarked. "The raggeder and more squalid the creature, the more polite and the softer Mr. Chesnut grows." James Chesnut was taking the prudent path. Indeed, it was a wise policy to show attentiveness and magnanimity—hand a poor neighbor a generous loan on request, lend some slaves for a special need, or offer other favors out of neighborliness—all signs of respect for the less well off. Such acts also displayed the benefactor's sense of honorable magnanimity.

The male elite were also solicitous of the status as well as feelings of the ladies but for quite different reasons. A sign of their status was how well disposed they were to the female sex. They were to show regard for those in their social class and perhaps shower compliments as thick as snow. Nonetheless, the women of the Old South were all subject to the more negative character of honor. Their position in the hierarchy was determined in large part by the "shall-nots": they were supposed to exhibit a reserved demeanor, not frankness; chasteness, not aggressiveness; submission to male authorities, not self-expression; confinement to home, hearth, and bedroom, not public and immodest exposure. Some plantation ladies, however, were most outspoken even outside the home. A number of them ruled over their husbands or families and set the parlor proprieties with an iron glove—as occasion might demand. Some might even serve as guardians, not just of larders but money as well. For these characteristics they could escape frowns or exclusion, particularly if they framed their justifications as merely fulfilling the wishes of absent or deceased husbands.

For young upper-class virgins, the acquisition of a spouse was paramount. Of course, heiresses were much in demand whether beautiful or homely. Parents had considerable sway over daughters in the choosing of mates. For women not to have a husband was a matter of pity among friends and anguish among relations. The childless woman was another source of commiseration and diminished respect. Widows of fortune, though, gained a degree of independence and might even run a plantation or open a shop. The development of religious interest and greater church attendance in the rural Old South gave women a new avenue for self-expression. Pious women could not only assist the work of their pastors but also scold with impunity the menfolk whose drinking, gambling, or other sins of the flesh caught the women's attention. As their men insisted, a chief female duty was to assure the purity and integrity of the bloodline. "Amalgamation," that is, white women's cohabitation with a black, was thought to be the height of disgrace that could lead to black overlordship and white subjection.

Education for women of the genteel caste was still rather modest compared with that of their northern counterparts. The aim was to train the young maidens in those areas pleasing to men—instruction in music and singing, sewing, painting pictures, and the like, along with lessons in reading and writing. French was the preferred language for young ladies. Literacy was fashionable, and poor grammar and spelling were sure signs of social and intellectual inferiority. With common schools spotty throughout much of the agrarian South, lower-class girls received little encouragement to advance educationally. By and large the young girls' first obligation was to assist their mothers in the kitchen, garden, and field. After all, women of the rural nonslaveholding class were not expected to preside over teas. Rather, they had to work alongside their fathers and brothers if sowing and harvesting required their hands. It was a hard life, albeit one with integrity. Like their wealthier female neighbors, they could not get pregnant before marriage without subjection to public censure and fearful shame.

To conclude this sketch of southern honor and social class, it should be noted that the code was losing its preeminence even as the storm clouds of war approached. A town life, civic institutional advances, and a middle class were growing as the southern economy developed during the midcentury years. These factors were replacing the older notions of honor to a degree. Yet, in the slave states, the national crisis over slavery and abolitionism required the full assertion of the slogans and symbols of honor, particularly when news arrived of antislavery Abraham Lincoln's election to the presidency. Weldon Edwards of North Carolina expressed a common sentiment in November 1860. He wrote, "Our honor, dignity, self-respect demand it at *whatever cost.*" With enormous self-confidence that the male ethic of martial truculence helped to promote, the Fire-Eaters, as they were called, led the way into the hell of a disastrous war. After four bloody and destructive years that consequence left the South deprived of slaveholding, the wealth that ownership had made possible, and a male population much depleted. Honor, too, was much diminished as the Rebel veterans tried to rebuild their lives and their economy.

BERTRAM WYATT-BROWN
University of Florida, Emeritus

Edward L. Ayers, *Vengeance and Justice: Crime and Punishment in the 19th-Century American South* (1983); Peter Berger, Brigitte Berger, and Hansfried Kellner, *The Homeless Mind: Modernization and Consciousness* (1973); Pierre Bourdieu, in *Honor and Shame: The Values of Mediterranean Society*, ed. J. G. Peristiany (1965); Kenneth S. Greenberg, *Honor and Slavery* (1997); Bertram Wyatt-Brown, *Southern Honor: Ethics and Behavior in the Old South* (1982), *The Shaping of Southern Culture: Honor, Grace, and War, 1760s–1880s* (2000).

Humor

In 1728 William Byrd II—Virginian and planter—described his common neighbors as cadaverous pork-eaters with no work ethic and fewer manners. They were an idle lot, he wrote in his posthumously published *History of the Dividing Line betwixt Virginia and North Carolina*, much given to smoking the local tobacco, loafing, mangling the King's English, and not much else. It is a funny book, and it set the pattern for what might be called the patrician style in southern humor for two centuries and more. By the 21st century, however, Georgia comedian Jeff Foxworthy had turned the same subjects into a contrary ideal, a populist alternative, with his Blue Collar Comedy Tour and best-selling books on how to be a redneck and love it. "You might be a redneck if," he announces, "your richest relative buys a new house and you have to help take the wheels off of it." Between Byrd and Foxworthy stands a long lineage of fools, bear eaters, con men, crackers, knaves, mighty hunters, seducers, and generally troublesome innocents that include Ransy Sniffle, Sut Lovingood, Huck Finn, Jeeter Lester, Will Stockdale, Barney Fife, and Larry the Cable Guy. Alongside them, in turn, stand Brer Rabbit, Stepin Fetchit, and girls who live at the post office. At the other end of the social scale are shabby-rich belles whose breeding is so refined that, in Florence King's terms, "No matter which sex I went to bed with, I never smoked on the street." Southern humor is complicated, and it is intimately related to social class.

The fact that this dual tradition in southern humor is the creation primarily of educated, middle-class, frequently urban and professional white males tends to reinforce certain assumptions about southern social structure. Whether such men wrote of their subjects to humiliate them (as Byrd certainly did) or to treat them as exuberant specimens of the democratic spirit, the gap between the genteel storyteller and his bumptious subjects has defined the style of southern humor. It echoes the patrician and populist divide not only in southern literature but in southern politics and social structure generally. The South, we are told, is (or was until the 1950s) an unequal triangle of elite whites, crackers, and black folk. Inside this triangle, humor functions to celebrate or castigate the basic incongruities of being southern. If, furthermore, humor serves to isolate threats and neutralize them (as Henri Bergson claimed), then southern humor is a veritable battlefield of class warfare. How else, one could ask, could an educated southerner insulate himself from the foolery around him, unless he made fun of it? How else could poor folk fight back?

But humor is not so single-minded, and social class is not so tidy. Humor's tools are parody and irony as well as humiliation, and its objects are often the humorist and his audience, not some third party. Moreover, in the American experience "class" itself is as much a matter of cultural values and attitudes as it is income or occupation—status groups rather than hierarchies. In the South, as in the nation, these attitudes and status groups have been in constant flux, so permeable and open to mobility that the southern gentleman and redneck alike have been works in progress since the colonial era. Southern humorists have lived in the gray zone between patrician and populist, and they have used their art to negotiate class identities as well as to poke fun at them.

This ambiguity was first evident in the Old Southwest (today's Deep South) between 1830 and 1860. There, an extraordinary group of amateur humorists produced tales of fights, revival meetings, alligator rassling, and horse trades—the stuff of rural folk and plain whites—plus stories of the bench and bar, courtship, the hunt, and other, more town-oriented themes. Through them all ran the confidence man, the shapeshifter who could be both patrician and populist as the occasion demanded. These humorists wrote for local newspapers such as the *New Orleans Picayune* or the *St. Louis Reveille*, as well as William T. Porter's New York sporting journal, the *Spirit of the Times*, and they created iconic figures in American humor. A. B. Longstreet's "Ransy Sniffle," Johnson J. Hooper's "Simon Suggs," and, above all, George Washington Harris's "Sut Lovingood" rank among the finest inventions in American humor. The stories were often told in a "frame" style, whereby a gentleman introduced a rougher character who told the tale in his own dialect, then turned it back over to the gentleman at the end. It was a safe technique by which the patrician could take on a separate identity to treat subjects that were not in that age available in polite fiction. No subject—not violence, not gross behaviors, not even sex—was taboo. Mark Twain brought the form to literary perfection in *Huckleberry Finn*, and William Faulkner adapted it in serious works and in his comic tale "Spotted Horses."

This was ripe territory and a good style for exploring class identities and status anxieties, and it is testament to the richness of southwestern humor that virtually everyone got a comeuppance, including the tale-tellers. On one hand, the stories can be viewed as relentless put-downs of the rubes and hayseeds, whose antics were truly revolting to more refined tastes. They are the first expressions of what might be called the "southern grotesque," warped, even sick, manifestations of the effects of poverty and universal suffrage. Simon Suggs stuffs gunpowder into his mother's pipe; Sut Lovingood is nothing but "a nat'ral born durned fool" who likes to stuff lizards up the parson's pant legs and watch him whoop. On the other hand, the stories can be seen as vehicles of masculine escape—comic vacations from the stress of being proper and restrained. What white-collar male has not fantasized about breaking his routine and blowing off steam? At still another level, such stories inverted social codes by using the brag and boast of the ripsnorter to parody the self-important chivalry of the gentleman. Hence, the violence of the street fighter and his cocksure strutting found its parallel in the highly ritualized ceremonies surrounding a gentleman's duel, a parallel that Longstreet displayed to good effect in "The Fight." Similarly, Thomas Bangs Thorpe explored the connections between the mighty hunter's confrontation with nature and the gentry's more effete approach to hunting in such tales as "The Big Bear of Arkansas." Hooper's con man Simon Suggs feeds off the pretensions of the upwardly mobile as well as the gullibility of the simpleton. That the tales were written largely by lawyers, journalists, doctors, and such—that is, men who were neither patricians nor plain folk—suggests that these were middle-class expressions of irony and perhaps even anxiety in a rapidly shifting social landscape. The antebellum southern professional was part of a somewhat marginal group, closely allied with the planter class yet temperamentally part of a rising bourgeoisie that was national and market oriented. Such a man existed on the cusp of the patrician and populist styles, and it is this incongruity that gives his humor its wonderfully keen, even subversive, edge.

The edge dulled, however, after the Civil War. Twain adapted the basic elements of southwestern humor, especially its use of language, conning, grotesque characters, and exaggeration, but Twain was a self-conscious artist with a wider, wholly American, audience in mind. Southwestern humor gave way to local color: pleasant tales about strange characters down the road, all wrapped up in a nostalgic package that itself was hand-in-glove with the rising mythology of the Lost Cause. "Bill Arp" (Charles Henry Smith) was as good as any of them, but as an ironist he bears little resemblance to his forebears. Interestingly, the exception that proves the rule were women humorists such as Ida McClellan Moore who began to use local color to explore their own worlds and, notably, humorists such as Joel Chandler Harris (a white) and Charles W. Chesnutt (a black) who began to open up the rich heritage of African American humor. While the women poked fun at the domestic scene, Harris and his peers focused on the trickster—the expert at "puttin' on ole massa." In one sense these tales were a chronicle of how southern blacks had successfully conned the whites; in another sense they were nostalgic projections of a time when race relations were presumably stable and threats to white authority were supposedly minimized. They re-create a world that never was. Still, it is ironic that southern humor lost its subversiveness at precisely the moment that sharecropping and poverty were inventing southern populism. There is no populist equivalent of Sut Lovingood.

There it stood until the 1920s, at which point several things conspired to bring back southern humor, make it socially relevant again, and transform it. By that point, H. L. Mencken (a southerner himself of sorts, being from Baltimore) had dismissed the whole region as a "Sahara of the Bozart"; he and his friends despaired at any cultural sophistication among southerners even as Faulkner, Allen Tate, and Robert Penn Warren were about to prove him utterly wrong. The "serious" literature of the "southern gothic," the "tortured South," or whatever name captures its essence, is a subject in itself but not one, oddly, far removed from the rediscovery of the southern grotesque—the kind of foolishness that the southwestern humorists had captured so beautifully.

A case in point is Erskine Caldwell. His *Tobacco Road*, for example, may be seen at one level as a tragic affair of poverty, inbreeding, and oxlike stupidity among the southern dirt poor. Caldwell's Jeeter Lester is Sut Lovingood gone wholly to seed and an object of polite pity and scorn. But it is important to remember that Caldwell was himself directly descended from the southwestern tradition: he was educated, middle class, the son of a Presbyterian minister, and he wrote in a plain, straightforward, "realistic" style that echoed Harris and Hooper. He had, like them, a moralist's notions of what was wrong with the South. Jeeter would not exist if cooperative farming and a little schooling were introduced, and from that angle Caldwell adopted both the elitist pose of the patrician and the social activism of the populist. At the same time, the absurdities of the Lesters' experience were ribald excess itself, a comic parody of southern notions of pride, agrarian virtue, and evangelical religion that anyone should have recognized as farce, but few did. Ralph Ellison, for example, doubled up with laughter upon seeing a stage performance of *Tobacco Road* in New York. Having been forced to play the fool as a black man in Alabama, it convulsed him to see Jeeter Lester, a poor white, play the fool on stage. The northern white audience did not get it, but Ellison, a black southerner, did. This was satire in the service of protest. It dissolved the lines between black and white and made him, he said, more aware of "our common humanity."

But even as the gap between poor and rich in the South became, in Roosevelt's terms, the nation's number one problem, national anxieties and the pull of the Lost Cause brought on a second wave of nostalgia. The publication and filming of Margaret Mitchell's *Gone with the Wind* in the late 1930s made the Old South, not the New, very fashionable in a time of extreme social stress. In these romanticized fantasies, class conflict and racial tension disappeared in a national wave of yearning for the supposedly simpler world of the hierarchical past. Perhaps the finest example of the South's nostalgic pull, as regards humor, was Walt Disney's live and animated rendition of the Remus tales in *Song of the South* (1946), wherein the Brer Rabbit tales were expertly rendered into lovable cartoons, while a chuckling old black man entertained his young white adorers. Artistically the film is masterful; as a characterization of race relations, it is antique.

Audiences, however, lapped it up, and southern humor became a national commodity, a vehicle for urban fantasies and status anxieties—a sort of stage on which southern stereotypes could be used to address national, even global, issues. Since World War II, "southern" humor has proliferated through rapidly changing types of media that have expertly blended the patrician and populist styles, often at the hands of nonsoutherners. Consider the humble comic strip, wherein Snuffy Smith, Pogo, Lil' Abner, Shoe, and a host of others have provided daily commentary on any number of social issues, mostly geared to the middle class and spoken in the unthreatening lingo of the southern populist. "We have met the enemy and he is us," quipped Walt Kelly's Pogo, an Okefenokee possum, in terms that addressed national obsessions with consumerism and pollution. On the other hand, Daisy Mae's raw sexuality and Lil' Abner's laziness reflected the morning pipedreams of commuters rushing to their jobs in glass-front office buildings. Ironically, Lil' Abner's creator was a

Connecticut Yankee, Alfred G. Caplin—aka Al Capp—as was Pogo's Kelly. Snuffy Smith was the offspring of Billy DeBeck, of south Chicago.

This appropriation of southern voices and stereotypes is nowhere more blatant than in television and cinema, and it has generally pursued one of two paths. The nostalgic strain was evident during the 1960s with TV's *The Andy Griffith Show*, a gentle family sitcom starring Andy Griffith (who made his mark, as we shall see, as a stand-up comic). Here the world was orderly, mostly white, nonviolent, and largely sexless—given Andy's widowed state. By portraying a single-parent home, lovable drunks, and bulletless deputies (Don Knotts's Barney Fife), *The Andy Griffith Show* and its clones offered an anodyne to depersonalization, dysfunctional families, and corporate stress nationwide. Its farcical counterpart, *The Beverly Hillbillies*, used Buddy Ebsen's Jed Clampett as a variation on the southern grotesque to mock the pretensions of consumerism and status hunting. One or both of these shows was on the air weekly from 1960 to 1971, and they endure in reruns.

A second use of southern stereotypes appeared as the reborn rebel, the southern outlaw. Again the South served as metaphor for a national mood of rebelliousness and escapism. Movies such as *Smoky and the Bandit* and television series such as *The Dukes of Hazzard* mated Nashville-style country music with NASCAR culture in wild, farcical comedies squarely designed to discharge modern frustrations with bureaucracy and authority. William Byrd's Virginia aristocrat devolved into Jackie Gleason's Buford T. Justice or Sorrell Brooke's Boss Hogg. That these films were creations of a corporate culture based in New York and Los Angeles is no small irony. That there were few if any blacks in them and that women generally appeared as full-busted Daisy Maes suggests a real urge for escapism among the modern American middle class. That they tore up cars (a symbol of bourgeois success), mocked authority (at a time when politicians were running on law-and-order platforms), and praised the con artist (when the modern family was working two jobs to put children through day camps and college) suggests the degree to which American status striving had given way to ambivalence.

It was becoming fashionable, in other words, to be redneck—a complete inversion of William Byrd's colonial perspective and a triumph, in a sense, of the populist over the patrician. The change was evident in the evolution of the southern stand-up comic—a more authentically southern humorous voice, albeit one with national appeal. Again, the evolution of media technology proved crucial. Vaudeville and nightclub acts had been around for some time, but the popularization of the long-playing record during the 1950s enabled comedians to find a national outlet, and the foremost of these were two: Andy Griffith and Brother Dave Gardner. Griffith offered the traditional route. *What It Was, Was Football* (1953) was the first "southern" comic album to become a national hit. In it, Griffith virtually reinvented Twain's Huck Finn, offering pithy challenges to the rituals of middle-class popular culture (e.g., football) and highbrow art (a satire on Shakespeare) that made him an instant celebrity. He reprised the role as Will Stockdale in the stage and film versions of Mac Hyman's hilarious *No Time for Sergeants* (1954) and then went on to television. (Ironically, his finest performance was as "Lonesome Rhodes," the country-boy-turned-kingmaker in Elia Kazan's *A Face in the Crowd*, which is part southern satire and part Greek tragedy and all comment on the power of mass media.) Griffith's success paved the way for a reawakening of the local color school, chiefly through the comedy of Jerry Clower, Justin Wilson, and others.

Gardner was more complex. Thoroughly antiestablishment, he fit in well with the hip counterculture of the late 1950s and was an item among intellectuals North and South throughout the 1960s for his clever wordplay, long pointless stories told in the southwestern tradition, and his fanciful forays into mysticism. "When we leave the realm of dualities, that's when we commence to swing," he said. Audiences had to work to understand statements like that, but clearly he had transcended the typical good-ole-boy syndrome, and his open embrace of drugs and Eastern philosophy was decidedly Hollywood, not Holly Springs. "I'm sick and tired of poor folks," he quipped. "I remember that I's brought up in that stroke, and the first piece of light bread I ever seen was thowed off the back of a CCC truck. Actually, that's why I have come to entertain the rich—the poor already have something to look forward to." One critic has noted that as Gardner maligned "'inferiors' he boosted the egos of members of the audience, assuring them that *they* were certainly not 'common' peckerwoods, but unique, lovable 'Children of Splendor.'" Gardner could be virulently racist. "Let 'em go to school," he said of desegregation. "We did, and we didn't learn nothin'." Still, when Gardner spoke in dialect, it was hard to tell if he was mocking poor blacks or poor whites. Thus did class and race, superiority and inferiority, provincialism and cosmopolitanism, all blend into one.

In the meantime, southern women writers were exploring their roots and their anxieties in short stories, novels, and essays that form in their own way a feminine counterweight to the southwestern frontier school. Flannery O'Connor's writings are often unsparingly bleak, yet there is a powerful strain of satire and irony running through them all, with her versions of the southern grotesque in full form. *Wiseblood* may be the grimmest funny book since *Tobacco*

Road, and its antihero, Hazel Motes, the most distorted poor white since Sut Lovingood. At a far gentler level, Eudora Welty's books and short stories explore the boundaries of class and race in nuanced prose that has inspired a new generation of southern women writers, among them Lee Smith and Fannie Flagg. Bailey White took the soft voice of southern gentility to National Public Radio in a series of sketches that merged the oral tradition with local color and transcended class. Florence King, on the other hand, could be acidly blunt about social distinctions. "Like all members of the shabby genteel class," she wrote, "I hated low-class people. Being a shabby genteel southerner only intensified this prejudice; we are bottomless wells of aristocratic disdain and empty thimbles of aristocratic power. All we can do is badmouth poor white trash."

However, badmouthing the poor white has become profitable. Ambiguity over roots and status has found modern form in the Blue Collar Comedy Tour: Foxworthy, Ron White, Bill Engval, and Dan Whitney (Larry the Cable Guy). The humor represented by the Tour offers fairly common variations on ethnic stereotyping, and as such it is representative of what might be called a comedic "first strike"—adopting a posture of inferiority as a means of turning the satire on its head. "Blue Collar" has taken "redneck" and moved it upscale to appeal to ordinary working people who may have poor folk in their backgrounds but who have themselves achieved a level of respectability. At $50 per ticket the audience is not poor, and Foxworthy's jokes and Larry's butt crack denote a social class that their listeners have worked hard to escape. "You might be a redneck if you mow your grass and find a car." It's funny, but no one in the audience would allow their yards to deteriorate that far—although they may have relatives or ancestors that fit the bill. At the same time, the audience (which is emphatically national and not simply confined to the South) knows well that it is not part of the quiche-and-chardonnay set. Redneck humor thus becomes a thumb in the eye of the sophisticated, and "blue collar" becomes its own status statement. Knowing that they will never join the ranks of the power elite, and anxious not to fall to the level of their poor forebears, the members of Foxworthy's audience can listen to redneck jokes and get the laugh on everyone, including themselves.

It is nervous laughter all the same. The humor of Blue Collar, Brother Dave, Andy Griffith, et al. has been enacted as a southern voice on a national stage, but the anxieties it addresses are wholly American. "Southern" has been appropriated as a code word for larger discontents and aspirations. "Class" no longer has the comforting stability it once demanded, if indeed its demands were ever met. Patrician has lost out to populist, but even that has not relieved status anxieties as modern stress ups the ante for staying in the game. At least people are still laughing.

JOHN MAYFIELD
Samford University

Roy Blount Jr., *Roy Blount's Book of Southern Humor* (1994); James C. Cobb, *Journal of Southern History* (February 2000); Ralph Ellison, *Going to the Territory* (1986); Richard Gray, *Writing the South: Ideas of an American Region* (1986); Robert C. Hauhart, *Journal of Cultural Research* (July 2008); M. Thomas Inge and Edward J. Piacentino, eds., *The Humor of the Old South* (2001), *Southern Frontier Humor: An Anthology* (2010); James H. Justus, *Fetching the Old Southwest: Humorous Writing from Longstreeet to Twain* (2004); Florence King, *Confessions of a Failed Southern Lady* (1985); Jack Temple Kirby, *Media-Made Dixie: The South in the American Imagination* (1986); William E. Lightfoot, *Southern Quarterly* (Spring 1996); Kenneth S. Lynn, *Mark Twain and Southwestern Humor* (1959); John Mayfield, *Counterfeit Gentlemen: Manhood and Humor in the Old South* (2009); Edward J. Piacentino, ed., *The Enduring Legacy of Old Southwest Humor* (2006); John Shelton Reed et al., *Southern Cultures* (Summer 1995).

Industrialization and Deindustrialization

In 1850 South Carolina textile magnate William Gregg pointed to the "thousands of ignorant, degraded white people among us" and promised that building "a manufacturing village of shanties in practically any healthy part of the state" virtually guaranteed "crowds of these poor people around you seeking employment at half the compensation given to operatives at the North." Little did he know that his observation foreshadowed the importance and plight of an abundant, economically marginalized and therefore eminently expendable labor force in southern industrial development over roughly the next 150 years.

For antebellum investors, the question had largely been one of putting their capital into producing cotton or processing it into cloth, but coupled with the disruption of the Civil War, the end of the antebellum cotton boom seemed at first to diminish the attractiveness of the latter prospect. The entire South boasted only 10,000 textile workers in 1870—roughly the same number as in 1860. Yet, as the crusade to build an industrial "New South" gained momentum in the 1880s, the number of southerners working in the textile industry grew explosively, reaching almost 100,000 by 1900. Textile plants could operate anywhere there was a stream with sufficient flow to provide waterpower, and the increasing availability first of steam power in the 1890s and then of electricity a bit later expanded the geographic possibilities dramatically.

Single men might pursue jobs with the railroad, in the coalfields or lumber camps, or in the emerging steel industry around Birmingham, but for married men millwork meant keeping their families intact and possibly even laboring side by side. For all its flaws, "mill village" housing was clearly a step up from what they had left behind in the countryside, and the escape from rural isolation was especially attractive for younger couples. A quarter to a third of textile operatives were 15 years old or younger in 1900, but the educational opportunities for younger children afforded by larger, more-progressive employers in their mill villages were also generally superior to what could be had for rural farm children.

Although pushed by the increasingly dismal prospect of lifelong tenancy and pulled by the allure of a steady paycheck, men found the decision to go into the mill or factory was often still an agonizing one; in a sense, it suggested failure as a farmer in a society where farming and masculinity remained tightly intertwined. In *Tobacco Road* Erskine Caldwell's Jeeter Lester spurns "them durn cotton mills" as "no place for a man to be" and declares it "a hell of a job for a man to spend his time winding strings on spools." Journalist Ben Robertson saw the pluses definitely outweighing the minuses for one of the tenant families who gave up farming for what was called "public work" in one of the mills dotting the South Carolina upstate: "The whistle blew for them at half past four o'clock and at six their work started, six to six was their shift. It was a hard life for a family accustomed to the open, but Saturday was payday—every Saturday." In many cases brutal economic realities ultimately made the choice for farmers like the Union County, S.C., man, who, after selling his cotton at five and a half cents a pound in 1914, found he could not even "pay the fertilizer bill and eat." At that point he knew "wherever I would go, whatever I did, I couldn't make it worse than this."

For all the chances for economic advancement that it offered, becoming what local town residents called one of the "mill people" often put you on the wrong side of a social divide that was nearly as unbreachable as the one between blacks and whites. In journalist Clarence Cason's view, Alabama mill workers were treated little differently from blacks when they came to town. "Mainly they seemed to buy snuff and stick candy, but the clerks never paid much attention to them one way or the other. They were just the cotton mill people."

The mill people were acutely aware of the prejudices they faced and occasionally rallied behind their self-styled political champions, such as South Carolina's Cole Blease. Although they were generally not overtly aggressive in asserting themselves when they were slighted or denigrated individually, extensive oral history research has revealed that they not only maintained their individual and communal dignity and pride—"Mill people is the best people in the world," more than one operative declared—but created and sustained a strong social network that functioned much "like a family."

Still, if the case for the development of class consciousness among southern workers had to rest on the success of organized labor in the region, then the case would seem a weak one indeed. This is not to say that southern workers did not lash out when management sought to cut their already meager wages or impose the "stretch out" or other techniques to wring more production from them without raising their compensation. Gastonia, N.C., is synonymous with the labor conflicts of the 1920s, and southern workers effectively precipitated the great textile strike of 1934; however, the textile industry was a stiff challenge for union organizers in the South, owing to determined, often ruthless opposition from management and the availability of a huge surplus of workers generated by agricultural mechanization.

The United Mine Workers had much better luck in organizing the southern coal fields, and World War II brought not only federal contracts for southern manufacturers but protections and guarantees for workers. Across the region, union membership more than doubled from roughly 500,000 in 1938 to more than 1 million a decade later, but postwar organizing efforts quickly ran afoul of the double bugaboo of white racial anxieties and Cold War fears of communist subversion. A typical piece of antiunion propaganda warned, "If they come in you will share the same restroom with Negroes and work side by side with them. It comes right out of Russia and is pure communism and nothing else." There is no denying that such rhetoric, trumpeted by chambers of commerce, newspapers, politicians, and even preachers (such as the one who warned that "CIO" meant "Christ Is Out!") had an effect on workers steeped in segregation, rabid anticommunism, and the scriptures.

Yet, neither rigid cultural conservatism nor the absence of working-class consciousness sufficed to explain the fact that union membership as a share of the workforce in the South stood at 50 percent of the nonsouthern average in 1964, roughly where it had been in 1939. Arguments that union-averse southern workers were simply blind to their own economic interest could not have been farther off base, for they understood full well why new employers had come in and offered them the regular jobs with regular paychecks that their parents never had. The meaning was certainly not lost on them when textile factories responded to successful organizing drives in Huntsville, Ala., and Darlington, S.C., in the mid-1950s by simply shutting the plants down. Explaining why his fellow employees had resoundingly rejected a collective bargaining agreement, one southern worker simply noted, "For some this was their first job ever. This was the first time they had ever seen a paycheck in their lives, and they didn't want to do anything to lose it." Every former Confederate state had right-to-work laws in place by 1954 save for Louisiana, which finally fell in line in 1976. In the ardently antiunion Carolina Piedmont, even at the end of the 20th century, a plant manager had no compunction about admitting that when he heard of a worker harboring union sympathies, he took him aside and threatened to "fire his ass and make sure that neither he, nor any member of his family, ever works in this county again." Such blatant disregard for worker rights went a long way toward explaining why, in 2008, union members accounted for roughly 3 to 5 percent of the workforce in the Carolinas, Georgia, Texas, and Virginia, figures that even with a sharp decline in union membership nationwide still fell well shy of half the national average of over 12.4 percent.

Save for lumber and steel, before the civil rights movement employment in southern industry was reserved overwhelmingly for whites, who, for example, claimed 90 percent of new manufacturing jobs created in South Carolina between 1940 and 1964. Contrary to the arguments of liberal economists, the general and long-standing availability of ample numbers of white workers eager to work at essentially the same starting wages as blacks had meant that it typically cost southern employers practically nothing to hire only whites. But by the mid-1960s, as more and better jobs became available to whites, labor market conditions forced employers who had long refused to hire blacks to choose between labor shortages and the higher wages that would be necessary to hold on to white employees. For traditionally lily-white industries like textiles that were losing large numbers of white workers to the more attractive job opportunities that became available during the 1960s, the civil rights movement had actually been, as more than one plant manager admitted, "a blessing in disguise" because it allowed them to hire black workers, "and if anybody wanted to complain about it . . . you could place the blame on the government."

Because blacks (and later Latinos) had come in behind whites who had moved to better positions in newer plants, they were concentrated heavily in the low-wage, low-skill jobs. These positions were generally the first to go when global competition from cheaper labor markets forced mass plant closings in the textile and apparel industries during the 1980s and beyond, although whites held a solid majority of the jobs that were vanishing. With sewing machine operators in North Carolina earning about as much in an hour as their counterparts in Bangladesh made in a week, it was clear that, although the South's labor costs may have remained low by North American standards, in the global economy they were anything but. As the pace of industrial outmigration quickened in the wake of the North American Free Trade Agreement (1994), North Carolina lost 35 percent, Mississippi 28 percent, and South Carolina 25 percent of their manufacturing jobs between 1996 and 2006, while eight other southern states suffered losses in the range of 19 to 24 percent.

Because of the peculiarly dispersed pattern of manufacturing activity in the region, 7 of the 10 states with the nation's highest concentrations of nonmetropolitan manufacturing-dependent counties were in the South in 1979, and 20 years later the South accounted for nearly all such counties that were also classified as "low wage." As a result, some of the worst suffering inflicted by the industrial exodus came in rural areas with little economic resiliency. Having kept taxes to a minimum in order to appease their now-departed industrial guests, these communities whose mortgaged futures have now gone even farther south or east lacked the educated workforce and physical infrastructure to compete for more dynamic, better-paying industries. Meanwhile, with their towns withering around them, members of an abandoned proletariat often too old to learn a new skill or to relocate found that the only employment available to them was tearing down their old workplaces—a task far less formidable than rebuilding the shattered self-esteem and dashed hopes of a people whose needs and feelings hardly seemed to count for more at the end of the South's industrial odyssey than they had at the beginning.

JAMES C. COBB
University of Georgia

James C. Cobb, *The Selling of the South: The Southern Crusade for Industrial Development, 1936–1990* (1993), *Industrialization and Southern Society, 1877–1984* (1984); Jacquelyn Dowd Hall, James Leloudis, Robert Korstad, Mary Murphy, Lu Ann Jones, and Christopher B. Daly, *Like a Family: The Making of a Southern Cotton Mill World* (1987); Tom E. Terrill, *Journal of Economic History* (March 1976).

Industrialization, Employment, and Organized Labor

During the past 60 years, the demographic and employment profile of southern workers has changed dramatically, with the pace of change accelerating over the past two decades. Industrial expansion characterized the period from the end of the war into the 1980s. More recently, however, the South has undergone dramatic deindustrialization. Job growth has continued, with the rapid expansion of the professional and service sectors offsetting the loss of manufacturing employment. Workers with limited educational qualifications, however, have found wages and benefits in service employment inferior to those in the declining industrial category. Accompanying these trends has been a remarkable change in the ethnic profile of the southern working class with the recruitment of large numbers of Mexican and Central American workers for low-wage agricultural, food processing, and manual service employment. Throughout five decades of multifaceted change, however, the South's status as a bastion of antiunionism has remained steady.

In the four decades after the end of World War II, southern workers made significant gains. From the late 1950s to the late 1970s, the South added over 1.7 million workers in manufacturing. In the same period, southern employment in relatively high-wage electrical and transportation equipment manufacture grew from under 360,000 to over 850,000 and employment in contract construction, another high-wage occupation, more than doubled. By 1980 per capita income in the South in had climbed to 88 percent of the national average. The positive impact of civil rights legislation in expanding job opportunities for African Americans in the textile, pulp and paper, and food processing industries spurred some of this advance, especially during the 1970s. Despite these positive developments, however, most southern states continued to fall below national norms in key socioeconomic indicators. Thus, a survey published in 1988 revealed that industrial wage rates in every southern state fell below the national average. The South continued to trail the rest of the country in educational attainment, health care, and income; more than 40 percent of the nation's poor people lived in the South.

Since the 1980s, the pace of development has accelerated while its contours have changed. Industrial employment fell off sharply. Agricultural employment continued to shrink, as did jobs in mining and other extractive sectors. New industries such as poultry raising and processing emerged, employing thousands, many of them Latino. Southern companies pioneered in the vast expansion of low-wage retail employment while establishing patterns of labor use and management practices widely emulated elsewhere. Expanding high-tech and creative enterprises generated thousands of low-wage service, retail, and custodial jobs, most of them filled by black or Latino and/or female workers.

Indeed, the southern labor force became more ethnically diverse. In the 1990s the Latino population expanded, especially in Georgia and North Carolina, which together added 300,000 Latinos. In that decade, the Latino population doubled and more in six southern states. In 1980, 2.5 percent of the South's population was Latino; by the mid-2000s the figure had climbed to over 8 percent. A survey at the turn of the century found that 90 percent of farm workers were Latino, while other estimates put the number of immigrant workers in the expanding food processing industry at more than 300,000.

Beginning in the 1980s, deindustrialization came to the South with a vengeance. Global competition, national trade policies, and corporate relocation strategies devastated many southern communities. Between 2001 and 2004, more than 20 percent of the national decline in manufacturing jobs occurred in the South. Alabama, among the most industrialized of the southern states, lost one-eighth of its manufacturing jobs in the first two years of the new millennium. The number of jobs in the textile industry plummeted by 80 percent between 1973 and 2009.

The decline of manufacturing had a direct impact on organized labor's presence in the South. U.S. employers in a variety of manufacturing industries, who once looked to Dixie for low-wage and union-resistant workers, began shifting operations and opening new plants in Mexico, Central America, and Asia. In the seven largest southern industrial states, union membership in manufacturing enterprises dropped from 643,000 in 1983 to 183,000 a quarter century later, a decline of more than 70 percent. By 2009 in Florida, North Carolina, Tennessee, Virginia, and Alabama teachers and other public employees constituted a majority of all organized workers. Between 1983 and 2009, despite the modest gains in the numbers of unionized public employees, total union membership in the former Confederate states fell by more than 1 million.

Southern political and economic elites grew even more determined than in the past to fight worker organization. Of the 13 states with the lowest proportion of union membership, 10 are in the Confederate South; all 11 "Old South" states have constitutional or statutory provisions—so-called right-to-work laws—that bar union security arrangements. The expansion of the automobile industry into the South, which peaked in the 1980s, took place on a largely nonunion basis. Most of the new auto plants were located in rural areas, with few African Americans, who have generally proved more union prone than their white coworkers. In the mid-eighties, Nissan's success in thwarting an organizing effort on the part of the United Automobile Workers at its new plant in central Tennessee revealed the potency of antiunion sentiments among company officials, state and local government officials, and even rank-and-file workers. Meanwhile, the devastation of the textile and garment industries destroyed the modest union presence in these areas. Even the heavily unionized southern pulp and paper industry showed declining union representation, especially as newer plants came online.

Just as in the older industrial regions, a surge in service and retail work has accompanied the decline in relatively well-paid industrial work. As of 2009, by some calculations, at least 70 percent of wageworkers in the South were classified as service, retail, and white-collar workers. Most of the service-sector jobs created since the mid-1990s were at the lower end of the wage curve. Those concentrated in the low-wage sectors were disproportionately black, Latino, and/or female.

This expanding service, retail, health care, and entertainment sector, employing as it does over a million low wageworkers, would seem to be an inviting target for labor organizers. With some exceptions, however, organized labor has enjoyed few successes. Medical and elder care facilities, entertainment complexes, and other facilities with large numbers of service and custodial workers were largely resistant to unionization in the South. Harsh employer hostility, a flawed federal union representation process, racial and ethnic divisions, and poorly conducted organizing campaigns, along with the antagonism of state and local public officials, all contributed to the continuing low levels of union penetration in this sector.

Even during the heyday of organized labor's national strength, the 1950s and 1960s, the unions' inability to organize substantial numbers of workers in the South's signature industry, textiles, set the region apart from the postwar labor relations regime that emerged from the New Deal. Many observers then perceived the South's exception to the nation's relatively union-friendly postwar order as an anachronistic throwback to an earlier era of labor-management confrontation. By the 1980s, however, with organized labor's ranks diminishing virtually everywhere, the southern pattern began to seem prototypical rather than exceptional.

A combination of low wages, ruthless price cutting, careful cultivation of employee loyalty, and fierce resistance to organizing efforts has helped to limit organize labor's inroads into the expanding retail section in the South and elsewhere. In particular, Wal-Mart, along with other nonunion southern employers such as Publix markets, Home Depot, and Fed Ex, has relied on temporary, part-time, short-tenure workers whose lack of skills, education, and alternative sources of employment promote a labor relations regime that has featured low wages, meager benefits, and minimal job security. Indeed, the rise of Wal-Mart from its origins in northwestern Arkansas in the 1960s was a particularly successful example of what might be termed the "southernization" of the U.S. labor relations system. Using its enormous market power, the firm has imposed low-wage, cost-cutting production requirements on its increasingly dependent suppliers, both at home and abroad. Hostile to the regulatory policies associated with the New Deal order, Wal-Mart has repeatedly ignored or violated minimum wage, fair labor practices, and health and safety regulations. At the same time, it has been successful in combining advanced marketing and inventory control with labor policies designed to win the loyalty of its low-wage, largely female, workers (or "associates," in Wal-Mart parlance).

From Wal-Mart's inception in the early 1960s, founder Sam Walton saw the men and women from the rural, Upcountry South as an ideal source of labor. With low-wage expectations and few other employment opportunities, they were particularly responsive to Walton's quasi-paternalistic management style. Pep sessions, focus groups, one-on-one meetings, and other forms of in-store social control encouraged disdain for "outside" parties such as union organizers and government inspectors. At the same time, when confronted with union-organizing initiatives, Wal-Mart, along with other southern retailers, has been aggressive in isolating and punishing dissidents and resourceful in taking advantage of the ineffectiveness of federal labor law's putative guarantees of workers' right to organize.

Twenty years ago, historian and economist Ray Marshall, charting the expansion of industry in the South, speculated that, while the South would no doubt continue to trail the rest of the country with respect to the density of union presence, continuing economic development could well narrow the gap. In view of the region's rapid industrial expansion, "Union membership in the South," he suggested, "probably will continue to increase both absolutely and relative to the rest of the country." In fact, however, whereas he held out the possibility that economic growth might finally bring the South closer to national norms, it is the South's union avoidance and the labor relations regime pioneered by such southern retail leaders as Wal-Mart that have helped to set the patterns increasingly characteristic of the national economy as a whole.

ROBERT H. ZIEGER
University of Florida

Barry T. Hirsch, David A. Macpherson, and Wayne G. Vroman, *Monthly Labor Review* (July 2001); Nelson Lichtenstein, *The Retail Revolution: How Wal-Mart Created a Brave New World of Business* (2009); Timothy J. Minchin, *Fighting against the Odds: A History of Southern Labor since World War II* (2005); Bethany Moreton, *To Serve God and Wal-Mart: The Making of Christian Free Enterprise* (2010); Steve Striffler, *Chicken: The Dangerous Transformation of America's Favorite Food* (2005); Robert H. Zieger, ed., *Southern Labor in Transition, 1940–1995* (1997).

Jews

When significant numbers of Jews first settled in the South in the early 19th century, the plantation-owning elite dominated society. These early Jews were involved with trade and were concentrated in port cities such as Charleston, Savannah, and New Orleans. Economic success as merchants led several of them, including Mordecai Cohen and Nathan Nathans in Charleston, to acquire plantations and slaves, emulating the city's planter class. They were the exception, though, as most southern Jews remained in commercial trade well into the 20th century.

During the antebellum era, the planter elites saw petty trade as beneath them and looked down upon merchants. This view applied especially to Jewish merchants, who as recent immigrants from Central Europe, were also seen as outsiders. This attitude changed in the years after the Civil War as Jews assimilated to the culture of the region, and commerce and economic development became paramount during the New South era. Jews enjoyed tremendous economic mobility in the postwar years. For example, Leon Godchaux started out peddling in rural Louisiana in the 1840s and eventually opened a successful clothing store in New Orleans. Godchaux later purchased several sugar plantations, including some of which he had visited as a peddler 20 years earlier. Men like Godchaux embodied the commercial spirit of the New South that arose upon the ashes of the old plantation society. Southern Jews, though they were less than 1 percent of the population, played a key role in spreading the market economy throughout the region.

Jews emerged as economic and civic leaders in the New South. Jews were active in fraternal organizations like the Masons and were often involved in local government, serving as mayors and councilmen. Southern Jews were often boosters of the local economy and leaders of the business community. In North Carolina, brothers Moses and Ceasar Cone helped to transform Greensboro into a center of the southern textile industry. In Birmingham, Ala., Moses Joseph, Emil Loeb, and Adolph Loveman built the region's largest department store and were actively involved in civic affairs, helping to expand the local steel industry. Jewish women were involved in various middle-class women's organizations that focused on charity or community improvement.

Within southern Jewish communities, there were often ethnic and class distinctions between the earlier arriving and more assimilated Jews from Germany and Alsace and the Eastern European Jews who came over in the late 19th and early 20th centuries. By the early 20th century, "German" Jews were more likely to be native-born and own larger retail emporiums and department stores, whereas newly arriving Jewish immigrants from Russia tended to own small clothing or grocery stores that often catered to a working-class or African American clientele. In many cities, German Jews established social clubs that did not accept Eastern European Jews as members, mirroring the discrimination that kept these Jews out of some elite gentile clubs. They feared that association with these unassimilated foreigners would hurt their own social position. This desire to separate themselves from newly arriving Jewish immigrants was less true in smaller cities and towns, where there were not enough Jews to support such a distinction. After World War II, these internal divisions faded away.

Since World War II, southern Jews have largely moved out of the merchant class and into the professions. According to a 1984 study of Atlanta's Jewish community, 57 percent of primary wage earners were professionals. In recent decades, Jews have become fully integrated into southern society, so much so that most communal efforts now focus on preserving Jewish identity against the powerful trend of assimilation. Southern Jews now worry more about intermarriage, a clear sign of Jewish social acceptance, than anti-Semitism.

STUART ROCKOFF
Goldring/Woldenberg Institute of Southern Jewish Life

Eli N. Evans, *The Provincials: A Personal History of Jews in the South* (1973); Mark Greenberg and Marcie Cohen Ferris, eds., *Jewish Roots in Southern Soil* (2006); Steven Hertzberg, *Strangers within the Gated City: The Jews of Atlanta, 1845–1915* (1978); Steve Oney, *And the Dead Shall Rise: The Murder of Mary Phagan and the Lynching of Leo Frank* (2004); Theodore Rosengarten and Dale Rosengarten, eds., *Portion of the People: Three Hundred Years of Southern Jewish Life* (2002).

Labor, Geography of

Typically, the geographic origin point for U.S. worker activism and unionism is seen to have been the Northeast. For instance, Howard Zinn has detailed strikes by New York porters in the 1650s and by that city's bakers in 1741. Others have recounted strikes waged by printers, cabinetmakers, carpenters, shoemakers, and cordwainers in cities such as New York and Philadelphia in the 1780s and 1790s. In 1792 Philadelphia shoemakers were the first workers in the new nation to form a local craft union for collective bargaining purposes, and Philadelphia journeymen cordwainers were the first unionists to be convicted of engaging in a criminal conspiracy when they struck in 1806. In 1827, Philadelphia workers created the Mechanics Union of Trade Associations, usually cited as the first citywide labor council formed in the United States. This flowering of unionism in the Northeast has often been explained as mirroring the geography of manufacturing in the late colonial and early Republic period, when much craftwork was concentrated in cities, including Boston, Philadelphia, and New York. Within this narrative, the South, viewed as a largely agrarian society, has typically been thought of as a union-free space, a region largely devoid of worker organizations. Indeed, as Melton McLaurin has argued, because organized labor in the South prior to the New Deal era was rarely examined by 20th-century historians, two myths about southern workers have tended to persist: they are docile and tractable; and they are little interested in organized labor, the result of an ideology of individualism.

However, the reality of matters is quite different. Indeed, some of the earliest recorded strikes in U.S. history took place in the South. For instance, in 1746 carpenters in Savannah, Ga., struck for better working conditions, while in 1763 African American chimney sweeps in Charleston, S.C., "had the insolence, by a combination among themselves, to raise the usual prices, and to refuse doing their work" unless employers met "their exorbitant demands." Likewise, although the geography of unionism nationally has often been thought of as a reflection of the geography of industrial activity (which was largely concentrated in the North until the late 19th century), in fact there have also been important instances of agricultural workers forming labor organizations through which to defend their interests, including sugar workers in Louisiana who joined the Knights of Labor in the 1880s and, later, the Southern Tenant Farmers' Union. Finally, although the South has frequently been presented as a union-resistant space, a region whose workers hold decidedly antiunion views, southern workers have often been favorably disposed toward unions. In 1885, for instance, Texas boasted the third-largest number of Local Assemblies of the Knights of Labor (after Massachusetts and New York). More contemporaneously, polls have shown that southern workers are more positively inclined toward unionism than is perhaps popularly imagined. For instance, according to a Zogby International (2005) survey, although workers in all regions of the country indicated significant opposition to unionizing their own workplace, the proportion who held such views in the South was lower, at 50 percent of those surveyed, than it was in the eastern United States (61 percent) and the Central/Great Lakes Region (60 percent). Likewise, respondents who had the least favorable outlook toward unions were not southern workers but those living in the Central/Great Lakes region. Similarly, whereas 44 percent of workers in the East believed that unions were no longer necessary and 43 percent in the Central/Great Lakes region did so, in the South just 32 percent of workers believed this to be the case. Finally, according to polling conducted by the Service Employees' International Union, as a whole southern workers are some 20 percent more prounion than are workers in other regions.

When seeking to understand the geography of unionism across the South and the broader United States, various factors are worth considering, especially as these themselves vary spatially and interact differently in different places. One of these is undoubtedly the economic geography of different regions, with unionism historically being more strongly associated with certain types of occupation (e.g., steel manufacturing) than others (e.g., various types of service work). Likewise, a region's demographic makeup can play a role. For instance, across the nation polls have shown that African American women are currently the most prounion demographic group, followed (in descending order) by African American men, Hispanic women, Hispanic men, white women, and white men. Given that a higher proportion of the total U.S. African American population lives in the South than is the case for the total U.S. white population, this is likely to affect the geography of unionism across the country. At the same time, however, in 2005, 70 percent of southern workers, a higher proportion than in any other region, believed they have upward mobility at work, a belief that may reduce the desire to unionize. Equally, the legacy of unionism in particular regions can shape future patterns, as it creates what Bourdieu calls a *habitus*, wherein specific places may become reservoirs of certain ways of being, even after the original creators of these ways have died. Thus, the fact that workers who live in union households are more likely to support unions than are those who do not—a 2007 Gallup poll indicated that, of those who lived in a household with a union member, 82 percent approved and 15 percent disapproved of unions, whereas the corresponding figures for people living with no union members were 55 percent and 35 percent—means that areas with a history of unionism often develop a degree of geographic path dependence, which may help explain why they remain regions of union resilience for long periods of time. Understanding such geographic patterns can provide important insights into explaining the South's historical patterns of unionization, raising questions concerning whether it is its economic geography, or perhaps a (supposed) culture of antiunionism among workers, or perhaps a virulently antiunion stance by employers and their allies in state legislatures to which we must turn to explain the pattern of unionism found in the region, both historically and presently.

The manner in which the geography of economic organization, the geography of cultural and political practice, and the geography of demographic structure, among other things, come together to shape the geography of labor organizing in particular locations is a huge topic. Nevertheless, geography and spatial considerations have shaped unionism in a number of ways in the South. For instance, examining the spread of the Knights of Labor shows that some of their earliest organizing successes in the South were among coal miners and sugar workers. Although there are various reasons as to why this might be, at least some of the explanation undoubtedly lies in the microgeographies of the work in which such workers were engaged. For instance, in the case of organizing sugar workers, the fact that such workers labored in gangs meant that their spatial proximity to one another in the fields gave them opportunities to talk union in ways that cotton workers, who were typically dispersed across fields, did not necessarily have. Equally, the Knights' successes in the coalfields of Kentucky and Alabama in the 1870s undoubtedly had at least something to do with the mines' physical geography. Thus, unlike factories and offices, where work spaces can fairly easily be spatially engineered to provide employers an opportunity to keep an eye on workers, the underground nooks and crannies of the mines provided spaces where workers could organize beyond the bosses' watchful eyes—employers, in other words, could not make mines geographically legible in the ways in which they could other workplaces. Moreover, the fact that the particular geologies of coal deposits in different mines meant that skills in one region were not so easily transferrable to others discouraged geographic mobility by miners, which promoted the kinds of local identification and place-specific consciousness that are frequently necessary to encourage unionism.

Other spatial factors also shaped the spread of unionism across the South and the broader country. In particular, the region became increasingly geographically integrated in the years after the Civil War as the railroad and telegraph spread across the landscape. This geographic extension of the 19th century's transportation and communication network facilitated what Marx famously called the "annihilation of space by time" as faster journey and communication times allowed distances to be traversed in much shorter periods of time, such that union organizers could more easily travel across the region and news about disputes in one place could more readily spread elsewhere. Indeed, given the railroad's space-compressing nature, it is perhaps unsurprising that the railroad strike of 1877 was really the first national strike in the United States. Having its origin in a wage dispute in Martinsburg, W.Va., the strike very quickly spread down the train tracks until some 100,000 workers across the country had become involved, including Texas and Pacific Railroad workers in Marshall, Tex., whose strike action encouraged African American longshoremen in nearby Galveston to strike for (and secure) wages equal to those of their white colleagues.

If the physical movement of organizers is one way in which disputes might be spread geographically (a fact recognized by employers, who often try to keep organizers out of their local areas so as to ensure their workforces' geographic isolation from what they see as unionism's pernicious effects), another is through what has been called a "demonstration effect," wherein workers in one location take heart from the actions of those in another. One such instance of how a dispute quickly diffused across the South is that of the famous 1934 textile strike, until then the largest strike in history, which involved some

400,000 workers in New England, the mid-Atlantic states, and the South. For instance, when textile workers in Huntsville, Ala., went out on strike on 18 July 1934, within a short space of time news of their actions caused textile workers in nearby Florence, Anniston, Gadsden, and, ultimately, Birmingham likewise to strike. Across the South and elsewhere, the strike's spread frequently outpaced the physical movement of union organizers traveling from mill to mill to call out the workers, a fact that testifies to the impact of a demonstration effect on the strike's geographic diffusion.

In the post–World War II era geographic issues—especially the scalar politics of the legal landscape—likewise shaped the spatiality of unionism in the South. In particular, the antiunion 1947 Taft-Hartley Act, although a federal piece of legislation, had a significant impact upon the geography of unionism because it allowed individual states to pass right-to-work (RTW) laws that made it more difficult for unions to operate. The majority of the states that did so are located in the South and West, a fact that created an uneven regulatory landscape in which unions now had to operate. The passage of such state laws helped enshrine a political geography in the United States wherein the South increasingly operated as a region to which northern corporations could relocate their manufacturing operations to escape unions, a mass migration of industry termed the "Snowbelt to Sunbelt Shift." This uneven political landscape has had two important implications. First, clearly it has shaped the geography of unionism in the United States as myriad manufacturing plants have relocated from non-RTW states and as foreign manufacturers, including Japanese, Korean, and German automobile producers, have often chosen RTW states in which to build new plants. Second, though, the creation of such a union-free region has provided corporations with a space in which to experiment, free of "restrictive" union rules, with new sets of labor relations practices that, once "perfected," can then be exported to their plants in non-RTW states. Significantly, this is similar to how employers in Mexico have used that country's northern region, home to myriad union-free *maquila* plants, as a geographic laboratory in which to develop new forms of labor relations that are then diffused to the rest of the country where unions are more established but where such new practices are used to undermine them.

The geographic relationship between the national level and local practices, however, has been played out in another way. Specifically, in the postwar period many unions sought to develop nationwide contracts, both as a way to nationalize labor relations but also to get around some of the provisions of the Taft-Hartley Act, such as its prohibition on secondary picketing (parties to a national labor contract can strike in support of each other in ways that they cannot if they are merely seeking to support each others' local concerns). Many also engaged in pattern bargaining, in which unions would seek to impose the agreements they secured with one employer on others. As a result, many southern workers increasingly became tied into agreements negotiated in response to conditions in the Northeast or other regions where unions were stronger. The unions' goal was to secure the same high wages and working conditions for workers in all regions of the country as existed in those parts where they were strong. For example, in the case of the East Coast maritime cargo-handling industry, the International Longshoremen's Association (ILA) representing dockers in ports from Maine to Texas worked during the 1950s and 1960s to build a national agreement wherein all its members would be paid the same, regardless of the port in which they worked. The union's goal was, then, to spatially equalize wages and working conditions along the coast. However, although this worked well for two decades, by the 1980s the growth of nonunion docking in southern RTW ports meant that the national ILA could no longer sustain the pattern—shipping companies in southern ports increasingly began to turn to nonunion stevedoring firms to load and unload their cargoes, placing union operations at a competitive disadvantage. As a result, in 1986 several ILA local unions in Texas broke with the national leadership in New York, abandoned the national contract, and negotiated giveback local contracts as a way to ensure continued work in the face of nonunion competition. Put another way, despite two decades of successfully implementing national wage rates and labor standards, the ILA eventually succumbed to the economic and political geography of the industry, namely that southern ports are all located in RTW states. Mike Davis, with noteworthy geographic imagery, has referred to the breakup of such national agreements in a host of industries in the 1980s—longshoring, trucking, autos, steel—as representing a shrinking of the perimeter of unionism in the United States. The fact that no southern state has a union membership rate above the national average indicates that, as a whole, the region presently largely lies beyond that perimeter.

ANDREW HEROD
University of Georgia

Black Commentator, blackcommentator.com/going_south.html (27 June 2002); Pierre Bourdieu, *Distinction: A Social Critique of the Judgment of Taste* (1984); Jeremy Brecher, *Strike!* (1997); Mike Davis, *Prisoners of the American Dream: Politics and Economy in the History of the U.S. Working Class* (1986); Philip S. Foner, *History of the Labor Movement in the United States*, vol. 1 (1947, 1998); Jonathan Ezra Garlock, "A Structural Analysis of the Knights of Labor: A Prolegomenon to the History of the Producing Classes" (Ph.D. dissertation, University of Rochester, 1974); Enrique de la Garza Toledo, in *Handbook of Employment and Society: Working Space*, ed. Susan McGrath-Champ, Andrew Herod, and Al Rainnie (2010); Donald H. Grubbs, *Cry from the Cotton: The Southern Tenant Farmers' Union and the New Deal* (1971); Andrew Herod, ed., *Organizing the Landscape: Geographical Perspectives on Labor Unionism* (1998), *Political Geography* 16:2 (1997), *Labor Geographies: Workers and the Landscapes of Capitalism* (2001), in *Company Towns in the Americas: Landscape, Power, and Working-Class Communities*, ed. Oliver J. Dinius and Angela Vergara (2010); Christian W. Peck, *The Attitudes and Opinions of Unionized and Non-Unionized Workers Employed in Various Sectors of the Economy toward Organized Labor*, psrf.org/info/Nationwide_Attitudes_Toward_Unions_2005.pdf (August 2005); John A. Salmond, *The General Textile Strike of 1934: From Maine to Alabama* (2002); James C. Scott, *Seeing Like a State: How Certain Schemes to Improve the Human Condition Have Failed* (1998); Howard Zinn, *A People's History of the United States: 1492-Present* (1980, 2005).

Latinos

During the last two decades of the 20th century, Latino immigration represented a key demographic transformation across most of the South. Previously, the New South was a frontier to Latinos, with two exceptions, Texas and Florida. In 1980 the U.S. Census Bureau reported that the South was home to approximately 4.3 million Hispanics, with nearly 90 percent concentrated in parts of Florida and more broadly settled in Texas. By 2000 more than 11 million Hispanics were counted by the Census Bureau, with the 2009 population estimates for the South revealing a 47.9 percent increase to nearly 16.4 million Hispanics.

While the absolute increase in *nuevo* southerners is dramatic, the greater impact is related to the spreading of Latino newcomers outside of the former settlement zones. Consider that between 2000 and 2009 the number of Hispanics living outside of Texas and Florida nearly doubled, growing from 1.7 to 3.3 million residents. At the community level, this means urban and rural places across the region, long bypassed by ethnic immigrants, are receiving streams of Latino newcomers from other parts of the United States and international locations.

In turn, the arrival of these newcomers has complicated social relations and class structures attached to the black-white binary. In a region where skin color situates a person's class position, brown means "in-between" and quickly labels one as an outsider. As a result, Latinos risk discrimination from blacks and whites, alike.

Although Latinos share roots of Iberian colonization and are overwhelmingly Spanish speaking, they come from disparate nations and cultural groups. Moreover, their settlement experiences in the South vary widely. When Latinos settle in places such as south Florida or the Texas Metroplex, they connect into existing social frameworks that ease stresses and enable newcomers to settle in more quickly. In contrast, Latinos arriving in large parts of the Deep South, Appalachia, or Coastal Plains are often viewed as outsiders. And social infrastructure—family, church, and community—are absent.

Historically, temporary immigrant labor has been a key production tool in southern agriculture and forestry industries. Seasonally, waves of international laborers with temporary work permits augmented domestic farm workers across the South's agricultural landscapes, planting, pruning, or picking crops as needed. Since the middle of the 20th century, Latino workers have been a growing segment of this invisible agricultural workforce. These sojourners filled critical labor shortages during labor-intensive phases in the production process and then moved on to the next work site.

More recently, the rise of Sunbelt cities in metros such as northern Virginia, Atlanta, Charlotte, Nashville, Raleigh, Greenville-Spartanburg, Orlando, and Greensboro attracted large streams of Latino laborers, drawn by the rapid growth in low-wage service-sector jobs. During the earliest stages of the immigration process, the urban migrants often fit a "pioneer profile," that is, young male workers, absent families, expecting to temporarily live in the United States and then return home. With maturing immigration streams, the single male prototype has been replaced by families establishing homes, building communities, and connecting to local place.

As Latino immigrants have moved from temporarily occupying places toward establishing lives in urban neighborhoods and rural landscapes, nativists and xenophobes have resisted the newcomers. For them, ethnic immigration challenges the vestiges of racial and class privilege. Often, the hostility directed toward Latinos by right-wing groups is expressed through the invocation of place, represented by defense of community and culture. Public discourse around Latino immigrants uses metaphors like "invaders" or even "animals" to demonize Latino immigrants. The late senator Jesse Helms referred to Latinos as burglars breaking into a home (the country) to steal law-abiding citizens' property. Increasingly, the Ku Klux Klan and other white supremacist groups have shifted their hate speech toward brown-skinned Latino immigrants.

Where local and state governments are drawn into efforts to defend their communities against Latino settlers, the processes and ordinances are more sophisticated but carry similar themes. Across the South, some municipalities and counties have actively sought to discourage Latino settlement or control immigrant place-making activities. The range of government actions include bans on Spanish-language signage, requiring the speaking of English on job sites, restricting the location of *loncheras* (food vending trucks) along city streets, rewriting zoning rules to forbid multiple-family housing (presumably favored by Latinos), and outlawing day-labor hiring sites. In similar fashion, state governments have put in place legislation to restrict the issuance of drivers' licenses, deny access to public services and/or higher education, and punish employers hiring undocumented labor. The recent publicity surrounding the Arizona anti-immigrant legislation has attracted legislative supporters.

Although Latinos face strong hostility from conservatives in the public arena, southern business interests have been strong supporters of northward labor migration under the H-2A guest worker program and the North American Free Trade Agreement. During the economic boom of the last decades of the 20th century, Latino labor built the southern cities and sustained the rural industrial and agricultural economies. Throughout the region, employers view Latinos as hardworking bodies who are easily disciplined and controlled. In many instances, they are preferred over local African American workers. Limited or prejudiced views of brown-skinned newcomers lead to "work ethic" myths. Not unexpectedly, the overwhelming majority of international Latino migrants moving to the South come from working-class backgrounds and fill jobs in the blue-collar labor market. In urban North Carolina, for example, Latinos dominate trade and landscaping sectors.

The competition for construction, manufacturing, and service jobs between African Americans, who have traditionally dominated these job categories, and Latinos has created tensions between the communities. Some black leaders and scholars contend that Latino immigrants have displaced African American workers and kept wage levels low for all workers. As early as 1979 *Ebony* magazine warned that undocumented Mexican immigrants in Florida and North Carolina posed "a big threat to black workers." Many labor market researchers offer an alternative explanation. They report that Latinos are not displacing African Americans in low-wage jobs. Rather, immigrants are filling "replacement" jobs. In other words, immigrants are taking jobs that African Americans have bypassed because they pay the lowest wages and are the most dangerous or dirty.

The color line inextricably undergirds class status in the South and frames belonging and place. Among Latino immigrants, the importance of skin color is not entirely new. Ethnographic research finds that racializing or skin-color stereotypes affect attitudes even within the Latino community. For example, South American migrants look down upon Mexican and Central American migrants as being less intelligent, submissive, and better suited to physical labor. Ethnic origin, reflected in skin tone and physical appearance, is broadly stigmatized. Darker skin color and physical features are associated with Indo-Latino (Latinos with indigenous ancestry) or Afro-Latino (Latinos with African heritage) groups and are viewed by light-skinned Latinos as having a lower-class status.

Recent Latino immigrants, especially those with darker skin color, perceive greater discrimination from whites. Research comparing first-generation immigrant parents and U.S.-born children shows that the two groups view race and race relations differently. The first-generation perspective finds greater discrimination from white southerners and more favorable attitudes toward African Americans. In contrast, their children report less positive relations with African Americans. Other research has found that white-Latino relations are comparatively more positive than white-black relationships. These data suggest that Latinos are making faster gains toward achieving the privileges of whiteness. In turn, the economic and social advantages of whiteness provide even stronger incentives for Latinos to create social distance from African Americans.

Social justice issues for Latinos are very different from the traditional agenda of the South's civil rights movement. Among Latino activists, skin color or racial identification is far less significant for explaining discrimination or unequal treatment in the South than national origin or legal immigration status. Consequently, Latino immigration rights advocates appeal for solidarity based upon the underlying principle that we are "a nation of immigrants." But for many in the African American community, the implication that citizenship bestows privilege is unacceptable. They remind Latinos that the black experience in the South is indelibly linked to racism and oppression.

Efforts to bridge the divides between Latino and native southerners are often built along three lines. The first, collaborations of color, is structured around bringing together black southerners and Latinos based upon discrimination and their common experiences as people of color. Racial profiling by law enforcement, housing or employment discrimination based upon skin color, hate speech, or violent targeting by racist groups are examples of the issues that foster activist coalitions between black and brown southerners.

A second form of collaboration arises from seemingly race-neutral issues. However, there are often racial undertones related to de facto discrimination and white privilege when access or equity of public resources is examined.

Among the issues that bring together these coalitions are concerns arising from public school quality, inadequate health care, or environmental racism.

A final bridging framework is traditional class-based community organizing. Commonly associated with workplace conditions or labor organizing, working-class southerners will put aside racial or ethnic prejudices to address shop-floor working conditions or the benefits of workers. Recent union efforts to organize meat- and food-processing workers in parts of the region reflect this pan-ethnic activity.

OWEN J. FURUSETH
University of North Carolina at Charlotte

Fran Ansley and Jon Shefner, eds., *Global Connections, Local Receptions: New Latino Immigration to the Southeastern United States* (2009); Karen D. Johnson-Webb, *Recruiting Hispanic Labor: Immigrants in Non-Traditional Areas* (2003); William Kandel and John Cromartie, *New Patterns of Hispanic Settlement in Rural America* (2004); Raymond A. Mohl, in *Globalization and the American South*, ed. James C. Cobb and William Stueck (2005); Mary E. Odem and Elaine Lacy, eds., *Latino Immigrants and the Transformation of the U.S. South* (2009); Debra J. Schleef and H. B. Cavalcanti, *Latinos in Dixie: Class and Assimilation in Richmond, Virginia* (2009); Barbara Ellen Smith and Jamie Winders, *Transactions of the Institute of British Geographers* (January 2008); Heather A. Smith and Owen J. Furuseth, eds., *Latinos in the New South: Transformations of Place* (2006); Roberto Suro and Audrey Singer, *Latino Growth in Metropolitan America: Changing Patterns, New Locations* (2002).

Latino Workers

Finding an aspect of Latino workers' lives not informed by class in the South is difficult. Class influences who migrates and who does not, where Latinos settle, and what kinds of work they perform. Class informs which long-term residents live in neighborhoods with growing Latino populations, which do not, and how social relations in these areas play out. Class affects how attitudes toward immigrants form, who speaks for "the Latino/Hispanic community," and who in that community is spoken for. In short, whether we think of class as power relations, social stratification, or material wealth, the connections between Latino workers and class are deep and complicated in the South.

At its most basic, class, as both an individual condition and wider power relations, influences Latino decisions to migrate to the South. On an individual level, migrants typically have higher levels of education than those who stay and typically go where they can earn higher wages. On a more structural level, Latino migration is influenced by the effects of U.S. free-trade policies across

Mexican carrot girls, Edinburg (vicinity), Tex., 1939 (Russell Lee, photographer, Library of Congress [LC-USF33-011974-M1], Washington, D.C.)

Latin America, the bifurcated labor market of the U.S. service economy, Sunbelt cities' need for construction and service workers, and the expansion of meat processing into the rural South. Since the mid-1990s, these transformations, along with other social and political motivations, have drawn Latino men and women into the South's labor markets, where "Latino" and low-wage labor have become synonymous. This link is so tight that it is sometimes difficult to see Latino workers in the South as anything other than cheap labor. This understanding of Latino workers has material consequences for their subsequent efforts to make a place in southern locales.

Nearly every discussion of Latino workers in the South describes their arrival in the South as an economically driven migration. Young Latino workers, the story goes, were drawn to the South by labor shortages in industries seeking low-wage workers and, especially at the beginning, by labor recruitment. In the rural South, the combination of these factors made the geography of meat processing and the geography of Latino settlement one and the same. In southern cities, economic restructuring in the 1990s went hand in hand with the ethnic restructuring of local labor markets, making the South's growing service economy increasingly reliant on its growing immigrant population. Another factor driving Latino migration to the South is wages. In comparison to the wages Latino workers earned in Texas and southern California, wages in the South are higher, although on average lower than what native-born southerners earn in the same industries. Latino workers in the South are concentrated in construction, agriculture, meat processing, and some manufacturing, although Latina women also work in less visible jobs, such as housekeeping, and frequently move in and out of paid work. Latino workers in the South include skilled craftsmen, educators, professionals, and entrepreneurs; but most jobs held by Latino workers offer little hope of upward mobility.

Where did the jobs that Latino workers fill in the South come from? Some were newly created, as industries like meat processing expanded in the late 1980s and early 1990s and, through restructuring, grew to depend on Latino workers as cheap labor. In other cases, low-wage jobs were vacated by southern workers, as opportunities expanded elsewhere in the region. In still others, such as Arkansas, Latino workers replaced native-born workers, as growth in the native-born population itself slowed. In comparison to national patterns, Latino workers represent a smaller portion of overall growth in the South, where through the mid-2000s, job growth for native-born workers kept pace with job growth for Latino workers. Equally important, although Latino workers do not seem to have displaced native-born southern workers, this issue is complex. Public rhetoric, especially from employers, stresses that Latino workers fill jobs that native-born workers will not do. These jobs, however, may function as fallback jobs for working-class southerners, who lose an important safety net when such jobs are filled by Latino workers. This situation raises thorny questions about the class-specific impacts of Latino labor in the South and merits further attention, especially in the context of economic recession.

Across the South, Latino workers, particularly undocumented workers, face various forms of exploitation, perhaps most frequently through wage theft. Other forms of exploitation, although less extensive, are more severe, especially for agricultural workers. Because many agricultural workers are paid piecemeal rather than hourly wages, they are encouraged to work at frenetic paces and pay little attention to worker safety. Migrant workers often live in housing provided by employers and, if employed on a work visa, must stay on good terms with employers to remain legally in the United States. As a result, they often feel under constant surveillance and never at rest. All of these factors, as well as guest workers' limited labor protections, lead some scholars to argue that such workers live in the shadows of society and outside legal protection.

This vulnerability, especially for undocumented Latino workers, is arguably one of the traits that make them attractive as workers. Southern employers in agriculture, for example, often prefer "lone" Latino/as for their flexibility as workers. With family members and social responsibilities somewhere else, such workers are understood to be more motivated and more willing to work for longer hours at lower wages. As "lone" Latino workers settle out and begin families in the South, however, conflicts arise between employer expectations and worker desires, leading some agricultural employers to maintain compliant workers by frequently replacing them. In urban areas, where work is less seasonal, worker flexibility is maintained through subcontractors and temporary labor agencies, which farm out Latino workers to employers seeking short-term labor. This flexibility reaches its apex in day laborers, who wait for work—whatever kind and wherever it takes them. Through such practices, employers in the South exploit Latino workers' social and, in some cases, legal limbo and institutionalize new standards of labor flexibility across the region by pressing the limits of Latino/as as "disposable" workers.

Although Latino workers have higher rates of employment than native-born workers in the South, Latino workers also experience underemployment in the region. This fact, in combination with the lower wages that Latino workers receive, helps explain growing Latino poverty rates in the South, even as native-born poverty rates fall. It also helps explain the pattern of Latino workers' holding multiple jobs whose cumulative hours total more than a full-time workweek. Another way that Latino workers respond to both low wages and uncertain hours is by being mobile. Immediately following Hurricane Katrina in 2005, for example, Latino workers streamed to New Orleans and, in less than two years, constituted 10 percent of the city's population.

Within the workplace, Latino workers often encounter deeply segregated work spaces. In meat-processing plants, racial differences among and between line workers and supervisors are used to organize, and control, the workforce. Although the specifics of job competition between Latino and native-born workers in the South are unclear in part because Latinos are concentrated in specific industries, studies have documented resistance from some native-born workers over a Latino presence in their workplaces and a more general concern among some working-class southerners over Latino migration's impacts on their daily lives. For long-term residents in struggling southern communities, the entry of Latino workers into the labor force has sometimes been perceived as salt in the wounds of those who have experienced their own displacements from the labor market vis-à-vis globalization and other forces. This resentment, however, is not just about job competition but, instead, also reflects the ways that economic churning in the South and beyond is understood, *and responded to*, through the local presence of Latino workers.

Despite the vulnerabilities that they face, Latino workers have resisted poor treatment across the South. Guatemalan workers in a North Carolina chicken plant, for example, drew upon their own histories of indigenous resistance to take on unscrupulous employer practices through a wildcat strike. In east Tennessee, Mexican workers successfully organized a plant in response to ill treatment. There have also been initiatives to link, rather than draw lines between, the fates of Latino workers and those of native-born southern workers. Through activities such as worker-to-worker exchanges between Tennessee and Mexico, labor advocates have tried to place *local* economic changes and displacements experienced by southern workers within *global* economic transformations that drive both the outsourcing of southern jobs and the migration of Latin Americans to the South.

Although Latino men and women are drawn to the South for its economic opportunities, once there, many Latino/as decide to stay and, in staying, sometimes change their class position. For those who can find year-round work in the South, the combination of steady work, higher wages, and lower costs of living may enable a lifestyle impossible in places like southern California. In parts of the South, Latino workers can buy homes, automobiles, and other middle-class accoutrements and, thus, shift from working poor to middle class. For Latino workers in more precarious jobs, however, class status feels more fixed. In many southern states, Latinos constitute the majority of migrant workers and face not only low wages and irregular pay but also substandard housing. With few possibilities of upward mobility, such workers face uphill struggles in improving their living arrangements. Across southern communities, most Latino men and women settle in working-class black and white neighborhoods, making the story of Latino settlement a class-specific saga inflected by race. In these locales, Latino workers encounter preexisting class relations, which they potentially "dislocate" by magnifying differences among long-term residents. In Dalton, Ga., for example, opinions concerning the impacts of Mexican settlement differed along class lines, with white business elites praising the work ethic of Mexican *workers* and working-class white residents displaying more ambivalence toward the presence of Mexican *residents*.

This reality that workers are never just workers helps explain the complexity of class dynamics vis-à-vis Latinos in the South. Latino workers are also neighbors, consumers, political leaders, church members, and so on. These multiple ways of defining and seeing Latino workers potentially problematize defining characteristics of the South. First, the treatment of Latino workers destabilizes ideas about "southern hospitality." Although in the South, Latinos have been accepted, and praised, as *workers*, Latino men and women have yet to be accepted as community *members*. In Charlotte, for example, Latinos were welcomed so long as their labor was needed to build the city's skyline. Once that work was completed, public sentiment toward them changed. Across the South, the challenge remains how to transform the image of Latino workers as cheap, temporary labor into the reality of their place as contributing community members in southern locales, large and small.

Second, the mobility and flexibility demanded of Latino workers, in conjunction with the low wages and limited advancement opportunities they face, have implications for southern communities' futures more broadly. Across the South, Latino men and women are often recent arrivals to the United States with relatively low levels of education. Because the jobs they hold typically do not provide health care and because their work commitments leave little time for job training to move into better jobs that provide such benefits, the costs of social reproduction, of maintaining healthy workers and ensuring the reproduction of the next generation, are borne by everyone but southern employers. In this way, Latinos' class position as cheap labor is reproduced over time at the expense of Latino families, the Latin American communities from which they come, and the southern communities in which they live.

Finally, Latino workers complicate southern strategies of economic and community development. In a region with a long, and unsuccessful, history of investing in places, not workers, where does the perpetuation of an exploitable Latino workforce fit? As southern communities work to marginalize Latino residents through legislation and ordinances that limit services for undocumented residents, make it harder for immigrant children to attend college, and work to exclude undocumented residents from southern communities altogether, is the South investing in Latino workers as a future part of the regional workforce and social body or maintaining their status as "disposable" labor? This question becomes even more pressing in the context of the new generation of southern-born Latinos. Will these future workers face the same plight as their immigrant parents or experience a different, more fluid relationship between Latino, labor, and social mobility? Southern communities are answering this question about their future right now, and that future does not look so bright for soon-to-be Latino workers.

JAMIE WINDERS
Syracuse University

Fran Ansley and Susan Williams, in *Neither Separate Nor Equal: Women, Race, and Class in the South*, ed. Barbara Ellen Smith (1999); Jorge Atiles and Stephanie Bohon, *Southern Rural Sociology* 1:19 (2003); Carl Bankston III, *Southern Cultures* (Winter 2007); Mary Bauer, *Under Siege: Life for Low-Income Latinos in the South* (2009); Randy Capps et al., *A Profile of Immigrants in Arkansas: Executive Summary* (2007); David H. Ciscel, Barbara Ellen Smith, and Marcela Mendoza, *Journal of Economic Issues* (June 2003); Terry Easton, *Southern Spaces* (21 December 2007); Leon Fink,

The Maya of Morganton: Work and Community in the Nuevo New South (2003); Rubén Hernández-León and Víctor Zúñiga, in *New Destinations of Mexican Immigration in the United States*, ed. Víctor Zúñiga and Rubén Hernández-León (2005); William Kandel and John Cromartie, *New Patterns of Hispanic Settlement in Rural America* (2004); William Kandel and Emilio Parrado, *Population and Development Review* 31:3 (2005); Rakesh Kocchar et al., *The New South: The Context and Consequences of Rapid Population Growth* (2005); Josh McDaniel and Vanessa Casanova, *Southern Rural Sociology* 19:1 (2003); Emily Selby et al., *Gender, Place, and Culture* (2001); Barbara Ellen Smith and Jamie Winders, *Transactions of the Institute of British Geographers* (2008); Steve Striffler, *American Ethnologist* (November 2007); Qingfang Wang and Kavita Pandit, *Southeastern Geographer* (November 2003); Susan Williams and Barbara Ellen Smith, *Across Races and Nations* (2006).

Literature

In *To Kill a Mockingbird* Atticus Finch's white racial paternalism is matched, if not exceeded, by his bourgeois class paternalism. We tend to overlook the latter. His courtroom mocking of both Ewells, father and daughter, dooms his African American client to Jim Crow "justice," his daughter to a foiled rape, and his son to a broken arm. Harper Lee's novel is as illustrative of the ways class operates in southern literature as it purports to be about race. On the one hand, class appears as a static array of social types—a taxonomy. On the other, class in Lee's Maycomb, Ala., is a dynamic strategy for allotting status and—peculiar to its southern context—attributing guilt for racial injustice. Taxonomies of class are inert, like chemical elements displayed on a periodic table; they fail to show how class operates in fusion with race and gender—especially in southern writing, so drenched as it is with all three.

Both modes, taxonomic and dynamic, are visible in *To Kill a Mockingbird*. First, the Ewells appear in the category of the lumpenproletariat. They live beyond the pale of middle-class, small-town respectability—even by the reduced expectations of Depression-era Alabama. They live behind the town garbage dump in what was once a Negro cabin, the toxic zone where class and racial "others" threaten the white middle class. To fill spaces in the taxonomy of class, Lee provides a foil for the Ewells in the Cunningham clan: a redeemable proletariat, the Cunninghams honor class-specific behaviors in the strata above them, such as table manners and contracts for services. Cunninghams can be shamed into retreating from a lynching when they are called out by the middle-class Scout on the steps of the Maycomb jail.

At Tom Robinson's trial, Atticus Finch condescends too publicly to Robert E. Lee Ewell and his daughter Mayella, asserting his class superiority, pretending cordiality that eventually leads Ewell to glare at him with the stupid resentment of the lumpenproletariat, and Mayella throws down a gauntlet of race and gender that trumps her low-class status. Her speech to the jury does more than seal Tom Robinson's conviction and insure his death; it surreptitiously absolves the white bourgeoisie of complicity in the Jim Crow "formations" and "practices" that lead to both conviction and death. It was the poor whites who ultimately pulled the trigger; the legal system would have worked if it had not been for the poor whites. Maycomb, and generations of readers of *To Kill a Mockingbird*, might feel justified, but only because—in this southern text as in many others—class operates as a diversionary spillway: the real hatred, the real hardness of heart, the real incorrigible problem is not whiteness but *poor* whiteness.

There is no more fertile field for studying the operations of class than southern literature. From the colonial era to the 21st century, southern writers have continuously represented a full class array. The classic Marxist hierarchy still serves: classes are defined by the means of production they own, control, or lack. The aristocracy owns the land, and it sets in place the legal apparatus that maintains its heirs in perpetuity (the Wilkeses of *Gone with the Wind*). The bourgeoisie owns the commercial, financial, and manufacturing means of production (the Hubbards of *The Little Foxes*). The proletariat owns nothing but its physical labor power (the sharecroppers of *Let Us Now Praise Famous Men*). The petty bourgeoisie is the class of small self-employed farmers, business people, and professional service providers (Atticus Finch of *To Kill a Mockingbird* or his demonic counterpart, Jason Compson III of *The Sound and the Fury*). In terms taxonomic, then, the southern literary canon is comprehensive in its representations of social class.

Even the lumpenproletariat, what Marx called "the scum of the earth," are included in the southern class array. From William Byrd II's *History of the Dividing Line betwixt Virginia and North Carolina* (1728) onward, the southern lumpenproletariat appears both as object of morbid fascination and as not-so-veiled threat to the stability of society at large. The backcountry squatters encountered by Byrd and his party of aristocrats are presented as troubling and exotic. When they reappear in James Dickey's *Deliverance* (1970), their malformed and wretched bodies are no longer passive objects of the privileged gaze.

In the antebellum South, tales of southwestern humor present poor whites not so much as lumpenproletariat as "the folk." The folk of southwestern humor tales display a surplus of verve despite their deficit in education (a certain native cunning fills the void). Authors such as Thomas Bangs Thorpe (1815–78), Augustus Baldwin Longstreet (1790–1870), and George Washington

Harris (1814–69) supplied bourgeois and aristocratic readers with a barrage of crude but lively characters "humorously" free from the inhibitions of the educated and refined middle class, which consumed the stories in popular periodicals. After the Civil War, these crude folk were gentled by romanticizing local colorists such as Mary Noailles Murphree (1850–1922) and James Lane Allen (1849–1925), who found in the surviving white mountain people a kind of Anglo-Saxon roots culture to serve as a refuge from the industrial modernism overtaking U.S. cultural life in the late 19th and early 20th centuries. The local colorists' combination of race, cultural identity, and nostalgia would, like the primitives of the *Dividing Line*, prove viable again in television series such as *The Andy Griffith Show* (CBS, 1960–68) and *The Waltons* (CBS 1972–81).

In the 20th century, however, as national awareness of poverty and its pervasiveness spread in the United States during the Great Depression, depictions of the poor, rural white in southern literature became, on the one hand, more hard-edged and extreme and, on the other, more crucial to the middle-class white South's self-defense against charges of its complicity in the racism and social backwardness that shaped the popular image of the South. Bourgeois southern writers in the mid-20th century were concerned to distance themselves from the poor whites. The Vanderbilt Agrarians, in *I'll Take My Stand* (1930), took a notoriously conservative approach to class as well as to race, erasing the poor white and inserting the yeoman in his slot.

Notwithstanding the glorification of the leisured South espoused by the Agrarians, most poor whites in southern texts show up as specters of want. Erskine Caldwell's Lester clan in *Tobacco Road* (1932) is a particularly gothic example of the human primitive, ignorant of both agrarian "best practices" (Jeeter Lester torches land he fails to farm and dies in the conflagration) and the simple care and maintenance of industrial machinery (Dude Lester runs a new automobile into junk). The tenant farmers of James Agee and Walker Evans's *Let Us Now Praise Famous Men* (1941) are icons of class in southern literature. Indeed, both Agee's prose and Evans's black-and-white photographs tacitly grapple with the problems of representing the reality of poverty as a condition of permanent want. Evans's images—the iconic "Sharecropper Bud Fields and His Family, Hale Country, Alabama, 1936" is most familiar—tend to frame the accoutrements of poverty (poorly constructed cabins, cheap furniture, ragged clothing, malnourished bodies) in such a way as to distance the viewer from the camera's subjects, replacing class recognition with aesthetic admiration. Some of his images of the interiors of sharecropper shacks achieve a kind of visual beauty. Agee is similarly conflicted. On the one hand, the poor endure unending seasons of debt, debilitating work, physical misery, and hopelessness. On the other, the cheap fertilizer sack one woman converts to a housedress seems to Agee unchanged from classical Greece. In short, class could be and often was converted (by the alchemy of Agee's prose style or the more mundane chemistry of Evans's darkroom practices) into articles for consumption, thereby displacing social acknowledgment of poverty and class with the assumption that the poor are essentially, intractably other.

Still other southern writers put class in motion to perform ideological work. Margaret Mitchell's *Gone with the Wind* (1936), widely, if superficially, read as a paean to the aristocratic class in the South, sets the poor white class in motion to absorb the brunt of the guilt for racial antagonism. Racism in *Gone with the Wind* is undeniable; Mammy, Pork, Big Sam, Prissy, and the complete roster of African American presences in the novel circulate on the level of caricature. They are, as many critics have shown us, uniformly in support of white supremacy and the inescapableness of their own inferiority: Mammy cultivates Scarlett's whiteness by bathing her skin in buttermilk, and Big Sam eagerly renounces emancipation and hurries back to Tara after the war. If there is racism in the South, it inheres in the class of poor whites. Early in *Gone with the Wind*, Mitchell serves up class as the agent of infection and sexual promiscuity on the plantation. After evening prayers, Ellen O'Hara instructs her husband to dismiss the overseer. It is the Yankee overseer and the white-trash girl who threaten the plantation with sin. More overtly in the second half of *Gone with the Wind* — set during Reconstruction — class operates more virulently to insulate "the South" from illegal and immoral action. Mitchell supplies Scarlett with Archie, a poor, white refugee from the mountains, who frankly admits to hating all blacks. Race hatred is a function of class, a function extended in the second sequel to *Gone with the Wind*, Donald McCaig's *Rhett Butler's People* (2007), where Archie leads a particularly vicious lynch mob.

In southern literature more recent than *To Kill a Mockingbird* and *Gone with the Wind*, the class of poor whites customarily spoken for has found its own voices. Harry Crews's works, especially *Childhood: The Biography of a Place* (1995), begins to restore to the southern poor what the photographs of Walker Evans and the manipulative narrative politics of Lee and Mitchell have omitted: a dimensional emotional life, viable social rituals, cuisine rather than simply food, and glimpses of interracial identification as poor southerners rather than black or white southerners. Rick Bragg's memoirs, especially *All Over But the Shoutin'* (1998), extend Crews's poor white presence, sharply capturing feelings of economic vulnerability and endurance — as well as a measure of class payback in the form of Bragg's Pulitzer Prize and Neiman Fellowship. Dorothy Allison, in *Bastard Out of Carolina* (1992) and *Trash* (2002), has perhaps gone

further, creating an "aesthetics of trash" to assert the form of class consciousness known as "poor white" as noteworthy as the content.
MICHAEL KREYLING
Vanderbilt University

James Agee and Walker Evans, *Let Us Now Praise Famous Men* (1941); Sylvia Jenkins Cook, *From Tobacco Road to Route 66: The Southern Poor White in Southern Fiction* (1976); Wai Chee Dimock and Michael T. Gilmore, *Rethinking Class: Literary Studies and Social Formations* (1994); Larry J. Griffin and Robert R. Korstad, *Social Science History* (Winter 1995); Gavin Jones, *American Hungers: The Problem of Poverty in U.S. Literature, 1840-1945* (2008); Harper Lee, *To Kill a Mockingbird* (1960); Donald McCaig, *Rhett Butler's People* (2007); Margaret Mitchell, *Gone with the Wind* (1936); Merrill Maguire Skaggs, *The Folk of Southern Fiction* (1972); Twelve Southerners, *I'll Take My Stand* (1930).

Lynching

After being arrested for robbery and shooting a shopkeeper, Benjamin Minter was being taken on 6 December 1893 to jail in Selma, Dallas County, Ala., by three constables when they were overpowered by a mob who unceremoniously hanged Minter. That same day, a few hundred of miles east at Verdery, Abbeville County, S.C., Will Lawton, an accused robber, was captured by a mob, hanged, and his body riddled with over 500 bullets. The murders of Benjamin Minter and Will Lawton were not unusual; in fact, lynch law "justice" was a common occurrence in the American South, and not infrequent elsewhere. A lynching is an extralegal killing involving three or more perpetrators. Although hanging was a common form of mob execution, lynching is not limited to hanging; victims were at times burned at the stake, riddled with bullets, drowned, or dragged or beaten to death.

The magnitude of lynch violence, especially aggression that was directed toward African Americans, was unprecedented in the years after Reconstruction and did not become a rarity until well past mid-20th century. While there were lynchings before and after, the period from the 1880s through 1930 was the era of the lynch mob in which more than 3,200 southerners were victims of mob violence. The vast majority, 87 percent, of those was African American, overwhelmingly men. Women, of both races, represented less than 3 percent of the total number of victims. Although there were some instances of black-on-black mob violence, the most common occurrence, by far, was a black man being murdered by a white mob. From the early 1880s through the mid-1890s the toll of victims of lynchings increased annually owing to the reinstitution-

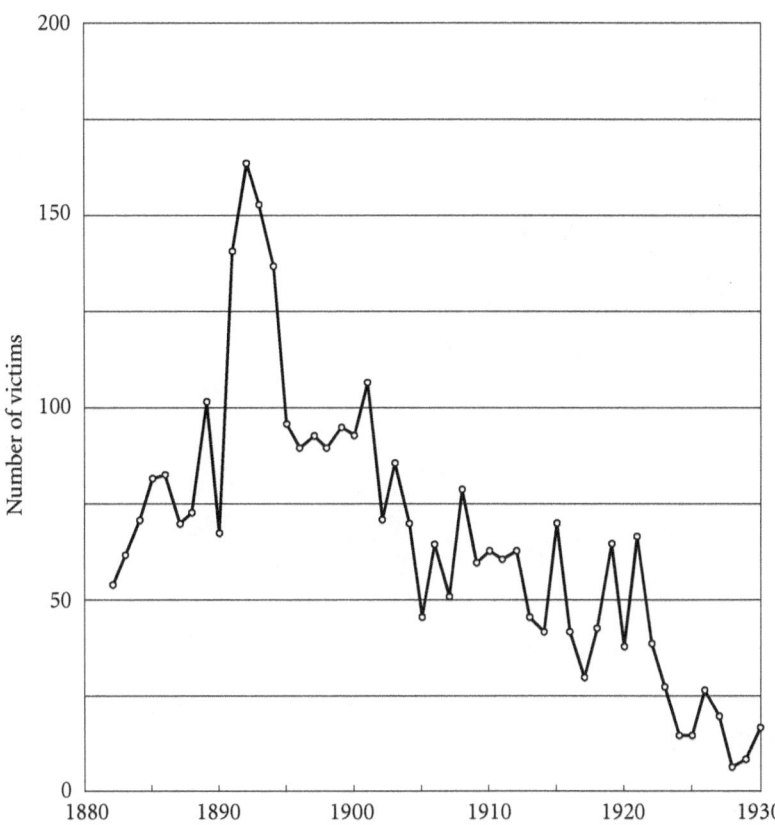

FIGURE 17. Victims of lynch mobs by year, 1882–1930.
Note: Totals for the states of Alabama, Arkansas, Florida, Georgia, Kentucky, Louisiana, Mississippi, North Carolina, South Carolina, Tennessee, and Virginia.
Source: E. M. Beck and Stewart Tolnay, "Confirmed Inventory of Southern Lynch Victims, 1882–1930" (2004).

alization of white supremacy, the intensification of radical racism, the need to leverage control over an essential black labor force, and stresses on the southern economic system.

During the peak of the frenzy, the years 1891–94, a southerner died at the hands of a mob every 2.4 days, on average. Figure 17 graphs the number of victims of lynch mobs annually. After the 1890s there was a general decline in lynchings, with only occasional episodes of heightened mob activity. This decrease is broadly attributed to a variety of factors, including a growing willingness of local and state officials to arrest and indict alleged lynchers, changes in agriculture that lessened the demand for control over black labor, an institutionalized caste system of Jim Crow segregation, improved professionalization

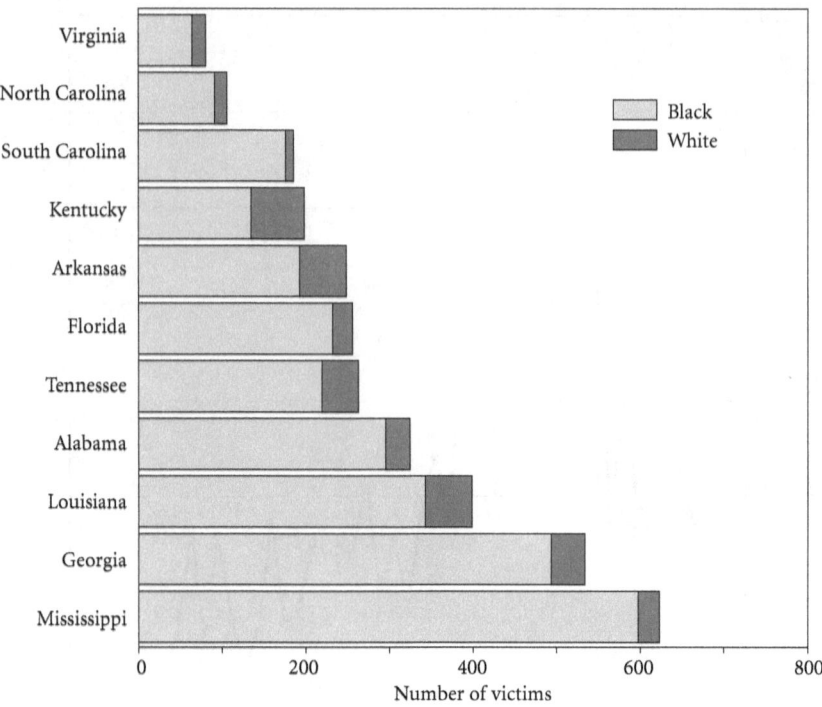

FIGURE 18. *Victims of lynch mobs by state, 1882–1930.*
Note: *All numbers of victims are incomplete estimates subject to revision as continuing research sheds new light on the scope of mob violence in the South.*
Source: *E. M. Beck and Stewart Tolnay, "Confirmed Inventory of Southern Lynch Victims, 1882–1930" (2004).*

of local police, an increasingly vocal antilynch movement both inside and outside the South, migration of blacks to the North and West, and shifts in public attitudes from approval to distain of mob violence.

Although all southern states witnessed many lynchings, almost half of the victims of mob violence were murdered in just three states: Mississippi, Georgia, and Louisiana (Figure 18). Virginia had the fewest documented lynchings, with less than 100. While most victims were African American men, the numbers of white victims of white mobs were also significant, estimated to be at least 375. Kentucky and Arkansas were unusual in the large proportion of white victims: 31 percent of Kentucky victims were white and 23 percent in Arkansas. This stands in stark contrast to Mississippi and Georgia where only 4 percent and 7 percent, respectively, of the victims were white.

Arguably the most significant of the white lynchings was that of Leo M. Frank near Marietta, Ga. Frank, a pencil plant manager, college graduate, a northerner, and a Jew, stood accused of murdering 13-year-old Mary Phagan, a working-class plant employee, a Christian, and a native-born southerner. After a sensational 1913 trial stoked with vitriolic anti-Semitism and classism, Frank was convicted and sentenced to death. Later there was question as to the evidence against Frank, and Gov. John M. Slaton commuted his sentence to life imprisonment. Yet in the early morning hours of 17 August 1915, he was taken from a prison near Milledgeville by a well-organized band calling itself the Knights of Mary Phagan and spirited to Marietta, where he was hanged. The trial and subsequent lynching of Leo Frank became international news, an embarrassment to many "New South" promoters, and the motivation for the creation of the Anti-Defamation League of the B'nai Brith.

The South's small white ethnic population was occasionally targeted for mob violence. In particular, a number of Italians met their death through lynch violence in Louisiana, Mississippi, and Florida. In fact, the South's largest lynching took place in New Orleans on 14 March 1891 when a large mob invaded the parish jail and lynched 11 Italians.

Lynch mobs almost always provided some rationalization for their actions. Frequently it was that the court system was either too slow or unsure in result, or that a jury trial was "too good" for the offender. Apologists for lynching often proclaimed that black men were a threat to white women and any assault, real or imagined, on a white woman must be dealt with swiftly and with deadly certainty. Research has shown, however, that the majority of victims had been accused of murder or attempted murder rather than sexual assault. Moreover, some victims were accused of no criminal offense but rather of violating the racial code of etiquette that proscribed that African Americans must remain subservient and acquiesce to white supremacy. Being "imprudent," "insolent," or not being sufficiently deferent, could, at times, be sufficient to result in a lynching.

Some defenders of lynching argued that lynch mobs were composed of uncontrollable local rabble, ruffians, drunks, and assorted misfits. Yet in many instances, newspapers commented that the lynchers were some of the "best citizens" in town. Particularly before 1900 it was not infrequent for white-owned newspapers to either support lynching explicitly or implicitly encourage mob violence by failing to condemn it. Further, some southern politicians were notorious for their race baiting. In a speech on 11 November 1911, South Carolina governor Cole Blease defended lynching and proclaimed that he would refuse to deploy state militia to protect any black men for alleged attacks on white women. Blease was not alone among well-known southern politicians who were apologists for mob violence that targeted the South's African

American population. Georgia's Tom Watson and James Vardaman of Mississippi were vociferous proponents of white supremacy and the violence that supported it.

Regardless of who actually participated directly in lynching, it is clear that in many regions of the South, political, religious, and civic leaders did little to curb mob violence until well into the 20th century. This official tolerance is likely a result of the fact that lynching served the purposes of diverse southern classes. On the one hand, poor whites benefited, economically, from the violent subjugation of the competing poor class of blacks. Lynching also helped to etch more clearly the racial caste, which, for poor whites, was essential for their claims of racial superiority. On the other hand, white landowners and employers profited from lynching because it served as a form of labor control over blacks, and the racial tension that it represented helped to prevent a coalition between poor whites and poor blacks.

Although research and data collection on averted lynchings is still in its infancy, there is mounting evidence that in addition to the thousands of successful lynchings, there were many hundreds, if not thousands, of lynchings that were foiled. Often mob plans were frustrated after they had become known and officials had removed the potential victim to a safe location. Particularly after 1900, state and local authorities showed increased willingness to enlist state or militia troops to protect likely targets of lynch mob violence. At other times, it was the action of a courageous sheriff that prevented a lynching, as was the case in November 1885 when 150 men approached the Oconee County, Ga., jail in Watkinsville and demanded G. C. Whitehead, a white man accused of murder. Sheriff Owenby refused and told the crowd that he would shoot anyone trying to break into his jail. Faced with such determination, the mob dispersed. The 1 December 1885 edition of the *Augusta Chronicle* newspaper concluded, "This is the sort of stuff a Sheriff should be made of."

By 1930 the annual number of lynchings was but a small fraction of yearly totals during the late 19th century, yet lynch violence did not end with the Great Depression. As the modern civil rights movement blossomed after World War II and white supremacy was being seriously questioned, there was an increase in mob violence often directed toward civil rights workers, their supporters, or even those who might question the prevailing racial order. In Georgia, for example, recent research suggests that 10 Georgians died in lynchings after 1945; most notably, on 25 July 1946, a mob of white men murdered two African American couples, Roger and Dorothy Malcom and George and Mae Murray Dorsey, at the Moore's Ford bridge between Walton and Oconee counties, Ga.; no indictments were ever issued, and the case remains open and under investigation. In Mississippi the number of victims was significantly larger, with the most publicized case being the murder of 14-year-old Emmett Louis Till in 1955; the April 1959 lynching of Charles Mack Parker in Poplarville; the Ku Klux Klan murders of Henry Dee and Charles Eddie Moore near Vicksburg in May 1964; the June Klan killing of Mickey Schwerner, James Earl Chaney, and Andrew Goodman, civil rights workers, in Neshoba County; and the 1966 Klan firebombing of the home of Vernon Dahmer, who later died of his wounds. In Alabama the most infamous of the modern-era lynchings was the Ku Klux Klan bombing of the 16th Street Baptist Church in Birmingham on 15 September 1963 that killed 12-year-old Denise McNair, 14-year-old Cynthia Wesley, 14-year-old Carol Robertson, and 10-year-old Addie Mae Collins.

Although lynching involved the murder of a particular person, it was a crime against the collective as well as against an individual. Since lynchers were rarely indicted, much less convicted, for their crimes, mob rule trumped criminal law and mobs could act with virtual impunity. This was a form of domestic terrorism that sent a powerful message of collective intimidation and social control to the community. This was especially true when white mobs killed African Americans and there were no consequences for the lynchers. The message to the black community was loud and unmistakable.

Lynching served a number of purposes in the racially and class-stratified society of the South. It served to control a large black laboring class, to emphasize the social superiority of whites, to punish suspected criminals, and to neutralize the political influence of African Americans. As the South changed, especially during the post–World War II era, the social and economic bases for lynching weakened. While the historical legacy of lynching continues to influence southern society, the deadly ritual itself is now part of the region's past.

E. M. BECK
University of Georgia

STEWART E. TOLNAY
University of Washington

James Allen, *Without Sanctuary: Lynching Photography in America* (2000); Bruce E. Baker, *This Mob Will Surely Take My Life: Lynchings in the Carolinas, 1871–1947* (2008); W. Fitzhugh Brundage, *Lynching in the New South: Georgia and Virginia, 1880–1930* (1992); David Jacobs, Jason T. Carmichael, and Stephanie L. Kent, *American Sociological Review* (August 2005); Ryan D. King, Steven F. Messner, and Robert D. Baller, *American Sociological Review* (October 2009); Steven F. Messner, Robert D. Baller, and Matthew P. Zevenbergen, *American Sociological Review* (August 2005); John Hammond Moore, *Carnival of Blood: Dueling, Lynching, and Murder* in South Carolina, 1880-1920 (2006); Vann R. Newkirk, *Lynching in North Carolina: A History, 1865-1941* (2009); Michael J. Pfeifer, *Rough Justice: Lynching and American Society, 1874-1947* (2004); Arthur F. Raper, *The Tragedy of Lynching* (1933); Stewart E. Tolnay and E. M. Beck, *Festival of Violence: An Analysis of Southern Lynchings, 1882-1930* (1995); Julius E. Thompson, *Lynchings in Mississippi: A History, 1865-1965* (2007); George C. Wright, *Racial Violence in Kentucky, 1865-1940: Lynchings, Mob Rule, and "Legal Lynchings"* (1990).

Middle Class, Development of

Few terms in the national lexicon possess as many different meanings as "middle class." Most Americans, including most southerners, have traditionally associated themselves with the broad middle class, regardless of wealth, occupation, or status. "Middle class" seems to be one of those terms that can mean a great deal if defined carefully, or mean very little if used nonchalantly. Even academic scholars, who spend much time and energy parsing language, have found it hard to employ the phrase with exactitude. Yet the widespread use of "middle class" as a descriptive term and a conceptual tool testifies to a broadly held view among academics and nonacademics that "middle class" connotes something deeply significant about the American experience, a phrase that when employed diligently reveals much about the nation, past and present.

Until recently, though, scholars questioned whether "middle class" was a useful concept for understanding the 19th- or early 20th-century South. Throughout much of the 1900s, when writers and scholars referred to a middle class, they almost always meant the middling yeomen farmers who lived within the slave South. Although Ulrich B. Phillips brought a more systematic approach to life on the plantation with his early 20th-century studies of slavery, Phillips was chiefly concerned with the plantation, large farms governed by wealthy white masters who owned more than 20 slaves. Not until the publication of Frank L. Owsley's 1949 *Plain Folk of the Old South* did scholars begin to take seriously the common whites who greatly outnumbered the region's planters. In fact, scholars have since estimated that masters holding more than 20 slaves composed perhaps less than 5 percent of the white population. Owsley shed light on the common white farmers, those who owned their own land but few or no slaves, and so by necessity his study focused on rural southerners. Owsley argued that these plain rural white folk played underappreciated political and economic roles in the slave South.

Owsley's middling rural farmers continued to attract the interest of historians, who found that yeomen harbored an ideology different from their planter neighbors. These small farmers were "middling" or "middle class" be-

A middle-class Tennessee couple on vacation, c. 1960 (Frank Collection, Mississippi Valley Collection, University of Memphis [Tennessee] Library)

cause they were neither as wealthy as planters nor as downtrodden as landless, laboring whites who toiled as day laborers or itinerant workers. Fairly confident that the yeomen composed the middling class of the Old South, scholars continued to refine our understanding of the southern social structure. James Oakes's work on slaveholding revealed that most masters held only small numbers of slaves, redirecting attention to what has been called "middle-class slaveholders." In *The Ruling Race* (1982), he demonstrated that these largely rural masters were politically influential and vital to the southern economy. Steven Hahn's landmark study *The Roots of Southern Populism* (1983) demonstrated that yeomen farmers, especially those in the mountainous regions of the South less reliant on slavery, feared becoming entrapped in the unpredictable marketplace and resisted industrialization. In the 1990s important works such as Bill Cecil-Fronsman's *Common Whites* (1992) and Stephanie McCurry's *Masters of Small Worlds* (1995) added considerable texture to our understanding of the plain folk and small farmers.

Thanks to such work, by 2000 historians had spent a great deal of energy in studying the rural middling yeomen and plain folk. Yet definitional problems persisted. To what extent did southern yeomen harbor a class consciousness, a sense that they were distinct from those above and those below them? Since by definition yeomen composed a rural middle class, what about professional and commercial interests in southern towns and cities? How numerous and influential were these middling professional and commercial southerners? Because discussions of class in the 19th-century South had largely been viewed in terms of whiteness, how did slaves fit into the region's social hierarchy?

Scholars have recently found that a middle class of professional and commercial men and women played a more prominent role in the history of the region than previously believed. Comprising professionals such as doctors, dentists, lawyers, clerks, and teachers, as well as commercially oriented occupations such as merchants, bankers, clerks, and shopkeepers, white middle-class southerners shaped the urban areas of the South from the end of the 18th century to the present day. Before the Civil War, the middle class was almost exclusively white, but after Emancipation an African American middle class began to form that also contributed a great deal to the region's economy, politics, and culture.

Beginning in the late 1700s, southern merchants and professionals, generally though not exclusively urban dwellers, formed organizations in which they identified themselves as a distinct class within the region. Today we are likely to categorize physicians as members of an upper class, but as scholars have demonstrated, doctors struggled for respect and status in the 19th century when ordinary folks were still suspicious of the validity and credibility of medicine as a field. Consequently doctors formed professional organizations and medical societies throughout the Old South to raise professional standards. Dentists formed their own professional organizations, and merchants formed chambers of commerce to advance their interests. The slave South, especially towns and cities, was alive with associations, societies, and clubs of all kinds that served the professional and cultural interests of the emerging middle class. From temperance societies to debating clubs to ethnic associations, the southern middle class formed a coherent and distinct identity by the 1850s. This southern middle-class ideology shared much with its antebellum northern counterpart but incorporated an attachment to slavery that distinguished southerners from professional and commercial northerners. The formation of a southern middle class before the Civil War shaped the region's economy and society, as professional and commercial southern whites pushed states to modernize their economies and cultures, from investing in railroads to expanding efforts in public education. However, the antebellum white southern middle class was not able to thwart secession and war, which would bring a rapid and catastrophic end to the middle-class agenda of cultural and economic modernization.

The devastation wrought by the war meant that not until the 1880s would the white southern middle class reemerge as a potent force in the region. The New South did not come rapidly out of the ashes of the Old South; rather the 1860s and 1870s were years of turmoil and debate over the region's direction now that slavery was dead. In the late 1800s and early 1900s the white middle-class search for labor on which to build this New South would lead to novel but crushing forms of work redolent of slavery. Sharecropping, tenant farming, prison labor, and other forms of peonage ensured that the white middle class would explore new forms of exploitation well into the 20th century, with devastating consequences for blacks and poor whites.

Even amid new forms of exploitation, a nascent African American middle class joined the white middle class, with important consequences for the New South. By the middle of the 20th century a new and influential black middle class pushed for respect and recognition, playing a vital role in the push for civil rights. Like the earlier white middle class, this emerging black middle class formed a distinct identity that found expression in a wide range of areas, from religion to consumer behavior to the formation of professional organizations. Yet, despite the emergence of a powerful and significant southern black middle class, the late 20th-century South simultaneously witnessed a revival of labor exploitation. The modern prosperity experienced by the South and its diverse black and white middle class is based in large part on nonunion wages and right-to-work laws that limit the working class's right to bargain collectively, as well as on the widespread use of prison laborers at a level not seen since the late 1800s.

JONATHAN DANIEL WELLS
Temple University

Frank L. Byrne, *Becoming Bourgeois: Merchant Culture in the South, 1820–1865* (2006); Bill Cecil-Fronsman, *Common Whites: Class and Culture in Antebellum North Carolina* (1992); Jennifer R. Green, *Military Education and the Emergence of the Middle Class in the Old South* (2008); Steven Hahn, *The Roots of Southern Populism: Yeoman Farmers and the Transformation of the Georgia Upcountry, 1850–1890* (1983); Stephanie McCurry, *Masters of Small Worlds: Yeoman Households, Gender Relations, and the Political Culture of the Antebellum South Carolina Low Country* (1995); James Oakes, *The Ruling Race: A History of American Slaveholders* (1982); Frank L. Owsley, *Plain Folk of the Old South* (1949); Jonathan Daniel Wells, *The Origins of the Southern Middle Class, 1800–1861* (2004).

Migration

Southern migration has been closely connected to social class throughout the region's history, as it has been elsewhere. Before 1940, landownership was the dominant determinant of rural social class in the South and had a strong influence on migration. Landowning families were tied to farms and to areas from year to year and, to some extent, across generations. In contrast, farm tenants, especially sharecroppers, were more mobile, often seeking improved terms from landowners in exchange for their labor. An extremely migratory landless class could threaten the efficiency and predictability of agricultural production for landowners who relied heavily on farm tenants and temporary laborers to raise and harvest their cash crops. As a result, the more politically powerful landowners employed a variety of strategies for restricting the movement of farm tenants. Vagrancy laws were used to arrest those who moved without the "permission" of their landlords. In addition, a system of peonage was created in which tenants were obligated to the same landowner from year to year through the debt that they accrued in the form of monetary advances or credit based on their share of the maturing crop. African American tenant farmers were especially vulnerable to these forms of labor control because of their political impotence and their greater exposure to mob violence. Despite these efforts to keep the landless from moving, levels of migration among sharecroppers and other tenants were considerably higher than those for landowners.

In southern towns and cities of this earlier time period, though southern social class was construed differently from how it was in the countryside, it was still related to geographic mobility. Traditional measures of human capital, such as education, occupation, and wealth, stratified urban society. While landed elites sometimes exerted strong political and economic influence in southern towns, a different set of actors, who were less directly rooted in the agricultural economy (e.g., doctors, bankers, teachers, nonagricultural laborers), constituted the urban class structure. Near the bottom of this social hierarchy was a population of unskilled workers who circulated between the rural and urban economies in search of employment. The relatively weak "rootedness" of these transient workers was an important commodity for the southern economy, and it contributed to their frequent movement from city to city or between the countryside and the city. Most of these moves were relatively short in distance and many were brief in duration. While county lines might be crossed, migration across state borders was less common for this group and exiting the South, altogether, was unusual. The urban elite (i.e., more educated, skilled workers) less often found it necessary to migrate in search of opportunity. Consistent with migration theory, however, when they did move, it was likely farther and for a longer time than was true of their lower-status neighbors.

Patterns of southern migration changed substantially during the second decade of the 20th century, but social class remained an important part of the phenomenon. Decades of economic marginalization for the landless in the agricultural economy, and limited possibilities for profitable employment among unskilled workers in the urban economy, created a pent-up potential for migration in search of opportunity. What had been missing for many southerners was an alternative economy that needed their labor. As the nation prepared to enter World War I, and when the United States sharply restricted immigration from Europe after the War, that alternative economy became available in the mills, factories, and shops of the urban North. The result was a massive exodus of population from the South, first toward the older metropolises in the northeast and north central regions, and eventually to the West as well.

This southern exodus, which is often referred to as the "Great Migration," included both blacks and whites, although a larger proportion of African Americans left the South. Early accounts presented unflattering profiles of the southern migrants. The white migrants were pejoratively referred to as "hillbillies" or "Okies," while the black migrants were portrayed as uncouth, illiterate sharecroppers. In fact, however, these depictions exaggerated the negative selection of southern interregional migrants, by social class. On average, those who left the South during the first three decades of the 20th century were actually more likely to be literate than their friends and neighbors who stayed behind, and many left from southern towns and cities, rather than directly from the farm. Still, it remains true that the Great Migration represented a powerful "safety valve" that helped to relieve pressure that had built up over the decades as a result of constrained economic opportunities, primarily among the lower strata of the southern class structure. This "pressure" was especially acute among southern African Americans, who were doubly handicapped by their disadvantaged class position and by their status as the subordinate population in a racial caste system.

Even as the Great Migration gained momentum after 1915, internal migration within the South continued. To some extent, the two migration patterns were linked. The economically destitute, and increasingly superfluous, landless population in the southern countryside often made their way to nearby towns and cities before they departed on their longer journeys to the North and West. And, as the Great Depression blunted somewhat the intensity of the Great Migration during the 1930s, the economically marginal population circulated within the South, seeking security wherever it could be found—sometimes in the very rural places they had abandoned. Although the popular image of the Great Depression might be bankers and Wall Street investors leaping from skyscraper windows, as in most economic crises it was those in the lower strata of the class structure who suffered most severely. For them, migration was sometimes their only hope for weathering the financial difficulties of the Great Depression.

World War II ushered in a new era of out-migration from the South. One stream of migration followed the same routes that were established during the earlier stage of the Great Migration—to the northeastern and north central regions—aided by networks of families and friends already there. The westward flow of migrants intensified sharply with the growth of war-related industries on the West Coast. Expanding mechanization of agricultural production, especially the introduction of the mechanical cotton harvester, displaced larger numbers of the landless rural population and thereby fed the pool of potential migrants who might seek better economic opportunities in the North and West, as well as in southern cities. The result of these forces was twofold—expanding urbanization of the southern population and a sharp increase in the number of southerners who left their region of birth during the Great Migration. The rural class structure that had prevailed in the South for many decades, consisting of a relatively small landed elite supported by a massive population of tenants and laborers, was fundamentally altered by the Great Migration. And, rural-to-urban migration, coupled with significant industrial development in southern cities, transformed urban class arrangements.

By the late 1960s (for whites) and the early 1970s (for blacks) the loss of southern population through net migration had ended. Reversing the pattern of a half century earlier, return and primary migration to the South increased as the economies of northern cities deteriorated, with the relocation of white population and many jobs to the suburbs. Unemployment and economic marginalization, much like that experienced by the lower and working classes of the South before the Great Migration, plagued the lower and working classes of Rust Belt cities. Those with the resources or familial connections to do so moved to the Sunbelt to take advantage of the economic opportunities that accompanied the growth of industrial and manufacturing employment in the South. This migration stream into the South was not composed entirely of displaced blue-collar laborers. The expanding southern economy also attracted professionals and highly skilled workers, who contributed to the growth of a larger and newer urban elite in many southern cities such as Atlanta, Charlotte, Birmingham, and Little Rock. Especially for African Americans, noneconomic forces also played a major role in the reversal of southern net migration during this time period. The civil rights movement resulted in greater freedom and expanded rights of citizenship for southern blacks. And, the threat of mob violence no longer reinforced de jure white supremacy. Many of these folks who were flowing into the South during the last quarter of the 20th century, laborers and professionals alike, had ancestral connections to the region, but many others did not (Figure 19). Thus, not only was the class structure of the South at the turn of the 21st century dramatically different from the class structure that prevailed at the turn of the 20th century, but the very nature of southern culture was also being transformed. Migration played a critical role in both.

Also contributing to demographic and cultural changes in the South is the rapid growth of the region's Latino population. Responding to a demand for inexpensive, unskilled workers, immigrants from Central and South America, many of them undocumented, have occupied an important place in various southern economic sectors, including poultry, forestry, light manufacturing, agriculture, and construction. From traditional "gateway cities," such as Miami, Atlanta, Houston, and New Orleans, the southern Latino population has dispersed throughout the region, following opportunities for employment. As a result, a regional population and class structure that historically consisted overwhelmingly of blacks and whites has recently growth more ethnically complex.

At the microlevel, geographic mobility by southerners has allowed indi-

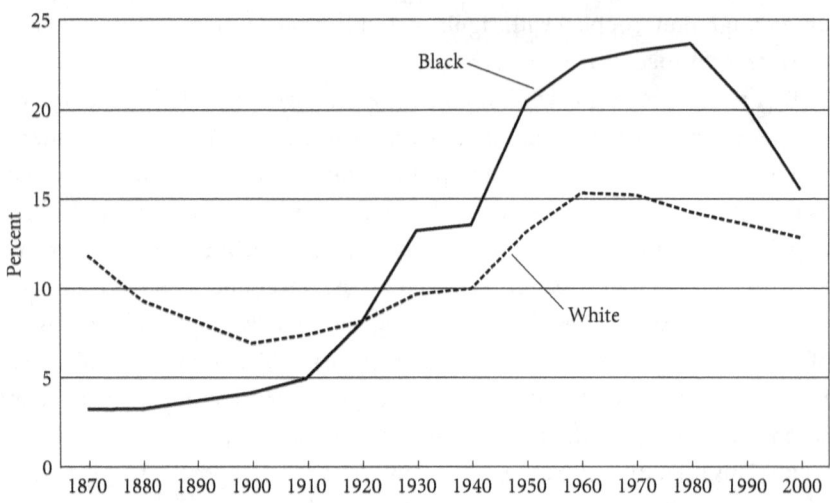

FIGURE 19. *Percentage of southern-born population residing in the non-South, by race, 1870–2000.*
Source: Integrated Public Use Microdata Series, 1870–2000, Minnesota Population Center (1890 values are interpolated).

viduals and families to seek upward social mobility by abandoning an area with little opportunity in favor of another area with more opportunity. Likewise, it has been a strategy for nonsoutherners to pursue socioeconomic opportunity within the South. At the macrolevel, migration streams have altered the South socially, economically, politically, and culturally through the selective processes that have moved population away from the region, as well as those that have brought population into the South.

STEWART E. TOLNAY
University of Washington

J. Trent Alexander, *Social Science History* (1998); Chad Berry, *Southern Migrants, Northern Exiles* (2000); William W. Falk, *Rooted in Place: Family and Belonging in a Southern Black Community* (2004); Neil Fligstein, *Going North: Migration of Blacks and Whites from the South, 1900–1950* (1981); James N. Gregory, *The Southern Diaspora: How Two Great Migrations Transformed Race, Region, and American Politics* (2005); Nicholas Lemann, *The Promised Land: The Great Migration and How It Changed America* (1991); Larry H. Long, *Migration and Residential Mobility in the United States* (1988); Jay R. Mandle, *The Roots of Black Poverty: The Southern Plantation Economy after the Civil War* (1978); Roger L. Ransom and Richard Sutch, *One Kind of Freedom: The Economic Consequences of Emancipation* (1977); Stewart E.

Tolnay, *The Bottom Rung: African American Family Life on Southern Farms* (1999), *Annual Review of Sociology* (2003).

Music

In 1928 Ulrich B. Phillips penned a piece for the *American Historical Review* entitled "The Central Theme of Southern History." He argued in the seminal essay that the South was "a land with a unity despite its diversity, with a people having common joys and common sorrows, and, above all, as to the white folk a people with a common resolve indomitably maintained—that it shall be and remain a white man's country." Ironically, Phillips's article emphasizing white supremacy and racial integrity appeared at the same time that Jimmie Rodgers, a white southern vocalist who had made his initial phonograph recordings in 1927, was attaining national prominence for his seemingly effortless musical blending of black spirituals, Appalachian ballads, rural blues, jazz, and Tin Pan Alley pop. It is unknown whether the prim and proper Phillips, an erudite professor of history at the University of Michigan, was familiar with the singing Mississippi brakeman later dubbed the "Father of Country Music"; the Georgia-born Phillips, a renowned scholar of the plantation and of slavery who could point to an aristocratic lineage on his mother's side, generally did not pay much attention to the "you 'uns" and the "we 'uns" that constituted the white southern yeomanry. There is little evidence, moreover, to suggest that he was very attentive to the sudden and rapid rise of country (hillbilly) or the blues (race music) within contemporary commercial music. Yet it is a certainty that Phillips, a rapt enthusiast of old plantation melodies who seemed out of place in the jazz age, was well aware of the tremendous impact the world over of modern, southern-derived, and African American–oriented syncopation. Historians, then, are left with the paradox that Phillips focused on locating the "central theme of southern history" at a time when racially charged musical genres associated with the region on a national and international front were taking center stage.

Indeed, for many, if there is a central theme of southern history, it is one tied to the perception that inhabitants of the region have had a propensity to produce, perform, and consume music in a manner and to a degree that distinguishes them from people elsewhere. Since at least the antebellum era, observers often have viewed the South as a faraway land of melody and melisma, a place where natives were as apt to break out in song as they were to talk or even breathe. Such impressions were due at least in part to the romantic imagery of "singing darkies" concocted by blackface minstrelsy, the nation's first popular music phenomenon and one that commenced and flourished in northern venues. In the years following the Civil War, the Fisk Jubilee Singers, dispatched on national and international tours to raise money for the Nashville-based educational institution that sponsored them, also contributed to the notion that southerners maintained a deep attachment to music. Finally, on the eve of large-scale commercial recording, musicologists and folklorists, steeped in the mistaken assumption that certain mountainous areas of the South served as isolated and untouched repositories of traditional Anglo-Saxon traits and pristine British ballads, set out on field expeditions that lent further credence to the perception that southerners had a unique relationship to music.

By the early 1920s, therefore, when talent scouts and assorted impresarios began seeking performers to record commercially, the South's well-established reputation as a musical Mecca marked it as a logical place to look. And as events over the next century demonstrated, the high regard in which the region was held musically was well founded. Beginning with the recording of acts such as Rodgers, Louis Armstrong, the Carter Family, Bessie Smith, Charley Patton, and Blind Lemon Jefferson, southerners and southern-derived genres remained central to the nation's production and consumption of commercial music. Any enumeration of musical styles that have emerged in the modern era is weighted heavily toward sources that emanated from the South: jazz, classic blues, rural blues, country music, western swing, black and white gospel, bluegrass, urban blues, honky-tonk, rhythm and blues, rockabilly, rock 'n' roll, Cajun, Tejana, and soul, to name only a few. It would be difficult to imagine any popular musical landscape without the styles listed above. Even less likely could one perceive a soundscape without historical actors such as Robert Johnson, Memphis Minnie, Muddy Waters, Bob Wills, Louis Jordan, Bill Monroe, Hank Williams, B. B. King, Loretta Lynn, Mahalia Jackson, Elvis Presley, Aretha Franklin, Sam Cooke, Ray Charles, Dolly Parton, and Tina Turner making music that was universally applicable and appealing. Southerners all, they and countless others both renowned and obscure helped cultivate a multifarious sound and image that spoke volumes about their regional roots.

As any cataloging would demonstrate, the South has churned out a wide variety of musical genres and personalities. And while several styles affiliated with folk or "roots music" certainly have gained widespread attention, such as those tethered to the blues or country music, in no way did they corner the musical market. Nearly all categories of music have thrived in Dixie, including those associated with classical, opera, fine art, and theater traditions. From the colonial era to the present, an appreciation for "good" music has provided the region's elite a tangible attestation of its elevated status. In 1762, for instance, the St. Cecilia Society, the oldest musical society in the United States, was founded in Charleston. New Orleans likewise achieved eminence as a cultural and musical center with the formation of an opera company and the building of an opera house. During the antebellum era, southern cities such as Charleston, New Orleans, Richmond, Memphis, and Natchez hosted concerts by European virtuosos like violinist Old Bull and soprano Jenny Lind. Southern native Louis Moreau Gottschalk became the most renowned American composer of the early 19th century. These pioneering proceedings served as a model for the years that followed. In the 20th century, major cities such as Nashville, Atlanta, Dallas, Houston, Charlotte, and Miami, as well as smaller municipalities, organized symphonies that catered to sophisticated tastes; not coincidently, the region produced figures such as William Levi Dawson, Lehman Engel, Samuel Jones, Leontyne Price, Wallingford Riegger, and William Grant Still, prominent musicians and composers whose talents and reputations compared favorably with anyone in the field.

Although classical, operatic, and theatrical legacies have been important to the region's musical development, the most recognized musicians to have emanated from the South undoubtedly were those who sprang from working-class traditions. People the world over have valued and venerated performers associated with musical styles that first gained a hearing not in symphony halls and musical conservatories but in juke joints, honky-tonks, bordellos, churches, and through radio, television, and the Internet. Such artists have captured the popular imagination at least in part because the music they produced generally did not require formal education and training to be appreciated or replicated. Most important, perhaps, the music's lyrical content addressed universal themes and issues that corresponded to the daily experiences and needs of ordinary people everywhere. Whether they represented joy or sorrow or were a response to freedom or oppression, the sounds of music seemed always to accompany work, play, and worship. Indeed, music was a constant presence in situations where people loved, laughed, cried, celebrated, mourned, lived, and died.

Most southerners, therefore, *were* musical people. This circumstance was a result of several factors. The region's two major demographic groups, British Celtic and West African, claimed age-old musical traditions (also influential were German, Czech, Polish, Hispanic, and French population pockets throughout the South). For British Celtic migrants, the large majority of whom were nonliterate, music, particularly ballads, provided a journalistic perspective of past as well as more recent events. In addition, they offered guides for morality, often producing narratives that described in graphic (and frequently superstitious) detail the harmful consequences of waywardness. Yet ballads, like other forms of Anglo-Celtic music brought to the region, also furnished entertainment, whether performed in the home or in areas of public amusement. Dancing to fiddle tunes during celebrations, such as weddings and community gatherings, for example, represented a standard practice, a piece of cultural baggage readily transplanted to the southern frontier. As for West Africans forcibly relocated to the slave South, their engagement with music was even more pronounced. In both individual and communal settings, music served as an important connection to another world, a spiritual realm where one's gods and ancestors dwelled in harmony. With its deep-seated emphasis on polyphonic and polyrhythmic tendencies, it also connected enslaved people to each other. Indeed, through the melodic sounds of voices and the rhythmic swinging and swaying of bodies, West African exiles were able to converge present with past and one to all in a manner that helped deny slavery's power to nullify a people and a culture.

The legacies established by West African and British migrants and their descendants were central to the evolution of southern music. Yet the rural and agricultural milieu from which the music emerged was also significant. Working behind a mule and plow, often separated by long distances from neighbors, farmers frequently sang out or hollered simply to hear a human voice. Sometimes those within earshot might even respond. If nothing else, such activities helped break the monotony of rural seclusion. The work songs and field hollers of slave laborers, in addition to establishing a regimented pace, likewise relieved the boredom that ensued from isolation and repetitious toil. Characterized by improvisation and the give-and-take of call and response between leader and chorus, the songs could reflect either a spiritual or a secular bent, referencing concerns or topics that all understood. For many who worked the land, whether it be their own or acreage that belonged to someone else, formal education received little attention and was routinely dismissed as unnecessary, superfluous, or out of reach. Inhabitants instead tended to rely on the spoken rather than the written word for their information, inspiration, and entertainment. It is no coincidence, then, that music flowed from a rural environment where public oratory, whether in the form of political speechifying, fire and brimstone preaching, or commodity auctioneering, played a very prominent role. It was a legacy that transferred easily to an urban milieu.

Most important to the South's musical evolution, however, has been the relationship of its people to power. In a region legendary for sustaining a rigid hierarchical social and governmental structure that favored the few while ignoring the many, the large majority of its citizens, both black and white, have possessed little real access to social, economic, or political authority and security. The ramifications of systemic discrimination along racial, class, and gender lines have been momentous. Enjoying little satisfaction associated with material acquisition, political prerogative, or social status, ordinary southerners turned to music, a cost-effective and seemingly apolitical means of enjoyment, release, creative sustenance, and self-expression. Unable to correspond personal worth and integrity with work, politics, or social status, they created an alternative space that privileged music as a means to articulate who they were and why they mattered.

Commercial or popular music of the modern era emerged at the same time as scientific management practices were being applied to the workplace. As work became more efficient, it likewise became more standardized and repetitive, thus causing alienated laborers to seek stimulation and meaning through popular entertainment. This dialectic, of course, was both liberating and limited. Significantly, it is a process of dissonance (what one does for a living) and harmony (how one lives by escaping) that has persisted into the new millennium, as corporate control and power continue to chip away at the autonomy of workers and citizens. Southerners can relate to this phenomenon in intimate and historical terms. And while they have demonstrated that music can provide a functional antidote to the depersonalization of modern life, they also have revealed that commercial entertainment in itself has rarely cured the structural and societal conditions that in many ways make the music necessary. Still, music certainly has made life more tolerable. Though not necessarily the elusive central theme of southern history, this may be one of its more enduring lessons.

MICHAEL T. BERTRAND
Tennessee State University

Lynn Abbott and Doug Seroff, *Ragged but Right: Black Traveling Shows, "Coon Songs," and the Dark Pathway to Blues and Jazz* (2007); William Barlow, *Looking Up at Down: The Emergence of Blues Culture* (1989); Michael T. Bertrand, *Race, Rock, and Elvis* (2004); Gavin James Campbell, *Music and the Making of a New South* (2003); Robert Cantwell, *Bluegrass Breakdown: The Making of the Old Southern Sound* (1984); Samuel Charters, *The Country Blues* (1959); Dena Epstein, *Sinful Tunes and Spirituals: Black Folk Music to the Civil War* (1977); David Evans, *Big Road Blues: Tradition and Creativity in the Folk Blues* (1987); Benjamin Filene, *Romancing the Folk: Public Memory and American Roots Music* (2000); James Goff Jr., *Close Harmony: A History of Southern Gospel* (2002); Charles Hamm, *Music in the New World* (1983); Anthony Heilbut, *The Gospel Sound: Good News and Bad Times* (1971); Patrick Huber, *Linthead Stomp: The Creation of Country Music in the Piedmont South* (2008); Charles Joyner, *Shared Traditions: Southern History and Folk Culture* (1999); Lawrence Levine, *Black Culture and Black Consciousness: Afro-American Folk Thought from Slavery to Freedom* (1977); Bill Malone, *Country Music USA* (3rd rev. ed., 2002), *Don't Get Above Your Raisin': Country Music and the Southern Working Class* (2002), with Dave Stricklin, *Southern Music, American Music* (2nd rev. ed., 2003); Grady McWhiney, *Cracker Culture: Celtic Ways in the Old South* (1988); Robert Palmer, *Deep Blues: A Musical and Cultural History of the Mississippi Delta* (1982); Robert Santelli et al., *American Roots Music* (2001); Frank Tirro, *Jazz: A History* (1977); Jeff Todd Titon, *Early Downhome Blues: A Musical and Cultural Analysis* (1977); Craig Werner, *A Change Is Gonna Come: Music, Race, and the Soul of America* (1998).

Place and Space

To speak of "the South" is to assert a place set apart. "What makes the South different" can be found in the ideas of place, space, and class—the global place the South has occupied in the international economy, the class structures that constrained the life chances of southerners and channeled the history of the South along certain paths, and the spaces constructed from material and memory left behind as the contested legacy of that history.

The South, of course, is not one place but many. What set the many Souths on their distinct paths, each different from the North, was plantation agriculture and racial slavery. As it expanded from Europe, the early modern capitalist economy created the plantation. New areas were drawn into the world economy and forced into specialized roles. Without precious metals, the export of only certain cash crops in North America met the requirements of the English mercantilist system, and those could be grown only in certain places.

The success of tobacco in Virginia and Maryland established the plantation and solidified slavery in North America. From its base in the Chesapeake, plantation society spread to new lands incorporated into the global economy. Yet the plantation system was on precarious economic footing until the cotton gin placed plantation slavery at the center of wealthy southerners' pursuit of profit and ensured that it would expand westward.

Not all natural places of the South, however, provided enough land for large-scale cultivation, soil conditions to support export crops, and sufficient accessibility to world markets to support plantation agriculture, but three spaces did. The Atlantic coast, easily accessible by water, constituted the eastern leg of the plantation zone. The interior lowlands stretching across Georgia, Alabama, and Mississippi, known as the Black Belt for its dark soil, formed the zone's southern portion. The alluvial land along the Mississippi, known as the Delta, formed the western part of the zone, stretching from New Orleans to Memphis. Between the Appalachian Mountains and the lowlands, east and west, lay a transitional area known variously as the Piedmont, Bluegrass, or Upcountry, neither best suited to nor geographically precluded from plantation agriculture.

In the lowlands, plantations growing export crops for the world market monopolized the majority of the best land. Wealthy planters, owners of dozens or even hundreds of slaves, formed the dominant economic and political elite. Captive African laborers formed the mass of cultivators, outnumbering non-elite whites consisting of town dwellers, small farmers, artisans, and overseers. Cut off spatially from world markets, smallholding yeomen in the Appalachian highlands farmed for subsistence first, arduously marketing any surplus when possible. The plantation was largely absent, but slave-owning elites were not. Migrant planters exploiting opportunities in the salt and iron industries and small slaveholding merchants formed the politically dominant upper class. In the Piedmont, a mixed society developed. Planters and their slaves settled in bottomlands, founding large estates geared toward commercial production. Yeoman established small holds. When situated near means of transportation, they pursued general farming and independent commodity production with household labor or a few slaves, forming the basis of an internal market. Small farmers and slaves in roughly equal numbers formed the mass of the population, yet planters formed the dominant elite politically, economically, and socially. Within these three geographic spaces, distinct political economies and class structures thus developed during the antebellum period.

Crises arising from conflicts among the great European powers during the early 19th century allowed American states leeway in economic development relatively free from the competitive pressures of the global economy. Dominant classes in the North and in the distinct regions of the South pursued different strategies of economic development. Elites in the plantation areas embraced export agriculture—fueling the English textile industry with cotton—wagering short-term profits against the threat of long-term dependence. Elites in the mixed economies of the Piedmont and the mountains pursued capitalist development including transportation, banking, commercial-industrial diversification, and the capture of internal markets. Where elites were large-scale slave owners, wealth in human beings was leveraged as a means to capital formation.

Although in no way inevitable, the antithetical development trajectories of North and South became sufficiently incompatible politically that secession and war were not avoided. The war itself increased the power of the federal state, developed corporate finance, and concentrated capital sufficiently to reorient the export economy to favor northeastern, rather than European, industrialization and capital formation.

The goal of Reconstruction was to create a "free labor" society from the ruins of plantation slavery, but the absence of land reform ensured that Emancipation would result in no revolutionary transformation of the class structure. The division of plantations into family-operated tenant farms merely encouraged the continued production of cash crops. Simultaneously, federal policy discouraged alternative paths of economic development. Banking reforms hampered the availability of credit in the South. Northern corporations completed ruined and bankrupt southern railroads and began carrying raw material north and manufactured goods south. Ultimately the end of the Civil War meant further pressure on the South to conform to the international division of labor.

The class structures of the three regions were transformed differently in response to this intensified economic pressure. Across the South, elites attempted to preserve their power and privilege in their particular niches of the restructured economy. The masses of white farmers lost the former independence of yeoman status while African American farmers were trapped in new machinery of racial coercion and debt bondage.

In the plantation regions, planters and their allies violently overthrew Reconstruction and reinvented the plantation economy with sharecropping but locked the region into a declining sector. The legal coercion of slavery was replaced by state-condoned racial violence, laws restricting labor mobility, and crop lien laws that advanced credit to tenants but prevented them from leaving landlords until all debts were paid.

In yeoman areas of the Deep South, white farmers were pulled increasingly into cash crop production as the only way to obtain the credit necessary to return their land to cultivation. Cycles of overproduction and agricultural depression fueled indebtedness and drove yeoman into tenancy. Planters remained dominant at the local level but locked themselves and the region into a declining agriculture.

In mixed regions such as the Piedmont, former planter elites continued a transition to capitalism and away from plantation agriculture. They were instrumental in industrialization in textiles, tobacco, and steel, driven by super exploitation of labor. The economic decline of the yeoman created a white working class. Racially split labor markets ensured low wages by confining the white working class to racially restrictive spaces such as cotton textile factories and black labor to tobacco factories. Planter-capitalists linked pools of local capital to invest in wholesaling that supplied credit to the stores and commissaries of the plantation South and used their profits to invest in industry to make the shoes, overalls, plow points, hardware, furniture, and fertilizer distributed to the southern market.

In Appalachia, local elites helped broker the entry of outside capital into the region to extract coal and timber resources. The decline of the yeomanry, the result more of population growth and the division of agricultural property, pushed native whites into the working class. In coal camps and company towns a similar mix of credit and coercion found in other areas of the South provided levers of control over the contentious workers. Displaced southern African Americans and European immigrants were recruited to divide worker solidarity and combat labor militancy in the coalfields.

Staple agriculture deteriorated in the early 20th century as the result of overproduction, increased global supply, and environmental crises brought on by monoculture. The response of a plantation system based on labor repression to declining profits was to increase levels of exploitation. Labor coercion and increased waves of racial violence helped propel the flight of much of the black agricultural labor force from the region in the Great Migration of the 1910s and 1920s. Southern politicians leveraged federal funds to build naval industries and military bases across the region but such measures did not forestall the complete collapse of the southern economy in the Great Depression.

The 1930s brought new waves of class conflict and federal intervention less welcomed by southern elites. New Deal agricultural reform policies established price supports, encouraged mechanization and a shift to less labor-intensive crops like soybeans and corn, and furthered rural outmigration. Industrial collapse spawned renewed militancy among southern workers. New Deal labor policies encouraged unionization of coal miners, but unionization drives failed in textile mills.

After World War II, African Americans used nonviolence to dismantle the state-sponsored coercion that lay at the heart of the plantation economy. The primary battlegrounds and the fiercest resistance were in the plantation areas. In the more "business-oriented" industrial regions, labor market discipline was central to maintaining elite control over labor and keeping wages low. Ultimately, however, the political revolution of the civil rights movement could not reverse the marginalization of the southern rural economy. Postwar labor militancy and the War on Poverty in Appalachia similarly failed to stem the structural decline of the economies. Increasingly, the plantation and mountain South (apart from the environmental effects of surface mining in the latter) have lost their character as distinct political economies and come to resemble the general impoverishment and decline of rural America with its high rates of structural unemployment, loss of working age population, and "brain drain." Deindustrialization and globalization have had much the same effect on southern industries, especially textiles and steel.

The legacy of distinct paths of development can still be seen, however, in the geography of southern urbanization. The poor and rural plantation and Appalachian subregions are encircled by a rim of urban, industrial, and commercial growth in "New South" or "Sunbelt" cities centered in the transitional regions. Military, tourism, second home, and retirement communities occupy specialized niches, but the hallmarks of the South's low-wage, labor-repressive capitalism persist. Working-class Latino migrants have augmented the labor force in agriculture and meat processing in rural areas and construction, domestic, and service work in metropolitan areas.

Just as the mansions of Charleston and Natchez are implicit monuments to the history of enslaved labor, vanishing sites of waged labor in coal camps and mill villages still bear traces of past exploitation as well. Southern class relations can also be traced in built environments outside the region. The skeletal remains of New England textile factories, for instance, embody the uncompensated labor of southern slaves, while the monumental libraries, museums, and universities of Pittsburgh and Chicago bear traces of the labor of southern miners who supplied the industries of those cities with coal. The point of being able to read class in the landscape is not to reduce all things southern to class but to see class everywhere.

ALAN DAHL
American University

DWIGHT B. BILLINGS
University of Kentucky

Dwight Billings, *Planters and the Making of a "New South"* (1980); Alan Dahl, "North of the South: Planters and the Transition to Capitalism in the Central Virginia Piedmont" (Ph.D. dissertation, University of Kentucky, 2010); Pete Daniel, *Breaking the Land: The Transformation of Cotton, Tobacco, and Rice Cultures since 1880* (1985); Steven Hahn, *The Roots of Southern Populism: Yeoman Farmers and the Transformation of the Georgia Upcountry, 1850–1890* (1983); Jonathan Wiener, *Social Origins of the New South: Alabama 1860–1885* (1979).

Political Behavior

Arguments about class and politics—about the power of social class to explain political behavior—have been ubiquitous since the coming of the Industrial Revolution. Different social classes possess different material interests, and these are always a potential seedbed for political conflict. Moreover, different social classes often experience the events of their time differently, giving them potentially conflicting impressions even of shared societal developments. Nevertheless, the study of southern politics has frequently proceeded without much attention to the place of class. Part of the explanation lies with the agricultural (and most definitely not industrial) economy of the Old South. Part of it lies with an analytic priority given to race—not class—in the New South. The combination has been implicitly hostile to a focus on class and politics in the region, and actively deleterious to an understanding of their relationship.

A regionally distinctive politics was already characteristic of the American South by the time the Industrial Revolution came to characterize the nation as a whole, in the late 19th century. The antebellum party system had been historically good at containing regional differences. Northern and southern Whigs faced off against northern and southern Democrats. Yet that system came apart in the 1850s, and in the aftermath of the Civil War, the party system that replaced it featured—in truth, was centrally characterized by—a regionally distinctive role for the South. In a sense, it was the one-party character of this major region that distinguished the national party system as a whole. As a result, from the 1870s through the 1960s, the United States had what might actually be described as a "three-party system," featuring northern Democrats, southern Democrats, and national Republicans.

Because the Industrial Revolution that swept through the Northeast and Midwest during the late 19th century essentially bypassed the South, the classic elements of an industrial politics—an organized working class and class-based policy concerns—largely bypassed the region as well. There were groups, organizations, and even political parties, as with the Redeemers, the Farmers Alliance, and the Populist Party, that gave expression to organized economic interests, thereby allowing chroniclers to argue over a kind of surrogate class politics. But even the iconic effort to apply systematic evidence to this phenomenon, from V. O. Key Jr. in his *Southern Politics in State and Nation* (1949), was limited by the absence of individual-level data—as well as by Key's belief that class could in effect just be overlaid on race for this type of analysis.

The coming of the Great Depression, and then of the New Deal as a policy response to it, brought class-based alignments all the way to the center of partisan politics outside the South. The new, diagnostic, and dominating feature of the New Deal party system was nothing less than the organizing role of social class. Yet an overwhelmingly agrarian economy still featured only intermittent divisions between large and small farms or between Lowcountry and Upcountry farming in the South itself, a pale agrarian echo of nonsouthern industrial cleavages. Beyond that, even these intermittent divisions were still

TABLE 7. *Social Class and the Coming of Southern Republicanism: The House*

Decade	Income Terciles			Total	Range High–Low
	Low	Mid	High		
1950s	40%	32%	25%	31%	−15
(N)	(80)	(59)	(100)	(239)	
1960s	31%	37%	44%	37%	+13
(N)	(137)	(113)	(122)	(372)	
1970s	34%	44%	50%	43%	+16
(N)	(184)	(217)	(201)	(602)	
1980s	34%	49%	53%	47%	+19
(N)	(131)	(202)	(230)	(563)	
1990s	40%	58%	64%	56%	+24
(N)	(225)	(270)	(338)	(833)	

Note: Entries are Republican percentage among all whites in contested districts.

further fuzzed by a unifying racial politics, emphasizing black disfranchisement. As a result, the persistence of a one-party South remained the great, continuing anomaly in this New Deal party system.

That was the situation in the immediate postwar period, when it became possible to use actual survey evidence to ask about class and politics among southerners as a whole, that is, as a general public rather than just as an aggregation of elites. The primary vehicle for doing so—the "gold standard" for such inquiries—was the American National Election Study, a national survey asking about policy preferences and political behavior in all presidential and most midterm elections after 1950. Accordingly, Table 7 looks at the vote for the U.S. House of Representatives, the national vote that is most revealing of partisan attachments, for contested seats gathered by decade across the half century following creation of the American National Election Studies (ANES). Table 7 is limited to white southerners, since there were so very few black southern voters in the early years of this table, though we shall turn to the latter in short order. Social class is assessed here by income tercile—top, middle, and bottom thirds by income.

The 1950s are effectively a picture of social class and voting behavior in the Old South, the world captured stereotypically by Key in his landmark *Southern Politics in State and Nation*. This is presumably a picture that would have characterized the region since the Civil War. What is distinctive about it is its class inversion. In the Old South, the rich were more Democratic, the poor more Republican. This is not just opposite to the usual argument about class interests and partisan alignment. It is opposite to the actual situation in the rest of the country. Yet it should probably be treated not so much as an inverse class effect but as a continued (and ossified) reflection of alignments internal to the South at the time of the Civil War. Appalachian areas, among the poorest parts of the South, were least sympathetic to secession in 1860. They remained least sympathetic to the southern Democratic Party a hundred years later.

This implicit class inversion was to change in the 1960s, to break up the southern Democratic ascendancy in the process, and ultimately to convert a Democratic bastion into a Republican stronghold. Economic development, so long delayed in the region as a whole, was under way beneath the surface of a static politics during the war years and was galloping ahead during the 1950s. By the 1960s its side effects were reaching politics in a manner difficult to ignore. Indeed, economic development and an associated politics of social class were first to bring the South into alignment with national patterns, then to take the relationship between class and politics to a higher level—a sharper division—than the same relationship for the nation as a whole.

In any case, the 1960s represented a dramatic break with the 1950s, and presumably with those many decades of politics beforehand. The 1960s are more commonly remembered as a decade of conflict over civil rights and cultural values. Seen through the lens of social class and political behavior, however, they are better viewed as the decade when the South finally rejoined the Union, and this change was to reconstitute not just southern but national politics thereafter. Now—and ever after, at least as this is written—the rich were more Republican, the poor more Democratic. This was still not the strongest class relationship to voting behavior itself. That would appear only in the 1990s, the decade of an actual Republican majority in congressional voting by white southerners. But it was the biggest shift from decade to decade in the entire postwar period. And it created the dynamic on which southern Republicanism would ride up thereafter.

Voting for president was always more volatile than voting for Congress, and it was also more responsive to occasional challenges from major independent candidates. On the other hand, the South had two major-party presidential candidates everywhere most of the time, so the changing impact of social class should be easier to see earlier, if the data can be made to offer a parallel comparison. To that end, Table 8 divides the southern presidential vote into old (i.e., established) Republican areas, those that that could offer a congressional candidate in the first year of the ANES, 1952, and new (i.e., emergent) Repub-

TABLE 8. *The Timing of a Class Reversal: The Presidency*

A. The 1950s

	Income Terciles			Range		
	Low	Mid	High	High–Low	Total	[N]
Old Republican areas	60%	58%	48%	−12	56%	[124]
New Republican areas	31%	44%	50%	+19	42%	[250]

B. The 1960s

	Income Terciles			Range		
	Low	Mid	High	High–Low	Total	[N]
Old Republican areas	44%	32%	57%	+13	46%	[112]
New Republican areas	35%	41%	55%	+20	42%	[240]

C. The 1970s

	Income Terciles			Range		
	Low	Mid	High	High–Low	Total	[N]
Old Republican areas	58%	67%	71%	+13	65%	[268]
New Republican areas	55%	63%	73%	+18	64%	[449]

Note: Entries are Republican percentage among all whites.

lican areas, either those lacking a Republican Party or those where it still could not produce a congressional challenger. This arrangement tells essentially the same story for the presidency as for Congress, with an even earlier beginning. In doing so, it underlines a set of major points about class and politics in the South.

In the 1950s (and not surprisingly), established Republican areas offered a better presidential vote than emergent areas. This is the "Total" column in Table 8A. Yet established areas also differed from emergent areas in their relationship between social class and political behavior. In the old areas, this relationship was still inverse: the rich more Democratic, the poor more Republican. In the new areas, it had already achieved the modern form: the poor more Democratic, the rich more Republican. In the 1960s a modest Republican edge for the established areas was still present, though old areas had already adopted the new class relationship—the same one that had characterized the non-South since the New Deal. By the 1970s there was simply no difference at all: the modern relationship between social class and political behavior characterized the entire South when the focus was voting for president.

When the vote for Congress and president are put back together, then, the following summary notes about social class and political behavior emerge:

- The great change in the relationship between class and politics in the South was the reversal of the old class inversion. This could be teased out of the presidential vote by the 1950s; it was inescapable in the congressional vote by the 1960s. It meant that Republican prospects were more or less guaranteed to rise as the South developed economically, acquiring an industrial, not an agricultural, economy.
- Yet there was much more to the class story than this. Indeed, the story was different in each of our income terciles:
    1. In the traditional class narrative, it is a mobilized working class that provides the crucial political dynamic. But in the American South, it was the upper-income tercile—the rich—that corrected the southern inversion. Class politics was driven from above, not from below.
    2. On the other hand, the story of a Republican majority was instead a story of middle-class politics. Only when the white southern middle class (our middle-income tercile) began to vote majority Republican did the overall partisan balance come to feature a different winner.
    3. Yet poor whites, our lower-income tercile, proved remarkably oblivious to this Republican attraction. They were instead the bedrock of white resistance to southern Republicanism. There is an impressionistic literature alleging that racial identity fostered Republican identification among precisely these voters. The data leave little room for any such effect. Regardless of their racial attitudes, their class attachments kept the poor white South in the Democratic Party.

After all that, two major parts of this story are still missing. One puts important limits on the influence of social class in southern politics. The other emphasizes the power of what remains, even after those limits are introduced. The first of these, that limiting influence, requires bringing black southerners into the picture. The second, a final emphasis on the power that class retains, requires bringing the rest of the country—the non-South—into this picture as well.

If the 1960s was the decade when the old class inversion was abandoned by southern whites, it was also the decade of the civil rights revolution, when southern blacks entered the electorate en masse. What must be said most directly about the political behavior of this new black electorate was that it produced a vote based overwhelmingly on racial identity, such that there was effectively no room left for a further contribution from social class. In the old southern politics, blacks had manifested strong (if practically limited) loyalties to the Republican Party, as a legacy of the Civil War and Reconstruction. These loyalties were already being seriously eroded by the time a politics of social class broke the hold of the Democratic Party on southern whites, courtesy of the New Deal, which provided critical economic aid to black as well as white southerners and which was administered in a more even-handed fashion than a southern regional politics would have tolerated.

The southern black vote in the ANES in the 1950s, as in the South as a political region, remained tiny. Yet survey data here, too, are consistent with a long political history in which it was northern Republicans, not southern Democrats, who had provided aid and comfort to southern blacks: there was still a very substantial Republican minority among black southerners. This minority was to be destroyed by the civil rights revolution. New black voters flooded into the southern electorate in the course of that revolution, and they arrived as full-fledged northern Democrats, not northern Republicans (Table 9A). As a result, a vote that was often more than nine-to-one Democratic on grounds of race left nearly no room for a further impact from social class. And indeed, there was none (Table 9B).

On the one hand, then, the class alignment associated with economic development did not reach into nearly all of the postwar South. Black southerners were effectively impervious. On the other hand, the power of the new relationship between class and politics in the white South—the class escalator for the Republican Party in southern politics—remained sufficient to pull that party into ultimate regional ascendancy. And the simplest way to appreciate this power is to note that by the 1960s the South had not only escaped the class inversion that characterized its politics for the previous hundred years. It had actually opened up a class gap in mass political behavior (the Republican vote in top versus bottom income terciles) that was larger than the parallel gap outside the South. This difference actually widened, rather than settling, during the 1980s and 1990s. So that in the end, a political region once noted for its suppression of the impact of social class was now distinctively characterized by that impact.

Current politics in the region are temporally incomplete, turbulent, and

TABLE 9. *The Demise of Black Republicanism and the Absence of a Class Effect*

A. Black Presidential Voting by Decade

Decade	% Republican	(N)
1950s	42%	(33)
1960s	3%	(74)
1970s	10%	(174)
1980s	9%	(130)
1990s	3%	(219)

B. Social Class and Partisan Voting

	Income Tercile		
1970s–1990s	Low	Mid	High
Presidency	92%	92%	93%
(N)	(290)	(128)	(61)

Note: Entries in B are Democratic percentage among black southerners.

thus inevitably lacking in the perspective necessary to assess the future political South. On the one hand, there are hints that the story of class and politics within the South has changed again. The class gap in Republican or Democratic support as between upper and lower income terciles has, for example, finally begun to recede. Moreover, this is largely due to increased Republican success, at long last, in the low-income tercile among southern whites. On the other hand, the problem of interpreting these developments at this point in time is effectively insurmountable, and the story of presidential politics in the South for the 2000s can show why this is so.

Among candidates, when southern politics is the focus, the 2000s has produced the two great aberrations in all of American history. That is, it has provided the first southern Republican nominee for president ever, in the person of George W. Bush, and it has—one election later—provided the first black major-party nominee, in the person of Barack Obama, who, even more significantly, won the presidency. To make matters worse, the 2000s has generated the greatest "foreign policy election" since the ANES began, in the election of 2004, along with the greatest "social welfare election" in that same period, in the election of 2008. The Great Recession after that further disrupted politics, but its meaning for class is uncertain. With four large and deviant sources of variation—when there are, in effect, only two data points, the two elections of 2004 and 2008—only seers and charlatans can claim to know what the 2000s have done to the relationship between class and politics in the American South.

BYRON E. SHAFER
University of Wisconsin at Madison

Stanley P. Berard, *Southern Democrats in the U.S. House of Representatives* (2001); James C. Cobb, *The Selling of the South: The Southern Crusade for Industrial Development, 1936–1990* (1993); Richard F. Fenno Jr., *Congress at the Grassroots: Representational Change in the South, 1970–1998* (2000); Hugh Davis Graham, *The Civil Rights Era: Origins and Development of National Policy, 1960–1972* (1990); V. O. Key Jr., *Southern Politics in State and Nation* (1949); Richard Nadeau and Harold W. Stanley, *American Journal of Political Science* 37 (1993); Richard G. Niemi, Harold W. Stanley, and Jean-Francois Godbout, *American Politics Research* (1 November 2004); Nicol C. Rae, *Southern Democrats* (1994); David W. Rohde, *American Review of Politics* (Spring 1996); Philip Scranton, ed., *The Second Wave: Southern Industrialization from the 1940s to the 1970s* (2001); Byron E. Shafer and Richard Johnston, *The End of Southern Exceptionalism: Class, Race, and Partisan Change in the Postwar South* (2006); Harvard Sitkoff, *The Struggle for Black Equality, 1954–1980* (1981); Bernard L. Weinstein, *Regional Growth and Decline in the United States* (1985).

Populist Movement

Populism in the South built on the antimonopolist and democratic ideology promulgated by the agrarian reform movements that emerged in the 1870s and included the Agricultural Wheel and the Farmers' Alliance. Made up of middling-level commercial farmers, subsistence farmers, and some tenants and sharecroppers, the white agricultural reformers made common cause with industrial workers and African American farmers. Such broad-based dissent was unprecedented in southern history and was all the more frightening to entrenched elites because of its claims as a class-based insurgency. Wheelers, Alliancemen, and Populists understood the role of class in terms of producerism, an ideology that pitted workers whose labor resulted in tangible commodities against the "plutocrats" who profited from the labor of others. However, agrarianism and the rural community were more complex than the ideological duality suggested, and conflicts within the movement often were based on competing ideas about class and social differences.

The first post–Civil War farm organization, the Patrons of Husbandry

(Grange), attracted more affluent planters and farmers who dominated positions of power within the organization. Although Grangers promoted cooperativism as the solution to chronic problems associated with farm costs and agricultural prices, they also advocated social programs designed to elevate rural life to mimic the cultural advantages perceived to be available in cities. Improved educational opportunities, construction of rural libraries, and the development of social graces were as important as markets in the programs of local Granges. For small farmers and tenants, the Grange offered few benefits, and membership declined throughout the South after the mid-1870s.

The Wheel and Alliance attracted some wealthier and better-educated men, but the organizations were largely characterized by smaller farmers and tenants who found themselves disadvantaged in the new postwar commodity markets where capital, not cotton, was king. The successors to the Grange self-consciously separated themselves from the bankers, lawyers, and merchants of nearby cities and towns, arguing that farm interests differed fundamentally from those of urban economic and political leaders. Their goals and demands made it clear that radical rural dissenters understood the new economy of industrial capitalism as subversive to the republican ideology articulated by Jefferson and Jackson. Popular election of U.S. senators, destruction of the National Bank, bimetallism, and regulation of transportation and communication were demands intended to restore power to the yeoman farmer and the worker.

If the agrarian organizations reinforced differences between urban and rural communities, they also bridged many traditional barriers. Farmers in the South, many of whom had served in the Confederate armies during the Civil War, recognized their common problems with farmers elsewhere in the nation. Although differences remained, particularly in regard to race, former enemies met in national conventions of the Wheel, Alliance, and People's Party to seek solutions to problems of production and markets. The potential for bridging the great national abyss disrupted carefully constructed one-party systems in both the North and the South. Outside the South, the Republican Party benefited from the social welfare system that existed under the umbrella of the Grand Army of the Republic. In the former Confederate states, racial hierarchy united white men of all classes under the banner of the Democratic Party. The agrarian insurgency threatened the entrenched elites everywhere. Opponents of the Wheel, the Alliance, and the People's Party ridiculed dissidents in pejorative terms and pressured the better-educated and wealthier members to recognize their own position among the "best men" and abandon the movement. Nevertheless, farmers voted across party lines to elect their own to local and state offices in 1890 and 1892 (a few members of Congress also claimed Populist affiliations). As rural voters abandoned the "party of their fathers" and moved into the Populist Party, they appeared poised to make additional political gains in 1896.

Local Wheels and Alliances organized around friendship and kinship networks and anchored their meetings within the rhetoric of religion. The sentiments expressed in the Sermon on the Mount defined the operating ideology of the agrarian movement. In the minds of farmers confronted with the depersonalization of industrial capitalism, the admonition to become their brother's keeper promised a more humane modernity. The sermons and prayers of country preachers reinforced the class-based demands of the rural insurgents. Meeting in rural churches and at rallies that mimicked familiar brush arbor meetings, agrarian leaders fostered the perception of a movement sanctioned by Holy Scripture and civic religion. The organizational structure of the Wheel and Alliance paralleled that of the Masonic lodges. Masons, Sunday School advocates, and agrarian dissidents frequently organized joint assemblies in which it could be difficult to distinguish one group from the other as speeches, songs, and calls for action overlapped in complex ways that promoted communal approaches to the issues raised by urban industrialization.

Rural dissidents demanded greater public participation in shaping the economic and political future of the nation. In their call for action, they opened the door for opponents to question their commitment to white male patriarchy. Few southern Wheelers, Alliancemen, and Populists called for woman suffrage or argued in favor of a larger political role for blacks. Nevertheless, women and blacks were more visible in the rural organizations than in other contemporary associations. Both the Wheel and Alliance permitted female membership; the Grange required women as members in order to obtain an organizing charter. Women served in minor offices and expressed their views in organizational publications. They claimed their membership as evidence of their partnership in the family farm, where they provided labor for production and reproduction and were instrumental in maintaining the social network that sustained small farm agriculture. White agricultural organizations never fully allied with African American farmers, but they made common cause in developing cooperative processing mills, boycotting the jute trust, and challenging tobacco and cotton purchasing practices. Meeting in segregated locals, the Colored Wheel and Colored Alliance felt the pressures against their participation from planter elites and within the larger agrarian associations. Ultimately, the racial and economic advantages that whites enjoyed created conflicts with black farmers that undermined their common rural concerns. African American farmers largely disappeared from the ranks of rural dissenters following the unsuccessful efforts by black sharecroppers and pickers to raise harvest wages in 1891.

Populist and agrarian demands for greater federal regulation of the new economy, implementation of electoral reforms to counteract elite control over legislation, and banking and currency laws that would give small producers and entrepreneurs easier access to credit ultimately found support in the middle-class programs of the Progressive Era and in New Deal legislation. The anticipated triumphs of 1896 failed to materialize as the Populists were subsumed into the campaign of the Great Commoner, William Jennings Bryan. The producerism view of class gave way to an industrial conceptualization of a permanent working class with no links to the agrarian world.

CONNIE L. LESTER
University of Central Florida

Joe Creech, *Righteous Indignation: Religion and the Populist Revolution* (2006); Michael Kazin, *The Populist Persuasion: An American History* (1995); Robert C. McMath, *American Populism: A Social History, 1877-1898* (1993); Charles Postel, *The Populist Vision* (2007); Catherine McNicol Stock, *Rural Radicals: Righteous Rage in the American Grain* (1996).

Poverty

Poverty and deprivation are persistent themes in southern society and culture. C. Vann Woodward, the great historian of the South, called poverty "a continuous and conspicuous feature of the southern experience." For a goodly portion of the 20th century, southern poverty was a national paradox—how in such a land of plenty could so many families, like the southerners written about so poignantly by James Agee in *Let Us Now Praise Famous Men*, have so little? Because the vast majority of African Americans lived in the South in the early 20th century, what Franklin Delano Roosevelt labeled the nation's number one "economic problem" in 1938—southern poverty—was closely intertwined with what Gunnar Myrdal called the "American Dilemma"—race. Television viewers during the horrific aftermath of Hurricane Katrina recalling the images of poor, black people clinging to rooftops in the 7th Ward of New Orleans or trapped in the Superdome might be forgiven for thinking that some things had not changed since 1938.

But much has, in fact, changed since 1938, including our understanding of the root causes of southern poverty. Many time-honored explanations of southern poverty—for example, that the South was poor because slavery or sharecropping somehow made it so—do not stand up to careful scrutiny. The

Iconic Walker Evans image of sharecropper Bud Fields and his family at home from Let Us Now Praise Famous Men, 1936 (Library of Congress [LC-USF342-8147-A], Washington, D.C.)

South was, indeed, once poor on average, but the key driving force behind southern poverty at the turn of the 20th century was a sharp reduction in income per person that occurred following the Civil War. Compared with post–World War II economic miracles such as in Germany or Japan, the economy in the South after World War II "converged" slowly on the rest of the nation during the first half of the 20th century. But Germany and Japan are the wrong reference standards to use to judge the performance of the southern economy. The rate at which living standards in the South converged with the rest of the nation was just about what could have been expected given the depth of the hole the southern economy had to dig itself out of after the Civil War. Since 1960 poverty rates in the South have declined sharply relative to the national average. The imagery from Katrina notwithstanding, the region is no longer a particularly relevant factor in poverty in the United States. Pockets of poverty, rural and urban, can be found throughout the South, sometimes in historically familiar places such as Appalachia and the Black Belt, but there is nothing distinctly southern about such pockets, for they can be found throughout the United States.

A widely used statistic measuring the economic well-being of a society is per person (or per capita) income. "Income" here refers to the value of all final

TABLE 10. *Selected Income Statistics, the South Relative to the Nation*

	Per Capita Income in the South/Per Capita Income in the United States	Percent of Individuals below the Poverty Line in the South	Southern Poverty Rate/ National Poverty Rate
1880	0.502	NA	NA
1900	0.506	NA	NA
1920	0.604	NA	NA
1940	0.603	NA	NA
1960	0.762	35.4%	1.58
1970	0.860	18.5%	1.47
1980	0.884	16.5%	1.27
1990	0.904	15.8%	1.17
2000	0.948	12.8%	1.13
2008	0.952	14.3%	1.08

Sources: Column 1, 1880–1990: Robert A. Margo, "The South as an Economic Problem," p. 172; 2000, 2008: http://www.census.gov/hhes/www/income/histinc/incpertoc.html, table P-7, "Regions—People (Both Sexes Combined) by Median and Mean Income," calculated by author from figures in column 5. Columns 2, 3: table 9, "Poverty by Regions," http://www.census.gov/hhes/www/poverty/histpov/perindex.html, calculated by author from columns 4 (All Regions, Percent Below Poverty) and column 13 (South, Percent Below Poverty). The figure for 1960 is an estimate for 1959. NA: not available (the census did not measure or estimate poverty for years prior to 1959).

goods and services produced in a given year—what economists call GNP, or gross national product. Living standards depend upon much more than income in this narrow sense, and the average may be an inadequate representation of the typical person if the distribution of income is highly unequal. These are important qualifications, to be sure, but they do not alter the thrust of comparisons between the South and the rest of the United States.

In 1900 per capita income in the South was about half of the national average (see Table 10). The consequences of poverty were everywhere to be seen in the South of the early 20th century. Southerners were less healthy on average, their life expectancy lower, and their children too often shoeless and prone to parasitic infections like hookworm. Material possessions, additionally, were fewer—fewer books per capita, rattier clothing, substandard housing, and the like. Because incomes, on the whole, were lower than in the rest of the nation, southerners thus spent less per capita on education, thereby helping to perpetuate low incomes across generations.

One explanation is that the South was poor around 1900 because it had always been so, and it was always so because slavery somehow retarded the "modernization" of the southern economy. According to this explanation, slavery was backward, and "precapitalistic" slave agriculture was less productive than free agriculture. American slavery was by no means solely a southern phenomenon, but it was embraced most fully in the states that formed the Confederacy of 1861.

The difficulty with the "slavery as root cause of southern poverty" explanation is that hard data suggest the opposite. The earliest regional estimates of per capita income are for the period from 1840 to 1860, and these show that the southern economy grew at about the national average before the Civil War. Moreover, while per capita income in the South was below the average in the Northeast, southern incomes were slightly higher than the levels prevailing in the Midwest. "Per capita" in this comparison includes slaves whose "income" (the value of food, clothing, shelter, and so on provided by masters) was indeed very low. Although one should keep in mind that incomes were distributed very unequally in the South, income per free (white) southerner circa 1860 was quite high by international standards—similar to levels in Germany or France in 1870, or Italy in 1900.

It is likely, too, that slavery, on balance, raised the level of income per white southerner before the Civil War. Recent research by economic historians establishes that labor productivity of slave farms in the South—the value of agricultural output per worker—was actually higher than labor productivity on free farms.

Although not all the sources of the productivity differential can be pinned down, certain key elements are known. The differential was not general but rather was confined to a small number of staple crops—cotton, tobacco, sugar, and rice. The differential cannot be accounted for by higher amounts of capital or land (quantity or fertility) per worker but rather was a pure productivity differential. Most importantly, the differential varied with the number of slaves: it was not present on smaller slave farms, but only after a certain threshold, around 16 slaves (measured in adult male equivalent workers) had been reached, that is, in large plantations.

This combination of elements has led economic historians to point the finger at the so-called gang system. Not unlike the factory system in manufacturing, the gang system utilized division of labor. Production tasks were subdivided and assigned to particular types of workers. There was a strict regimen, force was applied, and few workers, including children or women, were underutilized. The gang system was highly productive but was used only with enslaved labor—evidently, free labor was unwilling to work in the gang system.

Primarily because of the productivity gains associated with the gang system, slavery was economically profitable and, more important, viable. There is no reason to believe that slavery would have died out on economic grounds any time soon on the eve of the Civil War. Although the ownership of slaves engaged in gang labor was highly concentrated, the economic benefits derived from the system were spread quite diffusely. The price of cotton was lower than it would have been in the absence of slavery; consumers of shirts, blouses, and so on made from slave-grown cotton therefore paid lower prices, and thus benefited economically, because of slave labor. Slave owners purchased locally produced goods and services from free whites. In a hypothetical world without slavery, it is likely that, on average, free white southerners would have been poorer, not richer, before the Civil War, although the economic fortunes of particular individuals would have undoubtedly been different.

If the incomes of free whites were higher on average because of slavery, there is no evidence that any of the economic profits of the system trickled down to slaves and overwhelming evidence that the economic costs experienced by the enslaved were huge and long lasting. By modern standards, enslaved children were exceptionally malnourished, adversely affecting health at the time and later in life. With very few exceptions, slaves had little or no chances at wealth accumulation in land or other assets. Perhaps most important, most slaves reached adulthood unable to read or write. These deficits in physical capital and human capital adversely affected the economic mobility of generations of African Americans well into the 20th century.

Between 1860 and 1880, income per capita in the South declined very sharply, both in absolute terms and relative to the rest of the United States. As a result, although the southern economy grew more quickly in per capita terms than elsewhere in the United States from 1880 to 1940, this growth was not enough to close a still a large regional gap on the eve of World War II.

What caused the postbellum decline in per capita income? Economic historians have pinpointed three key causes. First, there was a large reduction in labor productivity in agriculture, and because agriculture was a substantial share of the South's total output, this reduced per capita income. Second, work effort among newly freed people declined, primarily among children and women. This decline is not surprising. Once free, former slaves choose to work less intensively than under slavery. Third, there was a decline in the rate of growth in the demand for southern cotton, as the South lost ground to other cotton-producing areas, such as India and Egypt. Although the relative merits of each factor are debated, most scholars believe that the decline in labor productivity was the chief culprit.

With Emancipation came a drastic rearrangement of employment relations in southern agriculture. Tenancy came to the fore, particularly sharecropping. A long intellectual tradition in social science views sharecropping as inefficient because sharecroppers appear to have had only partial incentives (they received only a share of any extra effort) to work hard or make investments in the land. Landlords are also said to have made sharecroppers "overproduce" cotton because cotton was readily marketable even though, as noted, growth in demand for southern cotton slowed after the Civil War. Frequently sharecroppers fell into debt peonage. Every year they had to start over again, borrowing necessities at the start of the year hopefully to be repaid out of the proceeds of the harvest.

However, while documentary and quantitative evidence establishes that the typical sharecropper was poor, it is a different matter entirely to claim that a person was poor because he was a sharecropper. The alleged inefficiencies associated with sharecropping contracts are more apparent than real because landlords had a countervailing incentive to supervise a sharecropper's work. Indeed, a case can be made that when unexpected conditions, such as poor weather, required some extra effort, sharecroppers had better incentives to respond than wage laborers who were paid regardless.

Farmers with limited experience or other skills (e.g., literacy) and a lack of capital to draw upon could find sharecropping (relatively) attractive because some of the riskiness inherent in agriculture was borne by the landlord, unlike farm owners who bore all of the risk. African Americans farmers were frequently in this position and were, in fact, disproportionately sharecroppers. Sharecropping was a way station, a rung, on the "agricultural ladder," requiring more experience and resources than wage labor but far less than farm ownership. With persistence and more than a little luck, a sharecropper might move up the ladder, eventually acquiring a farm. In fact, many did, including African Americans. In 1900 roughly 25 percent of African American farmers were owner-operators compared with hardly any in 1870.

Although sharecropping did not "cause" southern poverty, it nevertheless profoundly shaped social and class relations, along with race. Sharecroppers, particularly African Americans, were expected to behave in certain ways, mindful of their economic status and their place in the social order. Those who violated the social customs could face horrendous consequences especially if they were black—a beating or, worse, a noose.

If sharecropping did not cause the decline in labor productivity in postbellum southern agriculture, what did? The disappearance of the gang system was the most important culprit. Average farm size fell, a telltale sign that the economies of scale associated with gang production had been lost. The decline was compounded by a relatively high cost of capital after the Civil War, which made capital goods, such as mules and seed, expensive relative to labor.

After the initial decline in per capita income, why did the southern economy not recover more quickly? The issue here, in economic terms, is "convergence"—if a place has low income on average, certain economic forces should cause the economy to grow faster than those elsewhere, eventually narrowing differences in income across space. Examples of such forces are migration of capital and labor. After the Civil War, wages in the South were low relative to other parts of the United States, while the cost of capital was high. Labor should have left the South, while capital should have flowed to the region. The outflow of labor would have raised wages for those remaining behind, as would have the influx of capital.

Paradoxically, the outflow of labor from the South might have been greater had the South not been so poor. Migration, after all, is costly. The near poor are more likely to migrate than the very poor. Inadequate education plays a role here—better-educated southerners, black or white, were more likely to migrate from the region. Immigrant labor networks established during the antebellum period facilitated economic growth in the North after the Civil War. When immigration was abruptly cut off during World War I, southern workers, blacks especially, were able to "get a foot in the door" in northern factories.

However, while a variety of factors and institutions kept the southern economy from converging more quickly, thereby keeping southerners poorer than otherwise, there was little that was distinctively southern about this phenomenon. Outside of the South there were poorer states, such as Minnesota, where per capita income was very low relative to richer states, such as Connecticut. Indeed, circa 1900 the ratio of per capita income of Minnesota to Connecticut was about the same as income per capita of the South was relative to the rest of the nation. Yet the pace of economic convergence between poor and rich states outside the South during the first half of the 20th century was only somewhat faster than the pace of convergence between the South and the rest of the country. The primary reason why the South remained poor for so long was the depth of the decline in per capita income experienced after the Civil War, not anything special about its economic institutions.

Eventually the forces of convergence won out, and the southern economy began to substantially close the income gap with rest of the United States.

Southern convergence began after World War II and was especially rapid before 1960, a period that also encompassed substantial outmigration from the region. Agricultural productivity increased with mechanization, especially of cotton agriculture. It is widely believed that the invention and diffusion of reliable air-conditioning (which was preceded by electrification via such agencies as the Tennessee Valley Authority) also raised labor productivity, and thus incomes, in the South. Improvements in the region's public schools also fostered convergence by augmenting the supply of educated labor, which, as previously noted, was (and is) more geographically mobile.

The benefits of postwar economic growth were broad enough to trickle down through the income distribution so, as the southern economy grew, the proportion of southerners living in poverty declined sharply. The federal government began to monitor the poverty rate in the United States in the early 1960s. In 1959, the first year for which reliable national estimates are available, the poverty rate in the South was 35.4 percent—35 percent of southerners lived below the poverty line—compared with 22.4 percent for the country as a whole. Ten years later, the poverty rate in the South was cut in half, to 17.9 percent, and the gap with the rest of country had fallen to 5.8 percentage points. Further declines in southern poverty took place in the 1970s, absolutely and relative to other regions, but relatively little further change took place after 1980. In 2008, the most recent year of data, the poverty rate in the South was 14.3 percent, just slightly higher (8 percent) than in the country as a whole.

Declines in the southern poverty rate were especially important in narrowing the income gap between African Americans and whites. Although out-migration and economic growth were important factors in raising black incomes before 1960, recent work by Nobel Prize–winning economist James Heckman has established the critical role played by federal antidiscrimination legislation from the mid-1960s to mid-1970s. Antidiscrimination enforcement was disproportionately targeted at the South, and there is strong evidence that such enforcement raised the employment rates of African Americans in better-paying jobs. In recent decades the South has become a more reliable source of middle-class jobs for African Americans than other regions—in effect, the "New Promised Land."

Although "South" is no longer a synonym for poverty, the poor have not been banished from the southern scene. In the South, as elsewhere, poverty now has a quite different geography than it did a century ago. Today's poverty tends to be concentrated in blighted inner-city neighborhoods or remote rural hamlets whose residents are physically, socially, and economically segregated from the economic mainstream. Places of concentrated poverty are found everywhere in the United States today, not just in the South. The challenge today is to craft public policies that can attack the root causes of concentrated poverty, which are very different from the causes of southern poverty historically.

ROBERT A. MARGO
Boston University

John J. Donohue III and James Heckman, *Journal of Economic Literature* (December 1991); Robert W. Fogel, *Without Consent or Contract: The Rise and Fall of American Slavery* (1989); Robert A. Margo, in *The South as an American Problem*, ed. Larry J. Griffin and Don D. Doyle (1995); C. Vann Woodward, *The Burden of Southern History* (1960).

Race and Labor, since 1865

Since Emancipation, the question of race has been at the heart of organized labor's efforts in the South. As early as the 1860s, the nascent American labor movement confronted the dilemma that faced it well into the 20th century, namely whether to *exclude* black workers from unions as a means of limiting the labor supply or to *recruit* African Americans in behalf of common interests. The leaders of the American Federation of Labor (AFL, established 1886) often proclaimed the latter position, but in fact many of its affiliated unions, as well as the independent railroad brotherhoods, followed the former option. Most barred blacks from membership or relegated them to second-class status. Meanwhile, more inclusive organizations such as the Knights of Labor (KOL, founded 1869) and the Industrial Workers of the World (IWW, founded 1905), along with a handful of AFL unions, welcomed blacks, albeit with varying degrees of enthusiasm.

A more egalitarian strand of biracial organization emerged in the 1930s and 1940s, as the Congress of Industrial Organizations (CIO, established 1935-38), focused attention on the increasingly important role of black workers in the southern economy. Also important was the determination of black workers to form their own unions, sometimes apart from the mainstream labor movement. The most notable example of this development was the Brotherhood of Sleeping Car Porters, founded in 1925, which, under the leadership of Florida-born A. Philip Randolph, provided a base for labor and civil rights activism in southern communities. For most of the 1865-1980 period, racial factors were expressed as a black-white binary, but by the turn of the 21st century the presence of large numbers of Latino immigrant workers was complicating southern labor's historic narrative.

In the first decades of its existence, the AFL's ambivalent attitude toward inclusion of African Americans became clear. In 1891 the AFL convention castigated unions that "exclude from membership persons on account of race or color." Many of its affiliated unions, however, barred blacks, either outright or indirectly, sometimes through their control of municipal licensing ordinances. One important example was the International Association of Machinists (IAM), founded in Atlanta in 1888. The IAM initially barred blacks from membership but eventually accepted a technical modification of its constitution that left the policy of racial exclusion intact. Meanwhile, the pages of the *American Federationist*, the AFL's national organ, were peppered with dismissive commentary about black workers' suitability as unionists. White-controlled railroad unions in the South were aggressive in their attacks on African Americans, often using violence and intimidation to drive black firemen out of locomotive cabs and marginalize them in the roundhouses and repair shops. Such violence worked against hopes of class-based alliances across racial lines.

Despite long odds, biracial union activism sometimes emerged. The KOL, which flourished briefly in the mid-1880s, recruited thousands of black miners and agricultural workers. In the 1900s and 1910s, the IWW's militant industrial unionism attracted activists of both races who built short-lived biracial organizations in southwestern mines and timberlands. In the coal mines of Alabama and in the Gulf Coast ports, black and white workers practiced forms of biracial organization. The story in the Birmingham area, a rapidly expanding iron- and steel-producing center, however, was different and more characteristic. There, white metal and smelter workers excluded blacks from their unions and insisted that they remain in subordinate job categories.

During World War I opportunities for more equal treatment seemed at first possible. Federal agencies sometimes followed the logic of wartime mobilization to intervene in behalf of black workers in urban transport, laundries, and on the railroads, but the sudden end of the war aborted this tendency. With the government's backing, the brotherhoods quickly resumed efforts to drive blacks out of the operating trades.

The rise of the CIO in the 1930s and the labor demands of World War II, however, brought a more egalitarian brand of unionism to the South and increased hopes of working-class alliances among whites and blacks. Even before the birth of this federation of industrial unions in 1935, the United Mine Workers had reorganized itself in Alabama along biracial lines and the Southern Tenant Farmers' Union recruited impoverished agricultural workers of both races. CIO activists appreciated the key role played by black workers in southern industries and sought to challenge the conservative political orientation of the Solid South. Communists and other radicals organized wood workers, metal and smelter workers, tobacco and food processing workers, and others in integrated unions.

By the end of the war, the CIO could count about a quarter-million black members, perhaps half of them in the South. Even so, CIO activists found that they had to perform a balancing act in southern workplaces. Union-supported upgrading of black workers sometimes triggered violent resistance among the white majority. The textile industry, the South's largest by far, remained lily white, and white workers' resistance to Communist-oriented CIO affiliates in cigarette manufacture, food processing, and metalworking remained strong.

Challenged by the rival CIO, the AFL began cautiously to address the problems faced by black workers. To be sure, during the war affiliated unions that practiced blatant discrimination, notably in the booming shipyards and aircraft plants, flourished. Even so, AFL leaders aligned themselves verbally with the cause of racial equality. And some black workers in the South did find opportunities within segregated unions to attain leadership roles and to link their union activities to civil rights struggles in southern states and communities. By the end of the war, the AFL counted about 700,000 black members, more than 400,000 of them in southern states.

After the war, both labor federations sought to increase their southern membership. In the politically conservative postwar environment, however, neither was very successful. Moreover, as the issue of communism, both domestic and foreign, came to dominate public discourse, the leaders of the CIO distanced the industrial union body from its pro-Soviet affiliates, several of which had been in the forefront of biracial unionism.

Throughout the postwar period, the most significant developments affecting the relationship between organized labor and African American workers in the South involved the changing legal environment. Especially after passage of the Civil Rights Act of 1964, whose Title VII outlawed racial discrimination in employment, African American membership in unions representing southern pulp and paper workers, textile workers, and other industrial, transport, and service workers expanded owing in part to litigation brought by private parties and supported by the federal Equal Employment Opportunities Commission. In general, the national unions in these fields supported black workers' employment rights and welcomed African American workers into the unions. In many cases, however, on the local union level, African Americans found white fellow workers, along with managerial and supervisory personnel, hostile and resentful. In some cases, black workers, deeming their unions little more than agents of white privilege, petitioned the National Labor Relations Board to terminate union representation altogether.

Just as black workers made inroads into previously all-white industries and trades, employment patterns in the South began shifting away from these very sectors. Thus, for example, in the 1960s and 1970s, African Americans made major employment gains in the textile and pulp and paper industry and began to gain entry into skilled positions on the railroads and steel mills even as these industries began to shrink or to relocate. At the end of the century, the deindustrialization of the South accelerated, devastating southern unions in metalworking, transport, pulp and paper, and textiles and reversing employment gains African American workers had made.

African Americans in the South enjoyed somewhat more enduring success in the realm of public employment. In Memphis in the spring of 1968, Dr. Martin Luther King Jr. eloquently connected the efforts of the city's poorly paid and ill-treated sanitation workers to gain improved conditions, recognition of their union, and respect to the ongoing struggle for civil rights. Victory in the strike was, of course, tempered by the tragic murder of Dr. King in Memphis on April 4. Sanitation workers in other southern cities, along with hospital and other institutional workers, boosted minority membership in such unions as the American Federation of State, County, and Municipal Employees, Hospital Workers District 1199, and the Service Employees International Union (SEIU), organizations that stressed the connection between the civil rights movement and the efforts of low-skilled, poorly paid minority workers to gain both tangible improvements and greater respect on the job. The civil rights–labor connection, however, was fragile. Thus, for example, in 1977, Atlanta's African American Mayor Maynard Jackson fired striking sanitation workers wholesale, lest their rights-based activism jeopardize relations with the city's white-owned banks and corporate investors.

By the turn of the new century, the demographic profile of the southern working class was shifting dramatically. Whole new industries such as poultry raising and processing emerged, employing thousands, many of them recent Central American migrants. In 1980, 2.5 percent of the South's population was Hispanic; by the mid-2000s the figure had climbed to over 8 percent. Examples of multiethnic and black-Hispanic union activism did emerge, notably in the entertainment, senior care, and institutional medical sectors. In Florida, for example, SEIU pulled together multiethnic coalitions of church and civic organizations to support organizing campaigns among low-wage native and immigrant nursing home and health-care workers. At the same time, concerns about competition from immigrant workers and emotional public discourse over immigration reform highlighted perceived conflicts of interest between native black workers and their immigrant counterparts.

The history of the relationship between African Americans in the South and the American labor movement reveals a drift on the part of the latter toward ever-increasing degrees of acceptance and even cultivation. As organized labor's presence in the South (and nationally) has continued to shrink, a labor movement once characterized by racial exclusivism has become increasingly dependent on minority workers (and female workers), especially in the expanding service sector. There is thus an irony at the heart of the story of black workers and the labor movement in the South: even as organized labor has become more accommodating and progressive in its racial attitudes and policies, it has continued to diminish as a factor in southern life.

ROBERT H. ZIEGER
University of Florida

Michael K. Honey, *Going Down Jericho Road: The Memphis Strike, Martin Luther King's Last Campaign* (2007); Timothy J. Minchin, *Hiring the Black Worker: The Racial Integration of the Southern Textile Industry, 1960–1980* (1999); Robert H. Zieger, *For Jobs and Freedom: Race and Labor in America since 1865* (2007).

Racial Attitudes

Southern whites of all social classes internalized and acted on white supremacist ideology until at least the civil rights era, but class differences in the expression, precise content, and intensity of whites' racist beliefs were nevertheless unmistakable. Upper-class whites, for instance, frequently adopted a paternalistic (if thoroughly white supremacist) stance toward African Americans "in their charge," whereas the region's lower-strata whites more often openly expressed fear of blacks, extreme animosity toward them, and a strong desire for the physical separation of the races. Political and economic white elites, whatever their racial beliefs, also regularly used the often-violent "Negrophobia" of poor and economically insecure whites as a weapon against blacks and their white allies during times of racial insurgency and class conflict. Working-class southern whites and impoverished white farmers, again despite their racial opinions, moreover, sometimes (as in the Populist uprising and again in the 1930s) sought to transcend racial bigotry to forge strategic class alliances with African Americans. What African Americans themselves thought of whites of different classes is less visible for several reasons, but no less complex. Southern blacks often feared their white co-regionalists (especially violence-prone lower-strata whites), covertly expressed contempt for whites regardless of the latter's class status, sometimes looked to white elites for protection and patronage, and respected, allied themselves with, and felt genuine affection for others.

Precisely how each race felt about the other, and the extent of class differences in these feelings, is difficult to gauge, in part because scholars, at times lacking direct evidence, have had to infer racial beliefs from behavior and in part because of the messiness of the very notion of "racial attitude." When social scientists discuss attitudes, they usually mean consciously held favorable or unfavorable sentiments about, or assessments of, an inanimate object or idea (e.g., the American South), a group of people (e.g., southerners), or a specific individual (e.g., Dr. Martin Luther King Jr.). Although often grounded in and sometimes difficult to distinguish from an individual's understandings of factual truth, attitudes are properly understood as evaluations of, or opinions about, that perceived truth. Moreover, while attitudes are related both to one's personal moral standards and to social norms, which are peoples' understandings of society's behavioral prescriptions and proscriptions, they differ from both. Attitudes are important to study because they illuminate the belief systems of individuals and groups, because they predispose people to act in patterned ways, and because they powerfully condition future behavior, even if not always in a direct or precise way.

Racial attitudes are opinions about, or assessments of, issues or peoples that are explicitly understood in racial ways. Public pollsters have traced Americans' racial attitudes since the 1930s, and very systematic and nationally representative studies of such beliefs have been conducted by prestigious academic research organizations since the 1960s. One of the most respected social surveys eliciting racial attitudes is the General Social Survey (GSS), fielded by the National Opinion Research Center at the University of Chicago since 1972. Unlike many public polls, information collected by the GSS usually is derived from face-to-face interviews. Compared to data collected from computer-assisted telephone interviews (and certainly compared to self-selective Internet surveys), face-to-face interviews normally yield more accurate, more representative, and richer information about what people think about race. Coupling the data collected from the GSS and other scientific polls to theories of race relations, scholars have identified quite distinct kinds of racial attitudes. We describe and analyze six types here.

First are generalizations or stereotypes about races and racial differences. This type of racial attitude appears initially to be factually informed, but if "facts" are at all incorporated into racial stereotypes, they are done so in a highly selectively, biased fashion and then indiscriminately applied to all members of a racial group. Questions in the GSS that elicit racial stereotypes ask respondents to rate African Americans and whites on a "hardworking/lazy" scale.

Second are attitudes about the ideal social distance between the races. An example of a social distance question, again (as are the remaining questions we discuss) from the GSS, queries whites about their support for or opposition to a family member marrying an African American.

Third are attitudes about whether members of different races should be treated equally. Such opinions, known as "equality principles," are tapped in surveys by question such as, "If your party nominated an African American for President, would you vote for him if he were qualified for the job?"

Opinions about equality principles—specifically whites' beliefs that African Americans are not their biological or cultural equals—as well as whites' negative stereotypes about blacks and their desire for social distance from them, largely constitute what is commonly understood to be "racial prejudice." Prejudicial understandings and representations of African American spurred southern whites of all social classes to implement and fight to retain state-mandated racial segregation during the Jim Crow era. (Whites in the region also had other, nonprejudicial reasons to enact and enforce segregation laws—for instance, the elimination of economic and political competition.)

Fourth are attitudes about the execution of equality principles—that is, about if and how to ensure that the principle of equal treatment is implemented in law. One such implementation question in the GSS asks respondents if they would vote for a law mandating open housing or, instead, would vote to permit homeowners to sell their homes to whomever they wished, even if the homeowner chose not to sell to African Americans.

Fifth are attributions people make, or the beliefs they hold, about the causes of racial disparities in jobs, income, and housing between whites and African Americans. These "explanations," like racial stereotypes, appear on the surface to be factually based but are nonetheless inevitably evaluative and hence are accurately understood as racial attitudes. The GSS queries respondents about their beliefs about four putative causes of black material disadvantage: one evokes biological racism ("less inborn ability"), one targets blacks' alleged cultural deficiencies ("lack of motivation/willpower"), and two implicate racist institutional and systemic factors (lack of access to quality education, "discrimination").

Sixth are opinions about remedial or affirmative governmental action designed to reduce or eliminate post–civil rights racial inequalities. These attitudes go beyond either accepting general equality principles or supporting their implementation: affirmative action policies are intended to make up for past discrimination against African Americans and might require individuals or groups to trade strict numerical parity for racial equity and justice. One widely used affirmative action question asks respondents if they favor or oppose "preferential hiring and promotion" of African Americans.

Types of racial attitudes are empirically (if imperfectly) related to one another, and most people demonstrate some degree of consistency across these domains. Thus, for example, if one believes the primary cause of racial disparities is discrimination or a lack of educational opportunity, then one is more likely to favor affirmative actions to redress these wrongs. Conversely, if a white stereotypes African Americans as lazy or otherwise intrinsically inferior to whites, he is more likely to oppose a family member marrying an African American.

Opinions about the implementation of equality principles, affirmative action, and reasons for white advantage need not necessarily involve racial prejudice. For example, one may believe that property rights trump efforts to achieve racial equality (i.e., one should be able to sell one's house to whomever one wishes), or believe affirmative action policies themselves violate equality principles. Neither belief instances racial prejudice. But if, as many scholars argue, such opinions contribute, even unintentionally, to the persistence of America's long-standing and large racial inequalities—by delegitimizing remedial government policies, for example, or by denying the existence of racial discrimination, or by blaming blacks themselves for their plight—these attitudes, though nonprejudicial, nonetheless objectively harm the economic standing and life chances of people of color. Some scholars, therefore, label such beliefs "color-blind racism" or, especially if they are linked to attributions about African Americans' cultural deficits, "laissez-faire racism" to differentiate them from white supremacist ideology and overt racial prejudice.

Survey research has shown both that whites' expressed racial prejudice has markedly decreased since the 1970s, especially so in the South, and that their support for the implementation of equality principles and some remedial programs has increased over the same period. Part of the liberalization of whites' racial attitudes, however, may be less real than apparent because of the workings of a "social desirability" factor, whereby respondents tell interviewers what they, the respondents, believe is the socially acceptable response to racially charged questions rather than their true opinion. Still, social desirability is indicative of more liberal racial norms (e.g., even racial bigots know they are out of step with the cultural mainstream and attempt to mask their bigotry) and, in any case, is unlikely to have induced so substantial a shift in whites' racial sensibilities. Whites' support for affirmative action per se, on the other hand, has been consistently low for several decades, and they are less likely now than 30 years ago to believe discrimination against African Americans is the main reason for racial inequalities in housing, income, and the like. Less is known generally about the racial attitudes of African Americans or about class differences in racial opinions of either southern blacks or whites.

Different indicators of a person's social class will of course produce somewhat different estimates of how the class positions of individuals affect their racial attitudes. When we look at the last three General Social Surveys (2006, 2008, 2010), we find that subjective class identity—that is, where people place themselves in a class hierarchy (e.g., working class, middle class)—generally yields fewer class differences than we find with education, although the direction of the effects is usually the same for both class indicators.

Education is a crucial gauge of social class: it is both the best single expression of cultural capital (essentially competitively advantageous values, dispositions, knowledge, presentational and linguistic styles, and routines) and a major determinant, through both skill enhancement and credentials, of other dimensions of class, most particularly occupational placement and earnings. Advanced schooling also deepens one's stock of factual knowledge and usually is thought to induce greater cognitive openness and complexity, thus assisting the highly educated in questioning and rebuffing what passes for accepted wisdom.

Class differences in the racial attitudes of black and white southerners, as proxied by four categories of education attainment (did not graduate from high school, high school graduate, completed some college but did not graduate, and four or more years of college), are shown in Table 11 (African Americans) and Table 12 (whites). We combine the 2006, 2008, and 2010 GSSs to increase the number of respondents in the analysis (particularly important when focusing on subgroups defined by region and race) and thus the stability and reliability of the results.

The region's African Americans, unsurprisingly, espouse racial views that are substantially more "problack" and liberal than do southern whites. This is true for almost all attitudinal domains and educational levels in the tables. Racial differences in beliefs about racial stratification and in support for affirmative action are generally large, pointing to the difficulty of forming a biracial coalition committed to racial remediation. More germane for our purposes, however, is how southern blacks' educational credentials affect their racial opinions about members of both races (see Table 11). Although the class effects are neither universal across all questions (see, e.g., the results for presidential voting) nor generally large, they are patterned. African Americans with either a college diploma or some postgraduate work, when compared to other blacks in the region, less frequently stereotype blacks or whites as either lazy or hard-

TABLE 11. *Racial Attitudes of African Americas, U.S. South, 2006–2010*

Type of Racial Attitude/Question	Less Than High School	High School Graduate	Some College	College Graduate or Postgraduate
Racial stereotyping:				
blacks hardworking/lazy	45%/32%	40%/28%	31%/26%	34%/19%
whites hardworking/lazy	44%/21%	43%/21%	38%/20%	38%/15%
Social distance: opposed to family member marrying a black	NA	NA	NA	NA
Equality principle: vote for black presidential candidate	100%	98%	99%	100%
Implementation of equality principle: vote for open housing law	70%	79%	76%	82%
Reasons for racial inequalities/black disadvantage:				
discrimination	54%	62%	49%	67%
blacks have less inborn ability	22%	18%	11%	5%
lack of educational opportunity for blacks	46%	48%	46%	60%
blacks have insufficient motivation/willpower	57%	50%	51%	22%
Remedial government action: support for affirmative action	42%	40%	37%	54%
Number of respondents	57–96	89–132	73–133	35–67

Source: Analysis of GSS data from Tom W. Smith, Peter V. Marsden, Michael Hout, and Jibum Kim, *General Social Surveys, 1972–2010* [machine-readable data file]. Principal Investigator, Tom W. Smith; Co-Principal Investigators, Tom W. Smith; Co-Principal Investigators, Peter V. Marsden and Michael Hout, NORC ed. (Chicago: National Opinion Research Center, producer, 2005; Storrs, Conn.: Roper Center for Public Opinion Research, University of Connecticut, distributor). 1 data file (55,087 logical records) and 1 codebook (3,610 pp).

TABLE 12. *Racial Attitudes of Whites, U.S. South, 2006–2010*

Type of Racial Attitude/Question	Less Than High School	High School Graduate	Some College	College Graduate or Postgraduate
Racial stereotyping:				
blacks Hardworking/Lazy	19%/48%	15%/39%	15%/38%	16%/31%
whites Hardworking/Lazy	49%/21%	40%/12%	39%/11%	37%/11%
Social distance: opposed to family member marrying a black	46%	40%	35%	25%
Equality principle: vote for black presidential candidate	87%	92%	95%	97%
Implementation of equality principle: vote for open housing law	64%	62%	61%	67%
Reasons for racial inequalities/black disadvantage:				
discrimination	35%	20%	24%	25%
blacks have less inborn ability	22%	11%	7%	2%
lack of educational opportunity for blacks	34%	28%	33%	48%
Blacks have insufficient motivation/willpower	69%	64%	60%	41%
Remedial government action: support for affirmative action	22%	10%	8%	9%
Number of respondents	119–195	204–341	181–331	213–358

Source: Analysis of GSS data from Tom W. Smith, Peter V. Marsden, Michael Hout, Jibum Kim, *General Social Surveys, 1972–2010*. [machine-readable data file]. Principal Investigator, Tom W. Smith; Co-Principal Investigators, Peter V. Marsden and Michael Hout, NORC ed. (Chicago: National Opinion Research Center, producer, 2005; Storrs, Conn.: Roper Center for Public Opinion Research, University of Connecticut, distributor). 1 data file (55,087 logical records) and 1 codebook (3,610 pp).

working, more frequently say that discriminatory processes or constricted education opportunities are responsible for racial disparities in jobs and housing and less often fault blacks themselves (either their lack of "inborn ability" or their insufficient motivation), and more often support race-based affirmative action policies to compensate for past discrimination. Majorities of less highly educated African Americans, in fact, actually opposed affirmative action in the 2006–10 GSSs.

Thanks in part to the industrialization of the South's economy, the enforcement of civil rights legislation and subsequent government racial policies, and African Americans' continuing struggles to open avenues of socioeconomic success, the black class structure has become increasingly differentiated along schooling and work axes in the past three to four decades. As this process continues, African Americans are apt to become progressively more divided — at least in some particulars — in their racial opinions and policy preferences.

Southern whites, too, are divided in their attitudes about race by social class, occasionally in ways that parallel the African American experience (see Table 12). More highly educated whites, when compared to those with less formal schooling, less often stereotype members of either race; say they require less social distance from blacks, at least in terms of familial intermarriage; more frequently claim to be willing to vote for an African American presidential candidate; and more often say that stymied educational opportunity rather than the failings of African Americans (again, either biological or cultural) is the culprit behind racial inequalities in housing and the like. Of course, highly educated white southerners are likely to be more aware of current racial norms, which eschew overt prejudice, and thus more attuned to when and how to mask their own racial bigotry with a socially desirable response. But on the whole, this stratum of whites tends to be less conservative in its expressed racial beliefs: the attitudinal distance between the most and the least educated southern whites was, in 2006–10, often quite large, on the order of 20 percentage points or more (e.g., stereotyping blacks as lazy, opposing a family member marrying an African American, believing that blacks' lack of ability or their lack of will power causes their relative material disadvantage).

That said, highly educated southern whites, at least as we can judge from these and similar data, are hardly "racial liberals." Only 16 percent of them believed Africans Americans tend to be "hardworking" (almost twice as many believe blacks "lazy"), and 41 percent were willing to opine to a complete stranger (i.e., the GSS interviewer) that racial inequalities result from blacks' motivational deficits. Only about a quarter of most highly educated white southerners, additionally, attribute these disparities directly to discrimination, and fewer than 10 percent either "support" or "strongly support" affirmative action. In contrast, more than a third of southern whites with less than a high school education view discrimination as the main cause of racial inequalities, and the least educated, though not generally supportive of affirmative action, were nevertheless more than twice as likely as whites who have at least graduated from college to say they support this type of remedial racial policy (22 percent vs. 9 percent).

One interpretation of this somewhat contradictory pattern is that upper-strata, highly educated southern whites have jettisoned "old fashioned" prejudice and bigotry—no small accomplishment, to be sure—but, perhaps because of their very labor market and educational success—are unable to grasp the reality of racial discrimination and, correspondingly, are unwilling to fund the redistribution of opportunity from the racial "haves" to the racial "have-nots." If affirmative action is understood to be a zero-sum game, so that African Americans benefit at the expense of socially mobile, credentialed whites, highly educated whites' resistance to racial remediation via interventionist public or private policies is perhaps understandable: it is not in their perceived class interest to do so. Lower-strata southern whites, on the other hand, may think themselves victims of class discrimination and believe others—including racial "others"—are also captive of the workings of unfair, arbitrary institutions beyond their control and mostly inaccessible to the "left-behind" and forgotten. Hence, some form of policy intervention, in the minds of a small minority of this stratum of southern whites, may be more acceptable. Racial attitudes matter, even if, at root, they are not always only about "race."

LARRY J. GRIFFIN
PEGGY G. HARGIS
Georgia Southern University

Eduardo Bonilla-Silva, *Racism without Racists: Color-Blind Racism and the Persistence of Racial Inequality in the United States* (2003); Lawrence Goodwyn, *Democratic Promise: The Populist Moment in America* (1976); Larry J. Griffin and Kenneth Bollen, *American Sociological Review* (August 2009); Larry J. Griffin and Peggy G. Hargis, *Southern Cultures* (Fall 2008); Matthew O. Hunt, ed., *Race, Racial Attitudes, and Stratification Beliefs* (2011); Mary R. Jackman, *Social Science Quarterly* (1996); Donald R. Kinder and Nicholas Winter, *American Journal of Political Science* (April 2001); Jack Temple Kirby, *The Countercultural South* (2005); Maria Krysan, *Annual Review of Sociology* (2000); James H. Kuklinski, Michael D. Cobb, and Martin Gilens, *Journal of Politics* (May 1997); Gunnar Myrdal, *An American Dilemma: The Negro Problem and Modern Democracy* (1944); Howard Schuman, Charlotte Steeh, Lawrence Bobo, and Maria Kyrsan, *Racial Attitudes in America: Trends and Interpreta-*

tions (1997); David O. Sears, Jim Sidanius, and Lawrence Bobo, eds., *Racialized Politics: The Debate about Racism in America* (2000); Paul Sniderman and Edward G. Carmines, *Reaching beyond Race* (1997); Melvyn Stokes and Rick Halpern, *Race and Class in the American South since 1980* (1994); Steven A. Tuch and Michael Hughes, *Social Science Quarterly* (June 1996); Simo V. Virtanen and Leonie Huddy, *Journal of Politics* (May 1998); William J. Wilson, *The Declining Significance of Race: Blacks and Changing American Institutions* (1978); C. Vann Woodward, *The Strange Career of Jim Crow* (1974).

Radicalism

Although the South has tended toward conservatism in the popular mind, it has actually nurtured various strains of radicalism. While some of these have been right-wing extremist, the southern radicalism discussed here involves a set of beliefs or politics that advance the interests of the poor and working classes. A major expression of these ideas has been in the southern labor movement. Historically, southern radicals have also (though not always) embraced a kind of "race radicalism" that seeks to unite poorer whites with the region's subjugated African Americans in search of greater economic power.

Because virtual oligarchy characterized regional governance until far into the 20th century, any alliance of blacks and poor whites has long tended to provoke extreme fear in the region's aristocracy. This reaction dates as far back as Bacon's Rebellion (1676) on Virginia's western frontier. Although that uprising centered on conflicts with native tribes, the prospect of indentured servants uniting with African slaves against colonial authority provoked a larger uproar that hardened slave laws.

As slavery came under increasing fire after 1850 and its defenders grew more shrill, southern officials reacted hyperbolically to even a hint of black-white unity—as, for example, when white North Carolinian Hinton Rowan Helper authored "A Poor White's Opinion of Slavery" (1857), criticizing slavery for its oppressive effect on nonslaveholding white farmers and calling for its end. Helper's work was excoriated and banned regionally, and it fueled heightened secessionism in the South even as it stoked abolitionism in the North.

By the time of the Civil War, many critics of slavery had left or been driven from the South. Thus, relatively few white southerners embraced the "Radical Republican" Party in its quest for a biracial democracy during the Reconstruction era (1865–77). As the region started, haltingly, to industrialize in the final decades of the 19th century, unionization began, but the fierce repression that greeted the very idea of organized labor kept its successes small, and the region lacked the diversity of new immigrants that enlivened the rest of the nation.

Amid economic downturns of that era, radical agrarian movements like the Populists got some regional foothold to demand a greater voice for working-class rural people. Among these campaigns were some instances of black-white cooperation.

Yet such alliances tended to be short-lived owing to the widespread influence of white supremacist ideology, which, in addition to crystallizing racial segregation into a system of laws, kept southern race radicalism—in fact dissenting views generally—at a minimum until the 20th century. By then, and especially by the 1930s as the Great Depression crept over the region, more southerners began to cross the racial divide in search of common economic uplift. Many began as liberals, but became race radicals in the face of the heated opposition even modest biracialism often provoked.

Begun within many Protestant denominations in response to grinding urban poverty at the turn of the century in the nation's now-teeming cities, the "Social Gospel" movement promoted social action as part of Christians' responsibility to the less fortunate among them. The social gospel messages of justice and good works caught on in white churches in southern towns, and they inspired new interracial cooperation campaigns across the region. These ranged from modestly liberal, reform-minded groups such as Jessie Daniel Ames's Association of Southern Women for the Prevention of Lynching (1930) to more radical initiatives such as the Highlander Folk School, a leadership training center established in southeast Tennessee in 1932 to educate southern workers on the value of unionism and (later) racial cooperation. Based on the model of Danish cooperative education, the school was founded by three young white, native-born, southern radicals: Myles Horton, a teacher who worked with Highlander until his death in 1990; Don West, an itinerant poet, trade unionist, and sometimes Communist Party organizer; and James Dombrowski, a Methodist minister turned race radical. These three men, all of them idealists motivated by a combination of religious and socialist principles, would devote their lives to promulgating various strains of southern radicalism in search of greater economic and racial equity. These efforts gathered steam as the 20th century unfolded.

As the Great Depression exposed the shortcomings of U.S. capitalism and fascism spread across Europe, President Franklin D. Roosevelt liberalized the Democratic Party by expanding the role of government with a set of "New Deal" federal programs to put people to work and enhance social welfare. His administration became the first in U.S. history to give its support to trade unionism.

Southern unionism predated Roosevelt's endorsement, especially in border South West Virginia, where the United Mine Workers (UMW) had fought pitched battles to organize miners. In 1920 miners had clashed with coal operators and police in the closest thing to an armed "class war" in southern (or U.S.) history, and though blood had flowed freely, the UMW prevailed. With FDR's support, however, such labor struggles now expanded even into the former plantation South, where white supremacy often split workers' solidarity. The largely white, mostly female textile workforce of Gastonia, N.C., and other parts of the Piedmont South protested low wages and absentee northern owners in large-scale walkouts and strikes in the late 1920s and early 1930s. The strikes met with violent retribution and the unions were mostly crushed. Yet slain heroines like Gastonia's Ella May Wiggins (a singer-poet who led the walkout and sang and spoke at rallies) were memorialized in cultural forms such as novels and ballads that became part of southern radicalism and kept the saga of those struggles alive. Organizing among miners widened across the southern Appalachians as well.

These upsurges and many like them were part of another important source that boosted southern radicalism in this era—a new "Popular Front" policy initiated by the U.S. Communist Party (CP) to unite leftists with liberals and Roosevelt-style Democrats nationally for greater social reforms. Amid widespread economic suffering, the CP also identified black southerners as a possible vanguard of working-class revolt. Energized by the Depression, both the Socialist Party (SP) and the CP sent organizers south to organize blacks as well as whites into unions. Two of the most vibrant campaigns were the SP-inspired Southern Tenant Farmers' Union in Arkansas and the CP-led Alabama Share Croppers' Union. Such initiatives were brutally repressed by landowners and police. Yet by mobilizing agricultural workers—among the region's most downtrodden—they also inspired some middle-class, intellectual, and elite sympathizers. One was First Lady Eleanor Roosevelt, who encouraged her husband's liberalism, especially on matters of race. When a presidential commission on economic conditions in the South identified the region as "the nation's Number 1 economic problem," Eleanor Roosevelt attended a 1938 regional gathering in response that drew to Birmingham hundreds of southerners who supported the New Deal, trade unionism, and the expansion of social welfare. Although the conference was predominantly white and liberal, it attracted a significant number of blacks and a small contingent of socialists and communists—a diversity that provoked controversy.

That conference, which founded the Southern Conference for Human Welfare (SCHW), represented a turning point for the "Popular Front" in the South. Assembled to deal with class and economic inequities, attendees were immediately forced to confront the rigidly enforced boundaries that segregated blacks from whites by law in the region's industrial center when their first meeting was raided by the Birmingham police, who demanded segregated seating. Although forced to comply, the conferees vowed never to hold another segregated meeting, and Eleanor Roosevelt symbolically placed her chair between the two sections. While the SCHW was immediately lambasted as "communistic" and thus "un-American" by some southern journalists and elected officials, it garnered support among others. Along with black-led organizations such as the CP-inspired Southern Negro Youth Congress (SNYC, founded two years earlier amid similar controversies), the SCHW became an important outlet for southerners to cross the color line, especially as World War II heightened civil rights activity.

The "Southern Conference" never became a mass movement, but its opposition to segregation and demand for civil liberties in the region boosted southern trade unionism and laid the groundwork for the modern civil rights movement that was soon to follow. The SCHW lasted for only one decade, squelched by a chronic lack of funds and constant anticommunist attacks that gained more legitimacy in the postwar years as the Cold War increasingly cast social protest in a suspicious light and muted the upsurge of organized labor of the Depression–World War II years. Yet in 1946 SCHW spawned a sister organization—the Southern Conference Educational Fund (SCEF)—that persisted into the 1970s and focused more exclusively on the fight against segregation, becoming one of the prime sources of white southern support for African Americans' civil rights.

Directed by the same Jim Dombrowski who had helped to found Highlander in the 1930s, SCEF held regional conferences and circulated publications (including a monthly newsletter, the *Southern Patriot*) criticizing racial separation and hierarchy. Such critiques were highly marginalized in the 1950s as the Cold War produced a domestic anticommunist hysteria used by segregationists to prop up "Jim Crow" as it crumbled. Those tiny currents of dissent, however, sustained a southern white radicalism that would offer small but significant support to the black freedom movement that burst forth in December 1955 in a Montgomery, Ala., bus boycott, catapulting Rev. Martin Luther King Jr. to prominence. Race radicalism would soon reemerge fully and in new forms with a youth-led generation of mass civil rights movement in 1960 with nonviolent sit-ins across the region demanding an end to legal segregation.

The standard-bearer for southern radicalism as the 1960s dawned was the Student Nonviolent Coordinating Committee (or SNCC, pronounced "Snick"), an organization formed in the spring of 1960 and led by black college students who had spearheaded the scores of sit-ins that had swept Nashville, Atlanta, and other southern cities and towns since the decade began. While these youth were (by and large) not ideologically tied to communism or any particular ideology, their methods of nonviolent direct action and their commitment to a "beloved community" that transcended racial and other barriers and eschewed material comfort or even safety in favor of liberation marked them as radical. Another new element was the visibility of young white supporters in their ranks in spite of the fact that southern universities and colleges were routinely segregated. As the movement's "shock troops," SNCC youth pushed older leaders like King toward more radical agendas and led drives that more or less broke down segregation in southern public accommodations by late 1961. Their willingness to endure beatings, abuse, arrest, long confinements, and even death led them to tackle Mississippi—bastion of white supremacy—where their frontal assault on Jim Crow segregation helped to achieve the Civil Rights Act in 1964, followed by the Voting Rights Act in 1965. Their radical methods and commitments trained many and inspired many more young southerners later in the 1960s who applied similar tactics to oppose the Vietnam War, to usher in more freedoms on college campuses, and to support campaigns for black, Mexican American, Appalachian, women's, and later gay liberation. Activists of that generation also reinvented 1930s-style cultural activism in the form of alternative southern publications and music that advocated social justice.

Widespread white opposition and the intransigence of racism in southern institutions ate away at the interracial beloved community that SNCC originally sought, and a conservative white backlash to 1960s reforms found especially fertile ground in the South by the late 1970s, inspired in part by segregationist politicians such as former Alabama governor George Wallace. In the last decades of the 20th century, "Religious Right" ultraconservatism overtook the Social Gospel religious currents of earlier in the century; yet southern radicalism is still frequently informed by more socialist-minded strains of Christianity (an example of which is Atlanta's Open Door Community, a street ministry that since the 1980s has led local campaigns against homelessness and economic exploitation of day laborers). Although mass social protest declined in the region during the final quarter of the 20th century, southern radicalism found continued vibrancy in lasting cultural outlets (alternative newspapers, feminist bookstores, musical gatherings and theater troupes—some of which remained in existence into the 21st century); in antinuclear, antiviolence, union, and pro-environment crusades of the 1980s; and in a multiracial "Rainbow Coalition" movement that supported the African American Rev. Jesse Jackson's presidential campaigns in 1984 and 1988.

In spite of the South's much-touted conservatism in the 21st century, one outcome of the civil rights and civil liberties battles of the previous century has been greater legitimacy for dissenting voices than ever before in southern history. Although still not numerically large within the "Sunbelt South" and on occasion still subject to social sanction, today's southern radicals are considerably freer to criticize social injustices than were their predecessors. They range from southern affiliates of the radically prolabor "Jobs with Justice" to spontaneous protests against the Iraq wars to regional organizations such as Southerners on New Ground (SONG), formed in the 1990s by a biracial group of southern lesbians working on a range of issues related to class, race, the rights of immigrants and rural people, and the right to same-sex relationships. Southern race-radicalism still undergirds much of that contemporary activism.

CATHERINE FOSL
University of Louisville

Clayborne Carson, *In Struggle: SNCC and the Black Awakening of the 1960s* (1981); David Chalmers, *And the Crooked Places Made Straight: The Struggle for Social Change in the 1960s* (1991); Anthony P. Dunbar, *Against the Grain: Southern Radicals and Prophets, 1929–1959* (1981); Robin D. G. Kelley, *Hammer and Hoe: Alabama Communists during the Great Depression* (1990); Patricia Sullivan, *Days of Hope: Race and Democracy in the New Deal Era* (1996); Howard Zinn, *A People's History of the United States* (1980, 2010).

Radio, Television, and Film

Representations of social class in the South as depicted through radio, television, and film have focused primarily on either the top of the white social hierarchy, the plantation image, or the bottom of that hierarchy, the image of "poor whites" or hillbillies. As John Shelton Reed observed in his classic study of southern social types, "the class structure of the mythic South is peculiarly truncated." The cultural amnesia surrounding historical gradations in the South's social structure derived in part from a literary tradition dating back to colonial and antebellum observers who originated and then popularized the notion of a two-class South. Early silent films reinforced this binary understanding through their need to rely on stock types that would be easily recognized by the audience, and both films and radio drew on established types from stage productions, including vaudeville, minstrel shows, and adaptations of literary works. When television became the dominant medium in the second half of the 20th century, producers inherited the well-worn southern types and perpetuated them.

Depictions of the plantation South have featured a fairly consistent cast of elite white characters, including the gentleman, the colonel, the lady, and the belle. Though the romanticized view of the Old South captured in *Gone with the Wind* (1939) and a bevy of likeminded films in the first half of the 20th century gave way to more critical readings of the antebellum South in the wake of the civil rights movement, many of the stock plantation characters remained, thus legitimizing the myths even as newer films criticized the slave system. The plantation mythology included a variety of African American social types as well, including the mammy, Uncle Tom, and Sambo characters, but such types served to depict race relations in the South rather than address class considerations. Popular representations devoted even less attention to the nuanced class distinctions among black southerners than they did to those among whites. When nonelite white southerners appeared as part of the plantation myth, they were billed as "poor white trash," ranking lower in the social hierarchy than even plantation slaves, who were sometimes depicted as looking down on them.

A separate genre of representation in radio, television, and film has placed nonelite white southerners at the center of the story rather than on the periphery. Such whites appear in a variety of guises ranging from harmless to menacing and differentiated by considerations of geography and gender. Residents of the mountain South have most often been characterized as hillbillies. Male hillbillies have been depicted as backward, lazy, unkempt fools, mystified by the modern conveniences of urban life. The Clampetts of television's *The Beverly Hillbillies* (1962–71) provide examples of this type. Such hillbillies, often moonshiners by profession, are a nonthreatening source of comic relief. Female hillbillies have been characterized as more industrious than their male counterparts and as fountains of folk wisdom with a penchant for gossip. By creating Minnie Pearl, one of the *Grand Ole Opry*'s signature characters, comedienne Sarah Cannon personified this type, entertaining radio and television audiences alike. The *Grand Ole Opry* (1925–present) and similar barn dance radio programs featured not only the comic hillbilly but also the more serious mountaineer. This type was embodied by the Carter family of Virginia, whose traditional Appalachian ballads were first introduced to radio audiences through the 1927 Bristol sessions, record producer Ralph Peer's early effort to commercialize the music of the mountains. The mountaineer was devoted to family and religion, morally and racially innocent by virtue of geographic isolation, and, ultimately, tragic, an outmoded remnant of the region's past. Television's *The Waltons* (1972–81) showcased the simple virtues and strong family values of the mountaineer type, offering a bucolic retreat from modern American life. Though images of hillbillies could provide comic relief and idyllic escape, they could also inspire fear. Menacing hillbilly villains were depicted as violent, drunk, inbred, and depraved. The 1972 film *Deliverance* featured the most terrifying and memorable specimens of this type.

Early country music bore the label "hillbilly" and was associated with many of the negative stereotypes of the mountain South. Seeking to craft a more positive image to appeal to their working-class audience, many country music stars cultivated a western image, dressing as singing cowboys and cowgirls starting in the 1930s and 1940s. "Hillbilly" music fused with styles introduced from Texas to become known as "country and western" music before being labeled simply "country." Western imagery invoked an independent frontier existence free from the restrictions of urban life in the East, while the cowboy was a mythic figure from the American past rather than from the South. Country music stars, including Hank Williams and his Drifting Cowboys band, Loretta Lynn, and "outlaws" Willie Nelson and Waylon Jennings, adopted western styles at various points in their careers. As a character in country songs, the cowboy was a hard-drinking, hard-loving "good-timing man" whose exploits could turn a long-suffering "good-hearted woman" into a hardened honky-tonk angel.

The small-town and rural lowland South featured its own unique cast of characters. The residents of Dayton, Tenn.—who were lambasted by journalist H. L. Mencken during the 1925 Scopes trial as fundamentalist yokels driven by religious fervor and mob mentality—were immortalized in the 1960 film *Inherit the Wind*, based on a 1955 play of the same name, which used small-town southerners' devotion to "Old Time Religion" to make a statement about the excesses of McCarthyism. A more positive image of small-town southern life was showcased in the television show, *The Dukes of Hazzard* (1979–85). Though good old boys Bo and Luke Duke drove their car, the General Lee, too fast and enjoyed the occasional country song at the rowdy local bar, they also challenged the corruption of town authorities in the name of upholding their own vision of right and wrong. Family patriarch Uncle Jesse celebrated the values of family, country, and traditional morality. Meanwhile, Cousin Daisy represented a common female type, the good old girl, who was characterized as a buxom, competent beauty who could drive as fast as the boys. A more sinister type than the good old boy was the small-town redneck, who was similar to the menacing hillbilly. Rednecks were depicted as ignorant, violent, and, above all, racist. After the civil rights era, films, such as *Mississippi Burning* (1988) and *A Time to Kill* (1996), pictured violent rednecks motivated by racial hatred as the ultimate southern villains. Elsewhere, the label "redneck" has been adopted as an expression of pride, as in Gretchen Wilson's 2004 song "Redneck Woman," in which she reveled in her working-class status and declared her affinity for beer, honky-tonks, and pick-up trucks.

Hillbillies have been characterized as fools, yet those same fools have proved capable of revealing the materialism, greed, and corruption of urban life, as did the Clampetts and the Dukes. Mountaineers and their music have been celebrated as relics of the colonial American and even European past, as many folk songs have been traced back to British roots. The South has been viewed at times as a repository of traditional American values, such as devotion to country, family, and religion. Contemporary country music celebrates these values and, as such, has gained incredible popularity among conservative middle-class Americans nationwide. Finally, through the image of the depraved hillbilly or the violent racist, the working-class white southern male continues to serve as a scapegoat for the racial sins of white southerners of all classes and for those of the nation as a whole.

LEEANN G. REYNOLDS
Samford University

Dwight B. Billings, Gurney Norman, and Katherine Ledford, eds., *Confronting Appalachian Stereotypes: Back Talk from an American Region* (1999); Edward D. C. Campbell Jr., *The Celluloid South: Hollywood and the Southern Myth* (1981); Allison Graham, *Framing the South: Hollywood, Television, and Race during the Civil Rights Struggle* (2001); Jack Temple Kirby, *Media-Made Dixie: The South in the American Imagination* (1986); Kristine M. McCusker, *Lonesome Cowgirls and Honky-Tonk Angels: The Women of Barn Dance Radio* (2008); John Shelton Reed, *Southern Folk, Plain and Fancy: Native White Social Types* (1986); Cecelia Tichi, ed., *Reading Country Music: Steel Guitars, Opry Stars, and Honky-Tonk Bars* (1998); J. W. Williamson, *Hillbillyland: What the Movies Did to the Mountains and What the Mountains Did to the Movies* (1995).

Reconstruction and Redemption

Few periods in U.S. history have undergone more radical historiographical revisions than the decade and a half following Confederate defeat, bemoaned as the "Tragic Era" by southern apologists at the start of the 20th century and celebrated as an "Unfinished Revolution" at the end. Although historians continue to debate periodization, they conventionally define Reconstruction as beginning with the end of hostilities in 1865 and concluding in 1877, when the last former Confederate states were readmitted to the Union and President Rutherford B. Hayes committed to the final withdrawal of federal troops from the South. Redemption, the term white southerners gave to the reestablishment of conservative control over state and local governments, was generally complete by 1870. As the name suggests, the Redeemers who led this political counter-revolution cast themselves as saviors delivering the South from incompetent and illegitimate Reconstruction governments. Developments in electoral politics punctuated the broader struggle over the future of labor organization in the post-Emancipation South, but they did not determine the outcome directly. Nevertheless, these political benchmarks provide important sites for examining the extent to which the Civil War changed the class dynamics of the region.

The destruction of slavery presented a profound challenge to the antebellum social order. Long before the Civil War, defenders of the South had shifted from bemoaning slavery as a necessary evil, to celebrating it as the indispensable foundation of a distinctive political economy that forestalled class conflict. In one of the most pointed articulations of this view, South Carolina politician James Henry Hammond argued that by creating a racially distinct mud-sill class of laborers perpetually excluded from political participation, slavery provided both prosperity and political stability to the region. Embedded in his analysis was the assumption that there were only two meaningful classes in the South: slaves and free white men. Although empirically flawed, this characterization was politically invaluable in justifying the disproportionate political power of southern elites. It flattened distinctions among landless whites, yeoman farmers, and large slaveholding planters, ignored the presence of free black southerners, and failed even to entertain the possibility of women's independent interests. Instead, it imbued white manhood with extraordinary political significance, as both conferring rights and creating common interests that superseded economic differences. By making the defense of slavery synonymous with the defense of region and domestic order, this view of southern society anticipated secession.

The progress of the Civil War itself sharply challenged the belief that slavery had knit southern society together with uncommonly stable bonds of organic mutual interest. Rather than sustaining the Confederacy, enslaved southerners rose up to play a decisive role in Emancipation and Union victory. Small but tenacious pockets of white unionism within the Confederacy revealed competing political priorities shaped in part by economic interests. Wartime hardship and local violence threw the differences among white southerners into sharp relief and brought challenges to gender hierarchy and community comity. The political coalitions that emerged during Reconstruction revealed dramatic ruptures in the old political economy of the South and suggested that economic interests, along with masculine privilege, could provide a compelling basis for mobilizing citizens across racial lines in the wake of Confederate defeat.

Many freedpeople identified land as the just compensation for generations of uncompensated labor, and the greatest assurance of meaningful freedom. The architects of federal Reconstruction policy largely demurred from using land redistribution to directly transform the class structure of the region and instead identified universal male suffrage as a critical bulwark for protecting freedpeople's rights and political competition. The state constitutional conventions that met between 1867 and 1869 suggest that even such relatively modest changes held radical potential. Made up of former slaves, recent northern transplants, and native whites (both longtime unionists and recent Republican converts), the derisively labeled "Black and Tan" conventions themselves were a vivid demonstration of transformed political possibilities. The new state constitutions they produced demonstrated a broad challenge to old racial and class hierarchies. They prohibited racial and property qualifications for voting and holding office, modified tax structures, provided protections for working men including homestead exemptions for debtors, and, crucially, provided for publicly funded common schooling. Although burdened by debt, postwar disorder, and political violence, the interracial political coalitions forged during Reconstruction demonstrated that political mobilization could coalesce around concerns other than race. Without persistent and strong support from the federal government, however, these state governments proved vulnerable to Redeemers' political strategies that often relied on a potent mix of violence and appeals to racial solidarity.

Labor, as much as the meaning of citizenship, was at the center of Reconstruction conflict and the class organization of the region. These struggles overflow the banks of the conventional periodization of Reconstruction and Redemption and demonstrate considerable continuity in African American political practices from the antebellum era through the 20th century. While northern Republicans sought to establish a free labor economy, with contracts and wages governing the exchange of labor, southerners revealed a range of expectations that were not always sympathetic with this vision. Although conflicts over post-Emancipation labor organization varied dramatically across the South, they fundamentally pit former slaveholders, anxious to preserve as much of the old prerogatives of mastery as possible, against freedpeople, committed to exercising autonomy in their familial and economic lives. From voting and office holding, to organizing strikes and using courts to challenge employers, Emancipation greatly expanded the tools available to freedpeople for negotiating their working lives. The absence of land redistribution made labor mobility the most powerful weapon in freedpeople's arsenals and made gathering family members into economically productive households the frontline of Reconstruction conflict.

The labor patterns that emerged in the post–Civil War South defy easy categorization and suggest that the end of slavery did not precipitate a uniform transition to wage labor. Sharecropping and tenancy, the systems of agricultural production that became synonymous with the economic stagnation of the 20th-century South, in the post-Emancipation context emerged as a compromise between the interests of former slaves and former masters. Former masters lost their ability to employ the most intrusive forms of labor compulsion, but continued to exercise power as landlords to reduce labor competition and labor costs. Freedpeople escaped the most intensive surveillance and unrestrained violence of slavery and gained a greater measure of autonomy in organizing labor, frequently along kinship lines. In the same period, a different set of developments contributed to a rise in tenancy rates among white southern farmers as well as black. Historians suggest that the costs of wartime destruction drove yeoman farmers away from self-sustaining food production toward greater cotton production at an inauspicious moment in the global cotton marketplace. The vulnerabilities of market-oriented production contributed to the loss of landownership and a rise in tenancy and sharecropping. The common economic plight of many black and white farmers in the 1870s and 1880s rarely drove political reform in the region. Instead, the political legacies of Redemption bore fruit in policies hostile to the interests of much of the region's population.

From the earliest days of Reconstruction, violence played an important part in white resistance to Emancipation and Union victory. Freedpeople who attempted to demand wages, attend school, exercise the right to vote, or even simply claim children from former masters all risked violent reprisals from reactionary whites who interpreted their actions as illegitimate assaults on the social order of the South. The success of the Redeemers' efforts to topple state Reconstruction governments depended on their ability to harness these dispersed assertions of white supremacy in daily life to the larger project of restoring white home rule. For a time, the Ku Klux Klan's targeting of Republicans provoked an effective federal response that curtailed their power through prosecutions and expanded federal military presence, notably at election times. As northern commitment to Reconstruction waned in the 1870s, however, the persistence of white political violence made the costs of political activism high for African Americans and for whites who joined them in support of the Republican Party. Violence made White Leagues' appeals for white unity in voting out Republican governments compelling. Although Republican governments had promised protections for workingmen in the South through changes in law and the role of government, Redeemers appealed to the common prerogatives of white manhood grounded in the republican producer ideology of the antebellum era. That is, they cast themselves as restoring the old order whose foundation lay in natural hierarchies of gender and race.

Although Redeemers' appeals for white solidarity downplayed class differences among white men, their policies once in office tended to serve the interests of elites in the region. They reduced the provision of state services, most vividly in minimal and uneven funding of schools. They pursued policies that resulted in the disfranchisement of large swathes of white and black voters through property and educational requirements. They were innovative in developing new forms of labor coercion, notably in the convict lease system that demonstrated new forms of institutionalized racism and helped propel the modernization of the southern economy through the construction of railroads. Although a wide-angle survey of Reconstruction and Redemption in the South reveals significant changes in the political economy of the region, it remained sharply tilted toward the interests of elites. In this regard, developments in the South were consonant with a national shift toward using the state to protect the interests of property against the interests of working citizens in the late 19th century. Nevertheless, counternarratives abound. In the years following the end of Reconstruction, the Readjusters in Virginia succeeded in building a biracial political coalition that advanced progressive policies, and domestic workers in southern cities staged strikes to demand better pay. Although Reconstruction did not upend the class organization of the South, even the systematic restriction of citizens' rights through Jim Crow laws could not entirely negate the legacies of self-assertion and collective organization that defined the period.

CATHERINE JONES
University of California at Santa Cruz

Thomas J. Brown, ed., *Reconstructions: New Perspectives on the Postbellum United States* (2006); Jane Dailey, *Before Jim Crow: The Politics of Race in Postemancipation Virginia* (2000); Laura F. Edwards, *Gendered Strife and Confusion: The Political Culture of Reconstruction* (1997); Eric Foner, *Reconstruction: America's Unfinished Revolution, 1863–1877* (1988); Lacy K. Ford, ed., *A Companion to the Civil War and Reconstruction* (2005); Steven Hahn, *A Nation under Our Feet: Black Political Struggles in the Rural South from Slavery to the Great Migration* (2003); Richard L. Hume and Jerry B. Gough, *Blacks, Carpetbaggers, and Scalawags: The Constitutional Conventions of Radical Reconstruction* (2008); Tera W. Hunter, *"To 'Joy My Freedom": Southern*

Black Women's Lives and Labors after the Civil War (1997); Stephen Kantrowitz, *Ben Tillman and the Reconstruction of White Supremacy* (2000); Michael Perman, *The Road to Redemption: Southern Politics, 1869-1879* (1984); Heather Cox Richardson, *The Death of Reconstruction: Race, Labor, and Politics in the Post-Civil War North* (2001); Jonathan Wiener, *Social Origins of the New South: Alabama, 1860-65* (1978); C. Vann Woodward, *Origins of the New South, 1877-1913* (1951, 1971).

Religion

Religion varies by region of the country and contributes significantly to regional distinctiveness. Baptists, Methodists, and fundamentalists are common in the South, while Catholics and Jews, relative to the Northeast and except in some locales, are less so. Religion also varies by social class. Writing at the end of the 1920s, H. Richard Niebuhr was among the first scholars to rank religious organizations in the United States based upon the socioeconomic status of their members. He showed that denominations and other religious groups drew their adherents from relatively distinct socioeconomic levels and that these life worlds influenced religious beliefs and practices. Subsequent community studies in the South by Liston Pope and John Dollard confirmed that the churches of the region were segregated not only by race but by class as well.

Nationally, a system of religious stratification still favors a white, upper-class "Protestant Establishment" (Episcopalians, Presbyterians, Congregationalists) that is overrepresented in the leadership of business, political, and educational institutions, but Catholics and Jews have experienced substantial upward social mobility. Jews, in fact, rank as the highest religious group nationally in terms of educational attainment, income, and occupational prestige. Mainline Protestant denominations such as Methodists and Lutherans rank in the middle range of socioeconomic variables, whereas white Baptists—along with other evangelicals, fundamentalists, and Pentecostals—rank near the bottom of the national religious hierarchy, but generally above black Baptists. In the South, however, where roughly one-fifth of religious believers identify with Baptist traditions, Southern Baptists rank higher than in other regions.

In the colonial era, planters in the Tidewater South—much like their Congregational counterparts in New England—attempted to shore up their power and privilege by legally establishing the Anglican Church as a state church, requiring compulsory attendance and collecting mandatory tithes from the entire population while restricting the civil and political rights of nonmembers. Presbyterians initially were the dominant dissenting religious group in the southern backcountry, especially among elites, but the rapid growth of Baptist and Methodist denominations among the common folk, especially in frontier areas of the South, challenged the hegemony of both elite religious groups and contributed to the disestablishment of religion in the region.

Itinerant clergy in the case of the Methodists ("circuit riders") and untrained ("called") preachers in the case of the Baptists proved more adaptable to recruiting denominational members in frontier conditions than did those religious groups, like the Presbyterians, that demanded seminary training for its ministers. Methodism and various Baptist groups thus spread rapidly among lower and middle classes throughout the rural South, carrying with them evangelical beliefs and worship styles that promoted social leveling and democracy (at least among whites), individualism, emotional "heart-felt" and "born-again" religion, and enthusiastic worship. They were fueled by the revivalism of the Second Great Awakening, and camp-meeting style religiosity became a powerful force throughout the region.

In addition to attracting class-based memberships, religious organizations often serve as vehicles for the defense or challenge of social privilege. Among the classical sociologists, Karl Marx stressed the palliative effects of religion for the oppressed. Max Weber argued that massive inequalities in the civilizations that gave rise to the great world religions created the need for religious legitimation in the form of theodicies to explain either prosperity or suffering. Religious beliefs and affiliation may thus justify the status quo and encourage quiescence or, conversely, legitimate opposition to social inequalities. The southern Bible Belt has seen far more of the former than of the latter.

Although early evangelical leaders and church builders in the South were initially opposed to slaveholding, their eventual accommodation to the region's peculiar institution profoundly shaped southern religiosity in the antebellum era and well beyond. The religious defense of slavery reinforced the economic and political hegemony of wealthy landowning and slave-owning classes; encouraged the complicity of nonslaveholding whites in the injustices of white supremacy, class inequality, and the slave system; led to schisms within national Protestant denominations while giving rise to one of the region's largest and most influential denominations, the Southern Baptist Convention; and, more generally, led to the South's enduring alliance of religious, social, and political conservatism. Ultimately, the religious accommodation to slavery imposed blinders on southern believers that diverted attention from a wide range of social injustices and public evils—stressing instead private morality and blunting the prophetic resources of religious traditions that otherwise might have been brought to bear against class inequality and caste exploitation.

Secession, war, and defeat did not chasten conservative white southern religion. In the postbellum era, the white church remained a pillar of racial segregation and class inequality. The Myth of the Lost Cause functioned as a uniquely southern civil religion of defeat that likewise affirmed the righteousness of southern institutions and blunted social criticism. In contrast, however, African Americans produced distinctive forms of southern religion in slavery and afterward that kept alive their hopes for justice and liberation. The black church affirmed the dignity and humanity of its members, provided opportunities for personal and leadership development that other class- and race-based institutions denied, and ultimately—in the civil rights movement—provided one of the South's most effective ideological and organizational vehicles for mobilizing progressive social transformation.

The postbellum era was the era not only of Jim Crow but also of extensive southern industrialization. Here too, in the so-called but misnamed New South, the southern white church remained a bulwark of conservatism. The power and privilege of the region's traditionally dominant classes were exercised anew as former planter elites built new industries such as textile manufacturing but accommodated them to the class norms and racial exclusions of the Old South. In his classic study of religion and social class in Gaston County, N.C., Liston Pope described a tripartite and largely class-segregated religious environment that included—in roughly equal proportions—a remnant of traditional rural or farmer churches (dominated by small farm owners but also including farm tenants) and uptown or county seat churches (peopled predominantly by rising commercial, professional, and management classes) alongside the numerically predominant working-class churches of the mill villages, many of them built, financed, and controlled by industrialists. Each type tended to support the socioeconomic status quo, and quiescence reigned. Uptown churches of the upper and middle classes sanctified the prevailing economic arrangements and the virtues essential for business success. Working-class churches tended to extend compensatory spiritual and emotional escape from oppressive work conditions and encourage the temperance and discipline favored by employers. When textile workers attempted, briefly, to unionize in the 1930s, the churches provided powerful opposition.

Industrialists who built company churches tended to favor Methodism since the Episcopal structure of that denomination, along with sympathetic bishops and district supervisors, made the dismissal of clergy sympathetic to unions relatively easy. When the new working class and displaced rural poor built their own churches, however, these tended to be sectarian and Pentecostal. Although they, too, tended to encourage quiescence rather than direct opposition to class inequality and social reform, Pentecostalism was nonetheless the

South's greatest class-based religious movement of the 20th century. Following in the path of earlier Wesleyan Holiness and Restorationist movements that challenged the upward mobility and worldly accommodation of Protestant evangelicalism, it transmuted social marginality and exclusion into virtues, created spaces that affirmed the worth of the dispossessed (black and white alike), facilitated emotional escape and temporary transcendence from oppressive social conditions, and created sacred spaces where otherwise discredited groups, including women and African Americans, could develop and exercise spiritual leadership. Nor did Pentecostals inevitably oppose social reform. In the Appalachian South, for instance, Pentecostals sometimes contributed to leadership in union struggles, economic justice, and more recently—under the rubric of "creation care"—environmentalism.

Thus, it would be one-sided to say that southern religion has always and only contributed to the maintenance of class and racial caste inequality. While southern religion—led by Jerry Falwell, Pat Robertson, and others—is best known outside the region for its contribution to contemporary New Right Christian politics, undercurrents of southern religiosity helped to ignite powerful agrarian reform movements such as the Farmers' Alliance and Populism in the late 19th century. Among white urban middle classes in the same era, religion spurred temperance, prohibition, and charity but also antilynching and anti-child labor movements. Later, middle-class white churchmen and -women provided an impetus to reform race relations through such organizations as the Commission on Interracial Cooperation, while middle-class black women had championed racial uplift among African Americans well before the black church became a potent force for social change in the mid-20th century civil rights and antipoverty movements.

Finally, some scholars contend that social mobility, an overall rise in American educational levels, and declining allegiance to traditional denominations are leading to the restructuring of religion in the United States and, possibly, the diminishment of class distinctions among religious groups. Possible support for this thesis in the South comes from the remarkable growth of megachurches, which appear to be somewhat more racially and class inclusive than earlier organizations, and from smaller exurban churches where local exclusivity is being challenged by incorporation into expanding metropolitan zones that encourage accommodation to increasingly diverse populations. New immigrants from Latin America and Asia are also changing the social class composition of churches in some regions of the South—whether by working-class and often-undocumented migrants from Mexico and Central America, or highly educated, business, and professional migrants from Cuba, India, and

Korea. Even so, recent national surveys affirm remarkable continuities in the association between religious membership and class position, suggesting that religion's role in the future of southern inequality—and challenges to it—is far from spent.

DWIGHT B. BILLINGS
WALTER H. BOWER
University of Kentucky

Dwight B. Billings, *American Journal of Sociology* (July 1990); John Dollard, *Caste and Class in a Southern Town* (1937); John R. Earle, Dean D. Knudsen, and Donald W. Shriver Jr., *Spindles and Spires* (1976); Nancy Eiesland, *A Particular Place: Urban Restructuring and Religious Ecology in a Southern Exurb* (2000); Mary Ann Hinsdale, Helen M. Lewis, and S. Maxine Waller, *It Comes from the People: Community Development and Local Theology* (1995); Christine Leigh Heyrman, *Southern Cross: The Beginnings of the Bible Belt* (1997); Donald G. Mathews, *Religion in the Old South* (1977); H. Richard Niebuhr, *The Social Sources of Denominationalism* (1929); Liston Pope, *Millhands and Preachers* (1942); Christian Smith and Robert Faris, *Journal for the Scientific Study of Religion* (March 2005).

Secession, the Confederacy, and the Civil War

Variations of social class have never been very prominent in images of the South during the Civil War era. The black-white racial divide and the North-South regional conflict have loomed much larger, thanks in part to romanticized postwar portrayals of a white South resolutely united against northerners outside the South and African Americans within it. However, class was always a significant feature of southern society. This is especially true if the master-slave relationship is viewed as one of class as well as race. But even within white southern society there were important class divisions, especially the basic distinction between white southerners who owned slaves and those who did not.

The antebellum South's latent class fractures were mostly contained by a hegemonic slaveholding elite. Slavery not only shaped socioeconomic relations between black slaves and white masters but also influenced class relations between white southerners. The wealth and prestige afforded by slavery enabled slaveholders to control the political and economic life of the antebellum South. But because the Old South was a democracy—for white men, at least—wealthy slaveholders had to take lower-class white men into account. There were some signs of embryonic class conflict. In his 1857 book *The Impending Crisis of the South*, for instance, the North Carolinian Hinton Rowan Helper railed against the detrimental effects of the slave system on the economic position of white southerners who did not own slaves. But for the most part nonslaveholding white southerners acquiesced in the slaveholding regime prior to the Civil War. They did so for a number of reasons: many of them aspired to slaveholding status themselves; they often benefited from the economic system that had formed around slavery, relying on local planters to gin their cotton or transport their goods to market; they shared with slaveholders a "republican" political ideology, valuing their liberty and personal independence, and viewing the ownership of productive property—in land or slaves or both—as the basis of that independence. Perhaps most importantly, white southerners could all benefit socially, economically, and psychologically from what the eminent scholar W. E. B. Du Bois termed the "wages of whiteness." A shared interest in white supremacy brought white southerners of all social classes together and ensured that the most visible fault line in southern society was race rather than class.

Even so, class lines within white society did exist, and they became more significant than ever during the crises of secession and the Civil War. Facing the external enemy of the North, as well as the threat of slave resistance at home, the southern elite needed the support of other social classes more desperately than ever. Hence, in 1860 the Louisiana editor J. D. B. De Bow felt the need to write a pamphlet with the revealing title *The Interest in Slavery of the Southern Non-Slaveholder*. On the eve of secession, southern slaveholders were clearly aware of the danger of class divisions and responded with arguments designed to achieve cross-class unity among whites.

In 1860–61 there was a rough correlation between social class and support for secession: viewing the South as a whole, secession was most popular in districts with higher rates of slaveholding. Despite countless exceptions—Louisiana sugar planters, for instance, who valued the Union because its protective tariffs made them internationally competitive, or wealthy, conservative, ex-Whig slaveholders committed to the status quo and worried that secession would render slavery less rather than more safe—this correlation indicated that economic and social interest in the preservation of slavery drove secession. Indeed, one study found evidence that wealthy Georgia slaveholders supported secession in response not only to the external challenge from the North but also to internal, class-based challenges to their leadership from white nonslaveholders at home. Secession offered them an opportunity to consolidate slaveholder authority. Another study found that young, ambitious men of the slaveholding class in Alabama and Mississippi were most likely to support secession, viewing it as a means to secure the expansion of the slaveholding regime. Among other things, they believed expansion would further integrate nonslaveholding white southerners into the slaveholders' regime. As for middle-class southerners—urban merchants, lawyers, and the like—recent research has found that they were generally not strong supporters of secession to begin with, but that they typically accepted secession and the Confederate regime once it was in place.

In the opening months of the war, white men from all social classes volunteered to fight for the new Confederacy. There were many white southerners who still opposed secession, particularly in the region's low-slaveholding mountainous areas, but there was little overt class-based conflict. This changed, however, particularly after the spring of 1862, when the Confederate government instituted national conscription. This policy, combined with onerous taxation and the impressment of goods, generated widespread dissent that was often expressed in class terms. Poorer nonslaveholding white families increasingly believed that they were being forced to bear a disproportionate burden for the war effort. For example, they objected to the Confederate policy that allowed the wealthy to pay a substitute to fight in their place, and the so-called 20-nigger law that exempted from service one white southern man to control every 20 slaves. All of this led to complaints of a "rich man's war and a poor man's fight." Deteriorating economic circumstances exacerbated such complaints. In the second half of the Civil War, dissent increased considerably, centered in the same mountainous regions that had always been ambivalent about secession and the Confederacy. This dissent was often class based. Poor white women wrote to state and national officials demanding that their husbands and sons be released from the army and asking for other changes in Confederate policy that would equalize wartime hardships across class lines. The same frustrations led to a number of food riots, most famously in Richmond in April 1863, which vented popular resentment at iniquitous government policies and the profiteering of merchants and other villainous "speculators."

Even more significant was the dissent of slaves. Taking advantage of the instability of war and the approach of Union troops, slaves rebelled against the institution of slavery in a variety of ways, ranging from escape and enlistment in the Union army to more everyday defiance of masters' authority. Long ago W. E. B. Du Bois described these acts as a "General Strike," conveying the economic and social class valences of slaves' actions. As most recent historians have agreed, slaves' wartime resistance had an even greater impact on the defeat of the Confederacy than did the class-based dissent of nonslaveholding white southerners.

Both slave resistance and the Confederacy's white class divisions were sidelined by a Lost Cause vision of a harmonious South, united across lines of class, gender, and sometimes even race against the northern enemy. Largely obscured were the countless black-white conflicts, both overt and otherwise, that contradicted slave owners' claims of a happy, loyal slave population. Largely obscured were the divergent attitudes toward slavery, secession, and especially the Confederate war effort that produced the seeds of class tensions within white society. Beginning in the mid-20th century, cracks of class as well as race began slowly to reappear in historians' portrayals of the Confederacy, and in our own time they are beginning to emerge into broader public consciousness as well.

PAUL QUIGLEY
University of Edinburgh

John Ashworth, *Slavery, Capitalism, and Politics in the Antebellum Republic*, 2 vols. (1995–2008); William L. Barney, *The Secessionist Impulse: Alabama and Mississippi in 1860* (1974); W. E. B. Du Bois, *Black Reconstruction in America* (1935); Wayne Durrill, *War of Another Kind: A Southern Community in the Great Rebellion* (1994); Paul D. Escott, *After Secession: Jefferson Davis and the Failure of Confederate Nationalism* (1992); William Freehling, *The Road to Disunion*, 2 vols. (1990–2007); Eugene D. Genovese, *The Political Economy of the Slave South: Studies in the Economy and Society of the Slave South* (1965); Steven Hahn, *A Nation under Our Feet: Black Political Struggles in the Rural South from Slavery to the Great Migration* (2003); Michael P. Johnson, *Toward a Patriarchal Republic: The Secession of Georgia* (1977); Georgia Lee Tatum, *Disloyalty in the Confederacy* (1934); Jonathan Daniel Wells, *The Origins of the Southern Middle Class, 1800–1861* (2004); David Williams, *Bitterly Divided: The South's Inner Civil War* (2008).

Sharecropping and Tenancy

Since the post–Civil War years the plantation landlord and the tenant farmer have been among the most prominent figures in the nation's perception of the South. They have been graphic symbols of the region's ruralism, poverty, and cultural backwardness and have exemplified the paternalism, exploitation, and social class dimensions of southern agriculture. And, indeed, until the mid-20th century these images reflected the reality of several million southerners whose lives were blighted by crop lien tenancy.

Tenancy was a response to the disorganization and poverty of southern agriculture following the Civil War, becoming widely established by about 1880. Former slaves and landless whites needed access to land and compensation as laborers, but landlords lacked money for wages. To organize production, landowners allowed these workers to farm plots of 20 to 40 acres on a crop-sharing basis. They also undertook the support of their tenants during the crop season by extending credit for food and living necessities, secured by liens on their

A landless sharecropping husband and wife in Mississippi, June/July 1937. (Dorothea Lange, photographer, Library of Congress [LC-USZ62-106936], Washington, D.C.)

portions of the crop. Often this credit was arranged through rural store owners, or furnish merchants, who were also general suppliers of feed, fertilizer, and implements. Planter-landlords with many tenants, however, frequently furnished then directly, through plantation commissaries. This crop-sharing and lien-financing system was necessitated by the South's dearth of farm production credit. It reflected the limitations of agricultural technology; this system sustained the large force of unskilled labor that was needed as long as cotton and tobacco remained unmechanized.

Relatively few of the South's landless farmers were independent cash renters; most were share tenants and sharecroppers. The latter two levels of tenancy were defined by the farmers' contributions to production, their need for subsistence credit, and how closely they were supervised by landlords. Share tenants often owned mules or equipment and might be able to supply some seed or fertilizer. Their furnishing needs varied, as did their supervision. Accordingly, their portions of the crop could be as much as two-thirds or three-fourths, less, of course, advances and interest. Sharecroppers, on the other hand, usually possessed no work stock or tools and contributed only labor. Dependent on lien credit for nearly all living necessities, and working under much supervision, they ordinarily received no more than half the crop, from which "furnishing" and interest were deducted.

In the chronically depressed southern agriculture of the late 19th century and the early 20th century, tenancy increased steadily as many farmers lost their land. It reached its peak in 1930, when the census counted 228,598 cash renters, 772,573 sharecroppers, and 795,527 other tenants (mostly share tenants) in 13 southern and border states. Tenancy was the dominant pattern in staple-crop production. In 1937 the President's Committee on Farm Tenancy estimated that tenants and croppers were 65 percent of all farmers in the Cotton Belt and 48 percent in tobacco regions. Approximately two-thirds of southern tenants were white, although among croppers, the lowest tenure group, the numbers of whites and blacks were about equal. Share tenants, croppers, and their families easily composed nearly half the 1930 southern farm population of 15.5 million.

Southern tenancy was the context for a culture of rural poverty. Tenants and croppers received some of the lowest incomes in America, rarely clearing more than a few hundred dollars per year. Their more common experience, especially in years of low crop prices, was to receive no net income at all because their shares of crops could not cover high-interest furnishing debts. These scant earnings kept rural southerners living right at the bottom of the national scale. Cotton and tobacco tenants lived in the fields they worked in pine-board cabins that lacked window glass, screens, electricity, plumbing, and even wells and privies. Thousands of families were without common household furnishings, stoves, mattresses, or adequate clothing and shoes. The poorest croppers subsisted on a furnish-store diet that relied heavily on salt pork, flour, and meal. Owning no cows or poultry and tending no gardens, they seldom consumed milk, eggs, or fresh vegetables. Malnutrition compounded wretched living conditions to make chronic illness a major feature of rural life, as malaria, pellagra, and hookworm infection stunted the development of children, shortened lives, and lowered the economic productivity of the poor.

Crop lien tenancy was both exploitive and paternalistic. One of the familiar figures of southern rural lore was the tight-fisted landlord who kept all accounts, charged exorbitant interest on advances, and took over his tenants' cotton for debts. As part of the local power structure, planters were in a position to make

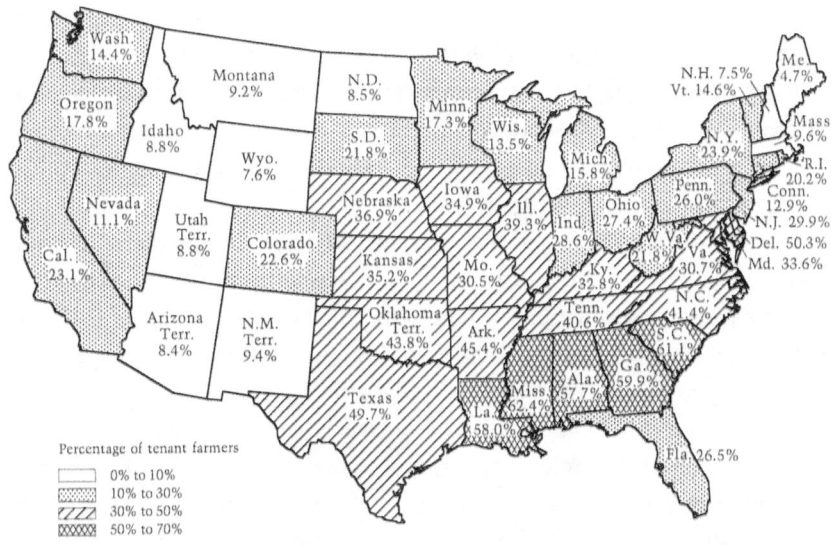

MAP 1. *Farm tenancy, 1890.* Source: George B. Tindall, America: A Narrative History, 2nd ed., vol. 2 (1988).

whatever settlements they wished, without challenge from illiterate tenants. Perhaps the greatest tragedy of this system was that exploitation was built into it. A landlord, hard-pressed by mortgage and tax obligations, production costs, and low crop prices, often could not profit without cutting as deeply as possible into his tenants' shares. Moreover, as planters extended credit, they also supervised tenants' farming, leaving the least skilled, especially, with little opportunity to develop competence and self-direction. Tenancy thus bred dependency among the poor.

Tenants had little security on the land. They worked under year-to-year verbal agreements that left landlords free to dispense with their services at settling time. With a great surplus of unskilled labor at hand, planters usually felt little need to hold dissatisfied or unwanted tenants. Most landless farmers were highly mobile, moving as often as every year or two. This transience was socially and economically wasteful; it deprived tenants of any role in their communities and reinforced illiteracy by preventing regular schooling of their children. It destroyed incentives to maintain farm property and contributed greatly to soil erosion.

The southern public's perception of tenancy conformed to traditional American views of poverty, which have been highly judgmental toward the poor. Rural poverty was so pervasive as to be the expected condition of landless farmers. Moreover, tenants and croppers were often seen as unworthy and shiftless people who had neither the ability nor the desire for self-improvement. Yet, at the same time, the assumption frequently expressed in the 1930s was that any ambitious, industrious farmer could work his way up an agricultural ladder, progressing from sharecropping to securer levels of tenancy, and then to small landownership. These persistent views were a major impediment to efforts to reduce rural poverty.

The Great Depression focused national attention on southern tenancy. Ironically, this public notice came as the system was beginning to break down. As hard times intensified, many landlords cut their own expenses by abandoning crop sharing, discontinuing furnishing, and converting to wage labor. This trend grew during the New Deal. Under the Agricultural Adjustment Administration (AAA), acreage-reduction contracts decreased labor needs, and, in effect, encouraged landlords to dispense with tenants to avoid sharing government payments with them. This impact of the AAA was brought forcefully to public attention after 1935 by the protests of the Southern Tenant Farmers' Union. Tenancy continued as a national issue as the New Deal attempted to alleviate rural poverty through federal relief, the Bankhead-Jones Farm Tenant Act of 1937, and the Farm Security Administration.

Sharecropping declined significantly in the 1930s, and in the following decades southern agriculture underwent massive changes that swept away crop lien tenancy. Mechanization was the most revolutionary development. From the 1930s onward the number of tractors on southern farms increased dramatically, and after World War II the cotton picker came into general use. Landlords employed wageworkers to meet their more limited labor needs and discarded outmoded crop-sharing arrangements. Crop and livestock diversification and chemical weed control made farming still less labor intensive. This transformation of southern agriculture was accompanied by a great exodus of the rural poor from the land and, in many cases, from the region.

PAUL E. MERTZ
University of Wisconsin at Stevens Point

James C. Cobb, *The Most Southern Place on Earth: The Mississippi Delta and the Roots of Regional Identity* (1992); David E. Conrad, *The Forgotten Farmers: The Story of Sharecroppers in the New Deal* (1965); Pete Daniel, *Breaking the Land: The Transformation of Cotton, Tobacco, and Rice Cultures since 1880* (1985); Gilbert C. Fite, *Cotton Fields No More: Southern Agriculture, 1865–1980* (1984); Charles S. Johnson, Edwin R. Embree, and Will W. Alexander, *The Collapse of Cotton Tenancy: A Summary of Field Studies and Statistical Surveys* (1935); Paul E. Mertz, *New Deal Policy and Southern Rural Poverty* (1978); Arthur F. Raper, *Preface to Peasantry: A Tale of Two Black Belt Coun-*

ties (1936); U.S. National Resources Committee, *Farm Tenancy: Report of the President's Committee* (1937); Rupert B. Vance, *Human Factors in Cotton Culture: A Study in the Social Geography of the American South* (1929); Jeannie Whayne, *A New Plantation South: Land, Labor, and Federal Favor in Twentieth-Century Arkansas* (1996); Thomas Jackson Woofter Jr., *Landlord and Tenant on the Cotton Plantation* (1936).

Slaveholders, Black

Some African Americans owned other blacks as slaves in the Old South, and in so doing they bequeathed to the study of southern society one of its more controversial topics. Some black men acquired land, slaves, and standing in civil affairs in early colonial times, most notably, perhaps, on the Eastern Shore of Virginia in the mid-1600s; those developments offer an intriguing glimpse of a path in American race relations that was ultimately not taken. Black slaveholding became a significant element in southern society only when the free black population grew in the wake of the American Revolution. The statistics for those decades are fairly clear if not widely known: in 1830, when free black slaveholding may have been near its peak, about 3,690 free, black southerners (including both blacks and people of mixed racial background, all of whom will here be referred to as "black") owned some 12,000 slaves. Both black slaveholders and slaves held by blacks were most numerous at that time in Louisiana, Virginia, Maryland, and South Carolina.

Loren Schweninger, the historian of southern black property holding, calculates that one free black family in every 14 in the Upper South owned at least one slave in 1830. The figure for free black families in the Lower South was one in four, though the distribution was uneven; Mississippi, Georgia, Alabama, and Florida had very few black slave owners and few free blacks overall, even as nearly a thousand blacks in Louisiana held slaves. People of mixed race were heavily represented among African American slave owners in the Lower South, where black slaveholding overall tended to stabilize or decline during the 20 years before the Civil War. In the Upper South, those same two decades saw a dramatic expansion in property holding in general among free blacks, yet ownership of slaves by that group declined, in part perhaps because a larger fraction of the prosperous free blacks now practiced skilled occupations and a smaller percentage owned farms. "Only a handful" of free blacks in North Carolina and points north owned slaves in the 1850s, Schweninger notes; measures that aimed to impede the acquisition of slaves by other blacks, such the one the legislature of Virginia adopted in 1858, may merely have ratified already existing socioeconomic trends.

The phenomenon of black slaveholding raises profound questions about the nature of southern society and the values of the region's black and white residents before the Civil War. Partly for that reason, historians have interpreted the data on black slaveholding in varying ways. Carter G. Woodson, pioneer historian of Afro-America, famously asserted that "the majority" of black southerners who owned slaves were motivated by "philanthropy," possessing only one or a few members of their own families. That judgment has been repeated casually and more sweepingly by many subsequent historians.

Citing Woodson, historians ranging chronologically and ideologically from Ulrich B. Phillips, a conservative who wrote about slavery in the 1910s and 1920s, through Kenneth M. Stampp, the liberal revisionist of the 1950s, and on to Ira Berlin in the 1970s, have suggested that black ownership of slaves typically was a legal fiction under which an already-free black southerner exercised technical ownership in order to protect a family member against perils that confronted newly freed blacks in the 19th-century South.

Virginia, for example, passed a law in 1806 that required African Americans liberated after that date to leave the state within a year. This law was rarely enforced, yet some black men and women who purchased their spouses or children from white masters chose not to liberate them formally, apparently seeking to eliminate even the remote possibility that their kin would be expelled from the state. Free black miller Philip Bowman of Prince Edward County bought his wife, Priscy, at a sheriff's auction in 1822 but kept her in technical bondage. He eventually bequeathed her person, along with a sum of money to support her after his death, to a trusted white employer. (The white man honored Bowman's wishes as long as the black man's monetary bequest lasted, but then sent Priscy Bowman to the county poorhouse.)

One trend in more recent historical writing has been to grant the importance of pro forma ownership by blacks of family members, yet at the same time to recognize that more than a few black slaveholders acquired human property for economic gain and treated enslaved persons much as white masters did. It is often difficult to say definitively whether benevolent or exploitative motives, or both, impelled a given black individual to become a slave owner; many historians from Woodson's time to the present have assumed that the greater the number of slaves a particular black individual owned, the more likely that the slaveholding in question was of the conventional kind aimed at making a profit. William Ellison, a prosperous free black cotton gin maker and planter in South Carolina, owned 63 slaves in 1860, making him one of the top-10 black slaveholders in the South. (The largest black-owned contingent of slaves in that year encompassed 152 persons held by a certain mother and her son in Louisiana.)

Thomas Day, a renowned black cabinetmaker in north-central North Carolina, at one time owned 14 slaves of various ages.

The documentary record that some wealthy black masters left behind makes clear that they profited from their ownership of slaves, buying and selling human property with no evident reservations. Even some free black southerners who purchased their own family members proved less than "philanthropic"; Woodson himself asserted that certain free black husbands bought their wives, "put them on probation for a few years, and if they did not find them satisfactory they would sell their wives as other slave holders disposed of Negroes."

Free black slaveholding presents varied faces depending on one's vantage point. The federal census of 1830 reveals that a free black man named William Daniel in Cumberland County, Va., held 32 slaves, while the other 14 free black slaveholders in the same county owned a total of 22 bondpeople; in every case but one, those smallholders held only one or two slaves each. Thus the "typical" black-owned *slave* in Cumberland (32 enslaved persons out of 54) belonged to a master who likely saw him or her mainly as an economic asset, at the very same time that the "typical" black slave*holder* in that county (at least 13 of 15 masters) was the presumably "philanthropic" pro forma owner of a family member. In the same year, each of the six black or mixed-race slaveholders in Iberville Parish, La., owned 18 blacks or more, with the two wealthiest individuals holding more than 40 each; in other southern counties, no black resident held more than one or two slaves, while in still other localities free black slaveholding did not exist.

Some historians have attempted to complicate or even challenge the assumption that large-scale black slaveholders necessarily behaved in an exploitative manner. They begin by saying, plausibly enough, that the relatively few blacks who attained prosperity in the Old South acquired slaves in part to show their white neighbors that they were reliable supporters of the southern status quo. The desire of a free black individual to reassure his white neighbors, however, did not necessarily mitigate, and might even aggravate, the treatment he meted out to his slaves.

Some writers go on to question outright the assumption that large-scale slaveholding by black masters was inherently exploitative. This view posits the existence of what might be dubbed "black Schindler's lists"—by analogy to the German industrialist who, during World War II, belonged to the Nazi party and earned large profits from slave labor, yet who also used his status and the autonomy that flowed from it to improve the condition of his enslaved workers. In this view, Thomas Day and other free blacks who owned sizable numbers of slaves earned profits and gained standing in the eyes of the white community even as they also provided a kind of refuge in which enslaved fellow blacks enjoyed a measure of well-being denied to most slaves.

Thus far, little evidence has been cited to substantiate the existence of "black Schindler's lists." Most intriguing, perhaps, are the facts that William Ellison and Thomas Day both sent their children to northern schools run by abolitionists, and that the Days apparently had antislavery friends in the North. These free blacks thus may have entertained misgivings about the morality of slavery, which in turn makes one wonder whether they should be categorized primarily as exploitative masters.

It is also worth noting that the two principal forms of wealth in the Old South were land and slaves; anyone who accumulated money—whether native southerner, northern or European newcomer, or the occasional prosperous free black—might well acquire slaves during the normal course of doing business. In Charleston, for example, the more real estate a free person of color owned, the more slaves he or she tended to possess. All in all, free black slaveholders in the Old South were numerous and diverse enough that the group may have contained at least some free black Schindlers even as it demonstrably encompassed some casual exploiters of fellow black southerners.

The relationship of free black slave ownership to social class is complicated. By 1800 at the latest, free blacks (including free people of mixed race) lived under varying conditions in different southern states; yet the group as a whole can be considered a racially defined subordinate social caste, which in turn was stratified according to wealth and social capital. Some historians say that the wealthiest black slaveholders constituted "the top of the bottom." That is true in the sense that they stood at the apex of a group—free black southerners—that faced social and civil disabilities unique to people of their color, such as exclusion from voting, serving on juries, and testifying against white defendants. Yet "top of the bottom" may understate the position of propertied free black southerners. Despite all the discrimination they faced, prosperous free blacks could and did come to be "greatly esteemed" and "respected" by whites who described them at the time, and they enjoyed greater material comfort than most members of the privileged race; even industrious free blacks of middling or modest income could gain recognition as "respectable" people in the eyes of their white neighbors.

For many in our own time, the most compelling question one might ask about black slaveholding revolves around the very definition of the word *respectable*. To what degree can one hold up a Thomas Day or a William Ellison as an exemplar of black achievement against formidable odds, and to what extent are those people's achievements adulterated by their having held fellow blacks in bondage? The phenomenon of black slaveholding contains subtle, troubling undertones, especially for those who would seek moral clarity in the lessons of the southern past.

MELVIN PATRICK ELY
College of William and Mary

Ira Berlin, *Slaves without Masters: The Free Negro in the Antebellum South* (1974); T. H. Breen and Stephen Innes, *"Myne Owne Ground": Race and Freedom on Virginia's Eastern Shore, 1640–1676* (1980); Melvin Patrick Ely, *Israel on the Appomattox: A Southern Experiment in Black Freedom from the 1790s through the Civil War* (2004); John Hope Franklin, *The Free Negro in North Carolina, 1790–1860* (1943); R. Halliburton Jr., *South Carolina Historical Magazine* (July 1975); Michael P. Johnson and James L. Roark, *Black Masters: A Free Family of Color in the Old South* (1984); Patricia Phillips Marshall and Jo Ramsay Leimenstoll, *Thomas Day: Master Craftsman and Free Man of Color* (2010); Research Department of the Association for the Study of Negro Life and History [Carter G. Woodson], *Journal of Negro History* (January 1924); Loren Schweninger, *Black Property Owners in the South, 1790–1915* (1990).

Slavery as a Class System

Slaves were property. This is what distinguished slavery as a class system from other forms of subordination: masters exercised power over slaves as a right of property. In principle, a feudal lord's power resided in his control of the land. In capitalism the employer rents the labor power of the worker in return for wages. But the slaveholder owns the slave outright and exercises power over the slave as a right of property. "Property in man" was the basis of slavery as a class system. This was generally true of all slave societies, but because slavery has flourished over many millennia in a variety of different settings, the class structures of slave societies have varied as well. Slavery in the American South was a class system based on property in human beings, but that is not all it was.

Southern slavery developed in particular circumstances, giving antebellum society's several distinctive characteristics. As was true across the hemisphere, for example, southern slavery was *racial* slavery. But it is crucial to understand what this does and does not reveal about southern slavery. Race tells us *who* the slaves were, but not *what* slavery was. Slavery was property in man; race became the primary criterion for enslavement. Put more simply, in the Old South only blacks could be held as property.

In the colonial South, slaves were generally classified within the laws of real estate, but with exceptions carved out to make slave property easier to buy and sell. With the development of capitalism, the ancient preeminence of land as the basis of the wealth declined and in its place the law of "personal property" took precedence. Stocks, bonds, bank notes, corporate charters—these were rapidly becoming the bases of wealth and class power in the antebellum North. The southern states, "in" if not "of" capitalist society, took advantage of this legal development beginning in the late 18th century by redefining slaves as a form of personal property. This gave the masters virtually unrestricted power to alienate and acquire slaves, power that was perhaps the signature attribute of the slaveholders as a class. Unlike the transfer of land and houses, which required elaborate legal documentation provided by the state, slaves as personal property could be bought and sold, almost literally, at the drop of a dime. Slave trading and slavery were thus inseparable elements of the same system. More to the point, the Atlantic and then the domestic slave trades were the ultimate expressions of the slaveholders' power over their slaves.

The right to command the labor of the slaves—the central element in the Old South's slave labor system—was at bottom a right of property. That right did not arise, for example, from the laws of family and marriage that gave husbands and fathers the power to command the labor of wives and children. Slaveholders commanded labor as a right of property—a right that readily violated patriarchal norms whenever a mistress exercised her power over a male slave or a child exercised the right of property over an adult slave. In one particular the distinction between slavery and patriarchy is especially clear. Domestic law was designed to make marriage difficult and divorce even more so. Once created, the relation of husband and wife was nearly impossible to break in the Old South. By contrast, slave families had no legal standing, and slave family life was notoriously unstable. Precisely because the slaves were the personal property of the owner, the master-slave relationship could be created or destroyed by means of a simple cash transaction. Thus the fact that the slaveholders' own families were organized on the basis of domestic patriarchy did not make slavery itself patriarchal—it was the contrast, not the similarity that stood out. Some slave societies protected slave marriages, but the southern slaveholders resisted it on the grounds that legalized slave marriages constituted a restraint on the master's rights of property.

Similarly, the relentless waves of human migration associated with slavery—across the Sahara, across the Atlantic, and in the 19th century halfway across the North American continent, from Chesapeake Bay to the Rio Grande—all of that movement was a function of the fact that the slaves were personal property. When Thomas Jefferson proposed revising Virginia law to shift slaves from "real" to "personal" property he justified it on the ground that slaves were, as he put it, "moveables."

If all slaves were property, not all property was commodified. In some slave societies, masters accumulated slaves as status symbols whose "value" had little or nothing to do with the price slaves could command on the market. The West African slaves who were slaughtered so they could accompany their deceased masters into the afterlife had little or no value as commodities. On the sugar plantations of Brazil and the Caribbean, slave mortality was so high that the labor force had to be constantly replenished by newly imported slaves from Africa. Once they got off the boats, sugar slaves ceased to be commodities; thereafter masters calculated their value in terms of the years of work slaves performed before they died. But in the American South, slaves were both property *and* commodities. The climate and work demands of most of the major crops—cotton, tobacco, wheat, hemp—made it possible for the slave population to reproduce itself, and by the early 19th century southern masters regularly calculated their annual returns on the basis of the crops slaves produced and the "increase" in the slave population itself. Hence, the robust domestic slave trade replaced the Atlantic trade after 1808.

One of the reasons England made the first successful transition to capitalism was that it had the strongest protections for the rights of property. Anglo-American slaveholders inherited that tradition. Moreover, English imperial officials allowed their colonists more home rule than did the French or the Spanish. As a result, southern slaveholders came close to exercising "absolute" property rights in their slaves. The American Revolution sealed the slaveholders' commitment to an unusually jealous regard for their inalienable rights of property. Thus the class power of the southern slaveholders over their slaves was truly remarkable by historical standards.

In one sense the southern slaveholders remained stuck in the late 18th-century world of near-absolute rights of property. The class structure that developed in the colonial South expanded dramatically but was not fundamentally transformed with the explosive growth of cotton in the 19th century. That structure, in its simplest form, placed the owners of human property on top, those who owned only landed property in the middle, and those who *were* property on the bottom. As capitalism developed in the North, different forms of property proliferated and with that proliferation came a recognition that the state could treat different forms of property in different ways. But the slaveholders, having taken advantage of the efflorescence of the law of personal property, dug in their heels by claiming that slave property was indistinguishable from other forms of property. This appeal to property rights had the singular advantage of winning the support of yeoman farmers who valued their landed independence. Property rights were, after all, property rights. The antislavery movement, by contrast, was based on the principle that the Constitution, though it respected the existence of slavery in the southern states, did not protect slavery as a right of property. This was the burden of Abraham Lincoln's famous speech at Cooper Union in February 1860: there is no such thing as a constitutional right of property in slaves. No wonder the slave states seceded when Lincoln was elected.

The dispute over slavery in the territories came down to precisely this issue: if a right of property was "expressly" recognized by the Constitution, as the slaveholders insisted, Congress could have no authority to prevent slaveholders from bringing their property into the western territories. By contrast, if the Constitution distinguished slaves from other forms of property—by always referring to slaves as "persons," for example—Congress was fully within its rights to discriminate against slave property. The emergence of a Republican Party dedicated to that proposition that there was no constitutional right of property in slaves represented a tremendous threat to the class power of the southern slaveholders.

That power had long been exercised in the national government. Far from withering in the wake of the American Revolution, the slaveholding class had flourished. It grew with cotton—expanding in numbers and in territorial scope. On the eve of the Civil War 400,000 slaveholders owned 4 million African Americans. Those slaves were distributed across the region as follows:

Alabama	435,132
Arkansas	111,104
Delaware	1,798
Florida	61,753
Georgia	462,230
Kentucky	225,490
Louisiana	332,520
Maryland	87,188
Mississippi	436,696
Missouri	114,965
North Carolina	331,081
South Carolina	402,541
Tennessee	275,784
Texas	180,388
Virginia	490,887

With that expansion of the slaveholding class came a corresponding increase in its political power. Slaves were counted for purposes of representation in the

House of Representatives, which in turn enhanced the slaveholders' power in the electoral college. For 75 years slaveholders or their advocates dominated the presidency and the Supreme Court. When they came under attack, the slaveholders had every reason to defend themselves by constant reference to their inalienable rights of property. When a major party arose in the 1850s expressly denying that there was any such a thing as a constitutional right of property, the slaveholders saw it for what it was. They were under attack, as a class. The abolition of slavery was the abolition of the slaveholding class.

JAMES OAKES
City University of New York

Ira Berlin, *Journal of American History* (March 2004); John W. Blessingame, *The Slave Community: Planation Life in the Antebellum South* (1972); Timothy H. Breen, *"Myne Own Ground": Race and Freedom on Virginia's Eastern Shore* (1980); David Brion Davis, *The Problem of Slavery in Western Culture* (1966); Carl N. Degler, *Neither Black Nor White: Slavery and Race Relations in Brazil and the United States* (1971); Robert W. Fogel, *Without Consent or Contract: The Rise and Fall of American Slavery* (1989); Eugene D. Genovese, *The Political Economy of Slavery: Studies in the Economy and Society of the Slave South* (1965), *Roll, Jordon, Roll: The World the Slaves Made* (1974), *The World the Slaveholders Made: Two Essays in Interpretation* (1975); Peter Kolchin, *American Slavery, 1619-1877* (1993); Melton McLaurin, *Celia, a Slave* (1991); Edmund S. Morgan, *American Slavery, American Freedom: The Ordeal of Colonial Virginia* (1975); Thomas D. Morris, *Southern Slavery and the Law, 1619-1860* (1996); James Oakes, *The Ruling Race: A History of American Slaveholders* (1982), *Slavery and Freedom: An Interpretation of the Old South* (1990); Orlando Patterson, *Slavery and Social Death* (1982); Kenneth Stampp, *The Peculiar Institution: Slavery in the Ante-Bellum South* (1956): Gavin Wright, *Slavery and American Economic Development* (2006).

Social Reform, 1932-1954

The recorded history of the Western Hemisphere is now well along into its sixth century. In the most generalized view of it, this history begins with the arrival by sea of European explorers along a vast "Indies" coastline of seemingly infinite length and impenetrable depth. It took 180 years for this Spanish-British-French-Dutch foothold on the North American continent to ripen into an independent country. By then, the fledgling United States of America, having remained all the while under the absolute dominion of European males, was entering nationhood as a broader amalgam of men and women than could be found in any of its contributing countries and territories. The first census, in 1790, counted close to 4 million people in the 13 colonies-turned-states. Most were Europeans spawned from half a dozen linguistic streams; the rest— roughly one of every six—were people of African descent, their forebears having been forcibly abducted for slave labor. Also present, but not counted, were perhaps 4 million native inhabitants (a conservative estimate) in scores of tribal and linguistic configurations.

In its 1776 Declaration of Independence from Great Britain, and in other founding documents, such as the Constitution (1787) and the Bill of Rights (1791), the United States had given expression to a set of ideals and values— democracy, freedom, justice, equality—intended to set it apart from the royalist and feudal empires out of which it had risen. The nation's original motto, *E pluribus unum* (Out of many, one), was inscribed in Latin on the Great Seal of the United States in 1776, and that spirit of unity and perpetual renewal brought an endless stream of immigrants to these shores.

But after eight decades of nationhood, America (as it had come to be popularly called) was threatened by an internal crisis rooted in the contradiction between the ideal of liberty and the reality of slavery. Although the trade in slaves from Africa had been outlawed in 1808, the practice of slaveholding continued to flourish, especially in the 11 southernmost states (among 33 in the nation at that time), and they joined in a rebellion against the Union in 1861, fueled in large measure by their determination to retain slavery.

Ahead of the Union's 1865 victory in that war, President Abraham Lincoln issued a proclamation freeing all slaves in the rebel states. As a condition of rejoining the nation, the defeated states had to agree to that mandate and ratify amendments to the Constitution guaranteeing equal protection of the laws. But the Union's 12-year program of "reconstruction" designed to make equality the legal standard in every state was not successful, particularly in the South. By the end of the century, a more subtle form of discrimination—"separate but equal" segregation—had been affirmed by the Supreme Court. It was quickly written into law across the South and became common practice in other states as well. These conditions prevailed until 1954, when the high court, in a unanimous decision, declared racial segregation laws to be unconstitutional.

The election of Franklin D. Roosevelt to the presidency in 1932 ushered in a generation of quickening social change in America, and although it was perhaps more gradual in the South, it was nonetheless profound and historic. Even though relations between the races and between the upper and lower classes of southern people were not dramatically transformed in the years between 1932 and 1954, that time was a vital and perhaps essential prelude to all that was to follow. In hindsight, it now seems fair to say that the prospects for elevation of the southern underclass, black and white, brightened more in that 22-year period than in all the years since the end of Reconstruction in 1877.

In the 1930s attorneys of the National Association for the Advancement of Colored People (NAACP) began to challenge racial discrimination in voting rights, in access to higher education, and in the administration of criminal justice. James Weldon Johnson, Charles H. Houston, Walter White, William H. Hastie, and Thurgood Marshall—each with roots both in Africa and in the South—spearheaded these NAACP ventures. An Atlanta-based biracial group, the Commission on Interracial Cooperation, founded in 1918, gave voice to Will Alexander, Jessie Daniel Ames, and other white progressives, as well as to black educators Benjamin Mays, Charles S. Johnson, Mary McLeod Bethune, and others.

Dozens of progressive southerners planned and carried out a biracial gathering of thousands at the Southern Conference for Human Welfare in Birmingham in 1938, and their efforts had a carryover effect that lasted into the civil rights era. The southern labor movement produced several strong advocates of desegregation in this time, among them H. L. Mitchell of Tennessee and Lucy Randolph Mason of Virginia—whites from opposite ends of the economic spectrum—as well as A. Philip Randolph, a Floridian who founded the all-black Pullman Porters Union, and Hosea Hudson, a black steelworker in Alabama. Higher education in the region, though tightly segregated, brought a host of prominent figures into the quest for racial equality, including Frank Porter Graham, Arthur Raper, Katharine Du Pre Lumpkin, and Alva W. Taylor from the white institutions and Horace Mann Bond, Charlotte Hawkins Brown, and Gordon B. Hancock from the black ones.

Elective politics was a closed field to African American southerners in that time, and white politicians typically hewed to the segregation line; among the handful of exceptions were Sen. Hugo Black of Alabama and two congressmen, Maury Maverick of Texas and Claude Pepper of Florida. By the 1940s, governors Ellis Arnall of Georgia and Jim Folsom of Alabama dared to venture toward race reforms. Few white men in the business world, in the field of journalism, or even in the organized church spoke out for racial justice in the 1930s, and those who did were soon isolated or driven out.

Even so, there were some prophetic voices in the ranks, men and women of the pen or the cloth or the soapbox who kept calling the South to its common destiny with the nation: Clarence Jordan and George Mitchell of Georgia; Septima Clark of South Carolina; Thomas Sancton of Louisiana; Howard Kester of the Committee of Southern Churchmen; Paul Green and W. J. Cash of North Carolina; Myles Horton, Don West, and James Dombrowski of the Highlander Folk School in Tennessee, to name a few.

By the finely calibrated gauge of history, this liberal remnant, which could not have counted more than a few thousand southern men and women in the first half of the 20th century, was influential out of all proportion to its number. After the eventual fall of Jim Crow segregation, when it was easier to acknowledge and even celebrate their visionary contributions, a belated twilight glow fell upon some of them. Here are a random few illustrative examples.

Zora Neale Hurston, raised in the all-black town of Eatonville, Fla., in the twilight of the 19th century, found her way along an improbable route to fame and notoriety as a novelist, folklorist, and caustic social observer. She earned elite credentials in New York as an anthropologist, found a prominent place for herself among the literati (whom she mockingly tagged the "niggerati") in the Harlem Renaissance of the 1920s, conducted ethnographic studies in the Caribbean region, and wrote about the rural laborers of Florida and the South for the Federal Writers Project during the Great Depression. Her 1937 novel, *Their Eyes Were Watching God*, was criticized by black writers of that time as a bruising burlesque of the hard lives of the unchained African American masses, but today, Hurston's work is praised for its honesty, and the artist-scholar herself as a fearless and far-sighted champion of the poor. Ironically, she died one among them, in a Florida home for the indigent, in 1960.

Lillian Smith was also born in a small town in north Florida (Jasper) near the end of the 19th century, but there her similarity to Hurston ends. Brought up in a prominent white family (her father was a civic-minded businessman), Smith spent significant portions of her young adult life as a student of music, a teacher in southern mountain schools, and as the director of music at a Methodist school for girls in China. When she was almost 30, she succeeded her father at the helm of a camp for girls in the mountains of north Georgia. It was from that unlikely base that Lillian Smith came into her own as a writer. Her 1944 novel, *Strange Fruit*, about an interracial romance in the South, brought her instant fame and lifelong notoriety; possibly even more sensational, at least in her native South, was *Killers of the Dream* (1949), a searing nonfiction assessment of the psychological damage done to all, but especially to whites, by racial discrimination. Until her death in 1966, Lillian Smith was a steadfast advocate of race and gender equality.

Aubrey Williams was a social worker in the Midwest when he was recruited for the welfare and relief task force of the Roosevelt New Deal in 1933, but his roots ran deep in the rural Alabama underclass. His plantation-owning grandfather had freed his slaves as an act of conscience five years before the Civil War, in consequence of which the family survived the war landless and impoverished. Aubrey, born in 1890 in a small town near Birmingham, somehow found his way into a Tennessee college without benefit of a high school diploma, and resourceful self-sufficiency marked his rise from there. He directed the National Youth Administration under FDR and was nominated in 1945 to lead the New Deal's massive program of rural electrification, but 19 of the South's 22 Senate Democrats saw to his defeat, calling him "a prolabor leftist" and a "communist sympathizer" who had "renounced the divinity of Christ." Williams went home to Alabama, where he founded a progressive newspaper for farmers and generally supported the cause of the South's beleaguered rural workers, white and black, until his death in 1965.

John H. McCray and Osceola McKaine founded the Progressive Democratic Party (PDP) in South Carolina in 1944 as a protest against their continued exclusion from the state's Jim Crow politics after the U.S. Supreme Court had ruled that all-white primary elections were unconstitutional. The PDP sent a biracial delegation to the Democratic National Convention in Chicago that summer (it was denied admission) and got McKaine on the fall ballot as a candidate for the U.S. Senate. For their audacity, the two black leaders were harassed and threatened; McCray, who published a weekly newspaper, even spent several months in prison after he was convicted of publishing "defamatory material." Still, their fight to end segregation had long-term inspirational potency; 20 years later, Fannie Lou Hamer and others led the Mississippi Freedom Democratic Party to challenge another national party convention, after which, in 1965, the federal Voting Rights Act became the climactic legislative achievement of the civil rights movement.

Southerners such as these showed by word and deed in the years before *Brown* that, notwithstanding their region's tragic history, they foresaw a future in which a richly diverse citizenry would enjoy an appreciable measure of equity in their public and private lives. At no time did these native sons and daughters have the numbers or the power to bring about what they envisioned. But had it not been for their courageous public advocacy of equal justice under law, the post-1954 movement for social change might have come too late to avert another civil war, this time not between geographic regions but between light and dark, rich and poor. The social reforms of 1933–54, however modest and fragile, provided the vital foundation for the broader social revolution that followed, and continues now, in the South and across the nation.

JOHN EGERTON
Nashville, Tennessee

Anthony P. Dunbar, *Against the Grain: Southern Radicals and Prophets, 1929–1959* (1981); John Egerton, *Speak Now against the Day: The Generation before the Civil Rights Movement in the South* (1994); Glenda Elizabeth Gilmore, *Defying Dixie: The Radical Roots of Civil Rights, 1919–1950* (2008); Patricia Sullivan, *Days of Hope: Race and Democracy in the New Deal Era* (1996).

Southern Identity

When scholars use the notion of "southern identity," they have in mind two very different but interdependent processes, one pertaining to the collective definition of the region and the other to the social psychology of regional identification. On the question of collective definition, what it means to be a southerner is a complex and historically shifting consequence of imposition of laws, images, stereotypes, and the like by powerful forces in the public arena (such as military victors, political majorities, the federal government, and the media) and negotiation of meaning among and between southerners and others. On the question of the social psychology of regionalism, why individuals identify themselves as "southerners"—whatever the collective meaning of the identity—is, on the other hand, a function of choices they make, choices, however, constrained by people's social positions.

One of the most important social positions individuals occupy is their social class location. Generally, class location and social status affect a variety of our actions and attitudes, from religious preferences to child-rearing patterns to political behavior. Do class and status, however, shape how southerners think of themselves in regional terms? There are several ways to go about answering this question. One method—the use of representative public opinion polls—offers systematic statistical evidence about how large numbers of randomly chosen southerners think about themselves in regional terms.

The best public opinion poll data on southern identity comes from a series of 19 representative surveys conducted by the University of North Carolina between 1991 and 2001. Known as the Southern Focus Polls (SFP), they include, cumulatively, the responses of about 17,600 southerners (defined as inhabitants of the former Confederate states plus Kentucky and Oklahoma). All polls asked respondents living in the South an identically worded question: "Do you consider yourself a southerner, or not?" Responses to this question thus indicate if the SFP respondents categorize themselves as members of a regional group, itself understood by sociologist John Shelton Reed (who helped design the polls) as "a reference group, a cognitive entity that people use to orient themselves."

Overall, we find that most of people who lived in the region, 75 percent or so, thought of themselves as southerners. This was true for both African

Americans and whites (though less so for other races and ethnicities). Income of region's residents (at least during 1991–2001) did not generally affect their identity claims; that is, individuals, again black or white, situated in the lowest income category or the highest, or somewhere in the middle of the income distribution, equally claimed to be southern (again, about 75 percent or so). From 1997 through 2001, the SFP also asked respondents who claimed to be southern how important their southern identity was to them. For whites, income had little effect on the salience of this identity: about 65 percent of whites who embraced their regional identity believed it either "very" or "somewhat" important, regardless of income. Higher-income African Americans were somewhat less likely than their lower-income peers to view their southern identity as important, but the differences were small and statistically insignificant.

When we shift attention to the consequences of educational attainment, an indicator of social class that places greater emphasis on the cultural dimension of class location than income, we find that highly educated residents of the South less frequently define themselves in regional terms. Thus, for whites, of southerners without a high school degree, 83 percent claim to be southern; only 67 percent of those who have graduated from college or have completed postgraduate studies do so. The pattern is similar for African Americans, albeit less pronounced (81 versus 76 percent). Sociologists have found that educational attainment often induces or reflects cosmopolitanism rather than parochialism (and thus perhaps regionalist sentiment) and a critical stance toward one's own culture. Highly educated southerners, too, may have been more frequently exposed to negative representations of the South and thus simply believe that they do not fit traditional images of what a southerner is. Among those who claim a southern identity, moreover, highly educated southerners of both races less often state that the identity is "very important."

The Southern Focus Polls, then, indicate that social class—especially education—does appear to affect modestly the likelihood that people in the South choose to claim a southern identity and the salience self-defined southerners place on their regional identities. But these same polls also show that such effects are eclipsed by much more powerful factors affecting identity choices—how long one has lived in the South, whether one has a self-perceived southern accent, in what part of the South one resides, and so on.

Most social surveys and opinion polls, however, are incapable of delving deeply into the consciousness of respondents and so do not help us understand what their regional identity means to them. In-depth interviews with a smaller number of targeted southerners are especially useful for addressing these questions. Though the people who are intensively interviewed are not representative of a nation, region, or social class (there simply are too few of them, and they are chosen at random), they may nonetheless constitute a sample of representative southerners.

Our in-depth interviews conducted in 2004-5 with 59 black and white southerners from various regions in the lowland and mountain South suggest that the meaning of southern identity both varies by social class and is racialized. They also indicate, in a way opinion polls generally cannot, just how complex are the linkages among social class, race, and regional identity. Departing a bit from the results of the SFP, for example, we found "elite" black southerners—that is, those with postgraduate degrees and high incomes—were accustomed to thinking about the South and about their own southern identity. Many of these highly educated African Americans expressed strong identification with the South and pride in their southernness—a pride, interviews tell us, often based on the history of racial struggle in the region and their people's ultimate triumph over Jim Crow segregation and oppression. In contrast, most African Americans with less education and lower income did not use the identity "southerner" as a reference group of importance. Traits that whites might associate with southerners, such as strong accents, living in rural areas, and eating southern foods, were often identified by these black southerners as "country" rather than southern. There is anecdotal evidence, moreover, that blacks in the South do not call themselves southern. In fact, many African Americans with lower levels of education and incomes appeared, when interviewed, initially uncertain as to what made one a "southerner" and stated that they had never really thought about being southern. Though they all ultimately concluded that they were "southern," regional affiliation was obviously not a basis of self-identification they frequently used, especially when compared to the significance they placed on their racial identity.

Class is also important for the identity of white southerners, but in ways that differ from how it affects the region's African Americans. In general, white southerners, regardless of their social class, were much more familiar with thinking about themselves in regional terms. No white southerners asked for clarification as to what made someone "southern." Whereas the majority of black southerners did not consider their regional identity to be very important, most white southerners moderately or strongly identified with the region. Commonalities among these whites abound. For example, most whites said that they enjoyed the food in the South, the friendly people, the laid-back lifestyle, and the "family values" of a bygone time, consequently romanticizing the "Old South."

Strong differences exist, however, in how white southerners of different social classes experienced and expressed their "southernness." On the one hand, white southerners with lower incomes and levels of education often strongly identified with the South and stated that the Confederate flag was a sign of southern heritage. They seemed more defensive of their heritage, often noting that jokes about the South really bothered them and that nonsoutherners looked down on the region. On the other hand, higher-status white southerners spoke of the importance of old family names, manners, and a genteel lifestyle that is now fading. Many middle- and upper-class whites, some large landowners, talked about the importance of preserving the land from development. They tended to acknowledge the racial wrongs of the past, but stated that they did not like to dwell on the negative aspects of the South's history. These affluent and highly educated whites also specifically stated that they neither identified with nor liked the "redneck," Confederate flag-waving image of the South and feared that nonsoutherners, unable or unwilling to distinguish among white southerners of different classes, would perceive them to be unintelligent. Through such social psychological mechanisms—as well, of course, through the concrete advantages conferred on them by way of their position, power, and prestige—higher-strata white southerners intentionally distance themselves and their definition of southern identity from stereotyped images of lower-strata and working-class white southerners.

LARRY J. GRIFFIN
Georgia Southern University

ASHLEY B. THOMPSON
Lynchburg College

James C. Cobb, *Away Down South: A History of Southern Identity* (2005); Larry J. Griffin, *Southern Cultures* (Fall 2006); Larry J. Griffin, Ashley B. Thompson, and Ranae J. Evenson, *Southern Cultures* (Spring 2005); Jack Temple Kirby, *The Countercultural South* (2005); John Shelton Reed, *Southerners: The Social Psychology of Sectionalism* (1983), *Southern Folk, Plain and Fancy* (1986); Carla D. Shirley, *Social Forces* (September 2010); Ashley B. Thompson, *Southern Identity: The Meaning, Practice, and Importance of Regional Identity* (2007).

Sports

The South has a rich sporting tradition that includes fishing and hunting, baseball, basketball, track and field, lacrosse, and equine sports among other athletic pursuits. A close look at any of these provides a picture of sports and social class in the South. But three activities in particular—Southeastern Conference (SEC) football, National Association for Stock Car Auto Racing (NASCAR), and the Masters golf tournament—illustrate the range of class-based sporting experiences that weave together the history of class and southern sports culture. All of these activities serve as rallying points, bringing people from diverse backgrounds together to root for their favorite teams and athletes, to celebrate triumphs, and to despair when rivals are victorious. Yet these three sports also reveal the fault lines of social class inequality, simultaneously shaped by hierarchies of race and gender that form the backdrop of social life in the American South.

Football, perhaps the most popular spectator sport throughout the United States, is revered in the South. Though Friday night high school games and Sunday afternoon NFL matches draw crowds, college football boasts the most fervent devotion, particularly among fans of SEC teams. When the Rebels of Ole Miss take the field, southern pride is on the line. Though the icons of southern culture are most prominently displayed by the Ole Miss faithful, fans throughout the SEC hold up their schools, and their teams' athletic performances, as representations of southern heritage and tradition. But at what cost? In the 1980s Mississippi's football coach blamed the fans' displays of the Confederate flag for the school's failure to attract talented African American recruits. This was just one part of the unfolding story of SEC football, southern culture, and race. For decades, SEC football staunchly defended a heritage and tradition of racial segregation. Throughout the 1950s and 1960s all-white SEC teams refused to compete against integrated teams from other regions. Only after these integrated teams began to dominate the national rankings did SEC schools, starting with the University of Kentucky in 1967, recruit black football players. In the end, the heritage of racial segregation was less sacred than the tradition of gridiron supremacy, and today's racially diverse SEC teams regularly dominate both the polls and the bowl games.

Outwardly it appears that SEC football unites southerners from all walks of life. On game days, the rich and poor alike dress in their teams' colors and proudly fly their schools' flags. Men and women of all races and ethnicities rally around their teams. However, a closer look at SEC football reveals persistent, structured inequality rooted in social class, race, and gender divisions. The Southeastern Conference, its member schools, head coaches, and corporate sponsors reap multimillion dollar payouts from a variety of revenue sources, including ticket sales, television broadcasting contracts, and merchandising. All too often, these economic victories are won on the backs of poor (and disproportionately black) athletes who may have been recruited despite records of low academic achievement and whose labor on the football field comes at the expense of their academic progress, often leading them to exhaust their athletic eligibility and their scholarships without earning college degrees. Though NCAA rules prohibit student athletes from enjoying the financial fruits of their athletic labor, most SEC football players are rewarded with heightened social status on campus. This same benefit rarely extends to female athletes, though women who play supporting roles for the men's football team, such as cheerleaders and the officially sanctioned campus hostesses, whose job it is to ensure that the next big recruit will be shown a good time during his on-campus visit, do accrue reflected glory. Thus, even as football serves as a cohesive force for the community, it simultaneously reinforces and reproduces the social class, race, and gender order.

Whereas football enjoys a fan base spread widely across the social spectrum, the sports of stock car racing and golf are both known for their class-based origins and appeal. According to NASCAR lore, the sport claims roots in the Appalachian mountain regions of the South, where moonshiners supposedly modified their cars in order to evade law enforcement as they transported bootleg whiskey across the treacherous roads. Founded in 1947 by Bill France Sr., NASCAR held its first sanctioned race at the Charlotte Speedway in June 1949. In the decades that followed, NASCAR maintained its reputation as a predominantly working-class, white male sport, and its most celebrated drivers (e.g., Richard Petty, Dale Earnhardt) have been those who highlighted their working-class roots. In 1961 African American driver Wendell Scott joined NASCAR's elite circuit, winning his first (and only) Grand National race in 1963. Yet nonwhite drivers remain few and far between, and nearly half a century later Scott remains the only black driver to have ever won a major NASCAR event. While NASCAR fans are overwhelmingly white, the organization proudly boasts that women make up nearly 40 percent of its followers. Still, female drivers are exceedingly rare and those who have managed to join the circuit, such as Liz Guthrie in 1977, were met with hostility both on the track and in the garage. Even as race and gender present clear obstacles to joining the NASCAR circuit, Guthrie herself pointed to money as the biggest obstacle. Racing is an expensive sport, and competitive drivers need to possess not only superb skills but also sponsors with deep pockets.

Both in the larger society and within the world of organized sports, money equates with power. NASCAR differs from other sports in the extreme degree of power wielded by the France family. Although players' unions exist in most major sports, the France family has managed on several occasions to repel efforts among NASCAR drivers to organize. To this day, NASCAR remains a family-owned and operated business and current CEO and chairman Brian France (grandson of Bill France Sr.) maintains strict control of the organization. Under Brian France's leadership, in the past few decades NASCAR has taken steps to increase its reach, extending beyond the South and looking to attract an upper-class, suburban market. In 2004 NASCAR replaced longtime sponsor R. J. Reynolds with Nextel Corporation, a deliberate move intended to distance itself from the tobacco industry and to increase its appeal among the more educated and technologically savvy consumer market. Even as it aspires to expand the demographics of its fan base, NASCAR continues to be associated with its white, working-class roots. This became clear with the emergence of a new political term, "NASCAR dads," used to denote southern, white, working-class, and lower-middle-class males who threw their support behind Republican George W. Bush in his 2004 presidential reelection bid.

Given the great profit to be reaped from commercialized sport, it stands to reason that every professional sports league would desire to widen its fan base. This is certainly true of the Professional Golf Association (PGA), which in recent years has realized significant gains thanks to the emergence of Tiger Woods as a dominant athlete whose multiracial and multicultural background holds global appeal. Though the PGA welcomes increased attention from those new to golf, the same is not necessarily true of the private clubs that host golf's major events. The Masters tournament, held at Augusta National in Augusta, Ga., every April, showcases southern charm and beauty. At a time when much of the northern hemisphere is still experiencing winter's chill, the course at Augusta National is resplendent with blooming azaleas, dogwoods, and magnolias. The PGA's telecast beckons all who watch to bask in the southern sunshine, yet actual tickets to the event are some of the hardest to come by in all sports. The event has been officially sold out since the early 1970s, and while a waiting list for tickets exists, no new names have been added since 1978 as it is said that the current list could not possibly be exhausted for several lifetimes. Still, the week of the Masters tournament holds the most promise for anyone wishing to glimpse the grounds of Augusta National. At all other times, visitors must be accompanied by a member. Since its inception in 1932, privacy and exclusivity have remained hallmarks of the elite club's identity. Though no membership list is available for public perusal, the club's most famous members have included golfing legend (and club cofounder) Bobby Jones and former U.S. president Dwight Eisenhower. Current members are said to include former Georgia senator Sam Nunn, CEO Jack Welch, investor Warren Buffett, and Microsoft founder Bill Gates.

With its members counted among the most prominent, wealthy, and powerful Americans, Augusta National remains a bastion of class elitism. In addition, Augusta National provides one of the more stark examples of the intersection of class, race, and gender in sports. Workers at the private club are predominantly African Americans from society's lower strata. For decades after the club's founding, even as white Augustans expressed an interest in working at the National, the club followed a practice of hiring only blacks as caddies, clubhouse attendants, and waiters. Not only are members wealthy and powerful, but they are overwhelmingly white. Responding to pressure from the PGA, which in 1990 made it clear that racially discriminatory clubs were at risk of losing the right to host major tournaments, in 1991 Augusta National admitted its first African American member. To this day, there are no female members. This fact became a national controversy in 2002 when Martha Burk, president of the Washington, D.C.–based National Council of Women's Organizations, protested. While Burk's campaign garnered worldwide attention, club president Hootie Johnson vocally resisted her charges of sexism and dismissed her as a "Yankee publicity seeker," suggesting that this was not only an issue of gender but also one of region and southern self-determination.

The South has a rich sporting tradition. While football, stock car racing, and golf represent only a small slice of sports in the South, each illustrates the paradox of social unity and division found within sports. Even as popular sports such as football bring people together, and as sports such as NASCAR and golf grow in spectatorship, they also reveal class relations infused with race and gender dimensions that work to maintain structures of inequality.

NANCY L. MALCOM
Georgia Southern University

Wes Borucki, in *Identities: Global Studies in Culture and Power* (2003); Liz Clarke, *One Helluva Ride: How NASCAR Swept the Nation* (2008); Jay Coakley, *Sports in Society* (2009); D. Stanley Eitzen, in *Sport in Contemporary Society*, ed. D. Stanley Eitzen (2005); Randal L. Hall, *North Carolina Historical Review* (July 2007); Douglas A. Hurt, *Southeastern Geographer* (May 2005); Charles H. Martin, in *Higher Education and the Civil Rights Movement: White Supremacy, Black Southerners, and College Campuses*, ed. Peter Wallenstein (2008); Dan Pierce, *Southern Cultures* (Summer 2001); Curt Sampson, *The Masters: Golf, Money, and Power in Augusta, Georgia* (1998); Monica K. Varner and J. David Knottnerus, *Sociological Inquiry* (Summer 2002).

Stereotypes, Female

The South, historically, was a patriarchal place, and stereotypes of southern women reflected the region's interest in supporting and maintaining traditional gender roles and the racial and class hierarchies that accompanied them. The model of southern womanhood was the white, upper-class genteel "southern lady," a staunch defender of both patriarchy and white supremacy. Emerging from the antebellum world of white privilege, connoting the leisure, wealth, and power of the planter classes, and changing but little for 100 years after the destruction of slavery, the respected and honored role of "lady" was not available to minority or working-class women. Whereas the stereotype of privileged white women suggested a place of honor and respect, women in marginalized groups fared much worse. Too powerless to define an image for themselves that percolated upward, they were stigmatized in pejorative and insulting ways. The upper classes characterized white working-class women as "crackers," "hillbillies," and (in more modern versions) "redneck mothers" or "trailer-park trash," and black women as "Jezebel," the seductress, or the servile "mammy." Latinas were stereotyped as "either the innocent, passive, virginal Madonna, as played by Natalie Wood as Maria [in *West Side Story*], or as the hot-blooded, fiery, sexy spitfire or whore, as played by Rita Moreno as Anita." All were judged against the ideal of the gracious, graceful, fashionably dressed, and well-mannered southern lady.

The ideal of "southern lady" was a public persona. Appearance mattered, and a lady must look her best in all situations. Not only must she be modestly attired and well coiffed, above all she must exhibit impeccable manners. She sat up straight and kept her knees primly together. She walked daintily, taking small, unhurried, steps, and walked most confidently when on the arm of a man. She did not stride, scratch herself, or dominate conversations—all things men did. She listened attentively, complimented frequently, and never interrupted. She was decorous, calm, and amiable. Her purpose was to put others at ease and build up social connections.

Likewise, a lady devoted herself to family. Her duty was to raise virtuous, patriotic citizens, all for the honor of her husband and the family's name. Her behavior and that of her children symbolized his success. A southern lady maintained regular contact with her own and her husband's family, preserved family traditions, either orally or in writing, and taught the children the family history. She entertained her husband's family and friends regularly, for a lady was also hospitable. To be a good hostess, she read widely in the classics and history. She exhibited an appreciation for culture and perhaps even mastered (to use a male term) a musical instrument, but a proper lady never upstaged or challenged men intellectually.

Key to a lady's image was sexual purity. A southern "belle" (a single young white woman), though she might be flirtatious and use her feminine wiles to catch the right mate, was sexually innocent and chaste. Upon marriage she became a "lady" and was expected to be faithful to her "lord and master." Lacking lust, she left sexual initiative to her husband. Men seeking sexually experienced and overtly sensuous women were expected to turn to prostitutes (the lowest classes) or to black women.

Another quality expected of a southern lady was piety. She professed faith in God, attended church regularly, and committed time to charitable and benevolent work. That black women of all classes dedicated just as much time to the church and spent much of their waking hours devoted to the care and upkeep of their families and neighbors (while simultaneously working full time) did not register on the consciousness of the powerful upper-class whites for whom black women toiled day in and day out for meager wages.

Though perceived as "delicate flowers" (indicating fragility as well as beauty), dependents in need of male protection, upper-class southern women were also seen as "Steel Magnolias" who were stronger than men—although they must keep this secret, out of deferential respect to men. They held home and hearth together regardless of any tragedy that might befall the family and the homestead, indeed, even the region (as during the Civil War). A lady contained a quiet strength and was not aggressive. She was a survivor, but she survived with dignity.

Exhibiting fitting respect for the "natural" distinctions between men and women, a proper lady was submissive to her husband and to patriarchal authority. She happily and willingly kept to her assigned domestic sphere. Economically dependent on men, she did not work for pay outside the home. Because politics was public and associated with men, a lady did not exhibit interest in worldly affairs, at least not in mixed "promiscuous" groups. If she influenced men, she did so gently and indirectly, through her role as moral guardian. She never contradicted a man, and if she expressed an opinion, it was "within a context that support[ed] southern traditionalism." Above all, southern ladies were status conscious and loyal to their class, cheerleaders for southern heritage, particularly the Lost Cause and white supremacy.

In the 20th century the trappings of a southern belle changed somewhat. A modern southern belle signed up for cotillion, tap, ballet, beauty pageants, the family's favorite sorority, and, before she was 20, served as a duchess or queen of some local festival or ball or another. A successful southern belle always wore a crown. Mardi Gras balls on the Gulf Coast have the debutantes making their appearance on the arms of older men. A southern belle's wedding was an over-the-top lavish affair, following which she joined an exclusive club such as the country club, the Junior League or other women's clubs that met at lunchtime, or (most importantly) a garden club.

Like their foremothers of the 1890s, the stereotypical 20th-century southern ladies were dedicated to the preservation of southern heritage and joined the United Daughters of the Confederacy. Only the younger generation of belles, who grew up after the civil rights movement of the 1960s, stopped referring to the Civil War as the "war between the states" or "the war of northern aggression." While many of the trappings of "ladyhood" continue to grip the personae of the southern woman, racism is increasingly receding as a venerable characteristic.

If upper-class white women personified the idealized notions of femininity in the South, black women embodied their opposite. Because upper-class whites did the defining, their prescription for appropriate gender behavior was accepted as the norm, and all deviations from it were derided or mocked. Because women of color could not afford to be leisured, they could not qualify as "ladies." Economic necessity required them to work with their hands, either outside their shacks alongside their husband and children in the fields or in servile labor outside the home. Because "lady" was synonymous with virtue, no one with illegitimate children qualified, and freedwomen all came out of slavery with illegitimate children. Upon their emancipation, freedwomen sought to legitimize their marriages and establish parental rights to their children, who frequently could not be located, but they were still powerless to change the image. Even black females born after 1865 to married parents fared little better in the southern mythology constructed by whites. Though African American leaders such as Mary Church Terrell encouraged the adoption of bourgeois values and culture among women of her race, they were powerless to alter the perception of the dominant group that black women were "Jezebels," or seductresses. Whites regarded ethnic women, including immigrants and women of color, as sexually promiscuous, unable to control their animalistic instincts. Their loss of sexual innocence at the hands of white men was therefore their own fault.

Another stock stereotype of black women was "mammy," a maternal, nurturing, domestic figure. Though a more positive portrayal, it was still a demeaning image that had the black woman as a subservient, faithful, and loyal servant to the privileged whites. The postbellum reconstruction of this figure came in the form of Aunt Jemima, the "slave in a box" developed by Quaker Oats in the 1890s. According to her "biographer," M. M. Manring, Aunt Jemima represents the "commodification of racial and gender inequality." Though rid of her bandanna by the late 1980s, Aunt Jemima remained a nonthreatening, asexual black woman happily serving white women. Both mammy and Aunt Jemima were satisfied with their positions. They implicitly supported white supremacy. Ironically, today, thanks to the feminist movement, there tends to be more respect among modern women of all races and classes for the black women of the past than for the southern lady. African American women, courageous in the face of seemingly insurmountable odds, held their families and communities together. One idol for modern women is Sojourner Truth, who embodied what women today perceive to be feminine virtue because she challenged the stereotypes of female incapacity. Ida B. Wells, Fannie Lou Hamer, Ella Baker, bell hooks, and Oprah Winfrey serve as role models for all women. The modern black superwoman, one commentator says, is "less of a woman in that she is less 'feminine' and helpless, she is really more of a woman in that she is the embodiment of Mother Earth, the quintessential mother with infinite sexual, life-giving, and nurturing reserves."

Latina women, caught in a culture that celebrated machismo (exaggerated masculinity), were stereotyped as weak and submissive to their husbands. While Latino culture today shows evidence of traditional patriarchy, research shows that there is tremendous variety of gender roles within Latino households, ranging from traditional to egalitarian, even in the division of domestic labor. The process of immigration itself often transforms traditional patriarchal patterns into more egalitarian ones, as the immigrants are influenced by the surrounding culture. Further, women in immigrant Latino families often work, which gives them a sense of autonomy and freedom, as well as the ability to leave abusive husbands.

Emmie Slattery in *Gone with the Wind* represents a traditional stereotype of lower-class white women: ignorant, unsophisticated, unlettered, narrow-minded, racist, and parochial. Women of this class characterized themselves quite differently: as hardworking and honest, friendly, familial, generous, self-sufficient, and neighborly. They resented that more cultured whites displaced racism onto them as a way of denying their own racism. In the modern era, when they have been in a position to do more of the defining themselves, these women have created a version of "redneck feminism" and the positive image of the "good old girl."

There is no stereotype of a southern middle-class woman, because, until very recently, the southern middle class seemed ill-defined. When it emerged, though, in some ways it conformed to other traditional southern values, it looked largely the same as bourgeoisie stereotypes elsewhere in the country.

All stereotypes represent exaggeration and, in the case of the "lady," an ideal image that few women upheld entirely. All stereotypes, too, reflect power arrangements in a given society. The people at the top, the cultural arbiters, invariably invent demeaning images of those "beneath" them. Yet the cultural output of the lower classes, particularly their stories, jokes, and songs, show that, rather than being respectful of the "better sort," they mocked and derided them, and regarded them as callous, selfish, and uncaring. But only one group was in a position to cement the image in the popular mind, and that was the people with money.

JANET ALLURED
McNeese State University

Caroline Matheny Dillman, ed., *Southern Women* (1988); Jacquelyn Dowd Hall, *Revolt against Chivalry: Jessie Daniel Ames and the Women's Campaign against Lynching* (1979); Anne Goodwyn Jones, *Tomorrow Is Another Day: The Woman Writer in the South, 1859-1936* (1987); Florence King, *Confessions of a Failed Southern Lady* (1985), *Southern Ladies and Gentlemen* (1975); M. M. Manring, *Slave in a Box: The Strange Career of Aunt Jemima* (1998); Sharon McKern, *Redneck Mothers, Good Ol' Girls, and Other Southern Belles* (1979); Anne Firor Scott, *The Southern Lady: From Pedestal to Politics, 1830-1930* (1970); Maryln Schwartz, *A Southern Belle Primer* (1991); Martha Solomon Watson, *Rhetoric and Public Affairs* (2009); Deborah Gray White, *Ar'n't I a Woman? Female Slaves in the Plantation South* (1985).

Stereotypes, Male

The Million Man March, Robert Bly's *Iron John*, the National Organization of Men Against Sexism, *Rambo*, the Coalition of Free Men, Radical Faeries, *Boys Don't Cry*, the Promise Keepers, RuPaul, and Comedy Central's the *Man Show*. Where they differ in cause, mission, storyline, and image, these events, organizations, products, and personalities have in common a few points. They are born of the late 20th century. Each represents a historically and culturally specific response to gender roles, mores, or representations in the United States. And together, they are part of the cultural and social backdrop to the development of men's studies, or masculinity studies, in the late 20th century in the United States, which steadily continues into the early 21st century. Central to this expanding field of inquiry are concepts about masculinity as a category of analysis, as well as stereotypes, archetypes, and self-concepts.

Illustrating the institutionalization of men's studies is the proliferation of books, journals, and professional conferences that emerged during the 1990s. Historical standards range from E. Anthony Rotundo's *American Manhood* (1993) to Michael Kimmel's *Manhood in America* (1995) to Gail Bederman's *Manliness and Civilization* (1995). In the social sciences, books and articles by Raewyn Connell, known commonly as R. W. Connell, and Joseph Pleck are canonical. The American Men's Studies Association, an intellectual outgrowth of the Men's Studies Task Group of the National Organization for Men, formed in 1991. A year later, the first volume of the *Journal of Men's Studies* was published, as was the first edition of Michael Flood's *Men's Bibliography*.

While the field of men's studies, an interdisciplinary endeavor, grows and evolves, its subject is rooted in the intellectual development of modern categories of gender and their relationships to notions of sex and sexuality. From the late 19th to the mid-20th century, a Western lineage of psychoanalysts and sexologists—notably Sigmund Freud, Karen Horney, and Alfred Kinsey—shaped prevailing theories about normative human sexual development, sex differences, and sex roles. Later, with the institutionalization of women and gender studies programs in U.S. colleges and universities during the 1970s and 1980s, feminist theory critiqued and challenged concepts about sex and gender. During the 1990s, as an increasing number of scholars in the humanities and social sciences incorporated poststructural and postmodern theories into their work, studies that critically examined concepts of masculinity proliferated. Some focused on stereotypes, archetypes, and representations, while others questioned the utility of gender as a social class or analytic concept.

Today, what might be considered subfields have emerged, among them the study of southern masculinity. Historian Craig Thompson Friend, for example, has edited two volumes dedicated to this subject, *Southern Manhood* (2004) with Lorri Glover, and its follow-up, *Southern Masculinity* (2009). Both tackle complex, sometimes contradictory, concepts of manhood, masculinity, and regional identity, spanning from ideals of manhood in the pre–Civil War South to southern manhood and masculinity from Reconstruction to civil rights, to diverse iterations in the early 21st century. Most of the work in this subfield highlights the various ways in which class, race, sexuality, and geography have shaped notions of gender throughout the late 19th and 20th centuries and focuses on historical moments of change and continuity.

Although definitions, boundaries, and exemplars of "maleness" and "southern" have shifted and changed, there are a few contexts that shape the contours of the subfield and its relationship to the larger body of work about manhood and masculinity. Scholarship on southern masculinity came about as a response to a lack of regional differentiation in national narratives about manhood and masculinity. As a result, the subfield has pushed inquiry into new intellectual and geographic terrains. The examination of relationships between masculinity and region have served not only to refine and modify narratives of American manhood but also to rethink gendered categories associated with male identity—from notions of "manhood" and "manliness" to "masculinity" to the ways that race, religion, class, and sexuality shape competing masculine ideals at various historical moments. Stereotypes range from the contemporary—the good ole boy, the gangsta, the NASCAR dad—to the antiquated—the Christian gentleman, the martial masculine, primitive masculinity. As southern masculinity scholarship has developed, early debates over notions of mastery, paternalism, and patriarchy have given way to questions about geographic and ideological identity boundaries, including culturally and racially diverse and conflicting modes of expression.

The intersection between race and masculinity provides another context, specifically the historical development of black and white race relations in the South. Humanities scholarship in the field offers detailed, well-documented examples of racialized constructions of southern manhood and masculinity across historical eras. From the 1870s to the 1930s, white communities across the South used public rituals of racial violence, namely lynching against African American men, as a galvanizing force to assert and maintain white patriarchy and supremacy. Utilizing one of the few institutions available to them—religion—southern black men conceptualized and enacted black masculinity and manhood through empowering depictions of Jesus Christ throughout the late 19th and 20th centuries. In the more recent past, tensions arose in Richmond, Va., over efforts to create a monument to honor tennis legend Arthur Ashe, thus showing how the legacy of race and racism structured southern public memory and notions of masculinity during and after the civil rights movement. The South, however, has a longer history of indigenous peoples of non-Caucasian or African decent, which further affects racialized constructions of gender. For example, across the Southeast during the late 19th century, Cherokee statesmen challenged concepts of Anglo-American manhood while creating empowering views of tribal manhood.

Another important context is class, especially as it relates to race and gender. Published in 1935, *Black Reconstruction in America* by W. E. B. Du Bois, a leading intellectual during the 20th century, was a forerunner in its use of class analysis and race. Du Bois examined the political economy of the South after Reconstruction, comparing disenfranchised, poor working classes of whites and recently freed blacks to the ultimate benefactors of the era's failed equalizing potential—a white propertied class. While scholars have debated he aftereffects of slavery on the unification of poor and wealthy whites, another historical moment highlights the intersections of class and race, as well as sex. Though the eugenics movement flourished in other areas of the country during the late 19th and early 20th centuries, sterilization laws were slower to be enacted and less common in the South, as a region, for multiple reasons. Nonetheless, across southern states, notions of white racial purity cast aspersions on poor white southerners and reified legal and extralegal attempts at maintaining bloodlines by race. In the past few decades, the South has become one of the fastest-growing areas in the country, though comparatively it maintains higher rates of poverty, which are disproportionately represented in rural areas and among African Americans.

Other contexts shaping southern masculine identity are religion and sexuality. As a region, the South has been historically homogeneous in religious belief practice, primarily Protestantism, though pockets of difference exist. Savannah, Ga., for example, is home to Mickve Israel, the third oldest Jewish congregation in the United States. Across the South during the late 19th and early 20th centuries, the "womanless wedding," a popular event in black and white communities nationwide operated as both a form of lighthearted entertainment and a social critique of prevailing gender roles, race relations, and sexual norms in family and community life, and often was enacted through local churches. In southern literature, Mississippi author William Alexander Percy negotiated white southern manhood in his writings, thus illustrating how place and mobility both facilitated and thwarted same-sex desires and relationships during the early to mid-20th centuries. Well documented are the ways in which white southern evangelicals, namely Southern Baptists, responded to a perceived threat of feminist ideology and the growing visibility of gay women and men to faith-based constructions of manhood and family roles during the late 20th century. Noted historian John Howard has focused much attention on relationships between sexuality, region, and law and the not-so-separate lines between church and state. His examination of the landmark *Bowers v. Hardwick* (1986) and *Lawrence v. Texas* (2003) cases explores changing notions of privacy, sexuality, and region in legal and popular narratives of sodomy in the South. Both southern-born legal cases had ethical, social, cultural, and political implications at the national level.

As scholarship on the South continues to reflect the textured and nuanced diversity of the region, it also contends with questions about what, if anything, makes "southern" distinct in terms of prevailing stereotypes, representations, and lived experiences. The same might be said of studies of masculinity and the South in relationship to scholarship about American manhood and masculinity. What is clear, regardless, is that concepts of masculinity are intimately tied to issues of race, class, power, and more. Newer and comparative studies will doubtlessly attend to stereotypes and self-concepts as they relate to the forces shaping life in the South in the 21st century, among them multinational corporation relocations, new migration shifts, economic uncertainties, persistent poverty, and conservative religious and political beliefs.

WESLEY CHENAULT
Auburn Avenue Research Library on African American Culture and History
Atlanta, Georgia

Lydia Plath and Sergio Lussana, eds., *Black and White Masculinity in the American South, 1800-2000* (2009); Riché Richardson, *Black Masculinity and the U.S. South: From Uncle Tom to Gangsta* (2007); Craig Thompson, ed., *Southern Masculinity: Perspectives on Manhood in the South since Reconstruction* (2009); Craig Thompson and Lorri Glover, eds., *Southern Manhood: Perspectives on Masculinity in the Old South* (2004); Trent Watts, ed., *White Masculinity in the Recent South* (2008).

Sunbelt South

During the 1970s some journalists and scholars began thinking and writing about the American South as part of a new regional phenomenon labeled the "Sunbelt." The term's popularity originated with political strategist Kevin Phillips in his book *The Emerging Republican Majority* (1969), which attributed Richard Nixon's victory in the 1968 presidential election to the rising strength of the Republican Party and conservative voters in southern and western states. A few years later, Kirkpatrick Sale's provocative book *Power Shift* (1975) contended that "the rise of the southern rim" had pulled political and economic power from the Northeast to the South and West. By the 1970s the Sunbelt concept quickly caught on among writers for magazines and newspapers as a journalistic shorthand for describing a cluster of powerful political, economic, and demographic changes that seemed to be reshaping the nation.

In the 1980s historians and social scientists began challenging the explanatory power of the Sunbelt thesis. They disputed the convergence of the traditionally distinctive South and West into a single region with shared characteristics. They also demonstrated that the growth patterns commonly associated with the Sunbelt thesis were not evenly distributed across the South or the West. In the South, for example, economically vibrant metropolitan areas showed up as "sun spots," while wide swaths of the region remained tied to a slow-growing, small-town agricultural economy that failed to share presumed Sunbelt prosperity. The Sunbelt boom of recent decades completely bypassed the Delta region of Mississippi and Arkansas, the "Black Belt" counties across central Alabama, and most of rural Appalachia. An elusive concept to begin with, Sunbelt imagery lost much of its luster by the beginning of the 21st century. Nevertheless, the term remains in common usage, even if scholars and journalists now recognize the bifurcation of the Sunbelt into southern and western growth areas with distinct demographic, economic, and cultural patterns.

Despite the debate over Sunbelt imagery and usage, the fact remains that the American South has experienced dramatic change over seven decades since 1940. In that year the South was described as an economic backwater of the nation typified by tenant farming, rural poverty, and economic stagnation. Just a few years earlier a New Deal report described the region as "the nation's Number One economic problem." The South badly lagged behind the rest of the United States in economic growth, personal income, education, health care, worker safety, indoor plumbing, and other measurable social statistics. It also had higher rates of infant mortality, illiteracy, homicide, suicide, and lynching. In 1940 the region was the least urbanized portion of the United States, lagging urban growth in the rest of the nation by 50 years. The South had a colonial economy dominated by absentee owners, mostly from the Northeast, who controlled key industries, resources, and access to capital and credit. Black and white divided southerners racially, and segregation remained deeply embedded in law and custom. The region lacked the economic energy, progressive politics, and ethnic diversity that shaped human activity in other sections of the country.

The South seemed an anomaly in the nation at large, but in 1940 the region stood poised on the brink of growth and change. The New Deal had mixed consequences for the South, undermining tenant farming by cutting cotton acreage, but new federal agencies imposed wage and labor standards, challenged the dominance of planter and mill owner elites, and encouraged a new leadership of business progressives. More significant, World War II launched the region on a trajectory of growth and change. The South became an important regional force in the wartime military machine, partially as a consequence of a purposeful policy of decentralizing bases, training, and war-production industries. In addition, a year-round temperate climate made the South an ideal location for naval and flight training. Large naval bases in Norfolk, Jacksonville, and Pensacola and huge airbases in Texas, Florida, and Alabama contributed to the big military presence. Aircraft factories in Georgia and Texas and shipbuilding in South Carolina, Florida, Alabama, and Mississippi dramatically altered labor markets and pumped up local economies. Some 40 percent of total wartime expenditures for military facilities and other infrastructure, such as airport expansion, went to southern states and cities, with much of the rest going to the West and Southwest. The federal government invested an additional $4–5 billion in southern war-production plants, substantially increasing the region's traditionally weak industrial capacity. The flood of federal dollars and a newer and larger workforce promoted urban development in the nation's least urban region. And the vast federal military and defense spending—a sort of "military remapping" of the nation—continued to sustain southern prosperity and urban growth into postwar decades, as the Cold War kept the United States in a permanent state of military readiness. The wartime stimulus set in motion patterns of dramatic change in a region where change came slowly and was often unwelcomed.

Economic growth and diversification over several decades brought modernization to the postwar South. Agriculture, mining, and textiles, traditionally key components of the southern economy, declined in the postwar era as part of a national economic transformation. Mechanization drove tenant farmers off the land. Older industries began outsourcing production to Central American and Asian nations or failed to compete with low-priced imports and shut down. Southern workers and communities—often small towns—suffered the consequences. The South was deindustrializing, but by the 1970s the region also experienced the rise of new industries such as electronics and computers, aircraft and aerospace production, biomedical research, medical services, banking and financial services, a rapidly growing real estate and construction sector, energy development, especially oil, and companies producing chemicals, pharmaceuticals, tires, carpets, machinery, and auto parts. These new industries emerged primarily in southern metropolitan centers, ranging from Charlotte, Atlanta, and Birmingham to New Orleans, Houston, Dallas, and Austin. As auto production closed down in the northern manufacturing belt, foreign auto companies invested in new car factories in Alabama, Kentucky, Tennessee, Georgia, North Carolina, and South Carolina. Major southern universities, especially urban public universities, filled an important gap in southern higher education and became significant innovators in technological training, medical research, and medical services. Benefiting from changing national consumption patterns, small southern towns became centers for food processing, especially poultry, hogs, beef, and farm-raised catfish. Nonunion labor, low wages, cheap land, low taxes, and state and local financial incentives drew foreign industrial investment. For example, by the 1990s the small city of Spartanburg, S.C., alone had attracted more than 50 foreign firms, including a huge BMW auto plant employing more than 3,500 workers. Northern and foreign economic investment boosted the South's Sunbelt image but also suggested at least the partial persistence of the South's colonial economy in the globalizing world of the 21st century.

Beginning in the 1940s a virtual demographic revolution began to reshape southern life. Responding to the mechanization of agriculture and new job opportunities, blacks and whites began moving off the farm and out of small towns, most heading north and west. Between 1940 and 2000, according to James N. Gregory's *The Southern Diaspora* (2005), an astonishing 22 million whites, blacks, and Latinos migrated out of the South. In addition, millions of rural and small-town black and white southerners sought urban job opportunities in their home region. Between 1940 and 1960, the proportion of southerners living in cities more than doubled, rising from 20 percent to almost 40 percent. Regional urban migrants rubbed shoulders with millions of northerner workers and retirees who began a postwar trek "down South," balancing regional population losses from northern migration. In the immediate postwar era the "amenities factor" drew older Americans to warmer climes such as Florida—the classic example of a Sunbelt state where sunshine mattered. One of the fastest-growing states throughout the entire 20th century, Florida advanced in population rank from 33rd in 1900 to 4th in 1990—a consequence of northern migration, military and defense spending, mild winters and air-conditioned summers, land development and boosterism, low taxes, Caribbean immigration, retirement financed by social security, and year-round golf, tennis, boating, and fishing. By the 1970s in-migrants also began pouring into other southern states such as Texas, Virginia, Georgia, and North Carolina. During that decade, for instance, thousands of Michigan's unemployed autoworkers found new oil service jobs in Houston, where they were labeled "blue platers" after Michigan's signature blue auto license plates. Good weather and good job climates in places such as Miami, Tampa, Atlanta, Charlotte, and Houston attracted millions of newcomers to the South over several decades and helped establish progrowth Sunbelt imagery by the 1980s.

As the Sunbelt states grew in population, the region's small and large cities exploded in population. In 1950 only Houston from the South ranked among the nation's top 10 cities in population. By 2010, the Sunbelt South boasted 8 of the nation's 20 largest cities—Houston, San Antonio, Dallas, Jacksonville, Austin, Fort Worth, Charlotte, and Memphis. With 2010 populations ranging from 5.2 to 6.4 million, Dallas–Fort Worth, Houston, Miami, Atlanta, and Washington, D.C., each ranked among the nation's top-10 metropolitan areas (central cities and their suburbs). Also by 2010, 5 of the 10 fastest-growing metros also had southern zip codes—places such as Palm Coast, Fla.; Raleigh, N.C.; Austin, Tex.; Fort Myers, Fla.; and Myrtle Beach, S.C. Skyscrapers, industrial parks, shopping malls, sprawling suburbs, and crawling traffic now characterize growing metropolitan areas across the region. The Sunbelt South's still unfinished demographic revolution brought southern urbanization close to national averages.

The Sunbelt South's new demography has been shaped not only by in-migration but also by immigration. Except for New Orleans, the South never experienced much European immigration during the industrial era of the 19th century. But the 20th century brought a surprising degree of immigration and ethnic diversity to the region. Mexicans and Mexican Americans have long composed a sizable proportion of population of Texas. Cubans, Nicaraguans, and Colombians, as well as Bahamians, Jamaicans, and Haitians, have altered south Florida's demographic profile. The South's distinctive immigrant groups also include Chinese in the Mississippi Delta region, Vietnamese fisherman along the Gulf Coast, Filipinos and Syrian-Lebanese in Jacksonville, Puerto Ricans in Orlando, Greeks and Italians in Birmingham, and immigrants from just about everywhere in Atlanta and Houston. Texas and Florida have large numbers of Asians, 965,000 and 455,000, respectively, in 2010. And since enactment of new immigration legislation in 1986, Latino immigrants, primarily from Mexico and Central America, have spread throughout the small towns and big cities of the Sunbelt South. Texas and Florida already had large Latino populations, but recent Mexican and Central American immigrants have especially concentrated in Georgia, North Carolina, Virginia, and virtually every big-city metropolitan area in the Sunbelt South. Black and white once defined the racial landscape of the American South, but multicultural and multiethnic now describe society in many parts of the Sunbelt South.

Political shifts accompanied the Sunbelt South's demographic and economic advances. For more than 100 years after the Civil War, the Democratic Party controlled southern politics. The rise of the Sunbelt coincided with the breakdown of the one-party system and the emergence of a new, powerful, conservative, and religiously evangelical southern Republicanism. Southern reaction to end of Jim Crow segregation and liberal Democratic support for the civil rights movement initiated the Sunbelt South's political transformation. Official segregation had ended, but race continued to shape the southern political landscape. School desegregation ordered by the U.S. Supreme Court triggered massive resistance throughout the South, as well as a massive outflow of middle-class whites from Sunbelt cities to outlying suburbs. Left behind during the suburban flight, blacks and Latinos became majorities in major southern cities by the 1970s and 1980s. Subsequently, minority political power led to the election of black mayors in New Orleans, Atlanta, Richmond, Charlotte, Birmingham, Memphis, Houston, Dallas, Savannah, Jackson, Miss., and Washington, D.C., and Latino mayors in Miami, Tampa, Austin, and San Antonio. In the aftermath of the civil rights movement, central-city and rural African Americans, Latinos (except in south Florida), and white liberals formed the basis of Democratic

Party strength in the region. Republican dominance drew essentially from conservative, white, mostly Protestant suburbanites, and small-town residents. The southern Democratic coalition showed strength during the 2008 presidential election, but by that time the one-party Democratic South had become a historic memory.

In politics and other areas, the Sunbelt label seemed to encapsulate southern change while continuing to differentiate the region from the rest of the nation. But many commentators have suggested that the South looks a lot like the rest of America, that it has lost its distinctiveness and blended with larger national patterns. Others challenged "the Americanization of the South" argument or "the End of Southern Exceptionalism" thesis, proclaiming instead the power of southern continuity and the persistence of distinctive regional culture.

More than cultural practice marks the modern South as distinctive. Scholars and statisticians have noted that murder rates in southern states and cities have been disproportionally higher than in the rest of the nation for more than a century. U.S. Census social statistics for 2004 and 2006 also document numerous other ways in which the South remains a markedly different region. On such national measures as percentage of high school graduates, percentage of college graduates, and median household income, most southern states clustered at the bottom of the scale, with only Virginia, Florida, and Georgia ranked in the middle range of all states. Reporting on the percentage of state population dependent on food stamps, percentage of people below the poverty level, percentage of children living in below-poverty-level households, and percentage lacking health insurance, the census found most southern states ranked highest among all states, once again with better rankings for peripheral southern states Virginia and Florida. On measures of infant mortality, violent crime, and environmental pollution, southern states ranked at the top of the list. In 2009 the U.S. Centers for Disease Control reported that southern states had higher rates of obesity than other states, a condition linked to poverty and low education levels as well as to higher rates of stroke, heart disease, and diabetes. Also in 2009 the Commonwealth Fund, a New York foundation, reported that 10 southern states ranked at or near the bottom of all states in levels of access to health care, prevention, and treatment. Several national studies in 2010 reported very poor rankings for southern states on such measures of well-being as child health, teenage births, premature childbirth, hunger among the elderly, environmental regulation, public transportation, and smoking. According to the U.S. Department of Justice, in 2007 most southern states fell into the top quartile of all states in the percentage of state population incarcerated in state or federal prisons. A 2010 study by the Death Penalty Information Center reported seven southern states among the top 10 for the number of executions between 1977 and 2010. All of these measures of social well-being, along with high rates of unemployment for most southern states, have been worsened by the Great Recession of 2008–11. These recent social statistics reveal that in many parts of the South—central cities, small towns, and rural areas—social conditions for poor and working-class people and for children and the elderly seemed reminiscent of conditions in 1940.

Big changes have rocked the South since the middle years of the 20th century—the civil rights revolution, the demographic transitions, the economic transformations, the shifting political landscape, urbanization, and immigration. But the consequences of change have been uneven. The image of the new Sunbelt South remains tied to population growth, economic dynamism, urban and suburban lifestyles, religious evangelicalism, and political conservatism. Less attention has been paid to another South, one marginalized by change and characterized by poverty, low wages, poor education, health concerns, and job insecurity. Not all is sunny in the Sunbelt South.

RAYMOND A. MOHL
University of Alabama at Birmingham

Carl Abbott, *The New Urban South: Growth and Politics in Sunbelt Cities* (1981); Numan V. Bartley, *The New South, 1945–1980: The Story of the South's Modernization* (1995); Richard M. Bernard and Bradley R. Rise, eds., *Sunbelt Cities: Politics and Growth since World War II* (1983); James C. Cobb, *The Selling of the South: The Southern Crusade for Industrial Development, 1936–1980* (1982), *The South and America since World War II* (2010); James C. Cobb and William Stueck, eds., *Globalization and the American South* (2005); Michael Dennis, *The New Economy and the Modern South* (2009); Wayne J. Flynt, *Dixie's Forgotten People: The South's Poor Whites* (1979, 2004); Dewey W. Grantham, *The South in Modern America: A Region at Odds* (1994); Matthew D. Lassiter, *The Silent Majority: Suburban Politics in the Sunbelt South* (2006); Matthew D. Lassiter and Joseph Crespino, eds., *The Myth of Southern Exceptionalism* (2010); Randall M. Miller and George E. Pozzetta, eds., *Shades of the Sunbelt: Essays on Ethnicity, Race, and the Urban South* (1988); Raymond A. Mohl, ed., *Searching for the Sunbelt: Historical Perspectives on a Region* (1990); Mary E. Odem and Elaine Lacy, eds., *Latino Immigrants and the Transformation of the U.S. South* (2009); Byron E. Shafer, *The End of Southern Exceptionalism: Class, Race, and Partisan Change in the Postwar South* (2009); Bruce J. Shulman, *From Cotton Belt to Sunbelt: Federal Policy, Economic Development, and the Transformation of the South, 1938–1980* (1991).

Tourism

In its early days, tourism in the South was an activity enjoyed almost entirely by the upper class. One had to have wealth and mobility to travel and the leisure time for it. Most southerners further down the social and economic ladder had neither. The lower classes also had to overcome the association of leisure with sloth, a widely held belief, reinforced by plantation owners, mill bosses, and Protestant preachers. The upper classes justified taking time off, if they felt any need to justify it at all, by pointing out that leisure was their reward for the work they had done to accumulate the wealth they enjoyed.

If that was not justification enough, elites stressed the benefits that came with travel. Health was high on the list of reasons they gave, which is why most of the early southern resorts were located close to hot mineral springs (Greenbrier in West Virginia and the Homestead in Virginia) or away from the malaria and miasma of the coast (Hendersonville, N.C., is still called "Little Charleston in the Mountains"). These and similar resorts provided comfortable lodging, good food, and other amenities that only the wealthy could afford. They also provided recreation, with balls, parties, gambling, bathing (as swimming was called well into the 20th century), and sports such as golf and tennis, all designed to appeal to the rarified tastes of the well to do. Publications such as *Health Resorts in the South* (1893) testify to the popularity of these places.

Railroads made travel to resorts easier, and developers built new and expanded facilities to meet the growing demand. The most famous of these was Henry Flagler, who laid track from Jacksonville to Miami and along it constructed exclusive hotels such as the Ponce de Leon in St. Augustine and the Breakers in Palm Beach. Most of the tourists Flagler attracted were from the North, a fact that, as much as their wealth, set them apart from run-of-the-mill southerners. But, no matter from whence they came, tourism was a form of entertainment enjoyed almost exclusively by the rich.

Then Henry Ford invented the Model T, and things began to change. Middle-class southerners now had the affordable mobility they had lacked, and during the prosperous 1920s they had money to travel for pleasure. They could not go far—vacation time was limited and the region's roads were poor—so they sought out attractions close by. Those who lived near the Atlantic coast went to Virginia Beach, Myrtle Beach, Tybee Island, and down into Florida. Those on the Gulf went to tourist hotels, cottages, and campgrounds on the islands off Texas and Louisiana and to coastal communities such as Gulfport, Miss., Gulf Shores, Ala., and the beaches west of Panama City, Fla. Inland southerners went to the mountains—the Appalachians, the Blue Ridge, the Great Smokies, and Ozarks. Meanwhile, the older, more exclusive resorts continued to attract the wealthy and a few who were pretending to be.

World War II changed things even more. Southerners who made it through Depression and war were ready to give up sacrifice and have a good time. Their dream, indeed the American dream, was a home, an automobile, and a good job that included two weeks' paid vacation. The G.I. Bill helped many achieve all three, and so they piled their baby boomer children into the car and hit the road.

It is hardly coincidental that as middle- and working-class southerners began to have the time, money, and mobility to tour and vacation, amusements designed to appeal to middle- and working-class tastes began to appear throughout the region. Nor is it coincidental that those amusements included entertainment for the children that middle- and working-class southerners were having in increasing numbers. In fact, in many places it seemed that the resorts were created for the children and adults were just invited to tag along.

So it followed that if the family wanted to vacation in the mountains the kids would have to "See Rock City." Opened to the public in 1932, after the war it became a go-to attraction for mobile southerners with a little money and, the more sophisticated snorted, not much taste. "Created by God, enhanced by man" was the theme, with enhancements that included "Mother Goose Village," "Fairyland Caverns," and the nation's first miniature golf course. The same love for lowbrow, child-focused entertainment turned Gatlinburg, Tenn., into a mecca for drive-in tourists. Calling itself "the Gateway to the Great Smokey Mountains," the community advertised access to rustic and scenic pleasures while creating just the opposite. The good old boys and girls and their boys and girls loved it.

The carnival atmosphere of such destinations was not accidental either, for promoters made a special effort to give middle- and working-class families the same sort of entertainment they enjoyed at the traveling shows that came to their towns and at county and state fairs. Of the many that successfully copied those amusements, none did it better than the promoters of Panama City Beach, Fla. (though Myrtle Beach, S.C., could surely hold its own). Panama City Beach was home of the Miracle Strip Amusement Park, with the "World's Longest and Fastest Roller Coaster," an arcade full of games, rides, and a fun house, and a chicken that told fortunes, plus a midway where a visitor could win a teddy bear. Nearby were other amusements, many of them—Petticoat Junction, Tombstone Territory—inspired by popular television shows, another acknowledgment of the form of entertainment that had become popular with their target audience.

As with most things southern, race played as important a role as class in shaping tourism, and there is no small irony in the unconfirmed rumor that many of the Miracle Strip rides were brought from a Birmingham amusement park that closed rather than integrate. Because of segregation, tourist opportunities for African Americans were limited. However, despite obvious obstacles, drive-to destinations such as Gulfside Assembly in Mississippi, Johnson Beach on the Florida Panhandle, and Atlantic Beach in South Carolina attracted black vacationers and day-trippers. Because their clientele came mostly from the black upper-middle and upper class, and because these resorts did not threaten the racial status quo outside their borders, most whites considered them a safety valve, a place where African Americans could vacation in something resembling a separate-but-equal atmosphere. Although Gulfside occasionally hosted integrated meetings, white Mississippians were not threatened and did not intervene.

This is not to suggest that the tasteless and tacky did not appeal to African Americans, for though most of those places were segregated, "South of the Border"—a South Carolina roadside attraction just off Interstate 95—was open to all races, though it did not advertise itself as such. If blacks wanted to visit the fake-Mexican border town with rides, a miniature golf course, souvenir shops, and the "largest sombrero in the world," they were welcomed—quietly. As the owner later said, "we checked only the color of their money, not their skins."

In a sense, the lowbrow amusements were also a safety valve for working-class whites, for they provided places where the ones who supposedly put the "redneck" in "redneck Riviera" could enjoy themselves without worrying about the boss or the preacher or, in some cases, the wife and kids. Which is why, in addition to the rides and games and thrills, these tourist enclaves often included bars and dance halls. Along the Gulf and Atlantic coasts were scores of communities that during the war entertained soldiers and sailors and airmen from nearby bases, and after the conflict these veterans often came back, sometimes with families, sometimes with friends, and turned what had once been an economy based on the military into an economy based on tourism.

However, the overall focus of middle- and working-class southern tourism was, and continues to be, family entertainment. As a result, resorts such as Dollywood, in the Tennessee mountains, and Branson, in the Missouri Ozarks, have become popular destinations. However, the ultimate family experience continues to be Disney World, where touring families from all over the South (and a goodly part of the North and Midwest) converge to enjoy the experience. Although the cost of these has priced many working-class families out of the market, saving up for a "trip to Disney" has become the goal for many.

While there is no doubt that more sophisticated southerners visit these amusements and enjoy them with their kids, when it comes to vacationing, the priorities of these folks differ from those farther down the social scale. According to a survey of its readers, *Southern Living*, which has been called the "how-to manual" for rising southerners, identified three main factors, other than price, that determined where they would vacation. They wanted scenery. They wanted good restaurants and comfortable lodging. And they liked to visit historical sites.

The search for history has often crossed class lines, for working-class southerners will visit Civil War battlefields almost as frequently as their middle-class counterparts; however, they are less attracted to the "Old South" imagery of historic homes or the colonial charm of Williamsburg. The opening of civil rights museums has given African American tourists more attractions to visit, and those tourists, like their white counterparts, are more from the middle class than from those below. If the more lowbrow want to visit a historical site, Graceland, the Elvis Presley home in Memphis, Tenn., is their kind of place.

Meanwhile, where are upper-class southerners going? Some get on a plane and fly to Europe, but many others are staying close to home. Interested in scenery combined with fine food and unique accommodations, they have also headed for the coast or to the mountains, but rather than going to Dollywood or Panama City Beach or even Disney World they isolate themselves in resort condominiums on the Carolina and Georgia barrier islands, in the rustic inns surrounding golf resorts in the mountains, and in coastal communities, some gated, some not, where they can buy or rent and enjoy amenities not available to others—and enjoy them with folks like themselves.

Though there are many of these resort communities sprinkled about the South, none is so clearly associated with both the affluence and the outlook of what might be called the New South elite than Seaside, on the Florida Panhandle. Conceived in an effort to recreate "old Florida," with wooden houses, screened porches, and oyster shell streets, Seaside was to be a "real town" with people from all walks of life living together in harmony. But the idea caught on, the houses became popular, and the upscale and affluent bought into the community. Homes became bigger, stores became fancier, and restaurants became trendier. Instead of a town, Seaside became a resort, and though its contributions to urban design are significant, for the people who bought there and who visit there it is a place, according to the *New York Times*, "as relentlessly tasteful as any place on the planet." Just the sort of place the better sort want to visit.

Similar communities have sprung up throughout the South, so Dixie's elite—white and, today, black—can vacation without fear of rubbing shoulders with the lower orders.

Just as it always has, class and affluence has determined where southern vacationers go and what they do when they get there. Likely as not, it always will.

HARVEY H. JACKSON III
Jacksonville State University

Ken Breslauer, *Roadside Paradise: The Golden Age of Florida's Tourist Attractions, 1929–1971* (2000); George H. Chapin, *Health Resorts of the South* (1893); Tim Hollis, *Dixie before Disney: 100 Years of Roadside Fun* (1999), *Florida's Miracle Strip: From Redneck Riviera to Emerald Coast* (2004); Harvey H. Jackson III, *Southern Cultures* (Spring 2010); Jeffrey Limerick, Nancy Ferguson, and Richard Oliver, eds., *America's Grand Resort Hotels* (1979); Brenden Martin, *Tourism in the Mountain South: A Double-Edged Sword* (2007); Gary Mormino, *Land of Sunshine, State of Dreams: A Social History of Modern Florida* (2005); Claudette Stager and Martha Carver, eds., *Looking beyond the Highway: Dixie Roads and Culture* (2006); Anthony J. Stanonis, ed., *Dixie Emporium: Tourism, Foodways, and Consumer Culture in the American South* (2008); Richard Starnes, ed., *Southern Journeys: Tourism, History, and Culture in the Modern South* (2003). Harvey H. Jackson III and Charles Reagan Wilson, eds., *Sports and Recreation*, vol. 16 of *The New Encyclopedia of Southern Culture* (2010), contains entries on most of the resorts and attractions mentioned here.

Upper Class, White

Few groups have so captivated the imagination of historians and the general public as the upper class of the Old South. It has been romanticized in movies and novels like Margaret Mitchell's *Gone with the Wind* and scrutinized by a distinguished and ideologically diverse cadre of scholars whose ranks include U. B. Phillips, Eugene Genovese and Elizabeth Fox-Genovese, James Oakes, and William K. Scarborough. The wealthiest and most prominent of the southern elite—men like James Henry Hammond and Stephen Duncan—cast long shadows on the South's historical landscape and have attracted the attention of biographers. Yet defining and discussing the upper class is something of a challenge. The economic terrain of the Old South was uneven and unstable. The upper class in the Upcountry paled in comparison to sugar planters and the Lowcountry elite, just as the economic and political clout of Virginia's grandees waned as their plantations declined and slavery spread into the Deep South. Moreover, simple economic measures cannot capture the complexity of upper-class identity—education, gender, notions of honor, and politics all shaped the counters of this influential group. It is, therefore, important to sketch lightly, recognizing that the shifting constellation of forces that continually made and remade the southern elite will continue to spark historians' imaginations and yield fresh insights.

Slave owners were the wealthiest class in the antebellum United States. A few statistics illustrate this point. In 1860 the nation's 12 wealthiest counties were in the South, and most of these counties boasted large concentrations of slaves. The county with the highest per capita wealth was Adams County, Miss., which was home to the fabulously wealthy "Natchez Nabobs." The fortunes amassed by slave owners dwarfed those of their countrymen. Historian Gavin Wright has calculated that the average slaveholder was more than five times wealthier than the typical northerner and more than 10 times richer than a southern yeoman farmer. As might be expected, slaveholders controlled a disproportionate share—some 90 to 95 percent—of the agricultural wealth in the South by 1860.

In the Old South, status and wealth stemmed, in large measure, from the ownership of land and slaves, and those who controlled the largest shares of these commodities constituted the upper class. Yet slaveholders were a diverse lot. On the eve of the Civil War, there were some 385,000 slaveowners in the United States, half of whom owned between one and five slaves. At the other end of the spectrum were the 12 percent of masters and mistresses whose ownership of 20 or more slaves qualified them as planters. Clearly, though, something more precise than owning slaves is needed to define the upper class. Scholars have traditionally described the Old South's economic hierarchy as a pyramid capped by planters with progressively broader—and lower—strata of middling and small slaveholders, yeoman farmers, tenants, landless free black and white laborers, and the enslaved. Although this hierarchy has been modified by recent studies of southern artisans and middle-class professionals, its basic contours still suffice.

Taking their cues from the pioneering work of Eugene D. Genovese, historians once viewed southern planters as possessing a premodern, precapitalist mindset. Although the complexity and nuance of Genovese's constantly evolving interpretation defies simplification, his most influential studies argued, in broad strokes, that southern planters developed a paternalistic ideology for managing their human chattels, one that emphasized the organic and reciprocal bonds between master and slaves. Genovese juxtaposed paternalism to the strain of capitalism developing in the North, which celebrated impersonal market relations and bourgeois individualism. Paternalism in turn bred an ambivalence toward economic progress. Planters, Genovese argued, were willing to forgo economic efficiency, rational management, and excessive profits to maintain stability in the Old South. Genovese's theses drew fire from scholars, including James Oakes and William Dusinberre, who depicted planters as acquisitive, shrewd businessmen whose management styles mimicked those of northern capitalists. More recently, Richard Follett has suggested that the resolution of this debate lies in a synthesis of the competing viewpoints. In his study of Louisiana's sugar masters, Follett found that planters were keenly interested in maximizing profits and managing their slaves in an efficient though ruthless manner. At the same time, however, they cloaked their actions in the language of paternalism and evinced a strong commitment to preserving the social hierarchy.

The southern gentry may have celebrated leisure and refinement, but most of its members were driven by a restless desire for wealth. The sprawling mansions that dot older plantation districts such as the Chesapeake, the Carolina Lowcountry, and Natchez were meant to convey a sense of stability, but these estates were the exception, not the rule. Planters' homes were often crude. In Alabama, Frederick Law Olmsted noted that "the large proportion of planters . . . live in log-houses, some of them very neat and comfortable, but frequently crude in construction . . . and wanting in many of the commonest conveniences." Planters moved across the South like locusts. They hacked plantations from the canebrake and forests, farmed them until the soil was "played out," then decamped for the next frontier. Because the South was wracked by bouts of speculative "fever," it was not uncommon for plantation districts to suffer heavy rates of out-migration. For example, Dallas County, Ala., witnessed a massive exodus of slave owners' sons in the 1850s. In the course of a decade, more than half of the planters' sons moved away, with even higher percentages of young men from middling and small slave-owning families leaving.

Planters were an enterprising lot. Their wealth may have been built on land and slaves, but their manifold business interests belie any notion of southern planters as simple agrarians. In Virginia, for example, the decline of tobacco cultivation in the early national period prompted many members of the gentry to embrace diversified agriculture and pursue a broad, diverse range of commercial and industrial undertakings. John Tayloe III may have owned more than 700 slaves, but he also operated mills and iron furnaces, dabbled in commercial real estate, and invested heavily in the Bank of the United States and several internal improvement projects. Natchez planter Dr. Stephen Duncan was among the largest slave owners in the South, but he also supported banks and invested hundreds of thousands in government bonds and railroads.

The realization that planters embraced certain elements of the emerging capitalist system, combined with the discovery of vibrant middle and working classes in the antebellum South, has inspired scholars to investigate other segments of the southern elite, most notably industrialists and merchants. In his study of South Carolina's Savannah River Valley, historian Tom Downey argues that the upper class, which historians have traditionally treated as being virtually synonymous with planters, was actually divided between agrarians and bankers, merchants, and industrialists.

These commercial interests had considerable clout, especially at the municipal and state levels. Merchants secured the passage of a law that made limited liability partnerships possible and ordinances that outlawed itinerant peddlers. For their part, factory owners dammed rivers and brushed aside local artisans to become the dominant force in the local economy. Whether Downey's findings are applicable to the larger South remains to be seen, but they do suggest that the southern upper class—however defined—shared in the broader Market Revolution that was reshaping the antebellum economy.

MAX L. GRIVNO
University of Southern Mississippi

Tom Downey, *Planting a Capitalist South: Masters, Merchants, and Manufacturers in the Southern Interior* (2006); William Dusinberre, *Them Dark Days: Slavery in the American Rice Swamps* (1996); Richard Follett, *The Sugar Masters: Planters and Slaves in Louisiana's Cane World, 1820–1860* (2005); Elizabeth Fox-Genovese, *Within the Plantation Household: Black and White Women in the Old South* (1988); Eugene D. Genovese, *The World the Slaveholders Made: Two Essays in Interpretation* (1969), *Roll, Jordan, Roll: The World the Slaves Made* (1972); Laura Croghan Kamoie, *Irons in the Fire: The Business History of the Tayloe Family and Virginia's Gentry, 1700–1860* (2007); James Oakes, *The Ruling Race: A History of American Slaveholders* (1982); William Kauffman Scarborough, *Masters of the Big House: Elite Slaveholders of the Mid-Nineteenth Century South* (2003).

Urbanization

Urbanization describes the growth and expansion of cities and suburbs and the transformation of surrounding rural areas. The ongoing processes of urbanization are associated with increasing size, density, and diversity of human populations, along with changes in land use, economic activity, social composition, and cultural practices. Since World War II the U.S. population has become majority urban or metropolitan, with the South experiencing the greatest population increase. In 2008, 8 of the 10 fastest-growing metropolitan areas in the United States were located in the South.

Social and economic interactions in post–World War II southern cities reflect rural-urban migration, dismantling of Jim Crow, interregional and transnational relocation of jobs, transnational immigration, and rising levels of educational attainment. As a result of economic diversification and increased educational attainment, metropolitan areas have experienced growing opportunities for a professional middle class and for skilled workers. Consequently, present-day inhabitants of southern cities and suburbs include whites and African American rural migrants from the region; corporate employers, employees, and retirees from the Rust Belt; recent immigrants from Mexico and Latin America, as well as Asia and Africa; and a return migration of African Americans and whites (or their descendants) who left the region during the Great Migration. These patterns of urbanization and metropolitan sprawl challenge deeply held understandings about a region noted for its historical ties to agricultural production, an enduring regional identity, resistance to industrialization, and ambivalence about city life. It also challenges understandings about social class.

Today casinos, automobile manufacturing plants, medical centers, shopping malls, and upscale retirement communities constitute the built environment on land where cotton and tobacco grew for generations. Textile mills that once led industrialization in the region have moved overseas. Millworkers, members of the industrial working class sometimes disparagingly referred to as "lintheads," have had to find alternative low-wage nonunion employment; meanwhile, mill village homes have fallen into the hands of urban gentrifiers and commercial developers. Icons of 20th-century urbanization—skyscrapers—rise above expanding commercial districts in downtown Atlanta, Charlotte, Dallas, Houston, Miami, and Nashville. Nearby, moneyed suburban enclaves such as the Park Cities in north Dallas, Buckhead in Atlanta, Sugar Land in Houston, and Belle Meade in Nashville house millionaires and billionaires with financial interests in technology companies, transnational corporations, professional sports franchises, and media conglomerates and have transformed farms and small towns into sprawling suburbs.

Spatial inequality follows different patterns in southern cities. In Memphis, growth of jobs and housing has moved east, leaving pockets of poverty and prosperity within the central city. In Atlanta and Dallas, suburban wealth is concentrated in the north and west, but southern and eastern suburbs struggle with greater concentrations of poverty. Post–World War II trends of decentralization and metropolitan sprawl carried middle-class and working-class families away from central cities; since the 1990s, however, central cities have attracted young, childless adults. This is especially true in Memphis and Atlanta.

But gentrification often comes at the expense of low-income housing and displacement of working-class African American neighborhoods.

Socioeconomic distinctions between southern cities and suburbs never have been as great as differences between cities and suburbs in the Northeast and Midwest. However, southern cities and suburbs, like their counterparts in other regions, are stratified by class and race boundaries, and central cities continue to claim a disproportionate share of the poor. In the South, as it is throughout the country, the most disadvantaged populations experience higher rates of infant mortality, school disengagement, violent crime, property crime, and health consequences of environmental pollution and degradation. National comparisons, however, show that southern city dwellers fare much worse. The proportion of city dwellers living in extreme-poverty neighborhoods is far above the national average. In 2000 New Orleans ranked second nationally in percentage of poor people living in neighborhoods of concentrated poverty. As a result of Hurricane Katrina and the breaking of the levees, 38 of the city's 47 extreme-poverty census tracts were flooded. The disaster unveiled the reality of urban disparities and the consequences for the South's most marginalized and vulnerable people, especially women and minorities. In 2010 the top 20 cities with the highest crime rates in the United States included seven southern cities ranked from number 10 through 16: Birmingham, Baltimore, Memphis, New Orleans, Jackson, Little Rock, and Baton Rouge. Infant mortality, associated with high rates of poverty, low rates of educational attainment, and limited access to health care, also stands out. Memphis has the highest infant mortality rate in the United States, and infant mortality in the mid-South is often compared to that of developing nations.

Despite impressive social and economic gains, particularly in affluent neighborhoods, Atlanta, like other American cities, continues to report high poverty rates, especially among African Americans, Latinos, and children. And Atlanta, along with New Orleans, Louisville, and Miami, ranks among the nation's top 10 large cities having high rates of concentrated poverty. Poor people living in disadvantaged neighborhoods segregated by low income face greater economic and social challenges than those living in neighborhoods where poverty is more dispersed.

The regional differential for urban problems is usually explained by a combination of cultural and structural factors. For some time, patterns of violence have been associated with a culture of interpersonal violence that was transported to the South from the British Isles, shaped by frontier experiences, and became entrenched as part of the southern way of life. Others point to the southern region's legacy of structurally embedded disadvantage, created by slavery, sharecropping, and segregation. That legacy has been complicated further by federal urban redevelopment programs that have produced varied results. Many of them have disrupted urban cores by destroying schools, residences, churches, and businesses in low-income communities and replacing them with expressways and housing projects. Metropolitan growth and sprawl have created pockets of distress as well as areas of prosperity within cities. By the 1970s urban problems in the centers of southern cities began to mirror urban crises in nonsouthern cities such as Los Angeles, Philadelphia, and Detroit—places identified with higher rates of unemployment, pollution, and crime. The spatial mismatch between metropolitan job growth and people left behind in urban cores in the South is similar to cities in other parts of the United States. But the region's institutional foundation of social inequality and structural shifts produced by uneven development produce and reproduce patterns of inequality.

Growth was the mantra of the New South era and has been the pride of the civic and commercial elite for more than a century. Business and property owners, especially members of religious institutions, civic clubs, and voluntary organizations who formed the leadership base in cities and towns, have promoted their visions of economic development and urban expansion. Bankers, merchants, brokers, lawyers, and entrepreneurs, as representatives of the major economic interests of southern communities, have played prominent and influential roles in shaping attitudes about urban growth and prosperity as well as policies. Their ideas, primarily reflecting the goals and concerns of white elites and promoted through major media and voluntary organizations, have influenced public officials, affected competitive strategies for economic development, and informed social policies. A black commercial elite emerged in some cities, particularly in Memphis, New Orleans, and Atlanta.

After the Civil War and Reconstruction, urban boosters, like Atlanta's Henry Grady, promoted southern towns to northern financiers and investors as bases for expanding railroad lines, building factories, and employing cheap, non-union labor. Although urban competition was a national phenomenon, this particular form of boosterism was prevalent in the South at the beginning of the 20th century. Southern municipalities competed with each other to recruit development by offering generous tax exemptions and bonds, often at the expense of public education and social programs. Many of these initiatives succeeded in attracting low-wage jobs for hiring displaced agricultural workers, but they failed to make the region more competitive by improving human capital.

During the Great Depression and World War II, federal dollars supported military bases, hydroelectric power development, and other economic stimulants that benefited southern towns and cities. In the postwar period, urban elites and boosters welcomed federal dollars for interstate highways and urban renewal. A succession of programs, such as the Title I Housing Act of 1949, the Community Development Block Grant in 1974, and the Urban Development Action Grant program in 1977, focused on businesses and jobs more than housing. Elected officials and chambers of commerce have promoted building airports, convention centers, hotels, sports arenas, and high-rise office buildings on urban landscapes. These projects typically have treated older and less affluent neighborhoods as "blighted" and in need of redevelopment, but redevelopment proposals often become contentious. Some have sparked neighborhood activism and fueled resistance.

One post–World War II development initiative, the plan for North Carolina's Research Triangle Park (RTP), has attracted widespread interest in a different type of economic development—the knowledge economy. The RTP was conceived as a means of diversifying the state's traditional industrial base, attracting high-technology industry, and creating employment for workers educated in science and engineering that were leaving the state. Faculty members from three universities—Duke University, the University of North Carolina, and North Carolina State University—the governor, and private funding launched the project in the 1950s. The RTP, founded in 1959, is now the largest research park in the world. The park has expanded to include 7,000 acres. The demands for housing and services for the 40,000 people who work there, and their families, have affected urbanization in the center of the state, especially in Raleigh, Durham, and Chapel Hill. The RTP serves as an economic development model for other areas, such as Memphis and Birmingham, where city leaders and public-private partnerships have intensified investment and participation in the knowledge economy.

WANDA RUSHING
University of Memphis

Alan Berube, "A New Metro Map," Brookings Institution (2010); Alan Berube and Elizabeth Kneebone, "Two Steps Back: City and Suburban Poverty Trends, 1999–2005," Brookings Institution (2006); Peter A. Coclanis, in *Globalization and the American South*, ed. James C. Cobb and William Stueck (2005); CQ Press, "City Crime Rankings, 2010–2011," os.cqpress.com/citycrime/2010/citycrime2010-2011.htm (2010); Pete Daniel, *Agricultural History* (Fall 1994); David R. Goldfield, *Cotton Fields to Skyscrapers: Southern City and Region* (1989); Bruce Katz, "Concentrated Poverty in New Orleans and other American Cities," Brookings Institution (4 August 2006);

Raymond A. Mohl, *Alabama Review* (October 2002); Wanda Rushing, *Memphis and the Paradox of Place: Globalization in the American South* (2009); T. Lynn Smith, in *The Urban South*, ed. Rupert B. Vance and Nicholas J. Demerath (1954); Stewart E. Tolnay, *Annual Review of Sociology* (2003).

Voting Rights

Voter discrimination based on racial identity and economic status is a dominant theme in the history of southern political culture. Since the settlement of the American colonies, disfranchised groups have attempted to gain access to the ballot box, which was oftentimes jealously guarded by the region's white elite. Although the lofty democratic ideals written down in the Declaration of Independence sprang from the mind of a Virginia planter, the landed gentry in the antebellum South was apprehensive about giving too much influence to the lower classes. Based on the charters drawn up during the colonial period, most franchise laws contained property and freehold qualifications that restricted voting and office holding to the upper strata of southern society. As the nation expanded, the settlers who moved westward protested against the provisions that placed the power in the hands of the plantation owners living on the eastern seaboard. These protests forced the ruling class to gradually reduce the property requirements for participation in the political process. During the Jacksonian era, southern state constitutions were democratized and suffrage was extended to all white males. Simultaneously, free blacks living in the South lost their right to vote, and most states in the North followed this example. Although the wealthy landowners still dominated the southern political scene at the outbreak of the Civil War, they could no longer ignore the demands of their less affluent white brethren.

After decisive northern victories at Gettysburg and Vicksburg in the summer of 1863 and the ongoing annexation of southern territory by U.S. troops, the federal government began outlining plans to bring former Confederate states back into the Union. In December of that year, Abraham Lincoln announced a limited Reconstruction program. Lincoln did not advocate suffrage for all African American males, but preferred to give the vote to a limited number of blacks, including those who fought for the North. The cause of voting rights for African Americans stagnated under Lincoln's successor, Andrew Johnson. Johnson's lenient attitude toward the southern rebels eventually led Congress to assume control over the Reconstruction process. The 1866 elections resulted in a great victory for the radical Republicans, who introduced important legislation aimed at giving the vote to blacks.

Under the leadership of the Republican Party, Congress passed two Reconstruction Acts, which divided the conquered South into five military districts, put the region under martial law, and ordered the army to oversee voter registration. Furthermore, the Republican majority on Capitol Hill submitted two amendments to the Constitution that were supposed to protect the rights of U.S. citizenship (the Fourteenth Amendment) and guarantee the ballot to all male citizens, including African American men (the Fifteenth Amendment). The Fourteenth Amendment was ratified in 1868, and ratification of the Fifteenth Amendment followed two years later. In addition to the enactment of the Thirteenth Amendment in 1865 and the Civil Rights Act of 1866, the laws passed during the period of Radical Reconstruction formed a major advance in the enfranchisement of racial minorities.

Of course, the South's white elite strongly disapproved of these congressional actions, which gave the right to vote to approximately 700,000 blacks and also increased the power of poor, landless whites. With the introduction of the Black Codes and the founding of the Ku Klux Klan, unreconstructed southerners tried to turn back the clock through legal and extralegal means. As the 1870s progressed, the plight of southern blacks worsened. Growing apathy in the North toward the enforcement of universal male suffrage in the former Confederacy, combined with white resistance in the South against the enfranchisement of African Americans, resulted in a steady deterioration of the programs initiated by the radical Republicans.

The symbolic end of Reconstruction came in 1877, when Democrats agreed to accept the disputed victory of Republican presidential candidate Rutherford B. Hayes in exchange for the promise that all federal troops would be withdrawn from the southern states. When the military left, the politics of Radical Reconstruction foundered and the Democratic Party assumed virtual control in the South. Even after the end of Reconstruction, blacks continued to participate in the political arena, although their rights were increasingly curtailed. Paradoxically, the Populist revolts that occurred during the last decade of the 19th century resulted in the almost complete disfranchisement of black southerners. The white elite tolerated African Americans in politics as long as they did not pose a serious threat to the interests of the upper echelons; when the Populist movement tried to unite blacks and poor whites on a platform that opposed the economic policies of the ruling class, southern leaders successfully stirred the flames of racism to break the interracial alliance of the Populists. Between 1890 and 1910, most southern states drafted new constitutions that deprived black citizens and a large segment of the poor white population of their political rights.

Since the Fifteenth Amendment prohibits voter discrimination on the basis of race, the Redeemers (southern Democrats who "redeemed" the former Confederate states from Republican rule) had to engineer novel strategies to reestablish white political supremacy. The framers of the new constitutions therefore included numerous clauses that appeared to be race neutral at first sight, but that nonetheless disfranchised practically all African Americans and a significant number of impoverished whites. The poll tax, literacy tests, and residence requirements formed the constitutional provisions that were specifically directed at the descendents of slaves, migrant workers, and the poor, thus restoring the authority of the plantation and business establishment. Another mechanism to secure white control was the grandfather clause, which exempted adult men who were registered as voters on or before 1 January 1867, as well as their male descendents, from literacy and property requirements. Because only a few African Americans were on the voting rolls at the beginning of Radical Reconstruction, the grandfather clause formed an effective method to limit their participation in elections. The introduction of the white primary by the southern wing of the Democratic Party further reduced the political influence of blacks.

At the beginning of the 20th century, a regime based on racial segregation and exclusive access to the ballot box was again firmly in place in the South. In 1909 the National Association for the Advancement of Colored People (NAACP) was founded, which took a leading role in the fight against the southern caste system. The NAACP initially targeted the most blatant forms of voter discrimination. The first success for the organization came in 1915, when the Supreme Court declared the grandfather clause unconstitutional. The 1944 decision of the Court in *Smith v. Allwright* formed another significant step toward regaining access to the southern ballot box. In this case, the Court ruled the white primary unlawful. Southern Democrats argued that their political party was a private organization and that they could therefore decide who was allowed to vote in its primaries. The Supreme Court disapproved of this standpoint, because the Democratic primary constituted the actual election in the one-party South.

After World War II the federal government became more responsive to black demands. African Americans who had moved from the South to the cities in the North started to form important voting blocs for both major parties, and southern apartheid was detrimental to America's desired appearance as the greatest democracy in the world, an image that gained renewed relevance during the Cold War. In 1948 President Truman asked Congress to pass a package of civil rights measures, including an anti–poll tax bill. A powerful coalition of conservative Republicans and southern Democrats on Capitol Hill prevented rapid enactment of such measures, however. In the end, the Judicial Branch again took the lead in the annulment of Jim Crow laws. The seminal 1954 decision of the Supreme Court in *Brown v. Board Education*, a case brought before the bench by the NAACP, invalidated racial segregation in public schools and cracked the legal edifice of the South's social system. Massive resistance against integration mounted in the southern states after the *Brown* ruling, prompting civil rights advocates to accelerate the drive for racial equality and the protection of constitutional liberties.

Although President Eisenhower was reticent about federal interference with local election customs, the White House did take the first steps toward the introduction of voting rights legislation in 1957. Not Eisenhower, but his attorney general, Herbert Brownell, submitted a proposal to Congress to improve the conditions of black voters in the South. Brownell not only abhorred the wave of violence rolling through the southern states after the *Brown* decision but also understood that the electoral support of African Americans might become critical in upcoming elections. Northern Democrats in Congress reasoned along similar lines, while party members from the South began to realize that their unyielding opposition to the basic democratic right of ballot was no longer tenable. Against this political background, Congress finally managed to pass the first comprehensive civil rights law since the 1870s. The act, which was signed by Eisenhower on 9 September 1957, was the result of a compromise between different interest groups (including the southern Democrats) and therefore had a very limited character. Civil rights leaders nonetheless hailed the bill as a victory for their cause, with the admission that the fight against disfranchisement in the South was far from over.

During the 1960s the movement for racial equality entered a more radical phase. Congress passed another moderate Civil Rights Act in 1960, but this kind of legislation no longer satisfied the new generation of civil rights workers. Whereas the NAACP attempted to achieve its goals through legislative and judicial means, young demonstrators turned to direct action to break the Jim Crow South. The Kennedy administration at first displayed an offhand attitude towards desegregation, but the unrelenting efforts of civil rights activists and the aggressive white backlash against them pressured Kennedy to take a clear stand on securing the franchise for southern blacks. Violent repercussions by law officers on peaceful demonstrators in Birmingham, Ala., during the spring of 1963 ultimately generated a substantial response from Washington. A few months before his death, the president announced that he would send to Congress civil rights legislation outlawing voter discrimination and segregation of public facilities. Kennedy's proposals were enacted in 1964 during the administration of his successor, Lyndon Baines Johnson. A year later, after local police forces had brutally assaulted civil rights activists in Selma, Ala., Johnson submitted a voting rights bill to a joint session of Congress. The president signed this bill into law on 6 August 1965.

The Voting Rights Act of 1965 (VRA) was the most important franchise law passed since the end of Reconstruction. Section 2 of the act prohibited any form of voter discrimination and banned mechanisms such as the literacy test that denied the ballot to certain parts of the electorate. Section 4 targeted specific areas in the United States with low voter registration and discriminatory ballot procedures. These parts of the country came under special scrutiny of the federal government; Section 5 of the VRA determined that locales identified by Section 4 could implement new voting laws only after either the U.S. attorney general or the District Court for the District of Columbia approved the proposed legislation. The act also authorized the use of federal registrars to enroll voters in jurisdictions that had systematically denied the ballot to selected groups in the past.

The primary objective of the VRA was obviously the termination of voting rights violations in the South, and the direct effects of the Act were particularly felt in this part of the nation. In 1964 around 35 percent of black adults in the South were registered; by 1969 this percentage had grown to almost 65. As a result, the number of black officials at all strata of government also increased. Another effect of the Voting Rights Act was the increase of white voter registration in the South, especially in areas with high concentrations of blacks. Since the passage of the act, white southerners increasingly started to vote for the Republican Party, causing a dramatic change of southern political culture. The solid Democratic South transformed into a region with a two-party structure. Although economic and demographic developments also played a critical role in the rise of the southern Republicans, race appears to be the decisive factor in the partisan division of the electorate in the South: blacks and a majority of Latinos vote for Democratic candidates, while the Republican Party primarily attracts white voters. At the start of the 21st century, a mobilized African American electorate joined by an adequate minority of white voters can decide elections in the South. During the 2008 presidential election, this coalition delivered Barack Obama 55 southern electoral votes.

The fact that three southern states, Florida, North Carolina, and Virginia, went to a black Democratic candidate in 2008 demonstrates the major impact of the combined effort by the federal government and the civil rights movement to end voter discrimination in the South. In 2006 Congress extended the Voting Rights Act for another 25 years. This renewal of the act followed previous extensions in 1970, 1975, and 1982, when areas outside the South became part of Section 5 regulations and other minority groups received voter protection through the act's provisions. Even though the VRA has generally been hailed as landmark legislation by both liberals and conservatives, the bill has also received strong criticism in recent years. During the 2006 debate, southern Republicans objected to the situation that large parts of their region still fell under VRA regulations, despite the major progress the black population has made since 1965. In 2009 Chief Justice John Roberts expressed similar thoughts in a majority opinion about a case dealing with Section 5 of the act. The Supreme Court decided not to strike down this integral clause of the VRA, although Roberts considered federal intervention based on data from the 1960s a problematic issue. "The historic accomplishments of the Voting Rights Act are undeniable," he said, "but the Act now raises serious constitutional concerns." Congressional hearings preceding the reauthorization of the VRA in 2006 showed different concerns, however. These investigations proved that voter discrimination is still widespread in the United States and that strong protection of the franchise is therefore necessary. Even in the South, where the Voting Rights Act added millions to the registration rolls, structural inequalities between black and white persist. Considering the critical role of the Supreme Court in breaking the legal barriers of southern racism, it would be striking if the Judicial Branch would now take the lead in limiting the reach of federal voting rights legislation.

MAARTEN ZWIERS
University of Groningen, the Netherlands

Earl Black and Merle Black, *The Rise of Southern Republicans* (2002); Charles S. Bullock III and Ronald Keith Gaddie, *The Triumph of Voting Rights in the South* (2009); Chandler Davidson and Bernard Grofman, eds., *Quiet Revolution in the South: The Impact of the Voting Rights Act, 1965-1990* (1994); Keith M. Finley, *Delaying the Dream: Southern Senators and the Fight against Civil Rights, 1938-1965* (2008); J. Morgan Kousser, *The Shaping of Southern Politics: Suffrage Restriction and the Establishment of the One-Party South, 1880-1910* (1974); Steven F. Lawson, *Black Ballots: Voting Rights in the South, 1944-1969* (1976); Robert Mann, *When Freedom Would Triumph: The Civil Rights Struggle in Congress, 1954-1968* (2007); William G. Shade, *Democratizing the Old Dominion: Virginia and the Second Party System, 1824-1861* (1996).

Welfare and Charity

Poverty and the attempt to alleviate its effects through governmental programs and private charity have a long history in the southern states. Initially imitating English Poor Laws, southern colonies assigned local parishes the task of caring for those without family support or adequate income. They hastened vagabonds on their way and paid families to board the local indigent and handicapped. The 18th century saw the rise of some municipal poorhouses and orphanages, as well as a few institutions established by private philanthropists.

The early 19th century, however, brought a dramatic increase in the number and types of both public and private institutions. Called "indoor relief," such institutions provided minimal services and often assigned residents including children to menial work and domestic service. Benevolent societies organized by middle-class women, religious denominations, or craftsmen and artisans provided "outdoor relief": food, firewood, or funds for those in crisis. Women's organizations like the Charleston Benevolent Society sought to alleviate the poverty of widows and their children. Some have argued that the growth of proslavery ideology in the South fostered the desire to elevate poor whites against the lowest classes: free blacks and, of course, slaves. The white rural poor had little recourse to any kind of assistance save asking the local planter to exercise his paternalistic nature and provide seed, livestock, or cash for the needy plaintiff.

Whereas the southern colonies or states had been the richest in the New World and early America, the post–Civil War South led the nation in lowest per capita income and highest number of families living below the poverty line. Following Emancipation, African Americans remained overwhelmingly poor in both rural and urban areas. Informal segregation gave way to formal Jim Crow laws beginning in the 1880s, which led African Americans to found their own benevolent societies, orphanages, and schools. The urban reforms of the Progressive Era largely overlooked African American citizens. While the movement in northern states emphasized problems caused by industrialization and immigration, in the South it tended toward moral reform movements such as temperance, prohibition, and prostitution. It fully embraced segregation. Although the national economy flourished in the 1920s, the South languished, leading tens of thousands of African Americans to migrate to the urban centers outside the region.

Devastating floods followed by years of drought brought the southern farmer to his knees. The New Deal programs of the 1930s designed to assist those crushed by the Great Depression served primarily to benefit large landowners and displace black and white sharecroppers from their work and their homes. Protest movements and food riots resulted. The Social Security Act of 1935 promised financial stability to some southerners but not those who worked in domestic service or agriculture. Southern poverty remained high. Modifications to Social Security in 1939 meant that states could provide assistance to widows and children through Aid to Dependent Children (ADC, later AFDC).

The "War on Poverty" under President Lyndon Johnson expanded the federal role in addressing rural poverty and in trying to reshape urban ghettos. Although many southern governors opposed these initiatives, most southern towns and cities profited from some form of job-training program, Head Start, federal aid to public schools, subsidized housing projects, and expanded welfare initiatives. Many complained about the requirements for minority participation in community planning and affirmative action hiring policies. Scholars disagree on the lasting impact on the poor of these "Great Society" programs. The Clinton administration, pressured by fiscal conservatives in Congress, promised to develop comprehensive plans to enable welfare recipients to join the workforce. This "welfare to work" program took the form of the 1996 Personal Responsibility and Work Opportunity Reconciliation Act (PRWORA), which ended federal welfare programs, provided block grants to the states to provide job-training and educational grants, while transitioning recipients into the workforce. Successive administrations whittled down the training programs, leaving states to decide how to fund those not qualified for social security or federal disability but still unable to support themselves. In rural areas with few opportunities for employment, poor families had no recourse.

As many manufacturing jobs moved overseas in the 1990s, followed by the housing crash and general recession that began in 2008, both public and private agencies became overburdened with applications for assistance. The recession resulted in significantly lower tax revenues in the southern states; bare coffers meant cuts in basic social services and in higher education. With the gap between the upper class and lower class in America continuing to widen, opportunities to rise from poverty remain few.

GAIL S. MURRAY
Rhodes College

Anne Marie Cammisa, *From Rhetoric to Reform? Welfare Policy in American Politics* (1998); Jane Henrici, ed., *Doing Without: Women and Work after Welfare Reform* (2006); Michael Katz, *In the Shadow of the Poorhouse: A Social History of Welfare in America* (1986); Timothy Lockley, *Welfare and Charity in the Antebellum South* (2007); James T. Patterson, *America's Struggle against Poverty, 1900–1980* (1981).

Women, White, Working-Class

Working-class white southerners, and working-class white women in particular, are often seen as a class only marginally less exploited by elite southerners than African American southerners. Others disagree and argue for essential solidarity among white southern classes. Racism, economic disparity, and a long history of Jacksonian democracy make easy characterization of class and gender relations in white southern society difficult.

Although plantation and small-scale agriculture dominated the southern economy for much of its history, increasing levels of industry and commercial farming have resulted in the white working class becoming an ever-increasing facet of southern history. Antebellum southern society valued independence based on landownership. Consequently, white men who worked for wages were looked upon as dependent and therefore not living up to the southern ideal. This opprobrium on wage labor was even more so for women because they lacked male relatives to prevent their dependence on wages. For example, during the panic of 1837, the city of Augusta, Ga., set up a sewing factory to aid poor women and children. Another observer described "the shrieks of poor women and children when they witness the destruction of property from which they derived their daily substance." Clearly the Old South ideal did not include white working-class women except for the most destitute elements of white society.

The majority of antebellum white southerners came from the small-farm yeomanry. Historian Stephanie McCurry argued that these men saw themselves as patriarchs controlling their enclosure and the women family members who resided there. Although planter classes dominated politically and economically, poorer whites in the Old South did not necessarily feel estranged from their wealthier neighbors. The planter classes were fluid, with members of extended families falling within both economic groupings. Economic interdependency of planters and yeomanry and the rise of universal white male suffrage in the Jacksonian era led to a *Herrenvolk* or whites-only democracy in spite of economic, social, and political tensions between southern white classes. Planters held most political offices, but still had to accommodate less affluent fellow citizens. The noted diarist Mary Chesnut complained about her planter husband entertaining a contingent of what she referred to as "sand hill tackies" as social equals.

Working-class white women existed in significant numbers in the Old South. Before the Civil War, the southern states possessed approximately 150 textile mills employing 10,696 workers in 1860. Sixty-three percent of these workers were female. In addition to textile mills, working-class women found employment in tobacco processing plants, as seamstresses, and occasionally as owners of small dress shops. Slightly more respectable occupations for antebellum southern women included running boardinghouses and teaching. In general these occupations were to be embraced only in the case of dire necessity.

The 1840s witnessed an increase in southern mill construction. William Gregg, who erected the pioneering textile mill in the South Carolina Piedmont in the 1840s, promoted his factory as a means of elevating the poorest elements of southern society. Gregg employed entire families, although as a dedicated paternalist he did provide schools and churches for his workers.

The Civil War brought profound changes to the lives of white southern women. The agricultural ideal remained, but economic reality forced changes to all classes of southern women. Poor women flocked to wartime production centers such as Richmond, Columbus, Atlanta, Augusta, Selma, and other southern cities. As more and more men went into the army, textile mills and government war plants, such as arsenals and clothing depots, employed thousands of working-class southern women.

The Confederacy employed hundreds of white working-class women and children in its arsenals. These women arsenal workers engaged in several labor strikes, and in some cases the strikes resulted in their demands being met. Over the course of the war, the women arsenal workers were one of the few groups of Confederate employees who received significant wage increases.

Working-class women also expended a great deal of low-wage effort in sewing for the Confederate and state governments during the Civil War. Paid for piecework, these women did not earn enough to support themselves on depreciating Confederate currency; it was, however, the only wage labor available to most poor southern women. As with the arsenal workers, newspapers and some members of the Confederate Congress extended sympathy for the "wives and mothers" of soldiers, but compensation remained absurdly low.

Voices from poor southern women during the Civil War are rare, but occasionally surface. One North Carolina woman complained that the money she received from sewing was so low that she could either "starve or go naked," while a laundress in Alabama complained that Confederate troops treated her as badly as did the Yankees. These vignettes reveal class tensions. They also reveal a lack of deference to the elite class and a belief in their equality on the part of the working-class women, both of which reflect the Jacksonian heritage of southern society.

Following the Civil War, working-class white women continued to participate in the labor force, especially in the New South textile mill expansion, but also in heretofore-restricted occupations such as clerking and teaching. The southern textile industry openly favored white operatives, with African Americans being hired to fill only the most undesirable positions. These "New South" mills continued the antebellum practice of using female labor, although often as part of a total family employment situation. As many of the yeoman class had lost their land in the post–Civil War years, textile mills usually followed William Gregg's example and hired the entire family. These late 19th- and early 20th-century mills often functioned as a community with less than rigorous industrial discipline. Mills reportedly shut down for baseball games and managers complained of frequent absenteeism. By the 1920s the mills had become far more demanding and no longer followed the paternalistic model. Hard-fought strikes broke out in the 1920s and 1930s in several southern textile mills.

The sharecropping system also drew in thousands of white women and children. Although the actual contract would be between a husband or father and the landowner, wives and daughters were expected to work the fields. One of the first questions a landowner asked a prospective tenant was the size of his family. The domestic sphere model of the Victorian period clearly did not extend to working-class women in the South or elsewhere.

Teaching, while marginally respectable, was something to be avoided by elite southern women, especially before the Civil War. Although some elite women worked as teachers in the antebellum South, most agreed with a young Virginia woman who wrote to her sister expressing her horror that their father expected them to be useful and put their education to good use by being teachers, without necessity. The Civil War feminized the teaching profession in the South. Women began networking about employment opportunities in various parts of the South. Single women soon dominated teaching; married women teachers did not become commonplace until the World War II era.

Migration also characterized the lives of many white southern working-class women in the 20th century. Some migrated to southern urban centers to find work in burgeoning industries, but large numbers also migrated out of the region. Less well known than their African American fellow migrants, white southerners migrated in large numbers to the industrial cities of the Midwest, beginning in the early 1900s and continuing until the 1970s. Unlike African Americans, who mostly migrated from the extensive agricultural regions of the Deep South, white migrants tended to come from the highlands of the Upper South. Like African Americans, these white migrants suffered from ridicule and discrimination, at least for the first generation.

Working-class women have provided the mainspring of southern industrialization. White women workers constituted the majority of antebellum textile operatives and, in the New South era, low-wage women employees proved crucial in making southern textile mills competitive. This trend carried over into the modern era with the rapid growth of light industries across the small towns and cities of the South. Some industries such as garment manufactures depended almost exclusively on low-wage white women employees. African American women joined this labor force in recent decades.

Some elite southerners disdained working-class white women, yet race solidarity remained a complicating factor. During the Jim Crow era, small-town white southerners all went to the same schools and often grew up with the same classmates from elementary through high school. Some scholars have suggested that poor whites were effectively "dewhitened," but this view underestimates the far greater social chasm of race. The racial caste system placed all whites, regardless of class, within the same caste. The heritage of Jacksonian democracy, combined with the racial caste system, at least partially counteracted the effects of social class hierarchy for white working-class women in the South.

GARY E. BRYANT
University of Houston

Edward L. Ayers, *The Promise of the New South: Life after Reconstruction* (1992); Gary E. Bryant, "Working Women in the Confederate South: White Women in the Paid Labor Force during the Civil War" (Ph.D. dissertation, University of Houston, 2008); W. J. Cash, *The Mind of the South* (1953); William J. Cooper and Thomas E. Terrill, *The American South: A History* (1990); Drew Gilpin Faust, *Mothers of Invention: Women of the Slaveholding South in the American Civil War* (1996); Neil Foley, *The White Scourge: Mexicans, Blacks, and Poor Whites in the Texas Cotton Culture* (1998); Clifford Kuhn, *Contesting the New South Order* (2001); Stephanie McCurry, *Masters of Small Worlds: Yeoman Households, Gender Relations, and the Political Culture of the Antebellum South Carolina Low Country* (1995); Frank Owsley, *The Plain Folk of the Old South* (1949); George Rable, *Civil Wars and the Crisis of Southern Nationalism* (1989); John A. Salmond, *Gastonia, 1929: The Story of the Loray Mill Strike* (1995); Harold Wilson, *Confederate Industry: Manufacturers and Quartermasters in the Civil War* (2002).

Women and Labor

Women have been integral, if at times unequal, partners in the labor movement in the South. Emerging from slavery and the gender-segregated and racialized socioeconomic caste system following the Civil War, the movement for organized labor arose in response to the paternalism and oppression imposed by new barons of manufacturing in the latter half of the 19th century. Even as they helped to rebuild the region, these early southern industrialists increased their wealth, eventually reaping profits of 30 to 75 percent in the textile industry alone. In many cases, the greed of the economic elites led to increasingly inhumane and oppressive working conditions for men, women, and children and greater class divisions. The labor movement provided both the philosophical and the practical means to address the widening class discrepancies. As early as the 1880s, the Knights of Labor, a national workers organization dedicated to equality for all men, women, and African Americans, enlisted as many as 50,000 women and nearly 10,000 African American workers of their 750,000 members nationally. Active in the South, the Knights of Labor supported child labor reform, an eight-hour workday, and equal pay for workers, among other progressive objectives.

The Knights were superseded by the better-funded American Federation of Labor, which by 1900 had sponsored organizing efforts in most major textile centers of the South and later extended its outreach to many small textile villages. Women had been a target audience for the organizers since the 19th century, when white women and children composed 60 percent of all textile workers. By 1923 two-thirds of the textile workforce consisted of white women, who were excluded from skilled and supervisory positions, usually reserved for white men. Because of the rampant paternalism, sexism, classism, harassment, and harsh working conditions imposed by the economic elite, white women workers understandably became enthusiastic and tireless union members and organizers.

In the textile industry, for example, women strikers and organizers were instrumental in the 1929 strikes in Elizabethton, Tenn., and in Gastonia, N.C. In the Elizabethton dispute, women were the instigators of the strike. These labor leaders were one step removed from a life of backbreaking poverty in subsistence farming in the nearby Appalachian Mountains. To combat the low wages, hard labor, increasing quotas, and strict rules imposed by the German-owned company, the women organized a walkout of all 3,000 workers at two rayon plants in Elizabethton.

Just a few weeks later, the infamous 1929 Loray Mill strike in Gastonia, N.C., began. The Gastonia strike is emblematic of the unrest and violence in southern textile communities and in the roles that women played in the labor movement in the South. From the outset of its organizing efforts in the early months of 1929 by the National Textile Workers Union, an affiliate of the Communist Party, women were central to the campaign, both as organizers sent from the

North and as local participants. In June 1929 police officers attacked a small group of picketing strikers, mostly women and children, brutally beating a number of them.

One of the Gaston County women, Ella May Wiggins, who grew up in logging camps in the Appalachian Mountains, became a national heroine of the labor movement. She was a local organizer, strike balladeer, and union speaker who also testified for the union in Washington. As the single mother of nine children, Wiggins had worked in oppressive conditions and saw the union as a means to improve the lot of her struggling family. When four of her children died, Wiggins penned the well-known ballad, "Mill Mother's Lament," to draw attention to her plight and that of many other women workers. In September, Wiggins was murdered by vigilantes as she traveled to a union meeting. Her death effectively ended the union effort in Gaston County at that time.

Later efforts to win equal rights for workers were also led by women. In *Civil Rights Unionism: Tobacco Workers and the Struggle for Democracy in the Mid-Twentieth-Century South*, labor historian Robert Korstad provides a study of the tobacco industry in Winston-Salem, N.C., in the 1940s. Korstad notes, "Winston-Salem was not only a city of blue-collar workers, it was a city of *women* workers." He also highlights the structures of racial capitalism, the political and racial oppression by white supremacist capitalists who controlled the city. However, the civil rights unionism—supported in large measure by women unionists—that emerged was based on solidarity with all workers, black and white. "They believed in the long run only an interracial labor movement could achieve their broader goals." With a social justice agenda of achieving civil rights and labor rights for all workers, the unionists hoped to ignite reform in the South.

In Henderson, N.C., in 1958, textile workers removed by a generation from the strikes of 1929 faced state-supported military opposition to the more than 1,000 strikers during a two-year dispute for improved working conditions. As in the Elizabethton and Gastonia conflicts, the state brought in armed militia to support company interests. In Henderson, the once-successful Textile Workers Union of America (TWUA) brought together black and white workers and provided equally for the strikers' needs, regardless of race. Women also assumed a major role in the strike, actively picketing and speaking at rallies in cities outside the South to garner support for the Henderson workers.

Although industries in the South had fostered a paternalistic racial and gender segregated class system, the Civil Rights Act of 1964 forced more equality among workers, most notably in the textile mills. African American women finally gained access to the better-paying production jobs in the textile plants, and many of these newly empowered women joined unions to address low wages, discrimination on the job, and working conditions, furthering the likelihood of achieving more democracy in the workplace. For example, at the Oneida Knitting Mills in Andrews, S.C., women constituted 85 percent and African American women were 75 percent of the workforce. A successful strike in 1973 reflected the burgeoning collective power of women of color in achieving the ideals of civil rights, women's rights, and workers' rights.

For many southern women, the labor movement continues to afford them a democratic process for negotiating power and effecting positive change for all people of the working class. Although union participation may not be a panacea to the disparities of gender difference at work, many women find that labor unions can be a source for empowerment and transcendence. Unions offer the possibility for women to achieve parity with men in nontraditional roles as they gain access to higher-paying, more autonomous, and more intellectually engaging work. As greater numbers of women assume leadership—both in the workplace and in the unions—they will enable other women and people of color to escape the pernicious effects of poverty and oppression.

Though both endeavored to overcome oppressive systems, the feminist and labor movements have not always worked together for the common good. The quest for political power is a function of both movements, but labor organizations have not always been advocates for women's rights. Under a patriarchal system, working women often were in no better position within the male-dominated labor movement than they were in the nonunion workplace. Diane Balser explains the connection between women's lack of power and patriarchal institutions: "Throughout the history of feminism there has been an understanding that gaining political power—in order to change society and control one's life—is essential to free women from oppression. Feminist leaders have generally believed, from the earliest stages of the movement, that institutionalized powerlessness underlies female servitude." Because of the rampant inequalities of women in the work world, unions now have a mandate to promote women's rights or risk alienating a large segment of their participant base. As Diane Balser notes, "Economic issues such as pay equity, the unionization of women workers, and increased social benefits have also become part of the larger women's liberation movement."

As these two movements come together to further the interests of working-class women, they have the power to forge a coalition with greater possibilities for improving the political power of all women. According to Balser, "Real economic power for women means organizing women in such a way that they can gain control over their economic lives, end inequality, and share fully in the society's material wealth and decision-making." Southern women's feminist activism and their work to make unions more inclusive and responsive to their interests and needs have resulted in women's empowerment and leadership within union power structures and politics. Thus unions have provided women workers with the greatest access to equality and social change in the southern workplace and have helped to alleviate the widening gulf of the wealthy and the working classes.

ROXANNE NEWTON
Mitchell Community College

Diane Balser, *Sisterhood and Solidarity: Feminism and Labor in Modern Times* (1987); Daniel J. Clark, *Like Night and Day: Unionization in a Southern Mill Town* (1997); Brent Glass, *The Textile Industry in North Carolina: A History* (1992); Jacquelyn Dowd Hall, James Leloudis, Robert Korstad, Mary Murphy, Lu Ann Jones, and Christopher B. Daly, *Like a Family: The Making of a Southern Cotton Mill World* (1987); Alice Kessler-Harris, *Women Have Always Worked: A Historical Overview* (1971); Robert Rodgers Korstad, *Civil Rights Unionism: Tobacco Workers and the Struggle for Democracy in the Mid-Twentieth-Century South* (2003); Timothy Minchin, *Fighting against the Odds: A History of Southern Labor since World War II* (2004); Roxanne Newton, *Women Workers on Strike: Narratives of Southern Women Unionists* (2006); Brigid O'Farrell and Joyce L. Kornbluh, *Rocking the Boat: Union Women's Voices, 1915–1975* (1996); John A. Salmond, *Gastonia, 1929: The Story of the Loray Mill Strike* (1995); Tom Tippett, *When Southern Labor Stirs* (1931).

Working Class, Black

Emancipation added more than 3.5 million African Americans to the South's free labor market. Well into the 20th century the vast majority worked on farms, while others served as a reserve labor force for the emerging southern industrial economy. Whether their labor was agricultural or industrial, compensated or coerced, black workers continually resisted the forces of white supremacy to secure better pay, better working conditions, and equality on the job. By necessity, their strategies were mostly covert, but with regularity they mounted overt, collective challenges to their employers' and white coworkers' efforts to consign them to second-tier status.

African Americans' hopes for freedom after the Civil War were tied up in their quest for landownership. Subsistence farming promised black families a degree of economic independence and social autonomy. By 1910 more than 200,000 black farmers had collectively acquired nearly 13 million acres of land. However, the majority were impoverished tenants or hired hands who were often paid in scrip redeemable only at plantation stores. Tied to their white landlords by chronic indebtedness and declining cotton prices, black families supplemented their income by providing household services to white families. Women and girls served as cooks, maids, nannies, and washerwomen, while men and boys worked as landscapers, drivers, and repairmen.

Defying plantation owners' efforts to keep them bound to the land, a growing number of black men found work in various southern industries, especially coal mining, meatpacking, iron and steel making, railroading, ship building, and forestry. These occupations generally offered cash, paid better than farm labor, and provided a greater measure of job control and camaraderie. Such was the case of the 164,000 black woodcutters and sawmill workers who made up about half of the workforce in southern lumber camps by 1900. Black industrial workers were, however, relegated to the dirtiest, most dangerous, and lowest-paying jobs. For instance, in iron mills in Birmingham, Ala., in the 1890s, African Americans occupied nearly 90 percent of those jobs that were considered to be unskilled, while their employers recruited white workers from the North for the highest-paying positions.

Through the 1920s, tens of thousands of black workers also fell victim to various convict lease programs in which southern state and local governments sold felons and petty offenders to private employers, who assumed responsibility for their incarceration. Prisoners repaid their debts to society by making profits for wealthy planters, lumber barons, and mining companies, under conditions that compared unfavorably to slavery. As southern industrialization fueled demand for black labor, the system's profitability drove up arrest and conviction rates for high crimes such as vagrancy and public drunkenness. Reports of torture, widespread disease, and deadly accidents, such as the 1911 Banner Mine explosion that killed 123 prisoners in Alabama, drew negative attention to the convict lease programs, but they were abolished only when companies found more cost-efficient ways of maintaining productivity. Prisoners continued to work on state-run prison farms and road gangs, as well as for private companies, though usually under the authority of prison officials.

Even the most immiserated black workers challenged their poor wages and working conditions through individual acts of resistance that included theft, spontaneous work stoppages and slowdowns, sabotage, and migration. Under cover of darkness, poor farm laborers escaped debt by abandoning their landlords in search of more favorable employment on other farms or in the industrializing cities of the South and the North. Scabbing—taking the jobs of striking workers—provided a rare opportunity for African Americans to break the color line in some southern industries.

In the face of ever-present threats of violence, black workers also organized collectively for fair wages and treatment. Several hundred laborers and tenant farmers, many of whom were women, carried out a series of strikes against wage cuts on the rice plantations near Beaufort, S.C., in 1876, and five years later, 3,000 Atlanta washerwomen did the same. Although most national labor organizations excluded black workers or treated them as subordinates, some unions attempted to organize southern workers on an equal basis, and a few even championed their cause. At its peak in the late 1880s, the Knights of Labor had a substantial black base among farmhands, sugar workers in Louisiana, and coal miners in Alabama and Tennessee.

During the 1930s and 1940s southern black workers joined unions such as the Brotherhood of Sleeping Car Porters, the Southern Tenant Farmers' Union, and the Food, Tobacco, Agricultural, and Allied Workers of America to advance political and social reforms that extended far beyond narrow economic goals. After World War II, however, the failure of "Operation Dixie"—the Congress of Industrial Organization's effort to organize the nonunion South—enervated these efforts to fuse civil rights and trade unionism until 1968, when Memphis's black sanitation workers overcame white opposition to establish American Federation of State, County, and Municipal Employees Local 1733.

Grassroots organizing and the civil rights reforms of the 1960s translated into substantial gains for black workers across the South. Class action lawsuits based on the Civil Rights Act of 1964 forced the major southern textile companies to end discriminatory employment practices that excluded black workers from all but the most menial jobs, and state and municipal governments opened up clerical, managerial, and public safety jobs to African Americans. The gains were undermined, however, by dramatic shifts in the economy since the 1970s. Most of the textile mills, for instance, closed because of foreign competition, and many other sectors of the southern economy were casualties of automation and managerial schemes that transformed full-time occupations into temporary work.

KIERAN TAYLOR
The Citadel

Eric Arnesen, *The Black Worker: Race, Labor, and Civil Rights since Emancipation* (2007); Douglas A. Blackmon, *Slavery by Another Name: The Re-enslavement of Black Americans from the Civil War to World War II* (2008); William H. Harris, *The Harder We Run: Black Workers since the Civil War* (1982); Robert H. Zieger, *For Jobs and Freedom: Race and Labor in America since 1865* (2007).

American Federation of Labor

From its founding convention in Columbus, Ohio, in 1886, until its merger with the Congress of Industrial Organizations (CIO) in 1955, the American Federation of Labor (AFL) had its deepest roots among white craft unionists in the North. Both of its longtime presidents, Samuel Gompers and William Green, hailed from outside the South, and the AFL leadership never fully committed to southern organizing campaigns. Yet the AFL figured significantly in southern labor history. In the early part of the 20th century, the United Mine Workers of America (UMWA) was the AFL's largest member union and was at the center of labor struggles in the rich bituminous mines of Alabama and West Virginia. By the 1930s the AFL had organized craft workers in the tobacco, paper, and longshore industries and, during World War II, the oil refining industry. In the World War II era the governors of Georgia, Alabama, Florida, and North Carolina courted the federation's favor, and the majority of its 700,000 African American members (10 percent of its total membership) lived in the South.

The AFL attracted black workers despite a long history of racist practices. Although the union's constitution prohibited exclusion of any worker on the basis of "color, creed, or nationality," most member unions still discriminated. The national union refused to force local unions to accept black workers as full members, so that the powerful, whites-only machinists' union and boilermakers' union gained its full acceptance. Gompers condemned racial exclusion as self-defeating for white labor rather than as an injustice to black workers. He held that trade unions could not afford to ignore or anger black workers, who constituted a large segment of the laboring classes. The AFL's seemingly inclusionary rhetoric on race led some black workers to conceive of the union as a potentially powerful ally. Yet black AFL members were often relegated to segregated unions, and, as racial lines hardened, Gompers increasingly cast African Americans as a "scab" race. The example of its role in southern child labor reform illustrates the federation's cynical use of race. Irene Ashby, whom Gompers hired to study child labor in Alabama cotton mills and to foment pro–child labor legislation, made the politically popular argument that mill labor deprived white children of an education, placing them at a disadvantage vis-à-vis black children, who were more likely to be in school. On this racial rather than class basis, the AFL allied with white southern reformers to demand protective legislation and compulsory education for white children.

Still, a number of black workers joined the AFL. Its segregated unions allowed black members to exercise leadership and to access coveted skilled jobs on the docks and in the mines. Also, dramatic episodes of interracial solidarity by AFL unions offered some hope to opponents of Jim Crow. The UMWA attracted miners en masse across lines of race, and interracial solidarity prevailed among striking carpenters in Bogalusa, La., in 1919 and iron and steel mills workers in 1918 in Birmingham, Ala. Finally, beginning in the 1930s, in response to the explosive growth of the inclusive, industrial CIO, the AFL made serious efforts to organize black workers and redoubled its energies after the 1944 Supreme Court ban on the white primary expanded the southern black electorate.

On the whole, the AFL's campaigns in textiles, a crucial southern industry, had mixed results at best. In part, cultural differences explain the problem. On the issue of child labor, Gompers took the more northern view of work and manhood, which held that the adult male in the household should earn a family wage—enough to sustain his whole family. Gompers believed that southern mills undermined the family wage by commanding the work of the entire family. In contrast, southern mill workers were more familiar with a family labor system; even children as young as four or five had worked on the farm to complete the daily tasks. Southern mills had adopted the family labor system as a means of persuading farm families to enter millwork. Moreover, the AFL-affiliated United Textile Workers of America focused its energies on the Northeast rather than the Piedmont region. This changed during World War I when massive wartime demand for textiles shifted the AFL's focus south, but a series of defeated strikes, as well as conflicts between craft and industrial unionists, gutted southern union support among textile workers. North Carolina unionists persuaded the AFL leadership to commit again to the South in 1929 and 1930; however, its reliance on a cooperative strategy with management and political favors from friendly state officials put it at odds with rank-and-file workers, in Danville, Va., and elsewhere, who saw the strike as their foremost weapon but lacked the AFL's financial backing.

After World War II, the fortunes of the AFL declined. It moved again to organize nonunion southern workers, who threatened the strength of organized northern workers. Although the southern populace often viewed the AFL as less radical than the CIO, southern employers successfully convinced many workers to avoid unionism altogether, especially in small textile towns, where mill owners exerted great control. In any case, unionism was never well established in the South and faced daunting prospects in the postwar political climate, which associated strikes and labor organizing with communism. Employers fiercely, and often successfully, attacked unionism. In the aircraft industry and other sectors, managers provoked strikes and then quickly moved to crush workers' unions with strikebreakers and antistrike injunctions. These defeats exacted a heavy toll on the entire union movement, in the South and therefore nationally, from which it has yet to recover.

THERESA CASE
ALLISON SANDLIN
University of Houston–Downtown

Herman D. Bloch, Journal of Negro History (July 1965); Gary M. Fink and Merl E. Reed, eds., Essays in Southern Labor History: Selected Papers, Southern Labor History Conference, 1976 (1977); Jacquelyn Dowd Hall, James Leloudis, Robert Korstad, Mary Murphy, Lu Ann Jones, and Christopher B. Daly, Like a Family: The Making of a Southern Cotton Mill World (1987); Timothy J. Minchin, *Fighting against the Odds: A History of Southern Labor since WWII* (2005); Shelley Sallee, *The Whiteness of Child Labor Reform in the New South* (2004); Melvyn Stokes and Rick Halpern, eds., *Race and Class in the American South since 1890* (1994); Robert H. Zieger, *For Jobs and Freedom: Race and Labor in America since 1865* (2007).

Anti-Semitism

The reputation of the region for bigotry, combined with the homogeneity of the most uniformly Protestant slice of the Western Hemisphere, was bound to stir the suspicion that hostility to Jews has been a noteworthy feature of southern society. Anti-Semitism has historically been integral to Christendom because the New Testament has been read as holding the coreligionists of Jesus responsible for his Crucifixion, and no section of the United States has been more pious or "Christ haunted." Add to the mix the xenophobia of white southerners, who commonly feared (in the phrase of W. J. Cash) the intrusion of "the intolerable Alien," and observers of the region have had every reason to expect that the mind of the South could not be detached from Judeophobia. That the Jewish minority in the former Confederacy has been statistically insignificant would not in itself constitute a barrier to anti-Semitism, which has existed—and sometimes even flourished—in countries where Jews are virtually absent. In 1915 the lynching of an Atlanta factory manager, Leo Frank, after he had been convicted two years earlier of a capital crime upon the testimony of a black witness, has constituted the most dramatic—and most lethal—piece of evidence of the religious prejudice infecting the South.

And yet the preponderance of recent studies on the experience of southern Jews has tended to minimize the impact of the animus or discrimination that they faced, especially in the smaller communities that valued the economic function of merchants and tradesmen. The Jews' commercial contributions have been widely acknowledged. Any consideration of southern anti-Semitism therefore needs to take into account the countervailing force of the respect and admiration that Jews elicited. They were welcomed as presumably direct links to a biblical past that Christians and Jews shared, as generally law-abiding and unthreatening neighbors, and above all as active participants in the aim of achieving prosperity in a notoriously impoverished section. Because virtually all Jews were white, they automatically belonged to the majority, whatever their sympathies for the racial minority that represented the chief object of southern bigotry. Academic scholarship has thus built upon the philosemitism highlighted in the articles of the Charlotte journalist Harry Golden and in the pioneering overview of Eli N. Evans's *The Provincials* (1973). Recent historians have tended to minimize Cash's claim in *The Mind of the South* (1941) that the reluctance of Jews to be fully absorbed into southern society, their insistence upon a right to sustain a sense of difference, made them objects of antagonism.

The social class that constituted

by far the lesser danger was the upper crust, which defined privilege largely in terms of social exclusivity. In the prestigious country clubs of cities such as Richmond and Atlanta, in the Krewes of a New Orleans that made the celebration of Mardi Gras so central to civic identity, membership could be denied to even the Jews whose wealth matched those families whose ancestry could be traced to, say, the colonial era. As elsewhere in the United States, from roughly the last third of the 19th century until the democratization that became pronounced after the Second World War, Jewish physicians could be denied hospital staffing privileges and Jewish attorneys could be excluded from the classiest law firms, regardless of merit or talent.

The aristocratic ethos that characterized the top was reflected in the complaint of W. W. Thornton, the chief academic officer of the University of Virginia, in 1890: "Jews certainly care less for what is embraced in the term culture than Christians who are equally well off. They are immersed in business and money-getting." Discrimination at Emory Dental School, for example, persisted as late as 1961; applicants were until then classified according to three categories: "Caucasian," "Jew," and "Other." In the expression of snobbery and in the desire to maintain an impenetrable monopoly upon its high status, the class that was socially dominant in Dixie (the First Families of Virginia, the planters, the Bourbons, and their descendants) behaved no differently from its counterparts elsewhere in America. Though no systematic study comparing different regions is extant, the obsession with preserving white supremacy in the South may well have made it less dedicated to puncturing the aspirations of Jews who sought inclusion in the governing classes.

The real danger came from below. Beginning about a decade after Union troops were withdrawn from the region, farmers saddled with heavy debts wrecked stores that Jewish supply merchants owned in several parishes of Louisiana and drove such businessmen from the state. In a few counties in southern Mississippi, nightriders torched dozens of farmhouses that Jewish landlords owned in the same era. Historian John Higham called these episodes "the first serious anti-Semitic demonstrations in American history." But whether the motives of these mobs were primarily economic, or were egregious eruptions of bigotry, cannot be ascertained, because of the frequency with which Jews engaged in the supply business and were believed to be taking advantage of the precariousness and desperation of small farmers as agricultural prices spiraled downward.

The social class that gave anti-Semitism a strikingly southern accent was the very constituency that formed the Second and Third Ku Klux Klans, the demographic pool from which lynch mobs could most readily be formed. It comprised the poor whites whom the most respectable elements tended to scorn and fear. Historian Leonard Dinnerstein's influential monograph on the trial and subsequent lynching of Leo Frank, for example, frames the episode as a crisis of modernization. The

New South required industrialization to participate in the competitive capitalism that the rest of the nation was pursuing, which meant tearing whites like the murdered Mary Phagan away from an agrarian economy and small-town tradition and making them toil in factories. Such uprooting, Dinnerstein argued, was bound to instill resentment and anxiety; and it is no accident that the Frank case came after the Populists' attacks upon the disturbing power of big cities and distant financial manipulation. The eclipse of agrarianism had the effect of moral and not merely geographic dislocation, as factories suddenly seemed poised to replace farms as sites where the burden of southern history would be borne. The demagoguery of Tom Watson, who had run on the Populist ticket and was wont to orchestrate what the historian Albert D. Kirwan called "the revolt of the rednecks," helped to seal the fate of the New York–bred Leo Frank. That the Knights of Mary Phagan became the inspiration for the revived Klan only confirmed the danger that a primitive and resentful class of poor whites posed to the security of southern Jewry.

American anti-Semitism almost entirely vanished in the decades immediate after the military defeat of the Third Reich, a regime that had revealed the genocidal consequences of Judeophobia. But the danger did not recede in the South, which confronted the challenge of the civil rights revolution. Very few of the region's Jews actively and publicly opposed racial segregation (or conspicuously championed the system of Jim Crow either). But the various Klan groups in particular could not help noticing that the national Jewish denominational groups and the defense agencies not only were liberal in orientation but were explicit advocates of racial equality. In 1958 members of the National States Rights Party, a fringe group of white supremacists, bombed the most prominent Reform synagogue in Atlanta. No one in the Temple was killed; and no one was convicted of the crime, which was unambiguously denounced by the white Atlanta establishment. Such crimes ensured that the most vehement and violence-prone foes of desegregation found themselves driven to the margins of public life. But such extremist groups, generally composed of poorly educated whites in low-status occupations, perpetuated into the 1960s and 1970s whatever tradition of lower-class and lower-middle-class rancor could be tapped against the Jews.

STEPHEN J. WHITFIELD
Brandeis University

Leonard Dinnerstein, *The Leo Frank Case* (1968); Melissa Faye Greene, *The Temple Bombing* (1996); John Higham, *Send These to Me: Jews and Other Immigrants in Urban America* (1975); Clive Webb, *Fight against Fear: Southern Jews and Black Civil Rights* (2001); Stephen J. Whitfield, *Voices of Jacob, Hands of Esau: Jews in American Life and Thought* (1984).

Appalachia

As officially defined by the federal government, the Appalachian Region consists of 420 counties in 13 states from New York to Mississippi and includes all of West Virginia. It is a highly diverse region of 205,000 square miles and 24.8 million people. As distinct from this region, "Appalachia" is an imagined place, a literary and political construction. Understanding the connections and dissimilarities between the Appalachian Region and Appalachia is a central intellectual aim of Appalachian Studies. The *Encyclopedia of Appalachia*, published in 2006, conveys both depth of this scholarship and the complexity of the region. Comprising 1,860 pages and more than 2,000 entries, it is comparable in size and scope to the original *Encyclopedia of Southern Culture* published in 1989.

Scholars generally agree that representations of Appalachia as a coherent region, distinct population, and homogeneous culture first became widespread in the last three decades of the 19th century when urban and industrial growth had seemingly bypassed the southern portions of the Appalachian Mountains. Although this area was actually undergoing rapid economic transformation through railroad building, timbering, and coal mining in those decades, it was typically pictured as isolated and backward. In the words of a magazine writer in the 1870s, Appalachia was "a strange land and a peculiar people," that is, an "other America" even then. Although some writers acknowledged the relative prosperity of valley residents and town dwellers in comparison to their counterparts who farmed steep slopes and narrow hollows, most accounts of that era ignored the great extent of economic diversity, social inequality, and social class differentiation that recent scholars have demonstrated. Instead, they repeated essentialized images of Appalachia as an undifferentiated "folk society" or "arrested frontier." Mountain folk could be pictured as heroic or benighted, deserving of uplift or displacement, depending upon the agenda and ambitions of writers and the interests for whom they spoke.

In contrast, representations of the social class composition of Appalachia became more predominant during the Great Depression. For instance, middle- and upper-class women active in the settlement house movement attempted to provide economic relief to low-income families (and preserve their own preferred versions of mountain culture) by helping to market homemade women's crafts as the products of part-time, domestic labor. Reformers in the Women's Bureau of the U.S. Department of Labor, however, attempted to define Appalachia's women artisans as exploited, full-time wage laborers and to regulate their wages and working conditions. During the same era, the American Left represented the labor insurgency of Appalachian coal miners as a potent symbol of imminent proletarian revolution in the United States and Appalachia as a zone of spontaneous class militancy. These class representations competed with older images of the lazy hillbilly or, in the case of the Tennessee Valley Authority's propaganda, the mountaineer as an obstacle to technocratic planning and engineering progress.

In the 1960s—when mechanization and massive unemployment momentarily displaced labor militancy and policy makers rediscovered poverty—representations of class took a backseat to old notions of the region's supposed folk culture that were retooled to portray Appalachia as a regionwide "culture of poverty." In the words of the region's new regime of economic development, the Appalachian Regional Commission, Appalachia was (again) "a region apart." Some scholars countered with the image of Appalachia as an exploited mineral colony, but neo-Marxists criticized this model of Appalachia as an internal colony by contending that regions do not exploit regions. Rather, they argued, classes exploit regions. Nonetheless, the rhetoric of insiders versus outsiders trumped both the rhetorics of class and of a subculture of poverty in popularity and inspired important grassroots movements for social and economic justice.

Today, in the Central Appalachian coalfields of West Virginia, Virginia, and Kentucky, a new form of class conflict is taking shape where a radical form of surface mining, known by its critics as mountaintop removal (MTR), has displaced thousands of workers while continuing to produce high levels of coal at the cost of extensive environmental damage. Here, middle-class environmentalists are allied with small property owners (many of them retired underground coal miners and their families) against MTR companies and their employees to defend mountains, steams, communities, jobs, and private homes from destruction.

DWIGHT B. BILLINGS
University of Kentucky

Rudy Abrahamson and Judy Haskell, eds., *The Encyclopedia of Appalachia* (2006); Jane Becker, *Selling Tradition: Appalachia and the Constructing of an American Folk, 1930-1940* (1998); Dwight Billings and Kathleen Blee, *The Road to Poverty: The Making of Wealth and Hardship in Appalachia* (2000); Shirley Burns, *Bringing Down the Mountains: The Impact of Mountaintop Removal on Southern West Virginia Communities* (2007); Ronald Eller, *Uneven Ground: Appalachia since 1945* (2008); National Committee for the Defense of Political Prisoners, *Harlan Miners Speak* (1932, 2008); Henry Shapiro, *Appalachia on Our Minds: The Southern Mountains and Mountaineers in the American Consciousness, 1870-1920* (1978).

Artisans

Although ignored by many scholars until quite recently, artisans were an important component of southern society from colonial settlement right through the Civil War. In the past 20 years, studies of artisan communities in Baltimore, Petersburg, the North Carolina backcountry, Georgia, the Chesapeake, and Charleston have shown that most regions of the colonial and antebellum South were home to populous communities of successful craftspeople who occupied a central place in the local economy and society.

An important consequence of their longtime neglect by historians is that artisans have often remained on the margins of discussion about class in a southern context. Indeed, many descriptions of southern class structure have not incorporated artisans into their narrative at all. So, where artisans have traditionally been viewed as a main component in a working-class or lower-middle-class sector of northern American society, this group in the

South is traditionally thought principally to have consisted of yeoman and their families. Thus, historians have mainly discussed social difference among the free white population by examining the divides between these yeomen and the rich plantation patriarchs of the Old South, groups whose status was then challenged by the rise of new capitalist plantation owners settling the Deep South after 1800. Recent historians, however, are now beginning to piece together a more complex picture of social class that fully incorporates artisans. As a result of their work, we now know that artisans were a core component of the South's middle classes. From the late colonial period through the antebellum era, successful craftsmen and craftswomen, especially in southern towns, engaged in entrepreneurial manufacturing activities to accumulate significant wealth and join merchants and professionals in the middling ranks. As members of a middle class, their experience was fundamentally different from that of poor white artisans and their free and enslaved black counterparts, who, from the 1740s until the Civil War, were engaged in a divisive struggle for work. With wealthier slaveholding artisans using economies of scale to keep costs low, poor whites were frequently driven to appeal to the authorities for controls on both the number of skilled slaves and the price of labor. Although poorer journeymen were often successful in their quest to obtain such regulation, laws were usually very badly enforced. At the same time, free black artisans' efforts to compete with their white counterparts were often stymied by the disadvantages of their color in a racist society.

The relationship between artisans and social class in the South is thus a complex one. When successful white artisans bought slaves and used their labor to create profitable enterprises, they helped to forge a southern middle class that often shared much with its northern counterpart, especially by the beginning of the 19th century. Yet, their success closed doors for slaveless whites and free blacks, whose residence in a slave society meant that it took working people longer to come together as a class and mount a coherent protest against their situation. So, while in some respects southern artisans shared an understanding of class and a particular social identity with Americans in other regions, there were important ways in which their experience of social difference remained specific to those slave societies that they inhabited.

EMMA HART
University of St. Andrews

L. Diane Barnes, *Artisan Workers in the Upper South: Petersburg, Virginia, 1820–1865* (2008); Michele Gillespie, *Free Labor in an Unfree World: White Artisans in Slaveholding Georgia, 1789–1860* (2000); Emma Hart, *Building Charleston: Town and Society in the Eighteenth-Century British Atlantic World* (2010); Johanna Miller Lewis, *Artisans in the North Carolina Backcountry* (1995); Howard B. Rock, Paul Gilje, and Robert Asher, eds., *American Artisans: Crafting Social Identity, 1750–1850* (1995); Seth Rockman, *Scraping By: Wage Labor, Slavery, and Survival in Early Baltimore* (2009); Jean Russo, *Free Workers in a Plan-*

tation Economy: Talbot County, Maryland, 1690–1759 (1989); Charles G. Steffen, *The Mechanics of Baltimore: Workers and Politics in the Age of Revolution, 1763–1812* (1984); Frank Towers, *The Urban South and the Coming of the Civil War* (2004); Richard Walsh, *Charleston's Sons of Liberty: A Study of the Artisans, 1763–1789* (1959); Jonathan Daniel Wells, *The Origins of the Southern Middle Class, 1800–1861* (2004).

Bacon's Rebellion

In 1676 Bacon's Rebellion broke out in colonial Virginia as a series of unauthorized attacks on neighboring Indian tribes by poor white farmers, joined by landless laborers, indentured servants, and African slaves. When opposed by Gov. William Berkeley, the insurgents turned on his government and the great planters who supported it, looting and torching their mansions and eventually burning Jamestown. Berkeley hanged 23 rebels when he regained control, but royal officials disapproved his conduct and removed him from office.

Bacon's Rebellion grew out of social tension in the last half of the 17th century, when a small number of influential Virginians monopolized most county and provincial offices, including membership in the county courts and the House of Burgesses, and used their power to obtain most of the colony's available land. By 1700 the top quartile of landowners claimed half the privately held acreage, rising to 70 to 90 percent in the most fertile tobacco-growing counties, and at least one estate reached 50,000 acres. These great planters cultivated portions of their estates with white indentured servants and a few African slaves but reserved most of their holdings for eventual resale. Unable to gain farms of their own in the older parts of the colony, servants who survived their terms of indenture sought land on Virginia's frontier, leading to violent quarrels with the region's Indians.

In the fall and winter of 1675–76, an escalating series of retaliatory raids blossomed into full-scale war between Susquehanna Indians and white settlers in the upper Rappahannock and Potomac valleys. When Gov. Berkley's defensive measures seemed ineffective, angry small farmers rallied around Nathaniel Bacon, a youthful, wealthy, and well-connected recent immigrant, and demanded that he lead an aggressive counterattack. Fearing a wider war, Berkeley refused him permission, but Bacon and his followers defied him by attacking what they called "all Indians in general," especially the "tributary" tribes living peacefully close to white settlements. Berkeley branded Bacon a rebel and raised his own army to regain control of the province. Throughout the summer of 1676 their marauding bands pursued each other and plundered their rivals' estates. Daringly, Bacon fed social upheaval with a cross-class alliance of Virginia's oppressed, rallying landless and smallholding whites and freeing slaves and servants who fled his opponents to join him. Insurgents burned Jamestown in this free-for-all, but their rebellion suddenly collapsed in October when Bacon died of a "bloody flux." Eight African slaves and 22 white servants were the last rebels to surrender.

Virginia's class relations shifted significantly in the decades following Bacon's Rebellion, as white solidarity displaced social alternatives. African slavery replaced indentured servitude, creating a laboring class that could not easily rebel. Virginia lawmakers intensified the stigma of race by strictly limiting the right of manumission, raising the penalties for interracial sex and marriage, and ruling that the children of enslaved mothers would be slaves as well, regardless of the race or status of their fathers. Conditions for poor whites simultaneously improved as land became more widely available, payments increased to indentured servants who completed their terms, poll taxes declined, and office seekers eagerly courted the favor of ordinary voters.

In the following century, a powerful planter gentry continued to dominate Virginia. Unlike their 17th-century predecessors, however, the contemporaries of George Washington and Thomas Jefferson relied on the labor of African slaves instead of white servants and counted on active support from small and middling whites who cherished their racial privileges and political freedoms and spurned alliances with people of color beneath them.

In his widely praised *American Slavery, American Freedom: The Ordeal of Colonial Virginia*, historian Edmund S. Morgan drew these trends together to suggest that Virginia's great planters created a prototypical southern society based on slavery, racism, and white power as part of a semiconscious strategy to defuse the explosive class dynamics that led to Bacon's Rebellion. The role of conscious strategy can be exaggerated, for slaves probably replaced servants for market-driven reasons, but the outcomes of Bacon's Rebellion point clearly nevertheless to the distinctive social relations of the Old South.

HARRY L. WATSON
University of North Carolina at Chapel Hill

John J. McCusker and Russell R. Menard, *The Economy of British America, 1607-1789* (1985); Edmund S. Morgan, *American Slavery, American Freedom: The Ordeal of Colonial Virginia* (1975); Anthony S. Parent Jr., *Foul Means: The Formation of a Slave Society in Virginia, 1660-1740* (2003); Wilcomb E. Washburn, *The Governor and the Rebel: A History of Bacon's Rebellion in Virginia* (1957).

Black Belt

The American South is unique for lots of reasons, none more so than the presence of a band of counties that have been majority or heavily black for as far back as anyone can remember. These counties largely but not entirely coincided with the presence of deep religious fervor (thus, "the Bible Belt"), the growth of cotton (thus "the Cotton Belt"), and proportionately large black populations (thus "the Black Belt"). Writing about the area in the 1930s—when there were roughly 200 majority black counties—Arthur Raper said, "The Black Belt includes the most fertile soil of the South and a disproportionate number of its poorest people. The ownership of the best land is in the hands of a comparatively small group of white families; landlessness and chronic dependence is the lot of more than half the white families and nearly nine-tenths of the colored." Fifty years later two *Atlanta Journal-Constitution* reporters described the area in similar terms, noting that "by almost every measure—industry, income, infant mortality, education, poverty, housing—the Black Belt badly trails the rest of the rural South." When historian James Cobb called the Mississippi Delta "the most southern place on Earth," it was precisely the extremes of white wealth and black poverty, coupled with social norms and customs that made it that way.

By 1990 there were just under 100 majority black counties in the Black Belt. By 2000 the number had actually increased slightly to 100. In the 2000 U.S. Census, African Americans constituted about 13 percent of the total U.S. population. Using this metric, counties that are "majority black" have four times as many black people in them as does the U.S. population. Jefferson County, Miss., was nearly all black in 2000 (population estimate was 88 percent). But using "majority black" gives a deceiving impression. If we lower the bar from majority black to 40 percent (roughly three times proportional representation), and again using 2000 U.S. Census data, we find 193 counties in that count. If we further lower the bar to 30 percent (just over two times proportional representation) or greater, we find a total of 330 counties. Even with lower levels, the larger sense of the region remains in place: the Black Belt is a band of counties that runs contiguously (one connected to the other) down the Maryland-Virginia eastern shore, through the Virginia-North Carolina Tidewater, the South Carolina-Georgia Lowcountry, then turns west through south-central Georgia, Alabama, Louisiana, and Mississippi before essentially forming the "buckle" on the "belt"—with heavily black counties following the Mississippi River south (through the plantation parishes of Louisiana all the way to New Orleans) and north all the way to Illinois. Yes, Illinois! This is not a place most people would consider in "the South" but, in fact, the culture one finds in its two southernmost counties—bordered by the Illinois River on one side and the Mississippi River on the other—are very "southern" in culture and history. Indeed, Cairo, Ill., was the site of an infamous race riot in the 1960s.

The Black Belt was the wellspring for much of the Great Migration, the largest internal migration in U.S. history, when millions of African Americans left the South for the North with its hope for better jobs, better living conditions, and better treatment in all ways. The Great Migration had largely played out by the late 1960s, and now, ironically, more African Americans are migrating to the South than from it. Scholars have noted that some migrants are truly returning to the South, those with southern roots who had one time moved away and were now coming home. These are the people most likely to move to the rural areas from which they once came and where their families still own land. But the more general pattern in the Black Belt is this: those counties with majority black populations will continue to slowly decline in absolute number, mostly owing to out-migration of younger people and the children (present or future) associated with them, thus making whites a proportionally larger part of the population. For historically black counties near large urban areas—indeed, virtually any urban area large enough to generate greater job prospects—local population change is more likely to come from white in-migration. This is especially notable in the Lowcountry where white population growth has been enormous. Conversely, the poorer the historically black county and the greater its proportion black population, the more likely it is to remain either majority black or heavily so.

With roughly 100 majority black counties and more than 300 that are at least 30 percent black, it is clear that the Black Belt's legacy will not soon go away. Instead, it will continue to evolve and change along with the society around it. The "New South" may be a term that was first heard shortly after the Civil War, but the ongoing sense of a South that will forever be "New" because of its changing demographics and social customs is a certainty. In this regard, the Black Belt will be no exception, although things there may be slower to change than elsewhere in the South (excluding, of course, the rural, nearly all-white upland South, which has also always known extreme poverty). For most U.S. citizens, the Black Belt, like rural America more generally, will remain a "forgotten place," albeit one of huge historical and contemporary significance for scholars and, one can only hope, for policy makers.

WILLIAM W. FALK
University of Maryland

Jim Auchmutey and Priscilla Painton, *Atlanta Journal-Constitution* (16 November 1986); James C. Cobb, *The Most Southern Place on Earth: The Mississippi Delta and the Roots of Regional Identity* (1992); William W. Falk, *Rooted in Place: Family and Belonging in a Southern Black Community* (2004); William W. Falk, Larry L. Hunt, and Matthew O. Hunt, *Rural Sociology* (December 2004); Thomas A. Lyson and William W. Falk, *Forgotten Places: Uneven Development in Rural America* (1993); Arthur Raper, *Preface to Peasantry: A Tale of Two Black Belt Counties* (1936); Carol B. Stack, *Call to Home: African Americans Reclaim the Rural South* (1996); Ronald C. Wimberly and Libby V. Morris, *The Black Belt Databook* (2001).

Bluegrass Music

Bluegrass music's representation of traditional music sounds and repertory (and culture) within a popular music framework contains class concerns at the heart of southern culture. This music's sound and style provided the soundtrack to much of the dramatic social change that transformed America and the South in the middle of the 20th century. Today, bluegrass retains its ties to rural lifestyles, if in a more symbolic way.

Many "first generation" bluegrass musicians and fans grew up in working-class environments throughout the American South. In their younger years Bill Monroe, Ralph and Carter Stanley, and many other notable musicians took part in farming or other manual labor. Many of these musicians moved to seek music work in cities as part of the greater rural exodus to urban areas offering industrial and manufacturing jobs during and after World War II.

Bill Clifton, part of the radio and recording scene in 1950s Virginia, is a higher-class exception. Born William Marburg to a wealthy Maryland family, Clifton created his pseudonym to prevent any association between his family and the "low-class" music he performed.

After bluegrass was established in the rural record and radio market and among recent immigrants from the rural South to urban areas, the music began to draw new attention and meanings. Bluegrass was touted as a sophisticated or even supercharged form of American folk music—some critics and observers favorably compared the style to jazz and other forms of American music. "Citybillies" and folk song clubs brought first-generation bluegrass musicians to perform at universities and to other venues and audiences in the growing folk scene.

By the early 1970s bluegrass festivals had emerged as the most significant centers for the celebration of bluegrass music and the development of its communities of musicians and fans. Here rural musicians, folksingers, mechanics, and graduate students created an unlikely community as they enjoyed the shared songs and sounds of bluegrass. The egalitarian mixing of regional, economic, and social class groups at festivals continues to the present, but divisions still exist. Distinctive regional styles draw markedly different crowds to festivals such as Rockygrass (Lyons, Colo.), the Hardly Strictly Bluegrass Festival (San Francisco, Calif.), and the Bill Monroe Bluegrass Music Festival (Bean Blossom, Ind.).

Bluegrass often expresses a "plain folks" identity, in the rural and idyllic lyrics of many songs and in the cultural practices that surround the music. The music's ensemble focus and participation dynamic make it intrinsically about community and social interaction. Bluegrass is often called a "picker's music" because many fans are—to some degree—also players.

Through its use of religious elements, comedy, and antiquated material, bluegrass musicians and other participants in the music continue traditions of down-to-earth humor and self-deprecation that have long enlivened and authenticated rural-based performances in America from early opera to the minstrel show and to much of country music. Bluegrass represents a turn toward tradition within country music, a movement that often highlights the style's links to rural life and working-class identity. The "country" lyrics, blue jeans, boots, and working-class poses of bluegrass may often be symbolic, but bluegrass's ecumenical scope affords performance and connoisseurship opportunities to both people who remain in the rural margin and those from urban and suburban milieus. Although spread far beyond the geographic region with which it shares a name, as well as the social situations in which it first sounded, bluegrass is still a southern music and an expression of working-class identity, but as musicians and audiences continue to transform the music in new ways, it plays within new resonances, meanings, and identities.

LEE BIDGOOD
East Tennessee State University

Bill C. Malone, *Don't Get Above Your Raisin': Country Music and the Southern Working Class* (2002); Neil V. Rosenberg, *Bluegrass: A History* (2005).

Blues Music

In the first edition of the *Encyclopedia of Southern Culture*, Charles Reagan Wilson wrote that "much of [southern] culture was created by the working poor, by people who were destitute only in worldly goods." Blues music, one of the region's most important working-class cultural achievements, began taking shape at the turn of the 20th century among the black sharecroppers of the Arkansas, Louisiana, Mississippi, and Tennessee deltas, where Bukka White said the blues started "back across them fields, you know, under them old trees, under them old log houses... right behind one of them mules." The rural genesis of the blues is evident in the transcriptions of folklorists such as the Lomaxes as well as the early recordings by Charley Patton, Son House, and other Delta blues musicians who ventured north to the studios. Heading into the commercial blues craze of the Great Depression, blues singers had modified traditional field hollers into the aab call and response format (wherein the first line is repeated plaintively and answered by a third line) and were drawing lyrical inspiration from their immediate surroundings (e.g., barnyard animals figured as sexual innuendo or veiled references to cruel boss men). These Delta musicians favored guitars and harmonicas for their versatility and portability. Scandalously humorous and often bitterly ironic, the blues could be both introverted, as when a singer conversed in solitude with his guitar, and extroverted, as at a Saturday night juke joint when the whole crowd laughed at the singer's sardonic jokes about a bigoted sheriff or being cheated by the plantation boss come harvest time.

In this light, the blues reflected the class consciousness of the South's proletariat: sharecroppers, loggers, and levee builders who delivered masses of raw materials to the modern capitalist market, but whose bonds of debt and frequent subjection to coerced labor bespoke a more feudal economic arrangement. Northern sociologists came to the Delta in the 1930s to study the plantation South's caste system, and leftist folklorists heard the repository of the black workers' resentment in black music. They reported their findings in books such as Lawrence Gellert's *Negro Songs of Protest* (1936). Huddie "Leadbelly" Ledbetter was brought by the Lomaxes to New York, where he commingled with Woody Guthrie and acquired the language of classism, writing the "Bourgeois Blues" in 1938.

As the rural black workers effected the Great Migration to northern cities during and after World War I, they remained subsistence earners: as factory laborers they earned cash, but little more than their immediate obligations to the marketplace for rent, food, clothing, and other essentials. Segregation in housing and the workplace hemmed them in; black workers had migrated "from plantation to ghetto." In the urban public houses and nightclubs—so often considered the incubators of class consciousness—the blues musicians retold the tales of the people's journey with songs such as "Detroit Bound Blues" and "Chicago Mill Blues." More often now they sat in front of pianos and hammered out barrelhouse tunes as they had in Deep Ellum, Storyville, Beale Street, and other black neighborhoods of the urban South; the guitar ceased to be the voice of the people until electric amplification became popular.

Blues music is chromatic—guitarists atonally bend strings between notes—and likewise blues culture bended racial and class lines; thinking of the blues as the exclusive purview of the black proletariat obscures the many traditions and techniques shared by Delta musicians and their white counterparts in the Mississippi hill country. Following Jimmie Rodgers's success with the trio of vocals, guitar, and violin (Rogers even recorded some traditional aab blues) in the late 1920s, the Mississippi Sheiks became one of the most popular black recording groups of the 1930s using the same formula, and Muddy Waters continued the practice with fiddler Son Sims at home on the Stovall Plantation. Market influences shaped the blues throughout. W. C. Handy was inspired by black folk guitarists in 1903, but the sheet music craze he initiated a decade later with "Memphis Blues" homogenized the Delta's music as young bluesmen copied Handy's style. When commercial recording picked up in the late 1920s, white record agents became both conduits to black speech and censors, sensitive to racial sensibilities and market demands. This had especially been the case for female vocalists rising from the medicine acts and minstrelsy shows; the common use of the term "vaudeville" to describe classic female blues testifies to the cross-racial commercial traditions that shaped blues divas like Ma Rainey and Bessie Smith.

That the blues developed as an expression of class consciousness among working-class blacks seems clear, but the blues phenomenon was not an exclusive creation of that social class. More accurately, blues music was a complex multiregional capitalist production marketed to and consumed by blacks during the Jim Crow era and became the basis of a multicultural phenomenon on both sides of the Atlantic during the civil rights era. The main theme of the blues' century of history has been its adaptability across social class, enthralling white youngsters in the form of Elvis Presley and Jerry Lee Lewis, and achieving canonical status among blues revivalists in England and northern Europe—a universalism captured by Alex Haley, in the forward to the previous edition of this encyclopedia: "Out of the historic cotton tillage sprang the involuntary field hollers, the shouts, and the moanin' low that have since produced such a cornucopia of music, played daily, on every continent."

R. A. LAWSON
Dean College

Blind Blake, "Detroit Bound Blues" (1928); David Evans, *Big Road Blues: Tradition and Creativity in the Folk Blues* (1982); Alan Lomax, *The Land Where the Blues Began* (1993); August Meier and Elliot Rudwick, *From Plantation to Ghetto: An Interpretive History of American Negroes* (1966); Peetie Wheatstraw, "Chicago Mill Blues" (1940).

Braden, Carl, and Anne McCarty
(CARL BRADEN, 1914–1975; ANNE MCCARTY, 1924–2006) ANTISEGREGATIONISTS.

Carl Braden and Anne McCarty Braden were among the modern civil rights movement's staunchest white southern allies. Despite numerous attempts in the Cold War years to discredit them as revolutionaries and "reds" because of their identification with Communist Party–led causes, the pair brought their left-wing perspectives and journalistic skills to civil rights and civil liberties campaigns in the South for almost three decades. Their commitment won them the respect of African American leaders such as Ella Baker and the Rev. Martin Luther King Jr., who referred specifically to Anne Braden as a white supporter in his 1963 "Letter from Birmingham Jail." After Carl's death, Anne Braden remained among the region's most outspoken white antiracist activists. Over nearly 60 years, she brought her message on the intransigence of racism and the responsibility of whites to combat it to almost every social justice movement in the South.

Natives of Louisville, Ky., the Bradens met there in 1947 as reporters on the daily newspaper. Anne McCarty—a decade younger than Carl Braden—had grown up in rigidly segregated Anniston, Ala., daughter of a middle-class, prosegregationist family. An idealistic Episcopal youth, Anne was never an activist until she teamed up with Carl, a labor journalist who had grown up poor, the son of Eugene Debs–style socialist trade unionists. Marrying in 1948, they immersed themselves in Henry Wallace's unsuccessful Progressive Party run for the presidency, then left mainstream journalism to write for Louisville's Local 236 of the Farm Equipment Workers Union (FE), part of the interracial left wing of the Congress of Industrial Organizations (CIO).

While the postwar labor movement splintered amid growing Cold War anticommunism, civil rights causes heated up. Repelled by racial hierarchy, the Bradens also saw the fight against segregation as the front line of working-class struggle in the South. Their rank-and-file local civil rights activism turned to regional notoriety when they helped to desegregate an all-white suburb of their border South city—an action that got them jailed and vilified nationally as communists. In May 1954, days before the U.S. Supreme Court condemned school segregation in *Brown v. Board of Education*, the pair acted as "fronts" for the purchase of a new suburban home by African Americans Andrew and Charlotte Wade, who had been stymied by segregated housing practices from purchasing a home on their own. A burning cross, gunshots, and unrelenting white hostility greeted the Wades, culminating in the dynamiting of their new home six weeks later one night while they were out.

When the chief investigator theorized that the purchase and subsequent violence had all been a communist plot to destabilize race relations, a local variation of the anticommunist hysteria known nationwide as "McCarthyism" ensued. In October 1954 the Bradens and five other whites were charged with "sedition," a vaguely defined charge that had lain inert in Kentucky law since its 1919 adoption during an earlier "Red Scare." After a sensationalized trial, Carl Braden—the perceived ringleader—was sentenced to 15 years' imprisonment. A paid FBI informant had connected him to the Communist Party, though not to the violence or any conspiracy. As the other defendants awaited trial, Carl served eight months and was out on bond when a Supreme Court decision invalidated state sedition laws as capricious. All charges were dropped in 1956, but the Bradens became pariahs, and the Wades were never again able to live in their house or see its assailants prosecuted.

By forcefully illustrating how dependent civil rights were on civil liberties, the sedition case strengthened the Bradens' relationship with the freedom movement farther south and with the beleaguered American Left as the couple traveled the nation publicizing how southern white politicians propped up segregation by silencing all dissent as communistic and disloyal. Blacklisted from local employment, they stayed in Louisville but took jobs as field organizers for the Southern Conference Educational Fund (SCEF), a small, New Orleans–based civil rights organization that had also been investigated as a "communist front" by committees of the U.S. Congress. Frequent excoriation in the press as seditionists and communists made them controversial figures even within the movement, but they also used every attack as a platform for condemning racial injustice.

In the years before southern civil rights violations made national news, the Bradens directed media attention to the burgeoning movement through SCEF's monthly newspaper, the *Southern Patriot*, and through pamphlets and press releases they wrote to expose racial injustices. In 1958 Anne Braden wrote *The Wall Between*, a memoir of their sedition case. One of the few books of its time to unpack the psychology of white southern racism from within, it became a finalist for the National Book Award. That same year, Carl Braden insisted on his First Amendment rights of free association and refused to answer questions at a U.S. House Committee on Un-American Activities (HUAC) hearing in Atlanta investigating the civil rights movement. That case went to the U.S. Supreme Court, but he lost his appeal and served a year in prison in 1961 for contempt of Congress.

In the 1960s the Bradens became respected elders to a younger generation now igniting a new student sit-in movement. When young blacks suggested that whites organize among themselves, Anne Braden defended the rise of "Black Power," and many young white activists associated with the "New Left" gravitated to SCEF. The Bradens faced a second sedition charge in 1967 in eastern Kentucky as a result of a SCEF campaign against strip mining. The challenge they mounted finally got the Kentucky sedition law declared unconstitutional.

Disillusionment and infighting in the New Left brought about SCEF's decline in 1973, but the Bradens continued organizing regionally on behalf of African

American activists under government attack, such as Angela Davis (Calif.) and the Wilmington Ten (N.C.). After her husband's 1975 death, Anne Braden helped form a new multiracial organization, the Southern Organizing Committee for Economic and Social Justice (SOC), which initiated battles against environmental racism. She became an instrumental southern voice in the two Jesse Jackson presidential campaigns of the 1980s and organized across racial divides in the new environmental, women's, and antinuclear movements of that decade, remaining a key figure in Louisville civil rights causes until her death at 81.

Both Bradens, but Anne in particular, became for many activists of the sixties generation and beyond a rare symbol of white southern resistance to segregation and racism. Despite the repression directed at them in the Cold War era, the couple never dissociated from Marxism, the Communist Party, or the left generally. Yet neither would they ever affirm, deny, or detail their relationship to the Communist Party, believing firmly that there should be no attacks on the left and that First Amendment principles should protect all such beliefs. Until the ends of their lives, they were unyielding in keeping the struggle against racism at the center of their activism, while connecting it to poverty, war, and other social ills.

CATHERINE FOSL
University of Louisville

Anne Braden, *The Wall Between* (1958, 1999); Catherine Fosl, *Subversive Southerner: Anne Braden and the Struggle for Racial Justice in the Cold War South* (2002, 2006); Barbara Ransby, *Ella Baker and the Black Radical Tradition: A Radical Democratic Vision* (2002).

Campbell, Will

(b. 1924) SOCIAL AND RELIGIOUS LEADER.

A son of the nation's most distinctive region, Will Davis Campbell abides no social distinctions. Born on 18 July 1924 in Amite County, Miss., Campbell learned the South's Jim Crow customs but soon grew to resist such social systems and conventions. By his own recounting, his nonconformity was the result of key experiences. In the early 1930s, for example, his Grandpa Bunt chastised the young Campbell for using a common epithet for an older African American neighbor. The impact of his grandfather's profession—that all are God's children and must be honored as such—altered the course of Campbell's life and thought. A decade later, while serving as a U.S. Army medic in the South Pacific, Howard Fast's *Freedom Road* led Campbell to see and reject the race baiting that the South's oligarchy used to protect its privilege. Whether segregated black or satirized poor white, the hope of the ostracized, Campbell learned from Fast, depended on their unity.

Returning from World War II, Campbell earned an undergraduate degree from Wake Forest (1948) and a ministerial degree from the Yale Divinity School (1952). After what he called his "pseudosophisticated period," Will and wife, Brenda, accepted the call to a Southern Baptist congregation in

Taylor, La. Already advocating progressive views on race, Campbell's ministry proved short-lived—especially after the Supreme Court's *Brown* decision. By July 1954 Campbell decided that "the Academy" better accommodated his views, and he became the director of Religious Life at the University of Mississippi. Some eight years before James Meredith successfully desegregated Ole Miss, Campbell labored creatively to breach the dividing, ivy-covered walls of racial hostility at the state's flagship university. After a couple tense years in Oxford, however, Campbell was again looking for a community to practice his reconciling vocation. This time Campbell looked outside the South.

In October 1956 Campbell became the associate executive director of the Department of Racial and Cultural Relations of the Division of Christian Life and Work of the National Council of Churches of Christ in the U.S.A. (NCC). Campbell was, in other words, the NCC's civil rights ombudsman in the South. Relocating to Nashville, Campbell threw himself into the major civil rights events of the late 1950s and early 1960s. He escorted the Little Rock Nine to classes at Central High School in 1957, and he participated in the Southern Christian Leadership Conference's founding meetings in Atlanta. In 1959–60, Campbell aided and advised James Lawson and Nashville students (Diane Nash, John Lewis, Bernard Lafayette, James Bevel, and Marion Berry) as they designed the sit-in movement and later sustained the Freedom Rides in 1961.

By 1962, however, Campbell had concluded that the pro-civil rights NCC was similar to the "steeple" in Louisiana and the University in Mississippi. He concluded, in fact, that all institutions are the same, that is, inherently evil. All institutions (governmental, academic, and ecclesiastical) manipulate individuals, creating adversaries so as to orchestrate and coerce their desired outcomes. The liberal NCC, for example, championed the cause of the African American by parodying and punishing the "redneck." Campbell maintained his ardor for human and civil rights, but recalled what he had learned 20 years earlier. The privileged manufacture social divisions to achieve their ends and outcomes. As Campbell explained in his *Race and Renewal of the Church*, this institutional ethic was the denial of Christian reconciliation (as described in 2 Corinthians 5).

All humans—irrespective of race, class, gender—are the same: a tragic confusion of myopic good intentions, avarice, and narcissism. Thus, attempts to mobilize the "good" against the "bad" are merely idolatrous. The self-ascribed "benevolent" believe they must defeat "those malevolent others" to control events and make history turn out correctly. Indeed, both the so-called Right and Left think and act according to the same idolatrous politic—the parties merely disagree over whom to pin their stigmatizing, derisive labels on. As Campbell would explain after Jonathan Daniels's murder near Selma, Ala., in August 1965, the good news is that "we're all bastards, but God loves us anyway."

For a time in the 1960s and 1970s,

Campbell and the Committee of Southern Churchmen offered one of the most scandalous, anarchistic venues in southern history in their journal, *Katallagete*. They illustrated what radical reconciliation looked like. Contributors and members were black and white, straight and gay, male and female, felons on the FBI's most wanted list, Klansmen, cloistered monks, and best-selling authors. None of these social distinctions, however, mattered. Given his iconoclastic vocation, Campbell has committed his life to provoking reconciled people to resist seductive powers that entice separation and division. He has called for sisters and brothers, irrespective of appearance, ideology, or social branding to *be* what God had made them—Reconciled!

RICHARD C. GOODE
Lipscomb University

Will D. Campbell, *Brother to a Dragonfly* (1977), *Writings on Reconciliation and Resistance* (2010); Will D. Campbell and Richard Goode, *Crashing the Idols* (2010); Thomas Connelly, *Will Campbell and the Soul of the South* (1982); Merrill Hawkins Jr., *Will Campbell: Radical Prophet of the South* (1997).

Child Labor

Until the mid-20th century, children were an integral part of the southern labor force. As early as 1618 the Virginia Company brought 100 poor children from London with the intention of binding them out as apprentices. Typical of the working children who appear in the historical record, these young people were bound with written contracts, called indentures, that served to establish the mutual obligations of child workers and their masters. Many more children worked on the land with the family, in the father's shop, and in the home with the mother. Lacking written documents pertaining to their work, much less is known about them.

The ancient institution of apprenticeship was remarkably flexible. Some children, at the behest of their parents, more or less voluntarily bound themselves to a master to learn a skilled trade. While not as fully developed in the South as in the North, craft apprenticeships in the 18th-century South appeared in the United Brethren settlements of North Carolina and workshops specializing in the carriage trade of Charleston. Other children, whose parents were deceased or unable to care for them, were bound out through local institutions or justices of the peace. These pauper or orphan apprentices often went on to learn trades, in the case of boys, and to work as domestic servants, in the case of girls. In early 19th-century New Orleans, both whites and free persons of color participated in formal apprenticeships. Elsewhere surviving records of African Americans in apprenticeship do not distinguish clearly between cases of long-term bound child labor and cases of training in a particular skill.

Enslaved children began intensive work in their early years. By age seven or eight they were expected to perform a variety of chores and within a few years worked alongside adult field hands. Consistent with 20th-century interviews with former slaves, price-by-age data from the mid-19th century indicated that slave children began to produce more than the costs of their upkeep around age eight. After enslaved young people began to work in the fields, their diets improved in terms of both calories and protein, which was necessary for them to carry out their grueling work. These dietary improvements also resulted in dramatic catch-up growth in their heights relative to modern standards, a phenomenon rarely seen in human history.

The industry best known for its employment of child laborers was cotton textiles. From the founding of the Graniteville Manufacturing Company in 1845, children constituted a large share of cotton mill workers and a large share of children worked in cotton mills. By 1909 more than half of children aged 10 to 15 in South Carolina, Alabama, and Mississippi, and nearly half in other southern states, worked. In the late 19th century about one-fourth of operatives in cotton textiles in the South were aged 10 to 15, roughly evenly divided between boys and girls. Girls primarily worked as spinners, a relatively demanding job, whereas boys primarily worked as doffers, taking away full bobbins and replacing them with empty ones. These jobs required little in the way of skill and paid poorly.

Child labor eventually declined, but the reasons for that decline are not completely clear. Compulsory school attendance laws reduced employment rates of youths only when combined with minimum age laws in manufacturing, and among southern states only Louisiana and Tennessee had minimum age laws in 1900. Later in North Carolina the state legislature passed a watered-down child-labor bill that had been written by manufacturers hoping to stave off more progressive legislation. Efforts to limit child labor at the federal level sparked opposition from southern manufacturers, and laws of 1916 and 1918 were eventually found unconstitutional by the Supreme Court. A proposed child labor amendment to the U.S. Constitution passed Congress in 1924 and was ratified that year by Arkansas and 12 years later by Kentucky, but only 26 other states joined them. When the federal Fair Labor Standards Act of 1938 finally limited child labor, there were relatively few children left in the labor force.

JOHN E. MURRAY
Rhodes College

Robert William Fogel and Stanley L. Engerman, *Time on the Cross: Evidence and Methods—A Supplement* (1974); David Galenson, *White Servitude in Colonial America: An Economic Analysis* (1981); Ruth Wallis Herndon and John E. Murray, eds., *Children Bound to Labor: The Pauper Apprentice System in Early America* (2009); Philip M. Holleran, *Social Science History* (Autumn 1997); Marie Jenkins Schwartz, *Born in Bondage: Growing Up Enslaved in the Antebellum South* (2000); Richard H. Steckel, *Journal of Economic History* (September 1986); Gavin Wright, *Old South, New South: Revolutions in the Southern Economy since the Civil War* (1986).

Citizens' Councils

Citizens' Councils and allied organizations—the Virginia Defenders of State Sovereignty and Individual Liberties, the Tennessee Federation for Constitutional Government, the North Carolina Patriots, and the Georgia States' Rights Council—were formed by white supremacists in the South to resist school desegregation. Appearing first in Mississippi in July 1954, this movement of "white-collar" or "country club" Klans spread rapidly into each of the 11 former Confederate states. Dedicated to "states' rights and racial integrity," the council movement, like the Confederacy itself, failed to overcome southern parochialism and thus never forged a united front. Yet a semblance of regional unity was provided in 1956 by the formation of the Mississippi-based Citizens' Councils of America, an informal confederation of the more viable southern organized resistance groups.

The councils' natural habitats were the old plantation areas of the Lower South, where the black population was most heavily concentrated and where white racial fears were highest. Except in Virginia, where organized resistance was endorsed by the Byrd machine, and Little Rock, where Gov. Orval Faubus was a supporter, councils or council-like groups enjoyed little success in the so-called rim South states. In Florida, North Carolina, Tennessee, and Texas, members of the white power structure rarely became closely identified with the groups. But in the Deep South—in Alabama, Louisiana, Mississippi, and South Carolina—councils won the support of high elected officials and of business and professional leaders. Here, where their power and prestige were greatest, Citizens' Councils officially eschewed violence. Individual members were sometimes implicated in terrorist acts, however, and the movement was instrumental in creating a climate of fear and reprisal in which few whites and even fewer blacks dared challenge the status quo. In Alabama and Mississippi, councils functioned as shadow governments.

There are no reliable membership figures, but the South-wide total probably never exceeded 250,000, though non-dues-paying sympathizers surely numbered many thousands more. Having rapidly expanded in the years immediately after *Brown v. Board of Education*, white resistance organizations gradually declined following the federal-state confrontation at Little Rock. In growing numbers whites recognized that some degree of school desegregation was inevitable. Remobilization campaigns in the 1960s failed, and by middecade membership even in Mississippi had dwindled to insignificance. Thereafter, diehard movement leaders turned their support to all-white private schools.

NEIL R. MCMILLEN
University of Southern Mississippi

Numan V. Bartley, *The Rise of Massive Resistance: Race and Politics in the South during the 1950s* (1969); Hodding Carter, *The South Strikes Back* (1959); Neil R. McMillen, *The Citizens' Council: Organized Resistance to the Second Reconstruction* (1971).

Civic and Historical Pageants and Pilgrimages

Beginning in the early years of the 20th century, southerners staged public productions in which they displayed, performed, interpreted, and improved upon the past. Civic and historical pageants featured ordinary citizens enacting time-honored stories about local and regional pasts, while home and garden pilgrimages invited visitors to experience the architecture, material culture, and bygone social relations associated with the antebellum South. Participants and other local residents solidified both social standing and local knowledge through the productions and constituted an intended audience of both spectacles as much as the tourists they ostensibly sought to educate and entertain.

Between the turn of the 20th century and World War II, southerners joined the nationwide craze for acting out dramatic episodes of local history in historical pageants—public celebrations of civic unity that featured large casts and emphasized timeless values and virtues. Growing out of progressive reform movements in public recreation and the fine arts and "antimodernist" sentiments that favored an idealized past over the uncertain present, pageants provided a vehicle for participants to locate themselves within accepted historical narratives, display group identities, express concern over the present state of affairs, and prescribe future behavior. In the segregated South, white southerners employed pageantry to express anxiety over the state of society—with its "uppity" Negroes and threats of social equality—by acting out "right" versions of the past. In grand displays of consensus that reinforced the social order and muted ethnic, class, and racial tensions, southern pageants asserted continuity with a supposedly stable and harmonious plantation past. African American productions that suggested otherwise—Emancipation Day and Fourth of July celebrations had been staged by freedpeople since the early years of Reconstruction, and W. E. B. Du Bois premiered his epic black history pageant *The Star of Ethiopia* in New York City in 1913—were therefore a source of distress to southern whites.

In the Jim Crow South, few pageant directors could resist the opportunity presented by historical pageants: the chance to rescript the southern past. Although some southern pageants looked to the future—the final episode of the Spartanburg (S.C.) Centennial Celebration buzzed with the prospect of Piedmont industrialization and the Reconstruction mantra, "Rebuild"—the vast majority gazed fondly backward on a past of near limitless peace and joy. The Old South of pageantry was one of generations of family and community living in harmony, and of blacks content with their place in the racial hierarchy. The stereotypical depiction of slave life was a staple of southern productions, with blacks depicted as comic simpletons happy under slavery. Coupling generic scenes and predictable structures suggested by the American Pageant Association ("Indians," "First Settler," "Colonial," "Civil War") with Lost Cause mythology that glorified and vindicated the Confederacy while idealizing the social order of the Old South, southern pageants were powerful representational vehicles for white southerners intent on influencing public memory.

Women figured prominently in all the productions, but especially in *tableaux vivants* in which they appeared in symbolic dances as "spirits" embodying community virtues. *Spirit of Columbia*, the South Carolina sesquicentennial celebration of 1936, featured the Spirit of Progress and the Spirit of History. In another typical pageant, the "sparkling and delicate" Spirit of the Antebellum South radiated "all the feeling of the Old Time South, its hospitality, its entertainment, and its feudal protection." Alabama Home Coming Week of 1926 included a beauty pageant in which young women vied for the pageant role of "Spirit of the South."

In an effort to claim gentility and reiterate the nation's Anglo-American identity, southerners wove Elizabethan rituals into pageant scripts, and these, too, featured women. Poet and dramatist Percy MacKaye infused both collegiate May Day rituals and civic pageants across the South with Maypole dances, May Queen pageants, and *tableaux vivants* that promoted remembrance of the South as an offshoot of European aristocracy. By casting descendants in the roles of their ancestors, southerners emphasized lineage and authenticated their connections to particular towns. In the end, the typical southern historical pageant amounted to an elaborate spectacle of social position that distorted history in favor of an idealized version of the past.

The southern pilgrimage movement that put colonial and antebellum homes on display to the fee-paying public got its start in 1929 when the Garden Club of Virginia opened notable gardens in order to raise funds for the restoration of gardens at Kenmore, home of Fielding and Betty Washington Lewis (sister of the first president), and at Stratford Hall, the birthplace of Confederate general Robert E. Lee. The first Virginia garden club had been organized at Warrenton in 1911, taking as its model the Garden Club of Philadelphia, and in the intervening years, seven additional Virginia clubs had formed. They were called "nosy, meddling women" by legislators, "a threat to progress" by utility companies, and "the scenic sisters" by billboard advertisers, but regard for garden club members improved when their Historic Garden Week proved a success. As the *Chicago Tribune* noted, "They are ladies of leisurely and melodious diction, and high grace of manner, but . . . they work."

Garden clubs across the region soon tried their hand at similar ventures. By calling a visit to a tour home or series of homes a pilgrimage—a religious term referring to a contemplative journey to a sacred destination undertaken with the expectation of transformation—southern garden clubs marketed Old South mystique. Putting antebellum homes, Confederate relics, and Civil War battle sites on display, and linking one site to the next, southern garden clubs created itineraries of romance and nostalgia, guideposts for pilgrims seeking transformation in the presence of holy shrines. The Natchez Garden Club in Mississippi was one of the first to adopt the concept. Faced with hosting a state convention of garden clubs in 1931 in the depths of the Depression, club president Katherine Balfour Miller opted to showcase the city's antebellum homes rather than its neglected gardens and convinced members to dress up in heirloom hoopskirts for the occasion. The gambit proved so popular that a weeklong pilgrimage opening 22 homes to the public was planned for the following year. Some 1,500 pilgrims from 37 states attended the first Natchez Pilgrimage of 1932, where local residents presented home tours, historical tableaux, a parade, a barbecue, a cotillion, a pageant, and a Confederate ball. In the years that followed, a social institution developed around the Natchez Pilgrimage and others like it: garden club members and their daughters received the public at tour homes, delivered interpretive talks, and starred in associated entertainments that were a source of status. The result was a system of race and class privilege linked to annual tourist productions about life in the Old South.

The 1930s saw explosive growth of the southern pilgrimage concept, with clubs from the hills of northern Mississippi to the Georgia coast initiating tours. Over time and across the region, the inspiration to preserve, display, narrate, and perform the southern past proved an economic lifeline for communities blessed with impressive architectural stock but burdened by the cost of preserving, restoring, and maintaining it. The multimillion dollar heritage tourism industry that exists today is the direct result of the imagination and hard work of southern women. The entrenched system of social privilege that resulted in part from this success is also their legacy.

ELIZABETH BRONWYN BOYD
Takoma Park, Maryland

Kathleen Clark, in *Where These Memories Grow*, ed. W. Fitzhugh Brundage (2000); David Glassberg, *American Historical Pageantry: The Uses of Tradition in the Early Twentieth Century* (1990); James Bland Martin, *Follow the Green Arrow: The History of the Garden Club of Virginia, 1920–1970* (1970).

Clubwomen

Although women began to join women's church auxiliaries, benevolence associations, and antislavery societies well before the Civil War, the rise of the women's club movement took place in the late 19th and early 20th centuries. Although the first women's club, Sorosis, formed in the 1860s in the North, most southern white and black women's clubs did not form until the 1890s and early 1900s. Separate state federations of women's clubs for white and black women quickly followed, and southern clubwomen also participated in the General Federation of Women's Clubs (GFWC) and the National Association of Colored Women (NACW). Many women's clubs began as literary associations and then branched out into social reform, providing services such as kindergartens, libraries, and playgrounds and lobbying for reforms in the schools, in the justice system, and in the workplace, with a particular focus on the needs of children and women.

Middle- to upper-middle-class women dominated both black and white women's clubs, particularly the wives of doctors, lawyers, and small business owners. African American teachers and the wives of businessmen, professionals, and college faculty disproportionately populated black clubs in southern cities. These women were wealthier than their African American neighbors and placed a premium on respectability. They pushed for women's clubs to focus on issues of the home, with a particular concern for protecting young women and defending black women from accusations of sexual immorality. This agenda sometimes led to tension between clubwomen and the objects of their reform, especially when clubwomen sought to control social behaviors such as dancing. Furthermore, they often tried to maintain exclusive membership policies. Yet black women's clubs could also be relatively inclusive of working-class African Americans, because the status of wealthy blacks did not protect them from racial oppression and their wealth was often relatively less secure than that of white clubwomen. Septima Clark, a teacher and civil rights activist, found clubs in Charleston to be far more exclusive and dominated by lighter-skinned women than those in Columbia, S.C., for example. Because many African American clubwomen worked outside the home, most often as teachers, they were empathetic to the problems working women faced, including childcare.

The makeup of white women's clubs in the South was similarly elite. Unlike black clubwomen, most white clubwomen did not work outside the home. They were married to doctors, lawyers, bankers, merchants, businessmen, and, in the Piedmont, cotton mill owners and bookkeepers. In comparison to the United Daughters of the Confederacy, fewer had husbands who were planters or farmers. Not surprisingly, white clubwomen also faced criticism for their desire to impose their standards on poor families, especially in mill towns. They advocated industrial education for whites in the schools on the basis that it was in the best interest of poor, often rural whites. They did not, however, acknowledge that it would also yield better laborers in the mill businesses their husbands ran, nor did they find it problematic to advocate the same manual training for poor whites as they did for African Americans (as opposed to higher education) to keep blacks "in their place." Yet, most progressive women who led the social reforms efforts in clubs also exhibited a genuine desire to benefit the poor. White women's clubs were also socially exclusive. Clubs with names such as Over the Teacups and the Thursday Club met in members' homes during the workday, where they shared tea and refreshments as they discussed literature, art, and current events. The format of club meetings therefore tended to reinforce social barriers.

While both black and white women's clubs accomplished a tremendous amount of progressive social reform, they did so as socially exclusive organizations that at times reinforced class tension. Significantly, the most rigid barrier to membership in a women's club was race: women's clubs in the South were completely segregated, and black women were not allowed to participate in the GFWC biennial meetings. Rather, they participated in the

NACW. Ironically, both black and white southern clubwomen sometimes felt stigmatized in the national organizations for their regional identity, even though their wealth and status mirrored that of clubwomen in the north.

JOAN MARIE JOHNSON
Northeastern Illinois University

> Karen J. Blair, *The Clubwoman as Feminist: True Womanhood Redefined, 1868–1914* (1980); Joan Marie Johnson, *Southern Ladies, New Women: Race, Region, and Clubwomen in South Carolina, 1890–1930* (2004); Kibibi Voloria Mack, *Parlor Ladies and Ebony Drudges: African American Women, Class, and Work in a South Carolina Community* (1999); Deborah Gray White, *Too Heavy a Load: Black Women in Defense of Themselves, 1894–1994* (1999).

Coal and Iron Workers

The growth of coal mining and iron and steel production in the late 19th and early 20th centuries depended upon black workers and white workers. Prior to the Civil War, southern coalmines and iron foundries rented slaves and hired some free black labor. Generally white workers held supervisory and skilled jobs. As long as management maintained this racial division of work, recognizing white workers' claims to the best jobs in coalmines and iron mills, relations between capital and labor remained cooperative. If white managers challenged the racial status quo by employing blacks in occupations whites claimed as their own, white workers mounted protests not only to defend their jobs but also to defend white supremacy generally. By framing such conflicts in racial rather than class terms, white workers mobilized support in their communities during conflict with management.

This pattern continued and intensified as the industry expanded after the Civil War and as African Americans asserted their rights as free men. In the mines and steel plants of the postwar South, whites established control of the best jobs, while enforcing practices designed to hold blacks in the least desirable jobs available. White workers believed that in a biracial industry they must maintain control of the racial line as a defense against management challenges to white supremacy in the workplace. Management recognized the powerful appeal of the idea of white supremacy and most of the time reconciled itself to the racial division of work, despite the additional labor costs white workplace privilege imposed. During economic downturns, or when white workers went on strike over wages and working conditions, management attempted to exploit the tension that existed between whites and blacks, who resented white workers' monopoly of the best jobs. Many African Americans took advantage of conflict between white labor and white capital to improve their position in industry by taking the jobs of white strikers. Organized workers, especially in coalmining, attempted to limit strikebreaking by black workers by including them in their unions, albeit as unequal partners. Blacks who joined these biracial unions hoped to loosen white control of the occupational ladder, but unions controlled

Coal miners, Birmingham, Ala., 1937 (Arthur Rothstein, photographer, Library of Congress [LC-USF33-002399-M4], Washington, D.C.)

by whites, with only a few exceptions, offered little substantive change in the racial division of work. Indeed, as the steel industry became more organized in the 1930s, segregation in plants and mines became even more institutionalized. Not until the 1970s and 1980s, when the federal government filed suits against companies and labor unions under the Civil Rights Act of 1964, did segregation and discrimination in the work place come to an end.

Scholars continue to debate the nature of class and race relations in the iron and steel industry. Many continue to argue that management fostered racial division among workers as part of a "divide and conquer" strategy. Others counter this argument with evidence of racially discriminatory union work rules and white workers' use of the ideology of white supremacy to challenge employers who violated the racial mores of the community. White workers believed that it was in their interest to control the black labor force in order to limit threats to their monopoly of the best jobs in the mines and steel plants of the South. Their strategy withstood repeated challenges for more than a century.

HENRY M. MCKIVEN JR.
University of South Alabama

Herbert Gutman, *Work, Culture, and Society in Industrializing America* (1977); Brian Kelly, *Race, Class, and Power in the Alabama Coalfields, 1908-21* (2001); Daniel Letwin, *The Challenge of Interracial Unionism: Alabama Coalminers, 1878-1921* (1998); David Lewis, *Sloss Furnaces and the Rise of the Birmingham District: An Industrial Epic* (1994); Henry M. McKiven Jr., *Iron and Steel: Race, Class, and Community in Birmingham, Alabama, 1875-1920* (1995); Robert J. Norrell,

Journal of American History (December 1986); Robert H. Woodrum, *Everybody Was Black down There: Race and Industrial Change in the Alabama Coalfields* (2007).

Congress of Industrial Organizations

From the CIO's (Committee on Industrial Organization, 1935–38; Congress of Industrial Organizations, 1938–55) inception in 1935, its leaders regarded promotion of industrial unionism in the South as essential to organized labor's political and economic objectives. Expansion southward would protect gains achieved in northern industry from low-wage southern competition. A growing union presence in the South would also advance civil rights for African Americans and weaken the political and legislative stranglehold of conservative southern politicians.

The cotton textile industry was the key to CIO fortunes in the South. By the 1930s about 450,000 men and women toiled in southern mills, most of them strung out along the Piedmont from southern Virginia to northern Alabama. In March 1937 the CIO created a Textile Workers Organizing Committee (TWOC), in an effort to bring union organization to textile workers. However, its efforts in Virginia, the Carolinas, and the Deep South achieved little before its termination in 1939. Employer resistance, hostile public officials, and the sharp economic downturn of the late 1930s proved fatal, along with the caution and diffidence of most textile workers.

During World War II the CIO did make inroads into the South. TWOC, now renamed the Textile Workers Union of America, gained recognition in some southern sites. CIO unions organized oil workers, furniture workers, tobacco workers, shipyard workers, and metal industry workers, often on a biracial basis. At the end of the war, the CIO could count about 225,000 members in southern states, about 30,000 of them textile workers.

In March 1946 CIO leaders created a Southern Organizing Campaign (SOC) with a budget of more than a million dollars. That summer, it dispatched more than 200 organizers across the South, most of them targeting the textile industry. From the start, however, the CIO campaign stumbled. The decentralized character of the textile industry necessitated a difficult and expensive mill-by-mill organizing agenda. Efforts to recruit textile workers encountered the same problems that had stymied TWOC's efforts a decade before.

Critics argued that the SOC should bypass the textile industry and concentrate on industries and locations with heavy black representation. From its inception in 1935, the CIO had supported civil rights for African Americans, but in the South its representatives often found that identification with blacks and with civil rights alienated white workers. Thus SOC leaders downplayed the CIO's racial agenda, stressing instead the improvements in wages and working conditions that union organization would bring all workers.

In October 1946 SOC suffered a crushing defeat at the large Cannon Mills in North Carolina. Employers throughout the industry colluded with law enforcement authorities to harass

Congress of Industrial Organizations pickets in Greensboro, Ga., 1941 (Jack Delano, photographer, Library of Congress [LC-USF-33-20926-M2], Washington, D.C.)

unionists. They also used selective wage increases and minor improvements in working conditions to undercut the union appeal. For all intents and purposes, by the end of 1946 the southern campaign was moribund.

The CIO suffered other setbacks as well. In 1949–50 the CIO ejected a number of its affiliated unions charged with being pro-Soviet. These included a Food, Tobacco, and Allied workers organization that had built strong biracial unions in several southern cities. The result of the anticommunist campaign was the ending of union representation for thousands of tobacco and food processing workers. Even the small gains in cotton textiles disappeared. In 1951 TWUA lost its bargaining rights at the Dan River Mills in Virginia, home of what had been its largest southern local union. Throughout the 1950s the weak tide of union representation in this key industrial sector ebbed even further.

By the time of the CIO's merger with the larger AFL in 1955, its presence in the South was limited, with its unions in the pulp and paper industry constituting a rare case of success. CIO political operatives continued to work in southern states to increase voter registration, especially among blacks, and to support liberal southern politicians. Even here, however, CIO representatives faced tough going. Indeed, many white workers denounced organized labor for its support of civil rights legislation and its efforts to promote desegregation in union and workplace affairs.

ROBERT H. ZIEGER
University of Florida

Barbara Griffith, *The Crisis of American Labor: Operation Dixie and the Defeat of* the CIO (1988); Michael K. Honey, *Southern Labor and Black Civil Rights: Organizing Memphis Workers* (1993); Robert H. Zieger, *The CIO: 1935-1955* (1995), in *Labor in the Modern South*, ed. Glenn T. Eskew (2001).

Convict Lease System and Peonage

The convict lease system was the means by which southern states dealt with their post–Civil War prisoners. Under this regimen, convicts were leased to individuals or corporations, who thus acquired a captive labor force and at the same time agreed to supervise it. As a result, the industrial landscape of the New South was dotted with prison work camps and stockades, home to inmates who were overwhelmingly (roughly 90 percent) African American. At their worst, these facilities afforded examples of human misery that shocked contemporaries and gave southern corrections a bad reputation.

Apologists pointed out that the state governments were impoverished, that penitentiaries erected before the war were destroyed, and that state and local officials had no reliable mechanism of control over recently freed black populations. In fact, models for privately run prisons were already in place. As early as 1825, Kentucky had leased its inmates to a businessman who sought to turn the penitentiary at Frankfort into a factory. In 1846 Alabama legislators leased the "Walls" at Wetumpka to the first of a series of entrepreneurs. The lure of turning a debit into a credit through off-site labor appealed to postwar officials, Republicans and former Confederates alike.

The convict lease system should be understood as a child of slavery. White southerners (and many northerners) believed that African Americans needed the tutelage of their former masters—that left to their own devices, freedmen would fall into idleness and crime. Judges imbued with these beliefs found themselves dealing with a range of behaviors (from genuinely criminal acts to mere rudeness) that once would have been handled extralegally by plantation discipline. In the post-Reconstruction world such offenses were punished by hard labor for the state or county. Judges of the period exercised considerable discretion in sentencing, taking into account the labor needs of sheriffs or lessees. Sentences tended to be long. Of 1,200 convicts leased by Georgia in 1880, more than 500 were serving terms of 10 years or more. In Texas, with more than 2,300 incarcerated in 1882, only two men were sentenced for less than 10 years.

By the 1880s several states had given their convicts over to large corporations. This had the merit of administrative simplicity and was also financially attractive. Georgia in 1876 divided 1,100 prisoners among three companies, each of which agreed to pay the state $25,000 per year. Tennessee and Alabama made their arrangements with the Tennessee Coal and Iron Company (TCI). In 1890 more than 800 Alabama convicts worked in TCI mines, for which the state was paid more than $180,000—six percent of its yearly income. It would be an oversimplification to argue that the South was following the "Prussian Road" of authoritarian development. On the other hand—in light of many alliances between entrepreneurs and ultraconservative Bourbon politicians — it is true that racial ideology and law converged for the benefit of New South industrialists. The latter gained both cheap labor and a readymade strikebreaking force.

Yet the concentration of convicts made them more visible to journalists, reformers, and other critics of the system. An assertion made during the period was that convict leasing was worse than slavery—that, as Women's Christian Temperance Union leader Julia Tutwiler said in 1890, it had all of slavery's evils without the personal contact and paternalism that she viewed as "ameliorating features." She was right to think that most lessees had few occasions to look upon their laborers as individuals and only the slightest economic motives to promote their welfare. The frequency of escapes was such that camp managers tended to fire lenient guards and to employ shackles and close confinement whenever possible. The results were poor sanitation and scandalously high mortality from disease and accidents. While 1 to 2 percent of northern prisoners died each year, death rates of 15 percent were not unknown in the South.

Critics of the system were a diverse group, including the African American leaders Booker T. Washington, W. E. B. Du Bois, and Mary Church Terrell, white women activists like Tutwiler and Georgia's Rebecca Felton, agrarian politicians and labor activists who opposed corporate power, and an intriguing number of well-placed, otherwise conventional whites who can be called "Bourbon reformers." The most celebrated of the latter was the Louisiana writer George Washington Cable, whose nonfiction work eloquently denounced racial discrimination and southern penal practices. These disparate elements did accomplish certain reforms in the 1880s and 1890s.

Administratively, these years saw the creation of stronger state regulatory boards, staffed by men who were acquainted with professional organizations such as the National Prison Association. Through these boards (and with persistent lobbying by women's organizations) the states mandated improved standards of housing, diet, and healthcare and began to provide educational facilities for inmates. During the same period the states began to exclude female prisoners and minors from the camps, placing them in separate facilities. By the turn of the century, reformist and anticorporate influences were strong enough to put some states on the road to ending the lease system, initially by working convicts on state-owned farms. A leader in this development was Mississippi, which took steps to abolish the lease system in its 1890 constitution (interestingly, the same constitution that effectively disfranchised black voters) and had opened Parchman Farm by 1901.

For all these improvements the convict lease system was irretrievably flawed. This is evident in the career of R. H. Dawson, chief inspector of the Alabama Department of Corrections (1883–96). A true Bourbon reformer, Dawson saw himself as a mediator between the convicts and TCI, the state's chief lessee. Each prisoner was expected to produce 4,000 pounds of usable coal per day; Dawson worked to insure honest time keeping and decent living conditions. To improve morale and fend off vice he distributed writing materials and encouraged letter writing. Thus miners could stay in touch with their families and more easily report corporate rule breaking. He gave each convict a card with two dates written on it: the date of the man's full-sentence release and the date of his "short-time" release for good behavior. For several years Dawson's methods seemed to work, and the convicts each had a fighting chance to survive prison—and to leave it with coal-mining skills, which many proceeded to put to use.

Yet in the 1890s TCI officials steadily undermined Dawson's achievements. Guards goaded prisoners into riots that wrecked their "short-time" status. Company bosses bribed or pressured inmates into overtime work in exchange for company scrip that fueled gambling and black market activities. Clearly, the lessees preferred to handle overburdened, dissolute men, and Dawson concluded that the kind of order he was promoting—prison run as a school of discipline—could not take hold within the convict lease system. Governor Thomas Goode Jones (1890–94) agreed, and under his administration the state prepared to shift its corrections to Mississippi-style prison farming. However, the Panic of 1893 touched off a crisis of state finance, and Jones's successors preserved the always-profitable mining lease.

The eventual decline of convict leasing came about as a result of several factors: middle-class concerns over child labor, illiteracy, and public health; election of progressive Democrats such as Georgia's governor Hoke Smith (a major actor in that state's 1908 abolition of the lease); and the "good roads" movement in Georgia, North Carolina, and other states, which shifted convict labor to the highways under state control. State sponsorship of private unfree labor ended with Alabama's 1928 laws terminating the convict lease. But public laws had little to do with the survival of a parallel regime—peonage—still very much alive in the 1930s.

Large numbers of African American farmers were sharecroppers who paid the landowner half their crops in addition to the value of supplies received. Declining prices of staple crops almost insured that such men (and their white counterparts) fell deeper in debt each year, thus creating a class of hopeless debtors. When plantation owners compelled tenants to work out their debts, the result was peonage. Across the region, contract labor laws criminalized breach of contract, opening the way for shadowy collaborations between planters and local law enforcement. Under this system a justice of the peace would arrange for a defaulting debtor to be arrested and fined on charges that might or might not be entered on his books. The landowner would appear, pay the fine, and be granted custody. Now the peon had to work out the fine (and the rest of his indebtedness) or risk another arrest. Though such practices appear (correctly) to modern eyes as a crude restoration of master-slave relations, they also meshed perfectly with a long-lived stereotype of black folk and poor whites alike—that the working classes must be forced to work.

Peonage was widespread in the "cotton belt," in Florida's turpentine camps, and in other settings of isolation and poverty. Nonetheless in the early 1900s a number of federal officials, most of whom were Republicans, joined forces with black spokesmen and a sprinkling of Bourbon reformers to challenge these practices. Acting under an 1867 statute, U.S. attorneys brought cases before District Judges Charles Swayne (Florida), Thomas Goode Jones (Alabama), Emory Speer (Georgia), and Jacob Trieber (Arkansas). Their greatest success came in Alabama, where Judge Jones and Booker T. Washington quietly supported a state case, *Alonzo Bailey v. Alabama* (1911), in which the U.S. Supreme Court overturned Alabama's contract labor law. Subsequently (*U.S. v. Reynolds*, 1914) the high court also struck down Alabama's practice of assigning prisoners to private citizens. Still, these victories did not end peonage. So long as debt reigned supreme, so long as planters and industrialists were patrons of local lawmen, the corrupt regime could flourish.

PAUL M. PRUITT JR.
Bounds Law Library
University of Alabama

Brent Jude Aucoin, "'A Rift in the Clouds': Southern Federal Judges and African-American Civil Rights, 1885–1915" (Ph.D. dissertation, University of Arkansas, 1999); Mary Ellen Curtin, *Black Prisoners and Their World: Alabama, 1865–1900* (2000); Pete Daniel, *The Shadow of Slavery: Peonage in the South, 1901–1969* (1990); Matthew J. Mancini, *One Dies, Get Another: Convict Leasing in the American South, 1866–1928* (1996); Blake McKelvey, *American Prisons: A History of Good Intentions* (1977); David M. Oshinsky, *Worse Than Slavery: Parchman Farm and the Ordeal of Jim Crow Justice* (1996); Paul M. Pruitt Jr., *Reviews in American History* (September 2001); Hilda Jane Zimmerman, "Penal Systems and Penal Reforms in the South since the Civil War" (Ph.D. dissertation, University of North Carolina, 1947).

Country Music

Country music is commonly portrayed as the music of the southern white working class, as its "white man's blues" and "workin' man blues" nicknames suggest. In reality, the class contours of country music's production, consumption, and thematic content have been far more complex than such characterizations suggest. Country music listenership has always transcended the working class, more so than ever after the 1990s, when country became the most popular radio format in the U.S. Moreover, it has frequently appealed to middle-class aesthetic and cultural values in its content and marketing. And yet, country maintains a deeply (white) working-class image and serves as a resource for audiences to express working class as a lived identity.

The class composition of country's producers and audiences has been ambiguous since its emergence as a commercial genre. In the late 1920s and early 1930s old-time (or hillbilly) music was aimed primarily at rural dwellers and rural-to-urban migrants of the South and Midwest. In areas such as the Piedmont, it has been interpreted as a response to the changing social structure of the New South, the musical expression of an emergent industrial working class taking shape in the region's cotton mills and factories. In the Southwest, country music's associations with oilfield honky-tonks and impoverished Dust Bowl "Okies" further emphasized the genre's working-class image. Iconic artists from Jimmie Rodgers to Hank Williams all projected working-man personae, and in California, Woody Guthrie regularly articulated class grievances on his popular country radio show. At the same time, however, producers of old-time radio shows such as WLS's *National Barn Dance* imagined an audience of prosperous farmers and small-town merchants. They explicitly worked to make the genre consistent with middle-class tastes, especially by mobilizing Victorian gender norms that connoted respectability. Fan mail to radio performers of the era confirms that projecting a middle-class image of respectability was also important to significant parts of the country audience, even when they identified as working-class.

The tension between working-class pride and middle-class aesthetics has remained a defining feature of the genre. In the 1960s, for example, the Country Music Association undertook a concerted campaign to counter the popular perception that the genre appealed mainly to lower-class whites, in large part because convincing advertisers that the country audience commanded significant disposable income was critical to securing radio airplay for the format.

Nonetheless, political and cultural observers on both the left and the right associated country with a disaffected white working class and declared it the music of the Silent Majority. Scholars remained conflicted as well, arguing that country music was a central factor in the "southernization" of an increasingly conservative American working class, and that, while it appealed to working-class whites, it worked against class formation by avoiding overt protest in favor of a fatalistic, individualized "class unconsciousness."

More recently, a number of scholars have argued that country's class appeal has genuinely changed to become more objectively middle class, in part because much of its audience participated in the upward mobility and suburbanization of the post–World War II era and in part because the format converged to a significant degree with adult-oriented pop in the 1990s. Although some surveys have shown that the country audience of the 21st century is actually more affluent than that for any other radio format, songs from "Workin' Man Ph.D." to "Redneck Woman" nonetheless continue to focus on working-class experience. Moreover, ethnographic research in communities as diverse as the rural environs of Austin, Tex., and the blue-collar neighborhoods of Detroit demonstrates that many white working-class Americans continue to shape their class identity in part through the practice of listening to and playing country music.

DIANE PECKNOLD
University of Louisville

Aaron Fox, *Real Country: Music and Language in Working-Class Culture* (2004); James Gregory, *Journal of Labor History* (May 1998); Pamela Grundy, *Journal of American History* (March 1995); John Hartigan, *Racial Situations: Class Predicaments of Whiteness in Detroit* (1999); Patrick Huber, *Linthead Stomp: The Creation of Country Music in the Piedmont South* (2008); Peter La Chapelle, *Proud to Be an Okie: Cultural Politics, Country Music, and Migration to Southern California* (2007); Bill C. Malone, *Don't Get Above Your Raisin': Country Music and the Southern Working Class* (2002); Kristine M. McCusker, *Lonesome Cowgirls and Honky-Tonk Angels: The Women of Barn Dance Radio* (2008); Melton A. McLaurin and Richard Peterson, eds., *You Wrote My Life: Lyrical Themes in Country Music* (1992); Diane Pecknold, *The Selling Sound: The Rise of the Country Music Industry* (2007).

Desertion during the Civil War

Desertion was an important reason for Confederate defeat. In official terms, Confederates distinguished desertion from absence without leave by the soldier's motivation, not the length of absence. According to the best authority, Ella Lonn, 104,428 Confederates deserted, although this is surely an undercount because of the breakdown in recordkeeping in the last half year of war. Officially, 31,056, or about 30 percent, returned to the army either voluntarily or involuntarily.

In a random sample of soldiers in Lee's army, some 15.5 percent of all soldiers in Lee's army deserted at any given time, and the percentage is an undercount. By Lee's own admission, in February and March 1865 his army lost approximately 120 men per day to desertion, yet with rare exceptions, only soldiers who deserted to Federal lines are recorded in compiled service records during those months. The Confederate Government offered amnesty on a few occasions, and one in every six deserters in the sample (16.4 percent) returned to the army. There are no official numbers, but it is possible more than 100 deserters were executed. Wartime hardships, losses, and faltering morale influenced whether and when soldiers fled the army. In addition, opportunity was a critical factor. Soldiers who served in an army more than a few hundred miles from home had little hope of making it back there. Poorer soldiers (middle- and poor-class were more than 1.5 times more likely), cavalrymen (57 percent more likely than artillerymen and 22 percent more likely than infantrymen), older troops (median age three years more), married men (31 percent more likely than single men), and fatherhood (80 percent more likely than childless) proved to be the most powerful issues in determining who deserted. Deserters were less likely to suffer combat wounds.

Desertion increased steadily by quarter and also by year. In Lee's army, for example, more men deserted from April through June than from January through March; that number rose from July through September and peaked from October through December. Each year, desertion increased over the previous one as well, until numbers exploded in the last quarter of 1864 and January until April 1865. For Lee's army, once Lincoln won reelection and

Sherman began his destructive march through Georgia, morale broke down, and soldiers abandoned the army in droves. Forced to choose between the well-being of family members and service in Confederate ranks, thousands upon thousands chose their families.

To maintain troop strength for the upcoming spring campaign season, the Confederate Congress in April 1862 passed Conscription Act. It retained those already in uniform for two more years and required states to maintain percentages of troops based on population and to do so through a draft of individuals from 18 to 35 years of age, if necessary. Over the next couple of years, the Confederate Government extended draft age to 17 and 45 as a high, with men from 45 to 50 serving in the state reserve, and extended the length of service for "the war." States did not enforce the law until late summer of 1862. Exemptions for certain occupations as well as one adult male in a household with 20 or more slaves existed (later changed to 15). Individuals could purchase substitutes, which benefited the wealthy. In fact, at Camp Lee, the rendezvous depot for the Army of Northern Virginia, only 2 percent of the drafted men received an exemption for 20 (or 15) slaves. But numbers did not matter. It bothered people that the wealthy could secure an exemption when poorer people could not do so. By the end of 1864, the Bureau for Conscription proposed that it terminate its service. The Confederacy had run out of men except 16-year olds coming of age.

More than half of those called out were exempted from service for health or occupation reasons. Large numbers of draft-age Confederates refused to serve. Some did so in protest against the unfairness of the law, favoring wealthy over the middle and poor classes. Most, however, simply did not want to serve. They did not support the Confederacy enough to enter the army, had other priorities, or objected for other personal reasons. The Appalachian Mountains became a hotbed of draft resisters' hangouts, although in North Carolina, a state that narrowly voted to secede, draft resisters congregated in the Piedmont region as well.

Since draft resistance and desertion could be punishable by death, both groups often merged to form gangs for protection, drawing on sympathetic community members and violent resistance for protection. Local militiamen (themselves exempted from conscription) usually could not handle these armed gangs and the Confederate army had to detach veteran soldiers on numerous occasions to battle deserters and draft resisters.

JOSEPH T. GLATTHAAR
University of North Carolina at Chapel Hill

Adam H. Domby, "'Loyal to the Core from the First to the Last': Remembering the Inner Civil War of Forsyth County, North Carolina, 1862–1876" (M.A. thesis, University of North Carolina at Chapel Hill, 2011); Joseph T. Glatthaar, *General Lee's Army: A History of the Army of Northern Virginia* (2008), *Soldiering in the Army of Northern Virginia: A Portrait of the Troops Who Served under Robert E. Lee* (2011); Ella Lonn, *Desertion during the Civil War* (1928); Mark A. Weitz, *A Higher Duty: Desertion among Georgia Troops during the Civil War* (2000).

Fraternal Orders

Fraternal Societies have played an important role in shaping the behavior, beliefs, and personal identities of individuals in the American South. Groups such as the Freemasons, the Odd Fellows, the Modern Woodmen of America, the Improved Order of Red Men, and hundreds of other voluntary, oath-bound organizations have tutored individuals in systems of thought and have bestowed symbolic identities and fictive familial relationships upon their members. Although some fraternal organizations promoted ethnic solidarity, fiscal responsibility through insurance, nativism, or other values, the initiation of new members constituted the central activity of most groups. Fraternalism in the South can be traced to the establishment of Masonic lodges in coastal cities in the first half of the 18th century, but the movement reached its greatest popularity and influence in the years between 1865 and 1930.

Fraternalism has appealed to southerners of both European and African descent, although until the final decades of the 20th century blacks and whites rarely belonged to the same organizations. Instead, parallel systems of lodges developed in many communities, such as the Independent Order of Odd Fellows for whites and the Grand United Order of Odd Fellows for blacks or the similarly divided Ancient Arabic Order Nobles of the Mystic Shrine and Ancient Egyptian Arabic Order Nobles of the Mystic Shrine, in which men practiced similar rituals and promoted comparable ethical systems but did not communicate or engage in fraternal brotherhood. A number of fraternal organizations, such as the Grand United Order of Galilean Fisherman or the Knights of Tabor, were found exclusively within the African American community and without comparable groups across the color line.

In both the white and the black communities, fraternal organizations sorted individuals along class and gender lines while simultaneously inspiring individuals to improve themselves by aspiring to comply with fraternal ideals of righteousness, personal responsibility, and thrift. Individuals of elevated social status could afford the initiation fees and annual financial obligations of the Mystic Shrine, for example, while those of lesser economic means might find fraternal fulfillment within the Woodmen of the World. Women participated in fraternalism through groups such as the Pythian Sisters and the Daughters of Rebekah.

In the decades surrounding the turn of the 20th century, fraternal organizations such as the Woodmen or the Knights of Columbus provided insurance benefits to individuals who might not otherwise have been able to afford such economic protection. In the middle decades of the 20th century, businessmen and professionals frequently abandoned fraternal orders and sought sociability among members of their own class within service organizations such as Rotary and Kiwanis, which emphasized networking and philanthropy while deemphasizing rituals. Other organizations, such as the Benevolent and Protective Order of Elks and the Loyal Order of Moose, jettisoned their fraternal trappings in the 20th century and became lower-middle-class social organizations largely organized around serving alcohol within private clubhouses.

WILLIAM D. MOORE
University of North Carolina at Wilmington

Alan Axelrod, ed., *The International Encyclopedia of Secret Societies and Fraternal Orders* (1997); David T. Beito, *From Mutual Aid to the Welfare State: Fraternal Societies and Social Services, 1890–1967* (1999); Jeffrey A. Charles, *Service Clubs in American Society: Rotary, Kiwanis, and Lions* (1993); William L. Fox, *Lodge of the Double-Headed Eagle: Two Centuries of Scottish Rite Freemasonry in America's Southern Jurisdiction* (1997); Nina Mjagkij, ed., *Organizing Black America: An Encyclopedia of African American Associations* (2001); Theda Skocpol, Ariane Liazos, and Marshall Ganz, *What A Mighty Power We Can Be: African American Fraternal Groups in Struggle for Racial Equality* (2006); Mark A. Tabbert, *American Freemasons: Three Centuries of Building Communities* (2005).

Freedmen's Bureau

The Bureau of Refugees, Freedmen, and Abandoned Lands, more commonly know as the Freedmen's Bureau, was a federal agency established to help southern blacks transition from their lives as slaves to free individuals. The Freedmen's Bureau was an unprecedented foray by the federal government into the sphere of social welfare and an effort to reshape the entire social and economic order of the South.

A key function of the bureau, especially in the beginning, was to provide temporary relief for the suffering of destitute freedmen. The bureau provided rations for those most in need as a result of the abandonment of plantations, poor crop yields, and unemployment. This aid was taken advantage of by a staggering number of both freedmen and refugees. As Eric Foner states in his *Reconstruction: America's Unfinished Revolution, 1863–1877*, in "the first 15 months following the war, the Bureau issued more than 13 million rations, two thirds to blacks." In a similar vein the bureau also provided medical care to the recently freed slaves. The bureau played a large role in providing basic health care and trying to stem pandemics. The bureau also assumed operations of hospitals established by the Army during the war and established dispensaries providing basic medical care and drugs free of charge, or at a nominal cost. The Bureau "managed in the early years of Reconstruction to treat an estimated half million suffering freedmen, as well as a smaller but significant number of whites," says Foner.

Although the immediate goal of the bureau was short-term relief, much of its efforts were focused on the longer-term transformation of former slaves into independent property owners. As initially devised the bureau would help make this a reality by allocating confiscated land, ensuring legal rights, and helping to establish schools for blacks all across the South.

During the course of the Civil War, the U.S. Army took control of a good deal of land that had been confiscated or abandoned by the Confederacy. In January 1865 General William T. Sherman issued an order that set aside the Sea Islands and lands from South Carolina to Florida for blacks to settle 40 acres of land and receive the loan of horses and mules from the Army. Although the promise of "forty acres and a mule" was written into the bureau law, the widespread implementation of this policy was quickly thwarted. In the summer of 1865, President Andrew Johnson issued pardons restoring the property of many Confederates. Johnson's actions took away what many felt was the freedmen's best chance at economic protection and self-sufficiency.

One of the duties the bureau did engage in was ensuring equal treatment according to the law. Bureau agents had judicial authority in the South and individually adjudicated a wide variety of disputes when it was deemed the civil courts would not ensure a fair trial. In addition to these judicial functions, the bureau also helped legitimize slave marriages; presided over freedmen marriage ceremonies in areas where black marriages were obstructed; helped file the claims of black soldiers for back pay, pensions, and bounties; and helped draw up work contracts to help facilitate the hiring of freedmen. The bureau helped planters and freedmen draft contracts on mutually agreeable terms—negotiating several hundred thousand contracts. Once agreed upon, the agency tried to make sure both planter and worker lived up to their part of the agreement. Although bureau agents took much flack from both sides, modern research found that contracts seemed to be competitive and were reflective of soil conditions.

Another structural impediment to the advancement and empowerment of the freedmen was their lack of education. In the wake of the Nat Turner revolt, southern states enacted severe penalties prohibiting black education. When given their freedom, many former slaves lacked the literacy skills necessary to protect themselves from exploitation and to pursue many personal activities. Thus, emancipated slaves experienced a great demand for freedmen schools.

The bureau helped to establish black schools throughout the South. Much of the early work was done by philanthropic societies, but the bureau organized and coordinated their efforts. The agency allowed the use of many buildings in the Army's possession, helped transport a trove of teachers from the North, appropriated salaries for State Superintendents of Education, repaired and rented school buildings and used military taxes to pay teachers' salaries. These resources were used to great success as the bureau helped establish a vast network of schools. The number of bureau-aided day and night schools in operation grew to a maximum of 1,737, instructing 103,396 pupils. Many historians feel this function of the bureau was among its most successful by its establishment of schools and the change the bureau made in perceptions about black education.

The Freedmen's Bureau was a unique effort on the part of the federal government to deal with many of the root causes of economic inequalities between blacks and whites. The bureau's functions were many and its mission near impossible. Although the bureau did not accomplish all of its lofty goals, it made an undeniable impact and helped ensure that blacks did not return to a position of bondage.

WILLIAM TROOST
University of Southern California

Eric Foner, *Reconstruction: America's Unfinished Revolution, 1863–1877* (1988); Roger L. Ransom and Richard Sutch, *One Kind of Freedom: The Economic Consequences of Emancipation* (2001); Ralph Shlomowitz, *Agricultural History* (July 1979).

Gated Communities

Gated communities first arose in England in the 1800s. They were walled communities in London, communities intentionally kept apart from their neighbors. The American version was high-rise apartment buildings, especially the ones with a doorman, or walled estates (even if using dense hedges to accomplish the barrier). The doorman was a de facto sentry, monitoring who went in and out of the building. This kind of "secure" facility was not only for the rich, for in time one could find such places even in the poorest of urban neighborhoods—public housing projects. In the American South, there are, or were, comparably fewer high-rise condos or secured public housing projects than in other parts of the United States. Why? In the South, land was cheaper. It was easier and more cost-effective to build low-rise houses and/or apartments, whether for the rich or the poor. Despite these historical interregional differences, however, the South now shares with the West the distinction of having proportionately more gated communities. So when considering the South, what are these places? And where are they found?

In the West, gated communities are concentrated especially in southern California. One estimate in the 1990s was that fully one-half of all new housing worth more than $500,000 in that part of the state was found in gated communities. This included not only single-family houses but often townhouses and low-rise condominiums. Just as gated residences are unevenly distributed in California, the same thing is true in the South. Although a few may be found in high-end mountain resorts, most gated communities in the South are found in two places: in Texas, notably Dallas and Houston, and especially in coastal areas, primarily the Lowcountry of South Carolina and Georgia. The proliferation of gated communities is apparent to anyone traveling U.S. Highway 17, essentially the "Main Street" of the coast. In fact, one sees signs for such places when traveling on U.S. 17 in North Carolina, starting an hour or so before entering the outer limits to Myrtle Beach. From Myrtle Beach (at the northernmost end of the

South Carolina coast) to Amelia Island (at the northernmost end of Florida), gated communities are common. It is almost axiomatic: the more expensive the housing, the greater the likelihood it will be gated. Indeed, for new, expensive housing, gates are expected. But it is worth noting that in the Lowcountry, even very modest developments are sometimes gated—including some trailer parks.

The first place in the South where gating was normative was Hilton Head Island, South Carolina. In 1950 Hilton Head was difficult to reach from the mainland and its population racially was much as it had always been: nearly all-black (out of 1,125 residents in the 1950 U.S. Census, 1,100 were black, 25 were white). Hilton Head was developed starting in the 1960s. The targeted clientele were affluent people who could be attracted to Hilton Head's beaches and, at that time, its largely unspoiled ecology. The success of its developers is found in the 2000 census data: by then, nearly 40,000 people lived in Hilton Head year-round—2,800 black, 2,200 Latino, and 35,000 whites. Not only had Hilton Head changed demographically, but residentially it was nearly all gated; about 70 percent of all residential units are found in its gated neighborhoods.

Hilton Head also pioneered another unique aspect of many gated, southern communities: they were called "plantations." While Hilton Head itself had numerous plantations on it in the 1800s, most had long since been called "communities" (often with the former plantation owner's name attached). With its emergence as initially a seasonal resort and subsequently with considerable year-round residents, the name "plantation" was attached to every large development—seven in all. Their names were contrived and had little to do with Hilton Head's history. What the developers banked on (and were economically rewarded for) was that the word "plantation" would appeal to their target clientele: affluent whites.

Other developers up and down the Lowcountry subsequently adopted the Hilton Head strategy of gated communities with plantation monikers. Myrtle Beach, in South Carolina's Horry County, had never known either a heavily black population or places called "plantation." But its neighbor to the south, Georgetown, and the Waccamaw Peninsula (just north of it) were incredible concentrations of wealth during slavery, mostly owing to rice production. In these places, too, gated communities with plantation names (having little or nothing to do with local history) became commonplace. Very recently, in Myrtle Beach, a high-rise condominium development arose on the oceanfront. It's name? Island Palms Plantation.

Historically, gated communities were attractive for some buyers because they were thought to offer security, greater property values, and a heightened sense of community. Although some scholars have shown these things to be illusory, citation to them still arises when people are queried about why they chose to live there. This construction of barriers reflects the creation of "gatedness" as a mentality, which is the product of an "increased sense of fear and declining levels of trust." Driving along the coast, one finds little indication of this trend slowing appreciably. Gated communities have become normative on the southern landscape. Although emerging from areas that had no history of gated neighborhoods, many buyers (especially new northerners moving into the area) have come to expect not only the gates but the amenities that often come with them—especially country clubs. This has caused a kind of balkanization of the residents, what one observer called "gated ghettos," places choosing to be self-segregated. In fact, gated communities are primarily white enclaves, often of people who have moved from other areas of the country. The only black and brown people one is likely to find in the gated plantation development are mowing the grass, cleaning the house, or providing other services.

Because there are comparatively few truly wealthy people, gated developments for them can account for only a small part of gated places. The primary market seems to be upper-middle-class people, professionals whose incomes allow them considerable choice when it comes to housing. For many of these people, the choice is an easy one: gates or not? Well, why not? And demographically who are most of these people? College-educated, white, married couples with children or (as the academic literature also shows) older, empty nesters who are primarily seeking a considerably heightened sense of security and/or easy access to certain amenities (thus the common presence in coastal North Carolina and the Lowcountry of large gated developments with country clubs, tennis courts, pools, gyms, and other features encouraging an "active" lifestyle). Whites, although the vast majority of gated residents, are not the only ones. Upper-middle-class enclaves of gated residents may also be found in Prince Georges County, Md. (the greatest concentration of black wealth in the United States), and suburban Atlanta (a migration magnet attracting a disproportionate number of well-educated, affluent, married black couples). The strategy utilized by developers often emphasizes the lifestyle that is offered within the gates, not necessarily the gate itself. In this way, the gated communities are marketed toward a specific group and designed to meet the resident's desires through amenities and a homogeneous sense of community.

The gates that "guard" all of these places vary tremendously from one development to another. At the more expensive developments, the gates are usually constructed of heavier materials, and they either slide or swing open. Even without guards, this type of gating is common on a wide range of developments—to include some that are a far cry from the wealthy ones. At the low end, found at some modestly priced, seasonal developments but also at more working-class places such as trailer parks, it is common to see a "gate" that consists of nothing more than a two-by-four affixed to a metal bracket extending out from the small stand holding the motor that moves the gate up and down. These are the places where one is most likely to see broken gates, almost always a small piece of wood still affixed to the motorized arm—a sign that someone, whether visitor or often resident—simply pushed against the arm until it broke.

Gates are often accompanied by a large investment in security, be it security personnel, identification cards or codes for entry, guard shacks at entry points, and the use of cameras. The wealthiest developments are, predictably, the most likely to have not only gated entrances but a security staff housed in a small building adjacent to the gates. These places almost always have separate lanes for residents and visitors, with visitors gaining access only after being screened by a guard. Visitors and service workers may be required to display a pass while in the community to prove they have been screened. Gated communities with no guards are more common. These places usually have some combination of electronically read codes affixed to a sticker on one's vehicle or require using either a card or entering a code on a touch pad. Visitors must gain access by having an owner provide them with a pass of some kind or calling when at the gate to get buzzed in (the owner doing this remotely from his residence).

Part of the history of gating includes residential neighborhoods without gates that eventually decided they wanted to add them. The gate itself is an inviting feature of the landscape for those who can afford to live within its confines because the practice becomes symbolic of "status, class, safety, prestige, value." The history of gated communities—whether gated at the outset or subsequently—is replete with legal cases raising fundamental questions about not only entrance or exit but equally people's rights once there and as a jurisdictional issue: who is responsible for such services as police, fire, and highway maintenance.

The growth of gated communities is part of the changes sweeping the South brought about by migration to it. Wherever gated communities are found, they convey a sense of exclusivity—that those inside want to be there and are allowed to be there; those outside must get permission but are otherwise not wanted. What some scholars have called "forting up" raises a fundamental question: in the process of locking some people out, are they also locking some people in? Such a question brings to mind the famous Janis Joplin song, "Freedom's just another word for nothing left to lose." The South has long been known for its hospitality and friendliness—can these survive in a gated world?

WILLIAM W. FALK
University of Maryland

SUSAN WEBB
Coastal Carolina University

WILLIAM YAGATICH
University of Maryland

Edward James Blakely and Mary Gail Snyder, *Fortress America: Gated Communities in the United States* (1997); Matthew Burke, *Journal of American and Comparative Cultures* (Spring–Summer 2001); Ann Dupis and David Thorns, *Urban Policy and Research* (June 2008); Thomas Sanchez, Robert Lang, and Dawn Dhavale, *Journal of Housing Education and Research* (March 2005); Elena Vesselinov, *Sociological Forum* (September 2008).

General Textile Strike of 1934

The largest strike in U.S. history, the General Textile Strike of 1934 became an emblematic dispute for organized labor in the South. In the midst of the Great Depression, the strike began on Labor Day, prompting violent conflicts that would test President Franklin Roosevelt's New Deal and workers' faith in government regulation and employee self-determination. Mill workers believed that the new minimum $12 weekly pay and maximum 40-hour workweek would lead to better conditions and a living wage for their families. However, the industry-controlled National Recovery Act established codes that allowed mill owners to flout these laws with job reclassification, shortened workweeks, and illegal firing, blacklisting, and evictions. In addition, while workers' pay increased, production rates and layoffs increased drastically. Mill owners also imposed curtailments, such as higher rent for workers' housing and increased prices at mill stores. The strike lasted only 20 days, and in that time, the ill-prepared United Textile Workers of America (UTW) unsuccessfully endeavored to organize and support several hundred thousand strikers. The failure of the UTW and the subsequent mill owners' backlash against workers contributed to a regional opposition to organized labor.

ROXANNE NEWTON
Mitchell Community College

Jacquelyn Dowd Hall, James Leloudis, Robert Korstad, Mary Murphy, Lu Ann Jones, and Christopher B. Daly, *Like a Family: The Making of a Southern Cotton Mill World* (1987); John A. Salmond, *The General Textile Strike of 1934: From Maine to Alabama* (2002).

Geophagia and Pica

Geophagia (or geophagy) is the intentional consumption of earth. In Western culture, it is commonly labeled a pica, an eating disorder characterized by the consistent consumption of nonnutritive substances such as feces (coprophagy), starch (amylophagy), or wood (xylophagia). In 2000 a panel convened by the Agency for Toxic Substances and Disease Registry in Atlanta proposed to distinguish between geophagy (culturally sanctioned behavior) and soil-pica ("recurrent ingestion of unusually high amounts of soil . . . on the order of 1,000–5,000 milligrams per day"). Other differences between both behaviors include impacted populations (pica is more prevalent among children under six, geophagia is reportedly more prevalent among pregnant women), consumed material (surface soil, possibly contaminated, for pica versus clays found at a 18- to 36-inch depth), and health consequences (generally detrimental for pica and potentially beneficial for geophagy).

A universal though limited practice, geophagia has been documented in the United States, especially among African Americans in the South and American Indians in the Southwest. Its introduction is commonly attributed to African slaves, an erroneous assumption since American Indians practiced geophagy before the arrival of European settlers.

Although individuals of both sexes of all races and ages practice geophagia and pica, they are more frequent among particular categories, especially young children, southern women, pregnant women, and persons with mental disabilities. For instance, documented geophagia in several southern states (Alabama, Georgia, Louisiana, Mississippi, North Carolina, and Tennessee) occurs almost exclusively among rural African American females. They reportedly have been introduced to the practice by relatives and at their turn socialized their children to it.

Its assumed origin and practitioners have combined to ascribe geophagy a minority status in the United States and Western culture in general. Rurality, being female, and being black are traits traditionally associated with poverty, especially during the period (from the 1930s to the 1970s) when most studies of geophagia in the United States were conducted. In addition, a correlation between pica and malnutrition and reported low levels of education among dirt eaters contributed to tie the practice to poverty and low social class position.

So why do people eat dirt? Explanations of pica and geophagia remain tentative at best, even though along the years psychological, cultural, nutritional, physiological, and sensory hypotheses have been advanced. Whereas pica is universally and consistently labeled a pathology—a mental or eating disorder—geophagia is treated as both adaptive strategy and pathology. Iron- and calcium-deficiency have been offered as factors of geophagia among pregnant women who would find in clay much needed minerals. Other rationales include calming hunger pains, alleviating malnutrition, or being socialized to the practice.

Although the incidence of geophagia is difficult to measure, it is assumed to be declining. The urbanization of American society has greatly limited access to sources of dirt. Greater availability of health care and commercialization of nutritional supplements have arguably limited the need or compulsion to resort to eating dirt as a health regimen. Finally, the stigmatization of the practice, especially by the medical profession, has certainly limited its transmission.

JACQUES HENRY
University of Louisiana at Lafayette

Agency for Toxic Substances and Disease Registry, *Summary Report for the ATSDR Soil-Pica Workshop* (2001); Gerald N. Callaghan, *Emerging Infectious Diseases* (August 2003); P. Wenzel Geissler, *Africa* (2000); Jacques Henry and Alicia Matthews Kwong, *Deviant Behavior* (July–August 2005); Ran Knishinsky, *The Clay Cure: Natural Healing from the Earth* (1998); Ella P. Lacey, *Public Health Reports* (January–February 1990); Russell M. Reid, *Medical Anthropology* (1992); Donald Vermeer and Dennis A. Frate, *American Journal of Clinical Nutrition* (1979).

Global South

The "Global South," a concept as ambiguous as it is important, means different things to different constituencies. To many in the international community today, for example, the term is a more socially acceptable cognate for what used to be referred to variously as the "Third World," the "LDCs" (less developed countries), and even the "Developing World." That is to say, it is applied to nation-states or parts of nation-states that are poor in material terms and rank low on various socio-economic indicators. The term, used in this way, is generally credited to former West German chancellor Willy Brandt, chair of an international commission studying economic development that released the so-called Brandt Report in 1980, the formal title of which was *North-South: A Programme for Survival*. Because many of the poorest areas in the world were then (as today) located in the Southern Hemisphere, the term "Global South" began to be used as a sort of shorthand for any and all impoverished, exploited, economically dependent parts of the world.

To those interested in the American South, or, to be more precise, the southern part of what is now known as the United States, the adjective "global" means something different when modifying the (proper) noun "South." Here, the term refers to the region's varied connections to, and engagement with, other parts of the world, which connections and engagement are assumed to have increased markedly in a relative sense in recent decades.

To add two other layers of ambiguity to the mix, the southern part of the United States—or at least the poorer parts thereof—partakes of some of the characteristics of Brandt's "Global South," and in some ways the (American) South's connections to, and engagement with, other parts of the world were as great or greater 200 or 300 years ago than they are even during the phase of globalization in which we are living today. There is, in other words, a lot to think about when considering the seemingly straightforward formulation "the Global South."

This said, it is becoming increasingly clear to scholars that it would be a mistake to sever the link between "Global" and "South" for any period in the region's history. From the early 16th century on, Europeans and Africans were present in the southeast quadrant of what became the continental United States, commingling therein with various native groups, and the permanent colonies established in the region by the Spanish, French, and English/British must be seen as part of the global expansion of the European economy during the early modern period. Indeed, throughout the colonial period, the settlements established under European auspices, particularly those controlled by the English/British, articulated closely with the mother country and other parts of an increasingly integrated "Atlantic World." Moreover, such imperial and extra-imperial ties were not merely economic but social and cultural as well: people, products, capital, and ideas all circulated widely into and out of the region. And the South's early and intense links with other parts of the world could also be seen in the natural realm, via the circulation of pathogens, flora, fauna, and the like, part of a process Alfred Crosby famously labeled the Columbian Exchange.

The South's links with the world have

modulated since that time but have nonetheless been ongoing. During the period between 1790 and 1860, for example — roughly between the time of the Constitution and the coming of the Civil War — the value of exports from the South far exceeded the total for any other region in the country, and recent work by cultural and intellectual historians has demonstrated convincingly that at least some southerners were not only conversant with but also, in some cases, active participants in emerging transatlantic intellectual debates.

The South's defeat in the Civil War — and the many economic, social, and political concomitants arising therefrom — shocked the region in profound ways, leading to a prolonged attenuation of its relationships with the world. Some, in fact, would contend that this attenuation process lasted until World War II. To be sure, the relative poverty — and lack of education — characteristic of much of the population in the South over the course of the 75-year period after Appomattox placed certain constraints on the region's engagement with the world. Thus, the economically pinched region, lacking the same structure of opportunity as other sections of the United States, failed to attract many immigrants during this time of massive population flows into the United States. Even so, it needs to be remembered that throughout the period the South retained its strong economic ties with other countries, maintaining the highest regional export-output ratio in the United States and continuing to draw in outside capital. It bears noting as well that many of its intellectuals and artists benefited from and contributed to international cultural movements and modernism, most notably. Here, think Faulkner, the New Criticism, and jazz.

The South, then, was still part of the world even during the hardscrabble period between 1865 and 1941. With World War II, though, its global links and connections began to intensify across the board, and beginning in the postwar period the region became something of a poster child for and example par excellence of an increasingly global region. This is particularly true of the period since the 1960s, as more and more foreign multinationals established branch plants in the South and as more and more immigrants began to set down roots in the region. People, products, capital, technology, culture, and ideas — as well as microbes and, at times, pernicious ideologies — from around the world flowed into and out of the region. Today, then, the South, an expression of world historical forces at its birth, has come full circle and reestablished, unambiguously, its global bona fides.

PETER A. COCLANIS
University of North Carolina at Chapel Hill

James C. Cobb and William Stueck, eds., *Globalization and the American South* (2005); Peter A. Coclanis, *Home and the World: Perspectives on the Economic History of the American South* (2010); Joseph A. Fry, *Dixie Looks Abroad: The South and U.S. Foreign Relations, 1789–1973* (2002); James L. Peacock, *Grounded Globalism: How the U.S. South Embraces the World* (2007); James

Peacock, Harry L. Watson, and Carrie R. Matthews, eds., *The American South in a Global World* (2005).

Greenbackers

In the South, the "Greenbackers" were a social movement and political party that challenged white-supremacist governments from 1878 to 1884, through a coalition of poor white and African American farmers, sharecroppers, and wageworkers.

Greenbackers believed currency should consist of paper money issued by the state that was not based on gold. During the Civil War, the federal government issued "greenbacks" unredeemable for gold, inflating the money supply but not disastrously. Greenbackers had a "producerist" ideology. Value was created through productive labor of which money was merely the symbol. Metallic money allowed wealthy elites to manipulate its supply, which should reflect the amount of productive activity and the needs of the "people" defined as producers—farmers, artisans, manufacturers, and workers. The class of "producers" dependent on credit was pitted against "capitalists" and "monopolists" who controlled credit and used state privileges for private gain.

The postbellum economy created a new southern class structure. At the top were elite planters and elite merchants, bankers, corporate officials, and their political representatives in the largest towns. In the middle was a growing class of local merchants. Some lower classes owned productive property. Yeoman owned their land. Tenants, artisans, and mechanics owned only tools and work stock. Sharecroppers, wageworkers in mining, timber, and railroad industries, and agricultural laborers owned only their labor. Sharecroppers and agricultural laborers were disproportionately African Americans. Yeomen were overwhelmingly white.

Class struggle in the postbellum South centered on credit and commodity rather labor market relations. Yeoman were increasingly indebted to local merchants and forced to exclusively grow cash crops with falling prices to obtain credit. Planters defined crop lien laws that made sharecroppers' share of the crop a wage paid in kind at the end of the growing season. Elite planters had additional leverage on croppers by advancing rations, stock, and other necessary supplies on credit. Even miners were disciplined through the company store. To the poorest southerners, an ideology whose main concern was an increase in the supply of credit had the ring of truth.

The postbellum Republican government supported the gold standard and began retiring greenbacks, contracting the money supply and causing hardship for farmers and others reliant on credit, particularly in the South. A depression ensued in 1873, prompting the formation of the Greenback Party. After the Great Railroad Strike of 1877, the labor movement was drawn to the party, which became the Greenback-Labor Party (GLP).

In the South the depression fueled resentment among poor whites against

Reconstruction governments. This aided planters' recapture of state governments through terrorism and racist appeals. Though reducing taxes on land favored by yeoman, Redeemer governments continued many hated policies of the Republicans, including favors to railroads and corporations.

Planters' political allies were the "capitalists" and "monopolists" detested by small farmers. Ignoring yeoman concerns, Redeemer legislators focused on ensuring planters' control over the labor and crops of sharecroppers through changes to crop lien laws, making elective local offices appointed, and giving judges and sheriffs more power in enforcement of contracts.

An "anti-Redeemer" insurgency developed including the Greenback-Labor Party that was strongest in the hill country of the Lower South and the Old Southwest. Both Greenback ideology and shared class interests favored a biracial coalition among yeomen, croppers, and workers. Political necessity made it a reality and led to the third-party movement in areas where a viable opposition movement required black voters. The GLP organized segregated Greenback clubs and leaders but held integrated conventions.

The GLP sought to shift taxes from land to capital and supported regulation of railroad rates, issues crucial to yeoman. All debtors benefited from the proposed reform of lien laws, expansion of usury laws to include credit in-kind, greater jury oversight of contracts, and opposition to laws meant to decrease subsistence use rights of open land. African Americans influenced GLP opposition to laws of interest to landless workers—those meant to restrict labor mobility and the convict lease system. Finally, the GLP supported measures to ensure a free and fair vote and civil rights for blacks.

Political power increasingly meant alliance with the Republicans. In addition to the ideological inconsistency created by an alliance with the party of "hard money," cooperation with Republicans left Greenbackers open to the charges of a return to Reconstruction and "Negro rule." Ultimately, these racist appeals, intimidation, fraud, and political murder led to the defeat of the Greenbackers.

In producerist ideology, planters were in an ambiguous position. Greenbackers criticized elite planters as "aristocrats." Yet their inclusion in the producing classes obscured the fact that, increasingly, planters were also creditors. Having secured their control over labor and credit, planters assumed once again the mantle of "farmer," co-opted the money issue after the return to the gold standard in 1879, and implemented measures such as the "white primary" that evaded charges of being antidemocratic. This ambiguous role of planters continued to jeopardize the ability of farmers' movements to mobilize effective challenges to the southern political economy in the decades to come.

The history of the Greenbackers in the South demonstrates that, as long as African Americans retained voting, biracial working-class coalitions remained a possibility, requiring coercion to overcome. Second, it illustrates the role of ideology in interpreting class interests into political mobilization. On the one hand, producerist ideology helped define mutual interests among owning and landless segments of the lower classes. On the other, the same ideology obscured the nature of class oppositions, helping weaken class consciousness in the long run.

ALAN DAHL
American University

Edward Ayers, *The Promise of the New South* (1992); Sarah Babb, *American Journal of Sociology* (December 1996); Judith Barjenbruch, *Arkansas Historical Quarterly* (Summer 1977); Bruce G. Carruthers and Sarah Babb, *American Journal of Sociology* (May 1996); Matthew Hild, *Greenbackers, Knights of Labor, and Populists: Farmer-Labor Insurgency in the Late-Nineteenth-Century South* (2007); Paul Horton, *Journal of Southern History* (February 1991); Michael R. Hyman, *The Anti-Redeemers: Hill-Country Political Dissenters in the Lower South from Redemption to Populism* (1990); Morgan Kousser, *The Shaping of Southern Politics: Suffrage Restriction and the Establishment of the One-Party South, 1880–1910* (1974); Daniel Letwin, *Journal of Southern History* (August 1995); C. Vann Woodward, *Origins of the New South* (1951, 1971).

Hamer, Fannie Lou

(1917–1977) CIVIL RIGHTS ACTIVIST. The youngest of 20 children born to Jim and Ella Townsend, black sharecroppers in Montgomery County, Miss., Fannie Lou Townsend moved to Sunflower County, in the heart of the Delta, just after her second birthday. She picked her first cotton harvest as a six-year-old. Townsend was a gifted student, but she left Sunflower County's inferior black schools after the sixth grade to work on the Brandon plantation because her family desperately needed the money. She married Perry "Pap" Hamer in 1944; they sharecropped on the Marlow plantation just outside of Ruleville, not far from the plantation of U.S. senator James O. Eastland.

Thousands of African American women in the Mississippi Delta shared Fannie Lou Hamer's family and educational history, and therefore her life prospects. Taught by their own public school systems that educating them would be a waste of money, they certainly were not expected to bear the responsibilities of citizenship. Hamer, however, rose far above the expectations held by the white supremacist society into which she was born. By the time of her untimely death in 1977 Hamer had become the most influential poor person in America. The absolute embodiment of the Student Nonviolent Coordinating Committee (SNCC)'s "Let the People Decide" mantra, Hamer voiced a homegrown critique of the American political system that made Mississippi's white supremacy possible. In the process, she became a standard-bearer for the disfranchised and ignored black poor and provided an effective challenge to Mississippi elected officials, the leaders of the national Democratic Party, and President Lyndon B. Johnson. Millions of Americans came to appreciate her as what a fellow activist called the "prophet of hope for the sick and tired."

Hamer was 44 years old when she attended a SNCC workshop in Ruleville and learned she was eligible to vote.

She was one of dozens of Ruleville-area blacks who attempted to register in 1962 and became an indefatigable canvasser for black voters. Hamer's initial application was denied with the others, but she attempted to register again; she learned in 1963 that Sunflower County's registrar had accepted her application on her second attempt, though other would-be voters had to return to the county courthouse multiple times. Such was Hamer's determination and so fast was the pace of change during Mississippi's Freedom Summer that the first vote she cast, in 1964, was for herself in a Democratic primary race against incumbent U.S. representative Jamie Whitten. Hamer lost that race, but she, Victoria Gray, and Annie Devine challenged Whitten and the rest of Mississippi's delegation to the House on the grounds that African Americans had systematically been denied the ballot throughout the state.

Hamer was the recognized spokesperson of the Mississippi Freedom Democratic Party (MFDP), the integrated but majority-black group that organized during Freedom Summer to challenge the lily-white "regular" Mississippi delegation at the Democratic National Party convention in Atlantic City in August 1964. Hamer and the MFDP lost the challenge, but in a nationally televised, highly charged address before the party's Credentials Committee, Hamer rattled off a litany of injustices she had suffered simply because she wanted to vote. "All of this is on account [of] we want to register, to become first-class citizens, and if the Freedom Democratic Party is not seated now, I question America," she concluded. Hamer's electrifying testimony laid bare the radically democratic enterprise at the heart of the civil rights movement as she knew it. Her further challenge of the congressional delegation kept Mississippi racism in the nation's consciousness after the conclusion of Freedom Summer and highlighted black disfranchisement, which kept pressure on Johnson and the Congress to pass what would become the Voting Rights Act of 1965.

Hamer remained a nationally recognized philosopher of the black freedom struggle and a darling of the Left even after much of the civil rights movement disintegrated. She was an effective fundraiser for civil rights and voting rights causes and a sought-after speaker among social justice and feminist organizations throughout the decades of the 1960s and 1970s. The feminists, it must be said, were not quite sure what to make of Hamer when she told them she was not "hung up on this thing about liberating myself from the black man. . . . I got a black husband, six feet three, 240 pounds, with a 14 shoe, that I don't *want* to be liberated from." She also departed from feminist orthodoxy on abortion, but was fully committed to the principle that women should control their own lives and persons.

Hamer came to this position via hard-lived experience. Spending all her life in a society with an inhumanly racist health-care system and being a civil rights activist took a tremendous physical toll on her. She suffered from polio as a child and later wrote of recurrent childhood dreams about food, in which she found a piece of cornbread or an apple or orange to relieve her persistent hunger. Hamer saw a local doctor for treatment of a stomach cyst in 1961; he performed a hysterectomy without her knowledge or permission. She suffered and walked with a limp for the rest of her life following a beating she received in a Winona, Miss., jail on the way home from a citizenship education school in 1963. One of Hamer's adopted daughters died from the effects of malnutrition at the age of 22; her life might have been saved had not a local hospital refused to treat her because she was black. Hamer herself succumbed to the effects of diabetes, hypertension, cancer, and heart troubles at the age of 59, in 1977.

J. TODD MOYE
University of North Texas

Ed King, *Sojourners* (December 1982); Chana Kai Lee, *For Freedom's Sake: The Life of Fannie Lou Hamer* (1999); Kay Mills, *This Little Light of Mine: The Life of Fannie Lou Hamer* (1994); J. Todd Moye, *Let the People Decide: Black Freedom and White Resistance Organizing in Sunflower County, Mississippi, 1945–1986* (2004); Charles Payne, *I've Got the Light of Freedom: The Organizing Tradition and the Mississippi Freedom Struggle* (1995).

Highlander Folk School
(1932–1961)
Highlander Research and Education Center
(1961–)

The Highlander Research and Education Center (formerly named Highlander Folk School) is an education center for social change located in east Tennessee. Highlander has been in the forefront of social justice organizing in the South and nationally, playing a vital role in the southern labor movement, the civil rights movement, the environmental justice movement, and the global justice movement, among others.

Highlander Folk School began in 1932 on the Cumberland Plateau in Grundy County, Tenn. Highlander's founders, Myles Horton and Don West, were both from the South and had been inspired by the social gospel movement and the Danish Folk Schools. They decided to build a school for adult education in the South. Dr. Lillian Johnson had land and a community house outside Monteagle where she had been working to teach local people about cooperatives. She wanted to find someone else to take over her work and agreed to let Horton and West try out their new ideas for a year. After that year, she turned the site over to them to use for the long term.

The school first began working in the local Appalachian community, with a nursery school, efforts to build a cannery, and local education programs. As labor organizing grew in the region, Highlander responded to the community's needs and began conducting labor-organizing training, working with local Works Progress Administration workers and miners in the Davidson-Wilder community and Grundy County. Highlander's work branched out to the growing textile industry, which was organizing throughout the South. The staff offered labor education at the school and in locals throughout the region. Highlander facilitated and hosted workshops that focused on enhancing skills needed for union organizing.

Zilphia Johnson Horton was committed to also making culture an important part of how workshops were facilitated, and square dancing, music, and drama became part of the educational work. This tradition of integrating culture with social action is a strong thread in Highlander's educational model and continues today.

In the 1940s Highlander staff made the decision that workshops would be integrated, believing that economic justice could not be achieved as long as black and white workers were segregated. Highlander became increasingly involved in the civil rights movement, first by offering workshops around school desegregation and the *Brown v. Board of Education* decision.

In the mid-1950s Septima Clark, a teacher from Charleston, S.C., became education director at Highlander and worked with Esau Jenkins and Bernice Robinson to develop the Citizenship Schools on John's Island, one of the South Carolina Sea Islands. The Citizenship School model became a vital part of the civil rights movement by teaching thousands of African Americans to read and write, resulting in black students being able to pass literacy tests in order to attain their right to vote. The Citizenship School model of education, based on people's needs and experiences, was then replicated throughout the South.

Highlander supported work around school desegregation and hosted the first gathering for the student leaders of the sit-in movement in April 1960. Highlander continued to serve as a meeting site for Student Nonviolent Coordinating Committee (SNCC) members and their adviser, Ella Baker. Other leaders also met at Highlander, including Bernice Johnson Reagon, Fannie Lou Hamer, Rosa Parks, Anne Braden, and countless others who helped shape and move the civil rights movement forward.

From its very beginning, Highlander faced harassment from powerful economic and political forces who wanted to squelch labor and civil rights organizing in the South. In 1961 Tennessee revoked Highlander Folk School's charter and confiscated the 200-acre site, including 13 buildings. The charges included holding integrated gatherings.

The Citizenship School Program moved to the Southern Christian Leadership Conference (SCLC), to ensure its continuance. Highlander then changed its name to the Highlander Research and Education Center and relocated to Knoxville. It continued hosting civil rights gatherings but began to also refocus on working with groups in Appalachia. There was a resurgence of activity in Appalachia, which grew out of labor organizing, mining, and the federal War on Poverty.

In 1971 Highlander Research and Education Center moved to a farm on Bays Mountain in Jefferson County, Tenn., and built a workshop center, library, offices, and staff housing. Work in the 1970s and early 1980s was concentrated in Appalachia with efforts to reduce poverty, improve environmental conditions, and increase health and democracy. Staff worked to support health clinics, which were being built by the United Mine Workers of America. Furthermore, organizing against devastation caused by strip mining for coal escalated. Highlander worked with the Appalachian Alliance in 1979 and 1980 on a participatory research project that focused on landownership in Appalachia, documenting both the vast areas owned by corporations and the low tax base and control resulting from this pattern of ownership. Highlander became part of an international Participatory Research Network, which worked to challenge the hierarchical view that "knowledge" was what was learned in a formal education setting. Instead, participatory research focuses on the knowledge of community people to inform research and serve as researchers in order to determine solutions to their own issues.

In the 1990s Highlander recognized the region's changing demographics and the need to develop new leaders for social justice. The school developed new programs for immigrants and youth and supported lesbian/gay/bisexual/transgendered groups organizing in the region. Economic work also continued at Highlander, focusing on deindustrialization in the region and opposition to free-trade agreements such as the North American Free Trade Agreement. Highlander supported the creation of two statewide networks, the Tennessee Industrial Renewal Network, begun in 1989, and the Tennessee Immigrant and Refugee Rights Coalition, begun in 2002.

Highlander's work changes as the needs and organizing work of groups in the South and Appalachia change, but the core methodologies of popular education, cultural organizing, and participatory research continue. The school maintains its core beliefs that social change should be led by people directly affected by issues and that everyone has access to knowledge that is important in addressing injustice within their communities.

SUSAN WILLIAMS
Highlander Research and Education Center

Frank Adams, with Myles Horton, *Unearthing Seeds of Fire: The Idea of Highlander* (1975); John M. Glen, *Highlander: No Ordinary School* (1996); Myles Horton, with Herbert Kohl and Judith Kohl, *The Long Haul* (1997); Eliot Wigginton, ed., *Refuse to Stand Silently By: An Oral History of Grass Roots Social Activism in America, 1921–1964* (1991).

Hillbillies, Crackers, Rednecks, and White Trash

The myriad labels for poor and working-class white southerners have long been used as pejorative putdowns and embraced as markers of regional and cultural identity. Although vernacular usage almost certainly goes back in time much further, appearances in print of the dominant terms for these people on the social and economic fringe date back to at least the 18th century. The term "cracker" first appeared in the 1760s whereas "poor white trash" (often condensed to "po' white trash" or just "white trash") began to appear semiregularly in the 1830s, used first by African Americans to refer to nonslaveholding whites and then by wealthier whites as a means of stigmatizing and denigrating nonblacks they deemed beneath them. "Redneck" and "hillbilly" date only to the turn of the 20th century, both first appearing in the explicitly political context of supporters or opponents of southern politicians but quickly thereafter expanding to other social and cultural settings.

These derisive labels and other similar terms were intended to indicate a diet rooted in scarcity ("clay eater," "corn-cracker," "rabbit twister"), physical appearance and clothing that denoted hard and specifically working-class laboring conditions ("redneck," "wool hat," "lint head"), an animal-like existence on the economic and physical fringes of society ("brush ape," "ridge runner," "briar hopper"), ignorance and racism, and, in all cases, economic, genetic, and cultural impoverishment (best summed up by the pointed label "poor white trash"). These terms spread with working-class southern whites as they migrated to southern and midwestern urban centers in the mid-20th century. In the civil rights movement era of the 1950s and 1960s these descriptors, especially "cracker" and "redneck," were widely used in news accounts and by civil rights activists to emphasize the backward-looking racism of southern lawmen and townspeople who fought integration.

Despite signifying generally the same cultural meanings, "cracker," "redneck," "hillbilly," and "white trash," the four most common of these terms, each has a distinct historical trajectory and connotations. "Cracker" initially referred to the boastfulness and lawless attitudes of backcountry squatters of the late 18th century who were violating the ban on British colonists' settling of the trans-Appalachian West. By the turn of the 19th century, the term had extended to poor whites of the Georgia and Florida frontiers (perhaps because they were reliant on a diet of cracked corn or perhaps because of the cracking sounds of their whips as they drove livestock to market). By the early 20th century, the once primarily derogatory term evolved into an accepted, even celebrated, label of regional identity (as evidenced by the Atlanta Crackers minor-league baseball team, 1901–65, and its African American counterparts, the Atlanta Black Crackers, 1919–52). Nonetheless, in the late 20th century it could still easily be reapplied negatively, especially in the civil rights era, to instantly signify, to newspaper readers and television news viewers, racist intransigence and the potentiality for violence.

"Redneck" had an even more multifaceted provenance and significance. Initially it literally referred to the physical effect of exhausting outside agricultural labor and, later, to a general antiprogressive sensibility. It has therefore long been associated with poor dirt farmers both economically and politically (for instance, the hardscrabble supporters of Mississippi governor and later senator James Vardaman dubbed themselves "rednecks"). Slightly later, in the 1920s West Virginia mine wars when striking miners wore red bandanas, it was tied to radical unionization efforts. In the 1950s and 1960s it became synonymous with virulent racism and opposition to civil rights. Starting in the 1970s its meaning evolved again, as millions of the white working class (largely but not exclusively men) worked to redefine the term as a cultural identifier positioned in dual opposition to both the power and cultural values of the upper-middle class and what it perceived to be a welfare-dependent and minority underclass. In the decades since, the success of Jeff Foxworthy's *You Might Be a Redneck If . . .* joke books and comedy routines and similar cultural products have given it a more benign and broadly middle-class cultural meaning but still one that indicates racial whiteness and a resistance to intellectualism.

"Hillbilly" has proved to be the most ambiguous of these labels. Although ostensibly a term for residents of the southern mountains from the Ozarks to the Blue Ridge, the label has been applied to people and culture across the broad interior of the nation. It has been used simultaneously to evoke, on the one hand, degradation, violence, animalism, and carnality and, on the other, romanticized rurality, cultural and ethnic purity, pioneer heritage, and personal and communal independence and self-sufficiency. It thus has resonated most broadly with audiences both nationally and in the southern hill country and has been the most commonly used such label in popular culture. It has applied to country music (indeed, "hillbilly music" was the standard if at times contested term for the genre from the 1920s to the 1950s), a range of cartoons and comic strips, and the title of one of America's most popular and influential television shows (*The Beverly Hillbillies*). Both adopted and rejected by southern mountain folk living in and outside of the region, it retained in the early 21st century its fundamental ambivalence, if not the social bite it once held.

"Poor white trash," the crudest of these terms, is nonetheless still routinely used in televised comedy and talk shows and even general conversation. It also is the one that most starkly reveals the fundamental tensions in all these words between a supposed normative racial identity ("white") and an antinormative (indeed, uncivilized) cultural and social status and outlook. Throughout the early 19th century the term was employed for different purposes by African Americans, abolitionists, and slavery apologists and defenders, all of whom used the label to critique (explicitly or implicitly) or justify the institution of slavery and its impact on southern society. In the early 20th century, textile mill operators and middle-class progressives who were heavily shaped by the predominant Social Darwinist view of biological social determinism also used the concept as a way of culturally bounding poor whites as lazy, dirty, criminal, and imbecilic degenerates who threatened national progress. The term thus was a means to assert the unquestionable superiority of their own cultural value system. By the late 20th century the term had lost altogether its southern regional specificity, instead becoming a generalized if increasingly cartoonish critique of non–people of color who rejected middle-class standards of social advancement and ways of living. In the same manner as did its companion terms, it thus reinforced the "naturalness" of middle class sensibilities and justified economic inequality by blaming poor whites for their own lower social and economic status. Used as explanatory labels, these words thus were ultimately means of avoiding concerns about the failures of capitalism to truly benefit all in the society.

The explicitly political origins and consequences of these terms and their dominantly derogatory connotations, however, were hidden behind their ostensibly comical overtones, particularly for middle- and upper-class whites in positions of authority, but also, in a different context and with a different intent, for working-class whites and people of color. Accordingly, they have proved to be remarkably semantically and geographically malleable. As noted, since at least the 1970s, "hillbilly," "redneck," "cracker," and, more recently, even "poor white trash" have all been reappropriated by some working-class and lower-middle-class whites as badges of class and racial identity and pride. In this context, they mark opposition to (or at least distinction from) hegemonic middle-class social aspirations and norms and, less explicitly, to the relative gain in status of African Americans and other minority social groups. As these terms have been increasingly embraced by those they were intended to denigrate, they have stretched well beyond their southern origins and are now used and adopted around the United States and even Canada.

ANTHONY HARKINS
Western Kentucky University

Anthony Harkins, *Hillbilly: A Cultural History of an American Icon* (2004); Patrick Huber, *Southern Cultures* (Winter 1995); Matt Wray, *Not Quite White: White Trash and the Boundaries of Whiteness* (2006).

Horton, Myles

(1905–1990) EDUCATOR, ORGANIZER, SOCIAL ACTIVIST.
Myles Horton was born in a log cabin near Savannah, Tenn. He learned the value of Christian responsibility for others, the concept of social service for people of all social, economic, and racial backgrounds, and the transformative nature of education from his parents, both schoolteachers and later sharecroppers. These principles contributed to his lifelong efforts to cultivate social change in the South.

In 1924 Horton enrolled at Cumberland University in Lebanon, Tenn., to study religion and literature. At Cumberland, he railed against traditional practices, such as hazing and mandatory fraternal membership. Even more significant, Horton served as president of the school's YMCA, and in 1927 he attended a biracial YMCA conference in Nashville. He supported the idea of laborers forming unions and visited nearby mills to promote worker's rights. His prounion stance and his antisegregationist practices attracted criticism from school administrators.

In the summer of 1927 Horton directed a vacation Bible school program in Ozone, Tenn. To encourage community involvement, Horton asked the students' parents to participate in informal meetings to discuss social problems. At these well-attended forums, residents discussed local issues such as farming, health services, working conditions, and the economy. The success of these meetings, where attendees could freely voice their opinions and concerns, influenced Horton's emerging educational philosophy.

After graduation in 1928 he enrolled at Union Theological Seminary in New York City to study under Reinhold Niebuhr, a famed theologian. By this time, Horton identified himself as a socialist. After a short stint at Union, Horton enrolled as a graduate student in sociology at the University of Chicago. In 1931 Horton, intrigued by the Danish Folk School model as a way to inspire patriotism and civic pride, embarked on a trip to Denmark.

In the spring of 1932, after contemplating his educational theories overseas, he returned to Tennessee to establish a folk school in the southern mountains. While searching for a suitable location, Horton met Don West, another social activist with similar educational goals. That fall, Horton and Don West founded the Highlander Folk School in Monteagle, Tenn. Their interracial school offered adult educational programs designed to impart social, political, and economic change. After West's departure in 1934, Horton focused Highlander on supporting the emerging southern labor movement. Highlander trained activists and labor organizers throughout the Great Depression and other groups after World War II.

In the 1950s Highlander became a training center for many civil rights activists. Horton developed courses on school desegregation, voter rights, and methods of nonviolent protest. Visitors at Highlander included Martin Luther King Jr., Rosa Parks, Fannie Lou Hamer, Septima Clark, and Eleanor Roosevelt. This publicity had significant ramifications for Horton and Highlander. Numerous factions, including politicians, segregationists, and business owners, accused Horton of being a member of the Communist Party and operating a school espousing un-American values. Horton made several appearances before government-sponsored anticommunist investigatory committees and emerged somewhat unscathed. His school, however, was not as fortunate. In 1961 the state of Tennessee revoked the charter for the Highlander Folk School and later auctioned the Monteagle property.

Undeterred, Horton secured a charter from the state of Tennessee to preserve the school's concept. Following the state's seizure of the Monteagle property, Horton opened the Highlander Research and Education Center in Knoxville, where it remained for 10 years before relocating to its present location in New Market, Tenn. In the following decades, Horton developed community leadership training programs and courses on environmental and social issues plaguing Appalachian residents. His unique programs earned Horton and Highlander a 1982 Nobel Peace Prize nomination. Highlander is still a haven for activists fighting mountaintop removal coal mining practices and for other rural-based groups demanding access to services, such as health care, education, and transportation.

Horton died in 1990, leaving behind

an impressive legacy of using practical education and empowerment as a catalyst for social change. His training programs prepared generations of laborers, civil rights leaders, local activists, and community organizers to fight difficult struggles that often defied tradition and social acceptance. Horton's lifelong activism and incredible foresight into emerging challenges helped redefine social class in the South.

AARON D. PURCELL
Virginia Tech

John M. Glen, *Highlander: No Ordinary School* (1996); Aimee Isgrig Horton, *The Highlander Folk School: A History of Its Major Programs, 1932–1961* (1989); Myles Horton, *The Long Haul: An Autobiography* (1990); Dale Jacobs, ed., *The Myles Horton Reader: Education for Social Change* (2003).

Hunting and Fishing

Hunting and fishing continue to remain among the most enduring of all cherished antebellum traditions, flourishing vigorously within the protean atmosphere of cultural transformation that has become the distinguishing hallmark of the contemporary American South. Perhaps the most important reason for their perennial popularity is the tendency of those who hunt and fish together to develop a willingness to accept each other's differences as normal and positive extensions of nature's great wealth of diversity. In much the same way that the subtle arts of serious imaginative literature provide universally accessible avenues through which all can improve their understanding and appreciation of the human condition, the field arts of hunting and fishing provide a common code of morally responsible sportsmanship through which all of the South's social and racial distinctions can join in their shared, heightened understanding and appreciation of each other as fellow participants in the timeless rhythms of an enveloping natural world. Although not all scholars would agree, much evidence suggests that once joined together on this nonthreatening ground of mutual fascination with the fish, the game, and the streams and forests they inhabit, men and women of all ranks and races frequently find themselves eager to disregard their social identities and to celebrate instead their shared excitement and the gratifying rewards of a genuine communion with nature.

Since the antebellum South was the most ideal place to hunt in the true sportsman's style, it is not surprising that only 19 years after the appearance of *The American Shooter's Manual* (1827), the first full treatise on field sports written by an American, the Harvard-educated planter and dedicated sportsman William Elliott III brought out the first, book-length collection of sporting narratives and ideological assumptions regarding proper sporting etiquette as it should be observed in the South: *Carolina Sports by Land and Water* (1846). Elliott was no less insistent than his northern predecessors on the need to follow the proper forms, techniques, and morally accountable etiquette of the responsible sportsman, but he was also at pains to risk public censure by daringly stating his belief that, within the freemasonry of the hunt, even the rigid restraints of slavery were no bar to the true sportsman's recognition of the common humanity and the love of sport that he shared with his African American bondsmen.

More openly revealing of the virtues and nonaristocratic and African American sportsmen are the works of later, post-Reconstruction southern writers such as Caroline Gordon (*Aleck Maury, Sportsman*, 1934) and William Faulkner (*Go Down, Moses*, 1942). In Gordon's Depression-era novel we find that the major source of emotional warmth and paternal affection does not come from young Aleck's family of aristocratic sportsmen but from the African American servants on the Maurys' large farm. It is the towering, one-eyed black servant, Rafe, who takes Aleck on his most memorable hunt, and it is Rafe's kindness to the young Virginian and his love for the excitement of the chase that remain among Aleck's most cherished childhood memories. The much more fully rendered bond between Sam Fathers and the youthful Isaac McCaslin in Faulkner's *Go Down, Moses* is even more revealing of the cross-cultural friendships that can develop among those who hunt and fish together. As Faulkner's omniscient narrator says in the opening paragraphs of the all-important chapter 4, the hunting story he is about to tell is not a story of men locked into the reductive isolation of their own prejudices, but rather of men, "not white nor black nor red but men, hunters, with the will and hardihood to endure and the humility and skill to survive." Faulkner's vision of a community of hunters in touch with their environment in a still imperfect but ripening realm of sporting egalitarianism provides both a modernist and an agrarian corrective to the evils of social and racial injustice. Although William Elliott's early attempt in *Carolina Sports* to reveal how the sports of the field can foster a meaningful recognition of cross-cultural humanity is over a century and a half old, hunting and fishing remain of inestimable value as bringers together of sportsmen on both sides of seemingly uncrossable social and political barriers.

JACOB RIVERS
University of South Carolina

Daniel J. Herman, *Hunting and the American Imagination* (2001); Jesse Y. Kester, *The American Shooter's Manual* (1827); José Ortega y Gassett, *Meditations on Hunting* (1972); Nicolas W. Proctor, *Bathed in Blood: Hunting and Mastery in the Old South* (2002).

Indentured Servants

Indentured servitude describes a form of employment relationship common in 17th- and 18th-century North America. In this employment relationship, servants committed to serve their employer for a fixed period of years. Most servants entered into indentures as a way to finance the costs of transatlantic passage, which have been estimated to be roughly half a year's income for the young English laborers who made up the bulk of such migrants.

Lacking other resources to pay the costs of passage, migrants would enter into a contract with a merchant or ship's captain, who agreed to transport them to America in exchange for their commitment to work for a specified period of time. Upon arrival, the captain would recover his costs by selling the contract. In addition to transportation across the Atlantic, servants typically received room and board during their service and were promised a small cash payment on the completion of the term of service. The term "indenture" derives from the written contracts that recorded these agreements.

The use of indentures as a mechanism to finance migration was introduced by the Virginia Company in 1619 and appears to have arisen from a combination of two other types of employment relationships common in England at the time: service in husbandry, a form of annual employment for agricultural labor, and apprenticeship, a multiyear commitment in which children were contracted to work for a master for several years in exchange for training in a craft skill.

There are no comprehensive data documenting the composition of European migration to North America during the 17th and 18th centuries. However, it is commonly estimated that between half and two-thirds of immigrants arrived as indentured servants. Because of rapid rates of natural increase in the colonial population, the share of servants in the total labor force was much smaller than their proportion among arriving immigrants. Under reasonable demographic assumptions, by 1700 only about 10 percent of the white labor force in the Chesapeake region would have been indentured servants.

Archives of surviving indenture contracts have been analyzed in some detail by a number of scholars. Consistent with the existence of a well-functioning market, scholars have found that the terms of service varied with measurable personal characteristics that would be expected to influence individual productivity, as well as regional differences in the conditions of employment and temporal fluctuations in the supply of and demand for labor in different locations.

Market forces also appear to have been important in the transition from servant to slave labor in some parts of colonial North America. Because of harsh working conditions and high rates of mortality in the Caribbean and Lower South, African slaves made up the bulk of the labor force in these regions. During the 18th century, rising supplies of slaves combined with improved conditions in England contributed to a transition from servants to slaves as the primary source of labor in the Chesapeake region as well.

By the late colonial period the Middle Atlantic region was the primary destination for indentured servants. Although servants continued to arrive in small numbers after the Revolution, this form of labor died out in the United States by the early part of the 19th century. At the same time, legal thought on employment relationships was shifting in the wake of northern abolition of slavery. Drawing an increasingly sharp distinction between slave and free labor, courts in several northern states ruled that employers could not impose specific enforcement of a labor contract, thereby effectively undermining the legal basis for indentured servitude.

JOSHUA L. ROSENBLOOM
University of Kansas

Richard S. Dunn, in *Colonial British America: Essays in the New History of the Early Modern Era*, ed. Jack P. Greene and J. R. Pole; David W. Galenson, *White Servitude in Colonial America* (1981), *Journal of Economic History* (March 1984); Farley Grubb, *Journal of Economic History* (December 1985); Robert J. Steinfeld, *The Invention of Free Labor: The Employment Relationship in English and American Law and Culture, 1350–1870* (1991); Christopher Tomlins, *Freedom Bound: Law, Labor, and Civic Identity in Colonizing English America, 1580–1865* (2010).

Indian Removal, 1800–1840

When the invention of the cotton gin made upland cotton a viable cash crop for thousands of Upcountry settlers, Georgia and the territory that became the states of Mississippi and Alabama were home to 32,800 first people, 53,400 free people, and 30,000 enslaved people. By 1840, when the first postremoval censuses were taken, the same region was home to 922,000 free people and 737,000 enslaved people. Census takers failed to note any remaining Cherokees, Creeks, Choctaws, and Chickasaws because nearly all of them had been expelled from the region during the previous decade.

Why would state and federal governments forcibly expel people whose ancestors had inhabited the land for millennia? President Andrew Jackson had advocated removal since his days as the commander of the Tennessee militia in the Creek Civil War and cited the threat that so-called Indians posed to settler society as well as the incompatibility of the two cultures. Rather than await what everyone expected to be their inevitable extinction, Jackson believed that the federal government had to remove the indigenous people to the West where they could perpetuate their "race." Despite considerable opposition to the proposal in both houses, Jackson garnered enough congressional support to see the measure pass, and he signed the Indian Removal Act on 29 May 1830.

Choctaws were the first to experience removal under the auspices of the Indian Removal Act, and subsequent treaties with the Creeks in 1832, the Chickasaws in 1834, and the Cherokees in 1835 secured the removal of those nations and the cession of their land. All told, the federal and state governments expelled just more than 50,000 people from their homelands, some in chains, others at gunpoint, and acquired almost 30 million acres of land for settlement, taxation, and development. In the ongoing construction of a society whose citizens saw the world in terms of white freedom and black slavery, there was simply no place for "Indians."

The federal government kept no systematic records of the removals, so it is difficult to ascertain how many people died. Perhaps a third of removed Choctaws perished, while the tally of 4,000 Cherokee deaths on the Trail of Tears, one-quarter of the total number of Cherokees removed, is a likely estimate. Perhaps 10,000 Cherokees who would have lived or been born had removal not occurred were wiped from the face of the earth. Such death tolls must also be understood in the context of the loss of land. Indeed, for Choctaws, separation from their homeland meant for them death, and Choctaw conceptions of the West as a place where spirits were lost only compounded their misery, sense of loss, and despair for the future. One of their leaders, a man named George Washington Harkins, understood all of this. As he departed his homeland, his mother earth, on a steamer bound for Fort Smith, Ark., he mourned the total destruction of his people's world. "We found ourselves," he wrote from the ship's railing, "like a benighted stranger, following false guides until surrounded by fire and water—the fire is certain destruction, and a feeble hope was left of escaping by water."

For the Mississippi House Indian committee, however, the removals, the deaths, and the despair augured a new beginning, "the dawn of an era . . . when . . . this state would emerge from obscurity, and justifiably assume an equal character with her sister states of the Union." Indeed, to the United States, the removals were a triumph. Land had been opened for settlement, the "Indians" had been saved, and the unrelenting expansion into the West could continue unabated. But what did the South lose with the removals? Were the removals acts of ethnic cleansing akin to what happened in the Balkans in the late 20th century? And why are not "Indians" remembered in the same way that the slaves and planters of the early 19th-century South are? Is it because they were removed from our memories as well? Such questions suggest that even today we have failed to come to grips with what removal meant to the South then and what it means to the South today.

JAMES TAYLOR CARSON
Queens University

Donna Akers, *American Indian Culture and Research Journal* (1999); James Taylor Carson, *Searching for the Bright Path: The Mississippi Choctaws from Prehistory to Removal* (1999); Michael D. Green, *Politics of Indian Removal: Creek Government and Society in Crisis* (1982); Lucy Maddox, *Removals: Nineteenth-Century American Literature and the Politics of Indian Affairs* (1991); Ronald Satz, *American Indian Policy in the Jacksonian Era* (1975); Russell Thornton, in *Cherokee Removal: Before and After*, ed. William L. Anderson (1991).

Industrial Workers of the World

In the early 20th century the Industrial Workers of the World (IWW) emerged as an organization that represented the needs of the working-class population in the United States. Eugene Debs, leader of the American Socialist Party (ASP), led the movement to combine elements of socialism and labor unionism in a bid to alleviate the corporate exploitation of common workers. The new organization differed from traditional socialism in that the worker and not the state controlled the means of production, such as factories or mines. This syndicalist approach to labor unionism appealed to many immigrant workers, who had yet to achieve voting rights and therefore could not cast ballots for the ASP.

In 1905 Debs met with "Big Bill" Haywood, and Mary "Mother" Jones, along with hundreds of socialists, anarchists, and union organizers to convene the founding meeting of the IWW in Chicago. The new members created an inclusive organization that welcomed new members regardless of gender, race, or ethnic background. By recognizing that all workers shared similar experiences, they emphasized worker solidarity over any perceived differences. In order to achieve their unionization goals, Bill Haywood utilized "direct action" where laborers spread propaganda, held boycotts, or went on strike to obtain better working conditions.

Haywood and IWW quickly earned a reputation as rabble-rousers, which led to numerous confrontations with corporate security guards, local police, and the military during a series of strikes across the nation. Local officials often arrested IWW leaders during a strike, even charging Haywood with the murder of Idaho governor Frank Steunenberg. In 1913 officials in Charleston, S.C., also arrested the elderly Mother Jones for inciting a riot and murder after a strike in Muklow, W.Va. Other leaders, such as Joe Hill and Carlo Tresca, paid with their lives for advancing the cause of workers' rights.

A particularly contentious strike occurred during 1912, when the lumber workers near De Ridder, La., walked out over low wages and poor working conditions. The Southern Lumber Operators' Association responded by locking out all workers in the region and blacklisting any union members. With the help of local police and special deputies, the lumber operators forcefully broke up union meetings and then hired "scab" labor to replace the striking workers. Events came to a head near the Galloway Lumber Company in Graybow, La., when union members tried to protest against the replacement workers. Company officials opened fire on the protestors, which led to a short gun battle that left one special deputy and three union members dead, with nearly 50 people wounded. Mass arrests occurred in the aftermath of the fracas; however, court trials failed to convict anyone who participated in the incident.

During the 1930s the IWW also contributed to the Harlan County, Ky., coal strike. The miners had walked off the job in protest of unsafe working conditions, low wages, and the payment of wages in company script instead of dollars. Once again, the mine owners reacted to the demands of reform with violence. Special deputies clashed with striking miners, which led to two deaths and the arrest of strike leaders. The IWW helped the miners by paying for the legal defense of the workers.

The reason the IWW could only help finance the defense of the Kentucky miners stemmed from a loss of power. During the intervening years the federal government repressed the IWW for protesting American involvement in the First World War. Bill Haywood and nearly 200 other members were arrested under the Espionage Act and sentenced to jail. Haywood eventually fled the country for the Soviet Union, while many of the remaining members either were jailed during the postwar Palmer Raids or joined the American Communist Party. The IWW further lost support during the New Deal, when President Roosevelt supported the growth of unions and improved working conditions throughout the nation.

PAUL LUBOTINA
Middle Tennessee State University

Melvyn Dubofsky, *We Shall Be All: A History of the Industrial Workers of the World* (1988); Elizabeth G. Flynn, *Rebel Girl: An Autobiography, My First Life* (1973); Philip S. Foner, *History of the Labor Movement in the United States*, vol. 4: *The Industrial Workers of the World, 1905–1917* (1966); William D. Haywood, *Bill Haywood's Book: The Autobiography of William D. Haywood* (1983); Joyce L. Kornbluh, *Rebel Voices: An I.W.W. Anthology* (1964); J. Anthony Lukas, *Big Trouble: A Murder in a Small Town Sets Off a Struggle for the Soul of America* (1997); Nunzio Pernicone, *Carlo Tresca: Portrait of a Rebel* (2010).

In-Migration

Reduced out-migration of native southerners has been the most powerful factor contributing to the transformation of the modern South to a region of positive net migration. However, the return of northward migrants since the 1970s also has played a role in southern population growth.

Research on contemporary southern in-migration is primarily concerned with the flow of return migrants and their contribution to regional growth. Studies reveal that return migration by blacks accelerated after 1970; black, southern-born migrants living in the North were less likely than white, southern-born migrants to return to the South, but blacks were more likely than whites to return to their birth state; and return migrants accounted for between one-half and two-thirds of all blacks moving to the South.

Deteriorating conditions in northern cities and improving conditions in the South motivated post–World War II black return migration. Rising unemployment, crime, and inadequate housing were among the factors driving black southerners "home." As conditions in the North worsened, the relative attractiveness of the South increased. Businesses and industries that traditionally provided the well-paying, blue-collar jobs in northern cities relocated to the Sunbelt, and employment opportunities for African Americans in the South grew more abundant. Additionally, although attitudinal surveys show somewhat higher levels of racial prejudice among white southerners, civil rights legislation finally ended formal discrimination and segregation that had long plagued the South.

Whites, too, have returned to the South. Northward migrants began returning home during the Depression in the 1930s, and economic changes since the early 1980s have played a role in the return migration of white migrants. White southern out-migrants had a much higher rate of return even during the peak years of the Great Migration, and many out-migrants expected to return to the South. Ties to kin and place ranked high on the list of pulls home and were amplified by demographic factors; out-migrants were of retirement age, their parents were ailing, and their children moved into adulthood and initiated migration trajectories of their own.

Early research concluded southern-bound migrants had lower levels of education and employment and were more likely to have lower incomes than southern migrants who remained in the North. In contrast, recent research has found that return migrants were positively selected on characteristics such as education.

Not all southern places experienced the same magnitude or type of in-migration. Settlement patterns vary by race and gender and reflect different motivations. Black migration to the nonmetropolitan South increased with each passing decade, especially during the 1990s, yet these places experienced a net loss of college-educated residents. Older, less educated migrants moved to nonmetropolitan southern counties, whereas in-migrants to metro areas had more competitive socioeconomic characteristics (e.g., higher education). Knowledge about the social, political, and economic consequences of southern in-migration is limited and is a work in progress.

KATHERINE J. CURTIS
JACK DEWAARD
University of Wisconsin at Madison

Chad Berry, *Southern Migrants, Northern Exiles* (2000); John B. Cromartie, and Carol B. Stack, *Geographical Review* 79:3 (1989); William W. Falk, Larry L. Hunt, and Matthew O. Hunt, *Rural Sociology* 69:4 (2004); Anne S. Lee, *International Migration Review* 8:2 (1974); Stanley Lieberson, *American Journal of Sociology* 83:4 (1978); Larry H. Long and Kristin A. Hansen, *Demography* 12:4 (1975); John D. Kasarda, in *State of the Union: America in the 1990s*, vol. 1: *Economic Trends*, ed. Reynolds Farley (1995); Howard Schuman, Charlotte Steeh, Lawrence D. Bobo, and Maria Krysan, *Racial Attitudes in America: Trends and Interpretations* (1997); Carol Stack, *Call to Home: African Americans Reclaim the Rural South* (1996); William J. Wilson, *When Work Disappears: The World of the New Urban Poor* (1996).

Jacksonian Democracy

"Jacksonian democracy" was a major shift in American political culture associated with the presidency of Gen. Andrew Jackson (1829–37), in which the deferential republicanism of the founding era gave way to a sharp increase in voter turnout, the emergence of two mass-based political parties, a glorification of the wishes and wisdom of ordinary voters, and the growing power of mass electorates. Historians dispute the meaning and significance of Jacksonian democracy, with some arguing that the new political order merely replaced an older elite with party bosses, that Jacksonians were no more democratic than their opponents (and in some ways less), and that they did not disturb a fundamentally unequal social structure. Scholars agree, moreover, that democratizing changes began before Jackson's administration and were not limited to his movement. Particularly in the South, Jacksonian Democrats gave staunch support to slavery and Indian Removal and did not meet 21st-century standards of democracy. Nevertheless, the era of Jackson's presidency did see dramatic shifts in political culture that did lift the status of ordinary voters.

Even before the adoption of the U.S. Constitution, the American states proclaimed themselves republics that were based on the will of "the people," but often limited voting and office holding to white male landowners. Slaveholding planters held most political power in the South and claimed that their wealth, education, experience, and family connections gave them the wisdom and personal independence to put aside narrow personal interests for the sake of the common good. The electorate's task was selecting leaders from this elite and ratifying their decisions.

Beginning with independence and accelerating after 1815, social and economic change destabilized this deferential model of republicanism. In the older, south Atlantic states, coastal planters shared power with backcountry farmers to blunt the class and sectional antagonisms that had fueled 18th-century insurgencies, such as the North Carolina Regulation. Farther westward, migration disturbed social hierarchies while the expanding cotton economy fed ambitions and raised new fortunes that demanded recognition. Georgia opened the ballot to white male taxpayers as early as 1775, followed by Maryland in 1801 and South Carolina in 1808. As they entered the Union, the trans-Appalachian states generally opened voting to all white men, partly because uncertain land titles made restrictions impractical. By the time of Jackson's election, property requirements for voting were mostly extinct outside Virginia.

Events of Jackson's presidency intensified the impact of these changes. Jackson himself came from very modest circumstances on the Carolina frontier and rose to prominence by his own talents, determination, and self-taught military prowess. In the presidential election of 1824 the Tennessee general had led in popular and electoral votes, but lost the election through an alleged "corrupt bargain" in the House of Representatives. His outraged supporters concluded that ordinary voters could identify the common good far better than political elites and made vindication of the popular will a central theme of Jackson's successful canvass in the next election. These efforts lifted nationwide voter turnout from 26.5 percent of adult white males in 1824 to 56.3 percent in 1828, though actual levels varied widely by state. In the South, participation ranged from 27.6 percent in Virginia (where property requirements still prevailed) to 56.6 percent in Mississippi to 76.2 percent in Maryland.

Once in office, Jackson made popular democracy a thematic cornerstone of his presidency, glorifying majority rule, rewarding party loyalty over pedigree when making appointments, and challenging the financial privileges of the Bank of the United States. A large slaveholder, Jackson did not extend democratic privileges to women or racial minorities, however, most notoriously in expelling American Indians beyond the Mississippi.

The rise of mass-based two-party politics was a major dimension of Jacksonian democracy, but increased participation was not a spontaneous response to loosened restrictions on the ballot. Instead, beginning with Jackson's Democrats and spreading to the opposing Whigs, rival bands of political organizers used clear electoral alternatives, simple slogans, cheap publications, theatrical rallies, and free food and drink to recruit huge numbers of previously disengaged voters. The pattern climaxed in the tumultuous election of 1840, when national turnout reached 78.0 percent of adult white males and exceeded 80 percent in all but four of the slave states.

Mass political participation meant that no politician or policy—including the South's ultimate decision to secede from the Union—could succeed without appealing to the tastes and opinions of ordinary white men, though wealthy candidates could win elections by adopting a populist manner. Beyond this, the effect of Jacksonian politics on southern class structure was ambiguous. Jackson's party may have opened significant opportunities for poor and middling whites by supporting cheap prices for public lands, for example, but land speculators could benefit as well. Jackson's other policies did not challenge the planter elite, and voters did not consistently link their class interests with either party. In the upper South, the lowland plantation districts favored the Jacksonian Democrats while small farmers of the upland counties often preferred the Whigs. The exact opposite pattern prevailed in the lower South. Some historians have used the concept of "*Herrenvolk*" or "master race" democracy to describe the Jacksonians' dual practice of equality for white men and oppression for minorities. Others insist that racial privileges obscured but did not erode the inequalities that slavery created among whites. Fundamentally, it is apparent that Jacksonian democracy changed the tone and mechanisms of southern class relations far more than their underlying structure.

HARRY L. WATSON
University of North Carolina at Chapel Hill

Alexander Keyssar, *The Right to Vote: The Contested History of Democracy in the United States* (2000); Marc W. Kruman, *Parties and Politics in North Carolina, 1836–1865* (1983); Richard P. McCormick, *American Historical Review* (January 1960); J. Mills Thornton, *Politics and Power in a Slave Society: Alabama, 1800–1860* (1978).

Jazz

Jazz's most influential early style took shape in New Orleans after 1900. The city was afflicted by particularly virulent social divisions along the lines of race, ethnicity, and language, as well as income. Tensions between segregationist Anglo whites, new immigrants from Sicily and other parts of Europe, mixed-race Creoles of color, and non-Creole rural black migrants made New Orleans a turbulent city, fraught with economic inequality, violence, and racial discrimination. Before jazz took root, white Creoles tended to patronize the French opera, middle-class Anglo whites enjoyed mainstream popular songs, and Creoles of color set themselves apart from other African Americans by partaking of elite social functions and the Creole "society" orchestras that performed there. Jazz surmounted some of these divisions. A few Creole society orchestras and white brass bands incorporated blues harmonies and collective improvisation into their playing to create early jazz (although many continued to call it "ragtime," a more reputable term in the 1910s). Individual musicians and audience members crossed class and racial lines as well to experience the new music. On Mississippi riverboats, Creole musicians worked with young non-Creole black jazz players such as Louis Armstrong and Baby Dodds to blend styles into sophisticated new kinds of band improvisation. The cross-fertilization of musical styles in jazz across class and racial lines also occurred in other river cities, such as Memphis and St. Louis. Still, the castelike discrimination and poverty of these southern port towns encouraged musicians of color, as well as some whites (such as Sicilians in New Orleans), to move north to advance their careers.

In the 1920s many southern musicians migrated to the North. Their mass-produced recordings made jazz nationwide stylistically more "southern," but in the South these records made jazz (and popular music as a whole) more similar to the new homogeneous national sound. Jazz bands in the South adapted to national stylistic trends. Despite this, jazz in the region in the post–Great Migration years still reflected local class divisions. Some African American and white big bands adhered to the "sweet," smooth popular music style of Guy Lombardo and Lawrence Welk in order to maintain their bookings in elite hotels, country clubs, and prestigious venues. In contrast, other regional big bands of the 1930s and 1940s exploited the popular new "swing" style, which tended to unite audiences and break down social barriers. The big bands attracted youthful fans across class and racial lines, and radio stations exposed the entire regional listening audience to swing music and other predominantly African American styles, such as rhythm and blues and "jump blues," a precursor of rock and roll. These cross-fertilizing cultural trends would increase in prominence and play a role in the accelerated racial integration that accompanied the civil rights movement, but well into the 1960s Jim Crow laws kept white and black dancers physically separated at many jazz functions, and racist whites often heckled and harassed black band members. As in the North, many restaurants and dance halls chose to exclude African American customers and to treat black musicians who worked for them as second-class citizens. Players would be forced to enter performing venues through rear doors, seek lodging and meals in black neighborhoods (often in private households), and leave downtown business districts as soon as their gigs were completed. Since the best-educated and best-paid black musicians suffered the same fate as other players, it is clear that race trumped class in the South during the Swing era.

After World War II, the end of the big-band vogue caused both white and black jazz musicians to scramble for employment. Many of the jobs they found involved playing other, more commercially viable kinds of music. In New Orleans the business community's effort to attract tourists gradually melded with musicians' efforts to maintain the old "Dixieland" style (as well as newer jazz styles), and popular venues such as Preservation Hall provided some regular employment for players. Still, this development mostly benefited middle-class tourism promoters instead of the black working-class musicians who kept early jazz alive. Elsewhere in the South, though, the rise of the middle class because of the GI Bill and postwar prosperity and the creation of excellent jazz performance programs at some colleges and universities provided welcome and stable employment for some musicians. However, as in other parts of the country—and, indeed, around the world—jazz in the South lost most of its commercial viability and became dependent on a relatively small middle-class fan base to patronize it at schools, clubs, and festivals, as well as on public radio stations. Working-class musicians of the postwar generations have more commonly aligned their fortunes with lucrative contemporary popular styles such as rhythm and blues, soul, rock and roll, and hip-hop, rather than the increasingly academic and "classical" realm of jazz.

BURTON W. PERETTI
Western Connecticut State University

Danny Barker and Jack V. Buerkle, *Bourbon Street Black: The New Orleans Black Jazzman* (1974); Jason Berry, Jonathan Foose, and Tad Jones, *Up from the Cradle of Jazz: New Orleans Music since World War II* (1986); Thomas D. Brothers, *Louis Armstrong's New Orleans* (2006); Ted Gioia, *The History of Jazz* (1997); Burton W. Peretti, *The Creation of Jazz: Music, Race, and Culture in Urban America* (1992); Bruce Boyd Raeburn, *New Orleans Style and the Writing of American Jazz History* (2007); Tommy Sancton, *Song for My Fathers: A New Orleans Story in Black and White* (2006).

Kester, Howard Anderson
(1904–1977) ORGANIZER, PREACHER, SOCIAL ACTIVIST.

Howard Kester spent his childhood years in Martinsville, Va. At a young age he took careful note of the town's racial segregation, heard stories of lynching, and recognized the great influence of the Lost Cause of the Civil War on the residents of the community. At age 11, he and his family relocated to Beckley, W.Va., where he observed significant class struggle between miners and mine owners.

Religion played a crucial role in Kester's upbringing. His parents encouraged him to join the ministry, and in 1921 he enrolled at Lynchburg College in Virginia. Kester became active in the school's YMCA chapter, and in the summer of 1923 he participated in a YMCA-sponsored "Pilgrimage of Friendship" to parts of Europe still recovering from World War I. After a tour of the Jewish ghettos of Krakow and Warsaw, Poland, Kester declared that the harsh treatment of Jewish people in Europe was no different from the unequal treatment of African Americans in the United States. Kester took issue with the YMCA's practices of segregating its conferences and questioned the ability of church-based groups to enact significant social change.

Kester enrolled in the seminary program at Vanderbilt University, where he studied under Alva Taylor, a leader in the emerging Social Gospel movement, and he met other socially conscious seminary students, including Don West and Claude Williams. Taylor and his many students believed that segregation was incompatible with Christianity, and they looked to more radical methods to eliminate racial inequality. Kester believed that progress could be made only through militant interracialism, class struggle, and Christian radicalism.

With the onset of the Great Depression, Kester gravitated to the Socialist Party. His interactions with Socialist Party leader Norman Thomas and radical theologian Reinhold Niebuhr contributed to Kester's decision to join the Socialist Party in 1931. Kester organized Socialist Party branches in Tennessee and became close associates with fellow Socialist Party member H. L. Mitchell. During this period he also worked for the NAACP as an undercover operative to investigate lynching in the South.

In the early 1930s Kester focused his reform efforts on the plight of southern sharecroppers. Sharecropping in the South had created a class of poor landless famers, black and white, dependent on a small percentage of the return on the crops they grew on another person's land. The New Deal's Agricultural Adjustment Act of 1933, which raised prices by decreasing agricultural output, benefited landowners and ignored sharecroppers. Norman Thomas urged Socialist Party leaders and others to form an interracial union to represent the rights of the forgotten sharecroppers.

In July 1934, 11 white and seven black leaders founded the Southern Tenant Farmers' Union (STFU). As one of the early leaders of the STFU, Kester visited Arkansas to evaluate the spread of the Socialist Party and the effectiveness of the new union. The result of his investigations appeared in 1936 as the STFU-published book *Revolt among the Sharecroppers*. Kester's book outlined the origins of the STFU, questioned the intent of the New Deal programs, and urged sharecroppers to overcome their hardships by uniting and demanding change. The book resulted in greater attention for the STFU. The union spread across the Southeast and eventually to California.

In the late 1930s Kester left the STFU, largely because of his opposition to the union's affiliation with the Communist Party. A self-described "revolutionary socialist," Kester took a leadership role in other social activist groups, such as the Fellowship of Southern Churchman and the Committee on Economic and Racial Justice. After World War II, Kester took his message of interracialism and building a classless society to the classroom, working in several schools in South Carolina, North Carolina, and Illinois.

Kester's lengthy and uncompromising career as a social activist represents a lifelong effort to redefine, if not fully eliminate, social class in the South. He opposed racial discrimination and demanded equal consideration for the poor landless farmers, long before social activists of the 1960s emerged. Through his preaching, teaching, and writing, Howard Kester spread his gospel of racial and class equality to a wide audience.

AARON D. PURCELL
Virginia Tech

Robert H. Craig, *Religion and Radical Politics: An Alternative Christian Tradition in the United States* (1992); Anthony P. Dunbar, *Against the Grain: Southern Radicals and Prophets, 1929–1959* (1981); Howard Kester, *Revolt among the Sharecroppers* (1936); Robert F. Martin, *Howard Kester and the Struggle for Social Justice in the South, 1904–1977* (1991).

King, Martin Luther, Jr.

(1929–1968) CIVIL RIGHTS LEADER. Born into a middle-class black family in Atlanta, Ga., on 15 January 1929, Martin Luther King Jr. emerged as the key figure in the civil rights crusade that transformed the American South in the 1950s and 1960s. As a student at Atlanta's Morehouse College (1944–48), he majored in sociology and developed an intense interest in the behavior of social groups and the economic and cultural arrangements of southern society. King's education continued at Crozer Theological Seminary (1948–51) and Boston University (1951–55), where he studied trends in liberal Christian theology, philosophy, and ethics, while also engaging in an intellectual quest for a method to eliminate social evil. With a seminary degree and a Ph.D. from Boston, King lived remarkably free of material concerns and personified the intellectual-activist type that constituted the principal model for W. E. B. Du Bois's talented tenth leadership theory.

Although mindful of how poverty and economic injustice victimized both races in the South in his time, King understood the social stratification of the region largely in terms of the basic distinctions between powerful whites and powerless Negroes. Framing the struggle as essentially a clash between loveless power and powerless love, King rose to prominence in the Montgomery bus boycott in 1955–56, and he and his Southern Christian Leadership Conference (SCLC) later led nonviolent direct action campaigns for equal rights and social justice in Albany, Birmingham, St. Augustine, Selma, and other southern towns. King's celebrated "I Have a Dream" speech during the march on Washington on 28 August 1963 firmly established him as the most powerful leader of the black freedom struggle.

After receiving the Nobel Peace Prize in 1964, King moved toward a more enlightened and explicit globalism. Convinced that the struggle for basic civil and/or constitutional rights had been won with the Civil Rights Act of 1964 and the Voting Rights Bill of 1965, he turned more consciously toward economic justice and international peace issues. He saw the interconnectedness of racial oppression, class exploitation, and militarism and moved beyond integrated buses, lunch counters, and schools for blacks to highlight the need for basic structural changes within the capitalistic system. He recognized that economic justice was a more complex and costlier matter than civil rights and that poverty and economic powerlessness afflicted both people of color and whites. He prophetically critiqued the wealth and power of the white American elites and chided the black middle class for its neglect of and indifference toward what he labeled "the least of these." King also fought for the elimination of slum conditions in Chicago in 1965–66, launched a Poor People's Campaign in 1967, and participated in the Memphis Sanitation Strike in early 1968. His attacks on capitalism, his call for a radical redistribution of economic power, his assault on poverty and economic injustice in the so-called Third World, and his cry against his nation's misadventure in Vietnam were all aimed at the same structures of systemic social evil. King framed his vision in terms of the metaphors of "New South," "American Dream," and "World House," all of which embodied what he considered the highest human and ethical ideal—namely, the beloved community, or a completely integrated society and world based on love, justice, human dignity, and peace.

King's broadened social vision can be understood in terms of democratic socialism and the tactics of massive civil disobedience and nonviolent sabotage that he thought would be required to achieve this ideal. While traveling to Oslo, Norway, to receive the Nobel Prize, he saw democratic socialism at work in the Scandinavian countries. In King's estimation, democratic socialism, which he considered more consistent with the Christian ethic than both capitalism and communism, would allow for the nationalization of basic industries, massive federal expenditures to enhance center cities and to provide employment for residents, a guaranteed income for every adult citizen, and universal education and health care, thus amounting to the kind of sweeping economic and structural changes essential for the creation of a more just, inclusive, and peaceful society.

King was assassinated in Memphis, Tenn., on 4 April 1968, weeks before his planned Poor People's Campaign was launched. Economic justice and international peace remain as the core issues in his unfinished holy crusade. In the half century since his death, some conservative forces have increasingly sought to use him as a kind of sacred aura for their own political ends, and particularly in their attacks on affirmative action, immigration, reparations, and government spending for social programs.

LEWIS V. BALDWIN
Vanderbilt University

Lewis V. Baldwin, *The Voice of Conscience: The Church in the Mind of Martin Luther King, Jr.* (2010); Clayborne Carson, ed., *The Autobiography of Martin Luther King, Jr.* (1998); Kenneth L. Smith, *Journal of Ecumenical Studies* (Spring, 1989); William D. Watley, *Roots of Resistance: The Nonviolent Ethic of Martin Luther King, Jr.* (1985).

Knights of Labor

The Noble and Holy Order of the Knights of Labor swept across the United States in the 1880s, becoming the first national labor organization to reach extensively into the South. Established as a secret society by skilled Philadelphia garment workers in 1869, it remained below the radar of employers, politicians, and the media until the economic revival of the early 1880s. It embodied the features of 19th-century fraternal lodges—tight-knot bonding among members, elaborate rituals that expressed the order's values, and mutual insurance and support. To this familiar basis it added the features of labor organizations—collective bargaining, strikes, boycotts, and cooperatives. Even as a small organization, the Knights articulated an inclusive ideology, expressed by its motto "An Injury to One Is the Concern of All." It practiced the most inclusive trade unionism the United States had yet seen, taking in unskilled workers as well as skilled, women as well as men, immigrants as well as the native born, and blacks as well as whites. While many of its locals were "mixed" (in terms of skill and occupation) rather than "trade" (like the craft unions of the era), most consisted of single racial or gender groups (e.g., white men, black women).

When the economy rebounded from the depression of 1873-79, workers were eager to make up for the ground they had lost to layoffs, wage cuts, and short hours. In 1881 telegraphers organized by the Knights and employed by the newly created Western Union corporation struck for higher wages. When they were victorious, workers around the country became interested in the little-known organization. That same year the Knights sent a delegation to meet with Pope Leo, where it agreed to dispense with much of its secrecy in exchange for his issuing an encyclical encouraging American Catholics to join labor organizations. As the economy continued to grow in the early-mid 1880s, the membership of the Knights expanded rapidly. In addition to seeking wage increases, workers were increasingly motivated by the call for "the eight hour day," an issue championed by the Knights.

Into the 1880s the South was less industrialized than the North and had fewer factories and factory workers and fewer unions. The racial division of the southern workforce also mitigated against wide-scale labor organization. But in the mid-1880s the Knights exploded in the South, from Richmond's tobacco factories and iron mills to Alabama's coalfields and New Orleans' docks. The Knights gave voice to workers' frustrations and hopes. Its organizational framework of separate but equal locals insulated it, initially at least, from accusations by employers, politicians, and the media that it was, at heart, a stalking horse for "social equality." It was embraced by white and black workers alike. And when workers discovered that its tactics—strikes, boycotts, cooperatives, and even independent political action—could bring results, there seemed no stopping this labor organization.

Nowhere was the Knights of Labor more popular than in the former capital of the Confederacy, Richmond. Thousands of workers joined in 1885 and 1886, winning several strikes, initiating several cooperatives, and waging a boycott against flour barrels made by convict labor. In the spring of 1886, determined to build a new city hall with local materials, local labor, a union contract, union wages and the eight-hour day, and job opportunities for black workers, the Richmond Knights organized the Workingmen's Reform Party and swept control of the municipal government.

Months later, it hosted the national convention of the Knights of Labor, which brought thousands of labor activists to the city.

In the later 1880s, however, southern leaders of both the Republican and Democratic parties, with employers and newspaper editors, undermined the Knights. As the labor organization's power receded from politics, the workplace, and the wider community, black workers would be placed at the very bottom of the economic ladder, while white workers, though securely above their black counterparts, would earn wages well below those of their northern peers. The defeat of the Knights of Labor would leave a legacy detrimental to all southern workers.

PETER RACHLEFF
Macalester College

Leon Fink, *Workingmen's Democracy: The Knights of Labor and American Politics* (1985); Joseph Gerteis, *Class and the Color Line: Interracial Class Coalition in the Knights of Labor and the Populist Movement* (2007); Melton McLaurin, *The Knights of Labor in the South* (1978); Peter Rachleff, *Black Labor in Richmond, 1865–1890* (1989).

Ku Klux Klan and Other White Racist Organizations

Perhaps the most resonant representation of organized white racism in the United States, the Ku Klux Klan (KKK) refers not to a single organization but rather to a collection of groups bound by a common iconography and a militant and often violent adherence to white supremacy. The KKK's following has tended to rise and fall in cycles often referred to as "waves," the first of which occurred soon after the Civil War. A second wave peaked in the 1920s, with Klan membership numbering in the millions, and self-identified KKK groups also built sizable followings during the 1960s. Various incarnations have continued to mobilize since—often through blended affiliations with neo-Nazi, neo-Confederate, and Christian Identity organizations—but in small numbers and without significant impact on mainstream politics.

First formed in 1866 in Pulaski, Tenn., the Ku Klux Klan quickly evolved into a group that openly resisted the political, economic, and social changes associated with the postbellum Reconstruction era. With the significant support of Confederate veterans, and in concert with like-minded vigilante groups such as the Order of the Pale Faces and the Knights of the White Camellia, KKK chapters worked to consolidate support for white supremacy across the South, often through violent intimidation of black community leaders and the "carpetbaggers" and "scalawags" who supported them. Klan activity declined in the 1870s, in part owing to federal regulation of KKK violence. With the removal of Reconstruction reforms following the fall of Republican control in 1877 and the later emergence of Jim Crow–style racial segregation, the Klan largely disappeared.

Over the next three decades, occasional Klan-like groups such as the Red Shirts in South Carolina and the Mississippi Whitecaps drove black tenants off farmland and engaged in other acts of racial terror. The KKK itself, however, survived mostly in popular memory, bolstered by romanticized depictions of its first wave. The Atlanta premiere of D. W. Griffith's epic 1915 film *The Birth of a Nation*, which portrayed the Klansmen as heroic defenders of traditional southern values, provided occasion for a formal KKK revival. By the 1920s, with the nation beset by post–World War I nativist tendencies, along with racial and labor strife, an agricultural crisis, and the start of Prohibition, the Klan's focus on racial purity and patriotic "100 percent Americanism" resonated with many white Americans. Klan recruiters often successfully tailored the KKK's message to the concerns of local communities, framing the group as the solution to a variety of grievances shared by white Protestants who felt their economic and social capital weakening.

By the mid-1920s the KKK was a national force, with membership estimated at 3–5 million. Klan adherents came from both white- and blue-collar sectors and frequently included prominent community leaders. Scores of Klansmen were elected or appointed to local and state offices, and although vigilante violence still occurred, it was often subsumed by the group's populist civic character. Chapters often had ties to a range of fraternal and church groups and sometimes organized around issues such as law enforcement and good schools. These emphases have caused some historians to suggest that racism was not primary to the 1920s Klan, though the intersection of class and race issues in many localities aligned the KKK's civic efforts with its overarching white supremacist agenda.

The KKK began to lose momentum by the late 1920s, officially disbanding as a single organization in 1944. As civil rights activity intensified in the 1950s, at least eight self-styled Klan organizations competed for adherents across the South. Membership totaled more than 25,000 by the mid-1960s, with KKK groups thriving in areas marked by high levels of racial competition for jobs and political power. Unlike the second-wave KKK, professional workers rarely joined, with membership instead drawn primarily from small business owners and semiskilled blue-collar sectors.

The Klan was again in serious decline by the end of the 1960s, and the KKK and other white racist organizations have never again succeeded in building a mass following. Today, pockets of white supremacy can be found in many areas of the United States, with the Internet and "White Power" music scenes providing vehicles for global connections. Such groupings largely are sustained subculturally, through "hidden" social spaces where members build and maintain racist collective identities. While today's adherents tend to be diverse in terms of educational and economic background, the ideology that pervades white supremacist groups has retained a strong class character, often centered on conspiracy theories of racial threat to white hegemony.

DAVID CUNNINGHAM
Brandeis University

David Cunningham, *Klansville, U.S.A.: The Rise and Fall of the Civil Rights–Era's Largest KKK* (2012); Martin Durham, *White Rage: The Extreme Right and American Politics* (2007); Rory McVeigh, *The Rise of the Ku*

Klux Klan: Right-Wing Movements and National Politics (2009); Pete Simi and Robert Futrell, *American Swastika: Inside the White Power Movement's Hidden Spaces of Hate* (2010); Allen W. Trelease, *White Terror: The Ku Klux Klan Conspiracy and Southern Reconstruction* (1971).

Longshoremen

Tasked with loading and unloading the ships that connect the region to the rest of the world, longshoremen have historically occupied a special position in the economic, social, and political life of the South. In the eyes of many southerners, longshoremen were often viewed as untouchables characterized by strong backs and weak minds. Yet if the first of these characteristics was undoubtedly true, the same cannot be said for the second since longshoremen have long had to possess a great deal of skill and savvy in order to work safely. Furthermore, southern longshoremen's unions have proved to be among the most durable working-class organizations in a region defined by its antipathy toward labor.

In large part, the nature of the cargo handled by each port determined the stratification of the waterfront as well as the level of class consciousness exhibited by longshoremen. In some ports such as Baltimore, the multiplicity of goods passing through the city meant that no one group of workers dominated the docks; as such, it was often difficult to maintain a commonality of interest between longshoremen from different sectors. Elsewhere, however, dockworkers frequently rallied behind the leadership of those whose job it was to handle a single dominant product. In the region's largest ports—New Orleans and Galveston—it was a group known as cotton screwmen who were at the top of the waterfront hierarchy. Laboring with large jackscrews, these specialized longshoremen would compress and stow bales of cotton, often increasing shipping capacity by as much as 25 percent. Beginning in the 1860s, screwmen formed some of the first labor unions in the South in order to protect the high wages they commanded. Over time, these exclusionary craft unionists joined with organizations of less-skilled longshoremen in arrangements that often allowed dockworkers themselves to control the supply of labor on the waterfront. Under such circumstances, the otherwise despised longshoreman became a force to be reckoned with by employers and local leaders.

One of the most unique characteristics of southern longshoremen was the degree of racial cooperation that existed among them within most of the region's ports. Because the nature of longshore work was historically defined more by its dependence upon physical labor than skill, the southern waterfront served as a meeting place for African Americans, native whites, and immigrants. Under such circumstances, class solidarity frequently depended upon a certain level of understanding between the races. Although they studiously avoided challenging Jim Crow prohibitions against social equality, these groups did form a number of strong biracial union alliances in various southern ports as a means of countering economic exploitation during the late 19th and early 20th centuries. The most enduring example of this biracialism was to be found in New Orleans where black and white longshoremen's unions joined together to control working conditions on the city's docks for much of the period from 1879 to 1923. Similar arrangements, including work-sharing agreements designed to avoid racial competition, prevailed with varying degrees of success in other southern ports. This biracial economic power was so strong, in fact, that it even allowed many disenfranchised black dockworkers a say in the political process with slates of longshoremen-approved candidates controlling municipal government at various times in both New Orleans and Galveston. It was only when employers made a conscious effort to inflame racial hatred and undermine the longshoremen's unions that biracialism began to wane in the 1920s.

Although longshoremen still maintain a presence in southern ports, both their numbers and the power of their unions have been dramatically reduced in more recent years. Biracial waterfront unions continued to exist well into the 1960s and 1970s, but they were rarely capable of exercising the same type of cooperation and control that prevailed during earlier periods. Technology has also severely undermined the longshoremen's trade. Just as steam-powered cotton compresses made the skills of screwmen obsolete at the turn of the 20th century, the development of container ships after World War II fundamentally altered the nature of longshoring. What once required the muscle of thousands of longshoremen is today completed by much smaller numbers of specialized crane operators throughout the South.

JOSEPH ABEL
Rice University

Gregg Andrews, *Journal of Southern History* (August 2008); Eric Arnesen, *Waterfront Workers of New Orleans: Race, Class, and Politics, 1863-1923* (1991), in *Waterfront Workers: New Perspectives on Race and Class*, ed. Calvin Winslow (1998); Clifford Farrington, *Biracial Unions on Galveston's Waterfront, 1865-1925* (2007); Ernest Obadele-Starks, *Black Unionism in the Industrial South* (2000); Bruce Nelson, in *The CIO's Left-Led Unions*, ed. Steve Rosswurm (1992).

Lumber Workers

Lumber manufacturing employed more southerners than any other industry until the 1920s and rivaled textiles as the region's largest industrial employer into the 1950s. Lumber also employed more African Americans than any other industry, nationally, until the Second World War. The industry developed rapidly along the Atlantic and Gulf coasts and more slowly in Appalachia starting in the 1880s, spurred by the depletion of forests in the Northeast and Midwest and rising demand for lumber in housing construction. By 1930 nearly a quarter-million southerners worked in sawmill and logging operations, producing roughly one-third of all lumber consumed in the United States. Observing that historians have paid relatively little attention to the industry, Edward Ayers notes that "lumbering, more than any other industry captures the full scope of economic change in the

New South, its limitations as well as its impact."

One reason for the scholarly neglect of southern lumber workers was the chronic instability of the industry, caused by poor financing, unfavorable tax laws, and highly unsustainable "cut-out and get-out" logging practices. As a result, most southern workers viewed lumber employment as a temporary, often seasonal, source of cash that they used to supplement their primary income in farming. "I didn't know definitely at the time 'bout what the sawmills would bring me," recalled Alabama sharecropper Ned Cobb, noting that he took periodic sawmill jobs to meet specific financial needs such as paying for his wedding, buying a mule, or "to make a speck if I could and then go back to my farm." Employers often attributed such behavior to "shiftlessness" and lack of responsibility among their largely African American workforce, but it was a rational response to an industry that rarely remained in one location more than a few years. "Because the sawmills themselves were temporary, the work force was even more temporary and did not build up either the sense of self-identity or social visibility of the cotton mill people," writes historian Gavin Wright.

Lumber workers' reputation for "shiftlessness" persisted despite a move toward more sustainable logging practices and the development of more settled lumber towns in the 1920s and 1930s. Facing declining supplies of timber and a rising exodus of experienced lumber workers from the South, mill owners invested in tree farming, mechanical logging, and "welfare capitalist" strategies that were designed to stabilize their workforce. Ironically, while stability made lumber workers more visible to outside observers, it produced a large body of literature by Howard Odum, Zora Neale Hurston, and others who emphasized the transience of the industry's early years. Stability also facilitated the emergence of a small yet persistent union movement in the southern lumber industry, which had defeated organizing efforts in the 1880s and the 1910s. Although left-wing activists paid little attention to lumber unions during campaigns to organize southern textiles and mining in the 1930s, lumber workers were among the more enthusiastic supporters of southern organizing drives initiated by the Congress of Industrial Organizations during and shortly after the Second World War.

Despite the emergence of sizable lumber mill towns in the 1930s and 1940s, the industry declined rapidly in the postwar era. Sustainable logging practices failed to produce adequate timber supplies, forcing firms to shift toward pulp and paper production based on the use of young, fast-growing pine. Lumber companies also mechanized and, in many cases, closed to reduce their workforces and avoid negotiating with unions. The industry had nearly disappeared by the 1960s, eliminating the most important source of employment for southern men, particularly African Americans, in the early 20th-century South.

WILLIAM P. JONES
University of Wisconsin at Madison

Edward Ayers, *The Promise of the New South: Life after Reconstruction* (1992); William P. Jones, *The Tribe of Black Ulysses: African American Lumber Workers in the Jim Crow South* (2005); Gavin Wright, *Old South, New South: Revolutions in the Southern Economy since the Civil War* (1986).

Lumpkin, Grace

(1891–1980) WRITER AND ACTIVIST. Born in Milledgeville, Ga., to wealthy, conservative parents, Grace Lumpkin was an activist writer whose early works were well received by the Communist Party. Lumpkin's proletariat works include *To Make My Bread* (1932), *A Sign for Cain* (1935), *The Wedding* (1939), and *Full Circle* (1962). She grew up and resided in Georgia and South Carolina before moving to New York in the mid-1920s. Her first novel, *To Make My Bread*, is a tale of the hardships endured by Appalachian peoples and the social injustices they experienced. With this publication she found herself lauded by communists for her commentary on hardships in American culture during the Great Depression.

Initially a social realist and communist sympathizer, Lumpkin found herself increasingly distancing herself from ties she made with New York City literary circles after McCarthyism took hold. Her 10-year marriage to Mike Intrator also spurred her political backpedaling, as Intrator's standing with the party was questionable. After testifying to the U.S. Senate subcommittee, where she informed on her former communist associates, Grace returned to Columbia, S.C. There she fully embraced an anticommunist sentiment, which is revealed in the writings and speeches she produced until her death in 1980.

MISTY DAWN CARMICHAEL
Georgia State University

Barbara Foley, *Radical Representations: Politics and Form in U.S. Proletarian Fiction, 1929–1941* (1993); Jacquelyn Dowd Hall, *Journal of Southern History* (February 2003); Sherry Linkon and Bill Mullen, eds., *Radical Revisions: Rereading 1930s Culture* (1996).

Lumpkin, Katharine Du Pre

(1897–1988) WRITER AND ACTIVIST. Born on 22 December 1887 in Macon, Ga., to Annette and William Lumpkin, a Confederate Civil War veteran and lawyer, Katharine Du Pre Lumpkin grew up in a household that adamantly embraced the ideology of the Lost Cause. Her memoir, *The Making of a Southerner* (1946), portrays a southern tradition that she herself was very much a part of, and as such, it provides unique insights into the perspectives of white, southern, elite families, detailing the system of slavery, the hardships of the Civil War and Reconstruction, and the rationale behind Jim Crow from their point of view. After illustrating this mentality and how it affected her childhood, Lumpkin then describes how she, as an individual, came to question and then to ultimately reject the mythology of the Lost Cause, which served to buttress southern hierarchies of gender, race, and class.

In Richland County, S.C., where she and her family moved to farm when she was 11 years old, Lumpkin came into close contact with economically exploited working-class whites. Her contact in South Carolina with white poverty ignited what would later become her critical stance toward the ideology she was taught as a child. Additionally, her education played a large role in facilitating her thoughtful analysis of oppression in the South. From 1912 to 1915 Lumpkin attended Brenau College, in Gainesville, Ga., where she earned a bachelor's degree before attending Columbia University to study sociology. After earning a master's degree from Columbia, Lumpkin moved to the University of Wisconsin and earned a doctorate in economics in 1928. While receiving her postgraduate education outside of the region, Lumpkin periodically returned to the South, and for a time she worked as the national student secretary for the southern region of the YWCA, an interracial organization that further challenged many of the biases and taboos Lumpkin learned as a child.

After earning her doctorate, Lumpkin lived most of her adult life in the northeastern United States, and she taught economics and social science at several women's colleges, including Mount Holyoke and Smith. Much of her academic research and writing deals with labor issues and social reform, and Lumpkin herself spent periods of time working in mills and factories in order to inform this research. She used her position as a social scientist to argue against white supremacy, the devalued status of women, and economic exploitation in the United States.

Lumpkin's memoir, *The Making of a Southerner*, remains an essential work for anyone seeking to understand the ways in which white supremacy was justified and accepted by elite white southerners as well as the roles white women played in this process. As such, her memoir is often compared to Lillian Smith's *Killers of the Dream* as it not only provides insight into this process but also details the difficulties of rejecting an ideology that was so thoroughly ingrained.

AMY SCHMIDT
University of Mississippi

Darlene Clark Hine, Forward to Katharine Du Pre Lumpkin, *The Making of a Southerner* (1991); Fred Hobson, *But Now I See: The White Southern Racial Conversion Narrative* (1999); Carolyn Perry and Mary Louise Weaks, eds., *The History of Southern Women's Literature* (2002).

Mardi Gras

The celebration of Mardi Gras along the central Gulf Coast portions of Louisiana, Mississippi, and Alabama marks the region's historical and cultural difference from the rest of the South. Mardi Gras ("Fat Tuesday"), or Carnival ("fleshly excess"), is celebrated with costumed float parades, neighborhood marches, informal parties, and formal balls in New Orleans, Biloxi, and Mobile among other Gulf Coast cities. In contrast, a rural Louisiana Cajun and black Creole *courir de Mardi Gras* or Mardi Gras run is carried out by horseback-mounted revelers in over a dozen French-speaking communities of southwest Louisiana.

Mardi Gras is historically associated with French and Spanish populations along the Gulf Coast. How-

Order of Myths, Mobile's first and oldest Mardi Gras society, Mobile, Ala., February 2010 (Carol M. Highsmith, photographer, Library of Congress [LC-DIG-highsm-05309], Washington, D.C.)

ever, many ethnic groups now join in the traditional festive occasion, which falls in February or March prior to Ash Wednesday and 40 days before Easter. It has been speculated that the Mediterranean-Latin roots of Mardi Gras are to be found in the pre-Roman rites of spring and later Roman festival or ritual occasions such as Bacchanalia, Lupercalia, and Saturnalia. Over time such occasions became part of the Catholic liturgical calendar. Thus, the Gulf Coast Carnival season officially begins on 6 January, the Epiphany and Feast of Kings. On this date in New Orleans "King Cakes"—with a plastic miniature baby (representing the Baby Jesus) inside each and adorned in Mardi Gras colors of gold, purple, and green—are consumed in celebration. The season may be as short as three and a half weeks or as long as two months, depending upon the date of Easter. The culmination of Carnival is Mardi Gras day or Shrove Tuesday (referring to a time to be "shriven of one's sins"). The festive eating, dancing, and drinking associated with Mardi Gras are followed by the relative austerity and penitence of the Lenten period.

Just as Roman Catholicism absorbed earlier pre–Roman Carnival elements, so too the worldwide variations on Carnival now reflect regional cultural diversity. Thus, Gulf Coast Carnival, like Carnival in related societies of the Caribbean and Latin America, represents a syncretism of French/Spanish, Native American, and African/Afro-Caribbean performance styles and structures. That the earliest European settlers of the Gulf Coast celebrated Mardi Gras is verified by the explorer D'Iberville's naming of Mardi Gras

Bayou along the Mississippi in southern Louisiana. Informal parades and festive masquerades are reported to have occurred in major centers such as Mobile and New Orleans throughout the early 19th century, and by midcentury (1857 in New Orleans) officially sanctioned parades began.

The early public parades in New Orleans and Mobile were founded by the Anglo and Creole (French/Spanish) elites of both cities. In New Orleans such "krewes" as Comus, Momus, Proteus, and Rex continue from the 19th century into the present. Some krewes still utilize smaller antique floats depicting mythological scenes crafted in papier-mâché. These floats were originally drawn by mules, which were eventually replaced by tractors in the 1950s. The artwork found on newer floats is made of plastic.

Today as many as 60 different krewes parade in the roughly two-week period prior to and including Mardi Gras day. Some, such as Arabi and Argus, are quite recent and represent suburban neighborhoods. All parades throw doubloons (introduced in the early 1960s) and other plastic trinkets to the crowds that line such primary parade routes as St. Charles Avenue and Canal Street. The varied krewes both reflect and invert the social structure of New Orleans on a day when the upper classes play at being kings, fools, and mythological beings. Suburban middle classes may likewise assert their right to be royalty for a day. Elite old-line krewes maintain an aura of secrecy about the selection of their royalty and invitation to their balls and affiliated social events. The newer krewes such as Bacchus, on the other hand, charge admission to their open gatherings in the Superdome and elsewhere at the end of parades.

The Zulu parade of New Orleans's black middle-class and elite community, founded in 1909 as a reaction to white stereotypes of blacks as "savages," is a Carnival activity rivaled only by the Rex Parade on Mardi Gras day. Zulu members dress in grass skirts and "wooley wigs," put on blackface, and throw rubber spears and decorated coconuts to the delighted crowds. Working-class blacks, particularly those of Creole (French/Spanish) ancestry, also invoke white stereotypes of "wildness" by masquerading pridefully in stylized Plains Indians costumes.

The black "Mardi Gras Indians" are hierarchical groups of men with titles such as Big Chief, Spyboy, Wildman, and Lil' Chief who dress in elaborate bead and feather costumes weighing up to 100 pounds. After months of time and money invested in sewing costumes and practice sessions at local bars, a dozen or more "tribes" appear early on Mardi Gras day to sing, dance, and parade through back street neighborhoods. Some of these black Indians, with "tribe" names such as "Creole Wild West," "White Cloud Hunters," "Yellow Pocahontas," and "Wild Tchoupitoulas," do in fact have partial Native American ancestry and speak in mythological fashion about Indian spirits and customs. Their performance style, however, is essentially Afro-Caribbean, as expressed in competitive dance and song and the call-and-response chants that mark their foot parades. These chants are often based on a secret code language consisting of a group leader's call and responses such as "Hey pocky way" and "Ja ca mo feen non nay." They also use standard tunes such as "Lil' Liza Jane" and "Shoo Fly" to improvise tales of their daring and exploits as they "go to town" on Mardi Gras day.

While the Mardi Gras Indians and the Zulu parade utilize Mardi Gras to make statements about group pride through inverted stereotypes of Indian and African tribes, many blacks also work at the service of whites on Carnival, thereby reflecting the postcolonial social structure of New Orleans. Some, for example, lead horses for major white parades such as Rex and Momus. Others dress in pointed white hood and cloaks and carry torches called "flambeaux" that light the way for night parades of old elite krewes such as Comus.

Although smaller in scale and less widely known than New Orleans Carnival, Mardi Gras in Mobile has been celebrated in various ways since the beginning of the 19th century. The Cowbellions, an early parading group using cowbells and other noisemakers, formed in the 1830s and later ordered its costumes from Paris. During the Civil War, Mobile's public Mardi Gras ceased. It was revived in 1866 by a veteran named Joe Cain, who dressed that year as a mock Chickasaw Indian chief called "Slacabamorinico" and drove through the then-occupied city in a decorated wagon. On Sunday before the Mobile Carnival, Joe Cain is now commemorated with a jazz funeral procession. Various other Mobile krewes such as the Comic Cowboys and the Infant Mystics date to the 19th century. The Order of Myths, the oldest krewe (1867), was modeled after the early Cowbellions. The symbol of the Order of Myths, which is the last krewe to parade on Mardi Gras, is Folly chasing Death around a broken neoclassical column and flailing him with a golden pig bladder. Although this imagery symbolizes a general Mardi Gras theme of mirth's triumph over gloom, some suggest that the broken column originally alluded to the broken dreams of the Confederacy.

The large float parades in the Mardi Gras celebrations of Mobile and New Orleans represent Mediterranean and Caribbean traditions. In contrast, the Cajun and black Creole *courir de Mardi Gras* of rural southwest Louisiana reflects country French traditions brought by Acadians of Nova Scotia who came to Louisiana in the latter part of the 18th century. In a manner not unlike Christmas mumming in Europe and the West Indies, a band of masked male revelers goes from house to house on the open prairie land of southwest Louisiana. The men, on horses or flatbed trucks, dress as clowns, thieves, women, and devils. Some wear the traditional pointed capuchon hats with bells and streamers. The group is led by a capitaine who may wear an elegant silk costume in the Cajun bands or simple work clothes in some black Creole Mardi Gras bands. The Mardi Gras bands come as quasi vigilantes and clowns in search of charity, in the form of live chickens, rice, spices, grease, sausages, and other ingredients for a gumbo supper. The capitaine, standing apart from the group as a keeper of the law, tries to prevent the men from getting too disorderly or drunk and sees that they carry out their agreed-upon rounds for the day. At each visited farmstead, the capitaine or a flagman will visit ahead of the band to see if the household will receive the Mardi Gras. There is usually an affirmative response to the courtly request, *Voulez-vous recevoir cette band des Mardi Gras?* (Do you want to receive the Mardi Gras band?), whereupon the clowns are waved on to charge the house on horseback. After dismounting and dancing together (which men do only on Mardi Gras), a competitive chase is often held for a live chicken. (This chase is usually preceded by a song of request to the man or lady of the house.) The chicken chase involves a designated bird, or one tossed into the air, and is a hilarious spectacle as men in costume pursue elusive birds through the muddy rice fields of early spring, leaping fences and crossing pigsties. After a chicken is caught, it is killed and put with other spoils in a sack, which is sent back to town where the cooking begins at midday. As the Mardi Gras runners depart a house, they sing a word of thanks and invite the householders to the dance and communal supper to be held in town or at a rural club late in the night.

By the end of the afternoon the band heads back toward "the hub" or its starting point in rice- and soybean-growing and cattle-raising towns such as Mamou, Church Point, L'Anse Maigre, and Swords. The riders on horseback may enter at a gallop. Those who are sober enough entertain waiting crowds with stunts and various acts of bravado. The gumbo from the day's catch is served to the riders and the general public followed by a large dance ending at midnight and the beginning of the Lenten season.

The parallel black Creole Mardi Gras bands are often located near the Cajun towns in tiny rural settlements established in the 19th century by manumitted slaves and other people of color. The black Creole Mardi Gras celebrations are usually smaller (10 to 20 men), more intimate, and more traditional than today's Cajun courirs. The cowboy style of Cajun Mardi Gras has not taken hold in the black Creole community. For example, the black bands take great care not to trample house gardens or urinate in public while pursuing the fowl. Elders are helped down from their flatbed trucks by younger men, and the bands present themselves more as polite beggars than as vigilantes. The older Creoles especially take great stock in such details and are critical of young men who do not behave or sing properly. The Creole Mardi Gras song is similar to that of the Cajuns but is often performed in a call-response manner showing Afro-Caribbean influences. The usual response line to the leader's song is *Ouais mon / bon cher camarade* (Yes my / good dear friend).

While old traditions and Carnival groups continue, in recent years new Mardi Gras events and locales have emerged to meet new social concerns and issues. For example, in New Orleans gay krewes and their French Quarter costume contests have become highly visible. In New Orleans and Baton Rouge, the Krewe of Clones and the

Spanishtown Mardi Gras respectively have become avant-garde satires on Carnival itself and on Louisiana topics such as politics and pollution. Suburban Mardi Gras celebrations have sprung up with children included and excessive drunkenness or sexual suggestiveness excluded. Adjacent Anglo-American regions have also started Mardi Gras celebrations. Monroe, La., for example, held its first parade in 1985, and the celebration was criticized by local fundamentalist preachers as "devil worship."

Films such as *Always for Pleasure* (Les Blank, director, Flower Films, 1978) and *Fat Tuesday* (Armand Ruhlman, director, Goofy Gator productions, 1981) offer rich visual documentation of Mardi Gras. Whatever locale and shape Mardi Gras takes in the Gulf Coast region, it will continue to reflect the historical and contemporary cultural traditions of its celebrants.

NICHOLAS R. SPITZER
Smithsonian Institution

Always for Pleasure (Les Blank, producer, Flower Films, El Cerrito, Calif., 1978); Erwin Craighead, in *Mobile: Fact and Tradition* (1930); Munro Edmunson, *Caribbean Quarterly* (no. 3, 1956); Arthur La Cour and Stuart Landry, *New Orleans Masquerade: Chronicles of Carnival* (1952); Rosary H. O'Brien, "The New Orleans Carnival Organizations: Theatre of Prestige" (Ph.D. dissertation, University of California at Berkeley, 1973); Harry Oster and Revon Reed, *Louisiana Folklore Miscellany* (no. 1, 1960); Phyllis H. Rabbe, "Status and Its Impact: New Orleans Carnival, The Social Upper Class and Upper Class Power" (Ph.D. dissertation, Pennsylvania State University, 1973); Michael P. Smith, *Spirit World: Pattern in the Expressive Folk Culture of Afro-American New Orleans* (1984); Nicholas R. Spitzer, "Zydeco and Mardi Gras: Creole Identity and Performance Genres in Rural French Louisiana" (Ph.D. dissertation, University of Texas, 1986); Robert Tallant, *Mardi Gras* (1949); Calvin Trillin, *New Yorker* (20 June 1964); Perry Young, *The Mystick Krewe: Chronicles of Comus and His Kin* (1931).

Mason, Lucy Randolph
(1882–1959) ACTIVIST.

Lucy Randolph Mason was one of the leading labor organizers and civil rights activists of her generation. Born in Virginia in 1882, a descendant of statesman George Mason, Mason followed in her famous forebear's footsteps to guarantee racial equality, workers' rights, and union participation in the South. Mason's work for social justice began as a women's suffrage volunteer and then as an employee of the Richmond YWCA, where she focused on economic opportunity for African Americans and workers' rights and fair labor practices, leading to the publication of her book, *Standards for Workers in Southern Industry*, in 1931. She later served as general secretary of the influential National Consumers League, which helped enact the 1938 Fair Labor Standards Act. In 1932 John L. Lewis hired her as a public relations representative for the Congress of Industrial Organizations (CIO) in the South. During her 16-year tenure with the CIO, Mason was able to organize and promote unionism in dangerous environments. Armed with an unyielding and forthright manner, a reputation as a genteel southern woman, and an understanding of federal labor laws,

Mason negotiated successfully with hostile politicians, ministers, and law officers. Until her retirement in 1951, Mason endeavored to register black and white voters in the South and to unite interracial religious and labor organizations. She died in 1959.

ROXANNE NEWTON
Mitchell Community College

John A. Salmond, *Miss Lucy of the CIO: The Life and Times of Lucy Randolph Mason* (1988).

Memory, Appalachian

Memory connects us to the past. It is not a mirror of past events, but rather a process by which we make sense of what has happened in order to understand the present and plan the future. Memory is central to the construction of personal and social identities, including those based upon class, nation, and region. Because their occupational roles and social positions vary, social classes draw upon different experiences to construct memories. Also, class influences whether specific memories are accepted as useful representations of the past. Elites in Appalachia are more likely to be educated and hold positions of authority, and, as a result, they exercise greater control over the process of writing history and shaping official stories of the past. They are disproportionately interviewed by the media and memorialized by their communities. Elites also write memoirs, newspaper columns, and local histories. They produce and direct history pageants, participate in the local history and genealogical societies, and play key roles in the design, funding, and construction of memorials, museums, and heritage sites.

Although the struggle of "memory over forgetting" generally favors the elite, there are nevertheless organizations that document the memories of farmers, low-income, working-class and middle-class people in the region. These include Appalshop, an arts and cultural cooperative in Whitesburg, Ky.; oral history and archival programs at regional community colleges, liberal arts colleges, and universities; and journals, blogs, newsletters, and magazines, including *Now & Then*, *Appalachian Voices*, *Appalachian Journal*, *Appalachian Heritage*, *Goldenseal*, and the *Journal of Appalachian Studies*.

Documentary filmmakers, also, have focused on nonelite Appalachians, a tendency that sometimes causes controversy within the region. Critics complain that the media's selective focus on poverty results in stereotypical depictions of the region's residents as poor, violent, and psychologically troubled. Nevertheless, filmmakers have produced thought-provoking records of nonelite life in Appalachia, including *Harlan County, U.S.A.* (1976), *American Hollow* (1999), and *Country Boys* (2006).

Within the region, Appalshop has created documentaries of Appalachian folk medicine, furniture making, musicians, and other arts and crafts as well as critical examinations of community identity, power, and values, such as *Beyond Measure: Appalachian Culture and Economy* (1994), *Justice in the Coalfields* (1995), and *Stranger with a Camera* (2000).

In addition, Appalachian workers have used story and song to preserve memories for future generations. One of America's most famous folksongs concerns John Henry, an African American railroad worker who died while competing with a steam drill. This folk hero, based upon a convict laborer in Appalachia, has functioned as a symbol of working-class masculinity, labor radicalism, and American multiculturalism. Other songs about workers in Appalachia have also become well known beyond the region. Examples include "Dark as a Dungeon," "Sixteen Tons," "Which Side Are You On?," "Black Waters," "You'll Never Leave Harlan Alive," and "The L&N Don't Stop Here Anymore."

Memorialization of labor unionization conflict in Appalachia demonstrates the complex relationship between class and memory. At Blair Mountain, W.Va., in 1921, striking miners fought company-hired guards in the second largest armed struggle on U.S. soil. Antiunion Massey Energy, corporate sponsor of a memorial to these events, is currently bidding to strip-mine Blair Mountain in opposition to a coalition of archaeologists, citizens, and union miners who seek to place the site on the National Register of Historic Places.

Harlan County, Ky., engaged in bloody unionization struggles in the 1930s, a conflict that was documented by a committee led by Theodore Dreiser in *Harlan Miners Speak*. However, many people in the county, including miners, ignore and downplay this chapter of local history. Harlan folksinger Sarah Ogan Gunning's "I Hate the Capitalist System" provides a different account, even as this period fades from local memory.

In 1985–86, in Harlan County, social class played an important role in the construction and eventual reconstruction of a memorial to workers killed while mining coal. In the initial construction of the monument, its middle- and working-class proponents successfully negotiated elite opposition from a prominent coal-mining family by enlisting the aid of a rival elite family. However, in later years, local government leaders replaced the original monument with a design that reflected their own aesthetic tastes and political interests.

In another part of Appalachia (Ashe County, N.C.), local opponents of a dam project used music, a local festival modeled after family reunion traditions, and a local history pageant to solidify opposition to the construction of a dam on the New River. The local pageant, written by a local teacher and historian, built alliances across class lines and helped a conflicted community counter the bureaucratic and technical arguments supporting the dam.

Social class, community, and region structure memory in complicated ways in Appalachia. Yet, as in every region, the struggle to understand the meaning of the past and how best to commemorate it is of political and cultural importance in Appalachia.

SHAUNNA L. SCOTT
University of Kentucky

W. Fitzhugh Brundage, *The Southern Past: A Clash of Race and Memory* (2005); Richard Couto, in *Fighting Back in Appalachia: Traditions of Resistance and Change*, ed. Stephen Fisher (1993); Theodore Dreiser, *Harlan Miners Speak: A Report on Terrorism in the Kentucky Coalfields* (1932); William D. Forester, *Harlan County: The Turbulent Thirties* (1986); Stephen William Foster, *Past Is Another Country: Representation, Historical Consciousness, and Resistance in the Blue Ridge* (1988); Scott Reynolds Nelson, *Steel-Drivin' Man: The Untold Story of an American Legend* (2006); Alessandro Portelli, *The Death of Luigi Trastulli and Other Stories: Form and Meaning in Oral Histories* (1991); Shaunna L. Scott, *Two Sides to Everything: The Cultural Construction of Class Consciousness in Harlan County, Kentucky* (1995); Jay Winter, *Remembering War: The Great War between Memory and History in the Twentieth Century* (2006); Jack Wright, *Music of Coal: Mining Songs of the Appalachian Coalfields* (2007).

Migrant Workers

Migrant workers for agriculture, forestry, and fisheries emerged as distinct social classes during the period following the Civil War, when migrant crews seasonally supplemented the work of sharecroppers, tenant farmers, and debt peons. During the first decades of the 20th century, the demand for migrant workers grew with the increase in fruit and vegetable production along the eastern seaboard to supply urban markets, resulting in the development of southern- and Caribbean-based crews of African Americans, Mexican Americans, and Puerto Ricans. African Americans and Puerto Ricans, based primarily in Florida and Puerto Rico, supplied labor to farms, forests, and seafood plants as far north as Maine, whereas Mexican Americans, based in south Texas, supplied labor across the Midwest and Great Plains. World War II drew many of these migrant workers out of agriculture, forestry, and fisheries and into the defense industry, stimulating the U.S. federal government to develop a class of migrant workers that could supply wartime food needs. By constructing labor camps and sculpting guest worker programs to access foreign labor, federal officials assisted with recruiting and transporting migrant labor. Following the war, the U.S. government relinquished control of the migrant labor supply to grower associations and labor contractors.

Southern migrant labor began shifting from primarily domestic to primarily international supply regions during the 1960s and 1970s, creating an underclass of largely undocumented migrant workers from Mexico and Central America that continues today. Within the migrant labor force, upward mobility is limited to workers who can become labor contractors or supervisors, and the majority remains confined to class positions that provide relatively low annual incomes. Thirty percent of all farm workers have family incomes below federally established poverty levels. When undocumented, paid by the piece rather than hourly, and working for labor contractors rather than directly for companies, migrant labor's relationship to capital has been stripped of worker protections in the form of guaranteed minimum wages, unemployment insurance, and health and safety standards. These conditions lead to high annual labor turnover rates, with 16 percent of all those surveyed in the National Agricultural Worker Survey reporting that they plan to work in agriculture for fewer than two or three years. High labor turnover has also led many southern employers of seasonal workers to embrace guest worker programs. From 1943 to 1992 Florida sugar producers brought more than 8,000 workers from the Caribbean annually, and today mid-Atlantic tobacco growers, forestry companies, and seafood processors utilize several thousand guest workers from Mexico under temporary contracts.

In response to conditions of economic hardship facing migrant workers, several federal programs and networks of advocacy organizations have developed to provide migrant workers with legal services, food and medical assistance, education, job training, and other services. For many years, these organizations acted on behalf of migrant workers in lieu of collective bargaining. In North Carolina the Farm Labor Organizing Committee, after a prolonged boycott of Mt. Olive Pickles, signed a union agreement with the North Carolina Growers' Association, while the Coalition of Immokalee Workers forced a piece rate increase in Florida's tomato fields by organizing farm workers and boycotting Taco Bell and other large buyers of Florida tomatoes. Similar collective bargaining successes have not been achieved by migrant forestry or seafood workers, most of whom are temporary foreign guest workers carrying H-2B visas.

Migrant workers have occupied the lowest strata of the southern working class since the end of the Civil War. Every year, as migrant crew buses arrive throughout the South and as workers crowd into low-quality labor camps and other temporary housing, local newspapers print exposés about conditions in the fields, factories, forests, and labor camps and life on the road. Popular and scholarly books and documentaries, focusing on the plights of migrant workers, often lead to congressional investigations. Presidential commissions on migrant labor have been established to hold public hearings, fund research, and present information about the lives of migrant workers. No such efforts, unfortunately, have improved the lot of the migrant.

DAVID GRIFFITH
East Carolina University

Pete Daniel, *In the Shadow of Slavery: Debt Peonage in the U.S. South* (1972); David Griffith, *American Guestworkers: Jamaicans and Mexicans in the U.S. Labor Market* (2006); David Griffith and Ed Kissam, with Jeronimo Camposeco, Anna Garcia, Max Pfeffer, David Runsten, and Manuel Valdés Pizzini, *Working Poor: Farmworkers in the United States* (1995); Cindy Hahamovitch, *The Fruits of Their Labor: Atlantic Coast Farmworkers and the Making of Migrant Poverty, 1870-1945* (1997); U.S. Department of Labor, National Agricultural Worker Survey, Research Report 9 (2005).

Military Academies

Private and state military academies provided nonelite southerners with nearly 100 opportunities for secondary education in the antebellum South. Between 1840 and 1860, military schools educated more than 11,000 southern young men. These institutions offered a curriculum based around modern languages, mathematics, and the sciences rather than the classics, which antebellum universities stressed. This curriculum allowed young men to peruse the more economically practical vocational schooling. Fathers with professional careers utilized these schools to help ensure that their sons entered professional and white-collar occupations and to achieve social stability. Thus, military schools provided one avenue for the development and propagation of an emerging middle class in the Old South.

The United States Military Academy at West Point began educating Americans in 1802, and reform in the early 19th century created one of the new nation's best engineering schools. It enrolled young men from across the nation to serve in the U.S. Army, guaranteeing a federally funded education and years of employment, if not a career. Historians have debated whether southerners found particular resonance at West Point, but it is clear that the first state-funded military schools in the country appeared in the South. These schools had no connection to the armed forces, and only 5 percent of their matriculates entered military service before the Civil War. The Virginia Military Institute (VMI), created by the state legislature, opened in Lexington in 1839 and served as the model for many of the subsequent state institutions. The South Carolina Military Academy followed in 1842 with the Citadel in Charleston and the Arsenal in Columbia. Before the outbreak of Civil War in 1861, 12 southern states funded military academies or instituted cadet corps at their state universities. The list includes Kentucky in 1845, Arkansas in 1850, Georgia in 1851, Texas in 1854, and Delaware, Florida, Louisiana, and North Carolina in 1859.

In addition, more than 70 private schools adopted military cadet corps, although these schools offered a variety of curricula. Military schools often named themselves academies or institutes, terminology that represented a level of school anywhere from a grammar school to a university. Former West Point superintendent Alden Partridge founded the first private military school, and many of his New England school's early graduates moved below the Mason-Dixon Line to found other private literary and scientific military schools, including schools in St. Louis, Mo.; Raleigh, N.C.; and Portsmouth, Va. As the number of schools rose, their graduates opened at least 18 additional private military academies, including Kings Mountain Military Academy in Yorkville, S.C.

The elite nature of antebellum colleges and universities has been much explored, and southern state universities, epitomized by South Carolina College, remained bastions of the elite even after northern schools underwent democratic changes. Southern universities almost always required classical languages for entrance and throughout the degree program. In contrast, military schools represented a national movement for what was then called "practical education." Reformers called for schooling with vocational courses, such as bookkeeping, and with subjects that did not rely on years of tutoring, such as English. An increase in science offerings occurred nationwide (and part of schooling was even for both sexes). The growth of military education thus reflected both curricular reform and the expansion of schooling in the South and West that marked the era. Early and mid-19th-century educational changes not only created different courses and multiple types of institutions but also encouraged young men from the social and economic ranks below the elite to pursue secondary and higher education.

The private and state military academies of the antebellum South facilitated the development and perpetuation of a nascent middle class. Without a Marxist bourgeoisie, identifying a middle class in the pre–Civil War years must, by necessity, focus on men in the middle social and economic ranks. Examining the occupations of the schools' matriculates and families makes apparent their social class position as members of the emerging southern middle class. The developing class consisted of nonmanual workers in both entrepreneurial and managerial positions, including professionals. For the most part, although not exclusively, men worked and, perhaps more importantly, found their primary identification in nonagricultural occupations. In the largest survey of military school alumni, Jennifer R. Green found that 75 percent of the 368 fathers for whom occupational data are available reached their highest status in the professions and white-collar careers (ranging from attorneys, physicians, and clergy to clerks and bookkeepers). Military education maintained the social position in the middle rank as 78.9 percent of 744 cadets found their highest status in a professional or white-collar career. This labor and mobility pattern set alumni and the class apart from elite planters, yeomen, and plain folk.

In particular, military school students received more training for careers in education and engineering than young men in nonmilitary programs. They entered those two careers at greater rates than southern state university graduates. Indeed, more than one-quarter of all military academy alumni became teachers. Twelve percent of them worked as engineers or for the railroads, whereas less than 3 percent of their southern university educated peers did so.

As with any educational institution, military schools proved an environment where youth grow into men. At the schools, young men of similar social class formed personal connections that led to lifelong associations and networks. Superintendents consciously sought open positions in which to place their graduates, especially as teachers in the newly professionalizing career. Frances H. Smith of VMI, the best example of this networking, aided alumni teachers and military education into the 1880s. Alumni hired each other at their schools, and teachers contacted their alma maters for replacements when they left positions, ensuring employment for like-educated men. Furthermore, graduates joined associations, such as the Masons, to continue to cement bonds of affinity and class.

The group that selected military academies illustrates the development of the national and regional middle class with shared traits and values. Although a military school could have been chosen for military proclivity or location, limited resources, both monetary and social capital, appear to have been an equal or greater influence. Weber directs scholars to an analysis of social class based on access to and use of resources and lifestyle and cultural choices. Across the nation, the 19th-century middle class began stressing education and specialized knowledge in the learned professions to create social status for its members. Receiving similar educations and coming from similar backgrounds, it is unsurprising that southern cadets exhibited similar cultural values. They reflected a developing nonelite manhood alternative to, although not challenging to, traditional southern honor. They stressed self-discipline and industry, as did increasing portions of southern society and the northern middle class. They likewise accepted a southern Christian respectability that included mastery of themselves.

Much scholarship on southern military academies has focused on the production of soldiers for the Civil War or on their militarism. In part this trend reflects the major alterations that the institutions underwent after the war. Military academies ceased to fulfill the same class-centered role in education as they had prior to 1865. The Morrill Land Grant Act of 1862 provided for the creation of numerous state universities with military programs, such as Texas A&M. Private schools, including Virginia's Fishburne Military School, opened in the late 19th century and operated at the K–12 level. Public school systems and uniform curricula made insignificant military academies' particular emphasis on mathematics, for example, and created increased competition. The schools have diversified their student bodies, increasing African American, foreign, and female enrollment as the 20th century advanced. Cadets at state military colleges have profited by offering the Reserve Officers Training Corps, which permits officer entry into U.S. military service. Since 1997, VMI and the Citadel have been in the news not for social class concerns but for gender discrimination. They accepted coeducation to continue to receive state funding. Current cadets stress cultural and familial reasons for attendance, and studies of 20th- and 21st-century social class at military schools still need to be done.

JENNIFER R. GREEN
Central Michigan University

Bruce Allardice, *Civil War History* (December 1997); Rod Andrew Jr., *Long Gray Lines: The Southern Military School Tradition, 1839–1915* (2001); Peter S. Carmichael, *The Last Generation: Young Virginians in Peace, War, and Reunion* (2005); Jennifer R. Green, *Military Education and the Emerging Middle Class in the Old South* (2008); Lynwood M. Holland, *Georgia Historical Quarterly* (September 1959); Alexander Macaulay, *Marching in Step: Masculinity, Citizenship, and The Citadel in Post–World War II America* (2009);

A group of spinners, doffers, and others during the noon hour at the Riverside Cotton Mills, Danville, Va., 1911. Some here are surely under fourteen, but not many. (Lewis Wickes Hine, photographer, Library of Congress [LC-USZ62-77035] Washington, D.C.)

Robert F. Pace, *Halls of Honor: College Men in the Old South* (2004); Stephen A. Ross, *North Carolina Historical Review* (January 2002).

Mine, Mill, and Smelter Workers

Beginning in the 1960s, works such as F. Ray Marshall's *Labor in the South* began to analyze the development of organized labor movements throughout the southern states. Marshall argued that the protracted defense of slavery and late start in the industrialization process created a distinctly southern biracial working class that slowly transformed the region to resemble northern industrial zones. Though fewer in number, southern labor activists waged numerous, though often futile, attempts to improve wages and working conditions. Collected works such as Marc S. Miller's *Working Lives: The Southern Exposure History of Labor in the South* and Merl E. Reed's *Southern Workers and Their Unions, 1880–1975* provide detailed accounts of strikes in Birmingham steel works, Cumberland cloth mills, and Appalachian mining camps, plus a host of other industries that had emerged since the end of the Civil War.

The strikes often followed similar patterns, with factory owners or supervisors extracting a maximum amount of work from laborers while providing minimal salaries and often-dangerous working conditions. Throughout the first half of the 20th century, low wages relegated most workers to the brink of poverty as they languished without political representation in unincorporated company towns. When workers demanded changes, they encountered an entrenched class of factory owners who despised unions and went to great lengths to ensure that their employees did not organize collectively. They fired anyone attending a union meeting, blacklisted organizers, and removed disenchanted workers from company housing. Once a strike broke out, local police, special security guards, the military, or Ku Klux Klan members often attacked the discontented laborers, forcing them back into the desperate conditions that sparked the work stoppage in the first place.

John A. Salmond's *Southern Struggles: The Southern Labor Movement and the Civil Rights Struggle* examines three strikes that occurred in the Carolinas. Salmond's work compared early 20th-century white struggles to achieve economic and social justice with later African American movements that strove for racial equality. He concluded that unions provided a limited medium for integration as prejudices among workers prevented them from working effectively together to initiate reform. In *Gastonia, 1929: The Story of the Loray Mill Strike*, Salmond provides an insightful narrative of the violence surrounding one of the most contentious strikes to occur in the South. The book recounts local opposition to the communist-led National Textile Workers Union, under the leadership of Fred Beal, who organized the mill workers. The ensuing strike included gunfights along with murder trials for both workers and deputies.

Robert Shogan's *The Battle of Blair Mountain: The Story of America's Largest Labor Uprising*, another narrative, chronicles the United Mine Workers attempts to unionize the West Virginia coal fields. Miners fought special deputies, soldiers, and the Army Air Service. The combination of brute force and aerial bombardment crushed the union, which only deepened the acrimony between southern industry and organized labor.

Stories of individuals organizing the strikes can be found in David Lee McMullen's *Strike: The Radical Insurrections of Ellen Dawson*, Mary Harris Jones's *Autobiography of Mother Jones*, and Melvyn Dubofsky and Warren Van Tine's *John L. Lewis: A Biography*. Each provides details of union activities, insights on motivating and controlling angry workers, along with negotiations with company officials. Unions such as the Industrial Workers of the World, Knights of Labor, American Federation of Labor, Congress of Industrial Organizations, United Auto Workers, Ladies' Garment Workers, and United Tobacco Workers also have numerous books and articles recounting unionization struggles and strike activities of their members.

PAUL LUBOTINA
Middle Tennessee State University

Melvyn Dubofsky and Warren Van Tine, *John L. Lewis: A Biography* (1986); Mary Harris Jones, *Autobiography of Mother Jones* (2004); F. Ray Marshall, *Labor in the South* (1967); David Lee McMullen, *Strike: The Radical Insurrections of Ellen Dawson* (2010); Marc S. Miller, ed., *Working Lives: The Southern Exposure History of Labor in the South* (1980); Merl E. Reed, Leslie S. Hough, and Gary M. Fink, eds., *Southern Workers and Their Unions, 1880–1975* (1978);

John Salmond, *Gastonia, 1929: The Story of the Loray Mill Strike* (1995), *Southern Struggles: The Southern Labor Movement and the Civil Rights Struggle* (2004); Robert Shogan, *The Battle of Blair Mountain: The Story of America's Largest Labor Uprising* (2004).

Mitchell, H. L.

(1906–1989) UNION ACTIVIST. Harry Leland Mitchell was a union activist and one of the founders of the interracial Southern Tenant Farmers Union (STFU). He grew up in Halls, Tenn., not far from the Mississippi River. At age 11, Mitchell witnessed an angry mob burn a black man accused of raping a white woman. A few years later, he heard a socialist speech about uniting the masses for better wages and a better way of life. Those two events helped shape Mitchell's lifelong interest in unionization, racial and social equality, and the elimination of class structure in the South.

After graduating from high school, Mitchell began work as a sharecropper. Unsuccessful as a tenant farmer, Mitchell moved to Tyronza in northeast Arkansas in 1928 to operate a drycleaning business in the back room of his father's barbershop. His business thrived, and he quickly developed a rapport with both black and white farmers. Mitchell befriended Clay East, the owner of a nearby gas station.

Mitchell convinced East to join him as a member of the Socialist Party, and the two quickly organized a small group of likeminded radicals. During the early years of the Depression, Mitchell and East took an active role in politics and promoted Socialist Party candidates. Mitchell was most concerned with the inequities of the sharecropping system and the failures of the New Deal to improve the lives of landless farmers in the Mississippi Delta.

Sharecropping in the South had created a class of poor landless famers, black and white, dependent on a small percentage of the return on the crops they grew on another person's land. President Franklin D. Roosevelt intended the Agricultural Adjustment Act (AAA) of 1933 to help struggling farmers by decreasing agricultural output and raising prices. However, the AAA programs directly paid landowners to not plant crops, which meant that sharecroppers were unable to grow their own crops and support themselves.

The Socialist Party recognized an opportunity to mobilize the sharecroppers. In 1934 Norman Thomas, leader of the Socialist Party, visited Tyronza and met Mitchell and East. The pair drove Thomas to nearby plantation shacks of several white and black sharecroppers. After the visit, Thomas published his findings in *The Plight of the Share-Croppers* (1934) and suggested that Mitchell and East form a union of sharecroppers.

A few weeks after the visit, the Socialist Party of Arkansas held its annual meeting in Tyronza. At this meeting members elected Mitchell as the state secretary of the Socialist Party. By that summer Mitchell and others planned a meeting to organize an interracial union of sharecroppers. In July 1934, 11 white and seven black leaders met at a schoolhouse just outside of Tyronza and founded the Southern Tenant Farmers Union (STFU). The preamble to the union's constitution called for a return of "land to the landless." Branches of the STFU spread across the Southeast and eventually to California.

Mitchell served as executive secretary of the STFU for eight years. He recruited a number of influential radicals to the union, including Howard Kester, who wrote the STFU's most influential publication, *Revolt among the Sharecroppers* (1936). Mitchell opposed the STFU's growing affiliations with Communist Party members, but he continued to represent the needs of landless sharecroppers for the rest of the decade. After World War II the union changed its name to the National Farm Labor Union and moved its headquarters to Washington, D.C. Mitchell worked in the nation's capital for a dozen years as a lobbyist for struggling farmers. He spent the following decades organizing other unions to support farmers, skilled fishermen, meat cutters, and migrant workers.

Mitchell, a true grassroots socialist, spent his life trying to break down class boundaries in the cotton fields of the Mississippi Delta. His skills as an organizer and promoter for the STFU brought together a diverse group of stakeholders interested in social change. H. L. Mitchell's work as a union organizer for farmers crossed social, class, and racial lines and helped redefine southern society.

AARON D. PURCELL
Virginia Tech

Anthony P. Dunbar, *Against the Grain: Southern Radicals and Prophets, 1929–1959* (1981); Donald H. Grubbs, *Cry from the Cotton: The Southern Tenant Farmers' Union and the New Deal* (1971); Howard Kester, *Revolt among the Sharecroppers* (1936, 1997); H. L. Mitchell, *Mean Things Are Happening in This Land* (1979), *Roll the Union On* (1987); Samuel Howard Mitchell, *A Leader among the Sharecroppers, Migrants, and Farm Workers: H. L. Mitchell and Friends* (2007).

NASCAR

In December 1947 a group of racers and promoters met in a smoky barroom in Daytona Beach to forge a plan to oversee the explosive postwar growth of stock car racing. At the time, there were no professional sports teams in the South. That drought would not end until the Braves moved to Atlanta in 1966. The founders who created the National Association for Stock Car Auto Racing, or NASCAR, intended to give residents of the former Confederacy a home-grown sport to call their own.

For most of its first 50 years, NASCAR fans were "plain, ordinary working people," as NASCAR's first president, Bill France, described them. In the rural, sport-starved South, races drew cult-like followings. Saturday nights in small towns boomed with the roar of Ford V-8s, kicking up rooster tails of copper-colored dirt, smashing and crunching into each other—and, occasionally, into the crowds. It was a rough sport full of dangerous, lascivious men who would bash each other's cars on the track and settle scores afterward. Many of the sport's pioneers were moonshiners, who found that the skills they had developed as high-speed whiskey deliverymen translated perfectly to the red-dirt tracks of Dixie.

It made sense for the South to embrace this homemade, loud, and dirty sport and its rough-hewn, law-breaking stars. Fans considered stock car racing the cutting edge of the wild side to which they aspired, or at least admired.

The perception of NASCAR as being of and for southern, blue-collar "rednecks" lingered into the 21st century. But in 2001, when Dale Earnhardt died on the final lap of the Daytona 500, millions of Americans wept, and the prolonged mourning for Earnhardt—the sport's Elvis—opened the eyes of more than a few nonfans.

NASCAR had by then grown into a multibillion dollar industry whose popularity, thanks to savvy marketing and soaring corporate sponsorship, had expanded beyond the South, finding unlikely strongholds in Los Angeles, Las Vegas, Dallas, Kansas City, and Chicago. Its fan base had doubled in the 1990s and, with attendance growing at 10 percent a year, it remained the fastest-growing sport of the new millennium. No longer a second-tier event on ESPN2, races were televised nationally on NBC, TNT, and FOX; in 2007 they began airing on ABC and ESPN, part of a TV contract worth nearly $5 billion. NASCAR became an attraction for 80 million loyal fans—and the second most popular sport in America, with races that regularly attracted 200,000 spectators.

Though it had evolved from a rural, working man's domain, most fans were now college-educated, middle-aged, middle-class homeowners. Nearly half were women. Modern NASCAR races still were not as racially mixed as a professional football or baseball game, but the social mix was unexpectedly diverse, with businessmen and bikers in the grandstands, working-class and upper-class alike. NASCAR's red-white-and-blue logo became a recognizable part of American culture, splashed on cereal boxes in supermarket aisles, on magazine covers, beer cans, clothing, even leather recliners. The companies sponsoring race cars included Viagra and, reflective of NASCAR's growing female fan base, Brawny paper towels, Tide, and Betty Crocker.

In 2004 NASCAR's longtime top sponsor—cigarette maker R. J. Reynolds, which had been introduced to NASCAR in 1972 by a convicted moonshiner—was replaced by communications giant Nextel. When Nextel merged with Sprint, NASCAR's top racing series became known as the Sprint Cup, symbolizing not only the sport's modern era but the continuing decline of the South's ideological dominance of the sport.

Until 1988, when Georgia's Bill Elliot won NASCAR's top championship, every champion but one had come from Dixie. Since then, only two champs were southerners, including Dale Earnhardt. NASCAR legend Richard Petty declared in 2005 that "NASCAR is no longer a southern sport." And though some longtime fans bristle at the loss of their sport's southernness, NASCAR has continued to transcend class lines, reaching out to a wider audience. NASCAR welcomed Toyota to its racetracks in 2006 and continued to seek more female and minority drivers. (It was considered a major coup when popular Indy racer Danica Patrick agreed to compete in NASCAR in 2010.)

Another sign of NASCAR's shifting class appeal came when Nationwide Insurance replaced Anheuser Busch as sponsor of NASCAR's No. 2 series. Today's stars are handsome and charismatic, some of them college grads. They are also millionaire celebrities who appear in rock videos, date supermodels, and live in mansions. Corporate sponsors need such fresh-faced stars to appeal to consumers and help sell their products.

Superstar Jeff Gordon has acknowledged that NASCAR is "all about marketing," and some critics deride the cars as merely flying billboards. And yet, NASCAR remains as popular as ever. As one of the sport's co-creators said back in 1947, stock car racing is "kind of like country music. Nobody likes it except the public."

NEAL THOMPSON
Asheville, North Carolina

Liz Clarke, *One Helluva Ride: How NASCAR Swept the Nation* (2009), "NASCAR Boom Puts South in Rearview," *Washington Post* (20 November 2005); Scott Huler, *A Little Bit Sideways: One Week inside a NASCAR Winston Cup Team* (1999); Neal Thompson, *Driving with the Devil: Southern Moonshine, Detroit Wheels, and the Birth of NASCAR* (2006).

New Deal

Between the Civil War and World War II, two classes predominated in the rural South: large plantation owners and poor sharecroppers or tenant farmers. Compared to other U.S. labor systems, southern tenancy stood out as highly unequal in both class and racial terms. White planter-landlords exercised near-total social, economic, and political control over their tenants, whether black or white; African Americans lived under additional racial oppression. By the 1930s tenant families accounted for one-fourth of all southerners. Of the 2.3 million farmers in the South, well over half were landless (47 percent of whites, 79 percent of blacks), and most grew cotton. Southern agriculture did include other classes: subsistence producers and commercial family farmers (who worked their own land by themselves), particularly in tobacco, but plantations dominated the region. The New Deal operated within this racist, paternalistic, and labor-repressive social structure.

During the Great Depression the Roosevelt administration saw low commodity prices as the immediate farm crisis. Agrarian New Dealers developed a policy of agricultural adjustment, which sought to raise prices by limiting supply. The federal government paid farmers who decreased their acreage in selected crops. In addition, marketing agreements were set up for some commodities like tobacco. Although this marketing program benefited small tobacco farmers in the South, cotton still ruled the region. In its first year (1933) the New Deal took 10 million acres out of cotton alone. Since fewer acres meant decreased labor needs, planters throughout the Cotton South evicted thousands of destitute tenants. Many landless farmers sunk even lower in the class structure to become day laborers.

Moreover, landlords often refused to share the New Deal government payments with their farmers. In response, a group of black and white sharecroppers organized the Southern Tenant Farmers Union, which faced violent reaction from local planters. The union appealed for help to the U.S. Department of Agriculture, which housed a few liberal lawyers in its acreage-adjustment unit. In defiance of their superiors, the attorneys ruled in favor of the displaced and aggrieved tenants, against the planters, and were promptly fired—an incident that became known as the "purge of the liberals." Although the U.S. Department of Agriculture soon revised the adjustment program somewhat, it continued to subsidize large landowners, who were then able to begin mechanizing their farms.

The New Deal received heavy criticism for this dominant-class bias of its major agricultural program. Could it do anything for the rural poor? President Roosevelt responded by creating the Resettlement Administration, later renamed the Farm Security Administration. One of the least racist and least classist of the entire New Deal, this agency represented the interests of small farmers and tenants as well as farm laborers. Farm Security benefited more than a million poor farm families. This "war on poverty" was especially active in the South, where it rehabilitated run-down farms and farmsteads, provided extensive technical assistance (in farm management and home economics), allowed some sharecroppers to buy good land and new houses, built thousands of schools, and established all manner of cooperatives, including the first national group health plans. Though certainly not free of racism, the agency nonetheless challenged southern racial norms by substantially supporting African Americans.

Overall, the New Deal had profound class consequences in the rural South. Its main program of agricultural adjustment helped planter-landlords and harmed tenants, most of whom moved to the cities and became industrial wage laborers. By 1940 the South had lost nearly a third of its sharecroppers. Simultaneously, the Farm Security Administration assisted hundreds of thousands of poor southerners until planters and other conservatives abolished it in the mid-1940s. Thus the New Deal (along with World War II and new technologies) led to the rapid class transformation from coercive, labor-intensive plantations to mechanized capitalist farms. Within a single generation, tractors, operated by only a few wageworkers, replaced sharecropper shacks as icons on the southern landscape.

JESS GILBERT
University of Wisconsin at Madison

Anthony J. Badger, *The New Deal* (1989); Sidney Baldwin, *Poverty and Politics: The Rise and Decline of the Farm Security Administration* (1968); Pete Daniel, *Breaking the Land: The Transformation of Cotton, Rice, and Tobacco Cultures since 1880* (1985); Gilbert C. Fite, *Cotton Fields No More: Southern Agriculture, 1865–1980* (1984); Donald C. Grubbs, *Cry from the Cotton: The Southern Tenant Farmers Union and the New Deal* (1971); Howard Kester, *Revolt among the Sharecroppers* (1936, 1997); Jack Temple Kirby, *Rural Worlds Lost: The*

American South, 1920–1960 (1987); Paul E. Mertz, *New Deal Poverty and Southern Rural Poverty* (1978).

New South, 19th-Century

The American Civil War fundamentally changed the social structure of the 19th-century American South. These changes, however, came more from the emancipation of slaves than from the creation of new industries and economic opportunities in the postbellum South. New South boosters such as Henry Grady and Richard Edmonds led many southerners, and future historians, to believe that postwar southerners embraced industrialization, urbanization, and scientific agriculture, whereas their antebellum counterparts cared only about cash crops, commercial profit, and slavery. Many observers believed that the South lacked a middle class. According to this interpretation, only planters, poor whites, and slaves inhabited the antebellum South. New South boosters articulated the myth that factories, cities, and an urban middle class emerged only after the Civil War. Although many antebellum southerners worked within a plantation economy dominated by cotton, rice, sugar, and tobacco, many other entrepreneurial southerners invested in factories, shops, urban spaces, railroads, and other innovative projects. Wealthy and middle-class planters, yeoman farmers, and "plain folk" existed alongside a growing cadre of merchants, professionals, industrialists, and factory workers. This growing diversity became more pronounced during the 1850s and created regional economic momentum that spanned the Civil War and continued throughout the rest of the 19th century. The postbellum creed that espoused the successes of a New South failed to acknowledge economic growth and social diversity in the Old South.

The end of the Civil War and the subsequent emancipation of slaves in 1865 altered social barriers by allowing ex-slaves to gain status in a society that had denied them basic human rights for centuries. Fearful of this newfound freedom and the specter of tangible social status for ex-slaves, postbellum whites formed violent vigilante groups such as the Ku Klux Klan, which was led by economically powerful whites but appealed to many ordinary people, and supported the establishment of Jim Crow laws to minimize social and economic opportunities for African Americans. In response, the African American community developed a social structure that often mirrored what white southerners had created in agriculture, industry, and commerce — though most African Americans remained poor. White landlords used unfair contracts and credit to dominate mostly black sharecroppers and tenant farmers, and factory owners took advantage of the lack of organized labor in the South to exploit mostly white industrial workers. The ownership of land and the means of production replaced slavery as a benchmark for control in southern society.

The continuity and discontinuity of 19th-century southern culture influenced the development of social class within the South. Historiographical debates about the trajectory of southern history often failed to recognize that the status quo could coexist with societal change. The end of slavery marked a clear dividing line between antebellum and postbellum periods, and one that created new opportunities for many whites and African Americans of all social classes. Yet the continuation and growth of farming, industry, commerce, and urbanization highlighted a more constant force at work. With the burden of slavery removed and a need to produce quick capital, many southerners reinvested heavily in railroads, cotton mills, mining, metal production, lumber, and urban development as a way of reigniting a stagnant economy. Yet cotton still remained king in the South. Race, not class, remained the most important way of dividing southern society as demonstrated by the failure of the fledgling biracial populist movement in the late 19th century. As had been the custom since Bacon's Rebellion in 1676, wealthy farmers and factory owners used their economic power to gain political and social status and used it to influence their region's middle and working classes and maintain racial divisions. Despite facing racism, violence, and a culture of "separate but equal," postbellum African American southerners managed to begin the process of social and economic integration that would truly revolutionize southern culture. Although the South endured great change during the 19th century and its spokespersons promoted the image of a mythical New South to explain many of these changes, the conservative social structure of white society that had been created in the antebellum South remained mostly intact.

JOHN F. KVACH
University of Alabama at Huntsville

Dwight Billings Jr., *Planters and the Making of a "New South": Class, Politics, and Development in North Carolina* (1979); Susanna Delfino and Michele Gillespie, *Global Perspectives on Industrial Transformation in the American South* (2005); Steven Hahn, *The Roots of Southern Populism: Yeoman Farmers and the Transformation of the Georgia Upcountry, 1850-1890* (1983); J. Mills Thornton III, *Politics and Power in a Slave Society: Alabama, 1800-1860* (1978); Jonathan Daniel Wells, *The Origins of the Southern Middle Class, 1800-1861* (2004); C. Vann Woodward, *Origins of the New South, 1877-1913* (1951).

1938 Economic Report on the South

One of the most controversial writings of the 1930s, the *Report on Economic Conditions of the South*, crystallized a long-developing body of thought about the region's persistent poverty and underdevelopment. At the same time, as a product of Franklin Roosevelt's New Deal, it became a flashpoint for controversy, owing less to the report itself than to FDR's famous characterization of the South as "the Nation's No. 1 economic problem" and his attempt to use the report as a weapon in his increasingly contentious struggle with the southern conservative Democratic political establishment. Politically, the report, and the controversy it stirred, became a milestone in the increasing disaffection between the white South and the national Democratic Party. Economically, the report faithfully described a South hopelessly entangled in a mass of economic pathologies but failed to anticipate the region's postwar transformation.

Beginning with the Progressive Era, southerners had been developing a tradition of critical thinking about the socioeconomic problems of the region. By the 1920s that tradition had become institutionalized with the establishment by Howard W. Odum of the Institute for Research in Social Science at the University of North Carolina in Chapel Hill and the creation of the University of North Carolina Press. Moreover, the problems of the region had become topics of national interest, particularly with the onset of the Great Depression in 1929. Southern poverty and underdevelopment seemed to many outside the region to be dragging the nation down with it, and such important early New Deal programs as the Tennessee Valley Authority specifically targeted the region. The Democratic takeover of Washington in 1933 brought a number of well-educated and idealistic young southerners into the federal government, many of them inclined to blame the South's problems on "economic colonialism" and eager to use federal power to right what they saw as a serious regional imbalance.

Led by Georgian Clark Foreman, a group of these young New Dealers took the idea for what became the *Report* to FDR in early 1938. Facing a growing revolt against the New Deal by the southern wing of his party, FDR saw the proposal as a means of mobilizing popular southern support for the New Deal against his opponents and placed the project under Lowell Mellett's National Emergency Council. Foreman and Mellett assembled a team of southern New Dealers to write a 64-page pamphlet dealing with various aspects of southern underdevelopment: environmental degradation, inadequate human capital, dysfunctional governmental and economic institutions, and weak purchasing power. They then presented it to an advisory committee of southern activists headed by University of North Carolina president Frank Porter Graham. During this presentation, Roosevelt's characterization of the region as "the Nation's No. 1 economic problem" was leaked. Lacking the context of the as-yet-unfinished *Report*, FDR's southern Democratic political enemies readily mischaracterized it as an attack on the region and were able to blunt its effectiveness as a weapon against them in his attempted "purge" of them in 1938.

Nonetheless, the *Report*, when finally released, was effective in presenting the state of thinking on southern economic questions to a large regional audience. Some half a million copies were distributed by the end of 1938 to individuals and organizations across the South, while public and private agencies published versions supplemented with local data. Although the full report quickly came under attack from conservatives for exaggerating the degree of southern poverty and blaming it on institutions rather than individual inadequacy, its ideas had actually long been common currency among educated southerners.

Unfortunately, though, the *Report* offered no clear solutions to southern problems. FDR had requested for political reasons that solutions not be included, and by the late 1930s the most logical approach—a major infusion of federal funds—lacked support nationwide. Moreover, the ideas animating the creators of the *Report*—hostility to finance capital and outside exploitation, for instance—were critically softened by the advisory committee. Further, southerners themselves lacked consensus on internally based solutions. Finally, efforts at constructing a "liberal" approach, notably through the Southern Conference on Human Welfare, ran aground on the shoals of race. Focusing on what it deemed the common problems of white and black southerners, the *Report* had astoundingly little to say about southern race relations—a failure that throttled its long-term effectiveness when racial issues moved to the center of regional debate after World War II.

Race was not the only factor that stifled the *Report*'s long-term effectiveness. The remarkable postwar economic convergence of the South on the rest of the country, featuring the transformation of agriculture and a sharp increase in industrialization and urbanization, broke the tangle of pathology that as late as 1938 seemed to tie down the South like Gulliver. While many problems persisted, and new ones arose, the *Report* could not address this truly new South. In retrospect, the *Report* described a South that was on the verge of dissolution.

DAVID L. CARLTON
Vanderbilt University

PETER A. COCLANIS
University of North Carolina at Chapel Hill

Roger Biles, *The South and the New Deal* (1994); David L. Carlton and Peter A. Coclanis, eds., *Confronting Southern Poverty in the Great Depression: The Report on Economic Conditions of the South with Related Documents* (1996); Gerald W. Johnson, *The Wasted Land* (1937); Bruce J. Schulman, *From Cotton Belt to Sunbelt: Federal Policy, Economic Development, and the Transformation of the South, 1938–1980* (1991).

Oil Workers

The opening up of Texas oil fields at Corsicana in the 1890s brought oil workers from established fields in Pennsylvania, West Virginia, and Ohio to the South, an in-migration of industry veterans accelerated after 1900 by gigantic oil discoveries at Spindletop and other Texas, Louisiana, and Oklahoma locations. These experienced workers taught the indigenous workforce such essential jobs as rig and tank building, well drilling, and pipelining. As oil discoveries brought the petroleum industry to the countryside, farm boys readily adapted to the industry's physically demanding outdoor labor, employment offering higher wages and far more excitement than life on the farm. Many also adapted to a high degree of geographic mobility, since jobs were most plentiful and pay highest when new fields opened up and activity boomed. By the 1920s there were thousands of "boomers" who followed oil industry excitement through Texas, Louisiana, Oklahoma, and Arkansas. There was also a growing industrial workforce located in refining centers such as Beaumont–Port Arthur, Houston, and Baton Rouge. Refinery

Oil field workers taking time out to read the paper, Kilgore, Tex., 1936 (Russell Lee, photographer, Library of Congress [LC-USF33-012175-M2], Washington, D.C.)

workers had more in common with other urban manufacturing workers than with boomers. Refining work's settled nature allowed labor-union growth, which high labor mobility discouraged out in the oil fields; refinery employment levels were stable compared to those out in the field.

During the first half of the 20th century, young Anglo men formed the overwhelming majority of the oil field workforce, and they had their own lifestyle and culture. They endured rough living conditions, living in tents and shacks and dining in boardinghouses and cafés. Rig workers worked 12-hour "tours" or shifts. Work was dirty and dangerous; lost limbs and lives were common. So was intermittent unemployment, and workers moved from job to job. After hours workers drank, gambled, looked for commercial sex, and fought each other. With this rowdy, rough-and-tumble life went fiercely independent individualism, tolerance of physical discomfort, and willingness to take physical and economic risks. Often separated from family members, workers put a premium on loyalty to friends and helping those down on their luck. During the 1920s and 1930s major oil company employers tried to counteract high levels of labor turnover and poor living conditions by building company camps with worker housing. Appealing to married workers, the camps offered a lifestyle more like the suburbs than boomtowns. Workers who stayed with such employers moved with a network of friends from camp to camp, region to region.

After World War II, oil exploration and production advanced into Mississippi, Alabama, and Florida, and oil field work changed in many important ways. Drilling offshore in the Gulf of Mexico generated its own worker lifestyle. Company camps became a casualty of company cost cutting, but availability of mobile homes meant workers could take decent housing with them as they moved from location to location. As postwar road construction reached out to the oil fields and tours shortened to eight hours, workers could live in town and commute to work, making life easier for families. Technology and greater emphasis on safety made work less arduous and hazardous. However, greater use of automation in areas such as pumping, pipelining, and refining meant fewer jobs for workers in these occupations. As ever, downtimes in the industry meant many lost jobs. The most calamitous downturn came in the 1980s, when, in Texas alone, over 200,000 oil workers lost positions. One result of the downturn was a major demographic change in the workforce after 2000. Anglos have not returned to the oil fields in large numbers; especially in Texas, their places have been taken by Latino workers who have been more willing to accept the uncertainties and risks of the work than their Anglo counterparts. Whether they will redefine oil field life and culture remains to be seen.

DIANA DAVIDS HINTON
University of Texas of the Permian Basin

Diana Davids Hinton and Roger M. Olien, *Oil in Texas: The Gusher Age, 1895–1945* (2002); Gerald Lynch, *Roughnecks, Drillers, and Tool Pushers: Thirty-Three Years in the Oil Fields* (1987); Roger M. Olien and Diana Davids Olien, *Oil Booms: Social Change in Five Texas Towns* (1982), *Life in the Oil Fields* (1986); Bobby D. Weaver, *Oilfield Trash: Life and Labor in the Oil Patch* (2010).

Operation Dixie

In the spring of 1946 the Congress of Industrial Organizations (CIO) planned an ambitious assault on the South's reputation as a haven for low wages, antiunionism, and conservative, undemocratic politics. At stake were two important CIO goals: protect the hard-won collective bargaining achievements of unions in the remainder of the country, and support the full political participation of white and black working people in the region, which the CIO believed would transform southern politics and remove a major impediment to liberal social legislation. The ultimate failure of the CIO's Southern Organizing Committee was, in the judgment of one scholar, "the most important factor on which to focus to understand all of U.S. politics" after World War II.

The time certainly seemed propitious for the CIO campaign. Southern industry had taken giant strides forward as a result of wartime investments in shipbuilding, petroleum, chemical, steel, textile, and apparel plants, which added more than 800,000 manufacturing jobs for black and white workers. Government involvement in the wartime economy meant that a fair number of these jobs fell under the protections offered by federal regulations, creating favorable conditions for union growth. Meanwhile, the Depression had loosened the bonds that joined evangelical Protestantism to antiunionism. CIO organizer Lucy Mason, for one, applauded the changes occurring in Holiness and Pentecostal churches. Moreover, the CIO's political goals dovetailed with some of the concerns of returning servicemen, black and white, who objected to the closed system of one-party rule that discouraged broad participation and responsive government.

High expectations quickly dissipated, however. The southern economy, despite changes, still relied heavily upon low-wage, labor-intensive industries, such as garment making, textiles, and woodworking. Employers in these industries were willing to fight tooth and nail to maintain regional wage scales. Operation Dixie's plan to make textiles the initial focus of the campaign ran headlong into the South's most intransigent companies. The textile industry was a poor choice for another reason—it left out those in the region most desirous of joining unions, black workers. Instead, the CIO purposely downplayed efforts to build interracial unions, worried that talk of organizing blacks would result in race baiting from employers, politicians, and antiunion whites. Despite the cautious approach of Operation Dixie, opponents nevertheless charged that the CIO wanted to give white jobs to black workers, upend the racial order in the South, and promote "social equality."

The CIO also ran up against a rapidly changing postwar political environment. Anticommunism, which would soon be pervasive in American culture, was a useful tool for southern companies against unions from Operation Dixie's outset. The rival American Federation of Labor (AFL), which began its own southern organizing campaign, actually helped employers by labeling the CIO as filled with radicals. AFL organizers sought to benefit from such slogans as "Join the CIO and Help Build a Soviet America." Operation Dixie leaders, fearing the impact of such charges, tried to keep their distance from any sympathetic organization that could be tarred with the brush of anticommunism, but to no avail. In 1947, when a conservative U.S. Congress passed the Taft-Hartley Act, which required union officials to sign affidavits that they were not members of the Communist Party, the CIO took additional action to expel unions suspected of harboring communists. Such struggle within the houses of labor only confused many southern workers and made them suspicious of all unions.

Finally, Operation Dixie confronted southern mill workers who were making more money than ever. As a result of the Fair Labor Standards Act (1938) and the National War Labor Board, southern wages had risen without collective bargaining agreements. In the minds of many mill hands, the question was, What do we need a union for? Reinforcing this attitude was a religious culture that made workers fearful of "being yoked with unbelievers" in secular organizations. Then, in 1951, rival AFL and CIO unions in textiles engaged in a bitter battle that led to a disastrous strike, destroying several of the most important beachheads that unions had established.

Although Operation Dixie officially limped along until 1953, the seven-year campaign failed to repay the efforts and resources that the CIO expended. Historians debate the most important reasons for the failure, but the mix of poor CIO strategies, anticommunism, racial animosities, improving standards of living, intransigent employers, and a conservative social and political environment combined to doom the Southern Organizing Campaign, a defeat that had long-term implications for the American labor movement.

KEN FONES-WOLF
West Virginia University

Elizabeth Fones-Wolf and Ken Fones-Wolf, *Labor* (Spring 2009); Michael Goldfield, *The Color of Politics: Race and the Mainsprings of American Politics* (1997); Barbara Griffith, *The Crisis of American Labor: Operation Dixie and the Defeat of the CIO* (1988); Michael K. Honey, *Southern Labor and Black Civil Rights: Organizing Memphis Workers* (1993); Robert Rodgers Korstad, *Civil Rights Unionism: Tobacco Workers and the Struggle for Democracy in the Mid-Twentieth-Century South* (2003); Timothy J. Minchin, *What Do We Need a Union For? The TWUA in the South, 1945–1955* (1997); Bryant Simon, *Georgia Historical Quarterly* (Summer 1997).

Ozarks

Poverty has long been associated with the Ozarks, in fact and in stereotype. From the beginnings of European and Anglo-American settlement the region's rugged terrain and generally infertile soils helped shape a society short on material prosperity and long on practices of self-sufficiency. Even with the emergence of pockets of substantial economic growth and wealth in the latter half of the 20th century, the Ozark region retains vast stretches of territory marked by rural poverty, low educational attainment, and sparse hope for economic development.

The mid-American highland region delineated by geographers as the Ozarks covers approximately 40,000 square miles, more than 90 percent of it in Missouri and Arkansas. With a few exceptions on the fringes of the region, the Ozarks was not conducive to large-scale market agriculture and instead nurtured a largely self-sufficient farming culture based on open-range livestock raising, small-scale crop production, and, throughout much of the 19th century, extensive hunting and trapping. Most 19th-century Ozarks settlers came from the Protestant Upland South, where terrain and tradition had encouraged agricultural strategies that would prove conducive to the Ozarks. With the exception of German settlements along the northern and eastern fringes of the region, few foreign immigrants found their way to the rural Ozarks. The absence of plantation-style agriculture meant that comparatively few slave owners and slaves came to the region, and the post–Civil War black population of the region never exceeded 5 percent. Although residents of the Ozarks were rarely cut off from regional and national market forces, their relative isolation and modest means bred a reliance on handicraft production and a maintenance of traditional folkways that extended well into the 20th century in some locales.

In the early 20th century the "discovery" of folkways and traditions long abandoned in American areas more

Destitute tenant farmer's wife, Ozark Mountains, Arkansas, October 1935 (Ben Shahn, photographer, Library of Congress [LC-USF33-006066-M3], Washington, D.C.)

aligned with the economic mainstream led to competing images of the Ozarks. To some observers the region's rural inhabitants were backward, provincial, ignorant, and even barbarous, their economic poverty a reflection of their cultural poverty. To others the Ozarkers represented independence, nonconformity, and resourcefulness—American traits feared to be in decline in an increasingly urbanized and homogenized society. For the romantically inclined, the Ozarkers' handicraft skills, folk remedies, and traditional music were not just quaint relics of bygone days but markers of an "authentic" folk culture resisting the onslaught of industrializing America.

By the middle of the 20th century, even the most isolated reaches of the Ozarks were rapidly being integrated into the American economic and cultural mainstream. Handicrafts and folk music would remain points of interest for collectors and scholars and would prove valuable in the emerging world of heritage tourism, but they were quickly discarded by pragmatic Ozarks residents as they sought to take their place in the burgeoning American consumer society. Nevertheless, the region remained among the most impoverished in America, especially so in areas with overwhelmingly white populations. In 1949 the Ozarks vied with the Delta as the most impoverished region of Arkansas; 6 of that state's 10 poorest counties were in the Ozarks. The Ozark region accounted for all of Missouri's 10 poorest counties, with the aptly named Ozark County ranking dead last in per capita income.

There had always been pockets of comparative prosperity in the Ozarks, but the post–World War II era witnessed the emergence of areas of true wealth for the first time. Buoyed by the emergence of such Fortune 500 companies as Wal-Mart, Tyson Foods, and J. B. Hunt Trucking and bolstered by the presence of the University of Arkansas, the northwestern corner of Arkansas experienced tremendous economic and population growth in the last third of the 20th century and into the 21st. So, too, did the region's largest city, Springfield, Mo. The past half century has also brought thousands of retirees and affluent second-home owners to previously rural areas of the region. Still, outside of these noted oases of prosperity, the Ozarks remains a rural region with above-average rates of poverty, below-average levels of educational attainment, and limited economic opportunities. By 2007 the Ozarks still claimed 8 of Missouri's 10 poorest counties. The Delta had largely supplanted the Ozarks as the poorest region of Arkansas, with the latter region claiming only 3 of the 10 poorest counties; yet, with few exceptions, per capita incomes in Ozark counties continued to rank below the average in this poor state and well below national averages. Just as poverty has stubbornly clung to the region, so has the image of the impoverished yet resourceful hillbilly.

BROOKS BLEVINS
Missouri State University

Brooks Blevins, *Hill Folks: A History of Arkansas Ozarkers and Their Image* (2002); W. K. McNeil, *Ozark Country* (1995); Milton D. Rafferty, *The Ozarks: Land and Life* (2001).

Pellagra

Although pioneer nutritionist Casimir Funk believed that pellagra existed sporadically in America as early as 1880, Alabama reported the first epidemic during the summer of 1906, after which it soon spread rapidly across the South. Over the next five-year period there were nearly 16,000 cases with 39.1 percent mortality. The alarming death toll prompted action by the U.S. Public Health Service and Joseph Goldberger's indefatigable campaign to eradicate a disease characterized by the "four d's": dermatitis, diarrhea, dementia, and sometimes death. As early as 1914 Goldberger, observing pellagra in various institutional settings, concluded that it was a nutritional deficiency disease. Later, Goldberger, joined by North Carolinian George A. Wheeler and statistician Edgar Sydenstricker, made a series of field investigations into pellagra in seven cotton mill villages in South Carolina. Their painstaking work yielded important conclusions about the nature of the disease, the most important being that pellagra was essentially a socioeconomic disease related to low family income and available food supplies. Goldberger's team revealed a disease not of the poor but of the *very* poor.

But Goldberger's thesis did not easily persuade colleagues or community leaders in the South. The truth was hampered by the Thompson-McFadden Commission's report in 1912 that proclaimed the disease infectious in nature. The consequences of this much-touted scientific cul-de-sac would be persistently recited by Goldberger's oppo-

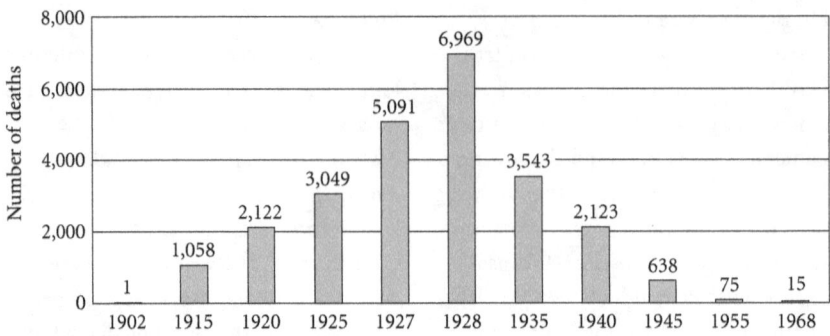

FIGURE 20. *Pellagra deaths in the United States*
Source: *U.S. Public Health Service Center for Disease Control, Atlanta, Ga.; and U.S. Vital Statistics, U.S. Bureau of the Census, Department of Commerce.*

nents like a well-worn catechism of faith because it told southern leaders (medical and otherwise) precisely what they wanted to hear: pellagra was *not* rooted in the socioeconomic conditions of the region but rather in the whimsy of microbes facilitated by bad habits, ignorance, and inattention to hygiene—the "lazy" disease. Meanwhile, pellagra rates climbed, reaching 170,000 cases by 1927 and exceeding 200,000 through 1930. Although Goldberger would die in 1929 without finding the specific cause of the disease (that would await Conrad Elvehjem's studies in the 1930s, which conclusively linked the disease to niacin deficiency), his nutritional deficiency thesis was, fortunately, generally accepted by 1927 when the Southern Medical Association passed a resolution in its favor. The next year pellagra mortality would reach an all-time high (see Figure 20). Yet naysayers persisted. Typical was Alabama physician William Partlow, who insisted that "the late Doctor Goldberger did not, nor has any one else proven pellagra to be due to a dietary deficiency."

Why the resistance? Goldberger's team knew that, for poor whites and blacks, life in the "new" human chattel-free agrarian South transformed into a slavery of a different kind, a color-blind bondage of economic dependence upon tenant farming under an equally merciless white master—cotton. But if the old agrarian ways of Dixie offered only the prospect of a dismal life under new arrangements, the so-called New South of business and industry was showing itself to be equally bereft of worthwhile returns. Indeed, the New South was built upon a bitter contradiction. Touting the benefits of modern diversified agriculture and industrial expansion, the New South stood upon the foundations of a low wage base managed by textile manufacturers and mining magnates quick to take advantage of the post-bellum opportunities offered by the vanquished region. Southern boosters proclaiming an "abundant supply of labor, thrifty, industrious, and one hundred percent American," belied an income only 60 to 70 percent that of other Americans. While tenant farmers were bound to their local stores and sundry shops through lines of credit that dropped them deeper and deeper into debt, factory and mine workers were frequently paid in company script redeemable only at the company store or at stores that accepted the company vouchers. This tied workers to the store inventory, which could be ample or limited, either way, and in the face of the most abundant store inventories, low wages and mounting debt forced even the most frugal families away from choice meats and fresh fruits and vegetables and toward cornmeal and biscuits (since 1878 produced by a roller-mill process that reduced the meal and flour's protein, ash, and vitamin content by 80 to 90 percent), molasses, syrup, fatback, and coffee, a menu tailor-made for pellagra. A similar scenario played out for sharecroppers and tenant farmers who were tied to the credit lines of landowners. Low wages and high debt bred pellagra.

Unfortunately, the challenge of pellagra would not prompt wide-scale action to eradicate poverty in the South. Instead, it was food enrichment incident to federal mandates issued during World War II that would end the southern scourge, a point clearly demonstrated in the precipitous decline in mortality rates by war's end.

MICHAEL A. FLANNERY
University of Alabama at Birmingham

Elizabeth W. Etheridge, *The Butterfly Caste: A Social History of Pellagra in the South* (1972); Casimir Funk, *The Vitamines* (1922); Joseph Goldberger, *Goldberger on Pellagra*, ed. Milton Terris (1964); Alan M. Kraut, *Goldberger's War: The Life and Work of a Public Health Crusader* (2003); Youngmee K. Park, Christopher T. Sempos, Curtis N. Barton, John E. Vanderveen, and Elizabeth A. Yetley, *American Journal of Public Health* (May 2000).

Poultry Workers

Since the earliest days of the southern poultry processing industry, social class has both divided and united the workers whose labor made cheap chicken a mainstay in the postwar American diet. Throughout the industry's long history, ranging from its 1930s origins to the early 21st century, the work of killing, cutting, and packing chickens has been distinctively southern, as a handful of states such as Georgia, North Carolina, and Arkansas have led and continue to lead the nation in poultry production. As such, the industry has been profoundly shaped by the particularities of southern labor history.

Although American farmers had long raised backyard flocks for eggs and meat, chicken was not a common staple in American kitchens in the early 20th century, with its consumption trailing far behind beef and pork. It was virtually unknown for farmers anywhere to produce exclusively poultry. In the days of the Great Depression, however, farmers in northern Virginia, north Georgia, and northwest Arkansas turned to chicken in hopes of diversification and profit. By World War II, however, poultry raising had become increasingly integrated and controlled by furnishing merchants, who provided farmers with the capital and chicks needed to cover the industry's high start-up costs—but in the process often bound farmers within the same networks of debt that had characterized cotton sharecropping.

Just as class tensions structured the raising of birds in the countryside, so also was the case within the urban processing plants that began appearing in the 1940s in a number of southern cities. Capitalizing on the exodus of tenants and croppers from the rural South in the wake of the New Deal, large-scale processors hired recent urban arrivals at desperately low wages. However, unlike their industrial predecessor, the cotton mill, poultry plants did not categorically exclude African Americans, though black workers often found themselves in the poorest-paying jobs and the least-comfortable areas of the plant. But if processors had hoped for a docile and pliable workforce, they began to face greater worker mobilization along class lines in the early 1950s. As national meatpacking unions pushed south after World War II, poultry workers demanded a right to organize, culminating in union drives and strikes across the region. Management responded predictably with intimidation and outright violence, crippling all but a few of the organization drives in the poultry towns. Unlike the beef and pork packinghouses of the Midwest, southern poultry workers would see no "golden age" in the decades after World War II.

Demographic change would also be crucial in deterring class-based allegiances among workers. Though the poultry labor force was predominantly white and male in its early years, expanding economic opportunities for white men in the 1950s and 1960s resulted in a growing African American and female presence in processing plants across the South. As workforces grew to be evenly split between whites and blacks and men and women, the wedge of civil rights mobilization in the 1960s and 1970s too often tended to widen the gap between workers of the two races, rather than unify them.

But demographic change was not limited only to black and white. In the early 1980s poultry processors began to recruit a new labor stream trickling into the South—Mexican and Central American workers seeking opportunities outside of both their lands of origin and traditional immigrant destinations such as Texas or California. Slowly at first but escalating during the 1990s, Latino workers grew from a minority to a majority in countless southern processing plants. Both white and black workers responded with friendly curiosity, unease, and resentment, and many were unsure how foreign-born workers would impact longer strategies of organization. Legal ambiguity and lack of documentation hampered many Latino workers' resistance strategies in the workplace, but foreign-born employees also brought to work unique forms of class mobilization that often operated outside of the formal American institution of the labor union. As workers today confront an industry divided by ethnicity, race, and gender, yet united in common goals of workplace safety and a living wage, the challenges of 21st-century labor organization hold both promise and uncertainty.

TORE C. OLSSON
University of Georgia

Leon Fink, *The Maya of Morganton: Work and Community in the Nuevo New South* (2003); Monica Gisolfi, *Agricultural History* (Spring 2006); David Griffith, in *Any Way You Cut It: Meat Processing and Small-Town America*, ed. Donald Stull, Michael Broadway, and David Griffith (1995); Steve Striffler, *Chicken: The Dangerous Transformation of America's Favorite Food* (2005).

Railroad Workers

Social class involves self-perception and identification as well as the perception of others. The relative material and political resources of a group also help to define one's social class. The history of southern railroad workers and social class during the period of massive railroad expansion, consolidation, and industry-state cooperation in the late 19th and early 20th centuries bolsters the view that in the South, in a more pronounced way than in the North, perception often mattered more than reality.

On the eve of the Civil War, two-thirds of railroad track in the United States lay in the North, where four out of five railroad workers labored. During the 1880s the nation's total mileage of track doubled, with much of that growth concentrated in the South, so that by 1890 railroads crossed nine out of 10 southern counties. Whether pressing into cities or remote towns, railroads brought an industrial workforce to build and maintain the track, depots, bridges, and machinery, to operate the trains, and to serve business people and travelers. Until World War II these industrial workers held a unique experience in common: their mass employment by large-scale corporations in the midst of a chiefly rural and agrarian region. However, the changing racial composition of the southern railroad labor force, set against the conflict-ridden backdrop of slavery, Emancipation, Reconstruction, and the nadir of American race relations, encouraged railroaders to identify racially rather than in class or occupational terms, despite the shared aspects of their work situations.

Antebellum southern railroads depended on thousands of enslaved workers for most manual- and service-labor needs. With Emancipation came a shift in the kinds of occupations open to whites and blacks. Although black railwaymen continued to work in the South in large numbers after the war (especially when compared to northern railways, which employed few black men during the 19th century), freedmen were forced out of firing and braking, positions to which white men lay claim because both were stepping-stones to the better-paid and more respectable work of engineers and conductors. By the late 19th century semiskilled and skilled labor was the near exclusive province of white men, many of whom joined the Brotherhood of Locomotive Firemen, the Brotherhoods of Locomotive Engineers, and the Order of Railway Conductors, all organizations that fiercely guarded entrance into more

Railroad workers, Port Barre, La., October 1938 (Russell Lee, photographer, Library of Congress [LC-USF33-011870-M4], Washington, D.C.)

skilled work, increasingly with the approval of railway companies.

The brotherhoods were national trade unions whose members identified racially as white and native-born. Indeed, the northern whites who populated many skilled positions on southern railways in the 19th century appear to have had no palliative effect on the intensity of the southern brotherhood men's race consciousness. The strong tendency of brotherhood men to measure their class status in terms of their place within a strict work hierarchy of race was also prevalent among less skilled white railwaymen, who equated the most servile, dirty, or otherwise undesirable kinds of work with black men. Certainly, white railwaymen's strong racial identification psychologically soothed men dependent on wages and engaged in grimy, hard labor in a post–Civil War cultural context that associated whiteness with self-ownership and an elevated status. However, it was also rooted in the exigency of labor competition. Brotherhood men identified against less skilled whites as well as blacks, promoting themselves as dignified, honest, sober, reliable labor so as to persuade railroad officials of their indispensability. Less skilled whites protected their racial privilege partly because they benefited from the opportunities for promotion denied to even the most able black workers.

Although usually relegated to the most burdensome forms of unskilled labor, many black laborers saw some promise in even the most backbreaking railroad work, such as section work, as it paid better than farm labor and allowed some room for extra income as seasonal employment. And, like white workers, black workers exercised leverage vis-à-vis their employers by moving from place to place, so that railroad companies complained frequently of labor shortages and, failing attempts to coerce workers to stay, were forced, to an extent, to improve workers' wages and conditions. While black newspapers and civil rights activists at times criticized the service jobs that black workers filled as demeaning, many porters and cooks appreciated this work's steadiness and relatively higher pay, despite the aggravations of serving a demanding and condescending white clientele. Black railroaders were accorded respect within black communities; among whites, semiskilled and skilled railroaders were more likely to be held in high regard.

Yet the harsh and frustrating realities of railroad labor seemed, to many railroad men, a violation of their rights and manhood. Railroaders in the yards, shops, and on the trains risked life and limb to make the tight, hurried, understaffed schedules ordered by management. As railroad companies teetered on the edges of bankruptcy, or failed altogether, managers rushed to drive down labor costs in order to pay the high price of railroad construction, operation, and maintenance. The dangers involved, as well as the job instability, deep pay cuts, and rigid, unresponsive bureaucracy that many railroaders experienced, led a number to protest across lines of race and skill during the 1880s under the banner of the Knights of Labor. White and black workers on Jay Gould's Southwest railway system in Texas and Arkansas struck in 1885 and then as Knights in 1886. In contrast to previous fraternal orders, the Knights accepted all workers as members, with the significant exception of the Chinese. In the South, Knights organized segregated assemblies and in no way directly challenged white supremacy but integrated the order's state and regional leadership and actively recruited and cooperated on an industrial basis.

The cross-racial Knights of Labor was a short-lived effort, in part disintegrating in the wake of the failed 1886 Southwest strike and some northern Knights' attempt to integrate accommodations at a national convention in Richmond, Va. Southern white Knights quit the union in response to the latter development especially. The decline of the Knights, the ascendancy of Social Darwinism, and the epidemic of antiblack violence in the South reinforced racial hierarchies on the railroads, so that the next influential mass union to form—the American Railroad Union—refused to adopt even segregated locals in the South and, along with the brotherhoods, waged vicious racist attacks on the character and intelligence of black railroaders in the hopes of driving them from braking and firing positions entirely, positions that black workers had reentered in large numbers beginning in the 1890s, at times as strikebreakers. In this effort, white railroaders largely failed, although they won support from local communities for their "race strikes" against black railwaymen. Still, the federal government, during and after its period of World War I–era intervention into the railroad industry, proved a poor protector of civil rights. Engineers and conductors in particular remained lily-white and male until the 1960s and early 1970s.

THERESA CASE
University of Houston–Downtown

Eric Arnesen, *Brotherhoods of Color: Black Railroad Workers and the Struggle for Equality* (2001); Edward L. Ayers, *The Promise of the New South: Life after Reconstruction* (1992); Theresa A. Case, *The Great Southwest Strike and Free Labor* (2010); Paul Fussell, *Class: A Guide through the American Status System* (1992); Walter Licht, *Working for the Railroad* (1983); Melvyn Stokes and Rich Halpern, *Race and Class in the American South since 1890* (1994); Paul Michel Taillon, *Good Reliable White Men: Railroad Brotherhoods, 1877–1917* (2009).

Raper, Arthur

(1899–1979) SOCIOLOGIST.
Throughout his life, Arthur Raper expressed a keen interest in the demarcations and consequences of social class. Born in 1899 on a North Carolina tobacco farm, Raper grew up in a community marked by widespread landownership. Nevertheless, as a teenager he became aware of social distinctions that existed within his home community and beyond. He began writing about racial and class barriers to equality while in graduate school at Chapel Hill.

In 1926 Raper moved to Atlanta with the Commission on Interracial Cooperation. He began investigating the mass exodus from the Black Belt through a comparative study of Georgia's Greene and Macon counties. In 1934 Raper updated his research in what would be published as *Preface to Peasantry*. He traced the characteristics of the families studied by race and tenure class, described overlapping racial and class attitudes and dynamics, and observed that many early rural New Deal initiatives, including the National Recovery Administration (NRA), perpetuated inequalities favoring large landowners at the expense of sharecroppers and tenant farmers.

In a paper entitled "The Southern Negro and the NRA" Raper described the lower wages and limited access to good jobs that African Americans had historically experienced. The traditional racial wage differential in the South had in turn lowered the wages of white workers. The Great Depression had caused many whites to seek what had been considered "Negro jobs," aggravating racial job competition and tension. While many African Americans had shared in NRA benefits, the NRA did not cover some categories of workers that included African Americans in large numbers, and numerous employers circumvented NRA codes, or discontinued marginal jobs in which blacks were employed.

In 1939 Raper went to work with Swedish social scientist Gunnar Myrdal on what would become *An American Dilemma*. Raper focused on the ways in which circumstances of race and class played out, particularly with regard to the justice system. For instance, he spent an entire day in Atlanta's police court, observing the range of treatment and sentencing defendants received depending on their race and class status.

Raper's next book, *Sharecroppers All*, coauthored with African American sociologist Ira Reid, explicitly addressed class. The book stated that most southern communities, whether rural or industrial, were essentially feudalistic. Wherever they were situated, working southerners were fundamentally "sharecroppers" in their assumption of risk without sharing in control, low wages, insecurity, "and lack of opportunity for self-direction and responsible participation in community affairs." The legacy of "race and attendant class demarcations" included the one-party system, the white primary, the poll tax, an impoverished population, and people "rendered socially sterile by race and class fears."

In 1940 Raper moved for two years to Greene County, as a participant-observer of an ambitious effort designed to improve diet and home farm production, upgrade working conditions in general, and reduce the dependency of "people as completely defeated and disinherited as anywhere in the lower South." Raper then worked for the U.S. Department of Agriculture, where his interests grew more national and international. In 1950 he coauthored *Rural Life in the United States*, writing the chapter on "Rural Social Differentials." He stated that social cleavages were especially pronounced at the local level. Status was largely determined by income, type of tenure, racial and national identity, education level, housing type, and participation in community affairs. In particular, it was "the class factor of racial identity that more than any one factor determines the social status of an individual or family." The ability to move from one social status to another was impeded by local practices and values. "Class factors," he continued, "have real meaning when differences in opportunities to secure an education, earn a livelihood, or participate in political matters make it 'natural' for some individuals and families to occupy lower positions while others readily remain at higher levels." The lower-class status of nonwhites became institutionalized as they received the least adequate housing and the poorest schools and suffered from segregation and political disfranchisement.

CLIFFORD KUHN
Georgia State University

Arthur F. Raper papers, Southern Historical Collection, University of North Carolina; Arthur F. Raper, *Preface to Peasantry: A Tale of Two Black Belt Counties* (1936), *Tenants of the Almighty* (1944); Arthur F. Raper and Ira De A. Reid, *Sharecroppers All* (1941); Daniel J. Singal, *The War Within: From Victorian to Modernist Thought in the South, 1919–1945* (1982); Carl C. Taylor et al. *Rural Life in the United States* (1950).

Rap Music

Rap music first appeared in the 1970s and early 1980s, predominantly in majority nonwhite, "inner city" communities of the urban North. Social class mixed with racial identity to inform rap music, making it a cultural expression of black and Latino youths living in the midst of continued race-based and class-based segregation, deindustrialization, and everyday experiences with violent crime, drug use, and policing. Although the inner cities of New York City and Chicago initially served as rap's creative centers, by the late 1980s

Los Angeles and Oakland also had their own unique rap scenes. Whether "East Coast" rap from the urban North or "West Coast" rap from urban California, rap music was a distinct musical genre, as rappers—also known as MCs and usually black men—gave lyrical or spoken-word deliveries over the top of synthesized, sampled, or looped beats and/or music. Much of the music sampled by southern rappers had some connection to past forms of black music, whether northern genres like soul and funk or southern genres like jazz, rock 'n' roll, gospel, or the blues. A wide variety of issues and interests—from racism to racial identity to communal solidarity and politics to street upbringings to sexual exploits to drug use to in-the-club or frivolity—defined the subject matter of rappers. Though grounded firmly in the social and racial experiences of minorities generally marginalized in urban America, the various messages and musical innovations of rap still made it incredibly popular and profitable by the late 1980s, as both independent and mass-market labels produced and distributed it to an audience of mostly young listeners.

In the South, early voices in rap music included Atlanta's Arrested Development, who became famous for its socially engaged and politically charged raps and its calls for black solidarity and class consciousness. 2 Live Crew, who came out of the "bass music" club scene of Miami, also attained commercial success, not so much for any class-based sensibilities but more for its controversial, sexually explicit lyrics and performances. Other rappers—such as New Orleans's Master P—emulated the slower beats, gangland subject matter, and profanity-laden, aggressive deliveries of West Coast "gangsta" and G-Funk rappers. In Houston, DJ Screw sold thousands of homemade mix tapes to his customers in the city's working-class black communities, while the Geto Boys represented an often hypermasculine portrait of gunplay, drug slinging, and death in the various ghettos of the so-called Capital of the Sunbelt.

Despite these early forays into rap music by black southerners, a distinct subgenre of American rap music known as "southern rap"—or "Dirty South" rap—did not take shape until the mid-1990s. A defining moment for southern rap came in 1995 when Atlanta-based rap group Goodie Mob released its first album, *Soul Food*. On this album, a song entitled "Dirty South" officially gave the southern rap genre its nickname. Since the song's release, exactly what made the South and southern rap "dirty" has meant many things to southern rappers, although in general its definition related to some cultural aspect based in social class. For some, it has meant a justice system and white-run society stacked against black men and women; for others, it has meant a down-and-out, southern black rebel identity on par with "redneck"; for others, it has meant a sense of sexual proclivity or a violent predisposition caused by both circumstance and choice. "Dirty" was often joined to a pride in being "southern," as seen in the expressive culture of southern rap. Most southern rappers emphasized their southern drawls—and, by proxy, their poverty-stricken or otherwise limited background—in their vocal deliveries, while others cast "down-home" folkways and "southern" preferences in music, fashion, drugs, liquor, food, cars, or sports teams as key elements of their class identity, personal distinctiveness, and popular appeal. Some southern rappers even appropriated the Confederate flag as a sign of their own "southern" identity and pride in "coming up southern." All in all, what made the South and its rappers "dirty" or "southern" was similar to what made the southern bluesmen of a previous generation "bad," yet desirable—a self-professed passion for telling the "truth" about the South's black underclass alongside a penchant for mythologizing those experiences and using such myths to "rise above" their social class, through either a fuller embrace of an in-your-face racial pride or a fuller pursuit of big-money commercial success.

OutKast, a duo of Atlanta rappers who quickly replaced Goodie Mob as the face of Dirty South rap in the 1990s, utilized all of these various meanings, all the while casting itself as an "outcast" in southern white society, in American social and political life, and in the national rap industry. OutKast's 1994 release *Southernplayalisticadillacmuzik* and 1996 effort *ATLiens* combined to sell over 2.5 million copies. OutKast's follow-up albums—*Stankonia* (2000), *Speakerboxx/The Love Below* (2003), and *Idlewild* (2006)—sold millions more and garnered OutKast wide praise and industry awards. In the midst of OutKast's breakout success, southern rap increasingly gained a major share in the national rap market. Master P and his No Limit label often featured rappers straight out of New Orleans's predominantly black wards, such as Mystikal, Silkk the Shocker, and C-Murder. New Orleans also served as the headquarters for Cash Money Records, founded by brothers Bryan and Ronald Williams and featuring Juvenile, B. G., the Hot Boys, and the Big Tymers. Inner city communities in Memphis contributed rappers like 8 Ball & MJG and Three 6 Mafia, while St. Louis offered party rapper Nelly. Ludacris and T. I. also emerged out of Atlanta as major mainstream rappers. Virginia Beach became the home base for the Neptunes (a duo of Pharrell Williams and Chad Hugo) and Timbaland, whose production work with southern and nonsouthern artists alike cemented their reputations as the region's premier hit-makers. Other subgenres in southern rap—such as New Orleans's jazz-influenced "bounce" music and the smooth-grooving "snap" music of Atlanta—emerged out of local black clubs and onto radio playlists and iPods nationwide. So did "crunk," a bass-heavy, call-and-response style of strip-club music popularized by Lil Jon and the East Side Boyz. "Rural rappers" or "hick-hoppers" like Field Mob, Nappy Roots, and Bubba Sparxxx added to southern rap's diversity, cutting songs accented with references to growing up "country"—and in Bubba Sparxxx's case, white—in the poorer parts of the rural South.

By the late 2000s southern rap was an established form of popular music. To some critics, however, new southern rappers like Soulja Boy, Lil Wayne, or Cowboy Troy—whose music attempted to combine rap and country—symbolized the overcommercialization of rap in general, where style and sellability trumped substance, innovation, and a distinct sense of social limitation and struggle. The notable lack of female rappers in the "Dirty South"—the exception being Missy Elliott—also seemed to point to a lack of artistic inclusiveness or outright sexism among southern rappers and labels. Still, it was readily apparent that the "Dirty South" was the "third coast" of a multibillion dollar, national rap music industry, one grounded in the social and economic station of the South's marginalized communities, yet capable of speaking to—and selling to—a much wider audience.

DARREN E. GREM
University of Georgia

Darren E. Grem, *Southern Cultures* (Winter 2006); Matt Miller, *Journal of Popular Music Studies* (August 2004), "Dirty Decade: Rap Music and the U.S. South, 1997–2007," *Southern Spaces*, online at http://www.southernspaces.org/contents/2008/miller/1a.htm; Roni Sarig, *Third Coast: Outkast, Timbaland, and How Hip-Hop Became a Southern Thing* (2007).

Readjusters

The Readjusters were a movement and political party in Virginia during the 1870s and 1880s that favored renegotiation of the state debt to maintain public services. Readjusterism represented the most significant biracial primarily lower-class coalition in the South between Reconstruction and the civil rights movement. Its defeat by a united upper class paved the way for suffrage restriction and the racial politics of Jim Crow.

Before the Civil War, Virginia's planter elite had begun to diversify into banking, commerce, and industry. With the business elite, the planters supported an active state role in capitalist development, especially railroads. To promote development, Virginia exchanged more marketable state bonds for those of the railroads, and a fourth of these bonds were held by upper-class Virginians. By 1845 Virginia was the nation's largest borrower, but, unlike other southern states, it had largely completed a rail network before the Civil War.

After the Civil War temporarily displaced the upper class from power, the freedpeople of Virginia actively asserted their rights. By 1867 African Americans secured civil rights, equal suffrage, and a new constitution that reoriented the role of government, establishing free public schooling and other social services.

By 1869 the Conservatives—the party of property, including the former planter elite—returned to power. In 1871 Conservatives passed the Funding Act pledging state revenue to service the antebellum debt. The depression of 1873 and widespread railroad bankruptcies made this nearly impossible. Conservatives refused to renegotiate the debt. Rather, they raised taxes that hit the masses hardest—including a poll tax linked to suffrage—and cut services. Half of the schools closed and 100,000 children were turned away. Citing honor, Funders' motives were more pragmatic. The Funding Act made bonds receivable at face value for taxes. For wealthy Virginians, bonds were as good as money.

The glaring inequity of the debt issue spawned the Readjuster movement in 1877. The Readjuster base consisted of three components: poor white farmers, many involved in the Grange; white urban workers, many immigrants; and African Americans, the most numerous bloc. The leadership of the movement was a mixture of political "outs" and some planters without capitalist investments. The most prominent figure, Gen. William Mahone, was a wealthy ex-Confederate railroad promoter and key organizer of the Conservative rise to power, although he never shared the pedigree of the upper class. Mahone used his money and organizational skills to help the Readjusters win control of the legislature in 1879, then the governor's office in 1881. As U.S. senator, Mahone gained access to more than 2,000 federal patronage jobs, solidifying the movement into a functioning party.

The Readjusters repudiated a third of the debt, slashed the interest rate, and revoked the tax privileges of bondholders. Readjusters cut property and liquor taxes, raised corporate taxes, and tightened collection of delinquent taxes. Increased revenues were directed to public education, services, and poor relief. Readjusters abolished flogging and payment of the poll tax as a provision for voting.

The progressive Readjuster program reflected African American voting and representation. By 1882, 15 Virginia legislators were black. African American teachers and administrators replaced white staff in black schools. Blacks were appointed to the school boards of Richmond and Petersburg. Black workers and professionals filled patronage positions. African Americans served on juries, as police officers, and even formed militias.

The Readjusters deflected the white supremacist rhetoric of the Conservatives in three general elections. But by 1883 a new centralized Democratic "Machine," able to mobilize the dense social and business networks connecting Virginia's local elites, peeled away enough white support to defeat the Readjusters. A riot in Danville provoked by white Democrats was used to increase white fears. The Democrats' victory was narrow and was consolidated only by a series of election laws effectively allowing vote rigging. African Americans went from 42 percent to 2 percent of the electorate by 1900. In 1902 the system was "legalized" through a new constitution. By midcentury only 1 percent of Virginians voted.

What sets the Readjusters apart from contemporary southern Independent movements, and even from the Populists, is the significant mobilization of African Americans. Unlike Radical Reconstruction, Readjusterism was not supported by the coercive power of the federal state. It was spawned by issues of debt familiar to the 21st century. The experience of Readjusterism emphasizes the historical agency of African Americans in the postbellum South, the willingness of common white people to join them in an anticapitalist coalition, the fluidity of southern racial politics, and the power of a united upper class as the force suppressing democracy.

ALAN DAHL
American University

Nelson Morehouse Blake, *William Mahone of Virginia: Soldier and Political Insurgent* (1935); Jane Dailey, *Before Jim Crow: The Politics of Race in Postemancipation Virginia* (2000); Jack P. Maddex, *The Virginia Conservative, 1867–1879: A Study in Reconstruction Politics* (1970); Allen W. Moger, *Virginia: Bourbonism to Byrd, 1870–1925* (1968); James Tice Moore, *Two Paths to the New South: The Virginia Debt Controversy, 1870–1883* (1974); Raymond H. Pulley, *Old Virginia Restored: An Interpretation of the Progressive Impulse, 1870–1930* (1968); C. Vann Woodward, *Origins of the New South, 1877–1913* (1951, 1971).

Regulator Movement

The Regulator movement (1766–71) was a farmer's reform movement in the North Carolina Piedmont. It aimed to hold corrupt government officials accountable and to create greater economic and political democracy in the area. At the movement's height, some 5,000 to 6,000 men, the great majority of free Piedmont males, took part in it. Regulators engaged in a variety of activities, some of them legal and some of them extralegal. Early in 1771 North Carolina's Gov. William Tryon defeated Piedmont farmers in a military battle, ending the Regulation.

The movement began in 1766 when a group of farmers started the Sandy Creek Association, named after the creek where most of the leaders lived. Leader and spokesman was Herman Husband, a Quaker who had moved from Cecil County, Md., and whose religiously inspired ideas about social justice became tremendously influential among Piedmont farmers. Early in 1768 members of the Sandy Creek Association joined with other reform-minded farmers. They called themselves "Regulators"—a name that indicated that they intended to "regulate" and reform government abuse.

Regulator grievances included difficulties in obtaining clear deeds to land, high legal costs and high taxes, the embezzlement of tax moneys, fee grabbing on the part of court officers, and the collusion between creditors and public officials. Initially farmers tried peaceful means of redress—they petitioned the governor and the Assembly, they took local officials to court, and they entered local elections.

Although the governor and Assembly were unsympathetic, and they did not succeed in getting corrupt officials convicted, the Regulators were surprisingly successful in the elections. They were outnumbered in the legislature, however, so their calls for a land bank, antispeculation laws, fair debt collection laws, court reform, more equitable taxation, secret ballots in elections, the right to instruct their representatives, and the disestablishment of the Anglican Church went unheeded.

When Regulators repeatedly tried such legal measures without results, they grew exasperated and began to resort to extralegal measures. They refused to pay taxes until they could be assured their money would not be embezzled, they repossessed property seized for public sale to satisfy debts and taxes, and they closed courts to prevent miscarriages of justice. They urged people to boycott the courts and resort to mediation.

Moreover, in September 1770, Regulators disrupted the Superior Court in Hillsborough, beat up a few lawyers and merchants, and destroyed the house of the most hated official in the Piedmont. The provincial authorities retaliated forcefully. The Assembly passed a sweeping Riot Act that gave Gov. William Tryon the authority and funds he needed to raise the militia and to march against the Regulators.

On 16 May 1771 about 1,100 militiamen confronted some 2,000 to 3,000 farmers on a field near Alamance Creek. The army was top heavy with officers, many of them leading eastern citizens who would in just a few short years lead the colony into independence. Two hours after the first shot was fired, 17 to 20 farmers were dead, along with 9 militiamen. More than 150 men on both sides were wounded. The next day, the governor ordered one Regulator hanged on the spot without benefit of trial. The governor then undertook a punitive march through the backcountry, burning fields, requisitioning produce and supplies, and forcing more than 6,400 men to take an oath of loyalty to the king. After a hasty trial, six more Regulators were hanged in Hillsborough in June. Some of the best-known Regulator leaders were outlawed and fled the province.

As a result of the violence and repression, the Regulation as an organized movement was crushed by the summer of 1771, though individually many people remained defiant and continued to support their leaders. Hundreds of families left the Piedmont in bitterness. Despite formidable odds, however, the Regulator dream of farmer independence and economic democracy persisted in pockets of the South, throughout the 19th century and beyond.

MARJOLEINE KARS
University of Maryland, Baltimore County

A. Roger Ekirch, *"Poor Carolina": Politics and Society in Colonial North Carolina, 1729-1776* (1981); Marjoleine Kars, *Breaking Loose Together: The Regulator Rebellion in Pre-Revolutionary North Carolina* (2002); William S. Powell, James K. Huhta, and Thomas J. Farnham, eds., *The Regulators in North Carolina: A Documentary History, 1759-1776* (1971).

Rock 'n' Roll

"Rock 'n' roll" describes the fusion of rhythm-and-blues, country, and gospel music that emerged from the South in the mid-1950s. Performed by artists such as Elvis Presley, Carl Perkins, Buddy Holly, Fats Domino, Little Richard, Jerry Lee Lewis, and Bill Haley and the Comets, the new music swept the country from 1955 until the early 1960s. Other than Haley, these artists hailed from working-class southern backgrounds and drew on vernacular musical styles associated with white and black southern working-class cultures. Because of its working-class, multiracial origins and its emergence at a time of great social, cultural, and economic change in the South, rock 'n' roll quickly became a polarizing cultural force with which all southern social classes were compelled to engage.

The southern white working-class generally interacted with African Americans more than other social classes did in the Jim Crow South, and the young white men who became the first rockers grew up absorbing black music from live encounters, radio, and records. Beyond drawing on black music, early rockers also imitated the clothing, slang, dance, and hairstyles of the black working class, much to the chagrin of the white southern middle class. Besides performers, other architects of rock 'n' roll such as Sam Phillips (owner of Memphis's Sun Records), also of southern working-class origins, drew on those working-class roots in crafting the rock 'n' roll sound and ethos. The southern white bourgeoisie accurately perceived that the new rock 'n' roll symbolized not just a musical genre, but an entire lifestyle and set of aesthetic, cultural, and social values derived in great measure from the southern black working class.

Although the performers and producers of rock 'n' roll were almost exclusively associated with the southern working class, the class demographics of the genre's consumers were considerably more complicated. Many white and black working-class and middle-class southern teens and college students enthusiastically supported rock 'n' roll by purchasing records, attending concerts, and listening to it on the radio. However, class-based audience preferences still existed within this continuum of fandom. One sociological study found that middle- or upper-class teens were more drawn to the music of Pat Boone, while working class teens were fans of Elvis Presley. Boone, a white rock 'n' roll artist from Florida, performed sanitized versions of vibrant recordings by other rock 'n' roll and rhythm-and-blues artists. His image was conspicuously defined by his clean-cut hairstyle, college education, early marriage, and conservative clothing. Boone was marketed to the middle class as a socially sanctioned alternative to the gyrating, heavily rhythmic, rebellious rock 'n' roll artists such as Presley.

Challenges to rock 'n' roll in the South came, predictably, from the white and black middle classes, which perceived an alarming threat to social norms embodied in the music and style of the southern working-class rockers. Educators, writers, politicians, and ministers delivered sermons and wrote articles describing the genre as "tribal," "primitive," and of "jungle" origins. Playing on the worst fears of midcentury white southerners, segregationist organizations even charged that consumption of rock 'n' roll led inexorably to miscegenation. Middle-class criticism of rock 'n' roll in the mid- and late 1950s echoed similar class-based objections to the risqué lyrics and infectious rhythms of rhythm-and-blues just a few years earlier.

The initial dominance of the artists and musical styles of the working-class South in the nation's rock 'n' roll scene was ended in the early 1960s by the Beatles' spreading fame and the stylistic diversification of rock music. A decade later, however, southern working-class rock artists once again emerged as a potent artistic force under the rubric of "southern rock." Avoiding the banal dance, love, and party-themed lyrics that characterized 1950s rock 'n' roll, these southern rockers articulated the sentiments of the postintegration southern white working class—a demographic increasingly marginalized from mainstream American culture and progress. The stance outlined in their songs, most famously in Lynyrd Skynyrd's "Sweet Home Alabama," valorized white rural southern masculine identity and conservative social values, emphasized the difficulty of preserving a traditional southern way of life in a postmodern world, aligned the artists with blue-collar workers, celebrated hard living, and employed Confederate and Christian iconography in an effort to project a working-class southern identity. Whether through musical gestures or lyrical content associated with black and white southern working classes, the class-based iconoclasm of rock 'n' roll and southern rock artists, targeting bourgeoisie social values, constitutes a vibrant cultural thread in the fabric of American popular music history.

CARRIE ALLEN
University of Houston–Downtown

Glenn C. Altschuler, *All Shook Up: How Rock 'n' Roll Changed America* (2003); Michael T. Bertrand, *Race, Rock, and Elvis* (2005); James C. Cobb, *Redefining Southern Culture: Mind and Identity in the Modern South* (1999); Pete Daniel, *Lost Revolutions: The South in the 1950s* (2000); Erika Doss, *Elvis Culture: Fans, Faith, and Image* (1999); Peter Guralnick, *Last Train to Memphis:* *The Rise of Elvis Presley* (1994); Mark Kemp, *Dixie Lullaby: A Story of Music, Race, and New Beginnings in a New South* (2004); Jack Temple Kirby, *Rural Worlds Lost: The American South, 1920–1960* (1987); Burgin Mathews, *Southern Cultures* (Fall 2009); Craig Mosher, *Popular Music and Society* 31:1 (2008).

Service Workers

Like most agricultural societies, the antebellum South was not home to a strict division between the provision of services and domestic production. Except on the largest plantations, the enslaved people, indentured servants, and wives who, under markedly different forms of subordination, performed services such as food preparation, cleaning, and intimate care were likely also to be producing goods for domestic consumption or for the market. Although white and black women shared experiences of work within slaveholding households, recent scholarship highlights the role of physical violence in white women's efforts to control slave labor.

Emancipation allowed some freedwomen to withdraw from domestic service for white families, preferring to work with and for their own families when possible. Home-based services such as laundering or dressmaking offered an alternative to cleaning, cooking, or childcare under white families' roofs. For the African American women who did work in domestic service in the 19th and 20th centuries, the intimacy and arbitrariness of supervision, and the lack of respect for their work, often overshadowed even demands for higher wages and shorter workweeks in a notoriously poorly paid job. In post-Reconstruction Atlanta, for example, professional laundresses strove to remove their labors from employers' houses to their own neighborhoods, where the washing could be performed among peers and away from white clients. Housecleaners who migrated from their southern homes to Washington, D.C., in the early 20th century went to great lengths to find work that allowed them to "live out"—that is, out from under their white employers' roofs—even at the cost of adding extra jobs to pay the rent.

Given the unpopularity of domestic service, and the refusal of employers to make the work more attractive with better conditions or higher pay, white southerners in Congress were particularly adamant that their states' pools of cheap labor not be compromised by social welfare legislation. Both agricultural and domestic workers were excluded from social insurance programs such as Social Security and unemployment insurance, and the protective maximum-hour legislation did not apply to women employed in others' homes. Neither the National Labor Relations Act nor the Fair Labor Standards Act applied to domestic employees.

World War II made clear just how unpopular domestic service work was under these conditions. War production and the federal prohibition of discrimination for contractors opened some new job categories to women, and though the demand for maids did not decrease, the supply diminished precipitously. In response, many service tasks moved from homes to institutions such as restaurants, hospitals, and hotels, where women of color and, increasingly, men of color again inherited the most physically demanding and ill remunerated of the tasks. With the federal redistribution of national wealth into the South facilitated by the Cold War military economy, a secondary tier of service work opened up in the South's burgeoning retail, tourism, and recreation industries. In the gleaming high-rises of "clean development" centers such as Houston, Atlanta, and Charlotte, white women especially entered low-wage clerical and secretarial jobs.

Southern service workers, however, did not universally accept the low valuations of their worth implied by the conditions they reported. Nationally, labor organizing was concentrated in cities and their factories. Yet in the service sector especially, the South was home to the kind of broad-based community organizing that today characterizes the healthiest national unions. With its intellectual foundation in broader human rights and its social base among activists and community members unified against white supremacy, the civil rights movement revitalized the national labor movement by way of public-sector and service unions. By the end of the 20th century the service sector had eclipsed manufacturing, agriculture, and extraction as the largest employer in the South, a shift that signaled a convergence with the national economy. Service occupations became the fastest-growing categories of employment in the country as well as the region, although southern states were particularly likely to see growth in the low end of service employment, among occupations such as retail clerk, food server, and home health aide.

BETHANY MORETON
University of Georgia

Evelyn Nakano Glenn, *Signs* (Autumn 1992); Thavolia Glymph, *Out of the House of Bondage: The Transformation of the Plantation Household* (2008); Michael Honey, *Going Down Jericho Road: The Memphis Strike, Martin Luther King's Last Campaign* (2007); Tera Hunter, *To 'Joy My Freedom: Southern Black Women's Lives and Labors after the Civil War* (1997); Larry Isaac and Lars Christiansen, *American Sociological Review* (October 2002); Nancy MacLean, *Freedom Is Not Enough: The Opening of the American Workplace* (2006).

Shape-Note Singing

The practice of singing from music using note heads of different shapes to indicate the degrees of the scale has long been entangled with perceptions of social class in the United States. The practice originated as an outgrowth of an 18th-century musical reform movement, based in New England, designed to improve congregational singing and promote musical literacy. Sometime in the 1790s in the middle Atlantic states the idea took hold of using differently shaped note heads to help teach ordinary people to sing music. In keeping with the then-prevailing British system of solfege, four shapes were devised, and first saw print in the *Easy Instructor* (1801). As European settlers moved south and west in the early 19th century, shape-note singing spread with them, and local composers tapped indigenous folk materials (African American and American Indian as well as various white ethnic strains) and the musical practices of the Second Great Awakening to create a distinctive body of American Indian hymnody.

Even as shape-note singing extended outward from New England, however, it was challenged by a new "Better Music Movement" that attacked it for being rude and primitive and called for a more refined style of music education along the most advanced (generally German) lines. Reformers such as Thomas Hastings and Lowell Mason hitched their wagon to the rising star of cultural hierarchy, as an expanding urban middle class in the Northeast, and later the Midwest, sought to culturally differentiate itself from rural popular culture. Thus the use of shaped notes was increasingly marginalized in the 19th century, primarily to the rural South. There it persisted among singers of the *Sacred Harp* and allied traditions, while moving from the early four-shape ("fasola") system to the Aiken seven-shape ("doremi") system; in the latter form, it provided the foundation for an indigenous southern publishing industry that by the late 19th century began to develop the more modern style nowadays referred to as "southern gospel."

Shape-note singing, though, continued to suffer from cultural condescension. It was excluded from mainstream musical instruction and generally fell into disuse except among the hardcore of fasola and similar singers, themselves reduced by defections from younger white southerners adopting more "modern" styles. Paradoxically, though, in the 20th century shape-note singing began to attract sympathetic interest from a segment of the urban elite itself. George Pullen Jackson, a Vanderbilt professor from a high-culture background in the urban "New South," "discovered" the "lost tonal tribe" of the "fasola folk" in the 1920s. The later folk revival of the 1950s and 1960s attracted attention from folk music enthusiasts and early-music advocates, who have since spread the oldest forms of shape-note singing (though not shape-note gospel) to urban settings across the anglophone world. This inversion of traditional cultural hierarchies often relies (more among consumers of the music than among participants) on the basic premises of those hierarchies: that shape-note singers are primitives, preserving in isolation an old, pure cultural tradition against "modern" inroads. In this regard, urban middle-class views of traditional singers can seem similar to older notions of southern mountain folk as "contemporary ancestors." Evocations by contemporary critics such as Greil Marcus of "the old, weird America" are a case in point.

Such views of traditional shape-note singers are, however, deeply misleading. Far from being a practice of marginalized people, shape-note singing, whether the older fasola or the newer gospel, appealed to a cross section of southern rural society. Stressing musical literacy, these styles perpetuated themselves through print materials (tune books, minutes, newspapers) and systems of highly organized conventions.

Leading shape-note advocates such as A. S. Kieffer of the *Musical Million* were knowledgeable in their advocacy. Singing-school masters and tune book compilers such as William Walker, B. F. White, and Joe S. James were prominent in their communities; shape-note gospel music publishers such as James D. Vaughan of Lawrenceburg, Tenn., were major New South entrepreneurs and innovators.

Finally, the question of class in shape-note singing is further complicated by the more recent revival of shape-note singing. While many of the revivalists originally filtered their understandings of the tradition through folk revival sensibilities, they soon came in contact with traditional singers, both migrants from the region and a new generation of singing-school masters teaching southern practice to the outlanders. Nowadays at major southern conventions, such as the National Sacred Harp Convention in Birmingham or the United Sacred Harp Convention, urban professionals from the South and the non-South sing with rural southerners from all walks of life, in both old classic "pine-box" churches and modern, stained-glass sanctuaries. Although the influx of urbanites has introduced some new tensions into the community of singers, those tensions have to do with culture and religion, not with social class. In the end, modern shape-note singing is not an expression of class boundaries, but a solvent of them.

DAVID L. CARLTON
Vanderbilt University

John Bealle, *Public Worship, Private Faith: Sacred Harp and American Folksong* (1997); Buell E. Cobb, *The Sacred Harp: A Tradition and Its Music* (1978); James R. Goff, *Close Harmony: A History of Southern Gospel* (2002); George Pullen Jackson, *White Spirituals of the Southern Uplands* (1933).

Share Croppers' Union and Southern Tenant Farmers' Union

In the decades after the end of Reconstruction, state governments in the South implemented economic policies that favored the interests of wealthy planters and business owners over those of poorer people. Low property taxes, limited public services, and labor legislation designed to maintain a cheap, docile labor force helped to encourage investment in the region but did little to improve living conditions for working-class southerners, white or black. The crop lien system trapped many sharecroppers and tenant farmers into a form of debt peonage that kept families working for the same employer year after year for no pay. Plantation owners used economic reprisals, intimidation, and violence to control workers and prevent them from organizing challenges to the system.

The Great Depression intensified the hardships that rural poor people endured and radicalized many other Americans as well. In 1931 Communist Party members who had been organizing workers in Birmingham, Ala., extended their efforts to the state's plantation regions in response to requests from black sharecroppers seeking to form a union. The Share Croppers' Union (SCU) was formed in August 1931 in Tallapoosa County and quickly spread to other parts of Alabama and to neighboring states. Mass strikes by union members secured some small wage increases and other concessions from plantation owners, inspiring more people to join the union. When the Agricultural Adjustment Act (1933) encouraged planters to take land out of production and evict sharecroppers or change their status to wage laborers to avoid sharing federal subsidies with them, many families turned to the SCU for help. By the mid-1930s the union had approximately 10,000 members in Alabama, Georgia, Louisiana, and Mississippi.

Plantation owners responded to the SCU's attempts to improve conditions for rural workers with a campaign of violence and terror aimed at destroying the union. Police and vigilantes disrupted union meetings, threatened and beat up union members, and murdered several SCU organizers. The union's communist affiliations made it an easy target for opponents who argued that its real goal was to incite African Americans to revolution. Progressive activists who might otherwise have supported the SCU's work were also wary of associating with the communists. In 1936 SCU leaders attempted to gain greater legitimacy by seeking an alliance with the National Farmers Union (NFU), an organization of white farmers that had grown out of the Farmers Alliance and Populist movements of the late 19th century. Leftist factions within the NFU saw an opportunity to strengthen their position in the union by encouraging black farmers to join, and in the late

1930s SCU locals transferred into the NFU. Although this change gave SCU members a voice in a national organization that was able to influence federal policy, at the local level union members continued to suffer from violent attacks and other forms of repression.

Similar problems beset the Southern Tenant Farmers' Union (STFU), an interracial union founded by socialists in Arkansas in 1934. When the STFU began publicizing planter abuses of New Deal agricultural programs and the displacement of thousands of sharecropping families from the land, white elites responded with the same forms of intimidation that their counterparts in other states had used against the SCU. Union members faced constant harassment, arrests, and attacks on their homes. Despite the dangers, organizers persevered and gained support from white northerners and some sympathetic government officials. The STFU drew national attention to rural poverty and the exploitative practices of plantation owners, attracting more than 20,000 members in Arkansas, Missouri, Oklahoma, Texas, and parts of Mississippi. Like the SCU, the STFU worked to secure better working conditions and fair treatment for tenant farmers, and it also lobbied for changes in federal policies that offered generous assistance to the nation's wealthiest landowners but did little to help families at the bottom of the agricultural ladder.

The combined efforts of the rural unions succeeded in persuading the federal government to modify some practices and pay more attention to the needs of tenants and small farmers. The Department of Agriculture expanded some of its loan programs so that more families could receive assistance and investigated complaints against landlords who cheated workers out of their share of subsidy payments. Plantation owners remained the dominant force in shaping agricultural policy and its implementation in the South, however, and the decades following the 1930s saw the continued displacement of poorer farm operators from the land. Farmers' unions were unable to prevent the decline of small farms and consolidation of landownership into fewer and fewer hands in the second half of the 20th century.

GRETA DE JONG
University of Nevada at Reno

David Eugene Conrad, *The Forgotten Farmers: The Story of Sharecroppers in the New Deal* (1965); Pete Daniel, *Breaking the Land: The Transformation of Cotton, Tobacco, and Rice Cultures since 1880* (1985); Donald Grubbs, *Cry from the Cotton: The Southern Tenant Farmers' Union and the New Deal* (1971); Robin D. G. Kelley, *Hammer and Hoe: Alabama Communists during the Great Depression* (1990); Jay R. Mandle, *The Roots of Black Poverty: The Southern Plantation Economy after the Civil War* (1978); Jeannie Whayne, *A New Plantation South: Land, Labor, and Federal Favor in Twentieth-Century Arkansas* (1996); Gavin Wright, *Old South, New South: Revolutions in the Southern Economy since the Civil War* (1986).

Socialism and Communism

Socialists and communists traditionally proposed radical socioeconomic alterations to benefit the proletariat. Socialists wanted the government to control the means of production and distribution and to allocate wealth on the basis of one's labor. Communists wanted the workers to control the means of production and distribution and to allocate wealth according to one's need. In the South, neither socialists nor communists sought such revolutionary reforms, but rather immediate benefits for the working class. Bourgeois opposition, red-baiting, and debates about race, however, hindered those efforts. The 250 Ruskin colonists who settled in Tennessee and Georgia in the 1890s in the Ruskin Commonwealth Association may have come closest to implementing pure socialism. Their utopian settlements, based on the teachings of English socialist John Ruskin, which included shared ownership and labor, emerged in 1894 but collapsed by 1901 as a result of infighting and poor planning.

The more common socialist reality is exemplified first by the Socialist Labor Party, which appeared contemporaneously with the Ruskin settlements. The party demanded government ownership of utilities, a shorter workday, and a progressive income tax. It organized workers in Houston, Dallas, San Antonio, and New Orleans in the 1890s, and by 1903 the *Southern Socialist* newspaper spread its agenda. Those efforts were hampered by the party's focus on class to the exclusion of race, however, and it never found a large following.

The Socialist Party of America was modestly more successful. Demanding government ownership of industry and the abolition of child labor, it won a small following in Louisiana by 1903, organized tenant farmers in Waco, Tex., by 1911, and operated several newspapers, notably the *Hallettsville Rebel* in Texas, which claimed a circulation of 25,000. It was inconsistent on race, however, at times subordinating it to and at others placing it as a precursor for proletarian unity. This inconsistency, combined with the Sedition and Espionage Acts and the nativist wave of the 1920s, undermined the party, and by 1932 it counted only 900 southern members.

Socialists achieved a modicum more success in 1932 when they organized the Southern Tenant Farmers' Union in Tyronza, Ark. Although few members understood the union's socialist ideology, they appreciated its efforts to aid the dispossessed, and by 1937 it numbered 30,000 supporters in seven states. Landowner attacks weakened the organization, however, and membership declined during the war years. In 1946 it joined the American Federation of Labor as the National Agricultural Workers Union, and socialist organizing in the South tapered off.

Communist efforts followed a similar trajectory, as the Communist Party of the United States of America entered the South through allied unions seeking economic improvement. The National Textile Workers Union organized a strike in Gastonia, N.C., in April 1929 centered on better wages and working conditions. The strike collapsed by June, in part a result of the failure to gain African American support, but organizing continued. In 1931 Alabama communists formed the Share Croppers' Union, demanding better pay and treatment. Despite landowner violence, by 1936 it claimed 10,000 members and had expanded into Mississippi and Louisiana. The failure to win white support, combined with a series of unsuccessful strikes, undermined the union, and it dissolved in 1937.

Communists made similar efforts to organize coal miners in Harlan County, Ky.; steelworkers in Birmingham, Ala.; cigar makers in Miami, Fla.; pecan shellers in San Antonio, Tex.; and tobacco workers in Winston-Salem, N.C. At the same time, the *Southern Worker* newspaper spread the party's agenda, unemployment councils helped those unable to find work, and the International Labor Defense provided legal assistance, notably defending the Scottsboro Boys and Angelo Herndon. None of those efforts achieved significant interracial cooperation, however, and communists were unable to create a unified proletarian movement.

In an attempt to generate interracial working-class unity, throughout the 1940s and 1950s communists participated in several civil rights organizations, including the Southern Negro Youth Congress, the Southern Conference for Human Welfare, and the Southern Conference Educational Fund. Those efforts, as well as continued organizing through affiliated unions and the Congress of Industrial Organizations, achieved only minimal gains. Worse, the campaigns facilitated segregationist attacks, which further inhibited working-class unity, and by the mid-1950s communist efforts in the South had dissipated.

Despite differing ideologies, both socialists and communists sought immediate gains for the proletariat rather than socioeconomic reform. Fear, bourgeois opposition, and the fact that for many southerners race trumped class ultimately prevented either movement from creating a substantive interracial working-class alliance, and southern workers were left to fend for themselves.

GREGORY S. TAYLOR
Chowan University

Numan Bartley, *The New South, 1945–1980* (1995); W. Fitzhugh Brundage, *A Socialist Utopia in the New South* (1996); W. J. Cash, *The Mind of the South* (1941); Philip Foner, *American Socialism and Black Americans* (1977); Glenda Elizabeth Gilmore, *Defying Dixie: The Radical Roots of Civil Rights, 1915–1950* (2008); Donald Grubbs, *Cry from the Cotton: The Southern Tenant Farmers' Union and the New Deal* (2000); Robin D. G. Kelley, *Hammer and Hoe: Alabama Communists during the Great Depression* (1990); Harvey Klehr, *The Heyday of American Communism* (1984); George Tindall, *The Emergence of the New South, 1913–1945* (1967).

Southern Conference for Human Welfare
(1938–1948)
Southern Conference Educational Fund
(1947–1977)

Although it is often seen as a bastion of conservatism, during the 1930s and early 1940s the South was one of the more politically liberal areas of the country. Progressive reformers were spurred on by the devastation of the Great Depression and encouraged by the liberal agenda of the New Deal. One of the most remarkable reform-minded organizations of the period was the

Southern Conference for Human Welfare (SCHW).

Founded in Birmingham in 1938, the SCHW brought together a broad array of reformers—journalists, academics, union leaders, and politicians—whose common purposes were social justice, improving race relations, and instituting electoral reforms. The organization was largely the brainchild of Joseph Gelders, an organizer for the International Labor Defense, and Lucy Randolph Mason, the public relations representative for the Congress of Industrial Organizations in the South. Gelders approached President Franklin D. Roosevelt with the idea of a regionwide conference focusing on the repression of civil liberties in the South. The president was receptive to the idea of the conference because he saw in it an opportunity to rally southern support for New Deal reforms, but his wife, Eleanor, always more reform-minded than her husband, became an immediate and enthusiastic supporter of the idea. The First Lady suggested the conference be broadened to address all of the South's problems, including segregation, low wages, and limited educational opportunities.

The SCHW held its inaugural meeting in Birmingham on 20 November 1938 and brought together the South's leading liberals, including Aubrey Williams of the Works Progress Administration, Mary McLeod Bethune, Supreme Court Justice Hugo Black, and James Dombrowski, one of the organizers of the Highlander Folk School. Eleanor Roosevelt was also in attendance.

Nearly 300 of the 1,200 delegates were African American, and the biracial nature of the meeting made the SCHW an easy target for its critics. The organization would also be continually plagued by accusations that it was a communist front. The fact that the SCHW welcomed African American members and had a strong prolabor stance made it a frequent target for anticommunist critics. If its critics proved to be a perennial problem for the SCHW, its finances were an even greater one. The 1939 meeting was cancelled because of funding problems, and maintaining the day-to-day operations of the organization proved nearly impossible. The SCHW's finances did not significantly improve until after World War II, when a series of fundraisers featuring celebrities brought in much-needed revenue. Encouraged by the organization's new growth, SCHW officers voted in 1946 to create the Southern Conference Educational Fund (SCEF), which would function as the educational wing of the SCHW. The SCEF was led by James Dombrowski, who also edited the SCEF's newspaper, the *Southern Patriot*. Whereas the SCHW tended to operate through traditional political channels, the SCEF functioned largely through teaching and publishing. The two also differed in their focus; whereas the parent organization had a broad agenda encompassing a number of reforms, the SCEF was focused exclusively on ending segregation in the South, which Dombrowski viewed as the most serious issue facing the region.

The SCEF grew as the SCHW faltered. Membership in the SCHW declined amid growing cries that the organization was a haven for radicals. The elder organization was eventually investigated by the House Un-American Activities Committee (HUAC), and in 1948 SCHW officers voted to end the organization.

The SCEF, which had been a separate organization since 1947, survived the SCHW for a number of years. Under Dombrowski's leadership, the SCEF became heavily involved in the burgeoning civil rights movement. Although the SCEF remained a biracial organization, it was particularly engaged in encouraging southern whites to resist segregation. The SCEF also worked closely with civil rights organizations such as the Southern Christian Leadership Conference (SCLC) and the Student Nonviolent Coordinating Committee (SNCC). From the mid- to late 1960s, when the civil rights movement became more focused on economic justice, the SCEF did as well, encouraging poor whites and African Americans to work together to improve economic conditions in their own communities.

Although it survived the SCHW by a number of years, the SCEF was also plagued by accusations that it was a communist front. Like its parent organization, the SCEF was repeatedly targeted by HUAC. It weathered such attacks for years, but was eventually undone internally, in much the same way as the SCHW had been. In the mid-1960s large numbers of young white volunteers joined the organization, shifting its membership away from the working class, which had always been its base. The new membership also led to a hodgepodge of ideologies, making it virtually impossible to form a coherent agenda. By 1973 the organization was effectively split, and in 1977 it ceased to exist altogether.

REBECCA WOODHAM
Wallace Community College–Dothan

John Egerton, *Speak Now against the Day: The Generation before the Civil Rights Movement in the South* (1994); Irwin Klibaner, *Conscience of a Troubled South: The Southern Conference Educational Fund, 1946–1966* (1989); Thomas Krueger, *And Promises to Keep: The Southern Conference for Human Welfare, 1938–1948* (1967).

Southern Regional Council

Founded in 1944, the Southern Regional Council (SRC) sought to alleviate racial injustice in the American South through expanded dialogue and cooperation between the races. Unlike the National Association for the Advancement of Colored People, the SRC did not pursue litigation aimed at dismantling segregation, nor did it organize grassroots protest in favor of civil rights. Rather, it focused on bringing white and black leaders together across the South to focus on issues that could alleviate racial injustice without fundamentally challenging the segregated, social structure of southern society. Such an approach hinged less on "human relations," noted Leslie Dunbar, than on "human resources," meaning that the SRC focused less on explicitly racial issues like integration than it did on structural issues contributing to racial injustice, issues such as jobs, social services, and education.

Because of its early focus on leadership elites, the SRC began as a distinctly upper-class institution, aimed at attracting predominantly white members of "commanding regional stature and authority." However, the organization lost a sizable segment of its membership in 1951, when it took a public stance against racial segregation. From that point onward, the SRC assumed a slightly less elite, but decidedly more inclusive, academic, and arguably middle-class status, including many more black members than originally envisioned. For much of the 1940s and 1950s, the SRC became the voice of many southern liberals, particularly white liberals who sought to improve race relations in the region without enlisting the federal government.

Foremost among the SRC's declared goals were research, information, and interracial dialogue, a project that the council pursued by sponsoring a series of studies on the South, including George McMillan's *Racial Violence and Law Enforcement* (1960), Howard Zinn's *Albany: A Study in National Responsibility* (1962), and James McBridde Dabbs's *Who Speaks for the South?* (1964). In 1962 the SRC mounted the massive Voter Education Project, aimed at facilitating the registration of black voters across the South—a project that dovetailed nicely with voter registration campaigns mounted by other grassroots civil rights organizations like the Student Nonviolent Coordinating Committee in places such as the Mississippi Delta in 1964 and Selma, Ala., in 1965.

ANDERS WALKER
Saint Louis University

Leslie W. Dunbar, ANNALS *of the American Academy of Political and Social Science* (January 1965).

Southern Student Organizing Committee

First formed in 1964, the Southern Student Organizing Committee (SSOC) was active throughout the decade, organizing white college students across the South around a range of progressive causes. Emerging as an extension of efforts by the Student Nonviolent Coordinating Committee (SNCC) to mobilize white student support for the civil rights movement, SSOC was formally launched at a meeting of student activists who traveled to Nashville that April. Its founding statement, entitled "We'll Take Our Stand" (a nod to the "I'll Take My Stand" manifesto penned in 1930 by the Nashville Agrarians), situated the group within a tradition of southern radicalism. Emphasizing a "determination to build together a New South which brings democracy and justice for all its people," the statement pledged to move outward from southern campuses to battle segregation, poverty, and elitist political control.

SSOC's base among white southern students filled a niche between SNCC's organizing efforts in black communities and Students for a Democratic Society's (SDS) national student movement. SSOC partnered directly with SNCC on several early projects and in 1964 established fraternal ties to SDS, which to that point had made only minimal inroads in the region. Funds provided by SNCC helped to launch the SSOC newsletter the *New Rebel*, which quickly evolved from a four-page stapled edition to a polished and widely respected publication. The group's first major activist initiative, undertaken in conjunction with the 1964 Mississippi Freedom Summer voter registration campaign, was the White Folks Project, in which SSOC adherents worked to build support for civil rights issues in white working-class communities along the Gulf Coast. While the project was by most accounts frustratingly ineffective, pushing the group toward its later base-building efforts on southern campuses, it was emblematic of SSOC's early civil rights focus.

Aided by a campus traveler who visited schools across the region to support local organizing efforts, SSOC quickly raised its profile, drawing students from 43 southern schools to its Atlanta conference in late 1964. The group's political orientation broadened as well, with new initiatives in 1965 and 1966 increasingly centered on antiwar, antidraft, and academic freedom issues. Later in the decade, two influential essays—Beverly Jones and Judith Brown's "Toward a Female Liberation Movement" and Lyn Wells's "American Women: Their Use and Abuse"—helped to fashion SSOC into a hub of women's liberation organizing.

This expansion in both size and political focus exacerbated tensions that had simmered within SSOC since its founding. The group's primary orientation to southern campuses clashed with the more radical class critiques that had motivated SSOC's interest in mobilizing among working-class whites. While particular projects—including a community initiative in a poor white neighborhood in North Nashville and labor organizing work in North Carolina textile mills—moved SSOC efforts away from campuses, its community-based focus was increasingly subsumed by student-centered programs. The group's distinctive orientation to the region also led to protracted debates over how—or whether—to draw on traditional southern symbols and embrace visions of southern distinctiveness. Such concerns fueled conflicts over the appropriateness of SSOC's founding emblem, which featured clasped black and white hands over the Confederate battle flag. Similar debates prompted the group to rename its *New Rebel* newsletter the *New South Student* in 1965.

As SSOC evolved from a coordinating committee with affiliates to a membership group with chapters in 1966, some of its most active adherents became increasingly oriented to local issues that were often disconnected from the regional and national focus of the group's officers. A 1968 restructuring effort failed to resolve those tensions, and in the face of a strong challenge by SDS, SSOC ultimately voted to disband in the summer of 1969. Despite this abrupt self-imposed exit, the group's legacy is estimable. Throughout the 1960s, SSOC was the primary organization advancing antiracist and other progressive causes among white southern students. Its reach extended to many smaller southern campuses that otherwise would have remained unexposed to progressive activism. Both its newsletter and affiliated underground publications, including Atlanta's *Great Speckled Bird* and Jackson's the *Kudzu*, were must-reads in southern leftist political circles. The group's efforts to organize poor and working-class whites, though halting, provided a model for subsequent interracial labor organizing campaigns. Indeed, in a region largely untapped by national student organizations such as SDS, SSOC was a primary conduit linking progressive southern students to the key national and global struggles of the era.

DAVID CUNNINGHAM
Brandeis University

Clayborne Carson, *In Struggle: SNCC and the Black Awakening of the 1960s* (1995); John McMillian and Paul Buhle, eds., *The New Left Revisited* (2003); Gregg L. Michel, *Struggle for a Better South: The Southern Student Organizing Committee, 1964-1969* (2004); Jack Newfield, *Motive* (March 1966).

Spiritual and Gospel Music

The frontier camp meetings of the early 19th-century South were the crucibles producing new forms of religious music that would come to be associated with the American South. Earlier, the colonial South had been mostly Anglican in religion, with psalms and classic British church hymns used in congregational singing that brought together parish communities aspiring to cross class lines. With the rise of evangelical Protestantism in the South after the American Revolution, believers found traditional psalms and hymns inadequate for the new religion's stress on individual conversion, and often-illiterate evangelicals could not use hymnbooks to guide their singing.

In response, camp meeting songs appeared. They were frequently narrative poems that traced the stages of conversion and assurance of salvation and portrayed the preachers, exhorters, young converts, and backsliders who were part of the open-air revivalism associated with early camp meetings.

The ethos of camp meeting songs was spiritually individualistic and egalitarian, it nurtured a postconversion sense of community, and it often drew from popular secular tunes. It appealed to rural, hardscrabble white farmers—and to their slaves. These were biracial affairs, and the presence of black exhorters and converts stamped evangelical music with early black influences, especially through the call-and-response singing, which had become typical of African American worshipers. In truth, there was a mutual exchange of influences, across racial lines, introducing blacks and whites to the sounds of each other's singing. Preachers sang out several lines of a camp meeting song, with the congregation repeating them, enabling worship to transcend illiterate congregants or the shortage of hymnbooks. Camp meeting songs often circulated in shaped-note form, whereby the shape of the note indicated its musical pitch—"fa" was a triangle, "sol" a circle, "la" a square, and "mi" a diamond. Singing schools became a training ground for shaped-note teachers who spread through the countryside, and tune books such as the *Sacred Harp* (1844) provided a musical repertoire for religious singing.

The camp meeting songs became a repository of white yeomen values in the South. The awareness of human sinfulness, the search for salvation, a radical spiritual individualism, a trust in the local congregational context for religious life, the fatalism that marked this vale of tears, the hope for the rewards of a just life in heaven, and the moralistic expectations of postconversion behavior—all marked the white yeomanry, not only with religious meanings but with broader cultural ways of dealing with life in the region.

African American spirituals emerged partly from the camp meetings but came to express a distinctive worldview for slaves. They were sacred folksongs that were sometimes also called anthems or jubilees. Creative slave preachers chanted sermons, and the spirituals grew out of preachers drawing from biblically based themes that expressed the sorrows and hopes of slaves. Spirituals drew especially from Old Testament stories and characters, showing God's identification with the oppressed and the ultimate hope of divine intervention in human affairs to bring liberation. They showed Jesus as a protector, comforter, friend, and redeemer, rather than a direct liberator. The Spirituals were typically otherworldly, but they also often had coded meanings: "freedom" was not just spiritual, and "steal away" did not just mean to seek refuge for prayer.

In the southern class system, hardscrabble white farmers who worked next to their slaves shared much in daily experience and in their sacred music. But slavery established not only a racial boundary but a class one as well, and in the praise sessions in slave quarters at night after work was done or at funerals, blacks used music to articulate a sense of identity. African inheritances emphasized the importance of body movement, while singing promoted preservation of the "ring shout," where slaves danced religion as well as sang it. Part of the distinctiveness of slave spirituals from white camp meeting songs was thus in performance—strong rhythms, percussive features such as stamping and hand clapping, improvised texts, and the call-and-response between song leader and responding chorus. White southerners knew the spirituals well before the Civil War, but other Americans did not, until Union troops in the South heard them and brought them to national attention. The first comprehensive collection was *Slave Songs of the United States* (1867).

After the Civil War, some elite African Americans distanced themselves from the spirituals. Black Methodist bishop Daniel Payne put them down as "cornfield ditties," but the masses of freed slaves continued to embrace them. Broader acceptance of spirituals by middle-class blacks came after they were reimagined in the sophisticated idiom of European choral music. The Fisk Jubilee Singers pioneered the concert performance of spirituals, with composers writing out the songs, the first examples of black sacred music that were not folk music spread by the oral tradition. Arrangers at black colleges now notated the songs in the musical language of European tradition and trained choirs performed the songs before appreciative northern and European audiences, often raising money for black education in the process. This was a social class change in the music, which moved beyond its rural, working-class folk origins and became a part of African American uplift activities aspiring to middle-class respectability in sacred music as well as in other social and cultural activities.

Denominational leaders in both black and white churches after the Civil War worked to raise the standards of sacred music. They stressed the importance of standardized denominational hymnbooks, training programs for song leaders, the use of choirs, and the employment of professional music ministers in churches wealthy enough to afford them—the latter being a clue that the entire denominational reform effort in sacred music was a class effort designed to move southern congregations away from spirited, informal, folk-based singing toward singing regarded as more dignified and consistent across congregations. Class-based controversies appeared in rural churches over musical instruments, particularly installation of organs. Organs were associated with wealthy urban churches, regarded as needless luxuries that reflected poorly on the moralistic self-denial favored by many southern evangelicals. One South Carolina preacher exclaimed of the organ: "I verily believe God will not suffer this *Beast* to rule in Baptist churches." He lamented that the embrace of this elite musical instrument seemed to spread, though, throughout the region.

Denominational reformers did not like a major trend in late 19th-century sacred music in the South, namely the spread of evangelistic music associated with northern urban revivalism. Gospel music had become defined by the 1870s in the publications of Ira Sankey, who was song leader for the era's leading evangelist, Chicago's Dwight Moody. Gospel music was assimilated to southern religious traditions when its revival songs were published in shaped-note form, enabling rural people to sing them in churches and at home. The Ruebush-Kieffer Company of Dayton, Va., and the Anthony J. Showalter publishing house in Dalton, Ga., led the way, with paperback hymnals that were used in country churches but were especially noteworthy for their role in the weekend singing conventions. The lyrics of southern gospel music were rooted in a biblically based theology that reflected the early camp meeting songs, with the wickedness of human nature, the need for salvation, and the joys of heaven still prominent. They were often nostalgic and sentimental songs of country churches, the family hearth, and spiritually nurturing mothers. Above all, the songs were about a comforting Savior, helping to create intimate possibilities for singers to know the love of Jesus. "What a Friend We Have in Jesus," "Washed in the Blood of the Lamb," and "In the Garden" are good examples. These songs permeated white working-class and middle-class culture in the South. In 1913 a seminary professor expressed his disdain for the songs, yet his sense was that they had become deeply rooted in the region: "Popular gospel hymns, sung with verve and vigor, may not satisfy the artistic taste of the cultured, but they serve the purpose of worship for the common man far better than more elevated efforts."

Black gospel music took distinctive shape through performance styles, with body rhythms, call-and-response patterns, and improvisations long characteristic of African-derived sacred music. More traditional churches and those well off financially did not embrace the emerging black gospel sounds that often came out of the northern ghetto experiences of the early 20th century. The songs of the Rev. Charles Albert Tindley, a black minister from Maryland, were a bridge from past to present, as he used folk imagery from the 19th-century slave experience to interpret the black experience in moving to the cities of the North. The golden age of black gospel music began in the 1930s, with the compositions of Georgia-born Thomas A. Dorsey. He and other composers transformed the congregational gospel hymns of Tindley into songs for church choirs, soloists, and ensembles, such as the Golden Gate Quartet, the Dixie Hummingbirds, and other black gospel groups. Pentecostal and Holiness churches became important religious traditions in the early 20th century, and they embraced black gospel music. They moved beyond traditional church piano and organ and embraced the tambourine, horns, and electric guitars as appropriate to a faith that sought the active workings of the spirit. The Church of God in Christ, centered in Memphis, Tenn., early supported services with new rhythmic intensity, and as its members became more socially and economically successful, they kept much of their lively sacred music culture despite rising to the middle class. White Pentecostal and Holiness churches also encouraged new sacred sounds, often leading to their influence on the popular music of such Pentecostal-raised performers as Elvis Presley and Jerry Lee Lewis.

Gospel music traditions experienced commercialization from the early 20th century. James Vaughan's publishing company in Lawrenceburg, Tenn., and the Stamps-Baxter Company in Jacksonville, Tex., blanketed the South with paperback hymnals, but they also pioneered in new ways to spread gospel music. They employed traveling quartet singers to market their songbooks, and they used radio, with Vaughan launching WOAN, one of the first broadcasting stations in Tennessee, and Stamps-Baxter sponsoring broadcasts over Dallas's KRLD beginning in 1937. Gospel performers such as the Blackwood Brothers, the Five Blind Boys of Mississippi, and Sister Rosetta Thorpe became regionally prominent celebrities who used gospel music for economic and cultural empowerment, escaping the cotton fields and textile mills, just as did southern performers of country music, the blues, or rock 'n' roll.

Country music has a long tradition of supporting sacred music, reflecting originally the outlook of working-class white southerners. The Carter Family's songbook of the upland South included songs documenting the hard times of such folk, such as "There's No Depression in Heaven," whose lyrics sang of "going where there's no depression, to a lovely land that's free from care." One strain of southern evangelicalism has a long history of speaking to the socially and economically disinherited, seeing the world as so corrupt that only the end of the world can bring new hope, seen in such songs as "This World Can't Stand Long," "We're Living in the Last Days Now," "Battle of Armageddon," and Ira Louvin's "Great Atomic Power." The Bailes Brothers "When Heaven Comes Down" was a lively song that combined apocalyptic passion with populist resentment, noting that in the earth's last days, "when Heaven comes down great mansions will burn" but their "little cabin, so close to the ground, will be a great mansion when Heaven comes down." Molly O'Day's "Tramp in the Street" was a socially conscious song that compared the suffering Christ to a homeless derelict.

Sacred music remains a vital tradition in the contemporary South. Christian contemporary music appeals to middle-class southerners, while package shows bring groups of performers with wide appeal on the same bill to community centers and larger church auditoriums. Sacred Harp singings are held periodically, and fifth Sunday singing conventions still take place in country courthouses and local churches. Family gospel singing is still highly prized among evangelicals, and religious music is heard on local radio stations across the South.

CHARLES REAGAN WILSON
University of Mississippi

Bob Darden, *People Get Ready! A New History of Black Gospel Music* (2005); Dana J. Epstein, *Sinful Tunes and Spirituals: Black Folk Music to the Civil War* (1977); James R. Goff, *Close Harmony: A History of Southern Gospel* (2002); Paul Harvey, *Redeeming the South: Religious Cultures and Racial Identities among Southern Baptists, 1865–1925* (1997); Anthony Heilbut, *The Gospel Sound: Good News and Bad Times* (1971); C. Eric Lincoln and Lawrence H. Mamiya, *The Black Church in the African American Experience* (1990); Bill C. Malone, *Don't Get Above Your Raisin': Country Music and the Southern Working Class* (2002).

Steelworkers

The history of steel highlights the unique way the region industrialized and unionized and the enduring centrality of race to class identities. The largest steelmaking facility in the antebellum South was the Tredegar Iron Works, in Richmond, Va. The mill employed close to 1,000 workers; half were black, many of them slaves. Richmond's demonstrated capacity to manufacture munitions helped make the Confederacy relocate its capitol from Montgomery. Tredegar made half the artillery pieces for the South and armor plate for the ill-fated css *Virginia*.

Following the war, another independent steel firm, the Tennessee Coal, Iron, and Railroad Company (TCI) sought to capitalize on the region's low wages and abundant supplies of iron ore and coal. By the 1890s TCI had become the second-largest steel producer in the country. During the 1907 panic U.S. Steel assumed control over the company. Southern historian C. Vann Woodward believed that TCI epitomized the ways that the North colonized the South. U.S. Steel protected its mills in Pittsburgh against the cheaper steel rolled in TCI facilities in Birmingham by means of a tariff placed on southern steel. U.S. Steel also maintained lower pay for TCI via a "southern differential." Other companies took advantage of competitive advantages offered by the South, such as Bethlehem, who developed a massive mill and shipyard in Baltimore.

The southern differential was ultimately eliminated in the early 1950s because of the efforts of the United Steel Workers of America (USWA). If steelmakers had been colonized by their northern competitors, southern workers were ultimately liberated by their counterparts across the Mason-Dixon Line. In 1937 the steel union led a successful strike at Jones and Laughlin in western Pennsylvania, which succeeded as a result of the aid of labor-friendly governor George Earle. A few weeks later, the union negotiated a national contract for all of U.S. Steel's facilities throughout the country.

Not unlike U.S. Steel itself, the USWA was a national and top-down organization. The union sought to make its influence felt in steel workers lives, and it helped raise wages, especially for the lowest-paid workers. In the South, that meant black workers disproportionately benefited from the union's work to uplift and standardize pay rates throughout all the national steel companies. That process of standardization and uplift culminated in the eradication of the southern differential. This is the argument traditionally advanced by the USWA in its own histories, and one echoed by some historians, such as Judith Stein.

The USWA was indeed a mighty force for uplift for its members, black and white, yet racial discrimination remained entrenched in steel. The USWA remained on the conservative side of Congress of Industrial Organizations unionism, and there is considerable evidence that the union consistently moved racial equality to the backburner. The key was the seniority system, which codified the inequities between black and white jobs. The USWA benefited from white antipathy to the communist-led International Union of Mine, Mill, and Smelters in the Birmingham-area iron ore mills; in 1949 the Ku Klux Klan joined a rally of white workers seeking to leave "Mine Mill" and join the USWA. By the early 1970s black members of the union (in both the South and North) sued the industry and the union and won some reforms to the seniority system. The benefits of affirmative action were short-lived, as the industry began to close mills. Steel workers paid the price for decades of lackluster investment by steel firms, as well as the government's liberalization of trade to the world market.

Yet a significant threat to union labor did not come from Korea or Japan, but from within the region: Nucor Steel. Founded in the mid-1960s, the company prided itself on an egalitarian corporate culture, with just five layers between the production floor and the CEO. Workers received bonuses linked to production that could equal their take-home pay, and the USWA never made any headway. Following the 1970s, companies using "mini mills" (that melted steel from scrap metal) took an increasing amount of market share from traditional steel firms. By the new millennium, their competitive advantage was disappearing, and Nucor joined other companies in protesting the "dumping" of Chinese steel into U.S. markets.

JOHN HINSHAW
Lebanon Valley College

Braddock Films, *Struggles in Steel: A Story of African American Steelworkers* (1996); Mark Reutter, *Making Steel: Sparrow's Point and the Rise and Ruin of American Might* (1988); Judith Stein, *Running Steel, Running America: Race, Economic Policy, and the Decline of Liberalism* (1998); C. Vann Woodward, *Origins of the New South, 1877–1913* (1971).

Textile Workers

The manufacture of textiles in the South began during the antebellum period in small family-owned factories that gave way to larger factories employing white men, although employment of women and children was not uncommon. Both Alamance County, N.C., and Graniteville, S.C., witnessed the development of a textile working class and later became textile centers that employed hundreds.

The working class that developed in southern textiles in the 1870s was made up of white, male yeoman farmers, tenants, and croppers who could not make a living on the farm. From 1880 to 1920, an era of industrial growth fueled by the boosterism of local civic leaders, many northern capitalists saw promise in the South and moved their mills to southern locales, such as Crown Mills in Dalton, Ga. (1885), Henrietta Mills in Rutherford County, N.C. (1887), and Pearl Cotton Mill in Durham, N.C. (1893). Local entrepreneurs built mills that became dominant economic forces, such as Dan River Mills in Danville, Va. (1882) and Fulton Bag and Cotton Mills in Atlanta (1889). Workers from failed farms—many from the Appalachian South—constituted the nucleus of the white textile working class. Synthetics factories controlled by cartelized European firms, such as Celanese in Cumberland, Md., and American Bemberg and North American Rayon in Elizabethton, Tenn., followed, building large factories that often employed thousands, including women, and dominated communities.

Factory owners in the South were paternalists who considered their workers children who needed "fathers" to care for them. Factory owners sought to keep mill workers dependent on them and away from the union organizer. One method included construction of "mill villages" (company-owned houses rented or sold to workers), which sponsored social events like baseball games and dances, as well as courses of instruction. Mill villages, such as Schoolfield outside of Danville, Va., and Cabbagetown in Atlanta, became the centers of mill life and culture, and outside community members readily identified occupants of the villages as textile workers and "lintheads." (Mill villages were less common in synthetics' production, although American Chatillon in Rome, Ga., and DuPont Rayon in Old Hickory, Tenn., had them.)

The role of mill villages in the lives of mill workers is complex. Not only symbols of paternalism and oppression, they also were centers of a vibrant

Child laborer in a textile mill, North Carolina, early 1900s (Lewis Hine, photographer, Albin O. Kuhn Library and Gallery, University of Maryland, Baltimore County)

worker culture that included transmission of oral tales and musical tunes and the flourishing of a women's culture. They were sites of opposition where union organizers enlisted members and where mill worker musicians such as Ella May Wiggins, Dorsey Dixon, and David McCarn sang their tunes of lamentation and revolution. Frequently denigrated as "lintheads" or "pitiable social types," mill workers also were heroic figures who stood up to the oppressive boss. Proletarian authors wrote fictional accounts that mirrored everyday struggles and violent strike encounters of workers. Notable are Fielding Burke's *Call Home the Heart* (1932), Grace Lumpkin's *To Make My Bread* (1932), and William Rollins's *The Shadow Before* (1934).

Violence was part of the culture of southern textile workers, especially from 1929 to 1935. Strikes in 1929 saw the murder of striker Ella May Wiggins at the Loray Mills in Gastonia, N.C., and in Marion, N.C., mill deputies and policemen murdered six mill workers. During the 1934 General Strike six workers in Honea Path, S.C., were killed, and National Guardsmen throughout Georgia forced strikers into detention camps. Memory of the strikes and the violence and bitterness they engendered has left indelible impressions on the participants. George Stoney and Judith Helfand found, when they interviewed surviving strikers and their friends and relatives in the 1980s for the video documentary *The Uprising of '34*, that memories still were raw, so that many refused to speak of the events of 1934.

Employment in the mills largely followed Jim Crow. Black males did not operate machines, but worked outside, unloading or taking apart bales of cotton. Black males might work on the inside as janitors, but black females rarely found millwork in any capacity. Sometimes they worked in a mill village as domestics for bosses or mill operatives.

Desegregation of textile mills followed the 1964 Civil Rights Act. Resistance by white workers—union or not—was common. In rare instances, such as the 1973 strike at Oneida Knitting Mills in Andrews and Lane, S.C., white and black workers cooperated in successful strike actions. But in many areas racial segregation and racist attitudes persisted, making it difficult for black workers to effect economic change and workplace justice.

Mill worker culture, symbolized by the (white) mill village, gradually disappeared from the South after World War II, as companies sold off housing and workers found homes in the suburbs. Industry-wide, since the 1980s, textile operations have continued to move production to regions of cheap labor and resources and weak unions. "Textile worker" as a distinctive social class has vanished from the southern scene, along with many of the jobs once performed by men and women who gave their lives to the mill.

MARIE TEDESCO
East Tennessee State University

Douglas Flamming, *Creating the Modern South: Millhands and Managers in Dalton, Georgia, 1884-1984* (1992); Jacquelyn Dowd Hall, James Leloudis, Robert Korstad, Mary Murphy, Lu Ann Jones, and Christopher B. Daly, *Like a Family: The Making of a Southern Cotton Mill World* (1987); Laura Hapke, *Daughters of the Great Depression: Women, Work, and Fiction in the American 1930s* (1995); Timothy J. Minchin, *Hiring the Black Worker: The Racial Integration of the Southern Textile Industry, 1960-1980* (1999); Tom Tippett, *When Southern Labor Stirs* (1929); Allen Tullos, *Habits of Industry: White Culture and the Transformation of the Carolina Piedmont* (1989).

Timber and Naval Stores

Work in southern pine forests for the collection of crude gum and the production of naval stores was, by necessity, among the first trades in the American South. Having depleted most of its own resources as early as the 17th century, Great Britain increasingly relied on the pine gum from its American colonies for the construction, maintenance, and caulking of its seafaring ships. The naval stores industry played an especially important role in the colonial Carolina economy in the 17th and 18th centuries, as slaves on plantations of pine exploited the trees for the pitch and tar that the British navy applied as sealant to the hulls of its ships. Though many small-scale white farmers maintained modest tracts of pine trees and produced naval stores for supplemental income, the labor-intensive method of extraction associated it primarily with African and African American slave labor in the antebellum South. The arduous mode of extraction, referred to in the industry's vernacular as "tapping" or "chipping," involved a unique scarification of the trees in which a tool called a bark hack was used to remove the bark and to tap into the "veins" of the

Hauling logs in Heard County, Ga., 1941 (Jack Delano, photographer, Library of Congress [LC-USF-34-43995D], Washington, D.C.)

trees' cambium layer. Once wounded, pine trees secrete resin onto the external surface of the wound, which acts as a protective coat to seal the opening, to prevent sap loss, and to resist exposure to pathogenic microorganisms. Workers scarred trees in V-shaped streaks down the length of the pine so as to channel the resin into a deep cavity called a "box," which was cut into the base of the tree. The V-shaped streaks, often measuring three feet or more in length, were referred to colloquially as "catfaces" for their resemblance to a cat's whiskers. After the resin had pooled in the box and congealed into gum, workers circulated through the woods and "dipped" the gum into large barrels for shipment.

After the Civil War, depletion of the forests in the Carolinas led to the industry's southerly migration to the pine belt region of southern Georgia and northern Florida, where the work became associated more with the production of turpentine and rosin than with naval stores. Though the industry became active in parts of Alabama, Mississippi, Louisiana, and east Texas during this time as well, the small towns along the Georgia-Florida border consistently served as the center of turpentine production in the United States.

In 1902 Dr. Charles H. Herty, a chemist at the University of Georgia, introduced his invention of the "cup-and-gutter" system of extraction, which averted the destructive method of "boxing" through the attachment of strips of galvanized tin ("gutters") that guided the resin into quart-sized cups, also tacked to the tree just below the catface. The new invention revolutionized the industry and facilitated the "turpentine boom" of the early 20th century, a period in which turpentine became a major ingredient in common household products like soaps, solvents, paints, varnishes, lamp oils, and a variety of salves and other medicinal items.

In southern Georgia and northern Florida, the industry continued to rely predominately on African American labor, much of which remained bound in a system of indentured servitude and debt peonage in turpentine camp communities. As some turpentine camps were notoriously harsher than others in their treatment of African American workers, life in the camps and labor in the turpentine woods are generally remembered as a period of racial oppression and maltreatment. The Works Progress Administration work of Stetson Kennedy and Zora Neale Hurston on an abnormally cruel Cross City, Fla., turpentine camp in the 1930s helped to popularize the somewhat overstated notion of turpentine camp brutality, though racial violence and abuses were indeed common in many camp communities.

Camps typically consisted of several different types of structures: tracts of worker housing often called "shanties," the housing of white producers and bosses, a commissary store that stocked workers' basic provisions, a small church and/or schoolhouse for workers and their families, a "jook" or juke joint for workers' social gatherings and nightlife activities, and a distillery where the pine gum was processed into the spirits of turpentine. Not all turpentine production occurred in the camp environment, however; many smaller producers maintained family-run turpentine operations, employing only a handful of African American workers or providing the labor themselves.

The turpentine industry remained strong through the 1940s and 1950s, but the latter half of the 20th century brought a series of changes that precipitated the industry's demise. Civil rights legislation that improved labor conditions for African Americans diminished the industry's profitability. Machinery and other technology that boosted many agricultural trades were impractical for the specialized tasks of the turpentine woods. A general economic trend of rural outsourcing and cheaper foreign labor led to a sharp decline in domestic turpentine production. High timber prices and rising labor costs weakened the industry's revenue stream. To make matters worse, the introduction of alternative industrial sources of turpentine rendered the substance obsolete. These hits devastated the industry. Whereas in 1950 there were 8,863 turpentine producers in the United States, this figure had fallen to just 1,222 by 1960. In the same period of time, the number of barrels of turpentine produced fell from 1,330,000 in 1950 to just 194,635 10 years later. At the midway point of the century, there were approximately 21,000 workers employed as turpentine hands; by 1960 there were just 3,300. By the mid-1970s few large-scale turpentine operations existed in the United States. Throughout the 1980s and 1990s, turpentining survived on the margins, mostly as contract labor on state and private land before becoming mere side work for individuals seeking supplemental income. The commercial production of turpentine in the United States officially came to an end in 2001, when the last bucket of pine gum was dipped in the forests of Soperton, Ga. Today, in the rural forest communities of China, Indonesia, Brazil, and several Mediterranean nations, turpentining remains a source of rural employment, but it is not the center of any economy as it was throughout the southern pine belt.

TIMOTHY C. PRIZER
University of North Carolina at Chapel Hill

Pamela Bordelon, *Go Gator and Muddy the Water: Writings by Zora Neale Hurston from the Federal Writers' Project* (1999); Lawrence S. Earley, *Looking for Longleaf: The Fall and Rise of an American Forest* (2006); Robert B. Outland III, *Tapping the Pines: The Naval Stores Industry in the American South* (2004); Timothy C. Prizer, *Pining for Turpentine: Critical Nostalgia, Memory, and Commemorative Expression in the Wake of Industrial Decline* (2009); Kenneth H. Thomas Jr., *McCranie's Turpentine Still* (1976).

Tobacco Workers

As the first cash crop in Virginia, tobacco provided the economic context for the initial construction of class relationships in the South. British indentured servants supplied the first tobacco workforce, but the presence of imported African labor offered another form of labor control. Codifying slavery in law as a permanent and inheritable condition, Virginia and Maryland established a class system by the early 1700s based upon African enslavement in which tobacco became a slave-produced crop. Tobacco cultivation produced a slave-owning planter elite, a larger group of small slave-owning family-farm producers, a class of tenant farmers, and an expanding slave trade. It fostered a racial ideology justifying enslavement, which interacted with a gendered system in which women of African ancestry labored in the fields while other women performed primarily domestic labor. A class system established within the tobacco economy simultaneously constructed a pattern of race and gender relations.

By the mid-19th century, tobacco manufacturing had emerged in Richmond using a mix of industrial slavery and waged labor. The disruptions of the Civil War inspired the further spread of small-scale manufacturing as new kinds of tobacco became available. Concentrated primarily in Virginia, North Carolina, and Kentucky, tobacco manufacturing shifted to wage labor while retaining elements of the preexisting patterns of gender and race with freedmen and freedwomen usually consigned to leaf preparation. As machines for the production of cigarettes came into use in the 1880s, those accorded "white skin privilege" within the postwar racial system operated the machines for the production of cigarettes and other tobacco products and, in the case of men, performed the more skilled operations including repair, thus adapting a

Assembly line work in a cigar factory, Louisville, Ky., 1931 (Photographic Archives, University of Louisville [Kentucky])

slave-based class system with its accompanying racial ideology and gender relationships to an industrial setting.

The first organization of tobacco unions in the South occurred among immigrant cigar makers in Florida in the 1870s and 1880s followed by the Knights of Labor in the midst of its rapid expansion in the mid-1880s. The Knights' efforts to organize all members of the producing classes irrespective of gender or race fostered the growth of assemblies in Richmond, Durham, Tampa, and other locations but could not be sustained. Founded in 1885, the Tobacco Workers International Union (TWIU) took up the task of organizing tobacco workers through segregated locals, while giving priority to the unionization of machine operators rather than the African American laborers and stemmers who processed the tobacco leaf. Its older colleague, the Cigar Makers' International Union (CMIU) began its own unsuccessful foray into Florida in 1890. Relying primarily on the use of the union label on tobacco products, the TWIU and the CMIU failed to organize successfully in the South for the next few decades.

The New Deal's prounion legislation brought a dramatic change in union fortunes in the 1930s, but not for the CMIU, whose membership had been undermined by the shift in consumer preference to cigarettes. The TWIU negotiated contracts with Brown & Williamson, Liggett & Myers, and the American Tobacco Company in Durham, Richmond, Petersburg, Louisville, Winston-Salem, and Reidsville. By 1937 the Congress of Industrial Organizations (CIO) established an agricultural workers' union that mounted a challenge to the segregationist practices of the TWIU. Forcing R. J. Reynolds to negotiate a contract in Winston-Salem, the CIO affiliate prodded the TWIU into more effective organization among African Americans. Destroyed by the impact of the Taft-Hartley Act and TWIU rivalry, the CIO veterans shifted their energies to civil rights. The decline in tobacco manufacturing in response to cancer fears further undermined tobacco unionization to force a merger between the TWIU and the Bakery and Confectionery Union in 1979. Despite some success in eliminating regressive aspects of a racial system that initially grew out of slave-based tobacco production, southern workers have yet to overcome the simultaneous effects of class, gendered subordination, and racial ideology, which made it difficult for tobacco workers to organize.

DOLORES E. JANIEWSKI
Victoria University of Wellington

T. H. Breen, *Tobacco Culture: The Mentality of the Great Tidewater Planters on the Eve of the Revolution* (2001); Kathleen M. Brown, *Good Wives, Nasty Wenches, and Anxious Patriarchs: Gender, Race, and Power in Colonial Virginia* (1996); Dolores E. Janiewski, *Sisterhood Denied: Race, Gender, and Class in a New South Community* (1985); Beverly W. Jones, *Feminist Studies* (Autumn 1984); Robert Rodgers Korstad, *Civil Rights Unionism: Tobacco Workers and the Struggle for Democracy in the Mid-Twentieth-Century South* (2003); Gerald E. Poyo, *Journal of American Ethnic History* (Spring 1986); Peter J. Rachleff, *Black Labor in the South: Richmond, Virginia, 1865–1890* (1984).

Washington, Booker T.

(1856–1915) EDUCATOR.

Booker T. (Taliaferro) Washington was arguably the most prominent advocate of education among southerners, especially African Americans, during the Progressive Era. Born in Virginia during the closing years of American slavery, Washington acquired an early appreciation for self-improvement. He attended Hampton Institute during the 1870s and subscribed to the principles of its founder, Samuel Chapman Armstrong, who stressed the salutary effects of manual labor regarding the building of good character. During this time, Washington dabbled in Republican politics and would later be a major broker of political patronage for blacks seeking public office. However, his real passion lay in education, which he assumed would help outfit African Americans for a useful role in the post-Emancipation South.

The greatest singular achievement of Washington was undoubtedly the founding of Tuskegee Institute in Alabama. Funded by sympathetic donors and constructed largely by the labor of students, this school became a symbol of black enterprise and upward mobility. Throughout his three decades as head of the institute, Washington sought to position Tuskegee as a producer of a new black middle class in the South, which would showcase itself as responsible accumulators of capital as well as avid consumers who could benefit the general economy. Just as significantly, this trained class of black entrepreneurs, teachers, mechanics, and farmers would be able to clearly demonstrate its value to white neighbors, many of whom were increasingly supportive of segregationist policies and black disfranchisement by the turn of the century. In Washington's view, whites who were skeptical of black aptitude needed only to witness African Americans participating conscientiously in wage labor and constructively advancing the economic interests of the South. Even if whites chose to repudiate integration (or "social equality"), Washington believed that they would be hard pressed to cede the fruits of citizenship to blacks whose honest labor exemplified the best in an emerging people. At its core, Tuskegee Institute was anchored in this logic of racial interdependence, which emphasized black achievement as being good for the South in general.

Though not unchallenged, Washington was the most prominent African American leader during the 20 years before his death in 1915. He had an unsurpassed ability to create networks of influence among white politicians, philanthropists, and other powerful people. Moreover, at a time when white hostility to black educational strivings was quite palpable in the South, Washington was still able to enhance the size and reputation of Tuskegee while aiding the development of other black institutions throughout the region. Despite these successes, his leadership endured a number of crises that would eventually eclipse both his national stature and his vision for black uplift. On various occasions, he was publicly taken to task by Harvard-trained sociologist W. E. B. Du Bois and other black spokesmen for being too silent in the face of disfranchisement, lynching, and Jim Crow legislation (though his personal papers, made public after his death, would confirm Washington's active, though secret, opposition to these infringements upon black rights). Some criticized his views on education as being more suited to preparing blacks for more plantation work than for jobs in an advanced, industrialized economy. To be fair, Washington, a vocal proponent of what some called vocational or industrial education, was not opposed to training in other fields, including the liberal arts. However, he did caution blacks to seek educational opportunities in those areas that would lead to realistic job prospects. At bottom, the conflict between Washington and his critics was more about the means for achieving first-class African American citizenship and less about the end itself.

Washington's advocacy of a rising social class of black teachers, tradesmen, and agriculturalists who would make themselves indispensable to southern progress did not die with him. Nonetheless, as the Great Migration and northern industries drew large numbers of blacks out of the South in the wake of World War I, competing visions of racial advancement further eroded the allure of his legacy. Still, even his critics conceded that he was largely right on the role that education would play in preparing the working class for the 20th century, though they differed with him on many other issues.

CLAUDE A. CLEGG III
Indiana University

Louis R. Harlan, *Booker T. Washington*, 2 vols. (1972 and 1983), ed., *The Booker T. Washington Papers*, 13 vols. (1972–84); David L. Lewis, *W. E. B. Du Bois: Biography of a Race, 1868–1919* (1993); Robert J. Norrell, *Up from History: The Life of Booker T. Washington* (2009); Booker T. Washington, *Up from Slavery* (1901).

Wells-Barnett, Ida B.

(1862–1931) JOURNALIST AND SOCIAL ACTIVIST.

For Ida B. Wells-Barnett, "southern culture" was an embattled site of identification. She was a native of Holly Springs, Miss., born a slave in 1862. There she attended Rust College, run by the American Missionary Association, and was strongly influenced by its "Yankee" teachers. Wells-Barnett was baptized in the Methodist Episcopal Church. After her parents' death in the yellow fever epidemic of 1878, she moved to Memphis, Tenn., around 1880 and lived there until 1892. That year, she published her most important writing, a pamphlet entitled *Southern Horrors: Lynch Law in All Its Phases*. This essay placed southern codes of honor in the horror of the lynching-for-rape scenario, part of a violent, morally hypocritical, crassly economic system of white supremacy. White men justified the murder of "bestial" black men by claiming the role of protectors of "weak" white women; Wells-Barnett proved that statistically, the rape charge was rarely in play during actual, documented lynchings. Instead, the cry rape was often a cover to punish black men who in any way challenged the social, political, or economic status quo of the South. She also pointed out that white women sometimes participated in both mob activity and consensual sex with black men. When a death threat appeared in print in 1893 because of Wells-Barnett's newspaper criticism of lynching and southern honor, the region became off limits and she left for the North. She returned only once, in 1917, to investigate the plight of 16 Arkansas farmers imprisoned for labor-organizing activity and sentenced to die in Helena, and then she went in disguise.

Ida B. Wells-Barnett became famous—to opponents, infamous—for her critique of the South, but she accomplished the work largely outside of it. In 1895 she settled in Chicago, Ill., married lawyer Ferdinand L. Barnett, and raised four children. She died there in 1931. She arguably achieved greatest prominence outside the United States during 1893 and 1894, when she traveled to England and Scotland to mobilize opposition to lynching in the United States. At strategic points, however, she referred to herself as a "southern girl, born and bred" or by the pen name "Exiled." Such identifications established her credibility as a native witness to history, especially since a black woman's moral authority was by definition suspect in U.S. society. After a difficult period of political retrenchment in Chicago and the brutal race riot of July 1919, Wells-Barnett again accented her southern roots and reached out to the progressive elements of the white South in renewed efforts toward interracial understanding in the region, but this offer likely did not even reach ears that had long since tuned her out.

Ironically, some of the best evidence of Ida B. Wells-Barnett's sparsely documented personal life dates from the 1880s, when she lived in Memphis and participated in a wide array of activities that mark her as a product of the post-Reconstruction New South. She left a diary dating from December 1885 to September 1887, and it provides vivid details of her life during this dynamic period. Entries describe a context not, perhaps, stereotypically "southern" or dominated by folkways. She studied Shakespeare and elocution, attended lectures by national figures like Dwight Moody, and was present at gender- and racially inclusive meetings of the Knights of Labor. The diary further documents her anger at injustice and violence directed at African Americans, some of which touched Wells-Barnett directly, as in her forced removal from a railroad "ladies" car. She was also the godmother of a child whose father was murdered, along with two business associates, during a conflict in the spring of 1892. This triple lynching in Memphis was a life-changing event that directed her attention to full time antimob violence protest.

Ida B. Wells-Barnett organized against southern violence outside of the region, resulting in scores of local antilynching committees and the founding the National Association of Colored Women (1896) and the National Association for the Advancement of Colored People (1909). Her efforts successfully positioned antilynching as a legitimate focus of national reform, but based in the urban North. In that context, individuals and groups more securely positioned than she by academic credentials, social status, or political connections in publishing, philanthropy, and government assumed leadership of the issue in the World War I era. Although Ida B. Wells-Barnett's southernness enabled her powerful voice to emerge in the 1890s, she became eclipsed by the competitive, money-driven, and consolidating trends that came to characterize social reform in the United States over her lifetime.

PATRICIA A. SCHECHTER
Portland State University

Miriam DeCosta-Willis, ed., *The Memphis Diary of Ida B. Wells: An Intimate Portrait of the Activist as a Young Woman* (1995); Trudier Harris, ed., *Selected Works of Ida B. Wells-Barnett* (1991); Patricia A. Schechter,

Ida B. Wells-Barnett and American Reform, 1880–1930 (2001); Ida B. Wells-Barnett, *Crusade for Justice: The Autobiography of Ida B. Wells*, ed. and intro. Alfreda M. Duster (1970).

West, Don
(1906–1992) POET, EDUCATOR, ACTIVIST, LABOR ORGANIZER.

Don West, who spent his youth in the mountains of northern Georgia among a family of subsistence farmers and sharecroppers, was a poet, educator, activist, and labor organizer committed to social change. His antebellum ancestors had opposed slavery and continued to advocate racial and ethnic equality after the Civil War. Even in his youth, West understood how race and social class divided the South.

In 1923 West enrolled at the Berry School, a high school for impoverished children in Rome, Ga. During his senior year, West organized a protest against the showing of the racist film *The Birth of a Nation* on campus. This activism got him expelled, and the school never awarded him a diploma. He was admitted to Lincoln Memorial University (LMU) in Harrogate, Tenn., and he studied with literature professor Harry Kroll and befriended classmates Jesse Stuart and James Still. As an undergraduate, West took an active role in nearby labor conflicts emerging from textile mills and mining camps.

By the late 1920s West decided that the ministry would provide him an effective way to reach the disenfranchised and disaffected. In 1929 he graduated from LMU and enrolled in the seminary at Vanderbilt University. In Nashville, West studied under Alva Taylor, a leader in the Social Gospel movement, and met other socially conscious seminary students, including Howard Kester and Claude Williams. Taylor and his many students believed that segregation was incompatible with Christianity, and they looked to more radical methods to achieve racial and social equality.

West's divinity thesis, directed by Taylor, focused on the patterns of development in Knott County, Ky., and emphasized the strong character of Appalachian people. While a seminary student, West began publishing his poetry. West's writings captured Appalachian folkways and delivered powerful political and social messages.

During the Depression, West's work as an educator and union organizer took a radical turn. West had spent a year in Denmark studying the country's folk school system and wanted to build similar programs in the United States. In 1932 West and Myles Horton founded the Highlander Folk School in Monteagle, Tenn. The interracial school trained people to become activists and labor organizers, while teaching the heritage of the Appalachian region. West adopted a militant approach to social change. Tempered first by the principles of the Socialist Party and then by the tenets of the Community Party, West favored radical measures to reach struggling Americans. Unsatisfied with the progress in Tennessee, West left Highlander in 1934 and during the rest of the decade he focused on political and labor organizing in Georgia and Kentucky.

After the Depression, West's writings reached a greater audience. His poems and short stories of Appalachian life contained distinct messages about equality, tolerance, freedom, and respect for others. West's *Clods of Southern Earth* (1946) became his most widely circulated book of poetry, reaching thousands of union members. That success led to a teaching position at Oglethorpe University in Atlanta.

In the post–World War II era, anticommunist investigators and newspaper editors labeled West as a communist sympathizer. West escaped significant incrimination during the McCarthy era, but he remained a target. His open advocacy of equal rights for African Americans and loud demands for greater rights for laborers, miners, and the downtrodden earned him many detractors.

In the 1960s West channeled his influence and energy into yet another educational program to impart social change, and he founded the Appalachian South Folklife Center at Pipestem, W.Va., in 1964. Much like Highlander, West's Pipestem school taught students the importance of Appalachian culture, racial and ethnic equality, and social activism. Pipestem brought together reformers and radicals from the 1930s and the 1960s, and remains an active school.

West lived long enough to see the results of his prodigious work. His union organizing brought greater rights to workers and the unemployed. Legalized segregation, and many of the racial inequities that defined social class in the South, evaporated during the civil rights movement. He helped to educate several generations of social activists and contributed to a new Appalachian consciousness. Through his organizing, writing, activism, and teaching, Don West helped redefine social class in the South.

AARON D. PURCELL
Virginia Tech

Anthony P. Dunbar, *Against the Grain: Southern Radicals and Prophets, 1929–1959* (1981); James J. Lorence, *A Hard Journey: The Life of Don West* (2007); Don West, *No Lonesome Road: Selected Prose and Poems*, ed. Jeff Biggers and George Brosi (2004), *Clods of Southern Earth* (1946).

Williams, Claude

(1895–1979) PREACHER, SOCIAL ACTIVIST, LABOR ORGANIZER.
Raised near Union City, Tenn., Claude Williams grew up in a family of sharecroppers. While he embraced the fundamental religious beliefs of his youth, Williams questioned the racism and economic disparity of the region. After working in the fields, on nearby Mississippi River boats, and on the railroad, Williams decided to become a preacher and enrolled at nearby Presbyterian affiliated Bethel College in McKenzie, Tenn. As a student, Williams questioned the church's conservative views on sociopolitical issues, but he applauded the denunciation of the wealthy classes by church leaders.

In 1924 Williams graduated and accepted a pastorate not far from Nashville. After several successful years as a preacher, he enrolled in summer courses at the Vanderbilt University seminary. Williams studied with Alva Taylor, a leader in the emerging

Social Gospel movement, and he met other socially conscious seminary students including Don West and Howard Kester. Taylor and his many students believed that segregation was incompatible with Christianity, and they looked to more radical methods to eliminate racial inequality. While a student, Williams attended a biracial conference in Waveland, Miss., and thereafter he committed himself to fighting segregation and racism through his preaching and organizing.

In 1930 Williams accepted a pastorate in the small mining community of Paris, Ark. For the next four years he became an articulate voice for the state's poor and marginalized people. By this time a confirmed socialist, he organized local miners into a union and participated in successful strikes. However, Williams's controversial sermons on issues of race and labor led to his dismissal by the Presbyterian Church in 1934. He next found work in Fort Smith, Ark., with the Workers Alliance, a New Deal program designed to help the unemployed. Local police arrested Williams after he led a demonstration of the unemployed through the streets of Fort Smith. After being released from jail, Williams relocated to Little Rock to focus on organizing sharecroppers.

Sharecropping in the South had created a class of poor landless famers, black and white, dependent on a small percentage of the return on the crops they grew on another person's land. The New Deal's Agricultural Adjustment Act of 1933, which raised prices by decreasing agricultural output, benefited landowners and ignored sharecroppers.

In July 1934, 11 white and seven black leaders founded the Southern Tenant Farmers' Union (STFU).

By 1935 Williams took an active role in the STFU alongside leaders including H. L. Mitchell and his Vanderbilt colleague, Howard Kester. The next year, Williams established the New Era School of Social Action and Prophetic Religion in Little Rock. The school became a regional training center for black and white labor organizers, especially those active in the STFU and the Workers Alliance. He also took over as director of Commonwealth College, a radical labor school in Mena, Ark.

By the mid-1930s he had joined the Communist Party. He wanted to expand STFU organizing and was willing to work with pro–Communist Party unions. Leaders of the STFU, such as Mitchell and Kester, opposed the union's connections with the Communist Party. In 1939 the STFU leadership voted to remove Williams from the union because of his communist tendencies.

A few months after his expulsion, Williams resigned as director of Commonwealth College to lead the People's Institute of Applied Religion (PIAR) in Detroit. PIAR offered interracial institutes for organizers, preachers, and recent immigrants. During the 1940s, PIAR expanded its programs to the South. Williams disbanded PIAR in 1949 because of pressure from anticommunist investigators, who hounded him through much of the McCarthy era. He retreated to a farm in rural Alabama, where he spent the next three decades.

Williams spent his life battling against white supremacy, intolerance, and class divisions in the South. His radical rhetoric and affiliations attracted a wide range of followers and many of his demands for racial equality came to fruition because of the civil rights movement. Williams challenged the social class system of the South by promoting equal rights for blacks and workers.

AARON D. PURCELL
Virginia Tech

Cedric Belfrage, *A Faith to Free the People* (1944); Robert H. Craig, *Religion and Radical Politics: An Alternative Christian Tradition in the United States* (1992); Anthony P. Dunbar, *Against the Grain: Southern Radicals and Prophets, 1929–1959* (1981); Donald H. Grubbs, *Cry from the Cotton: The Southern Tenant Farmers' Union and the New Deal* (1971); Samuel Hill, *On Jordan's Stormy Banks* (1983).

Yeomanry

During the 19th century, small, landowning, family farmers (the yeomanry) typically composed the single largest class of people across the South, yet their identity as a cohesive group remains largely illusory. Despite this, their significance during the first 100 years of the American republic as an "anonymous" yet critical class remains beyond question.

While a farming middle class existed in colonial America, it was Thomas Jefferson who identified the yeomen as an ideal and articulated their importance to the future of the American experiment. Accordingly, yeomen farmers required little from government other than freedom to access western lands. In return, yeomen employed their freedom in the service of sustainable agriculture and rewarded the republic with an independent class of voters. This agrarian worldview has led some to conclude that yeomen farmed only for subsistence and conceded market agriculture to the class of planters. However, 19th-century yeomen typically practiced a type of composite agriculture that favored household subsistence yet supplemented some market activity.

The longest-running question in yeomen historiography revolves around their class identity. Beginning with Frank Owsley's *Plain Folk of the Old South* (1949) historians generally agreed that, in addition to being self-working family farmers, yeomen must own land. The amount of land ranges from a few acres to around 200. Nevertheless, the critical distinction is ownership, and this always set yeomen apart from tenants and sharecroppers. The main disagreement about their class identity is the lack of consensus on the economic ceiling—especially the number of slaves owned. Was slave ownership compatible with this class status? At what point did a yeoman graduate to the next social class? Owsley suggested plain folk could own one to 10 slaves. Other scholars have offered rationales for accepting yeomen slave ownership somewhere in this range and even higher in rare cases. Overall, this lack of consensus on yeomen identity has rendered comparative studies especially problematic when exploring slave ownership but still fruitful when investigating the class as a group of self-working family farmers.

The other critical question about the yeomanry revolves around their general class consciousness and their specific support of planters during secession and the Civil War. A paucity of self-reflective sources has hampered solid conclusions about the yeomen's ideological convictions. However, an early 20th-century survey of aged Tennessee Confederate veterans concluded that no more than one out of three antebellum yeomen was aware of any class conflict. At the same time, recent scholarship suggests that yeomen who owned even one slave were quicker to support secession than those who owned none. Eventually, most southern yeomen saw the sectional conflict as an ultimate threat to their status and supported the war to preserve the only society that they knew.

In the postbellum era, yeomen found themselves in an increasingly unfavorable economic landscape that mandated farming primarily for capital rather than the composite model that sustained them before the war. Exponential growth of farm tenancy, increased global competition, and the stranglehold of the burgeoning financial and transportation industries collectively spurred an agrarian protest. The rhetoric that accompanied this unrest was polarized and pitted yeomen farmers against the business class. As conditions worsened, many yeomen joined grassroots agricultural societies that culminated with the populist movement of the 1890s. Despite the failure of populism, many of the yeomen's concerns would be addressed during the New Deal. However, 20th-century technology and growing urbanization heralded the demise of family farms and the statistical significance of the southern yeomanry. Although extinct as a contemporary social class, the yeomen ideal (self-sufficiency, family cooperation, and political independence) remains a potent mental icon of southern identity.

GARY T. EDWARDS
Arkansas State University

Fred Bailey, *Class and Tennessee's Confederate Generation* (1987); Steven Hahn, *The Roots of Southern Populism: Yeoman Farmers and the Transformation of the Georgia Upcountry, 1850–1900* (1982); Samuel Hyde, *Journal of Southern History* (November 2005); Stephanie McCurry, *Masters of Small Worlds: Yeoman Households, Gender Relations, and the Political Culture of the Antebellum South Carolina Low Country* (1995); Carl Osthaus, *Journal of Southern History* (November 2004); Frank Owsley, *Plain Folk of the Old South* (1949); Stephen A. West, *From Yeoman to Redneck in the South Carolina Upcountry, 1850–1915* (2008).

"You Might Be a Redneck If . . ."

"You might be a redneck if . . ." is a comedic tag line coined and made famous by southern comedian and television personality Jeff Foxworthy (b. 1958). Foxworthy has used the phrase to set up hundreds of one-liners that spoof the unsophisticated behavior, speech, and dress of rednecks—from dating practices ("You might be a redneck if . . . you go to family reunion looking for women") to lawn care ("You might be a redneck if . . . you have ever cut your grass and found a car"). In using such overblown stereotypes to depict redneck life, Foxworthy continues a long tradition of southern humorists representing the region as the home of crude, uneducated backwoods characters. It is a style of humor that stretches back to the South's frontier days and the writings of Augustus B. Longstreet, George Washington Harris, and Mark Twain.

Social class plays a major role in Foxworthy's humor. Playing to audiences composed largely of white suburbanites, many with rural roots, he evokes laughter by drawing cultural distinctions between redneck culture and the mainstream middle-class sensibilities. But it is a nervous laughter, according to sociologist Robert Hauhart, since redneck jokes sometimes strike close to home for many audience members. Foxworthy's emphasis on "you *might* be a redneck" exposes a middle-class anxiety over how narrowly some of us have avoided being a hick or how others of us could still become one. This anxiety perhaps mirrors the comedian's own background. Although Foxworthy grew up near Atlanta (in Hapeville, Ga.) and his father was an executive at IBM, he freely traces some jokes to the redneck exploits of his friends and family. He attributes "if you ever used your ironing board as a buffet table" to a Thanksgiving meal served by his mother-in-law.

Foxworthy first gained notoriety for his redneck jokes in the late 1980s and the early 1990s with the help of a successful stand-up comedy career and the release of several best-selling books and comedy albums. "You might be redneck" has since become an iconic phrase within the American lexicon while also fueling a merchandise industry that includes calendars, greeting cards, board games, coffee cups, and even a line of slot machines. Foxworthy has also inspired Internet adaptation and homage. Examples include "You might a redneck firefighter if you ever put out a cow chip fire," "You might be a redneck pagan if you buy incense and candles at Wal-Mart," and "You might be a redneck superhero if you got your powers from radioactive chewing tobacco."

The success of "You might be a redneck if . . ." was due, in no small part, to the close relationship that Foxworthy has with the country music industry. He was an opening act for Garth Brooks and Emmylou Harris and recorded *Redneck Games* with Alan Jackson. Rapid growth in the popularity of country music provided Foxworthy a national fan base interested in things rural, southern, and down-home. Also helpful was Foxworthy's own unassuming "good old boy" persona, which resonated with audiences beyond the American South. Foxworthy made plenty of room for nonsoutherners in his definition of redneck, suggesting that the unsophisticated could be found just about anywhere. Indeed, he first got the idea for his comedic theme while performing at a club in Michigan. He found that attached to the comedy club was a bowling alley with valet parking.

Historian James Cobb has pointed out that by the 1990s the word "redneck" had shifted from being an ethnic slur to being more of a term of endearment and a symbol of independence for identity-challenged white southerners. Foxworthy's humor operated within and contributed to this social milieu. Even as Foxworthy made fun of rednecks, he sympathetically held them up as challengers of social conformity and political correctness ("You might be a redneck if . . . you think 'recycling' means going back home"). Foxworthy's redneck humor was not immune to the country's racial politics. In 2001 two high school students in western New Jersey were suspended for wearing a T-shirt referencing some of Foxworthy's redneck one-liners. School officials suggested the word "redneck" was offensive to minorities and feared that the shirt would inflame racial tensions, although the courts ultimately ruled that the school had violated the students' free speech. The popularity of Foxworthy humor has created new places, including some outside the South, for talking about and even debating the social meaning of redneck.

DEREK H. ALDERMAN
East Carolina University

James C. Cobb, *Journal of Southern History* (February 2000); Michael Dunne and Sara Lewis Dunne, in *The Enduring Legacy of Old Southwest Humor*, ed. Edward J. Piacentino; Jeff Foxworthy, *The Final Helping of You Might Be a Redneck* (1999); Robert C. Hauhart, *Journal for Cultural Research* (July 2008).

INDEX OF CONTRIBUTORS

Abel, Joseph, 390
Alderman, Derek H., 472
Allen, Carrie, 437
Allured, Janet, 267

Baker, Bruce E., 85
Baldwin, Lewis V., 385
Beck, E. M., 166
Bertrand, Michael T., 181
Bidgood, Lee, 324
Billings, Dwight B., 186, 235, 317
Blevins, Brooks, 421
Bower, Walter H., 235
Boyd, Elizabeth Bronwyn, 334
Britt, Sam, 71
Bryant, Gary E., 303

Carlton, David L., 415, 441
Carmichael, Misty Dawn, 393
Carson, James Taylor, 375
Case, Theresa, 313, 427
Chenault, Wesley, 272
Clegg, Claude A., III, 464
Cobb, James C., 136
Coclanis, Peter A., 358, 415
Cunningham, David, 388, 449
Curtis, Katherine J., 378

Dahl, Alan, 186, 361, 434
De Boer, Tycho, 101
De Jong, Greta, 443
DeWaard, Jack, 378
Dixon, Marc, 66

Edwards, Gary T., 471
Egerton, John, 255
Ely, Melvin Patrick, 112, 247

Falk, William W., 322, 353
Flannery, Michael A., 423
Flynt, J. Wayne, 1
Fones-Wolf, Ken, 419
Fosl, Catherine, 222, 328
Frederick, Jeff, 92
Furuseth, Owen J., 152

Gilbert, Jess, 412
Glatthaar, Joseph T., 348
Goode, Richard C., 330
Green, Jennifer R., 403
Grem, Darren E., 431
Griffin, Larry J., 21, 213, 260
Griffith, David, 402
Grivno, Max L., 287

Hargis, Peggy G., 21, 213
Harkins, Anthony, 367
Harris, J. William, 87
Harrison, Daniel M., 80
Hart, Emma, 319
Henry, Jacques, 357
Herod, Andrew, 146
Hinshaw, John, 455
Hinton, Diana Davids, 417
Hoffschwelle, Mary S., 97

Isaac, Larry W., 80

Jackson, Harvey H., III, 283
Janiewski, Dolores E., 462
Johnson, Joan Marie, 337
Jones, Catherine, 230
Jones, William P., 391

Kars, Marjoleine, 436
Kreyling, Michael, 162

475

Kuhn, Clifford, 430
Kvach, John F., 414

Lawson, R. A., 326
Lester, Connie L., 198
Lubotina, Paul, 105, 376, 407

Malcom, Nancy L., 263
Margo, Robert A., 201
Mayfield, John, 128
McDonnell, Michael A., 61
McKiven, Henry M., Jr., 339
McMillen, Neil R., 333
Mertz, Paul E., 242
Mohl, Raymond A., 276
Moore, William D., 350
Moreton, Bethany, 439
Moye, J. Todd, 363
Murray, Gail S., 301
Murray, John E., 332

Newton, Roxanne, 306, 357, 399

Oakes, James, 251
Olsson, Tore C., 425

Pecknold, Diane, 346
Peretti, Burton W., 381
Prizer, Timothy C., 459
Pruitt, Paul M., Jr., 343
Purcell, Aaron D., 370, 383, 409, 468, 469

Quigley, Paul, 239

Rachleff, Peter, 386
Ragsdale, Rhonda, 78
Reynolds, LeeAnn G., 227
Rivers, Jacob, 372

Rockoff, Stuart, 144
Rosenbloom, Joshua L., 373
Rushing, Wanda, 290

Sandlin, Allison, 313
Sauceman, Fred W., 109
Schechter, Patricia A., 466
Schmidt, Amy, 393
Scott, Shaunna L., 400
Shafer, Byron E., 190
Smith, Barbara Ellen, 118
Spitzer, Nicholas R., 394

Taylor, Gregory S., 444
Taylor, Kieran, 310
Tedesco, Marie, 457
Thompson, Ashley B., 260
Thompson, Neal, 410
Tolnay, Stewart E., 166, 176
Troost, William, 351

Walker, Anders, 448
Walker, Melissa, 37
Watson, Harry L., 321, 379
Webb, Susan, 353
Wells, Jonathan Daniel, 172
Whitfield, Stephen J., 315
Williams, Susan, 365
Wilson, Charles Reagan, 451
Winders, Jamie, 156
Woodham, Rebecca, 446
Wyatt-Brown, Bertram, 122

Yagatich, William, 353

Zieger, Robert H., 140, 209, 341
Zwiers, Maarten, 295

INDEX

Page numbers in boldface refer to articles.

Adventures of Huckleberry Finn (Twain), 130
Affirmative action, 215–17, 220–21
Africa and Africans, 108, 183–84, 253
African Americans, 17, 27, 28, 66, 69, 93, 96, 139, 258, 260–62, 279–80, 322–24, 331, 334, 335, 354–55, 357–58, 363–64, 367, 373, 383–84, 399–400, 409–10, 430–31, 434–35, 447–49, 464–65, 466–67; antebellum era, 5; and new industrial order, 6–9; impact of World War II, 14; sharecroppers, 26, 58–59; civil rights movement, 30–32, 81–84, 328–30; labor force, 33–34, 37–38, 40, 43–45, 209–13, 303, 305–6, 339–40; class identification, 46–51; and American Revolution, 61–63; elite and middle class, **78–80**, 174–76; crime and punishment, 90–92; education, 98–100; immigrants, 106–7; foodways, 110–11; free, 112–18; and gender, 119–20; and honor, 122; employment, 141, 142–43; and unions, 142, 307, 313–14, 341–42, 408, 443; women, 148, 308–9, 337–39; and job competition, 154–55; literature, 165; lynching of, 166, 168–71; migration, 176, 177–79; music, 181, 326–27, 381–83, 431–32, 438, 451–54; economy, 188–89; politics, 191, 195–97; and Populist movement, 198, 200–201; poverty, 201, 206–8; racial attitudes, 213–21; radicalism, 222–27; and films, 228; and Reconstruction, 232–34; religion, 235, 237–38; and Civil War, 239–42; tenancy, 244; slaveholders, **247–51**; and reforms, 257–58; and football, 264, 266–67; female stereotypes, 268–69, 270–71; male stereotypes, 274–75; mayors, 280; tourism, 285–86; and urbanization, 291–92; voting rights, 295–300; and welfare and charity, 301; working-class, **310–12**; and child labor, 332; and convict lease system, 343–46; fraternal orders, 350; and Freedmen's Bureau, 351–53; and Greenback Party, 361–62; and Highlander Folk School, 366; and indentured servants, 374; in-migration, 378–79; and Martin Luther King Jr., 385–86; and Knights of Labor, 388; and Ku Klux Klan, 388; longshoremen, 390–91; lumber workers, 391–92; and Mardi Gras, 396–98; migrant workers, 402; and military academies, 406; and New South, 414–15; and Operation Dixie, 419–20; poultry workers, 426; railroad workers, 427–29; service workers, 439–40; and shape-note singing, 441; steelworkers, 456; textile workers, 458–59; and timber and naval stores, 459; tobacco workers, 462, 464
Agee, James, 164, 201
Agency for Toxic Substance and Disease Registry, 357
Agricultural Adjustment Administration (AGA), 246, 409, 443, 470
Agricultural Wheel, 198–200
Agriculture, **57–61**, 153; modernization, 59; mechanization, 60–61, 246, 278, 461; New Deal, 412–13
Aid to Dependent Children, 302
Alabama, 137, 149, 240; impact of Civil War, 6; and new industrial order, 8; income ratio, 38–39; and Great Depression, 60; and Knights of Labor, 66–67, 312; antiviolence laws, 67; crime and

477

punishment, 90; manumission, 114; industrialization, 142; literature, 162; lynching, 171; race and labor in, 210; free blacks, 247; social class, 289; convict lease programs, 311, 343; Mardi Gras, 394; oil fields, 417–18; pellagra, 423

Alabama Share Croppers' Union, 224

Alamance County, N.C., 457

Albany: A Study in National Responsibility (Zinn), 449

Aleck Maury, Sportsman (Gordon), 373

Alexander, Lamar, 100

Alexander, Will, 257

Allen, James Lane, 164

Allied Media Corporation, 74

Allison, Dorothy, 165–66

All Over But the Shoutin' (Bragg), 165

Alonzo Bailey v. Alabama, 346

Alsace, 145

Always for Pleasure (film), 399

American Cancer Society, 18

American Dilemma, An (Myrdal), 430

American Federationist, 210

American Federation of Labor (AFL), 11, 15, 67, 69, 81, 209–11, 307, **313–14**, 342, 420, 445

American Federation of State, County, and Municipal Employees, 212, 312

American Historical Review (Phillips), 181

American Hollow, 400

American Homecoming Act of 1987, 76

American Independent Party, 96

American Indians, 27, 101, 274, 321, 357–58, **375–76**, 441

American Manhood (Rotundo), 272

American Men's Studies Association, 272–73

American National Election Studies (ANES), 43–45, 192, 193–94, 197–98

American Railroad Union, 429

American Revolution, 4, **61–65**, 87, 253

American Shooter's Manual, The, 372

American Slavery, American Freedom (Morgan), 322

American Socialist Party (ASP), 376

American Tobacco Company, 464

"American Women: Their Use and Abuse" (L. Wells), 450

Ames, Jessie Daniel, 91, 223, 257

Andrews, S.C., 309

Andy Griffith Show, The, 133–34, 164

Anglican Church, 235

Anheuser Busch, 412

Anniston, Ala., 6, 66–67, 150

Antebellum era, 3–5, 145, 163, 175; music, 183; films, 228; religion, 236; slavery, 251–52; social class, 288–90; voting rights, 295; labor, 303–5; hunting, 372; military academies, 404–5; and New South, 414–15; railroad workers, 427; timber and naval stores, 459

Anti-Defamation League, 169

Anti-Semitism, **315–17**

Antiunionism, **66–71**

Antiviolence statutes, 67

Appalachia, 16, 77, 111, 153, 276, 283–84, **317–19**; memory, **400–401**

Appalachian Development Program, 16

Appalachian Heritage, 400

Appalachian Journal, 400

Appalachian Regional Commission, 319

Appalachian South Folklife Center, 469

Appomattox, surrender at, 93

Apprenticeship, 332

Arizona, 154

Arkansas: antiviolence laws, 67; right-to-work laws, 68; internment camps, 72–73; Latinos, 158; lynching, 168; Ozarks, 421–23

Arkansas Delta, 60

Armstrong, Louis, 182, 381–82

Arnall, Ellis, 257

Arrested Development, 432

Arsenal, 404

Artisans, **319–20**, 361

Ashby, Irene, 313

Ashe, Arthur, 274

Ashe County, N.C., 401

Asian Americans, **71–77**

Asian Indians, 73–76, 107–8

Asians, 27, 108
Association of Southern Women for the Prevention of Lynching, 223
Atlanta, Ga., 74, 83, 146, 210, 291–92, 312, 317, 355
Atlanta Journal-Constitution, 322–23
Augusta, Ga., 266, 303
Augusta Chronicle, 170
Augusta National, 266–67
Aunt Jemima, 270–71
Austin, Tex., 73
Austin Business Journal, 74
Autobiography of Mother Jones (Jones), 408
Automobile industry, 142
Ayers, Edward, 391–92

Bacon, Nathanial, 321
Bacon's Rebellion, 2, 57, 222, **321–22**, 415
Bailes Brothers, The, 455
Baker, Ella, 271, 328
Bakery and Confectionery Union, 464
Balser, Diane, 309–10
Baltimore, Md., 292
Bankhead-Jones Farm Tenancy Act of 1937, 13, 246
Bank of the United States, 380
Banner Mine explosion, 311
Baptists, 3, 62, 63, 72, 113, 117, 235–36
Bastard Out of Carolina (Allison), 165–66
Baton Rouge, La., 292, 398–99
Battle of Blair Mountain (Shogan), 408
Beal, Fred, 408
Beatles, 438–39
Beaufort, S.C, 312
Bederman, Gail, 272
Bell, Daniel, 41
Bergson, Henri, 129
Berkeley, William, 321
Berlin, Ira, 117, 248
Berry, Marion, 331
Bethune, Mary McLeod, 257, 447
"Better Music Movement," 441
Bevel, James, 331
Beverly Hillbillies, The, 133, 228–30

Beyond Measure: Appalachian Culture and Economy, 400
B. G., 433
Bible, 10
"Big Bear of Arkansas, The" (Thorpe), 130
Big Tymers, 433
Bilbo, Theodore, 10, 93, 121
Bill Haley and the Comets, 437
Birmingham, Ala., 6, 12, 13, 24, 83; steel, 137; Jews, 145; strikes, 150, 313–14; lynching, 171; race and labor in, 210; and radicalism, 224–25; reforms, 257; violence, 292; voting rights in, 298–99; iron mills, 311
Birth of a Nation, The (film), 389, 468
Black, Hugo, 14, 257, 447
Black Belt, 110, 186, 202, 276, **322–24**, 430
Black Codes, 90, 296
Black Reconstruction in America (Du Bois), 274
Blacks. *See* African Americans
Blackwood Brothers, 454
Blair Mountain, W.Va., 401
Blease, Cole, 10, 93, 137–38, 169–70
Bloom, Jack, 81, 82, 83
Blue Ridge, 283–84
Bluegrass music, **324–25**
Blues music, **326–27**
Bly, Robert, 272
Bogalusa, La., 313–14
Bond, Horace Mann, 257
Boon, Pat, 438
Bosnians, 107–8
"Bourbon Reformers," 344
Bourdieu, Pierre, 148
Bowers v. Hardwick, 275
Bowman, Philip, 248
Bowman, Priscy, 248
Boys Don't Cry (film), 272
BP oil spill, 104
Braden, Anne, 366
Braden, Carl, **328–30**
Bragg, Rick, 165
Brandt, Willy, 359

Brandt Report (*North-South: A Programme for Survival*), 359
Branson, Mo., 285
Brazil, 253
Bristol sessions, 228
British Celtic migrants, 183
Broadnax, Andrew, 84
Brooks, Garth, 473
Brooks, Sorrell, 133
Brotherhood of Locomotive Engineers, 427–28
Brotherhood of Locomotive Firemen, 427–28
Brotherhood of Sleeping Car Porters, 209, 312
Brotherhood of Timber Workers, 11
Brown, Charlotte Hawkins, 257
Brown, Judith, 450
Brown & Williamson, 464
Brownell, Herbert, 298
Brown v. Board of Education, 259, 298, 328, 331, 334, 366
Bryan, William Jennings, 201
Buddhists, 17
Buffet, Warren, 266
Bui doi (dust of life), 76
Burke, Fielding, 458
Burke, Martha, 267
Bus boycotts, 82
Bush, George H. W., 121
Bush, George W., 197, 266
Byrd, William, II, 128–29, 163–64
Byrd machine, 334
Byron, Lord, 123, 133

Cable, George Washington, 344
Cairo, Ill., 323
Caldwell, Erskine, 131, 137, 164
California, 353
Call Home the Heart (Burke), 458
Cambodians, 76
Campbell, Will, **330–32**
Cane, Joe, 397
Cannon, Sarah, 228

Cao, Joseph, 76
Caplin, Alfred G., 132–33
Caribbean islands, 253
Carolina Sports by Land and Water (Eliott), 372–73
Carpetbaggers, 93
Carroll, Etta, 58
Carter Family, 182, 228, 454
Cash, W. J., 257–58, 315
Cason, Clarence, 137
Catawba Valley, 77
Catholics, 17, 107–8, 235, 387
Catts, Sidney, 10
Cecil-Fronsman, Bill, 174
Central Americans, 140–41
"Central Theme of Southern History, The" (Phillips), 181
Chaney, James Earl, 171
Chapel Hill, N.C., 17
Charity, **301–2**
Charles, Ray, 182
Charleston, S.C., 70, 79, 83, 85, 115, 116, 147; music, 182–83; free blacks, 250; military academies, 404
Charlotte, N.C., 160
Charlotte Benevolent Society, 301
Charlotte Speedway, 265
Cherokee Indians, 375
Chesapeake, 87–88, 102, 112–13, 186, 289, 374
Chesnut, James, 126
Chesnut, Mary, 126, 303
Chesnutt, Charles W., 131
Chicago Tribune, 336
Childhood: The Biography of a Place (Crews), 165
Child labor, 8–9, 313–14, **332–33**
Chinese, 72, 108, 429
Choctaw Indians, 375–76
Christian American Association, 68
Cigar Makers' International Union (CMIU), 464
Citadel, 404, 406
Citizens' Council, 82, **333–34**

Citizenship Schools, 366
Civil Rights Act of 1866, 90, 296
Civil Rights Act of 1960, 298
Civil Rights Act of 1964, 83, 96, 211, 308–9, 312, 340, 385
Civil rights movement, 30–32, 66, 71, **80–85**, 86, 96, 139, 212, 317, 328–29, 364, 368, 371, 399; birth of modern, 14; since World War II, 17, 331; and unions, 70, 341; and black middle class, 175; and migration, 179; and economy, 189; politics, 196; radicalism, 225–27; and films, 228; political transformation, 280; and voting rights, 297–99; and labor, 308–9; and Highlander Folk School, 366; and Martin Luther King Jr., 385–86; and Ku Klux Klan, 389; and service workers, 440; and Southern Student Organizing Committee, 449; and textile workers, 459; and turpentine industry, 461
Civil Rights Unionism: Tobacco Workers and the Struggle for Democracy in the Mid-Twentieth-Century South (Korstad), 308
Civil War, 57–58, 86, 103, **239–42**; impact of, 6; and crime and punishment, 90; and agriculture, 187–88; and slavery, 231; and female labor, 304–5; desertion, **348–49**; and New South, 414
Clark, Septima, 257–58, 339, 366, 371
Class identity, 45–52
Class organization, 40–45
Class, Race, and the Civil Rights Movement (Bloom), 81, 82
Clay, Henry, 125
Clinton, Bill, 100; administration, 302
Clods of Southern Earth (West), 469
Clower, Jerry, 134
Clubwomen, **337–39**
C-Murder, 433
Coalition of Free Men, 272
Coalition of Immokalee Workers, 403
Coal workers, **339–40**
Cobb, James, 323, 473

Cobb, Ned, 392
Cohen, Mordecai, 144–45
Cold War, 225, 278
College of William and Mary, 97
Collins, Addie Mae, 171
Colonial era, 2, 106, 113, 235
Colored Alliance, 200
Colored Wheels, 200
Columbia, S.C., 404
Columbus, Ohio, 313
Comic strips, 132–33
Commission on Interracial Cooperation, 238, 257
Committee of Southern Churchmen, 331–32
Committee on Industrial Organization. *See* Congress of Industrial Organizations
Common Sense (Paine), 64
Commonwealth Fund, 281
Common Whites (Cecil-Fronsman), 174
Communist Party (CP) and communism, 12, 24, 138, 328–30, 371, 393, 410, **444–46**, 468, 470; and unions, 210–11, 342, 377; radicalism, 224–26; and female labor, 307–8; and strikes, 408; and Operation Dixie, 420; and Share Croppers' Union, 443
Community Development Block Grant, 294
Cone, Ceasar, 145
Cone, Moses, 145
Confederacy, **239–42**
Congregationalists, 235
Congress of Industrial Organizations (CIO), 13, 15, 41, 68, 69, 81, 209–11, 312, 313–14, 328, **341–42**, 399; and lumber workers, 392; Operation Dixie, 419–20; and Communism, 446; and steelworkers, 456; and tobacco unionization, 464
Connell, R. W., 272–73
Conscription Act, 349
Conservative Party (Va.), 434

"Contadini in Chicago: A Critique of the Uprooted" (Vecoli), 106
Convict lease system, 90–91, 96, 234, 311, **343–46**, 362
Convict servants, 63
Cooke, Sam, 182
Country Boys, 400
Country music, 19, **346–47**
Country Music Association, 347
Cowboy Troy, 433–34
"Crackers," **367–70**
Creek Indians, 375
Creoles, 381–82, 396–98
Crews, Harry, 165
Crime and punishment, **87–92**
Croatians, 107
Crosby, Alfred, 359
Cross City, Fla., 461
Cubans, 106–8
"Culture of personalism," 57

Dabbs, James McBridde, 449
Dahmer, Vernon, 171
Dallas, Tex., 291
Dallas County, Ala., 289
Dallas Morning News, 68
Dalton, Ga., 160
Daniel, William, 249
Daniels, Jonathan, 331
Danville, Va., 435
Darlington, S.C., 138
Davis, Angela, 330
Davis, Jefferson, 93
Dawson, R. H., 344–45
Dawson, William Levi, 183
Day, Thomas, 249–51
Dayton, Tenn., 229
Death Penalty Information Center, 281–82
DeBeck, Billy, 133
De Bow, J. D. B., 240
Debs, Eugene, 376
Dee, Henry, 171
Deindustrialization, 140, 141–42, **136–40**, 141–42, 278; and economy, 189

Deliverance (film), 163, 228–29
Duluth, Ga., 72
Demagogues, **92–97**
Democratic National Convention, 259
Democratic Party, 10, 17, 68, 123, 199, 280–81, 363, 416–17; antebellum era, 3–5; New Deal, 13–14, 223; class organization, 40; and civil rights movement, 82, 83; and crime and punishment, 90–91; demagogues, 92–93, 95–96; and party system, 191, 193–97; radicalism, 224; and voting rights, 296–99; and Knights of Labor, 388
Democratic socialism, 386
De Ridder, La., 377
Detroit, Mich., 83
Dew, Thomas R., 115
Dickey, James, 163
Dinnerstein, Leonard, 136–37
"Dirty South," 432–34
Discrimination, 145, 155–56, 221
Disney World, 285–86
Dixiecrat, 95–96
Dixon, Dorsey, 458
DJ Screw, 432
Dodds, Baby, 381–82
Dollard, John, 235
Dollywood, 285
Dombrowski, James, 223, 225, 257–58, 447–48
Domino, Fats, 437
Dorsey, George, 170–71
Dorsey, Mae Murray, 170–71
Dorsey, Thomas, 454
Douglass, Frederick, 123–24
Downey, Tom, 290
Dreiser, Theodore, 401
Dubofsky, Melvyn, 408
Du Bois, W. E. B., 240–41, 274, 335, 344, 385, 465
Ducktown, Tenn., 105
Dueling, 89, 124–25
Dukes of Hazard, The, 133, 229
Duke University, 294
Dunbar, Leslie, 448

Duncan, Stephen, 287, 289
Dunmore, Lord, 63
Durham, N.C., 17, 74
Dusinberre, William, 289

Earnhardt, Dale, 265, 411
East, Clay, 409
East Africans, 108
Easy Instructor, 441
Ebony (magazine), 154
Ebson, Buddy, 133
Economic Report on the South (1938), **415–17**
Edmonds, Richard, 414
Education, 27, 29, 86, **97–100**, 127–28, 217–21, 291, 352, 465–67
Edwards, Weldon, 128
Egerton, John, 111
8 Ball & MJG, 433
Eisenhower, Dwight D., 266, 298
Elizabethton, Tenn., 307–8
Elliott, Bill, 411
Elliott, Missy, 434
Elliott, William, 124, 372–73
Ellison, Ralph, 132
Ellison, William, 115, 248, 250–51
Elvehjem, Conrad, 424
Emerging Republican Majority, The, (Phillips), 276
Emory Dental School, 316
Emory University, 98
Employment, **140–44**
Encyclopedia of Appalachia, 318
Encyclopedia of Southern Culture, 23, 326, 327
Engel, Lehman, 183
England, 253
English Poor Laws, 301
Engval, Bill, 135
Environment, **101–5**
Episcopalians, 235
Equal Employment Opportunities Commission, 210
"Equality principles," 215–16
Ethnicity, **105–9**, 155–56

Evans, Eli N., 315
Evans, Walker, 164, 201

Face in the Crowd, A (Kazan), 134
Fair Labor Standards Act of 1938, 333, 399, 420, 440
Falwell, Jerry, 238
Farm Bureau, 12, 67
Farmers' Alliance, 10, 191, 198–200, 238
Farm Labor Organizing Committee, 403
Farm Security Administration, 246, 413
Fast, Howard, 330
Fat Tuesday (film), 399
Faubus, Orval, 334
Faulkner, William, 130, 131, 360, 373
Federal Emergency Relief Administration, 100
Fed Ex, 143
Felton, Rebecca, 344
Field Mob, 433
Fifteenth Amendment, 296–97
"Fight, The" (Longstreet), 130
Filipinos, 72
Film, **227–30**
Fire-Eaters, 128
Fishing, **372–73**
Fisk Jubilee Singers, 181–82, 452
Fisk University, 99
Five Blind Boys of Mississippi, 454
Flagg, Fannie, 135
Flagler, Henry, 283
Fleming, Cynthia Griggs, 84
Flood, Michael, 273
Florence, S.C., 83, 150
Florida: antiviolence laws, 67; right-to-work laws, 68; and unions, 70; Asian Indians, 73–74; Vietnamese, 76; environment, 103; immigrants, 108; and organized labor, 142, 212; Latinos, 152–53, 154, 212; lynching, 169; free blacks, 247; migration to, 279–80; tourism, 283–86; oil fields, 417–18; timber and naval stores, 460–61
Florida Agriculture and Mechanical University, 99

INDEX 483

Flynt, Wayne, 22, 24
Follett, Richard, 289
Folsom, Jim, 257
Foner, Eric, 351
Food, Tobacco, Agricultural, and Allied Workers of America, 312
Foodways, **109–12**
Football, 263–67
Ford, 410
Ford, Henry, 283
Foreman, Clark, 416
Fortune (magazine), 68
Fourteenth Amendment, 90, 296
Fox-Genovese, Elizabeth, 287
Foxworthy, Jeff, 128, 135, 369, 472–74
France, Bill, Jr., 265
France, Bill, Sr., 410
France, Brian, 265–66
Frank, Leo, 24, 108, 168–69, 315–16
Franklin, Aretha, 182
Franklin, John Hope, 115–16, 135–36
Fraternal orders, **350–51**
Free blacks, **112–18**, 123, 247–51, 288, 295, 301, 320, 339, 351–52, 427
Freedmen's Bureau, 7, **351–53**
Freedom Rides, 331
Freedom Road (Fast), 330
Freud, Sigmund, 273
Friend, Craig Thompson, 273
From the Other Side (Gabaccia), 108–9
Full Circle (G. Lumpkin), 393
Funding Act, 434–35
Funk, Casamir, 423

Gabaccia, Donna, 108–9
Gadsden, Ala., 13, 150
Galveston, Tex., 149, 390–91
Gang labor system, 205, 207
Gardner, Brother Dave, 134–35
Gaston County, N.C., 237, 308
Gastonia, N.C., 12, 138, 224, 307–8, 445, 458
Gastonia, 1929: The Story of the Loray Mill Strike (Salmond), 408
Gated communities, **353–56**

Gates, Bill, 266
Gatlinburg, Tenn., 284
Gelders, Joseph, 447
Gellert, Lawrence, 326
Gender, 108–9, **118–21**, 126–27, 148, 231; and female labor force, 32–35; and Populists, 200; and sports, 265, 267; and female stereotypes, **267–72**; and male stereotypes, **272–76**; and white working-class women, **303–6**; and female labor, **306–10**; and fraternal orders, 350; and female military academies, 406; and female poultry workers, 426; and female service workers, 439–40; and female textile workers, 457–59; and female tobacco workers, 462
General Federation of Women's Clubs (GFWC), 337–38
General Social Survey (GSS), 45, 53, 214, 217
General Textile Strike of 1934, **357–58**
Genovese, Eugene, 287–89
Geophagia, **357–58**
Georgetown, Va., 354
Georgia, 76, 102, 139–40, 240, 353; colonial era, 2; and new industrial order, 8; Korean immigrants, 72; Asian Indians, 74; Ku Klux Klan, 82; crime and punishment, 88–90; environment, 103; immigrants, 108; and employment, 141; lynching, 168, 170; free blacks, 247; tourism, 286; convict lease system, 343; and Jacksonian democracy, 380; strikes, 458; timber and naval stores, 460–61
Georgia Female College, 98
Georgia Institute of Technology, 99
Georgia States' Rights Council, 333–34
Germans, 106–7, 421
Germany, 145
Geto Boys, 432
GI Bill, 100, 284
Gleeson, Jackie, 133
Global South, **358–60**
Glover, Lorri, 273
Godchaux, Leon, 145

Go Down, Moses (Faulkner), 373
Goldberger, Joseph, 423–24
Golden, Harry, 315
Goldenseal, 400
Gold standard, 361
Gompers, Samuel, 313–14
Gone with the Wind (film), 123, 228
Gone with the Wind (Mitchell), 132, 163, 165, 271, 287
Goodman, Andrew, 171
Goody Mob, 432–33
Gordon, Caroline, 373
Gordon, Jeff, 412
Gospel music, **451–55**
Gottschalk, Louis Moreau, 183
Gould, Jay, 429
Graceland, 286
Grady, Henry, 293, 414
Graham, Frank Porter, 257, 416
Grandfather clause, 297
Grand Ole Opry, 228
Graniteville, S.C., 457
Graves, Lonnie, 59
Graybow, La., 377
Great Britain, 106–7
Great Depression: 12–16, 24, 60, 100, 109, 416, 430; literature, 164; migration, 178; economy, 189; politics, 191; radicalism, 223–24; and tenancy, 246; and welfare and charity, 301–2; and New Deal, 412; and Share Croppers' Union, 443
"Great Migration," 177, 189, 323, 326, 466
Great Recession of 2008, 11, 43, 197–98, 282
Great Speckled Bird, 451
Green, Jennifer, 405
Green, Paul, 257–58
Green, William, 313
Greenback-Labor Party, 9, **361–63**
Greensboro, N.C., 82, 145
Gregg, William, 136, 304–5
Gregory, James N., 279–80
Griffith, Andy, 133–35
Griffith, D. W., 389
Gulfport, Miss., 283–84

Gulf Shores, Ala., 283–84
Gunning, Sarah Ogan, 401
Guthrie, Liz, 265
Guthrie, Woody, 326, 347

H-2A guest worker program, 154
Hahn, Steven, 174
Haley, Alex, 327
Halletsville Rebel, 445
Hamer, Fannie Lou, 259, 271, **363–65**, 366, 371
Hammond, James Henry, 231, 287
Hampton University, 99
Hancock, Gordon B., 257
Handlin, Oscar, 106
Handy, W. C., 327
Harkins, George Washington, 376
Harlan County, Ky., 12, 105, 377, 401
Harlan County, U.S.A., 400
Harlan Miners Speak (Dreiser), 401
Harlem Renaissance, 79
Harris, Emmylou, 473
Harris, George Washington, 129–30, 163–64, 473
Harris, Joel Chandler, 131
Harvard Encyclopedia of American Ethnic Groups, 108
Hastie, William H., 257
Hastings, Thomas, 441
Hauhart, Robert, 473
Hayes, Rutherford B., 230, 296
Hays, Brooks, 14
Haywood, "Big Bill," 376–77
Health Resorts in the South, 283
Heckman, James, 208
Hefland, Judith, 458
Heflin, Tom, 93
Helms, Jesse, 153
Helper, Hinton Rowan, 222, 239–40
Henderson, N.C., 308
Hendersonville, N.C., 283
Henry, John, 401
Herndon, Angelo, 446
"*Herrenvolk*" democracy, 381

Herty, Charles H., 460
Higham, John, 316
Highlander Folk School, 12, 223, 225, 257–58, **365–67**, 371, 447, 468
Highlander Research and Education Center, **365–67**
Hill, Joe, 377
Hillbillies, 228–30, 318, **367–70**
Hilton Head Island, S.C., 354
Hindus, 17
History of the Dividing Line Betwixt Virginia and North Carolina (Byrd), 128, 163–64
Hmong, 72, 76–77
Holiness churches, 454
Holly, Buddy, 437
Home Depot, 143
Honea Path, S.C., 458
Honor, **122–28**
hooks, bell, 271
Hooper, Johnson J., 129–30, 131
Horney, Karen, 273
Horton, Myles, 223, 257–58, 365, **370–72**, 468
Horton, Zilphia Johnson, 366
Hot Boys, 433
House, Sam, 326
House of Representatives, 192, 254–55, 380
Houston, Charles H., 257
Houston, Sam, 125
Houston, Tex., 74, 279
Howard, John, 275
Hudson, Hosea, 257
Hugo, Chad, 433
Humor, **128–36**
Hundley, Daniel, 5
Hunting, **372–73**
Huntsville, Ala., 17, 138, 150
Hurston, Zora Neale, 258, 392, 461
Husband, Herman, 436
Huston, Felix, 125
Hyman, Mac, 134

IBM, 473
I'll Take My Stand, 164

Immigrants, 106–9, 212, 280; Jewish, 145–46; Latino, 153, 238; Asian, 238; and urbanization, 291; and longshoremen, 390
Immigration Act of 1965, 71
Impending Crisis of the South, The (Helper), 239–40
Indentured servants, 5, 112–13, 222, 321–22, **373–74**; and American Revolution, 61–63; and child labor, 332; and service workers, 439–41; and turpentine camps, 461; and tobacco workers, 462
Indian Americans, 72
Indian Asians. *See* Asian Indians
Indian Removal Act, **375**, 379
Industrialization, 25–27, 59–60, 103–4, **140–44**, 407
Industrial Revolution, 191
Industrial Workers of the World (IWW), 209–10, **376–77**
Inherit the Wind (film), 229
In-migration, 279–80, **378–79**
Institute for Research in Social Science, 416
Interest in Slavery of the Southern Non-Slaveholder, The (De Bow), 240
International Association of Machinists (IAM), 210
International Longshoremen's Association (ILA), 150
International Workers of the World, 81
Interracial marriage, 73
In the Shadow of Selma (Fleming), 84
Irish, 106–7
Iron John (Bly), 272
Iron workers, **339–40**
Italians, 106–8, 169

Jackson, Alan, 473
Jackson, Andrew, 199, **375**, 379
Jackson, George Pullen, 442
Jackson, Jesse, 226, 330
Jackson, Mahalia, 182
Jackson, Maynard, 212
Jackson, Miss., 292

Jacksonian democracy, **379-81**
Jacksonville, Fla., 66-67
James, Joe S., 442
Jamestown, Va., 321
Japanese, 72-73
Jazz music, **381-83**
Jefferson, Blind Lemon, 182
Jefferson, Thomas, 199, 252, 471
Jefferson Parish, La., 72
Jenkins, Esau, 366
Jennings, Waylon, 229
Jews, 17, 107-8, **144-46**, 235, 275, 315-17, 383
Jim Crow laws, 79, 83, 163, 225, 226, 234, 298, 414
Jindal, Bobby, 74
Job Corps, 16
Jobs with Justice, 227
John L. Louis: A Biography (Dubofsky and Van Tine), 408
Johnson, Andrew, 295, 352
Johnson, Charles S., 257
Johnson, Hootie, 267
Johnson, James Weldon, 257
Johnson, Lillian, 365
Johnson, Lyndon B., 298-99, 302, 363
Johnson, Olin, 14
Johnson, Robert, 182
Johnston, Joseph E., 125
Jones, Beverly, 450
Jones, Bobby, 266
Jones, Mary Harris "Mother," 120, 376-77, 408
Jones, Samuel, 183
Jones, Thomas Goode, 346
Joplin, Janis, 356
Jordon, Clarence, 257-58
Jordon, Louis, 182
Joseph, Moses, 145
Journal of Appalachian Studies, The, 400
Journal of Men's Studies (Flood), 273
Justice in the Coalfields, 400
Juvenile, 433

Katallagete, 332
Kazan, Elia, 134

Kelly, Walt, 132-33
Kennedy, John F., 298-99
Kennedy, Stetson, 461
Kentucky, 149, 319; effects of World War II on, 16; environment, 103; lynching, 168; convict lease system, 343; tobacco, 462
Kentucky Fried Chicken, 104
Kester, Howard Anderson, 257-58, **383-84**, 410, 468, 469-70
Key, V. O., Jr., 191-92
Key West, Fla., 10
Kia Motors, 72
Kieffer, A. S., 442
Killers of the Dream (Smith), 258
Kimmel, Michael, 272
King, B. B., 182
King, Florence, 128-29, 135
King, Martin Luther, Jr., 70, 83, 85, 328, 371, **385-86**; and unions, 212; racial attitudes, 214; radicalism, 225-26
Kinsey, Alfred, 273
Kirwan, Albert D., 317
Knights of Labor, 9, 66-67, 81, 147, 307, **386-88**, 467; and geography, 148-49; and minorities, 209-10; and railway workers, 429; and tobacco, 463
Knights of Mary Phagan, 169, 317
Knotts, Don, 133
Koreans, 72-73
Korstad, Robert, 308
Krispy Kreme Donuts, 104
Kroll, Harry, 468
Kudzu, 251
Ku Klux Klan, 82, 90, 108, 153, 171, **388-91**; and Reconstruction, 233, 296; anti-Semitism, 316-17; and strikes, 408; and New South, 414; and steelworkers, 456

Labor, 32-39; geography of, **146-51**; and race, since 1865, **209-13**
Labor in the South (Marshall), 407
Lafayette, Bernard, 331
Laotians, 76
Latinos/Latinas, 17, 28, 36, 73, 84, 108, **152-56**, 268, 271, 354-55; employment,

139, 141, 142–43; wages, 142–43; and gender, 148, 271; workers, **156–61**, 179; and economy, 190; and unions, 209, 212; migration, 279–80; mayors, 280; and urbanization, 291–92; voting rights, 299; oil workers, 419; poultry workers, 426; rap music, 431–32

Lawrence v. Texas, 275

Lawson, James, 331

Lawton, Will, 166

Ledbetter, Huddie "Leadbelly," 326

Lee, Harper, 162

Lee, Robert E., 336, 348

Liggett & Myers, 464

Leo (pope), 387

Let Us Now Praise Famous Men (Agee and Evans), 163, 164, 201

Lewis, Betty Washington, 336

Lewis, Fielding, 336

Lewis, Jerry Lee, 327, 437, 454

Lewis, John, 331, 399

Lewis, Ronald, 107

Liberia, 114

Lichtenstein, Nelson, 70

Lil Jon and the East Side Boyz, 433

Lil Wayne, 433–34

Lincoln, Abraham, 89, 127–28, 254, 256, 295, 348–49

Lind, Jenny, 183

Linnaeus, Carl, 105

Literacy, 27, 98–99, 117, 118, 127

Literature, 4–5, **162–66**

Little Foxes, The (Hellman), 163

Little Rock, Ark., 292, 331, 334

Loeb, Emil, 145

Lomax, Alan and John, 326

Lombardo, Guy, 382

Long, Huey, 15, 96

Longshoremen, **390–91**

Longstreet, A. B., 129–30, 163–64, 473

Lonn, Ella, 348

Louisiana, 240, 289, 316; and unionization, 10–11; and Knights of Labor, 66–67, 312; right-to-work laws, 70; Asians, 72; Asian Indians, 74; Vietnamese, 76; Ku Klux Klan, 82; and demagogues, 96; free blacks, 116–17; lynching, 168–69; black slaveholders, 247, 248; tourism, 283–84; planters, 289; Mardi Gras, 394

Louisiana territories, 72

Louisville, Ky., 292

Louvin, Ira, 455

Loveman, Adolph, 145

Ludacris, 433

Lumber industry, 103, **391–92**

Lumpkin, Grace, **393**, 458

Lumpkin, Katharine Du Pre, 257, **393–94**

Lutherans, 235

Lynchburg, Va., 66–67

Lynching, 11, 24, 91, 94–96, 108, **166–71**, 274, 315–16, 466–67

Lynn, Loretta, 182, 229

Lynyrd Skynyrd, 439

MacKaye, Percy, 336

Macon, Ga., 66–67

Mahone, William, 435

Making of a Southerner, The (K. Lumpkin), 393

Malcolm, Dorothy, 170–71

Malcolm, Roger, 170–71

Man Show, 272

Manhood in America (Kimmel), 272

Manila Village, La., 72

Manliness and Civilization (Bederman), 272

Manring, M. M., 270–71

Manumission, 113–16, 322

Marburg, William, 325

March on Washington, 21, 82, 385

Marcus, Greil, 442

Mardi Gras, **394–99**

Marietta, Ga., 168–69

Marion, N.C., 458

Market Revolution, 97

Marshall, F. Ray, 40, 144, 407

Marshall, Tex., 149

Marshall, Thurgood, 257

Martinsburg, W.Va., 149

Marx, Karl, and Marxism, 1, 3, 10, 24–25,

39–40, 149, 330; and literature, 163; and religion, 236
Maryland, 63, 64, 123; environment, 103; and manumission, 114; agriculture, 186; black slaveholders, 247; and Jacksonian democracy, 380; tobacco production, 462
Mary Sharp College, 98
Mason, George, 399
Mason, Lowell, 441
Mason, Lucy Randolph, 257, **399–400**, 420, 447
Masons, 145, 200
Massachusetts, 147
Massey Energy, 401
Master P, 432
Masters golf tournament, 263–64, 266
Masters of Small Worlds (McCurry), 174
Maverick, Maury, 257
Mays, Benjamin, 257
McCarn, David, 458
McCarthyism, 229, 328
McCarty, Anne, **328–30**
McCray, John H., 259
McCurry, Stephanie, 60, 174, 303
McKaine, Osceola, 259
McMillan, George, 449
McMullen, David Lee, 408
McNair, Denise, 171
Mechanics Union of Trade Associations, 146
Medical University of South Carolina, 70
Mellett, Lowell, 416
Melting pot theory, 106
Memphis, Tenn., 84, 212, 286, 291, 292, 312
Memphis Minnie (Lizzie Douglas), 182
Mencken, H. L., 131, 229
Men's Bibliography (Flood), 273
Men's Studies Task Group of the National Organization for Men, 272–73
Meredith, James, 331
Methodists, 3, 113, 235–37
Mexican Americans, 402
Mexicans, 106–8, 140–41
Miami, Fla., 292

Michigan, 279
Mickve Israel, 275
Middle class, **172–76**, 441, 465; development of, 13, 59–60; during World War II, 14–16; after World War II, 17–18; and social class, 31–32, 37; class identity, 45–51; African American, 78–79; and education, 98–100; and gender, 109; and humor, 128–34; artisans, 320; and music, 347, 382–83, 438; and military academies, 404–6; and NASCAR, 411; and New South, 414–15
Middle Easterners, 108
Migrant workers, **402–3**
Migration, 156–57, **176–80**, 207; slave, 252–53; southern, 279–80; and urbanization, 291; and female labor, 305; in-migration, **378–79**; and Jacksonian democracy, 380
Military academies, **403–6**
Milledgeville, Ga., 169
Miller, Katherine Balfour, 336–37
Miller, Mark S., 407
Million Man March, 272
"Mill Mother's Lament," 308
Mill villages, 457
Mind of the South, The (Cash), 315
Mine, Mill, and Smelter Union, 12
Mine, mill, and smelter workers, **407–8**
Mining, 278
Minter, Benjamin, 166
Miracle Strip Amusement Park, 284
Mississippi, 139–40, 240, 316, 344, 363–65; impact of Great Depression on, 12; agricultural employment, 26–27, antiviolence laws, 67; Asians, 72; Ku Klux Klan, 82; "whitecappers," 91; and manumission, 113–14; lynching, 168–69, 171; and radicalism, 226; free blacks, 247; tourism, 285; Mardi Gras, 391; oil fields, 417–18
Mississippi Burning (film), 229
Mississippi Delta, 186–87, 323
Mississippi Freedom Democratic Party (MFDP), 259, 364

Mississippi Sheiks, 327
Mississippi State University, 99
Missouri, 92, 421–23
Mitchell, George, 257–58
Mitchell, H. L., 257, **409–10**, 470
Mitchell, Margaret, 132
Mobile, Ala., 396, 397
Monroe, Bill, 182, 324
Monroe, La., 399
Montagnards (Mountain People), 76–77
Montgomery, Ala., 82, 84, 225
Montgomery bus boycott, 385
Moody, Dwight, 453, 467
Moore, Charles Eddie, 171
Moore, Ida McClellan, 131
Moreno, Rita, 268
Morgan, Edmund S., 322
Mormons, 17
Morrill Land Grant Act of 1862, 406
Mountaintop removal (MTR), 319
Mt. Olive Pickles, 403
Mount Vernon, 63
Muddy Waters (McKinley Morganfield), 182, 327
Muklow, W.Va., 377
Murfreesboro, Tenn., 108
Murphree, Mary Noailles, 164
Muse, Vance, 68
Music, 19, **181–85**; bluegrass, **324–25**; blues, **326–27**; country, **346–47**; rap, **431–34**; rock 'n' roll, **437–39**; spiritual and gospel, **451–55**
Musical Million, 442
Muslims, 17, 108
Myrdal, Gunnar, 201, 430
Myrtle Beach, S.C., 284, 354
Mystikal, 433

NAACP, 79, 91, 257, 297–98, 448, 467
Nappy Roots, 433
NASA, 100
NASCAR, 19, 93, 133, 263–67, 273–74, **410–12**
Nash, Diane, 331
Nashville, Tenn., 82

Natchez Pilgrimage, 337
Nathans, Nathan, 144–45
National Agriculture Workers Union, 445
National Association of Colored Women (NACW), 337–39, 467
National Association of Manufacturers (NAM), 67–68, 70
National Barn Dance, 347
National Council of Churches of Christ (NCC), 331
National Farmers Union (NFU), 443–44
National Farm Labor Union. *See* Southern Tenant Farmers Union
National Labor Relations Act, 440
National Labor Relations Board (NLRB), 67, 211
National Organization of Men Against Sexism, 272
National Public Radio, 19, 135
National Recovery Act, 357
National Recovery Administration (NRA), 430
National States Rights Party, 317
National Textile Workers Union, 307–8, 408, 445
National War Labor Board, 67–68, 420
National Youth Administration, 100
Nationwide Insurance, 412
Nat Turner Revolt, 352
Naval stores, **459–62**
Nelly, 79–80, 433
Nelson, Willie, 229
Neptunes, 433
New Deal, 12–16, 59, 67, 100, 110, 357, 377, **412–13**, 415–16, 430, 447; and labor, 143; and economy, 189; politics, 191–92, 194–95; and radicalism, 223, 224; and tenancy, 246, 277; and welfare and charity, 301–2; and tobacco, 464
New Era School of Social Action and Prophetic Religion, 470
New industrial order, 6–9
New Orleans, La., 72, 79, 85, 108, 145; waterfront workers, 81; Latinos, 159; lynching, 169; music, 182–83, 381;

poverty, 201; and urbanization, 292; longshoremen, 390; Mardi Gras, 395–97
New Orleans Picayune, 129–30
New Rebel, 449–50
New South, **414–15**
New South Student. See *New Rebel*
New Testament, 123
New York (state), 39, 147
New York, N.Y., 146
New York Times, 73, 286
Nextel Corporation, 266, 411
Niebuhr, H. Richard, 235
Niebuhr, Reinhold, 371
Nissan, 142
Nixon, Richard, 276
North American Free Trade Agreement, 139–40, 154
Northampton County, Va., 112
North Carolina, 41, 73, 76–77, 102, 139–40; impact of Civil War on, 6; and new industrial order, 8; and gender stereotypes, 24; and American Revolution, 62; and Knights of Labor, 66–67; crime and punishment, 87–88; and manumission, 113–15; employment, 141–42; Latinos, 154, 159; free blacks, 247; tourism, 286; and social class, 289; secession, 349; migrant workers, 403; strikes, 408; Regulator movement, 436–37; naval stores, 459–60; tobacco, 462
North Carolina Growers Association, 403
North Carolina Patriots, 333–34
North Carolina State University, 294
No Time for Sergeants (Hyman), 134
Now & Then, 400
Nucor Steel, 456–57
Nunn, Sam, 266

Oakes, James, 174, 287, 289
Oak Ridge National Laboratory, 100
Obama, Barack, 197
Occupational shifts, 27–29
O'Connor, Flannery, 134
O'Day, Molly, 455
Odum, Howard, 392, 416

Ohio, 88, 417
Oil workers, **417–19**
Oklahoma, 10, 92
Old Bull, 183
Old Testament, 123
Ole Miss. See University of Mississippi
Olmsted, Frederick Law, 289
Open Door Community, 226
Open range, 104
Operation Dixie, 41, 68, 312, **419–21**
Oral tradition, 86
Orangeburg, S.C., 82
Order of Railway Conductors, 427–29
Organized labor, 9–11, 82, 138, **140–44**, 146–47, 407–8
Outkast, 433
Owenby, Sheriff, 170
Owsley, Frank, 57, 172, 471
Ozarks, 283–84, 285, **421–23**

Page, John, 64
Pageants, **334–37**
Paine, Thomas, 64
Palm Beach, Fla., 283
Panama City, Fla., 283–84
Panama City Beach, Fla., 284
Parchman Farm (penitentiary), 91, 344
Parker, Charles Mack, 171
Parks, Rosa, 366, 371
Partlow, William, 424
Parton, Dolly, 182
Partridge, Alden, 404
Patrick, Danica, 412
Patrons of Husbandry (Grange), 198–99
Patterson, Orlando, 123
Patton, Charley, 182, 326
Payne, Daniel, 452
Pearl, Minnie, 228
Peer, Ralph, 228
Pellagra, **423–25**
Pennsylvania, 87, 417
Pentecostals, 235, 237–38, 454
Peonage, **343–46**, 443, 461
People's Institute of Applied Religion (PIAR), 470

People's Party, 199
Pepper, Claude, 257
Percy, William Alexander, 275
Perkins, Carl, 437
Personal Responsibility and Work Opportunity Reconciliation Act of 1996 (PRWORA), 302
Petty, Richard, 265, 411
Phagan, Mary, 168–69, 317
Philadelphia, Pa., 146
Phillips, Kevin, 276
Phillips, Sam, 438
Phillips, Ulrich B., 172, 181, 248, 287
Pica, **357–58**
Pilgrimages, **334–37**
Plain folk, 57–60, 174, 414
Plain Folk of the Old South (Owsley), 172, 471
Plantations, 227, 443–44
Planters, 40, 57–58, 60, 63, 82, 123, 126, 145, 240, 303, 434, 471–72; antebellum era, 3–5; impact of the Civil War on, 6; and new industrial order, 6; education, 98–99; and environment, 102–3; foodways, 111; social class, 172–74; and economy, 187–88; and tenancy, 233, 242–45; religion, 235, 237; and New Deal, 277, 412–13; paternalism, 287–89, 301; and convict lease programs, 311; and Bacon's Rebellion, 321–22; and Freedmen's Bureau, 352; and Greenback Party, 361; and Jacksonian Democrats, 379–80; and New South, 414; tobacco cultivation, 462
Playboy (magazine), 18
"Playing the dozens," 124
Pleck, Joseph, 272–73
Plight of the Share-Croppers (Thomas), 409
Poles, 107
Political behavior, **190–98**
Poor whites, 57; antebellum era, 3–5; impact of the Civil War on, 6; and new industrial order, 7–8; and environment, 102; image, 227–28; and New South, 414

"Poor White's Opinion of Slavery, A" (Helper), 222
Pope, Liston, 235, 237
Poplarville, Miss., 171
"Popular Front," 224
Populist Party and Populism, 9–11, 67, 81, 96, 223, 238, 317, 472; and party system, 191; as movement, **198–201**, 213; and voting rights, 296
Pork, 110
Porter, William T., 129
Poultry workers, **425–27**
Poverty, 109–12, **201–9**, 242, 244–46, 277, 292, 318–19, 358, 360, 416; and welfare and charity, 301–2; and migrant workers, 402; in Ozarks, 421–23
Power Shift (Sale), 276
Preface to Peasantry (Raper), 430
Prentiss, Seargent S., 125
Presbyterians, 72, 235
Presley, Elvis, 182, 286, 327, 437–38, 454
Pressman, Lee, 70
Price, Leontyne, 183
Professional Golf Association (PGA), 266
Progressive Democratic Party (PDP), 259, 328
Progressive Era, 11, 99, 301
Promise Keepers, 272
Protestants, 223
Proudhon, Pierre-Joseph, 10
Provincials, The (Evans), 315
Publix, 143
Puerto Ricans, 402
Pulaski, Tenn., 388

Quaker Oats, 270
Quakers, 113

Race and labor, **209–13**
Race and Renewal of the Church (Campbell), 331
Racial attitudes, 84, **213–21**
Racial Violence and Law Enforcement (George), 449
Radical Faeries, 272

Radicalism, **222–27**
Radical Republicans, 222
Radio, **227–30**
Railroad workers, **427–30**
Rainey, Ma, 327
Raleigh, N.C., 17, 74
Rambo (film), 272
Randolph, A. Philip, 209, 257
Randolph, John, 125
Randolph, Judith, 114
Randolph, Richard, 114
Raper, Arthur F., 59, 257, 322, **430–31**
Rap music, **431–34**
Readjusters, 234, **434–36**
Reagon, Bernice Johnson, 366
Reconstruction, 57–58, 93, **230–34**, 256, 295–96
Reconstruction: America's Unfinished Revolution 1863–1877 (Foner), 351
Redeemers and Redemption, 93, 191, **230–34**, 297, 362
Rednecks, 229–30, **367–70**, 411, 472–74
Reed, John Shelton, 17–18, 227, 260
Reed, Merl E., 407
Regulators and Regulator movement, 62, 88, **436–37**
Reid, Ira, 430–31
Reigger, Wallingford, 183
Religion, **235–39**. *See also individual religions*
Religious Right, 226
Report on Economic Conditions of the South, 415
Republican Party, 17, 90, 93, 105, 199, 232–34, 240, 276, 280–81, 346, 361–62; and party system, 191, 193–97; and radicalism, 222; and slaves, 254; and voting rights, 295–300; and convict lease system, 343; and Knights of Labor, 388
Research Triangle Park (RTP), 73, 294
Reserve Officer Training Corps, 406
Resettlement Administration, 12–13, 413
Revolt among the Sharecroppers (Kester), 410
Revolutionary War, 2, 6, 88

Reynolds, R. J., 266, 411, 464
Rhett Butler's People (McCaig), 165
Richmond, Va., 241, 274, 387, 429, 455, 462
Richmond Dispatch, 115
Right-to-work laws, 41, **66–71**, 139, 142, 150, 175–76
Rising Tide of Color against White World-Supremacy, The (Stoddard), 105–6
Roberts, John, 300
Robertson, Ben, 137
Robertson, Carol, 171
Robertson, Pat, 238
Robinson, Bernice, 366
Rock 'n' roll, **437–39**
Rodgers, Jimmie, 181–82, 327, 347
Rollins, William, 458
Roosevelt, Eleanor, 224–25, 371, 447
Roosevelt, Franklin Delano, 12–13, 67, 109, 132, 357, 377; and poverty, 201; reforms, 256; and Agricultural Adjustment Act, 409; New Deal, 412–13, 415–16; and Southern Conference for Human Welfare, 447
Roots of Southern Populism, The (Hahn), 174
Roth, Randolph, 87–89
Rotundo, E. Anthony, 272
Ruebush-Kieffer Company, 453
Ruling Race, The (Oakes), 174
RuPaul, 272
Rural Life in the United States (Raper et al.), 431
Ruskin, John, 445
Ruskin Commonwealth Association, 445
Russia, 145

Sacred Harp, 441, 451
Sahlins, Marshall, 23
Saigon, Vietnam, 76
St. Augustine, Fla., 283
St. Cecilia Society, 182–83
St. Louis Reveille, 129–30
St. Petersburg, Fla., 83
Sale, Kirkpatrick, 276
Salmond, John A., 408

Sanction, Thomas, 257–58
Sandy Creek Association, 436
Savannah, Ga., 147, 275
Scabbing, 311
Scalawags, 93
Scarborough, William K., 287
Schultz, Mark, 57
Schweninger, Loren, 116, 247
Schwerner, Mickey, 171
Scots-Irish, 107
Scott, Sir Walter, 123
Scott, Wendell, 265
Scottsboro, Ala., 12
Scottsboro Boys, 446
Secession, **239–42**
Second Great Awakening, 236
Sedition and Espionage Act, 445
Self-enslavement, 117
Self-purchase, 113
Selma, Ala., 166, 299
Selznick, David O., 123
Senn case, 67
Service Employees International Union (SEIU), 212
Service workers, **439–41**
Seven Years' War, 62
Shadow Before, The (Rollins), 458
Shape-note singing, **441–42**, 451
Share the Wealth program, 96
Sharecroppers All (Raper), 430–31
Share Croppers' Union, 12, **443–44**
Sharecropping, 7–8, 26, 58, 60, 81, 103, 163, 175, 176, 200, **242–46**, 409–10, 470, 471; and economy, 188; and poverty, 206–7; and Reconstruction, 233; female labor, 305; and music, 326; and Greenback Party, 361–62; and New Deal, 412; and New South, 414; and pellagra, 425; and Share Croppers' Union, 443
Sherman, William T., 348–49, 352
Shogan, Robert, 408
Showalter, Anthony J., 453
Sign for Cain, A (G. Lumpkin), 393
Silkk the Shocker, 433

Sims, Son, 327
16th Street Baptist Church, 171
Slaton, John M., 169
Slattery, Emmie, 271
Slave Songs of the United States, 452
Slaveholders, black, **247–51**
Slavery, 22, 80–81, 86, 87, 92–93, 112–17, 123–24, 127–28, 320, 357, 369, 393, 407, 471–72; colonial era, 2; antebellum era, 3–5; and American Revolution, 61–63; and social order, 78–79, 231–33; and immigrants, 106, 107; and foodways, 110–11; and social class, 172–75, 287–88; and economy, 186–88; and poverty, 204–5; and Bacon's Rebellion, 222, 321–22; and films, 228; and religion, 236–37; and Civil War, 239–42; and tenancy, 242; and class system, **251–55**; and reform, 256; and women, 270; and eugenics, 274–75; and welfare and charity, 301; and child labor, 333; and labor force, 339; and convict lease system, 343–44; and Freedmen's Bureau, 351; and indentured servants, 374; and Jacksonian Democrats, 379–81; and New South, 414–15; and Ozarks, 421; and service workers, 439; and spiritual music, 452, 454; and timber and naval stores, 459; and tobacco workers, 462–64
Smith, Bessie, 182, 327
Smith, Charles (Bill Arp), 131
Smith, Francis H., 405
Smith, Lee, 135
Smith, Lillian, 258
Smith-Hughes Act, 99
Smith-Lever Act, 99
Smith v. Allwright, 297
Smokey and the Bandit, 133
Smoky Mountains, 283–84, 285
"Social closure," 106
Social Darwinism, 105
Social Gospel movement, 223, 226
Socialist Party (SP) and socialism, 10, 24, 224, 384, 409, **444–46**, 468

Social reform, 1932–1954, **255–59**
Social Relations in Our Southern States (Hundley), 5
Social Security Act of 1935, 302
Song of the South (film), 132
Soulja Boy, 433–34
Sound and the Fury, The (Faulkner), 163
South Carolina, 41, 76, 102, 137, 139–40, 353; colonial era, 2; and impact of Civil War, 6; Ku Klux Klan, 82; crime and punishment, 88–89; and manumission, 113–14; black slaveholders, 247; tourism, 284–86; and social class, 289–90; and Jacksonian democracy, 380; strikes, 408; and pellagra, 423; and naval stores, 459–60
South Carolina College, 404
South Carolina Grand Council, 107
South Carolina Military Academy, 404, 406
Southeastern Conference (SEC), 19, 263–65
Southern Baptists, 235–36, 275
Southern Christian Leadership Conference (SCLC), 70, 83, 331, 366, 385
Southern Conference Educational Fund (SCEF), 225, 329, **446–48**
Southern Conference for Human Welfare (SCHW), 14, 224–25, 257, **446–48**
Southern Diaspora (Gregory), 279
Southerners on New Ground (SONG), 227
Southern Focus Polls (SFP), 260
Southern Horrors: Lynch Law in All Its Phases (Wells-Barnett), 466
Southern identity, **260–63**
Southern Living (magazine), 17, 105, 286
Southern Lumber Operator's Association, 377
Southern Manhood (Friend), 273
Southern Masculinity (Glover), 273
"Southern Negro and the NRA" (Raper), 430
Southern Negro Youth Congress (SNYC), 225

Southern Organizing Campaign (SOC), 341, 419–21
Southern Organizing Committee for Economic and Social Justice (SOC), 330
Southern Patriot, 225, 329, 447
Southern Politics in State and Nation (Key), 191–92
Southern Regional Council (SRC), **448–49**
Southern Socialist, 445
Southern States Industrial Council, 67
Southern Struggles (Salmond), 408
Southern Student Organizing Committee, **449–51**
Southern Tenant Farmers' Union (STFU), 12, 147, 210, 224, 246, 312, 409–10, 413, **443–44**, 445, 470
Southern Worker (Hundley), 12, 446
Southern Workers and Their Unions, 1880–1975 (M. Reed), 407
Spartanburg, S.C., 278
Sparxxx, Bubba, 433
Specie Circular Act, 57
Speer, Emory, 346
Spencer, Herbert, 105
Spirit of the Times, 129–30
Spiritual and gospel music, **451–55**
Sports, **263–67**
"Spotted Horses" (Faulkner), 130
Springfield, Mo., 423
Sprint, 411
Sprint Cup, 411
Stamp Act, 62
Stampp, Kenneth M., 248
Stamps-Baxter Company, 454
Standards for Workers in Southern Industry (L. Mason), 399
Stanley, Carter, 324
Stanley, Ralph, 324
Steelworkers, **455–57**
Steunenberg, Frank, 377
Stevenson, Brenda, 116
Still, James, 468
Still, William Grant, 183

Stoddard, Lothrop, 105–6
Stoney, George, 458
Strange Fruit (Smith), 258
Stranger with a Camera, 400
Strike: The Radical Insurrections of Ellen Dawson (McMullen), 408
Strip mining, 367, 401
Stuart, J. E. B., 123
Stuart, Jesse, 468
Student Nonviolent Coordinating Committee (SNCC), 225–26, 363, 449–50
Students for a Democratic Society (SDS), 449–50
Suffrage, 232, **295–300**
Suffragists, 120
Sunbelt South, **276–82**
Susquehanna Indians, 321
Swayne, Charles, 346
Sydenstricker, Edgar, 423
Systema Naturae (Linnaeus), 105

Taco Bell, 403
Taft-Hartley Act of 1947, 41, 68, 150–51, 420, 464
Tallahassee, Fla., 82
Talmadge, Eugene, 93, 121
Tampa, Fla., 10
Tate, Allen, 131
Tayloe, John, III, 289
Taylor, Alva W., 257, 383–84, 469–70
Taylor, Joe Gray, 110
Teaching, 305
Television, **227–30**
Tenant farming, **242–46**, 277, 278, 288, 361, 412, 414, 425, 443, 462, 471
Tennessee, 41, 370–71; and union organization, 24; convict lease system, 91, 343; and organized labor, 142; Latinos, 159–60; and Knights of Labor, 312; and Highlander Folk School, 365–66
Tennessee Coal and Iron Company (TCI), 91, 343–45, 455–56
Tennessee Federation for Constitutional Government, 333–34
Tennessee Valley Authority, 100, 318, 416

Terrell, Mary Church, 270, 344
Texas, 139, 147, 353, 445; and Socialist Party, 10; and unionization, 10–11; anti-violence laws, 67; Asians, 72, 73; Vietnamese, 76; environment, 103; immigrants, 108; Latinos, 152–53; tourism, 283–84; convict lease system, 343; oil fields, 417, 419
Texas and Pacific Railroad, 149
Textile industry, 237, 278, 312, 314, 391; paternalism, 119; and industrialization, 136–38, 139, 142, 143, 291; and Jews, 145; and strike, 149–50; and labor, 211–12, 341–42, **457–59**; and female labor, 303–10; and child labor, 333; and Operation Dixie, 420; and desegregation, 458
Textile Workers Organizing Committee (TWOC). *See* Textile Workers Union of America
Textile Workers Union of America (TWUA), 308, 341–42
Their Eyes Were Watching God (Hurston), 258
Thirteenth Amendment, 296
Thomas, Norman, 409
Thornhill case, 67
Thornton, W. W., 316
Thorp, Sister Rosetta, 454
Thorp, Thomas Bangs, 130, 163–64
Three 6 Mafia, 433
Thurmond, Strom, 94–96
T. I., 433
Tidewater South, 4, 235
Till, Emmett Louis, 171
Tillman, Ben, 93
Timbaland, 433
Timber, **459–62**
Time to Kill, A (film), 229
Tindley, Charles Albert, 454
Title I Housing Act of 1949, 294
Tobacco Road (Caldwell), 131–32, 134–35, 137, 164
Tobacco workers, **462–64**
Tobacco Workers International Union (TWIU), 463–64

To Kill a Mockingbird (Lee), 162, 165
To Make My Bread (G. Lumpkin), 393, 458
Tourism, **283–87**
"Toward a Female Liberation Movement" (Jones and Brown), 450
Trade unions, 39
Trail of Tears, 375
Transylvania University, 98
Trash (Allison), 165–66
Tredegar Iron Works, 455
Tresca, Carlo, 377
Trieber, Jacob, 346
Troy, Leo, 41
Truman, Harry, 95–96, 297–98
Truth, Sojourner, 271
Tryon, William, 436–37
Turner, Nat, 116, 352
Turner, Tina, 182
Turpentine production and camps, 459–62
Tuskegee Institute, 465
Tutwiler, Julia, 344
Twain, Mark, 130–31, 134, 473
2 Live Crew, 432

Unions and unionism, 22, 40–45, 83, 146–51, 156, 237, 312, 313–14, 341–42, 376–77, 399–400, 409, 469, 470; and immigrants, 107–8; and women, 120–21, 308–10; and industrialization, 138–39, 142–44; and New Deal, 189; and minorities, 209–13; radicalism, 222–25; and labor force, 339–40; Knights of Labor, 387; longshoremen, 390–91; lumber workers, 392; and Operation Dixie, 419–20; poultry workers, 426; railroad workers, 427–29; service workers, 440; Share Croppers' Union, 443–44; steelworkers, 456; textile workers, 457–59; tobacco workers, 463–64
United Automobile Workers, 142
United Daughters of the Confederacy, 270
United Mine Workers of America (UMWA), 11, 138, 210, 223–24, 313, 366–67, 408
U.S. Bureau of Labor, 41

U.S. Census Bureau, 25
U.S. Centers for Disease Control, 281
U.S. Department of Agriculture, 12, 60, 413, 431, 444
U.S. Department of Justice, 281
U.S. Department of Labor, Women's Bureau, 318
U.S. House Committee on Un-American Activities (HUAC), 329
United States Military Academy, 404
U.S. Supreme Court, 259, 280
U.S. v. Reynolds, 346
United Steel Workers of America (USWA), 456
United Textile Workers of America (UTW), 314, 357
University of Alabama, 97–98
University of Arkansas, 99
University of Georgia, 97–98
University of Kentucky, 264
University of Mississippi, 97–98, 264, 331; Ole Miss Rebels, 264
University of North Carolina, 97–98, 260, 294, 416
University of North Carolina Press, 416
University of South Carolina, 97–98
University of Tennessee, 97–98
University of Virginia, 97–98, 316
Upper class, white, **287–90**
Uprising of '34, 458
Uprooted, The (Handlin), 106
Urban Development Action Grant Program, 294
Urbanization, 29–30, **290–94**
Ursuline Academy, 97

Van Tine, Warren, 408
Vardaman, James, 93–96, 170, 368
Vaughan, James D., 442, 454
Vecoli, Rudolf, 106
Verdery, S.C., 166
Vicksburg, Miss., 66–67, 171
Vietnamese, 72, 76
Violence, 292, 298, 307–8, 458
Virginia, 89, 113–14, 139, 283, 319, 321–22,

334; colonial era, 2; and Bacon's Rebellion, 2; Tidewater, 4; and American Revolution, 62, 63, 64–65; Asian Indians, 74; crime and punishment, 87–89; immigrants, 108; free blacks, 116–17; and organized labor, 142; lynching, 168; agriculture, 186; and Reconstruciton, 234; black slaveholders, 247–48; slaves, 252; and social class, 287, 289; and Jacksonian democracy, 380; and Readjusters, 434–35; tobacco, 462
Virginia Defenders of State Sovereignty and Individual Liberties, 333–34
Virginia House of Burgesses, 107, 321
Virginia Military Institute (VMI), 98, 404
Voter Registration Project, 449
Voting rights, **295–300**
Voting Rights Act of 1965 (VRA), 83, 226, 259, 299, 364, 385

Wade, Andrew, 328
Wade, Charlotte, 328
Wages, 141–43, 157–61, 188–89, 224, 304
Wagner Act, 67
Walker, John G., 72
Walker, William, 442
Wallace, George C., 15, 93, 96, 226
Wallace, Henry, 328
Wall Between, The (Braden), 329
Wal-mart, 143–44
Walton, Sam, 143–44
Waltons, The, 164, 228
Warner, W. Lloyd, 2
War on Poverty, 16, 24, 302, 366
Warren, Robert Penn, 131
Washington, Booker T., 344, 346, **464–66**
Washington, George, 63, 133
Watkinsville, Ga., 170
Watson, Tom, 170, 317
Watts riots, 83
Webb, Jim, 121
Weber, Max, 1, 24–25, 106, 236, 406
Wedding, The (G. Lumpkin), 393
Welch, Jack, 266
Welfare, **301–2**

Welk, Lawrence, 382
Wells, Lynn, 450
Wells-Barnett, Ida B., 271, **466–67**
Welsh, 107
Welsh Americans (Lewis), 107
Welty, Eudora, 135
Wesley, Cynthia, 171
West, Don, 223, 258, 365, 371, 383–84, **468–69**
West Point (military academy), 404
West Point, Ga., 72
West Point, N.Y., 404
West Side Story (film), 268
West Virginia, 41, 283, 319; environment, 103, 105; immigrants, 107; and unionization, 408; oil fields, 417
Wheeler, George A., 423
Whig Party and Whigs, 3–4, 92, 123, 191, 380–81
White, B. F., 442
White, Bailey, 135
White, Bukka, 326
White, Ron, 135
White, Walter, 257
"Whitecappers," 91, 388
"White trash," **367–70**
Whitehead, G. C., 170
Whitney, Dan, 135
Whitton, Jamie, 364
Who Speaks for the South? (Dabbs), 449
Wiggins, Ella May, 224, 308, 458
Williams, Aubrey, 258–59, 447
Williams, Bryan, 433
Williams, Claude, 383–84, 468, **469–71**
Williams, Hank, 182, 229, 347
Williams, Pharrell, 433
Williams, Ronald, 433
Williamsburg, Va., 63, 286
Wills, Bob, 182
Wilmington Ten, 330
Wilson, Charles Reagan, 326
Wilson, Gretchen, 229–30
Wilson, Justin, 134
Winfrey, Oprah, 79, 270
Winston-Salem, N.C., 308, 464

Wiseblood, 134–35
Wood, Natalie, 268
Woods, Tiger, 266
Woodson, Carter G., 248–49
Woodward, C. Vann, 201, 455
Workers Alliance, 470
Working class, 347, 415
Working Lives (M. Miller), 407
Workingmen's Reform Party, 387–88
Works Progress Administration, 100, 365, 461
World War II, 277; impact of, 14–16; internment camps, 72–73; and civil rights movement, 81; and unions, 138; and migration, 178–79

Wright, Gavin, 288, 392
Wright, Richard, 111

Yeomen, 57, 126, 233, 253, 320, **471–72**; antebellum era, 3–4; impact of Civil War on, 6; and new industrial order, 8; and agriculture, 187–89; and social class, 288; and labor, 303, 305; and Greenback Party, 361–62; and New South, 414; and spiritual music, 451–52
"You Might Be a Redneck If . . . ," **472–74**
Young, Kenneth, 59

Zinn, Howard, 146, 449

www.ingramcontent.com/pod-product-compliance
Lightning Source LLC
Chambersburg PA
CBHW020631230426
43665CB00008B/124